"We have worked in the isolation of our homes when you needed us to and we have taken on a second job too when you needed that. Now we want to decide WHEN we work, HOW we work, and WHO we work for. We want to be able to decide NOT TO WORK AT ALL—like you."

— The campaign of *Wages for Housework*. Silvia Federici, New York, 1973.

365 Days of Invisible Work has been developed with several self-organized migrant domestic workers unions. We align ourselves with the urgent call for recognition and struggle for better working conditions. This calendar is dedicated to: The Indonesian Migrant Workers Union (Amsterdam), Justice for Domestic Workers (J4DW) (London) and Sindillar/Sindihogar (Barcelona). Thank you so much for your determination, solidarity, and militant work, which keeps on inspiring us deeply.

365 Days of Invisible Work assembles 365 images of home-work gathered by the Domestic Worker Photographer Network, a growing online community of amateur photographers, which currently consists of 161 contributors from different ages and fields, based in more than 50 locations from all over the world.

Inspired by the first Worker Photographers of the 1920s and 1930s, who took part with their cameras in the international labour movement, and in the spirit of the Domestic Worker Photographers, this calendar is commissioned by the Werker Collective in the service of a *Bilderkritik*, an image critique of 'everyday life' as we know it. This is another step, like many have done before, to call attention to the hegemonic structures that make reproductive work invisible and to disrupt the visual material that propels this invisibility in dominant media. As such, we may also begin to imagine counter-hegemonic ways of organizing life and work, an ongoing task in the struggle to liberate ourselves from what Marina Vishmidt describes as the libidinal experience of working that breaks us into the components: utility, terror, satisfaction, and marking time.

—Marc and Rogier of the Werker Collective, Amsterdam, 2017.

WORK BREAKS US, WE BREAK WORK.
A CORRESPONDENCE BETWEEN
MARINA VISHMIDT AND LISA JESCHKE

On 18 May 2017 at 23:01, Marina Vishmidt wrote:

Hi dear Lisa,

Here's a thing—I was wondering if you might feel like, or have any time to have a conversation with me about work? I thought maybe we could talk about work broken down into components, like utility, terror, satisfaction, and marking time. And also maybe, or perhaps centrally, how you think about it in your poetic, critical, and theatrical activities.

   I was thinking we could perform a series of divagations over email (since I can't think and speak at the same time)?

× ×

On 19 May 2017 at 14:48, Lisa Jeschke wrote:

Dear Marina,

Thanks very much for the invite, I'd love to. This breaking-up-
into-components you initiated as a structuring principle
(or method of destruction(?) "work breaks us, we break work,"
a ripping off of the felt that covers the scaffolding of the various
wheels of fortune) seems really useful to me. Could we develop
some propositions off of these? I did want to ask if you could
expand on the terms you chose (or one of them)?…

L × ×

On 28 May 2017 at 21:01, Marina Vishmidt wrote:

When I suggested that we could talk about work broken down
into the components utility, terror, satisfaction, and marking time,
it was a numinous attempt to describe an impression I had in the

process of trying to recall bits of dialogue from your theatre piece with Lucy Beynon, *The Tragedy of Theresa May* (a competition to the death between Ute, a middle manager and Theresa May impersonator, and Volker, her employee and horse). I think that particular combination pointed to its general ambience. "Components" for instance evokes the tiny increments sufficient to grow a paycheque above the boundary of what one worker would do to another worker, the "10p more" Ute is paid than Volker. Another is the disaggregation of a relationship into parts (mask, wig, hand-boots, isolated mouth evoked by the "Not I" section of the piece) even as the moments of service work, love, and cruelty cabaret seem to execute a different dynamic, that of fusing these components together.

Apart from trying to imagine my way into the performance through this search string, the four terms could also be seen as points on a libidinal map of the experience of working. "Utility" as task satisfaction, taking pride, feeling like the job needs to be done (regardless of the awful or senseless conditions of doing it), the utopia contained in the tiny job (see November 29).

"Terror" as whatever forces make sure you do the job you are paid or not paid to do, from structural to intimate violence (see May 3). "Satisfaction" is when you really do fuse with your mask, as with the Theresa May impersonation in the performance. "Marking time" is the terror of having nothing to do, the terror of this being all you will ever do. Marking as an assertion of power, that there is time and a subject elsewhere than this experience. Like the markings on a prison or bedroom wall, or keeping count in a game, marking as an attempt to control the pathos of a situation that is set up to work only so long as you have no control (see October 13). These all sound like behaviours of adaptation, and thus somehow can be read as more instrumental or studied than what I first meant by using them, which is to say, pre-defined components of work. Really it was about libidinal switches in the actual time of labour.

This question of measure and adjustment is something we can also see approached in the Domestic Worker Photographer Network project, where a lot of people have chosen to send images of their beds as the prime creative workspace.

From self-directed artist model (see March 25), to effulgent
disaster areas of equipment and fabric (see July 27), the bed
as a site of relaxation becomes a site of labour, and hence
of measure (see July 23). Yet, at the same time, its unmoderated
character is retained and maybe even curated. The home
in general can be thought about as this kind of excessive or
obsessional workplace, at least for 'creatives' if not for house-
workers (whether we see that as a division of tasks, labour
markets, or figures of class division), where there's nobody
to monitor how fiercely or laxly you've internalized capitalist
discipline—or, rather, competition, with now invisible and always
lower-waged others (see December 10).

On 29 May 2017 at 22:44, Lisa Jeschke wrote:

This disaggregation into components which you speak about
above also becomes strongly evident in the Domestic Worker
Photographer Network photographs, which often seem to zoom
in on the small props of the workers' lives, with even their own

body parts as objects disarticulated from themselves (see
December 11, June 16, or July 13). It also reads to me also like
an acknowledgement of how difficult—or currently undoable—
a full making-visible of work relations, either at home or at bound
work-place is. I mean that you couldn't give one defining image
of the degree of your humiliation, the web of relations to employers,
clients, unemployment agencies, or other workers you might
find yourself in. That's why the collection of images by so many
different contributors feels hurtfully, but necessarily incomplete.

   Coming back to the domesticity of what is shown by the
calendar: if one of its aims is to document the intrusion of work
into your bed, then in *The Tragedy of Theresa May* there's maybe
a reversal of that. The work-relation between middle manager
and employee is also already domestic, a love relation—not
as an extraneous plot conceit, but as something that's intrinsic
to this work-relation. Maybe in that sense the set-up of the performance is not entirely separate from the domestic situations
shown in the calendar, even if it re-externalizes what you called
internalized forms of capitalist discipline, doing this as a related

folding-out of insides. (These insides would not quite be feelings, but organs for example, starting with the tongue, and again only ever being parts.) Most clearly, it's an externalization of an excessive degree of internalized acquiescence: Volker doesn't deny she's a horse on all fours, but gives herself to her subjection so fully that her acquiescence becomes too acquiescent to be acquiescent. It pushes at related kinds of limit conditions where being too much of too little—too bland, too quiet, too mask-like, not sharing enough of what would be called a "personality"—can form into (an intended or not) misbehaviour or threat. As with Herman Melville's Bartleby, making your work-place more total than it would like to think it is, giving your all to it. But of course no one can *live* like that.

On 30 May 2017 at 10:31, Marina Vishmidt wrote:

You bring up the incipient aggression of an acquiescence that is "too much" or "too obscene," in shoving the disavowed in the face of the one who holds a whip, or hand over the sparkly

but shackled horse. This gives me two ideas: one is the fearful
dis-organizing (as in disintegrating or corrosive) quality of calling
attention to the invisible parameters of the situation as a means
to destroy it, or to seriously impede its reproduction. You could
include here naming reproductive labour as the transcendental
ground of wage labour, non-value (slavery or "non-work") as
the transcendental condition of surplus value (a dynamic internal
to surplus value itself of course), a killed non-human world
as the transcendental condition of industrial human life, work-
to-rule, smile strikes, human strikes—all the possible ways
of calling time on the intolerability of making the intolerable
tolerable. The other idea is the profound and often rapacious
self-pity of the manager, and how that makes a bid for re-
establishing humanity in a relationship where the conditions
for it no longer apply. In *The Tragedy of Theresa May*, you have
Volker rueing the fact that she has killed her slightly richer,
tired sister; it's a painful moment, because there you have
a dimension of solidarity or slowdown, conceivable in death,
but which was absolutely foreclosed in a life spent striving

to bully subordinates. This acquiescence also makes me think about how this reluctant companionship in a relation of subjugation, something that makes the intolerable slightly more tolerable, has two effective forms of morality: utility (this relationship is configured the way it is for reasons larger than ourselves, to get the job done) and sentiment (don't be so cruel and uncaring as to call me your boss or organize with your co-workers, I thought we were friends).

Another image that gets evoked here for me, is a *singspiel* by the Russian art group Chto Delat? I watched online maybe 10 years ago; in it they have a sort of sculpture that grows through and around different social classes in a pyramid. A sort of red venous structure of biological and social cohesion disavowing the antagonism that feeds it, the work depicts an impersonal circulation system of actually violent togetherness, the circulatory system of slow death.

On 30 May 2017 at 19:07, Lisa Jeschke wrote:

In terms of what you write about the solidarity conceivable in
death, I'd like to rewind to a moment in the performance when
the employee and the middle manager are still alive. I'm not sure
if in the following I'm referring to *The Tragedy of Theresa May*,
or speaking of any other similar (and similarly mediated)
situation in reality, so to set up a kind of extrapolated figuration:
perhaps in the relation between middle manager and employee
there is a dialectic going on whereby a first step to understand
a work situation means stating clearly the extreme chasm
between yourself and your middle manager. This is what you
speak of above, as a calling attention to the invisible parameters
of a situation as a means to destroy it: you, my middle manager,
do not share a world with me. But then, once that division is
clear, it seems that on the basis of a continued understanding
of that division there's still a sense of, or appeal to, a continual
flicker of a possible solidarity—if middle management was willing
to join in its abolition as middle management, in the undoing

of the workplace (why are you acting as a medium of the brutal
extraction of value when you too are subjected to that extraction?).
This situation is exactly where the self-pity you named comes in,
but which then does make solidarity inconceivable while they
are still alive, since the manager can't get over the fact of having
been antagonized against. In this situation the middle manager
can't possibly agree to undo their position of micro-power,
so they sentimentally utter what they think is an appeal to
a shared humanity—though this is really a curse fortifying
the division between a lowly employee and middle manager.

On 31 may 2017 at 19:48, Marina Vishmidt wrote:

As well as this, the undoing of the workplace through, for example,
the incentives to petty entrepreneurship offered by platform
capitals like Airbnb, which of course often means a bleed into
and saturation of all pores of personal and social life by income-
generating activities, i.e. work, however it is ideologized. We can
see that, for example, in the calendar's image of the storage

area titled "Mi Casa Es Su Casa," of the graphic designers—
one a tenant, one a landlord—who decided to rent out a bedroom
in the flat through Airbnb (see January 14). Monetizing this
'resource' in an attempt to avoid work, they of course generate
more work for themselves. These demands on time and energy
made by the decision to engage in an intensified exploitation of
self and others gives us a pitiful figure of the small business-owner.

On 1 June 2017 at 15:44, Lisa Jeschke wrote:

The manager's appeal to pity at the moment of their death as
paired with the notion that in the end we all die has been one
of the greatest trivialities of the history of theatre, keeping
culture together as an apparent end horizon that 'proves' we're
all already equal. Maybe even the definition of "the human" in
a liberal sense is only possible if thought from that final horizon:
as in, "don't worry too much about injustices, in the end we will
be levelled." It's a position that doesn't even need the promise
of an after-life to make the buy-off work. To aim for social equality

rather than assuming that the equality-of-death is equality-enough on the other hand would be to think that death is 'fully' socially produced. Not in the sense of an individualizing reprimand through behavioural control, as in cigarettes cause illness, but as a result of expenditures specific to an economic system. This would suggest something like: "No death is natural! All death is man-made!" Maybe that seems obvious, but I keep having to remind myself of the extent of what thinking backwards from death means in how our lives are produced. I've looked at some pictures of this Chto Delat *singspiel*, and it looks absolutely amazing. It's difficult to get a full sense of how it worked, but it makes me wonder if the organicist imagination of the right (the nation, the heart, blood pumping, etc.,) could be countered through an artificial, monstrous organicism. No life is natural either!

On 2 June 2017 at 01:54, Marina Vishmidt wrote:

No life is natural, no death is natural, no work is natural, neither is any means of avoiding work. Maybe this is also the somewhat

venerable question about where the alienation comes from,
or comes into alienated labour. Rendering that alienation less
natural requires some other type of alienation—like, what
mediates between the fragmentation of a body, selling its time
in parts and the fragmentation of a body in political theatre into
an array of polemical props. In this way, shedding the great
equivalence of human death as a natural rather than produced
outcome of a certain mode of production (maybe there is a
stronger set of connotation to "shedding" in German, I'm thinking
of Verena Stefan's book about her feminism, *Shedding and Literally
Dreaming*) could also go via thinking about measurement.
Measuring also becomes relevant not only since this conversation
will be published in a calendar depicting various forms of work
and its refusal, but also in light of your discussion of "the middle"
of middle management. The desire to measure, to see experience
rendered into an impersonal and non-contingent medium,
can be related to the desire for form. I'd connect that back
to the 'satisfaction' and 'utility' elements, or the power of an
aesthetic relation to your work. Here is Witold Gombrowicz:

Oh, the power of Form! Nations die because of it. It is the cause of wars. It creates something in us that is not of us. If you make light of it you'll never understand stupidity nor evil nor crime. It governs our slightest impulses. It is at the base of our collective life. This urgency of form and forming shows us that there isn't anything more primary than second nature, already…

This is why a giant red plush theatrical vine in the work of Chto Delat? is a less pernicious metaphor for social relations — however ominous its notes of organicism — than the social contract, where form encompasses errancy in a humanism predicated on exchange. Here the form of value, which is to say, not the type or kind of value, but its unicity, in for example the value form, is both the empty lynchpin of capitalist social life and the de-naturalizing force of forces in critical that is to say revolutionary thought. This form, that of value, and its emotional instruments of measurement — the forms of competition, debt, merit, love — also features strongly in *The Tragedy of Theresa May*.

Yes, I think the word "*Häutungen*" [moults] in Verena Stefan's book does have a more strongly bodily connotation than "shedding," in the sense that the emphasis seems placed on the subject removing her skin. Shedding seems more orientated towards the object that is being removed. But of course both terms wear the woman-snake constellation glowingly. As well as this, the continuous form "shedding" and the plural *"Häutungen"* seem equally less invested in exposing a core origin than in sketching a continual forwards-movement in time. As you put it, even the primordial appears alienated—natural history as a social history even in the everyday experience of my body. In terms of this layering of alienations you speak of—the twentieth-century usages of alienation (*Verfremdung* to de-naturalize *Entfremdung*) no longer feel entirely adequate to what can or could be done in the degree and multiplicity of alienation as an artistic and/or activist activity. Partly I mean this because it has sometimes been used in a formalist way, whereby artistic alienation of the everyday might be used as an end in and of itself rather than as a response to alienated labour. And then even in Brecht, where it is meant to be a direct response to alienated labour, retrospectively there is still a sense of the theatre being constructed as a slightly removed model.

By contrast, I think there is a much stronger sense of continuity between the alienation experienced in wage labour and in this case poetry in V. Spott's / A. French's *Click Away Close Door Say*, where the poetry appears not as a model for anything, but jumps right out of the work place and its mediations, as a violation of measure in poetry and a leaking in the inseparably physical and political senses. As an excess of form that comes right from within the workplace, it makes me think also about the essay "Oppose the Party 'Eight-Legged Essay'" by Mao in which he critiqued the way party members remained stuck in petty bourgeois forms, structuring their reports, meetings, and articles by, in his words, arranging "terms into A, B, C, D… as if setting up a Chinese drug store." Imagine Angela Merkel taking the act of writing so seriously as to realize that a problem central to how we live in Germany was that all CDU (Christian Democratic Union) party meetings, as well as all work-place meetings, are structured A, B, C, D.

Thinking about form in this way would imply that the staff meeting minutes or rota schedules at the work-place at issue and the poetry of *Click Away Close Door Say* take place on the same plane. It would also imply that they are in direct antagonism with one another—the book of poetry is neither more important (in the sense of culture), nor less important (in the sense of "it's just poetry") than the mediations we experience day by day in our relation to employment, unemployment, production, reproduction, and so on. If a staff meeting is as economic as it is cultural, then these poems are as economic as they are cultural, i.e. not mere superstructure, or model, or second-order level of representation: they're right there with us.

Werker 3 — Domestic Worker Photographer Network
(DWPN) is initiated by the Werker Collective
(Marc Roig Blesa and Rogier Delfos) with Casco –
Office for Art, Design and Theory, within the Grand
Domestic Revolution or GDR (2009 / 2010 – 2012),
a multi-faceted living research project exploring
the domestic sphere in order to imagine new forms
of living and working in common.

Eight *Bilderkritik* workshops analysing the images
from the DWPN were organised at Casco (Utrecht),
The Showroom (London), Tate Modern (London),
Tensta Konsthall (Stockholm), Can Felipa (Barcelona),
City of Women (Ljubljana), as a part of GDR
GOES-ON, Indisciplinadas (Madrid), Nine-to-Five
(Sant Marti Vell), 1st of May Library (Moscow) and at
Critical Studies / Sandberg Institute (Amsterdam).

Special thanks to the more than 200 contributors
to the Domestic Worker Photographer Network
and *Bilderkritik* workshops.

Concept: Werker Collective
(Rogier Delfos & Marc Roig Blesa)

Design: Werker Collective
with Steven Lenoir & Julie da Silva

Editors: Binna Choi, Yolande van der Heide

Contributors: Domestic Worker Photographer Network

Text: Lisa Jeschke and Marina Vishmidt

Online text: *Bilderkritik* participants, Steyn Bergs

Copy editing and proofreading: Tom Clark

Published by:

Spector Books
Harkortstraße 10
04107 Leipzig, Germany
www.spectorbooks.com

Casco – Office for Art, Design and Theory
Lange Nieuwstraat 7,
3512 PA Utrecht, The Netherlands
www.casco.art

Werker Collective
Geldersekade 74
1012BL Amsterdam, The Netherlands
www.werkermagazine.org

Distribution:

Germany, Austria: GVA, Gemeinsame
Verlagsauslieferung Göttingen GmbH&Co. KG,
www.gva-verlage.de

Switzerland: AVA Verlagsauslieferung AG, www.ava.ch

France, Belgium: Interart Paris, www.interart.fr

UK: Central Books Ltd, www.centralbooks.com

USA, Canada, Central and South America, Africa,
Asia: ARTBOOK/ D.A.P., www.artbook.com

South Korea: The Book Society,
www.thebooksociety.org

Australia, New Zealand: Perimeter Distribution,
www.perimeterdistribution.com

2017, Casco – Office for Art, Design and Theory,
Utrecht; Werker Magazine, Amsterdam; Spector
Books, Leipzig

First edition
Printed in The Netherlands

ISBN 978-3-95905-156-9

This publication is made possible by The Mondriaan Foundation & Creative Industries Fund NL. Casco's funders are the Mondriaan Foundation, Gemeente Utrecht, Doen Foundation through Arts Collabratory.

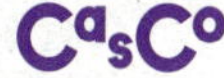
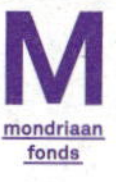
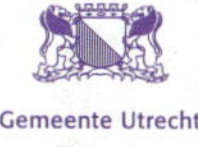
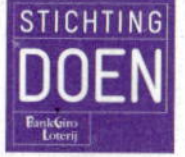
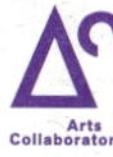

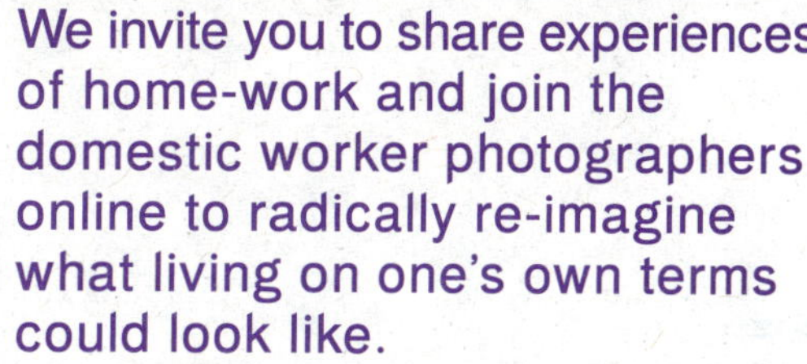

www.werkermagazine.org/domesticwork

the domestic worker visa is the life of migrant domestic workers. without rights and protection there is more abuse, exploitation, and trafficking. the domestic worker visa is the prevention of trafficking, it is a medicine that cures that disease. justice for domestic workers fights back to restore rights to the domestic worker visa.

domestic worker visa

DOMESTIC WORKER
VISA
PREVENTS
HUMAN TRAFFICKING

the tree of life. an acrylic painting made by the members of justice for domestic workers in the uk. it is a representation of our struggles and sorrows as individuals, in our own land, and as migrants in foreign countries who seek for a greener pasture, better living conditions, and a better future. some succeeded but many failed. we found comfort in our fellow domestic workers and as one, we fight against exploitation and human degradation, slavery, and isolation. regardless of age, gender, and race. we are one vision.

the tree of life

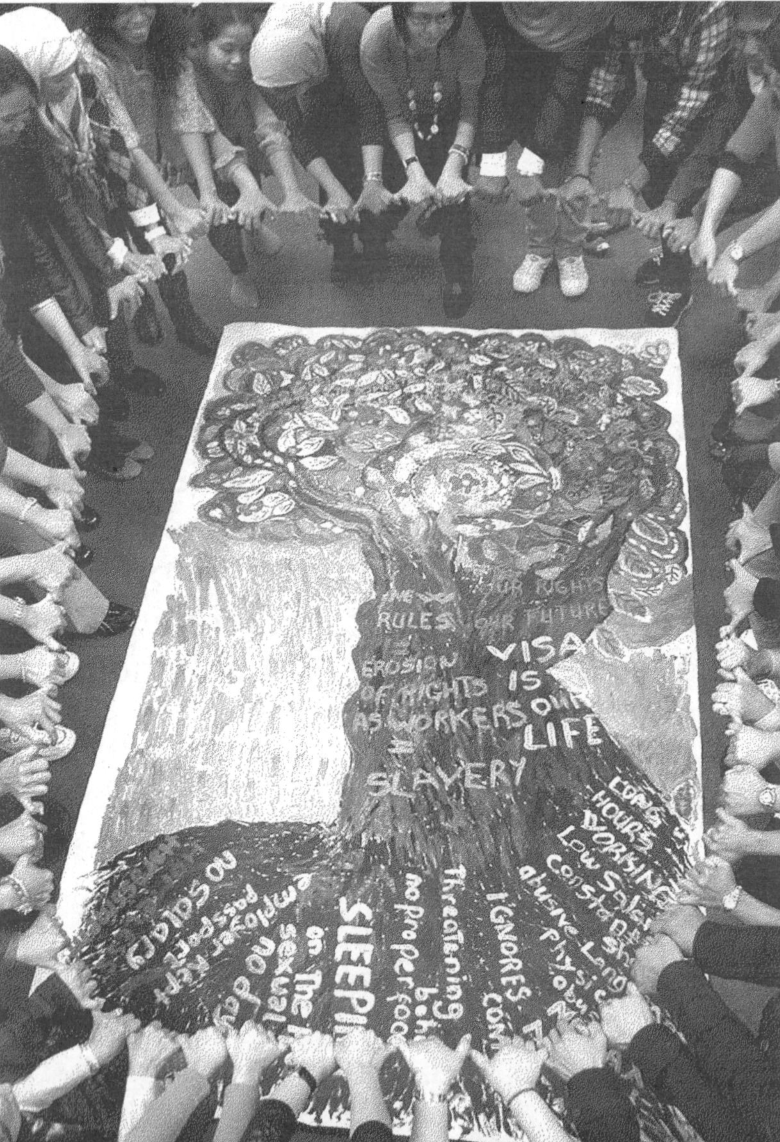
OUR RIGHTS
RULES OUR FUTURE
EROSION
OF RIGHTS
AS WORKERS OUR
VISA
IS
LIFE
SLAVERY
LONG
HOURS
WORKING
LOW SALARY
CONSTANT
ABUSIVE LONG
IGNORES
SLEEPING
ON THE
no proper food
Threatening
EMPLOYER KEEP
PASSPORT
NO SALARY

may 3

this is just one of the revelations
of being a domestic worker. my room
is a room of work. i wake up with
laundries and sleep with them at the
end of the day.

my day bedroom

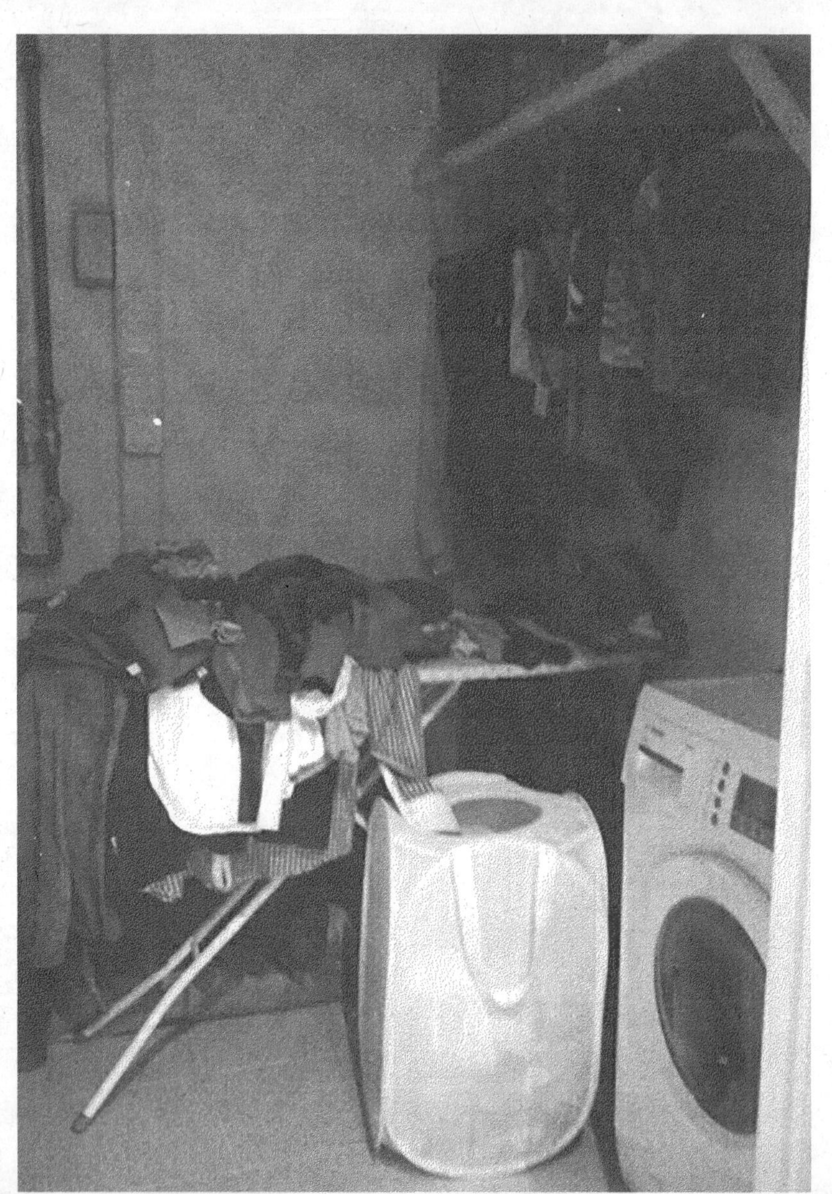

may 4

athiraman kannan jumped to his death
from the 147th floor of the world's
tallest building, the burj khalifa. from
india, he came to dubai to work as
a cleaner in the newly opened building.
in an attempt to honour his courageous
call for attention to be given to the
lives of migrant workers, i photographed
what i describe as a 'pop out city.'
these are spaces that are an attempt
at permanency and comfort in an
always vulnerable life as a migrant
worker. unlike the families they work
for, whose life exists behind walls,
their lives exist on the street, forging
new notions of 'the public.'
al naeem, 2011.

in memory of athiraman kannan

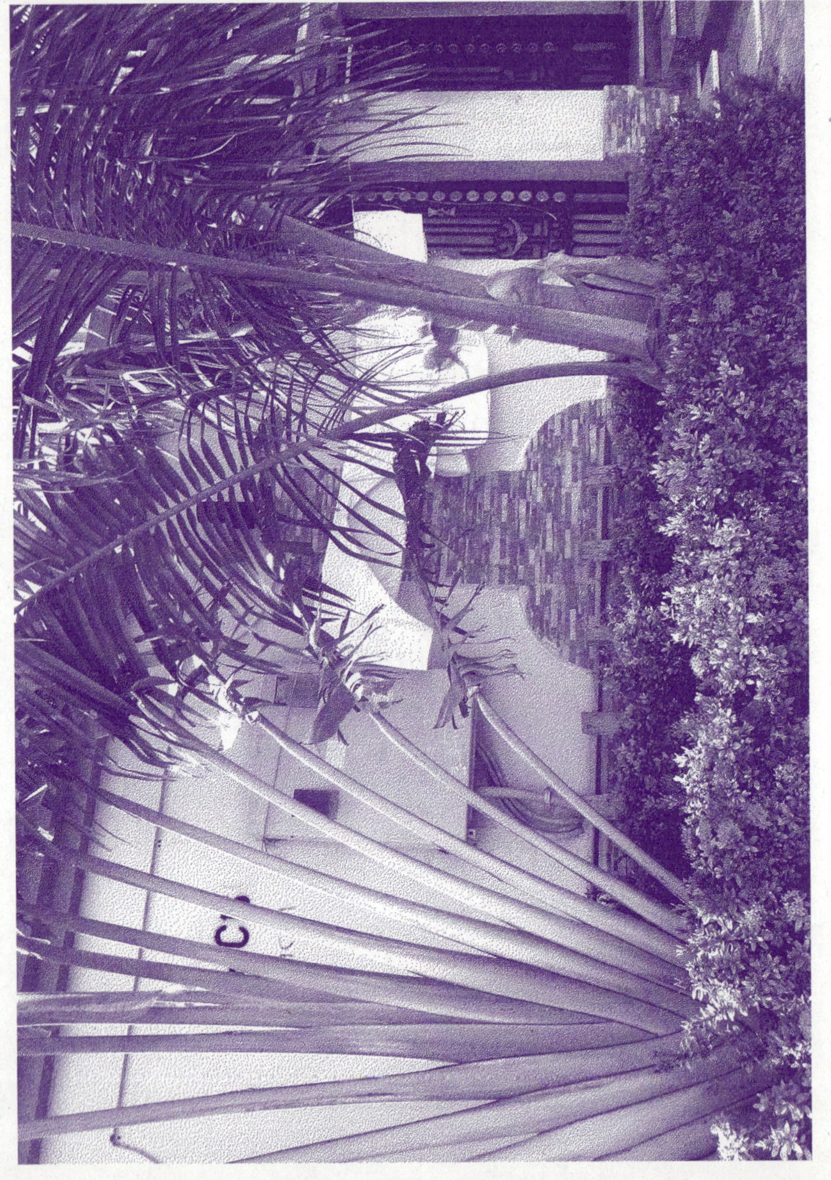

ninety-seven selected photographs
showing groups of wealthy peruvian
people in daily domestic situations.
in the background of each image one
can see either a figure or a deletion
of a domestic worker. all images have
been collected from the social network
site facebook.

97 house maids

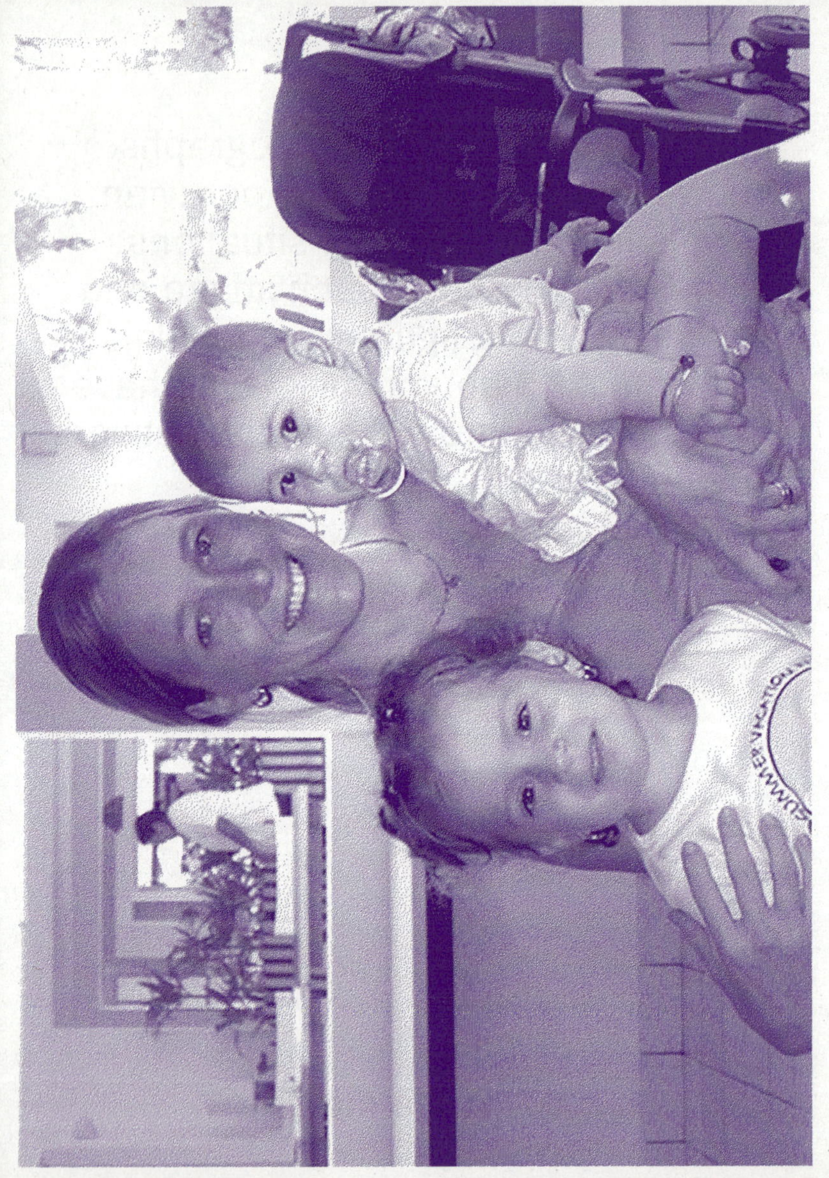

may 6

athiraman kannan jumped to his death
from the 147th floor of the world's
tallest building, the burj khalifa. from
india, he came to dubai to work as
a cleaner in the newly opened building.
in an attempt to honour his courageous
call for attention to be given to the
lives of migrant workers, i photographed
what i describe as a 'pop out city.'
these are spaces that are an attempt
at permanency and comfort in an
always vulnerable life as a migrant
worker. unlike the families they work
for, whose life exists behind walls,
their lives exist on the street, forging
new notions of 'the public.'
al naeem, 2011.

in memory of athiraman kannan

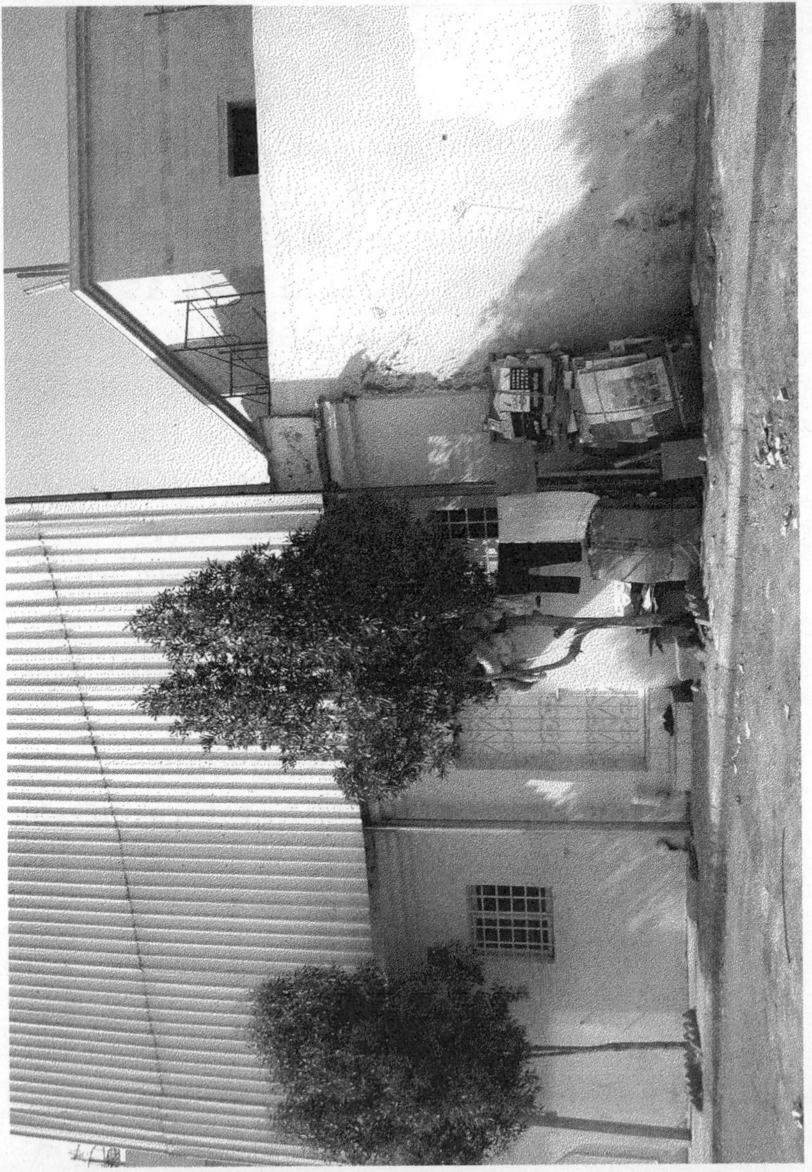

may 7

we are still working.

furniture shopping

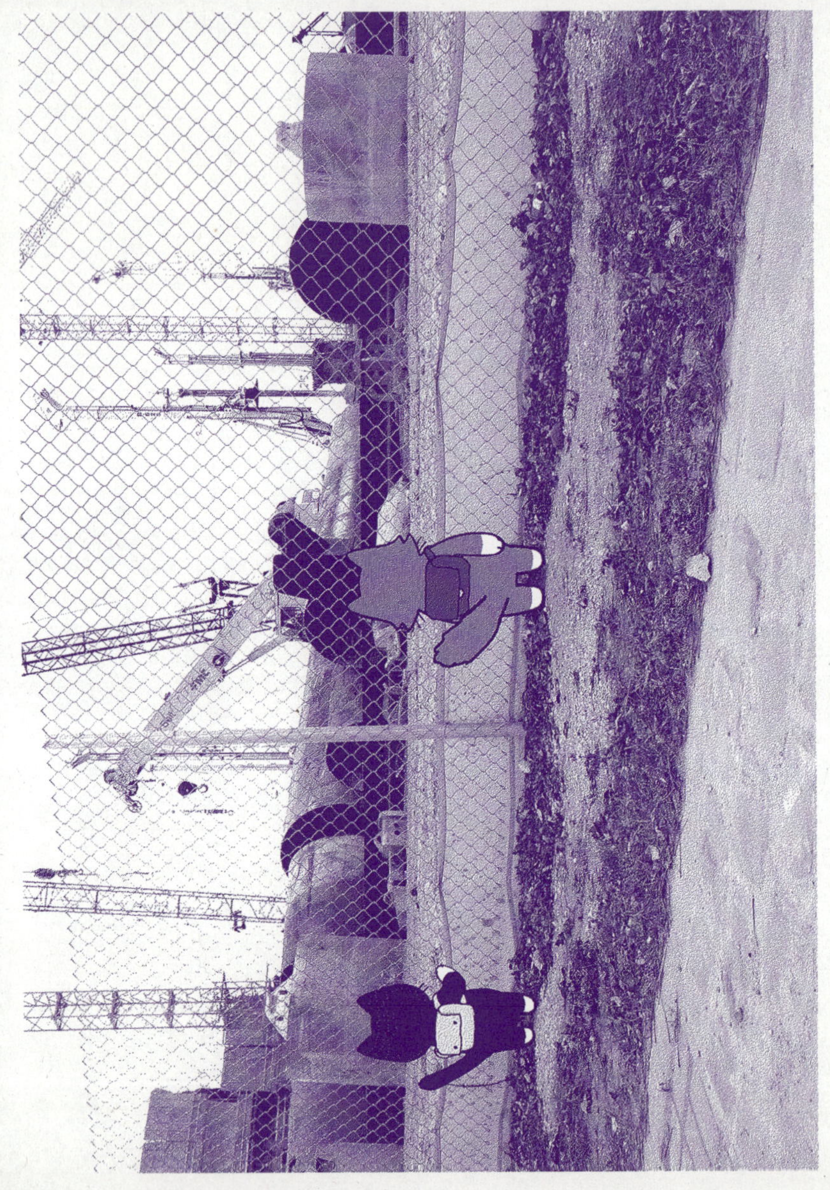

still from *tiempo real* [real time],
(2003), video, 43 min.

shopping

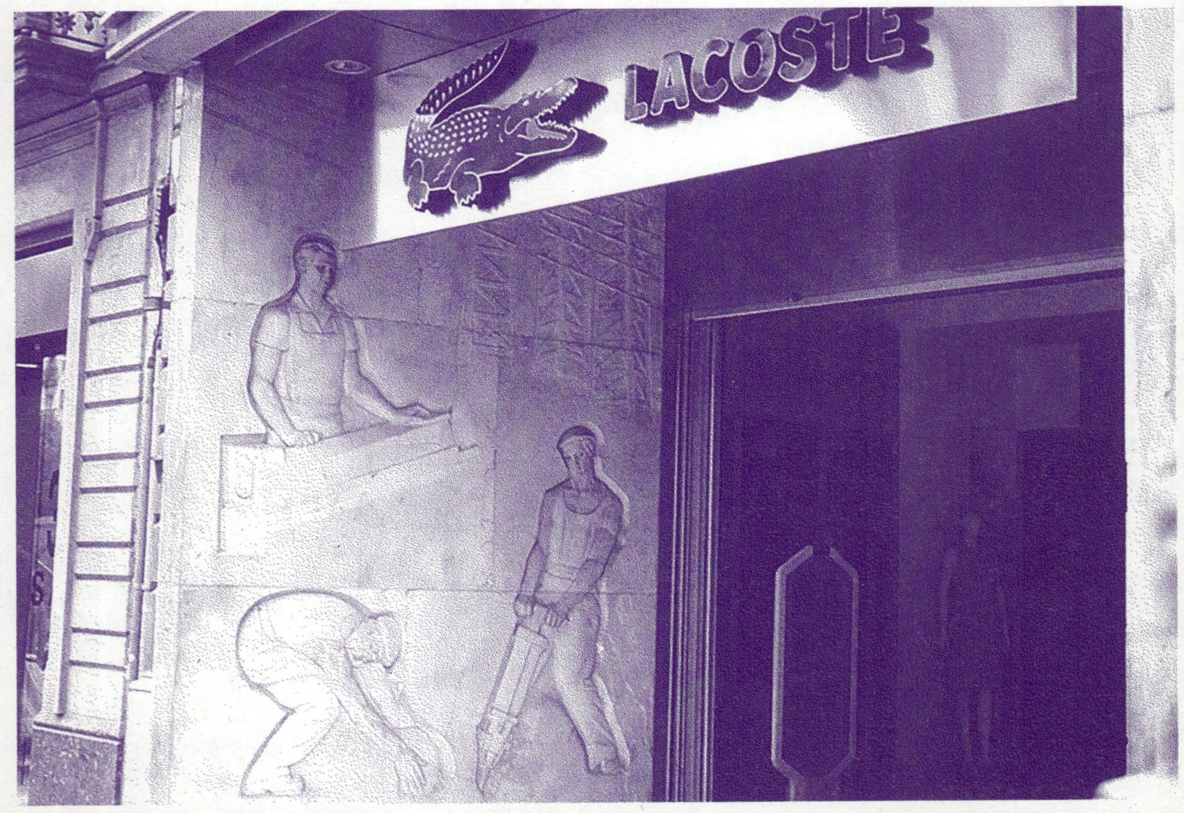

LACOSTE

may 9

the new leak

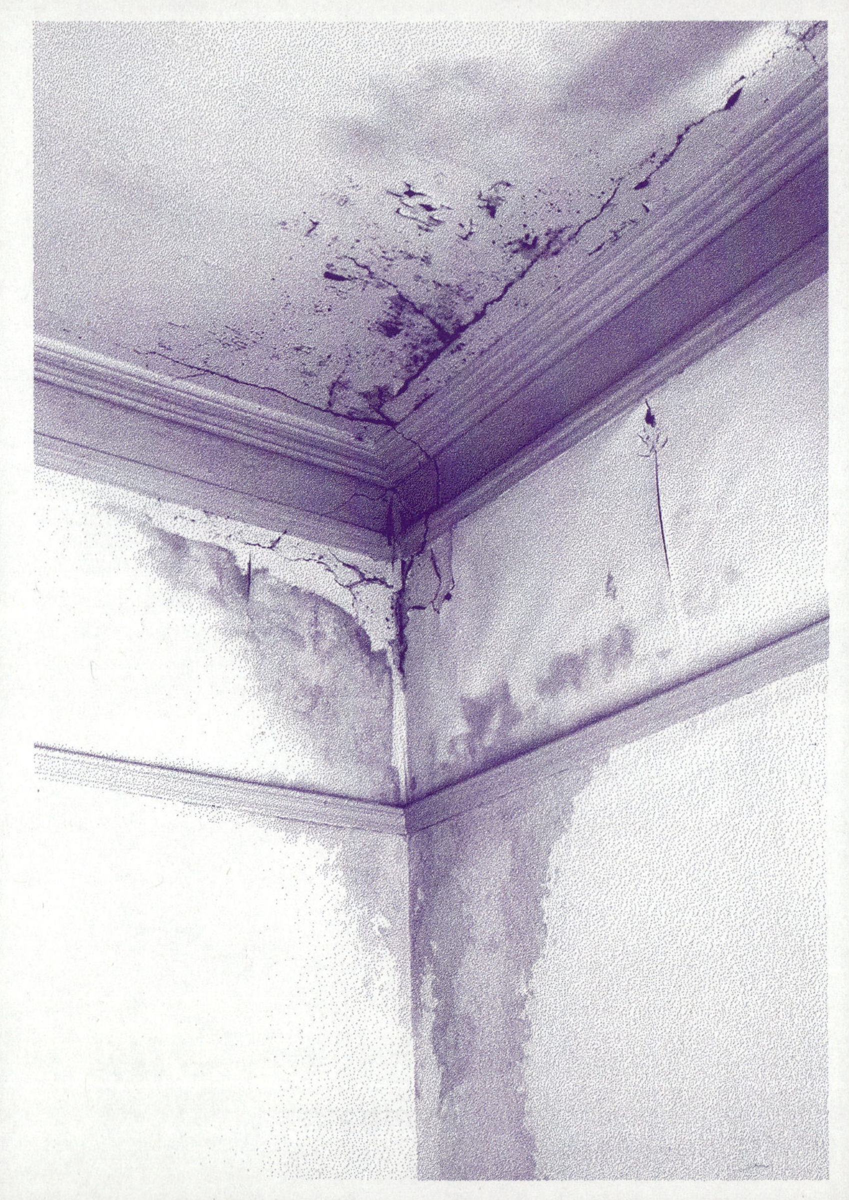

may 10

unfold the paper clip and use it like
a conventional nail cleaner.

nail cleaner

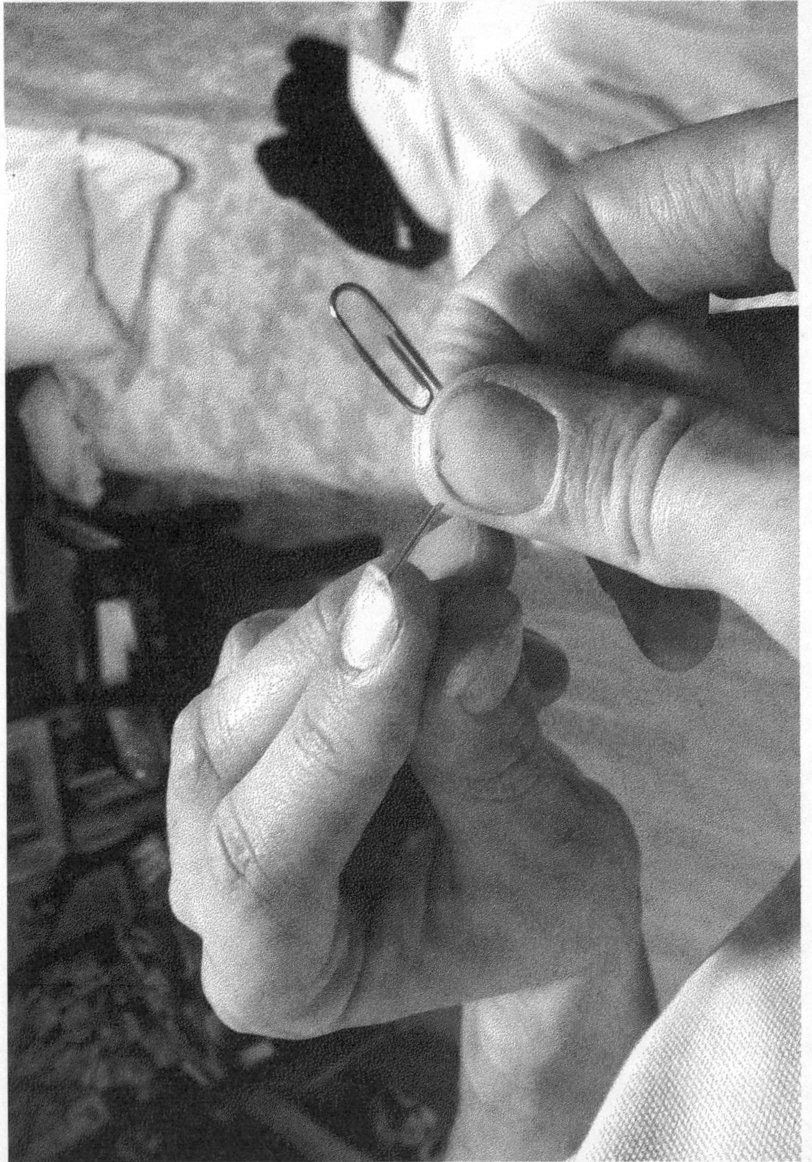

vicentica is 82 years old. her son
has bought her a washing machine,
but she still prefers to use the washing
place in the street. she needs a
domestic excuse to occupy the public
space. almenara, 1996.

washing place

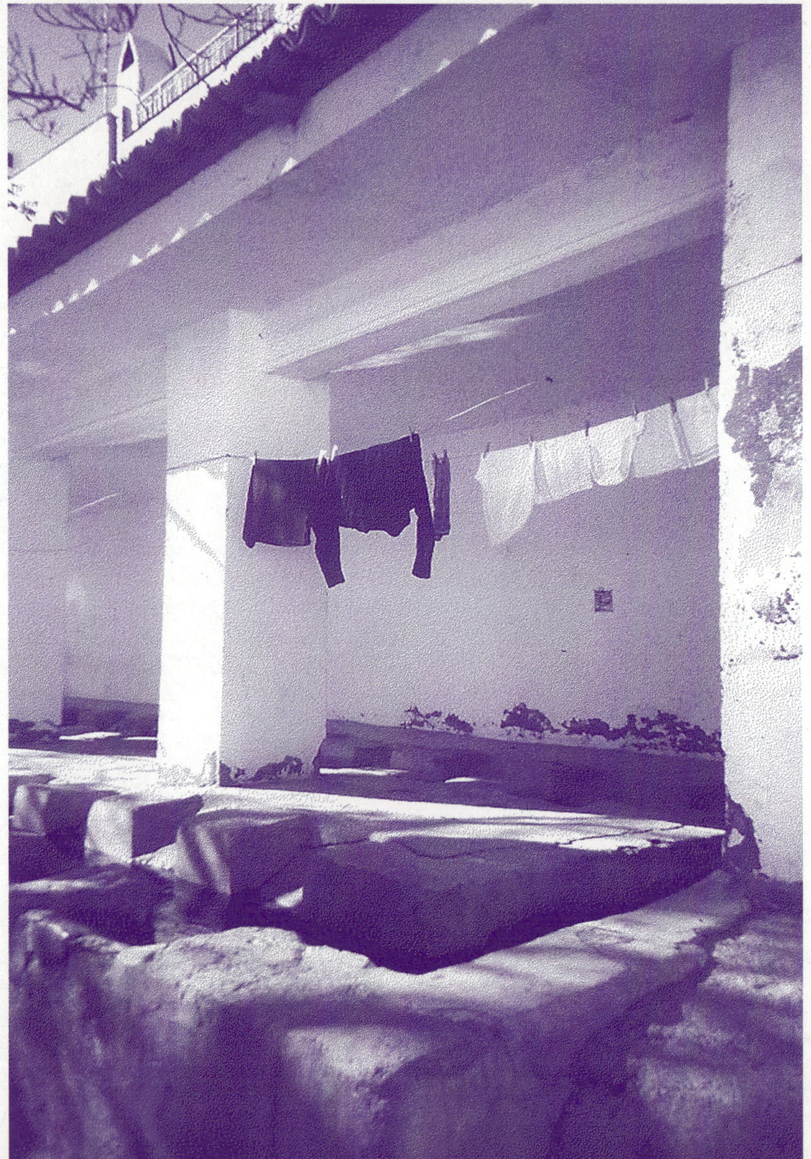

may 12

concrete, polyurethane, pine wood,
(2010). photo by thamanta.

creature comforts no. 1

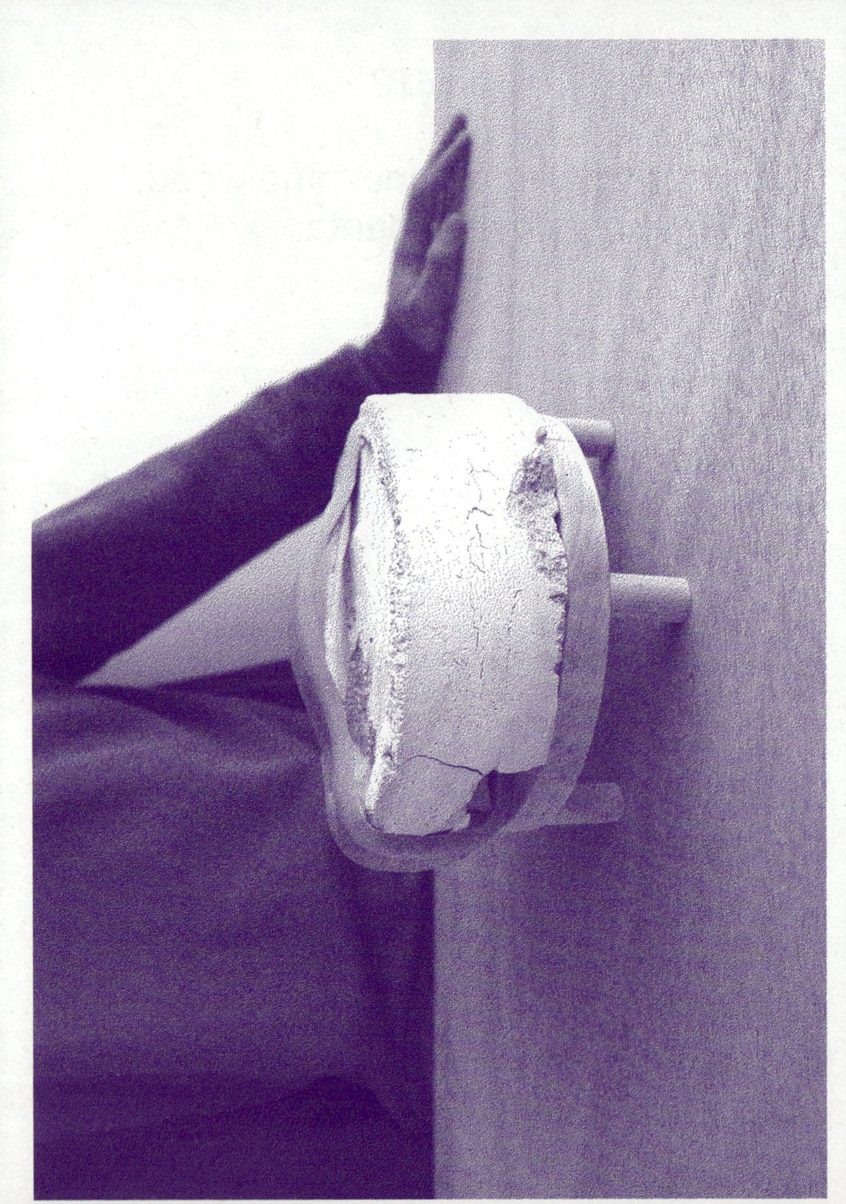

may 13

"qu'attendre de son métier?"

box office

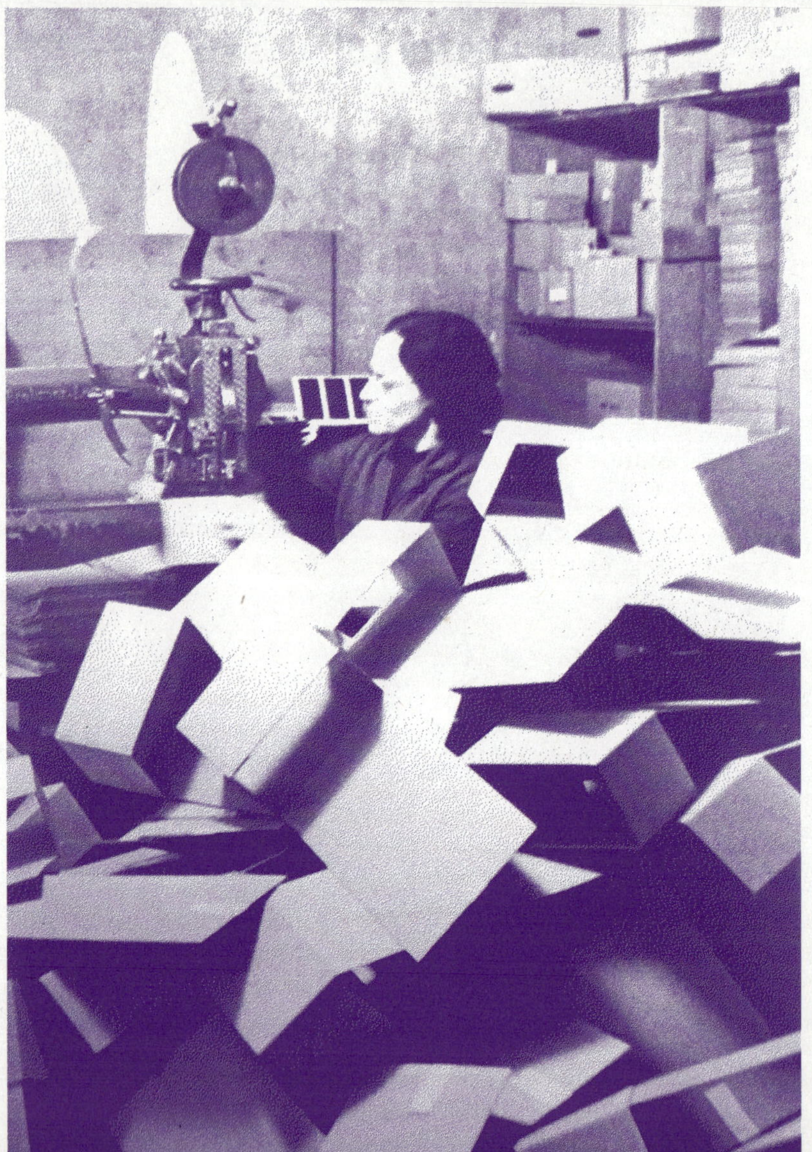

storm. leaks and moisture. even water
drops where they shouldn't be, the
owner shirks any repair. four layers
of paint have been completely useless.

rotting walls

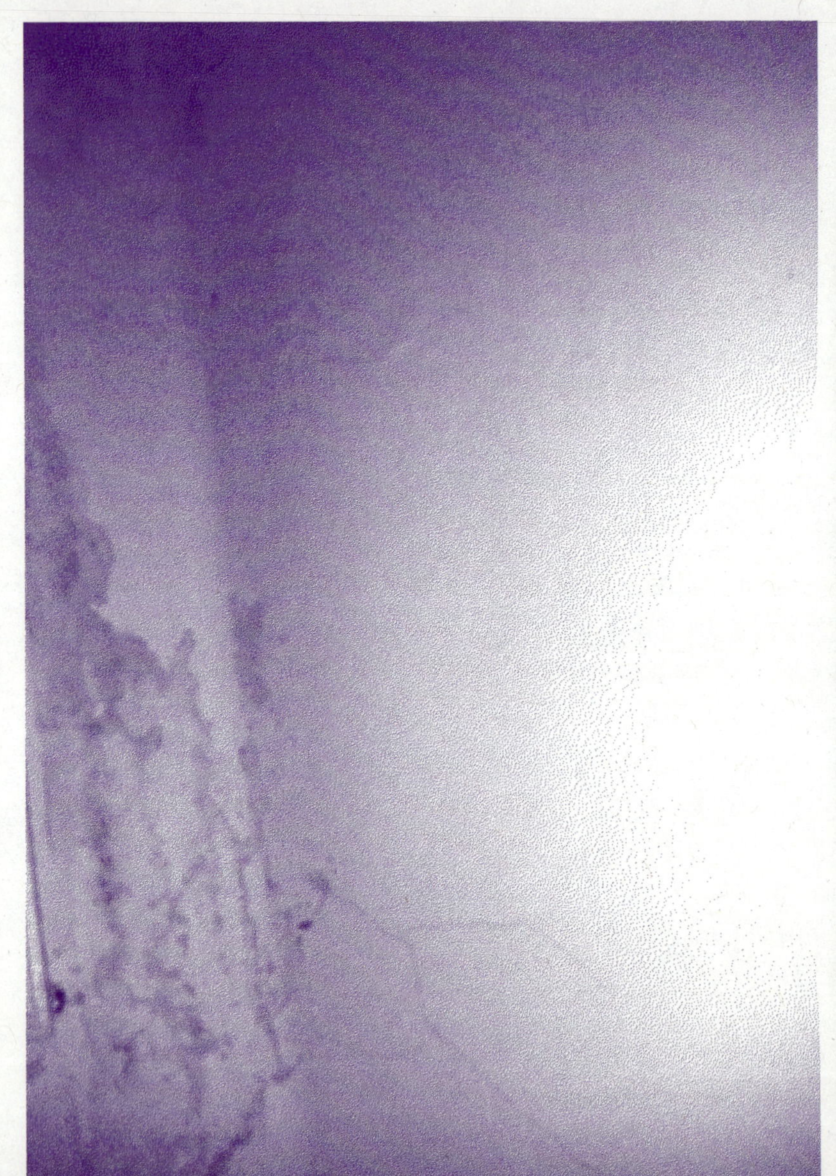

may 15

laundry

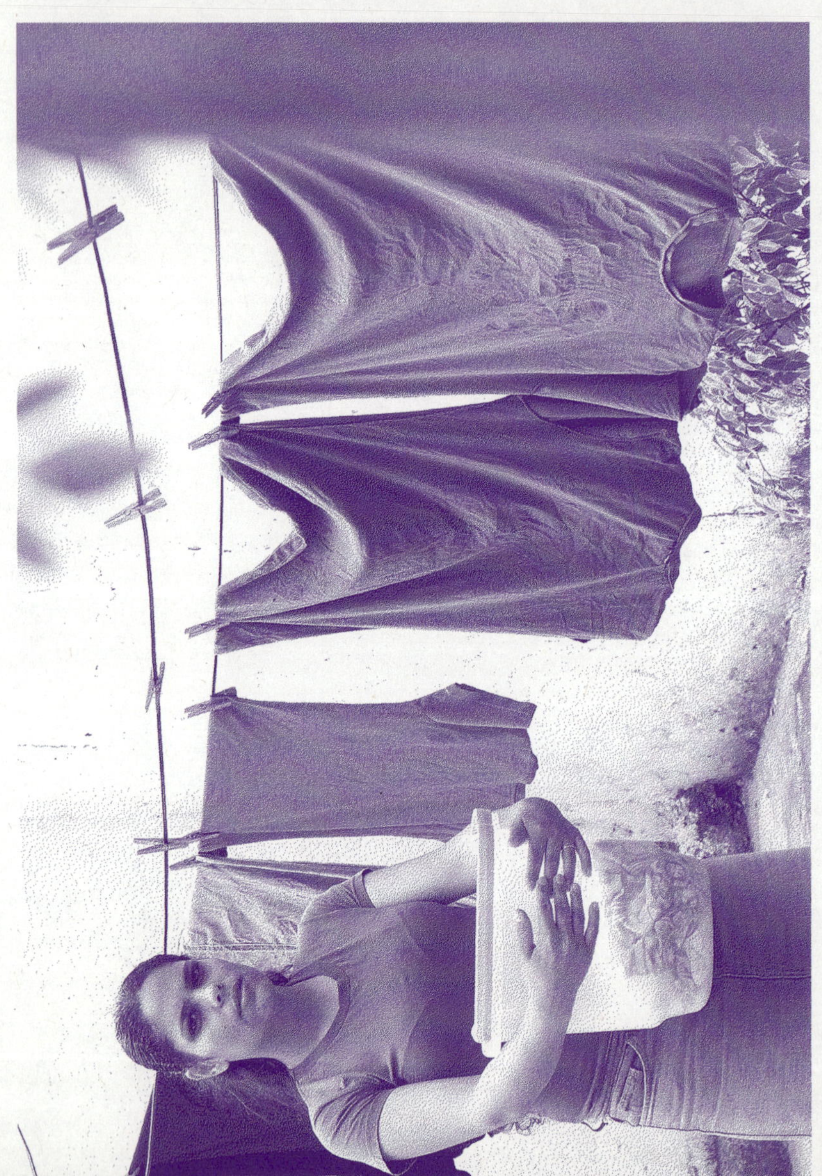

may 16

camp home—domestic exercise
and rehearsal.

stunts

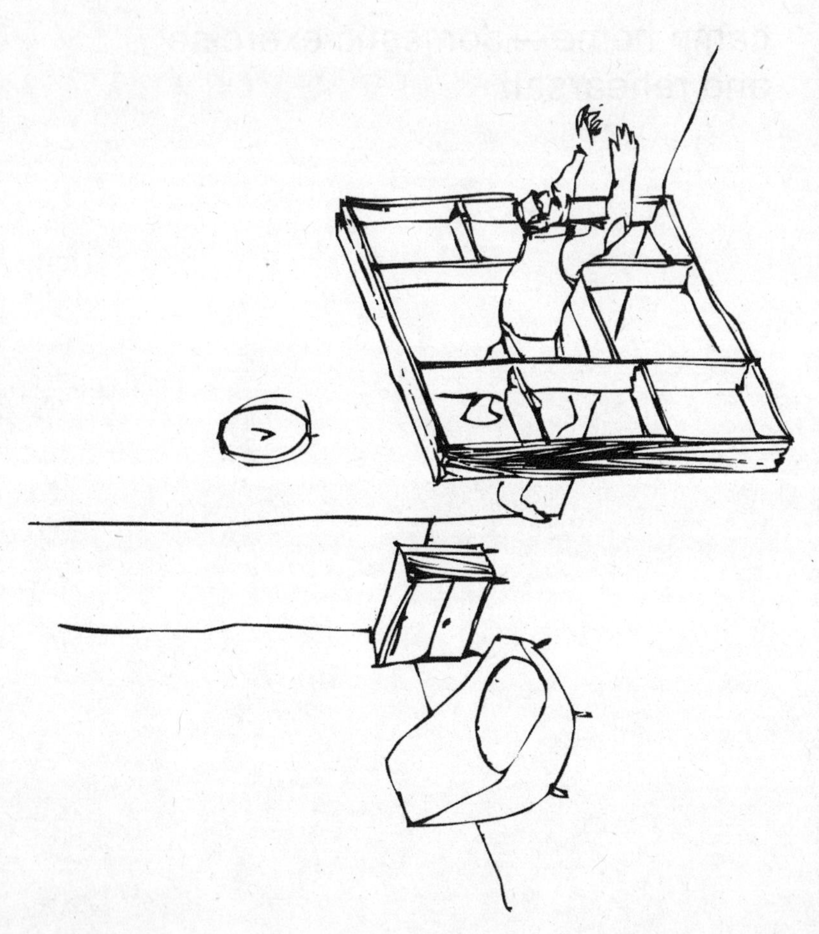

may 17

fossil fuel free material and tool
transport system for working in
the neighbourhood.

truckbarrow

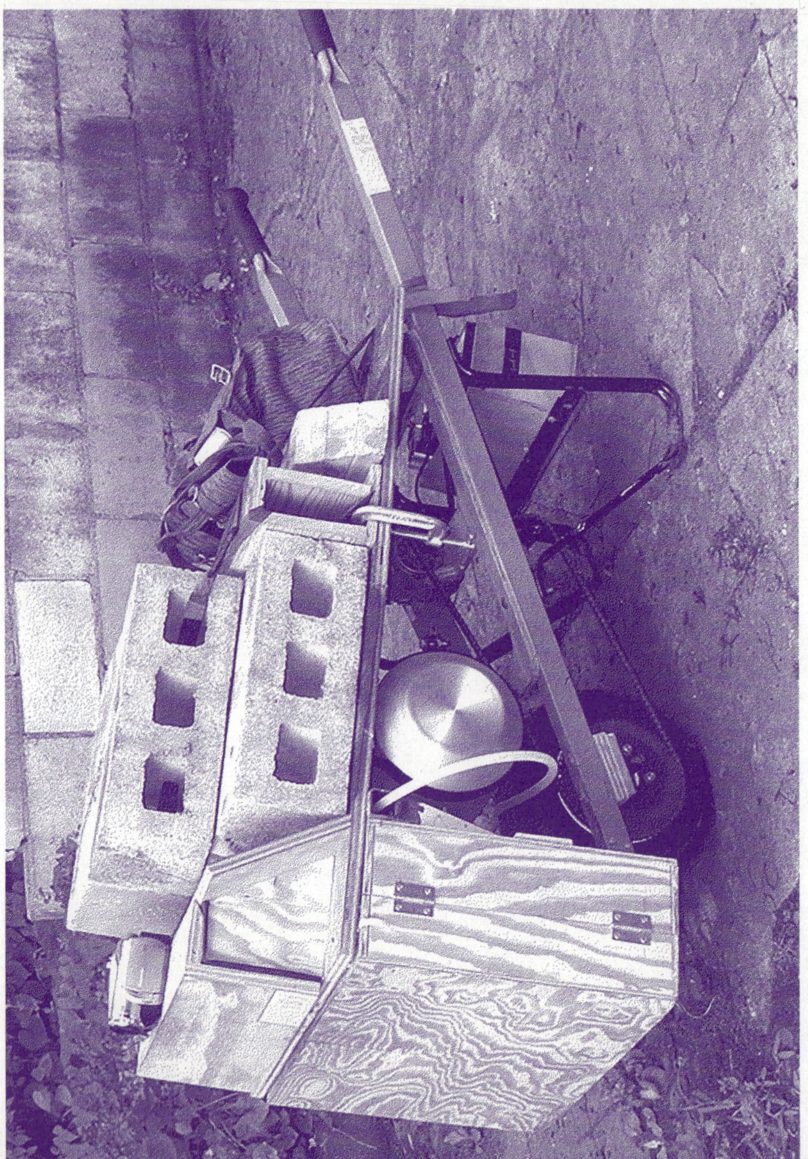

may 18

sindihogar joining the international
women's day demonstration.
barcelona, 2013.

manifestación 1 de mayo

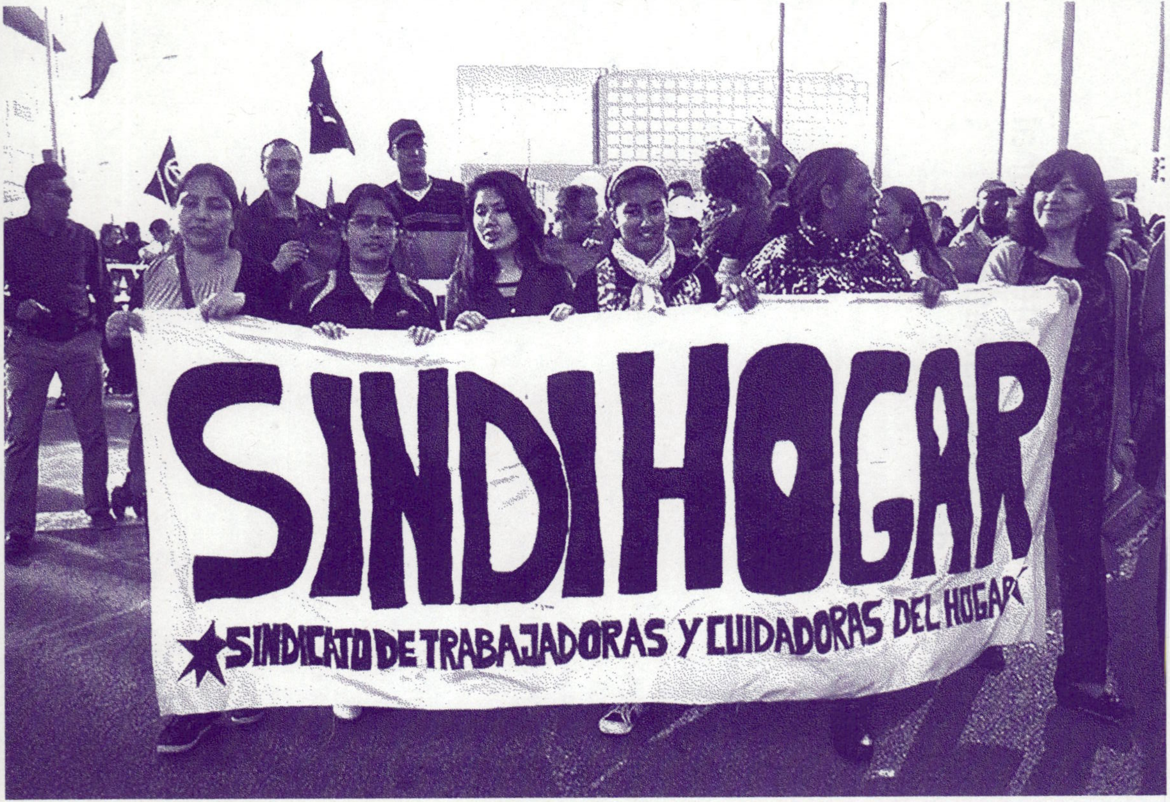

SINDIHOGAR
SINDICATO DE TRABAJADORAS Y CUIDADORAS DEL HOGAR

may 19

cultural workers move/migrate for residencies, exhibitions, appointments, teaching, internships, etc.

moving

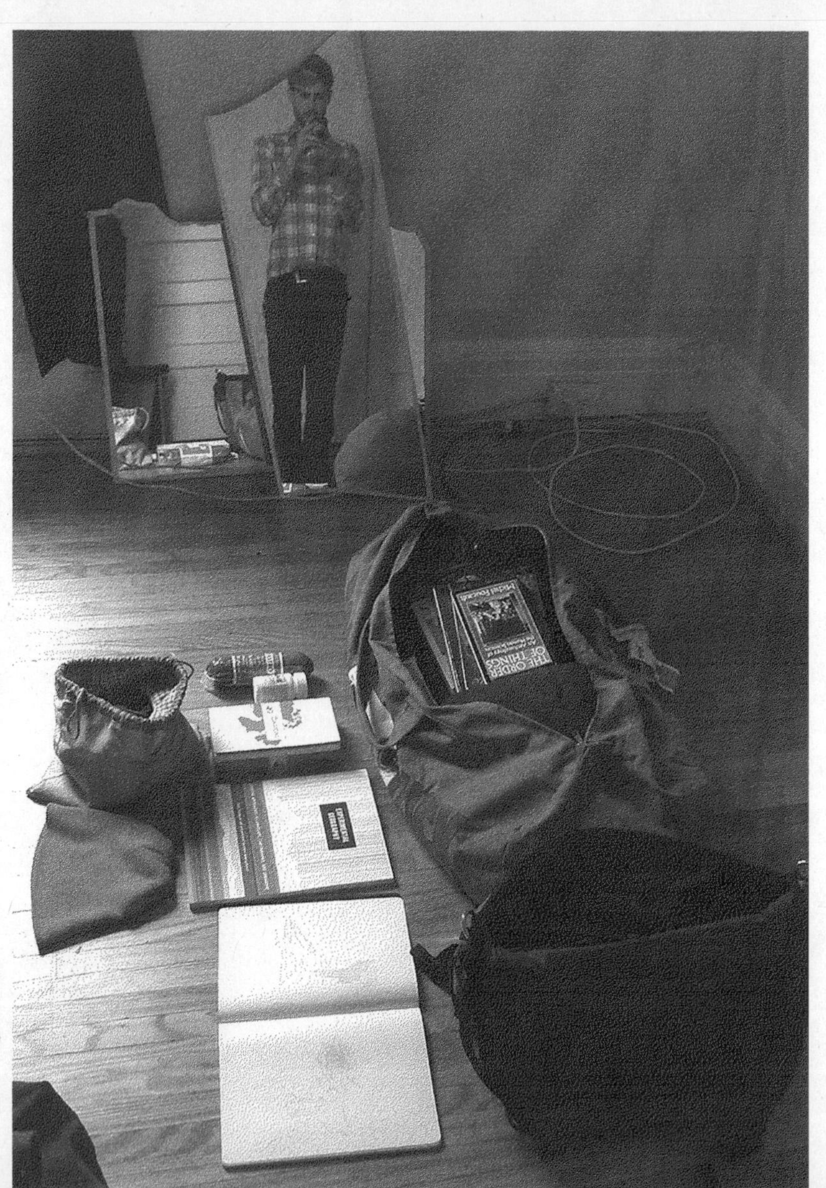

may 20

volkstuin.

gardening

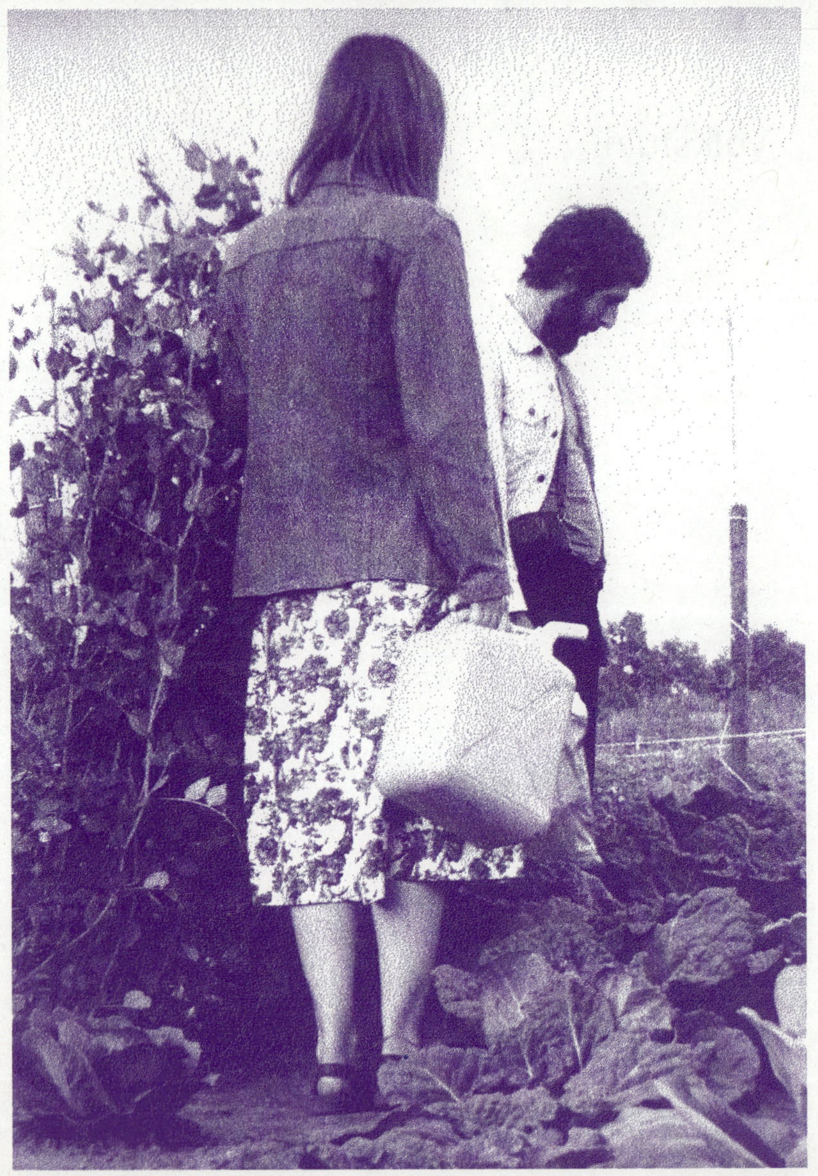

may 21

design your own functional home office.

home office

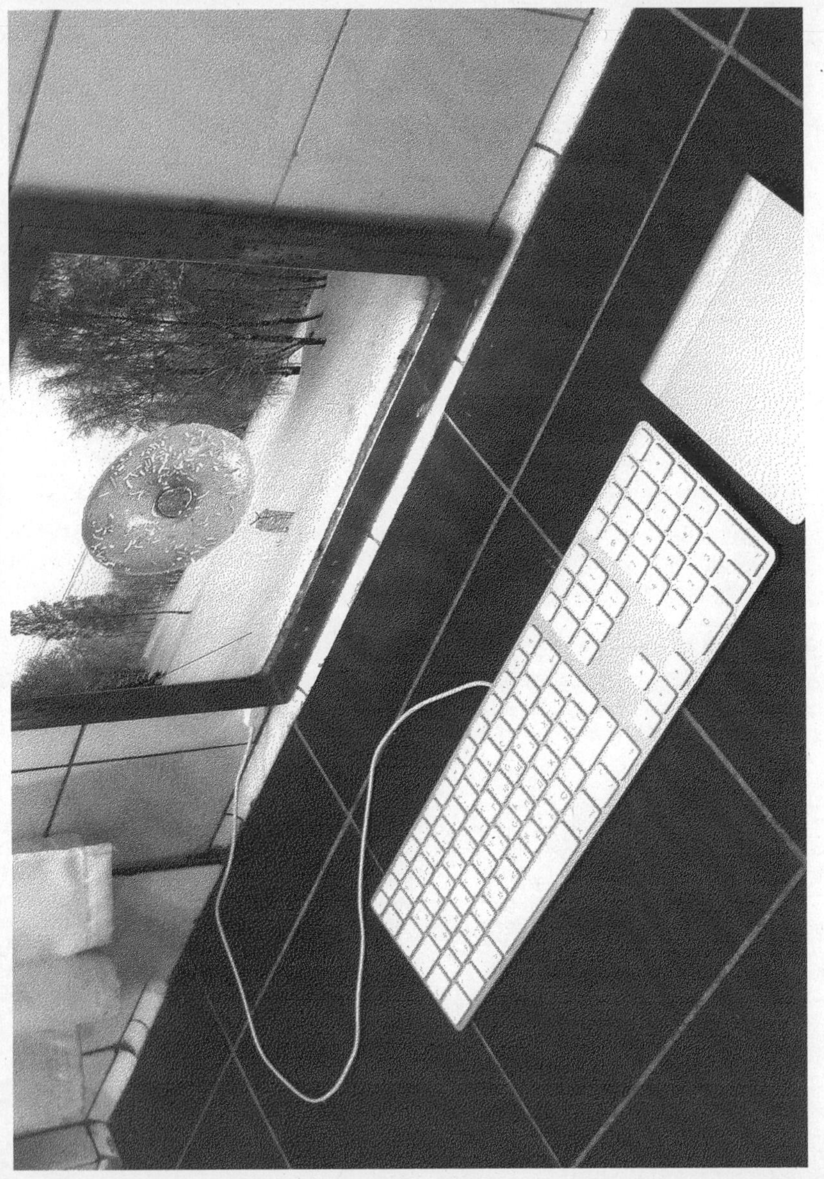

domestic workers have no future
if we are not recognized. our future
is in your hands… do something
for us. recognize our contribution!

recognition

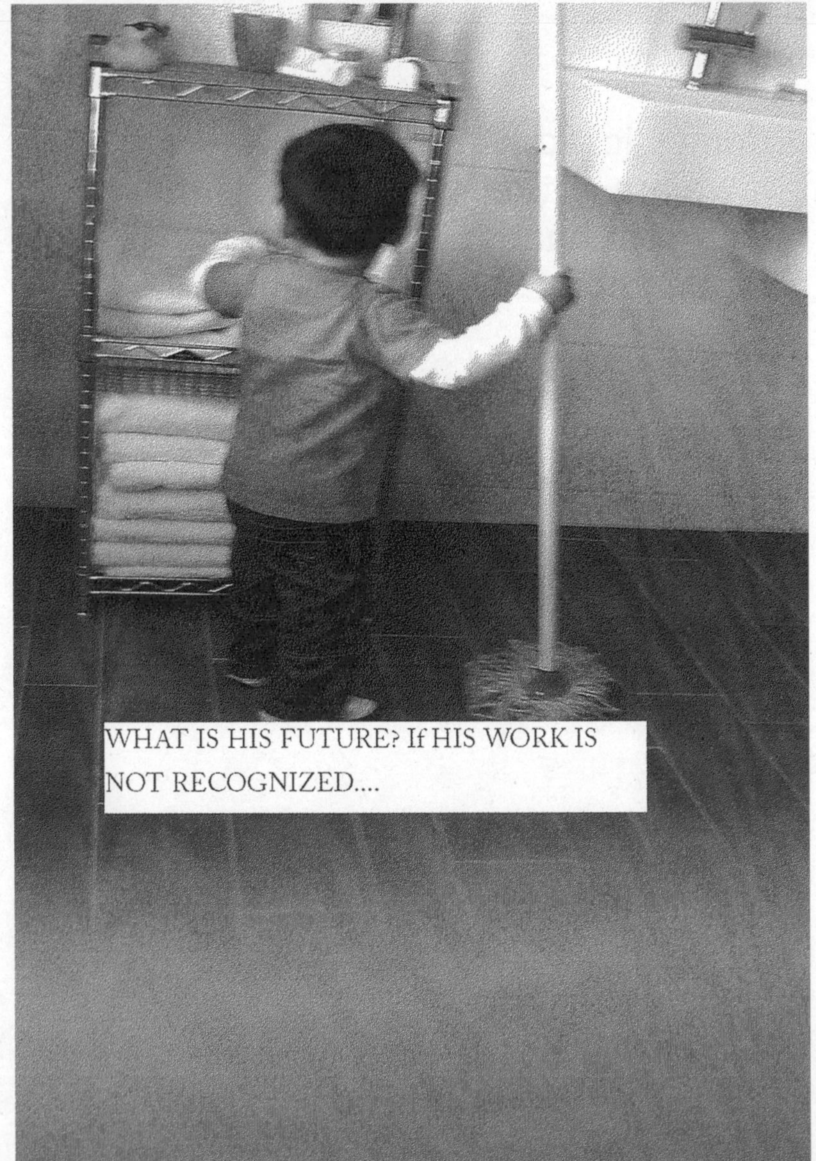
WHAT IS HIS FUTURE? If HIS WORK IS
NOT RECOGNIZED....

may 23

i need money to pay my rent so i work in a garden. it's hard work, much harder than i thought it would be!

warming up for saturday's gardening

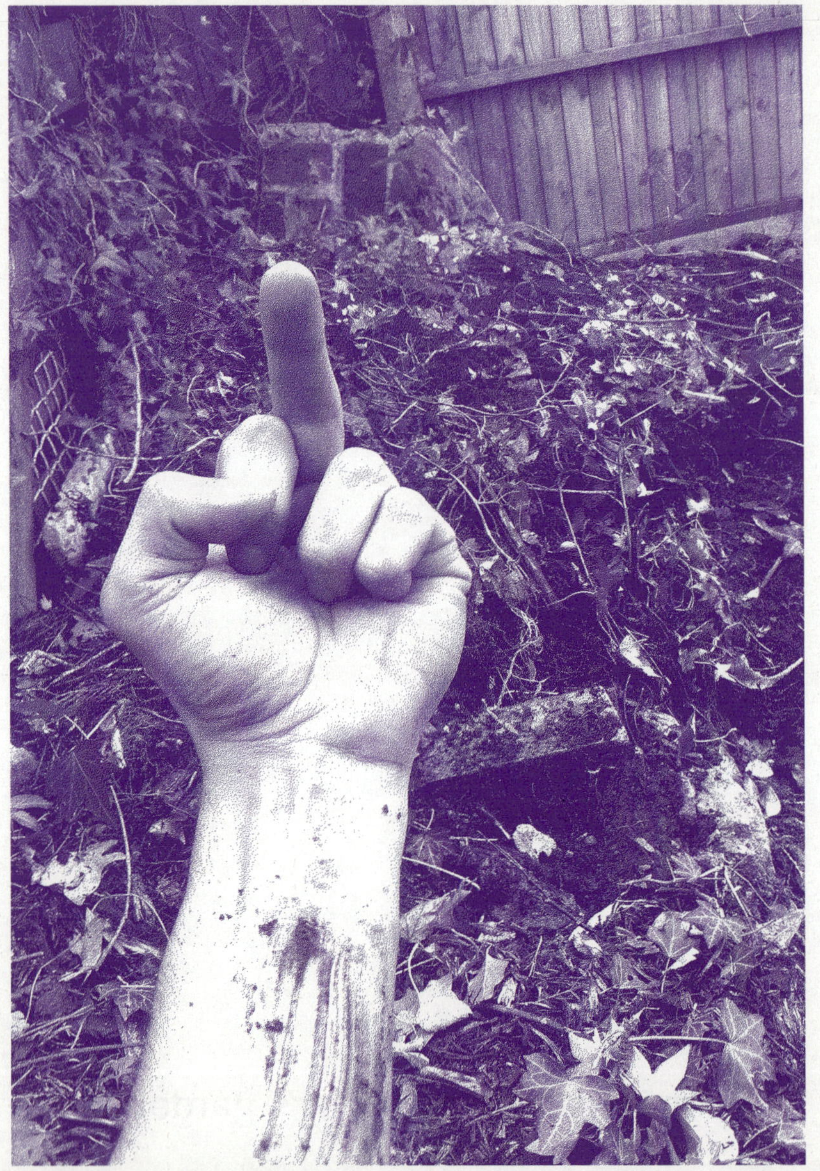

it's not my fault.

relax

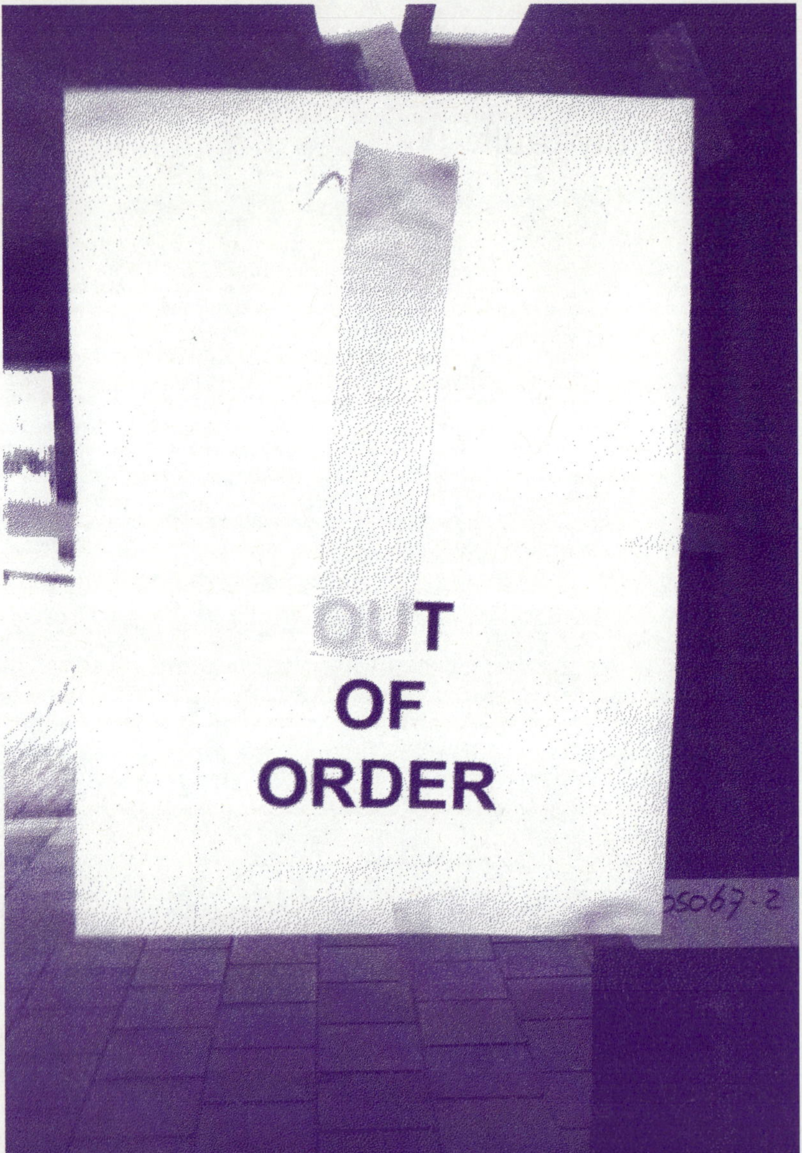

OUT
OF
ORDER

may 25

spread from "coqueteria: album de
intimidades de la mujer española"
(date unknown)

coqueteria

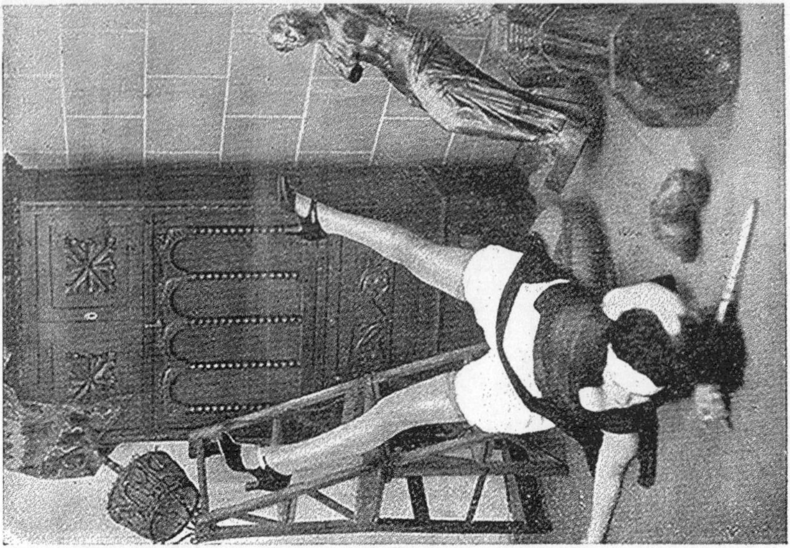

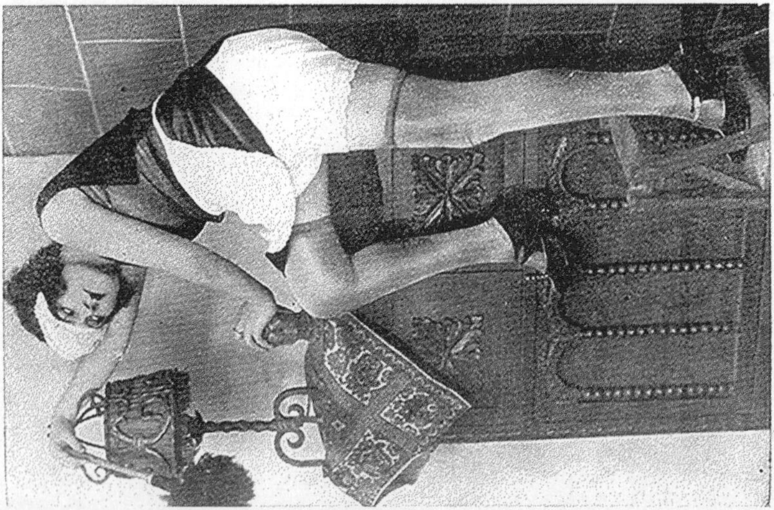

may 26

grandma on her way to the supermarket. this daily routine is keeping
her life busy.

food journey no. 1

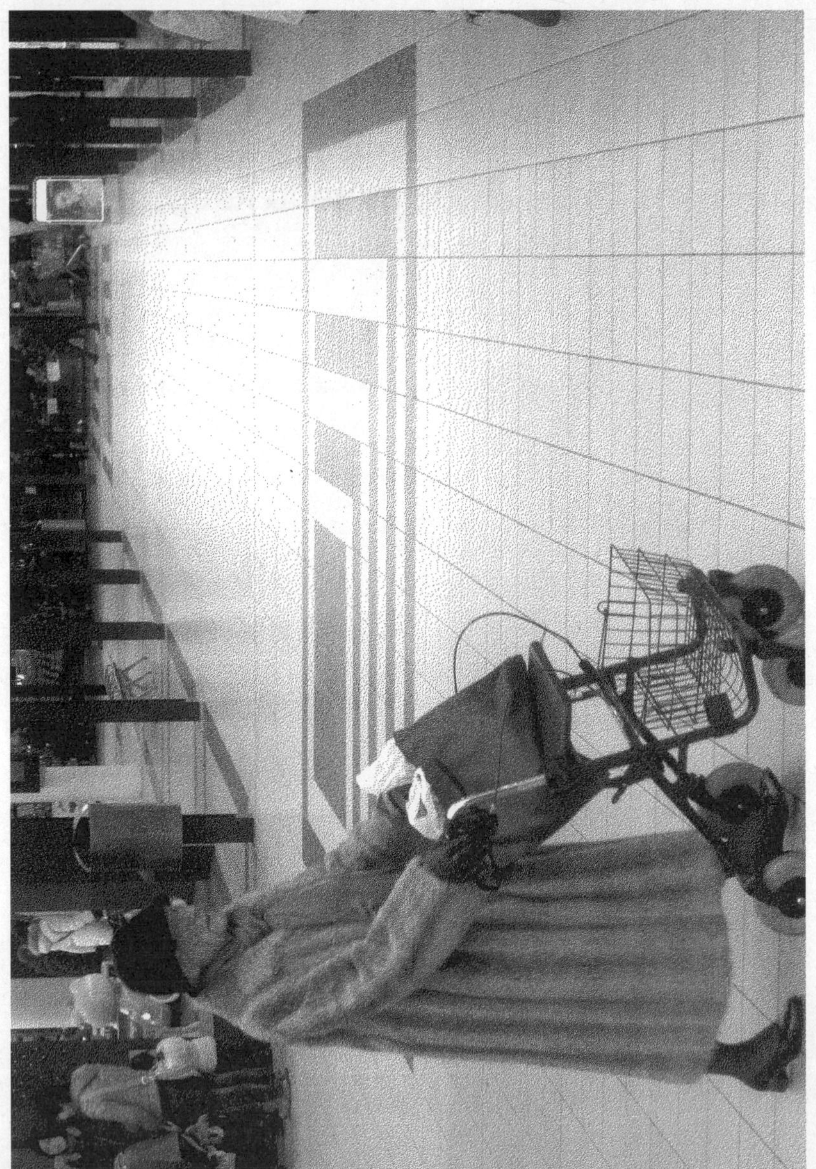

may 27

the french philosopher christine
de pizan constructing a house.

la cité des dames

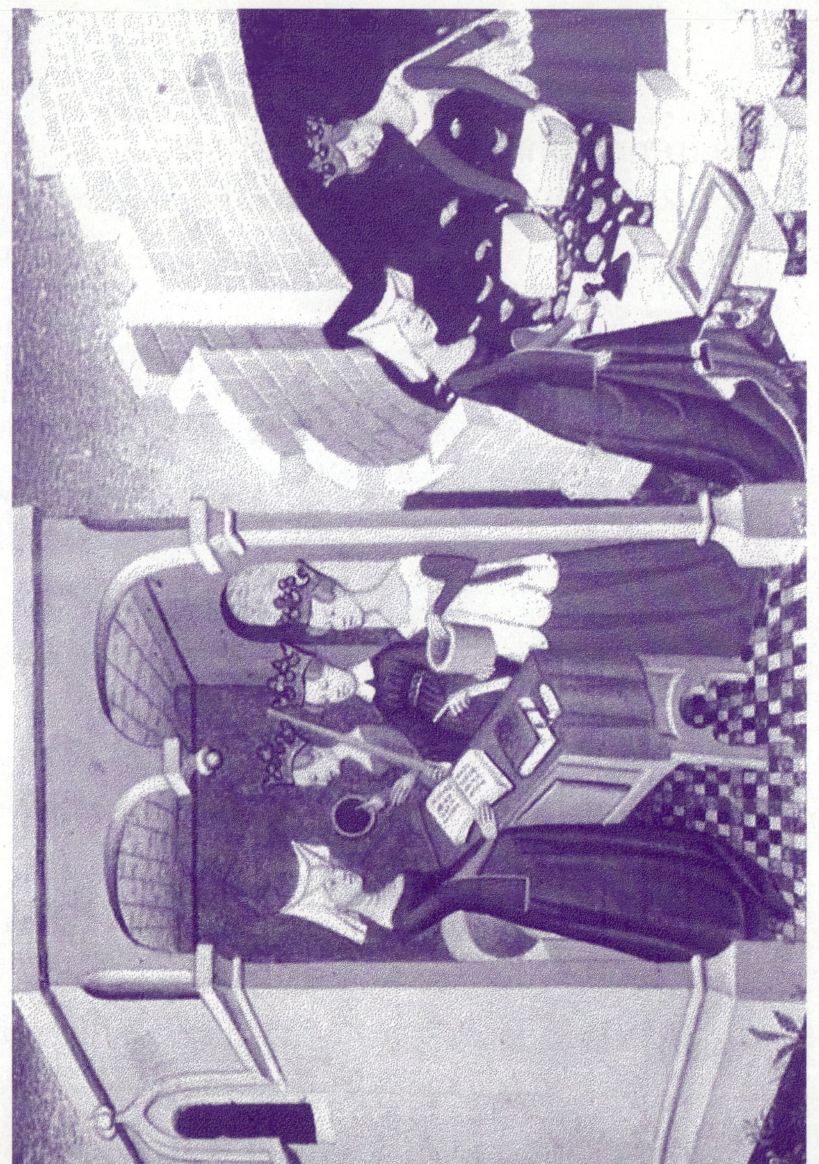

may 28

a rubbish bin behind a restaurant
for tourists on laclede's landing near
the st. louis arch. how nice of them
to label the can for those that might
think otherwise!

inedible

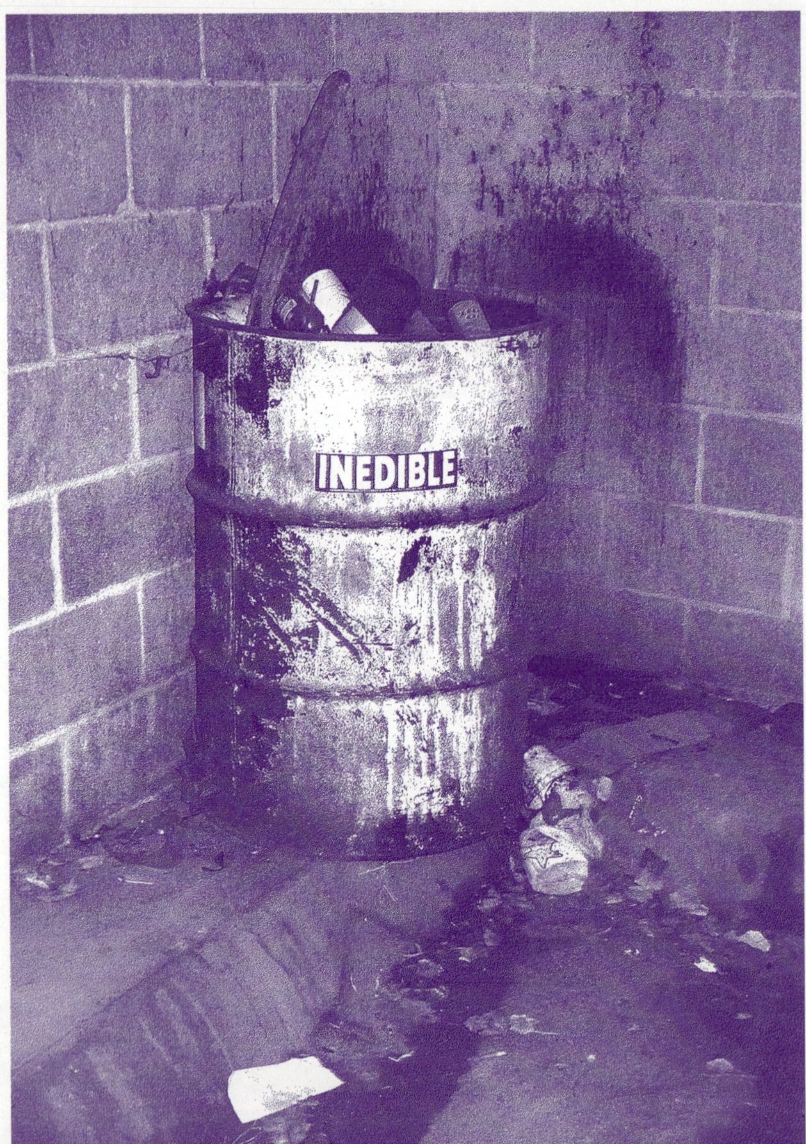
INEDIBLE

may 29

lush girl

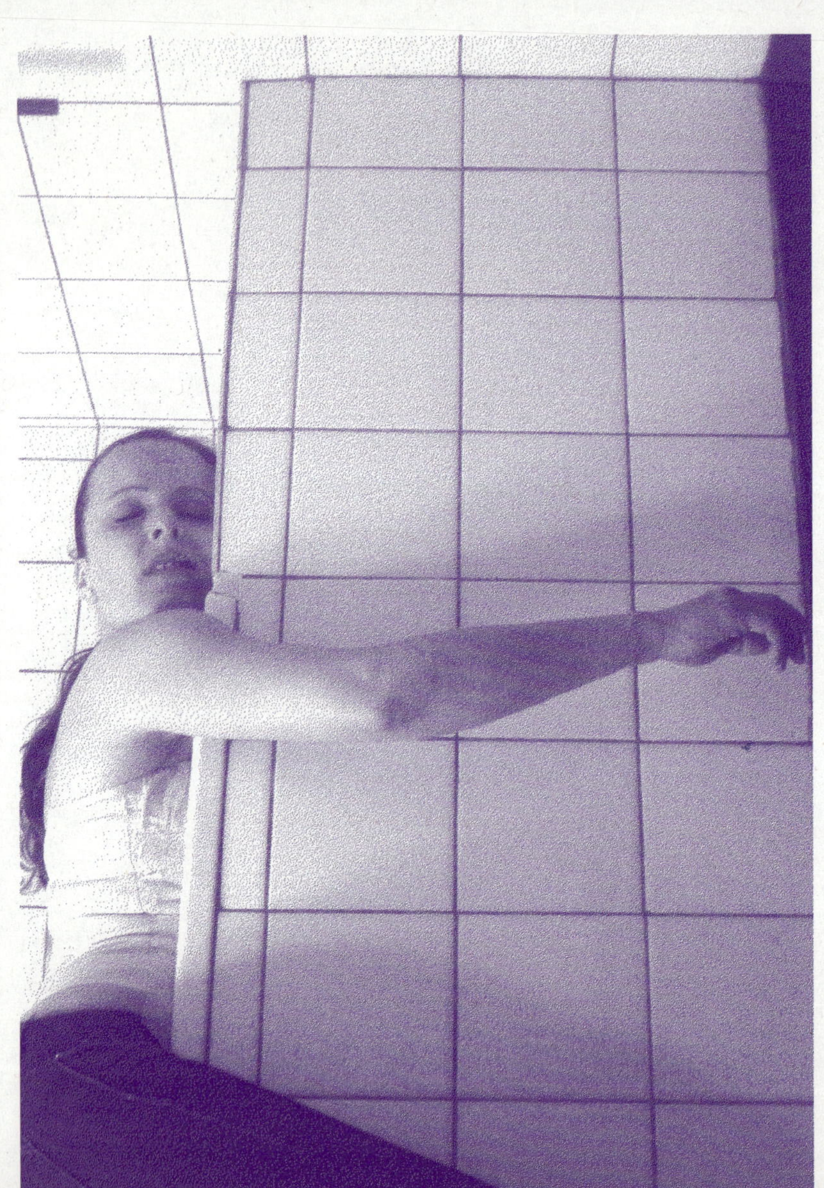

may 30

sabrina's dad baked a huge apple
pie for her birthday party. but she got
sick, so there was no party. we took
the cake to our studio and ate it in two
days between the five of us.

birthday cake

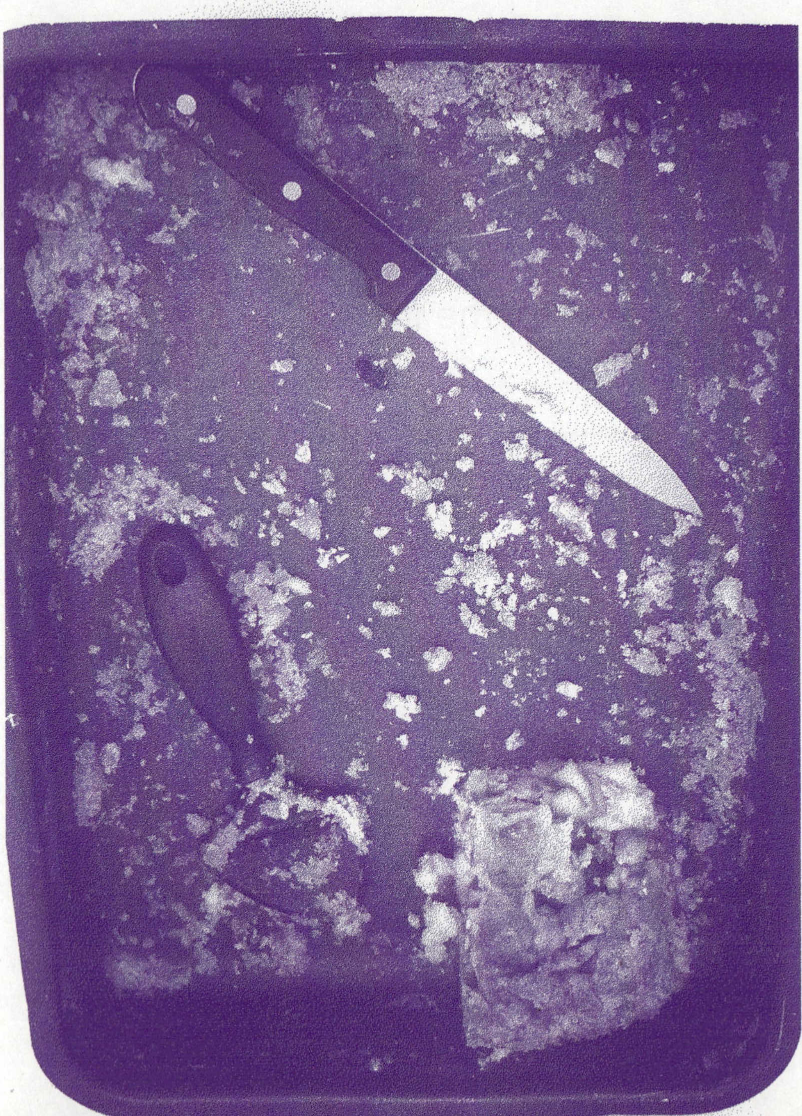

may 31

work break.

temporary housing in coldharbour

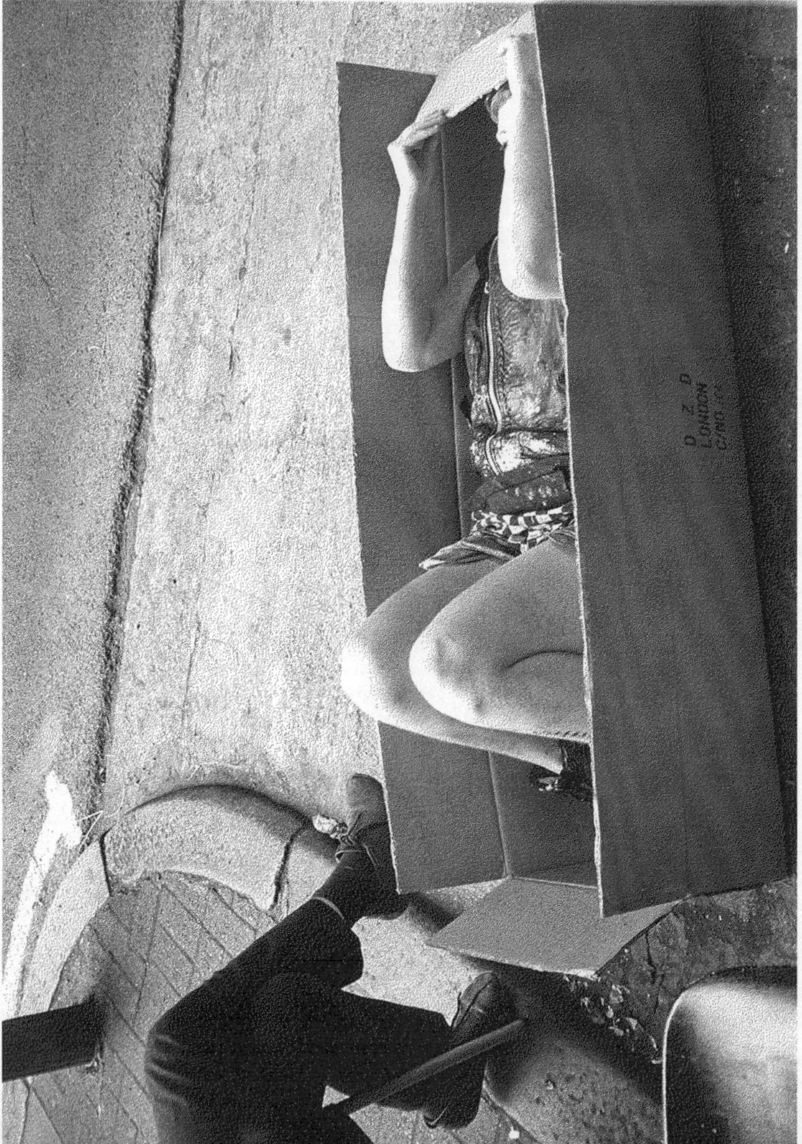

june 1

boy, sit down to pee!

thanks,
mum.

pee in pink

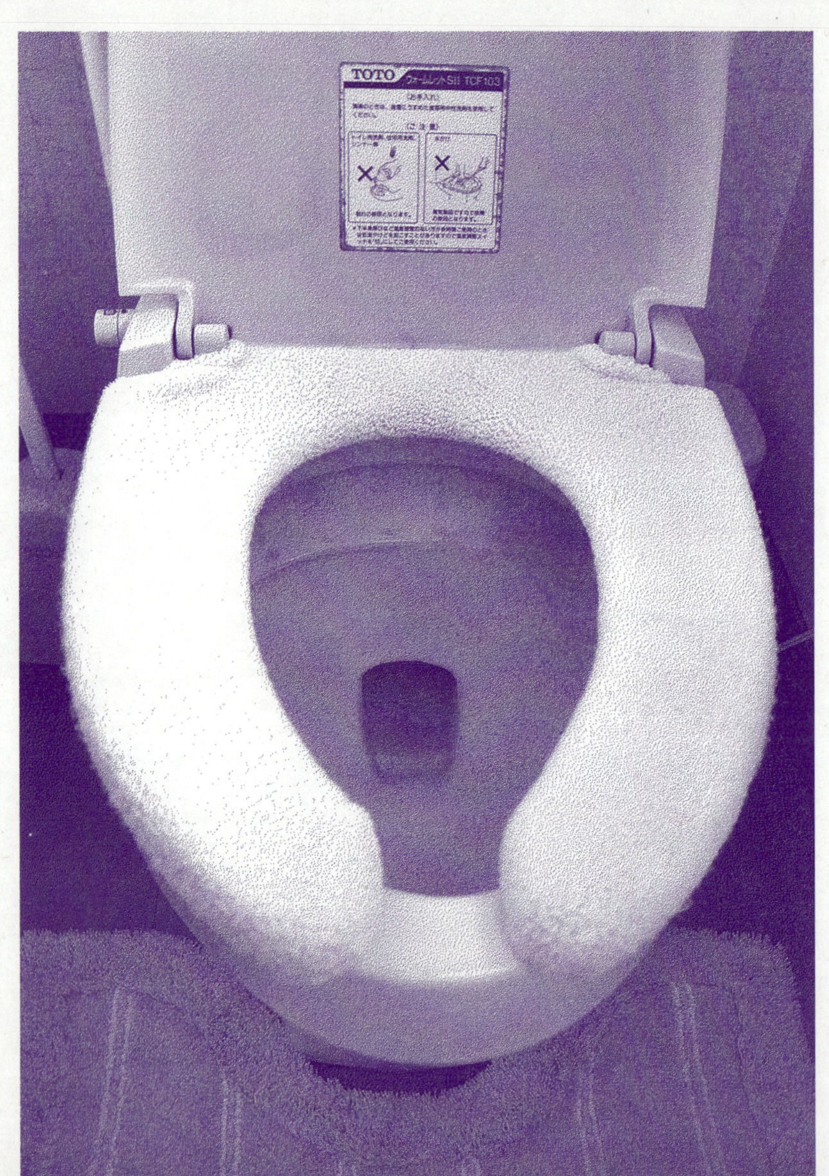

TOTO　フォームレットSII TCF103
お手入れ
ご注意

june 2

work-academy-party-bed,
work-academy-party-bed.

busy week

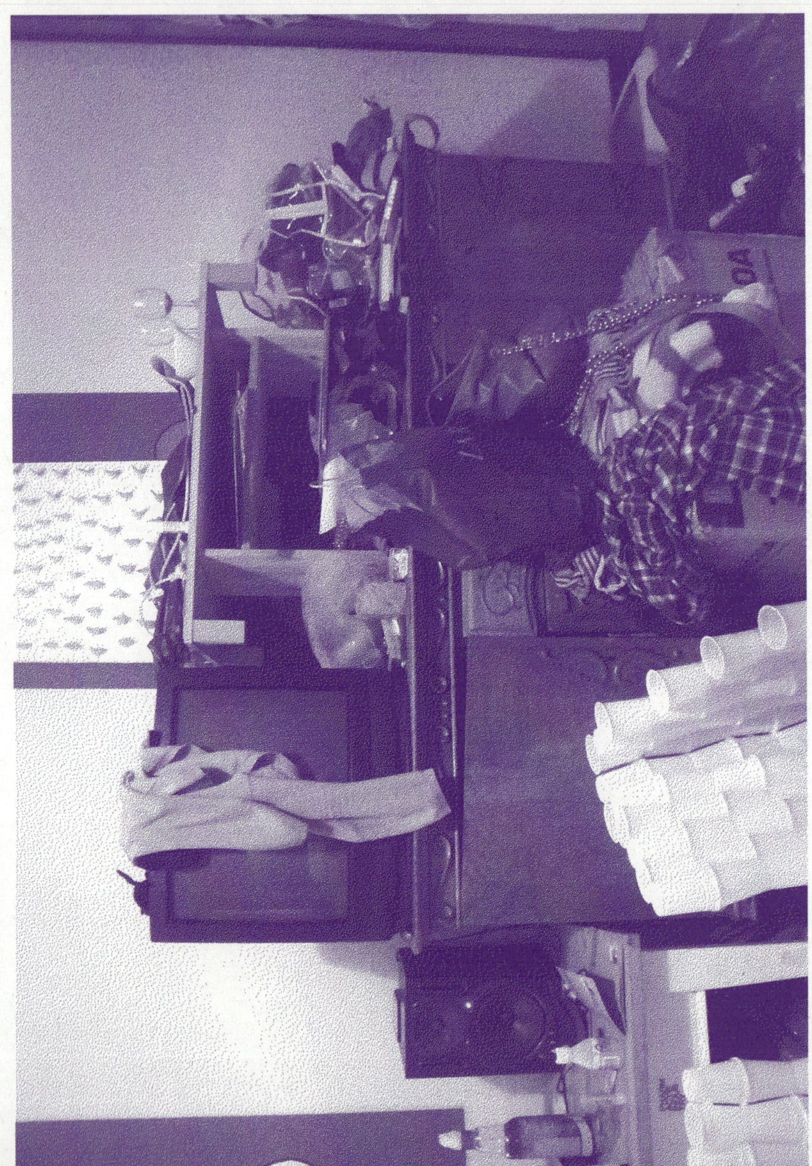

june 3

to be done not more than once
a month.

monday, hard cleaning

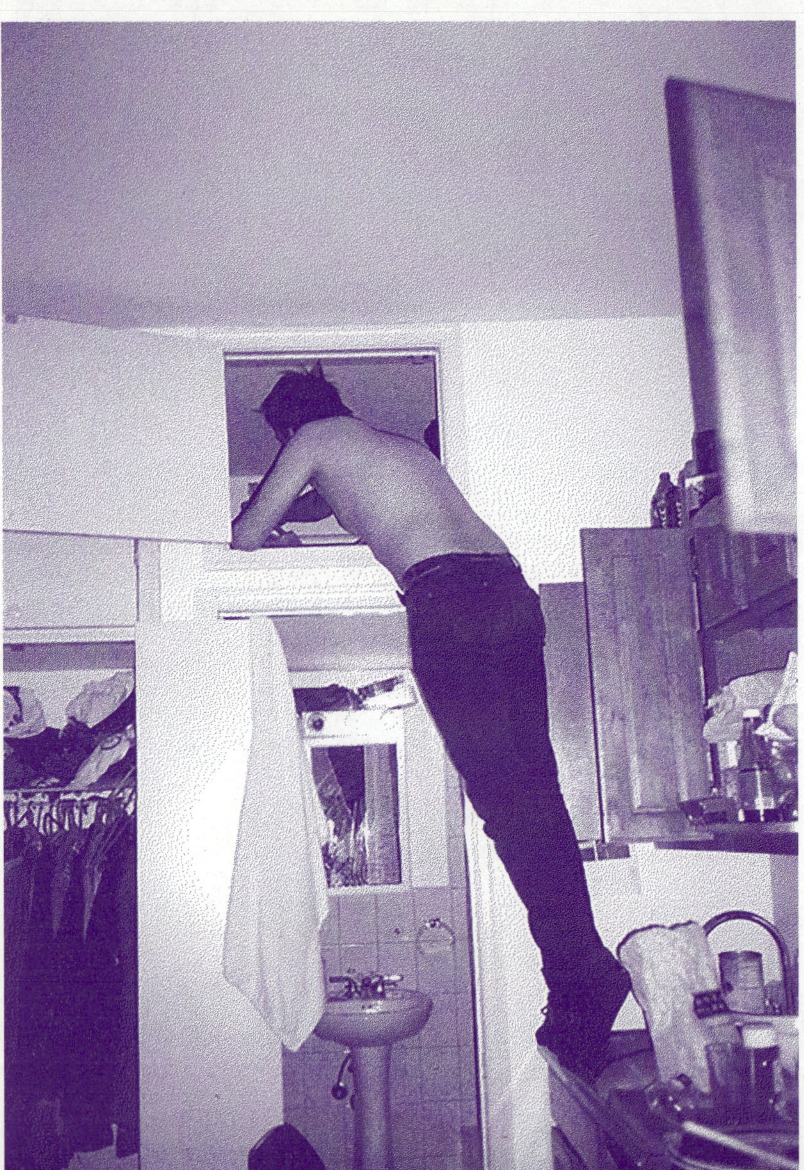

june 4

inscription on the wall: "the bathroom
is not a place for a dating."

st. petersburg communal bathroom

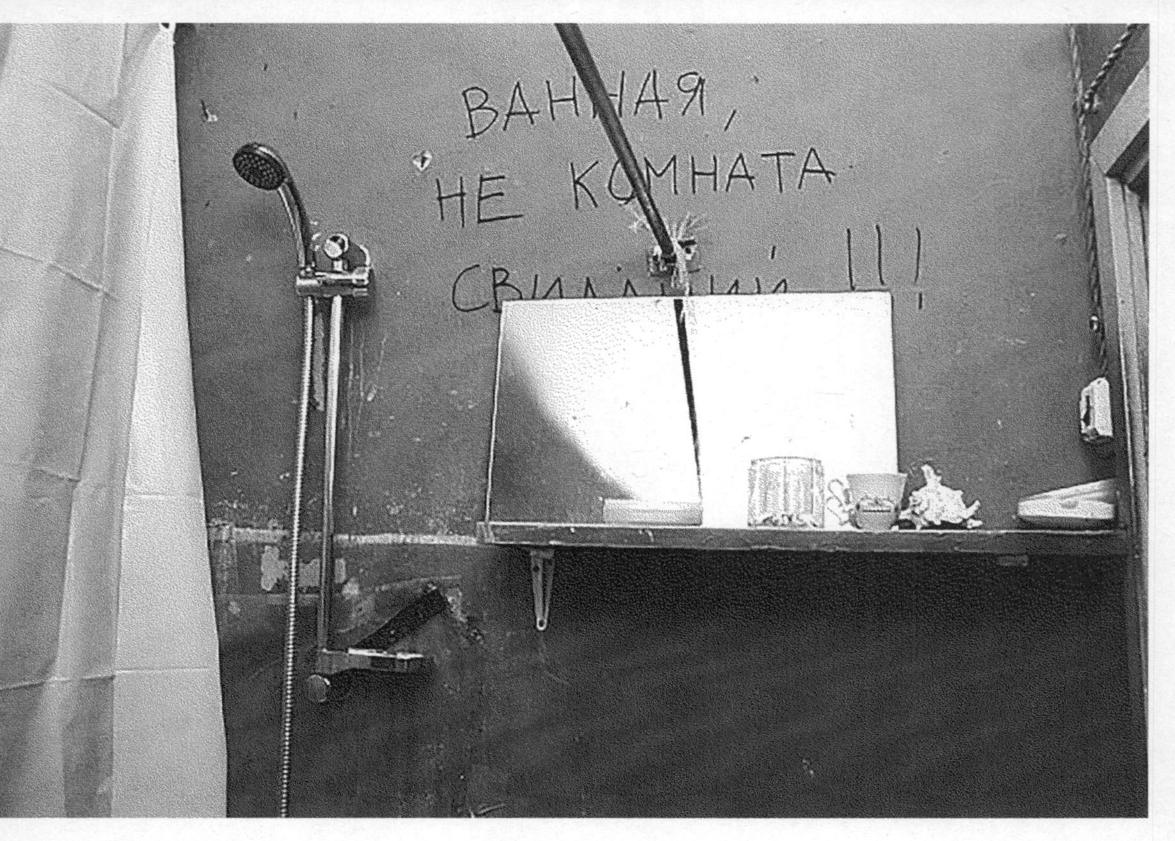

ВАННАЯ,
НЕ КОМНАТА
СВИДАНИЙ !!!

june 5

time for a surprise on the street.

oyster

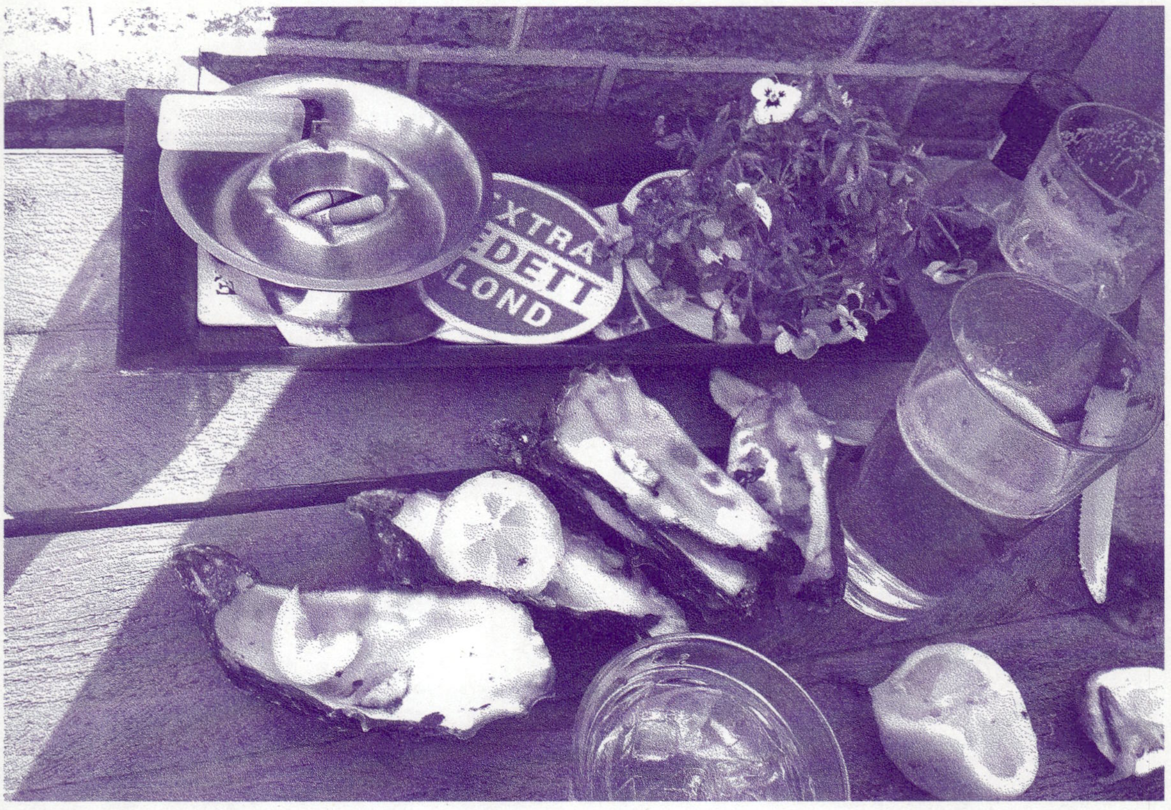

XTRA
DETT
LOND

june 6

sharks

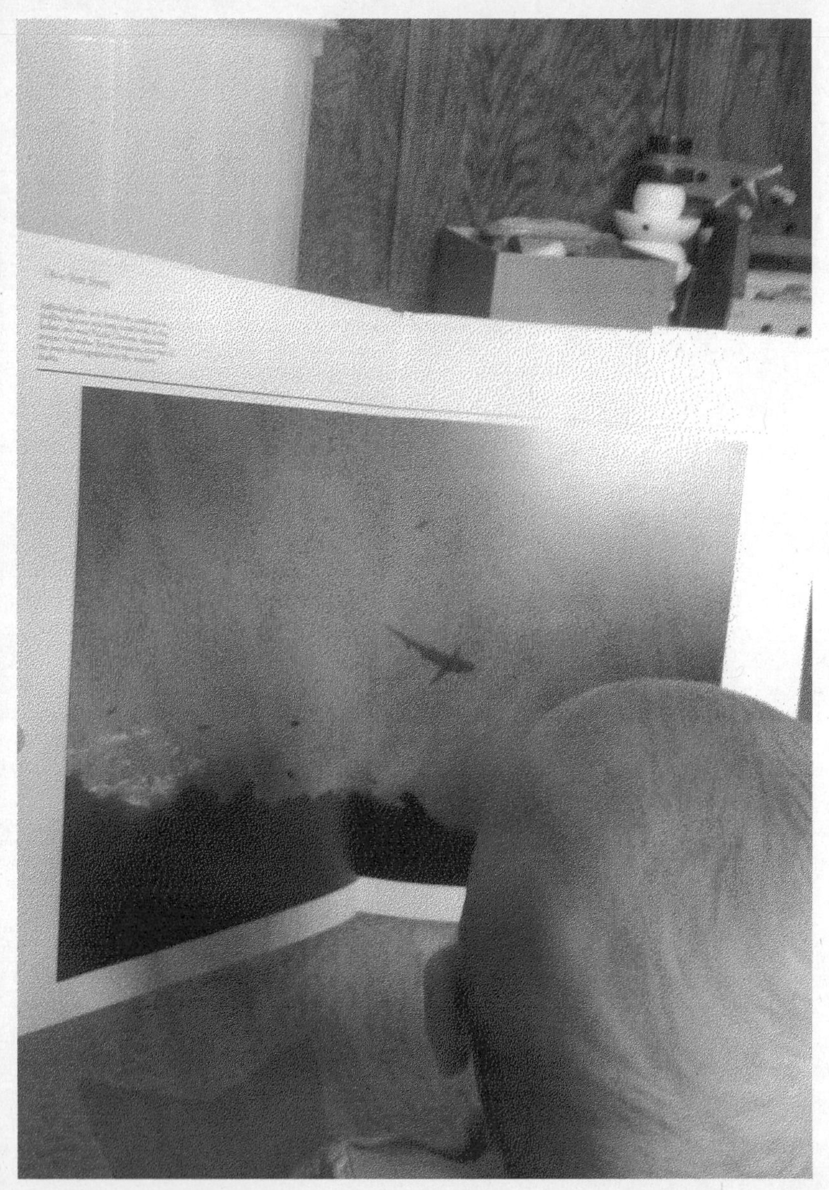

june 7

when you wake up and there is a war
into your living room and you feel
afraid of humans.

siesta

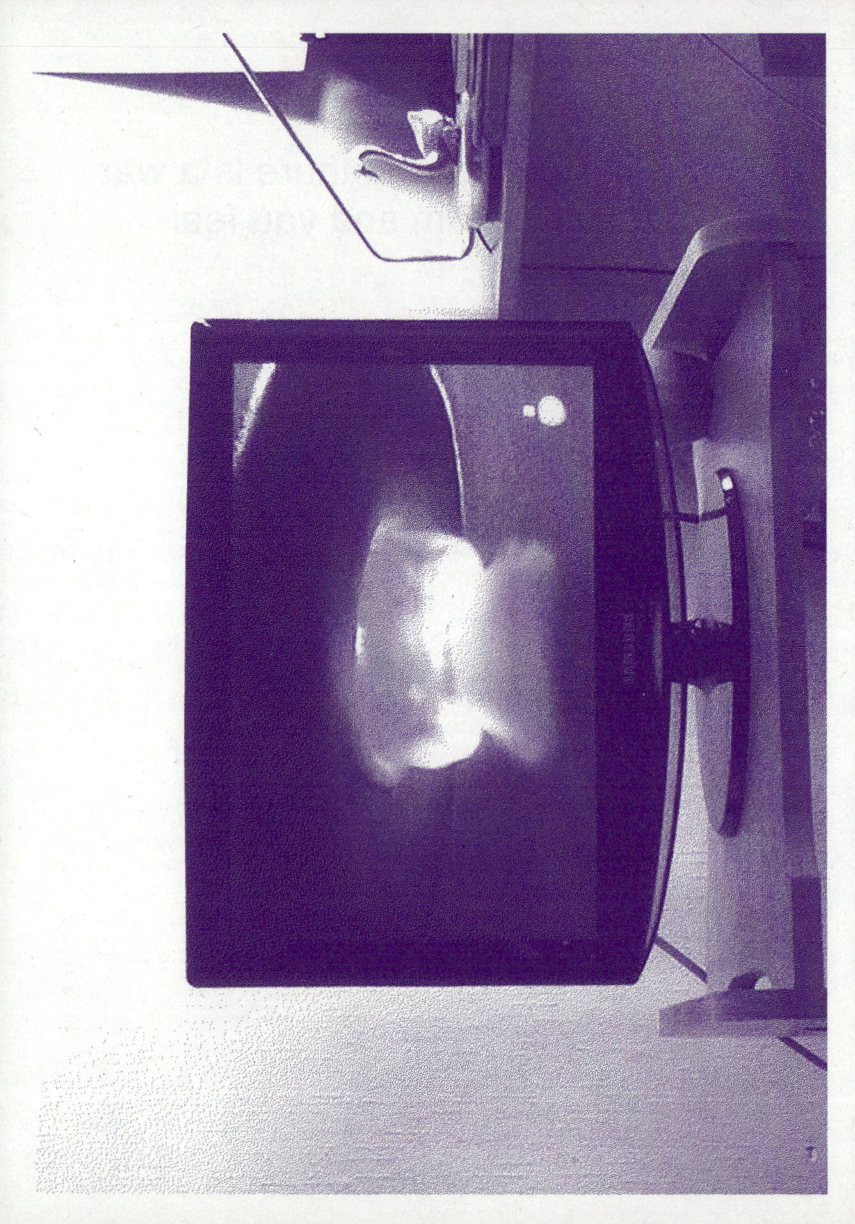

june 8

we often asked ourselves: is there life after being a migrant domestic worker? my answer is yes! but we need to work hard and be dedicated to achieve this. we also need to learn the basic mathematics of earnings - expenses = savings. every sunday during my day off i spend some time studying and some time volunteering serving my fellow domestic workers. i chose the entrepreneurship course because that is how i see myself after being a domestic worker. on my graduation day, i even received "the best business plan" award.

the domestic worker can be
an entrepreneur

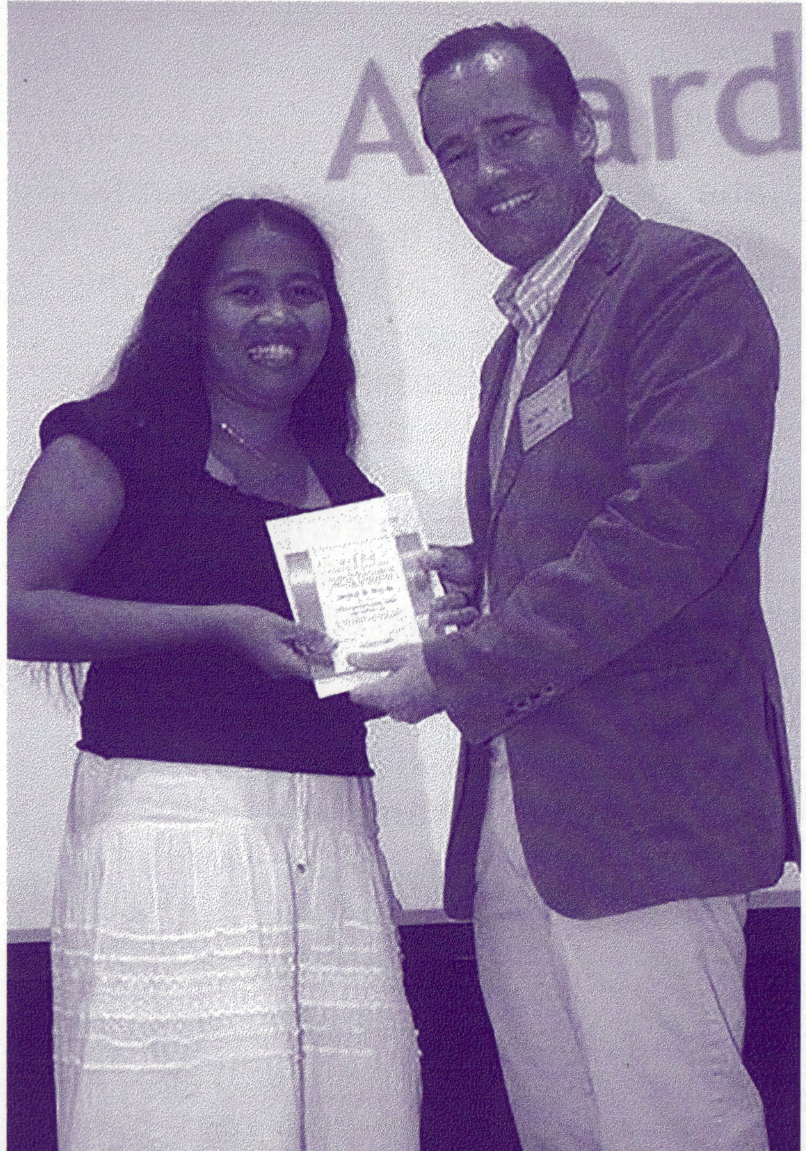
Award

june 9

my brother and me sharing a room.
cleaning it, before the cleaner comes.

the second photograph I ever took

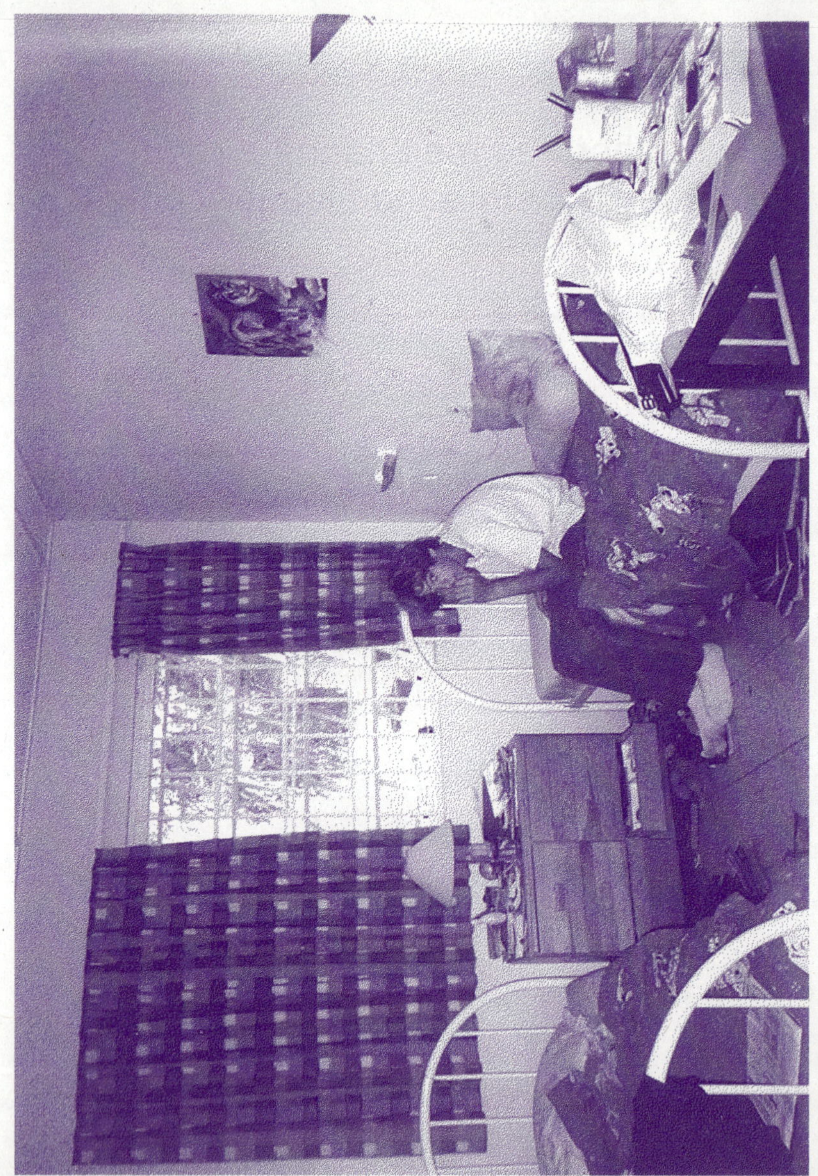

june 10

twenty pegs, twenty garments.

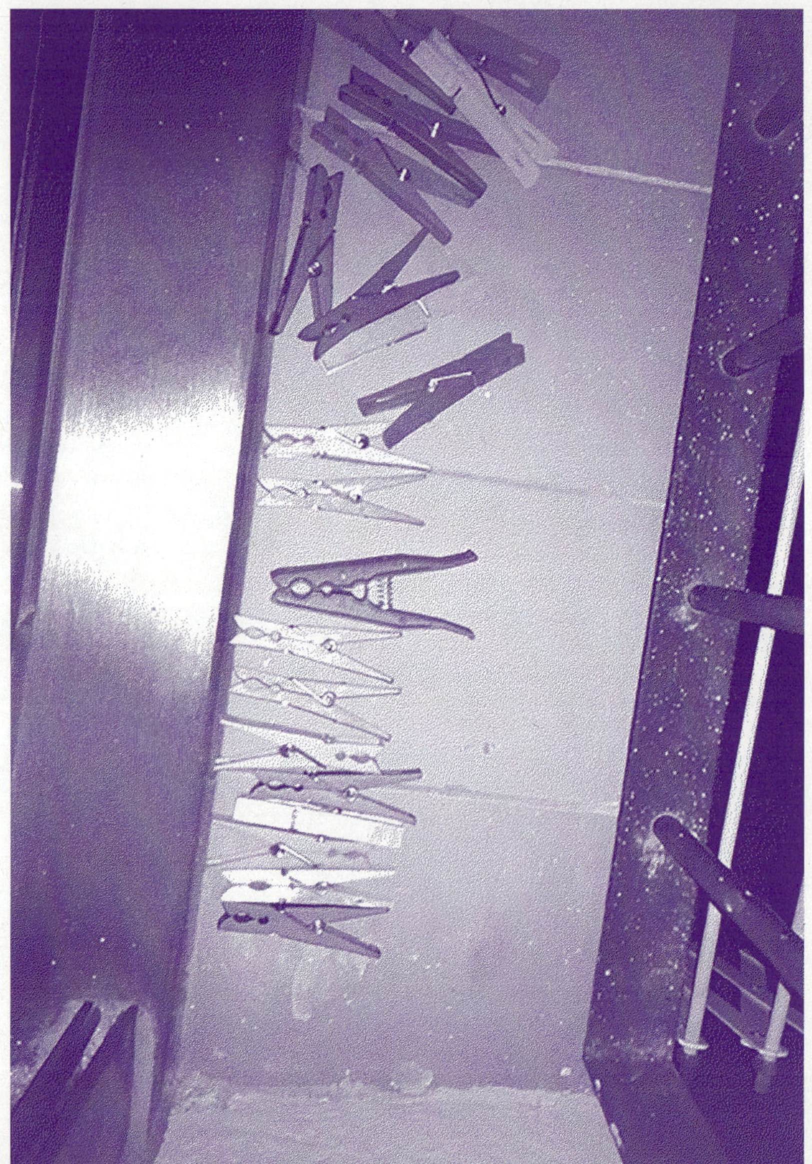

june 11

doing research at the new york public
library's picture collection.

american way of life, 1942

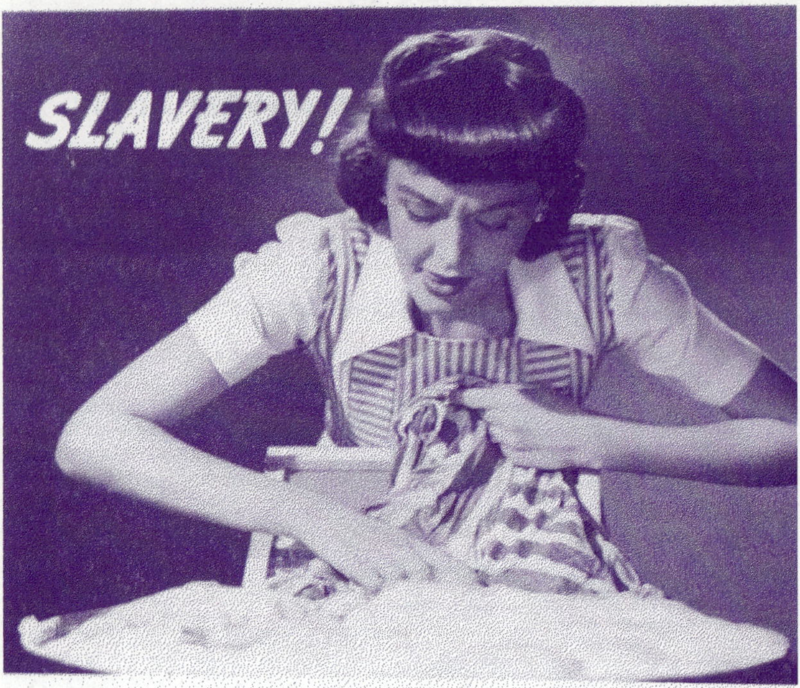

june 12

the moment that it's impossible to write
something intelligent unless you take
40 minutes to find the perfect sound-
track to your ideas.

cognitive capitalism

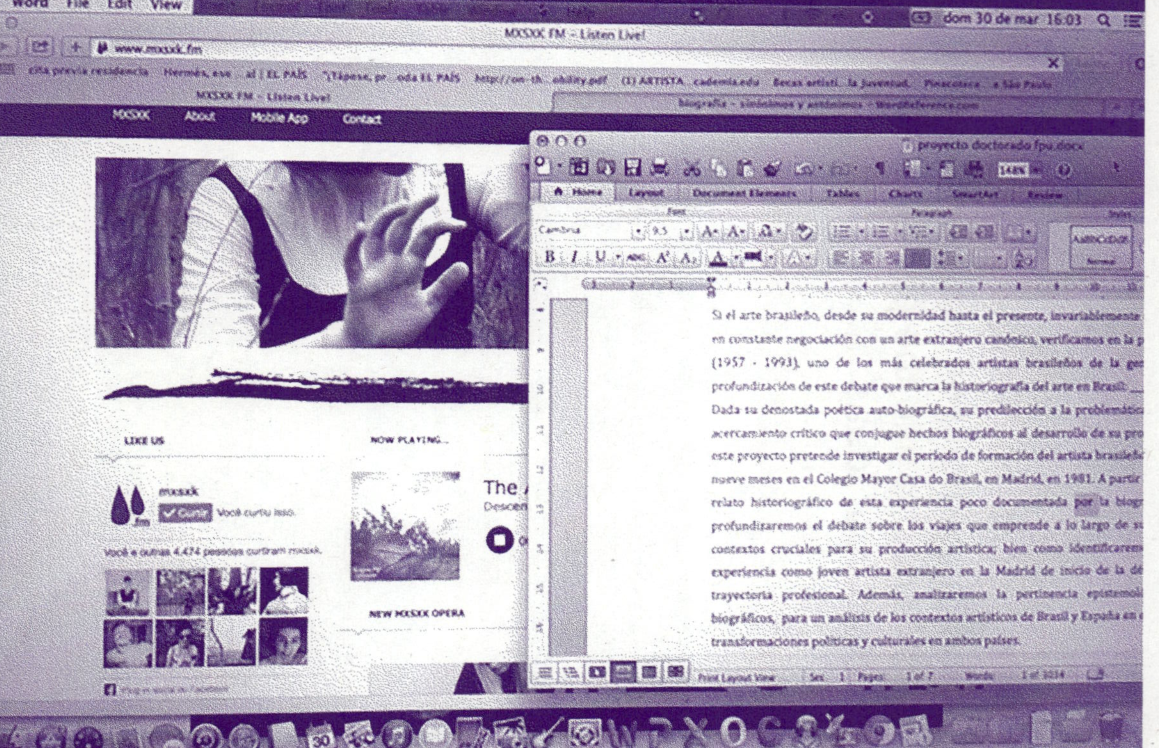

Word   File   Edit   View
dom 30 de mar 16:03
MXSXK FM - Listen Live!
www.mxsxk.fm
MXSXK   About   Mobile App   Contact
LIKE US
NOW PLAYING...
The A
NEW MXSXK OPERA
mxsxk
Você curtiu isso.
Você e outras 4.474 pessoas curtiram mxsxk.
proyecto doctorado fpu.docx
Home   Layout   Document Elements   Tables   Charts   SmartArt   Review
Cambria
B I U
Print Layout View   Sec 1   Pages   1 of 7   Words   1 of 1014
Si el arte brasileño, desde su modernidad hasta el presente, invariablemente
en constante negociación con un arte extranjero canónico, verificamos en la p
(1957 - 1993), uno de los más celebrados artistas brasileños de la gen
profundización de este debate que marca la historiografía del arte en Brasil.
Dada su denostada poética auto-biográfica, su predilección a la problemática
acercamiento crítico que conjuga hechos biográficos al desarrollo de su pro
este proyecto pretende investigar el período de formación del artista brasileño
nueve meses en el Colegio Mayor Casa do Brasil, en Madrid, en 1981. A partir
relato historiográfico de esta experiencia poco documentada por la biogr
profundizaremos el debate sobre los viajes que emprende a lo largo de su
contextos cruciales para su producción artística; bien como identificarem
experiencia como joven artista extranjero en la Madrid de inicio de la dé
trayectoria profesional. Además, analizaremos la pertinencia epistemol
biográficos, para un análisis de los contextos artísticos de Brasil y España en
transformaciones políticas y culturales en ambos países.

june 13

waiting for the appearance of a ghost
maid during a night time tour in the
attics of casa milà.

la pedrera horror story

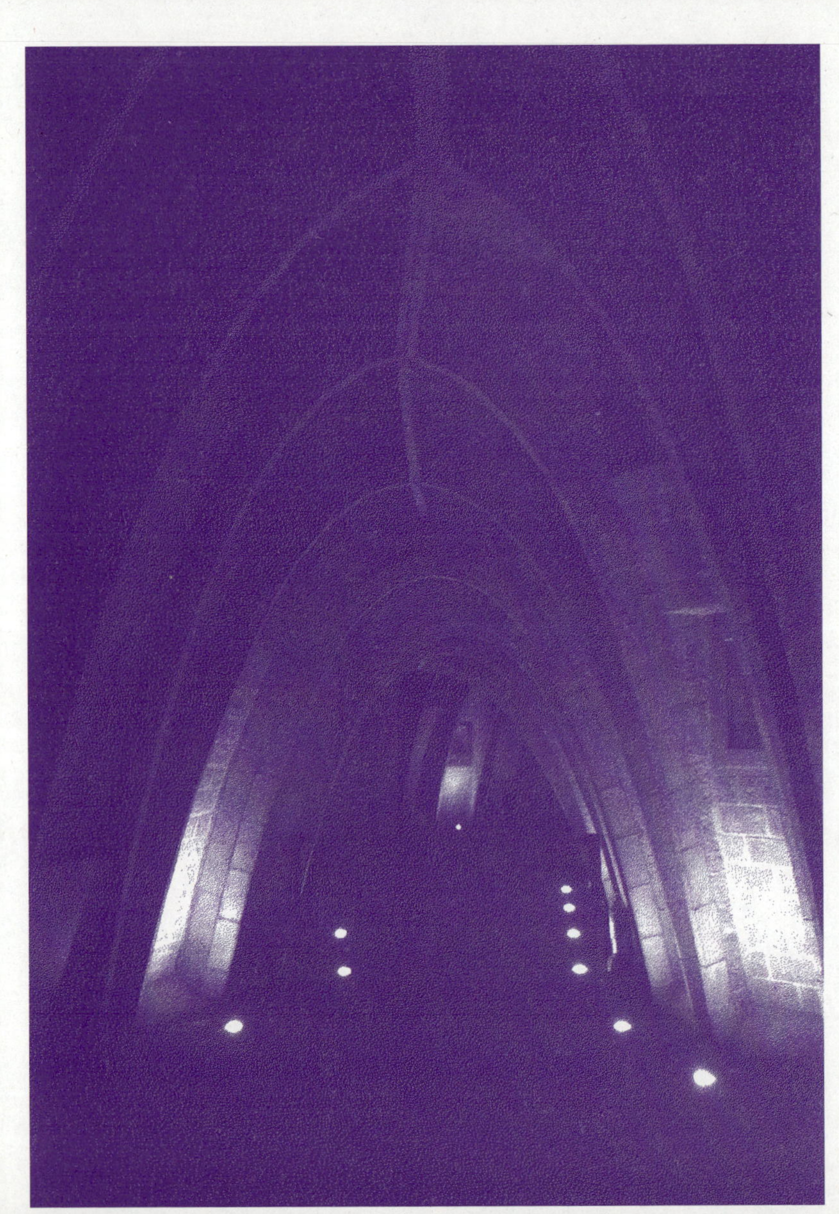

june 14

tumble dryer filter (img. 1) and dried
clothes in a tumble dryer (img. 2).
from the same drying sequence.

lint explorer

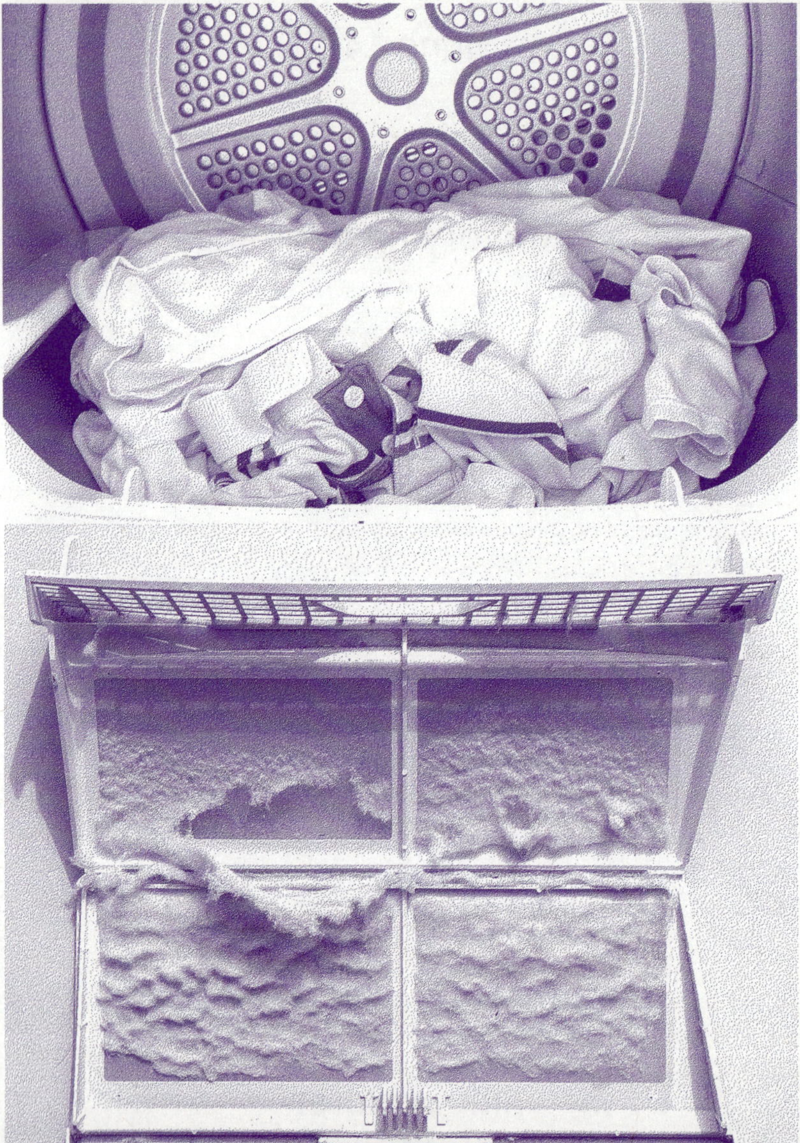

the midnight rangers: are you a person who can't sleep in the night? are you a nightwatcher? are you a nightstalker? a clubber? an insomniac? a streetpunk? whoever you are, you need something, someone to take care of you in the night when all 'the normals' sleep.
so, say thanks for all those people who work to serve anything you need till the dawn. some of them are working 24 hours, some started when the moon showed its face, some open their 'shop' at 00:00:00.

24 hours

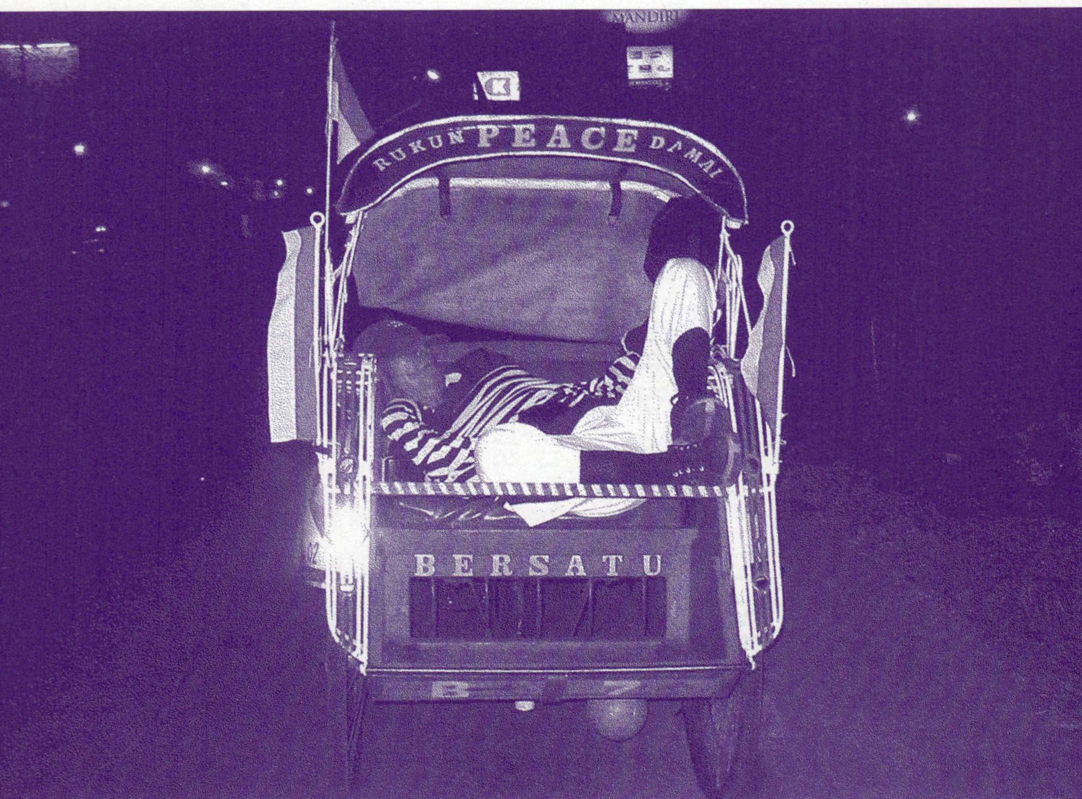

MANDIRI
RUKUN PEACE DAMAI
BERSATU

june 16

collective cocktail production
at the birthday party of my friend.

collective cooking

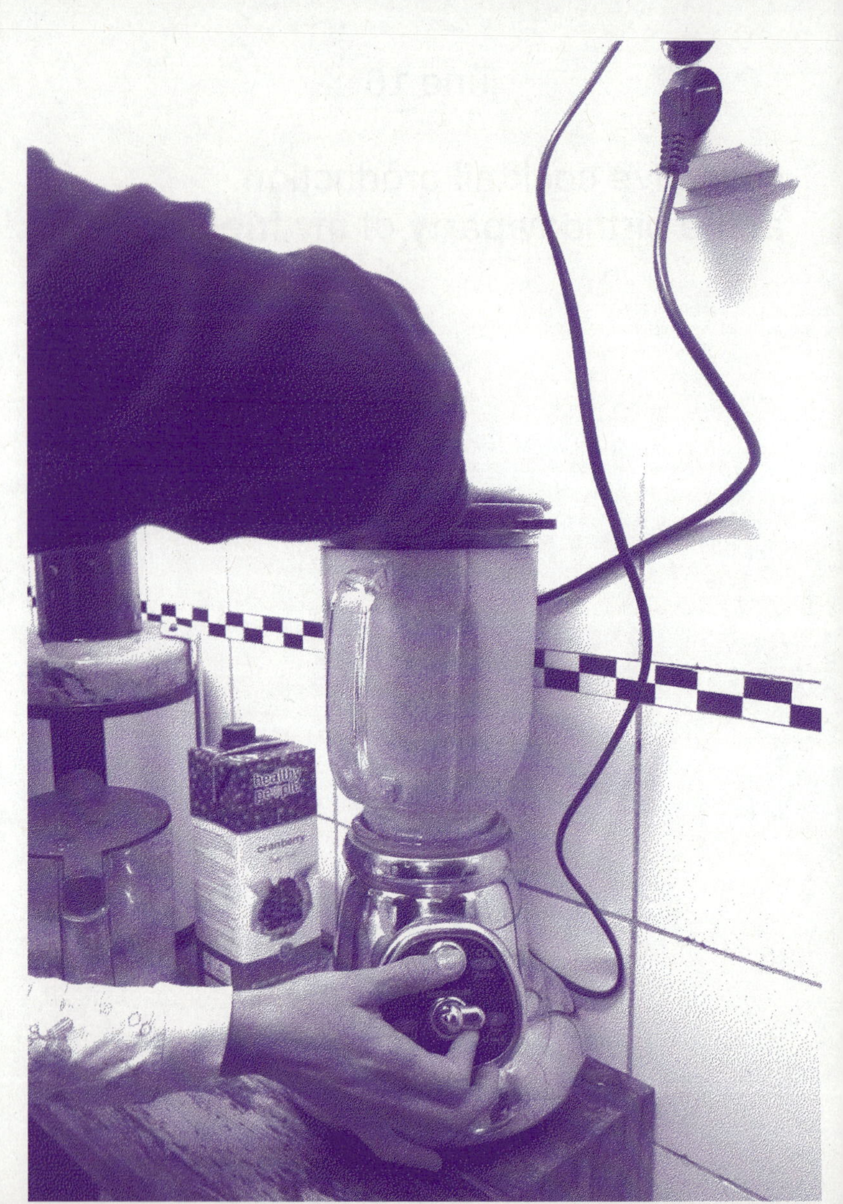

healthy
people
cranberry

june 17

truth will make you free

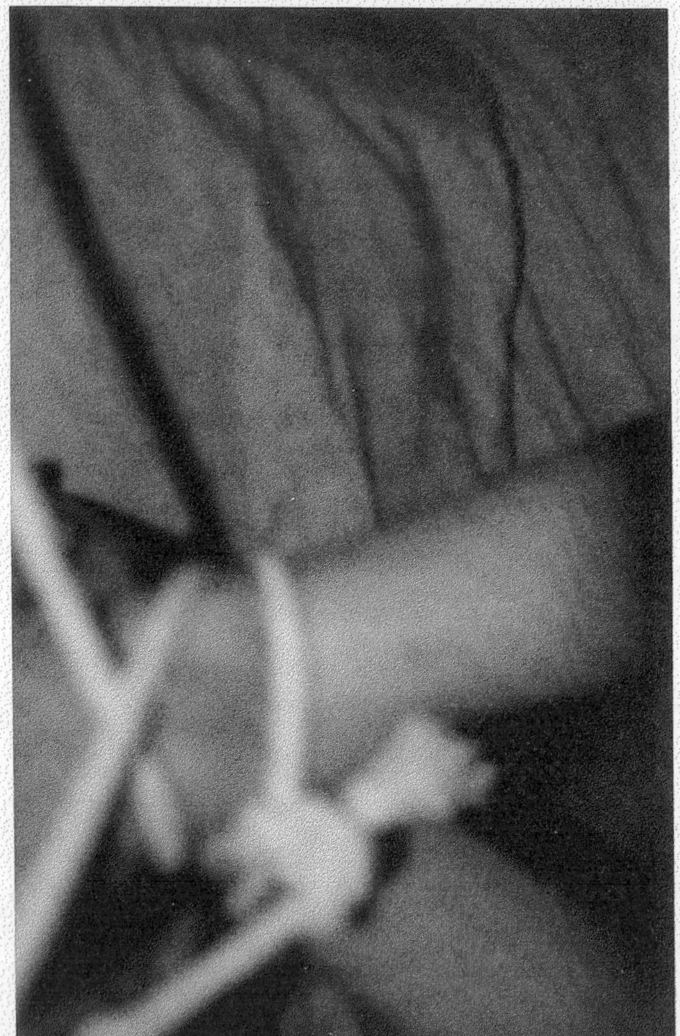

june 18

a handsome worker fails to construct
the billboard image effectively. it takes
him over an hour to compose the advert
in which his face and body are represented. his presence as a body is
shown rather than represented in this
labour. this performance was made on
24th june 2016 with a public audience
in london for the rca degree show.

billboard performance,
—
performing masculinity

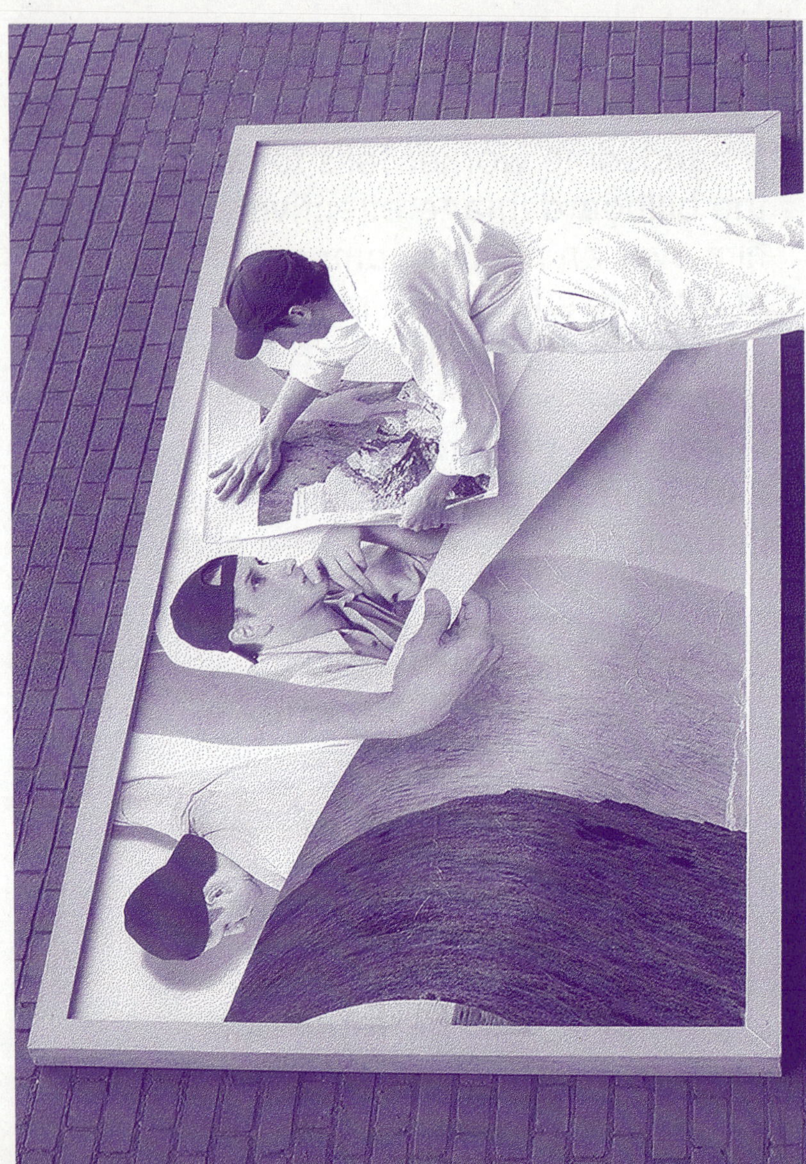

june 19

always use a step-stool to reach high places.

dutch treat

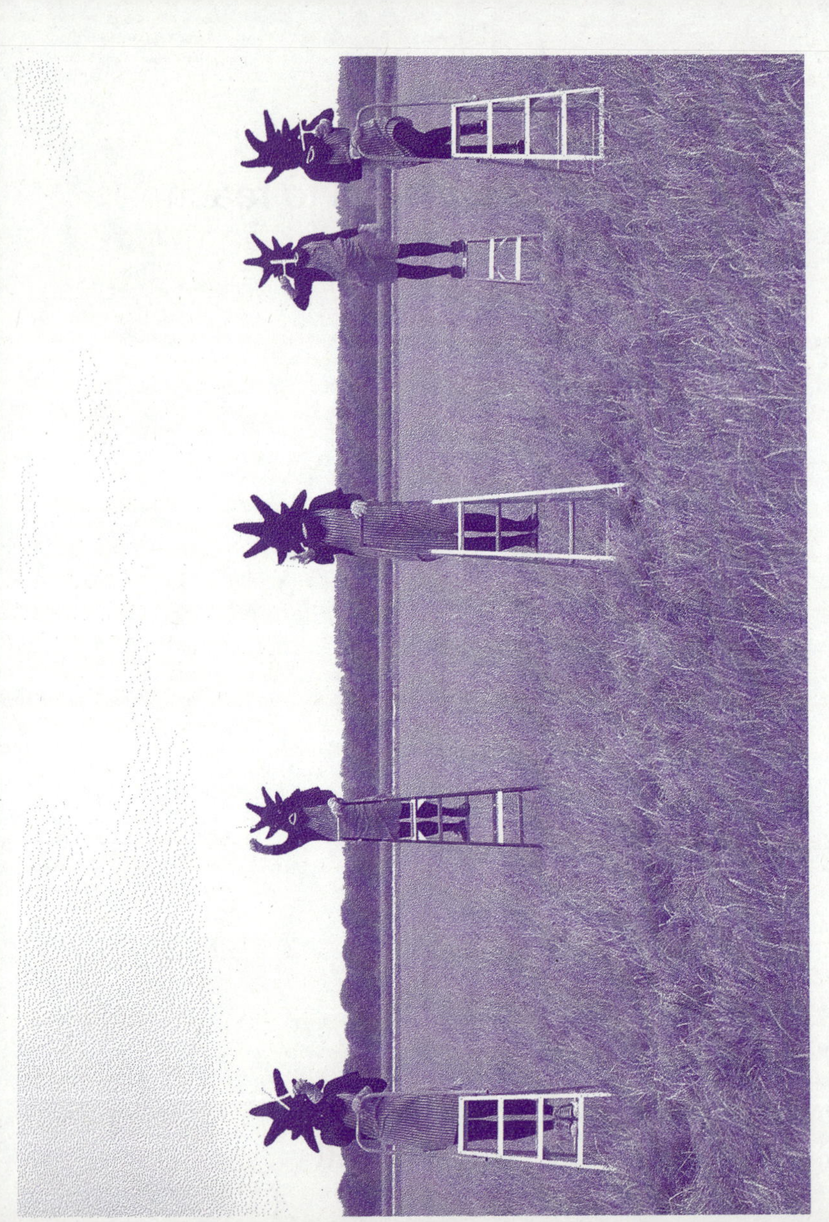

june 20

store local farmers' organic vegetables
for urban customers to pick them up.
if you have a urban space with a regular
opening schedule, offer it at no cost
to local farmers/customers as a picking
point and let monsanto burn in hell.

not going to the supermarket

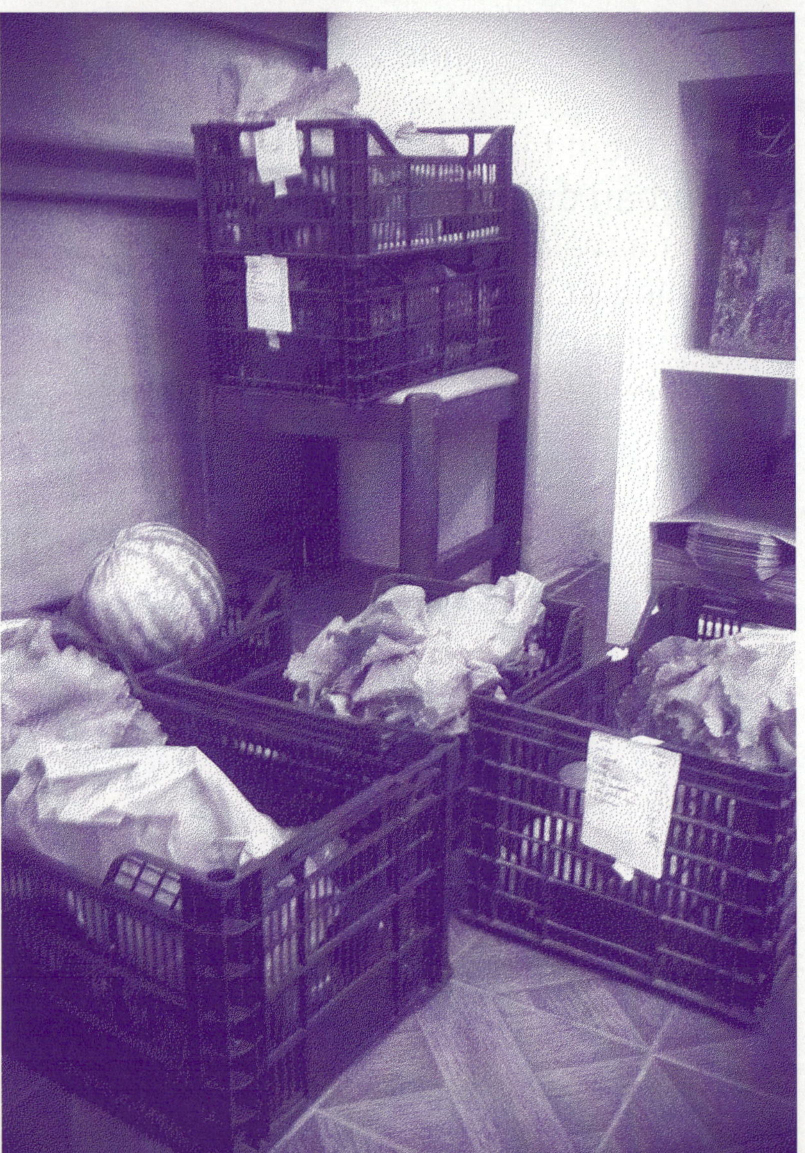

june 21

self-portrait with freedom and talent.

freedom

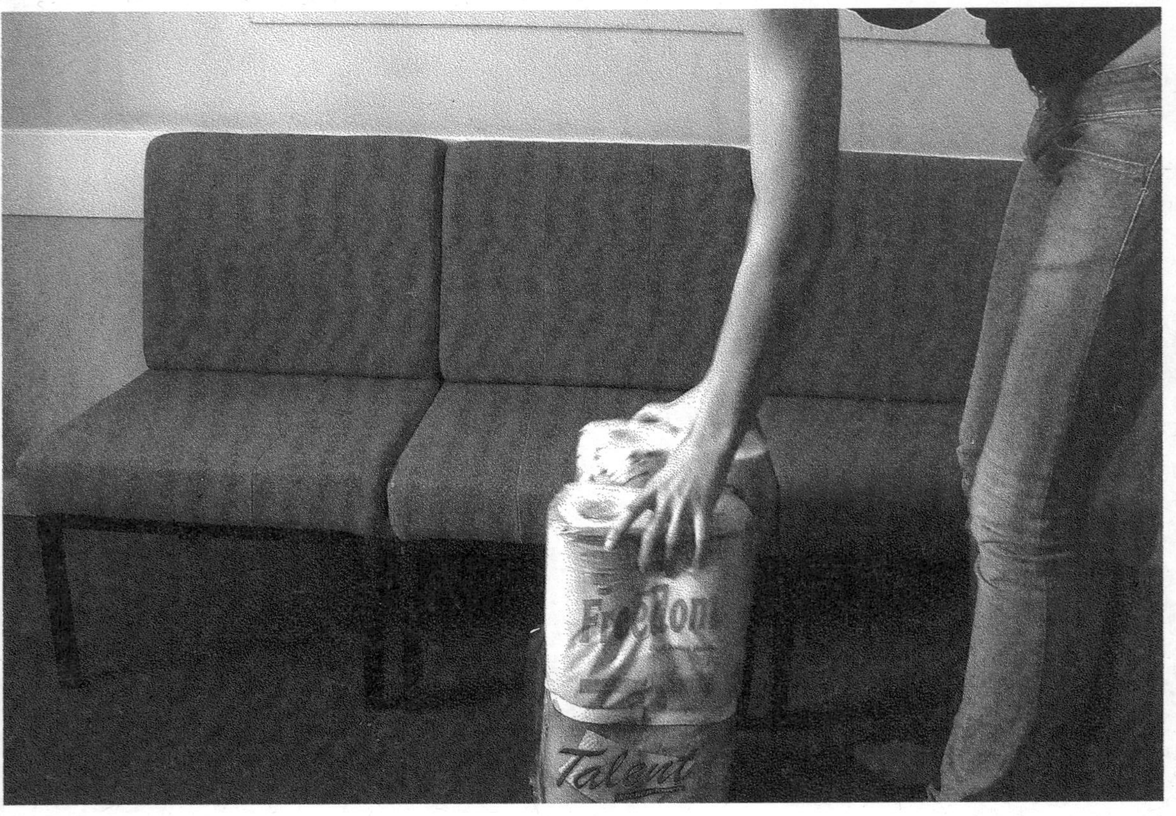
FreeTone
Talent

june 22

a meal bought by a lorry driver
in france.

dinner

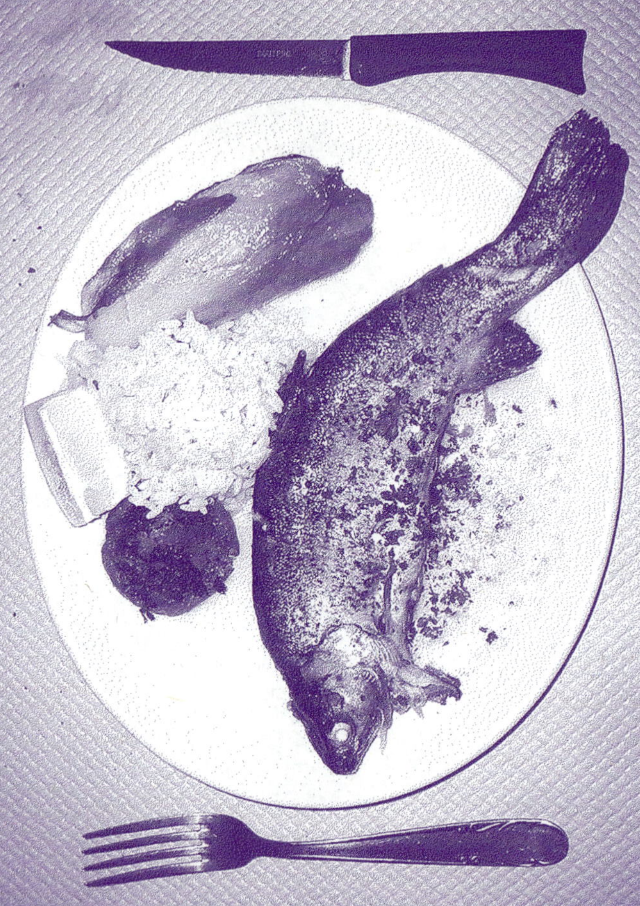

june 23

working in my mother's garden.
working on the land is some kind
anti-melancholy pill for me!

working on the land!

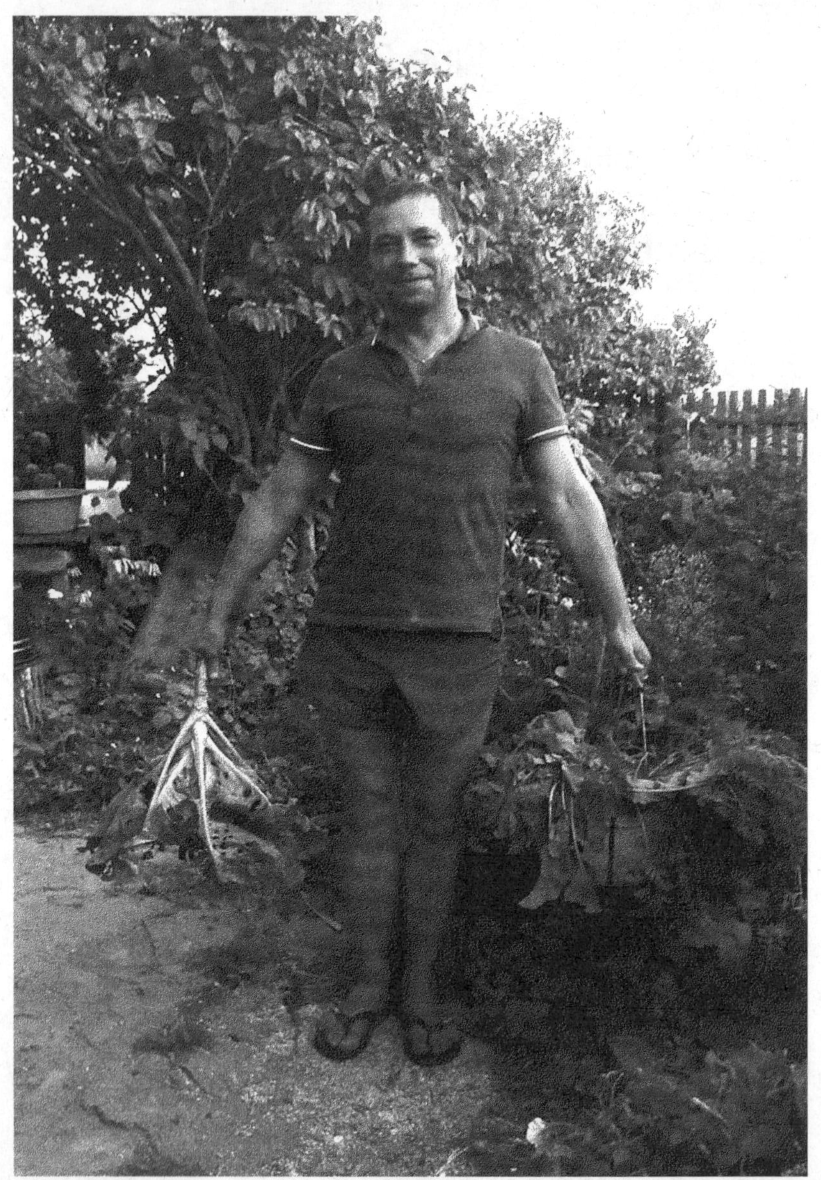

june 24

i can't remember what i was
doing there.

half-way under the bed

june 25

a gift of reflections and colours
for my eyes.

a gift for my eyes

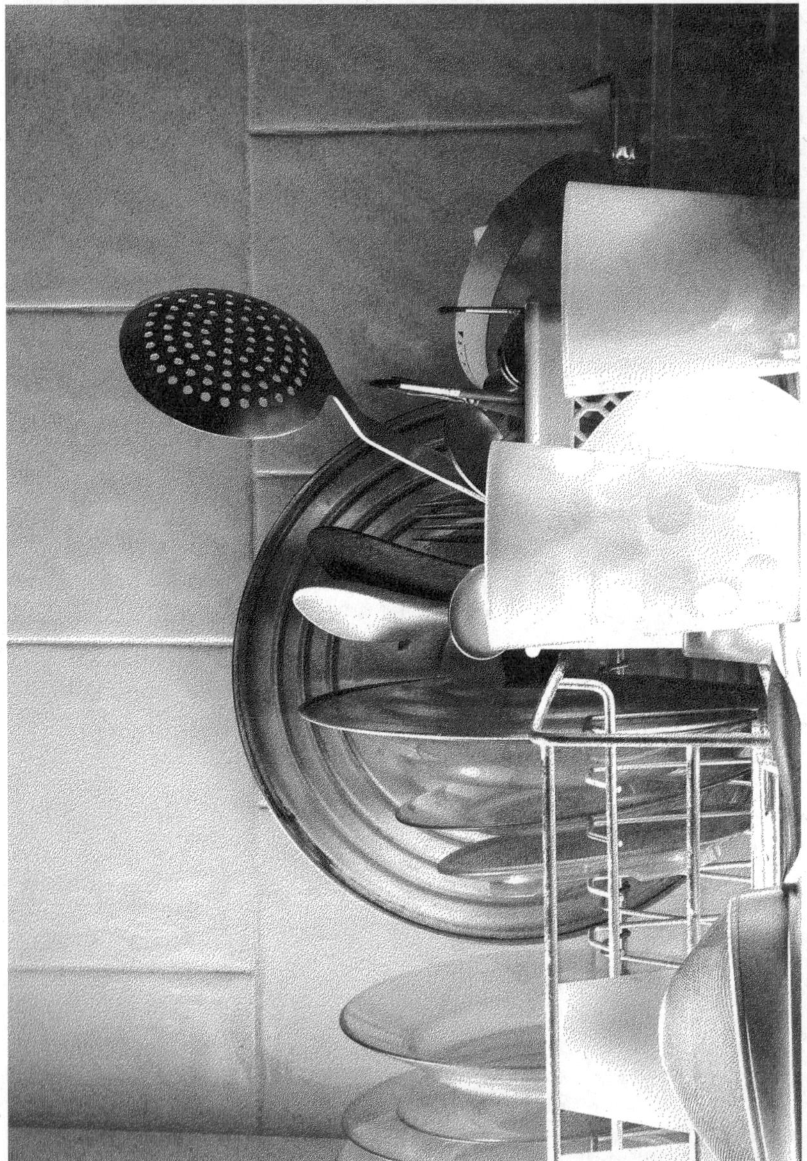

june 26

justice for domestic workers (j4dw) with
ask! (actie schone kunsten) creating
alliances at the showroom, london.

ask!

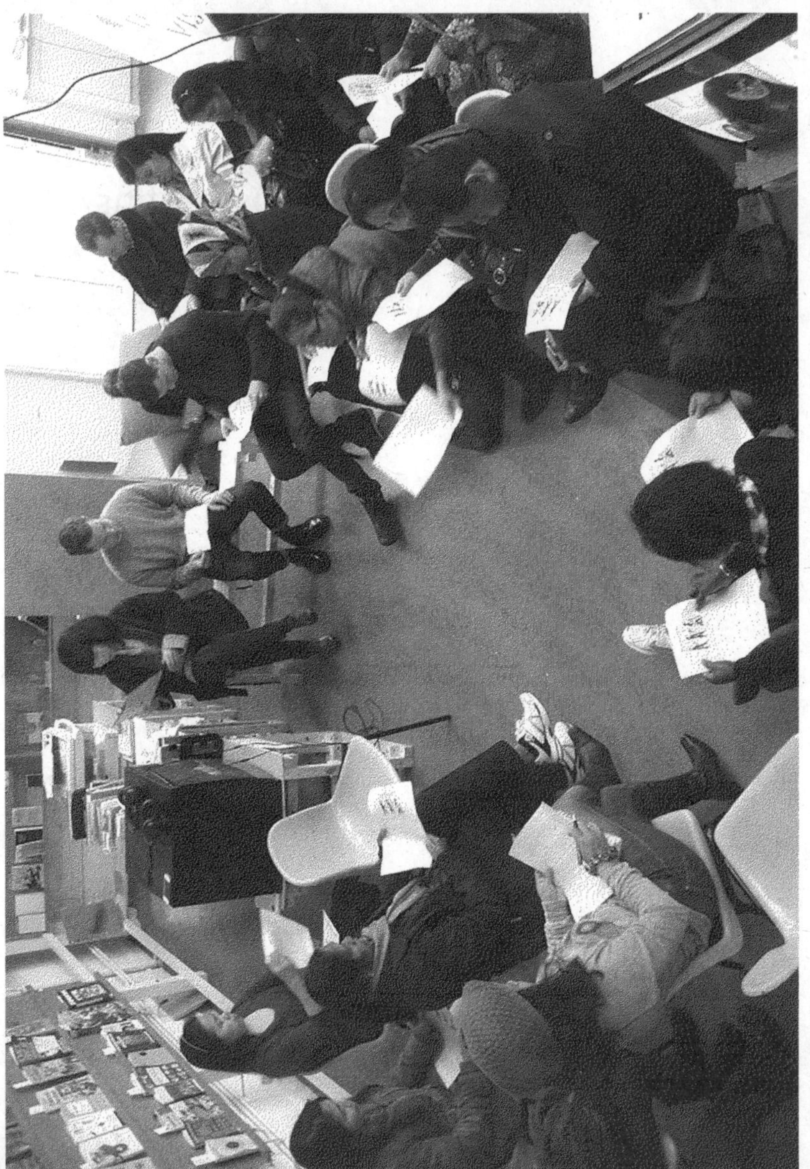

june 27

one second before getting started

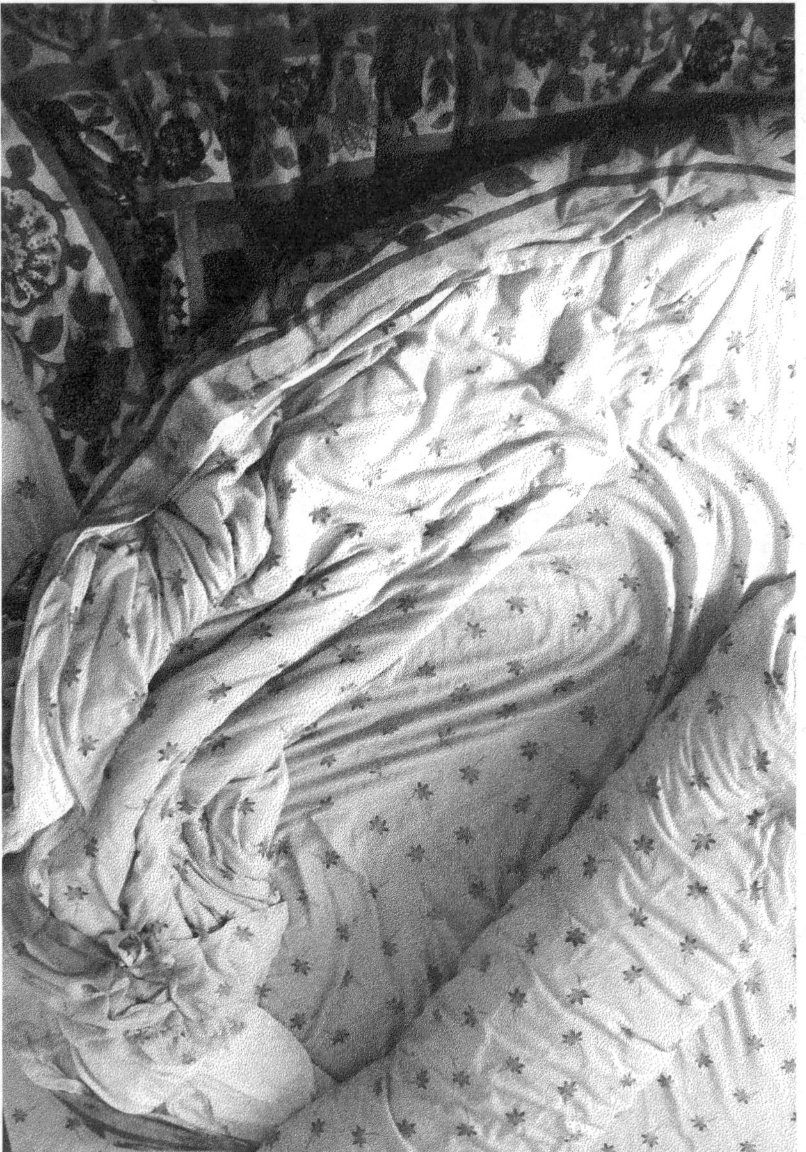

june 28

about to sit in bath.

i thought the water was warm enough

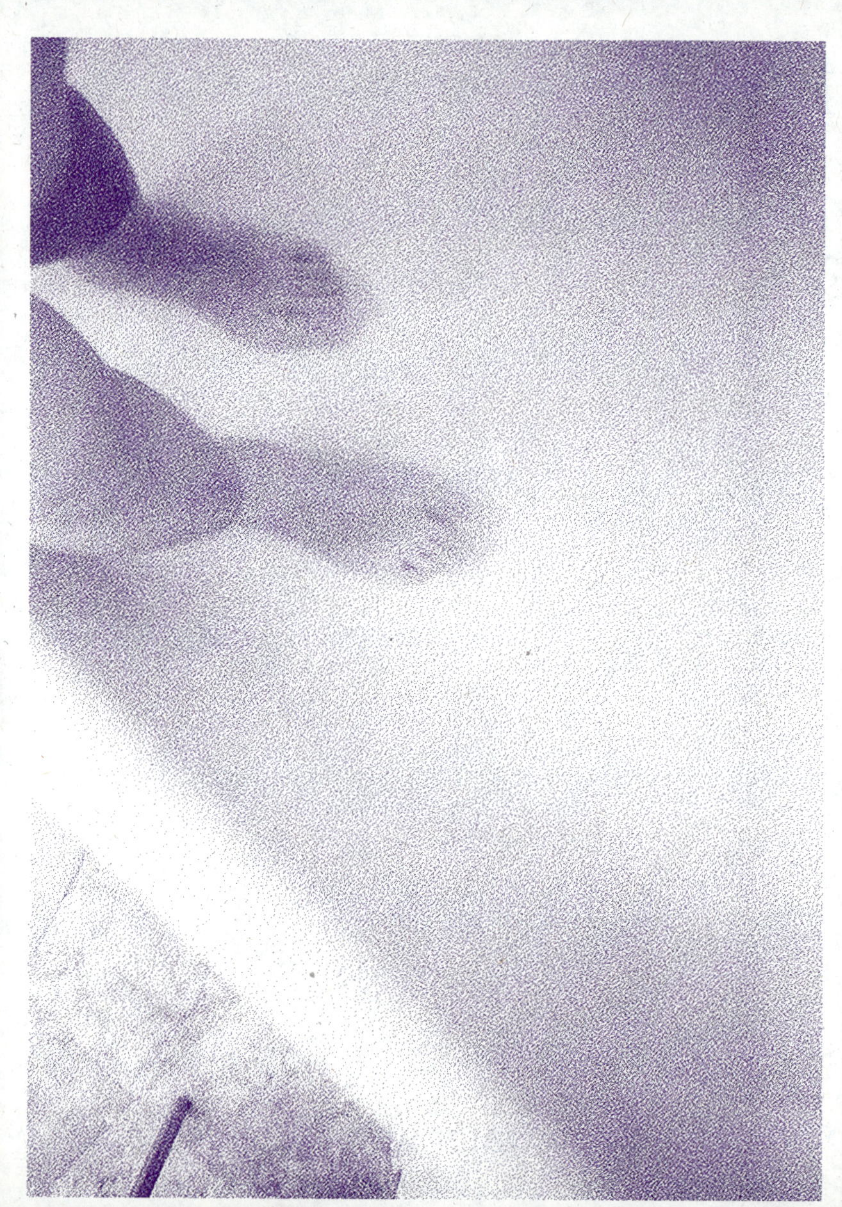

june 29

athiraman kannan jumped to his death
from the 147th floor of the world's
tallest building, the burj khalifa. from
india, he came to dubai to work as
a cleaner in the newly opened building.
in an attempt to honour his courageous
call for attention to be given to the
lives of migrant workers, i photographed
what i describe as a 'pop out city.'
these are spaces that are an attempt
at permanency and comfort in an
always vulnerable life as a migrant
worker. unlike the families they work
for, whose life exists behind walls,
their lives exist on the street, forging
new notions of 'the public.'
al naeem, 2011.

in memory of athiraman kannan

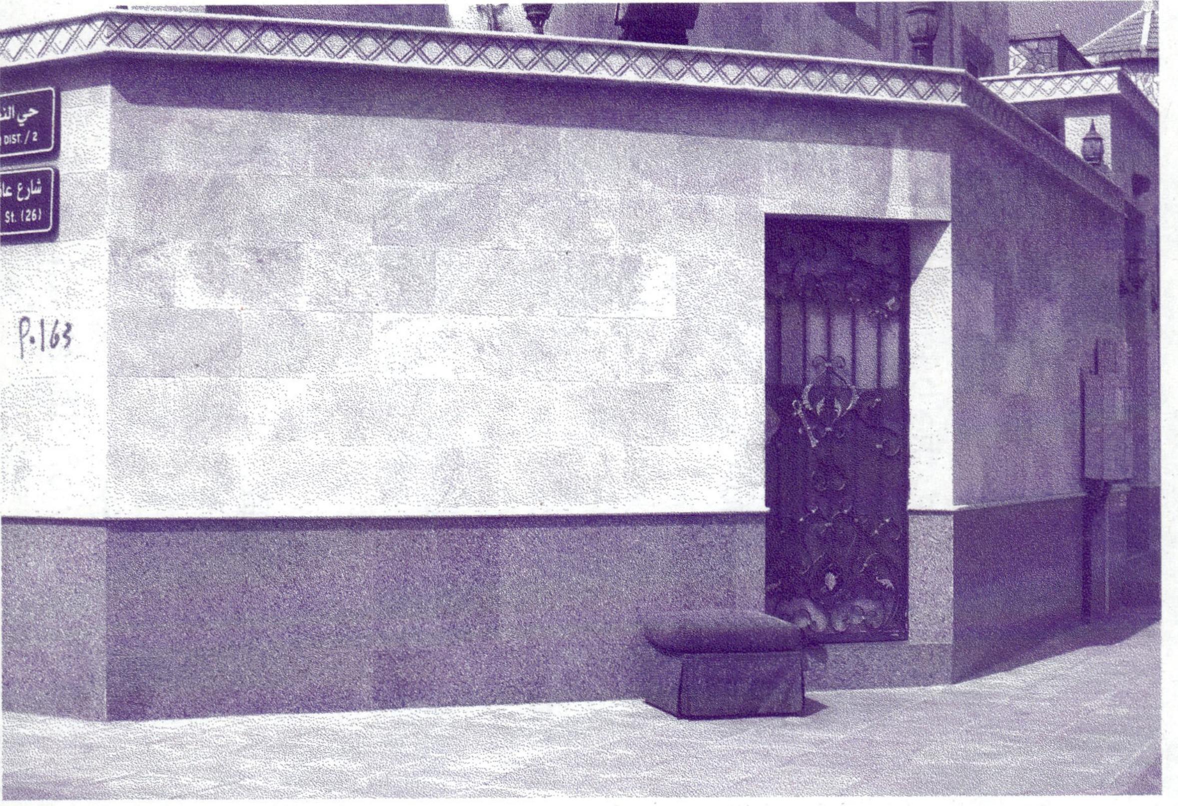
حي الن...
DIST. / 2
شارع عا...
St. (26)
P.163

last winter i saw so many lost gloves
i decided to take a picture whenever
i found one. i had this idea right after
winter was over. this is a typical
summer/early autumn glove. it is for
work, rather than avoiding the cold.
as cold comes, the woollen ones start
to appear in the city streets, lost on
public transportation, bus stops,
or swollen in the snow. when the sun
comes, they rise above the surface.

lost glove, early autumn

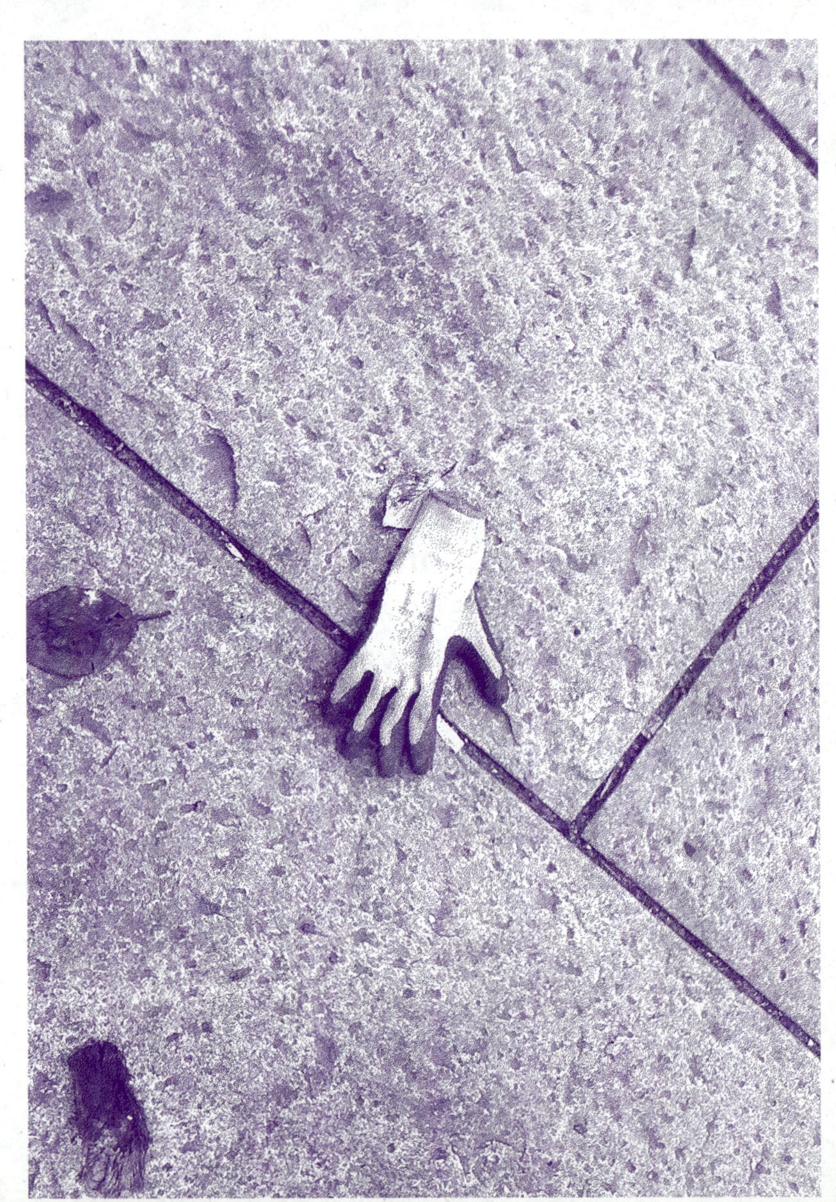

july 1

home, love, loneliness, desires,
pj harvey, wishes, melancholy, flowers,
woods, sad nature, music, body, pain,
hope, some places, some feelings…

the desperate kingdom of love

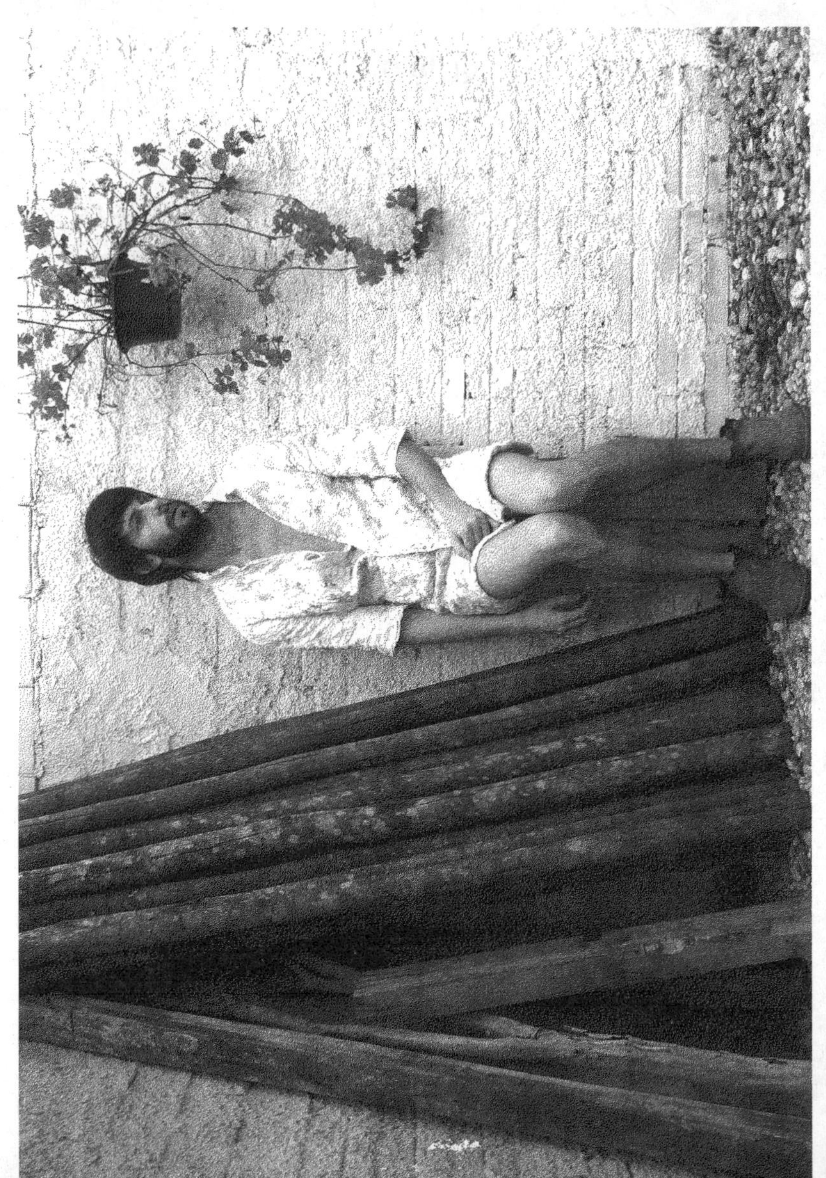

july 2

four people, two grants,
two exhibitions

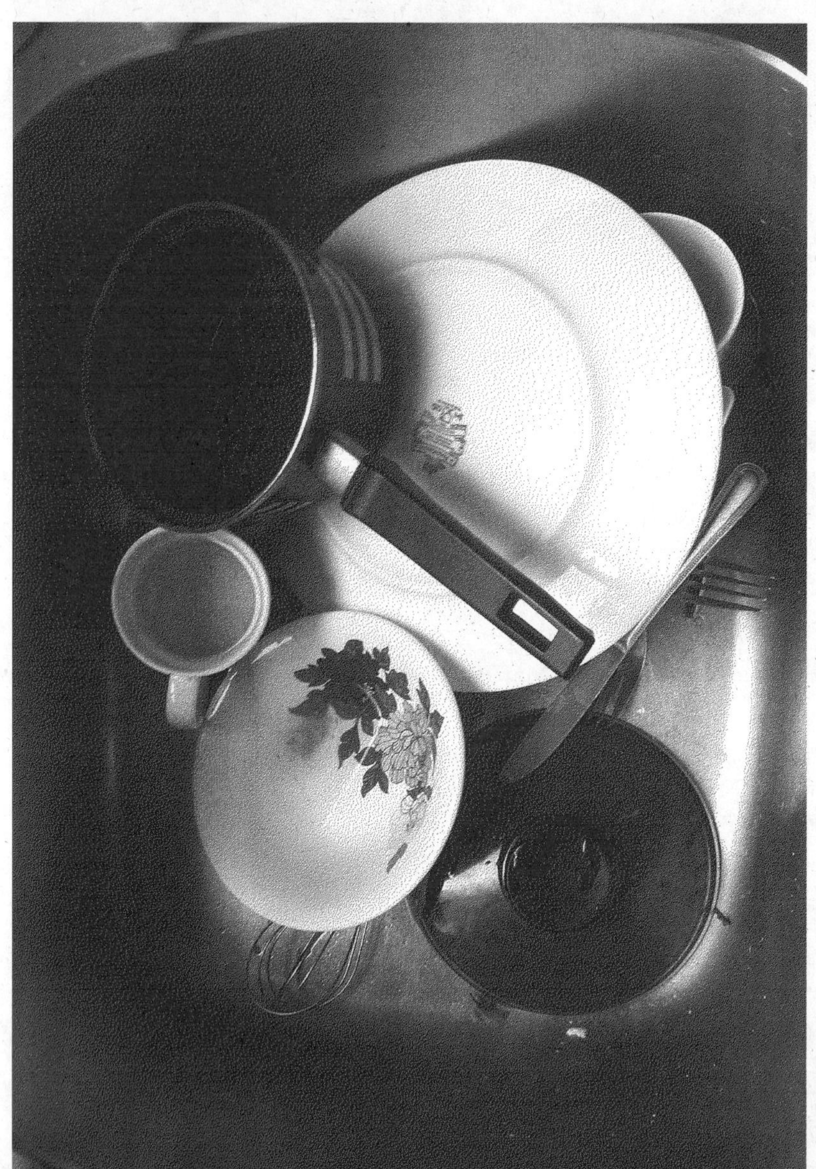

in the cave-houses quarter, women
hang out ropes of red peppers in front
of their houses. the pantry is outside.
almería, 2000.

inside/outside

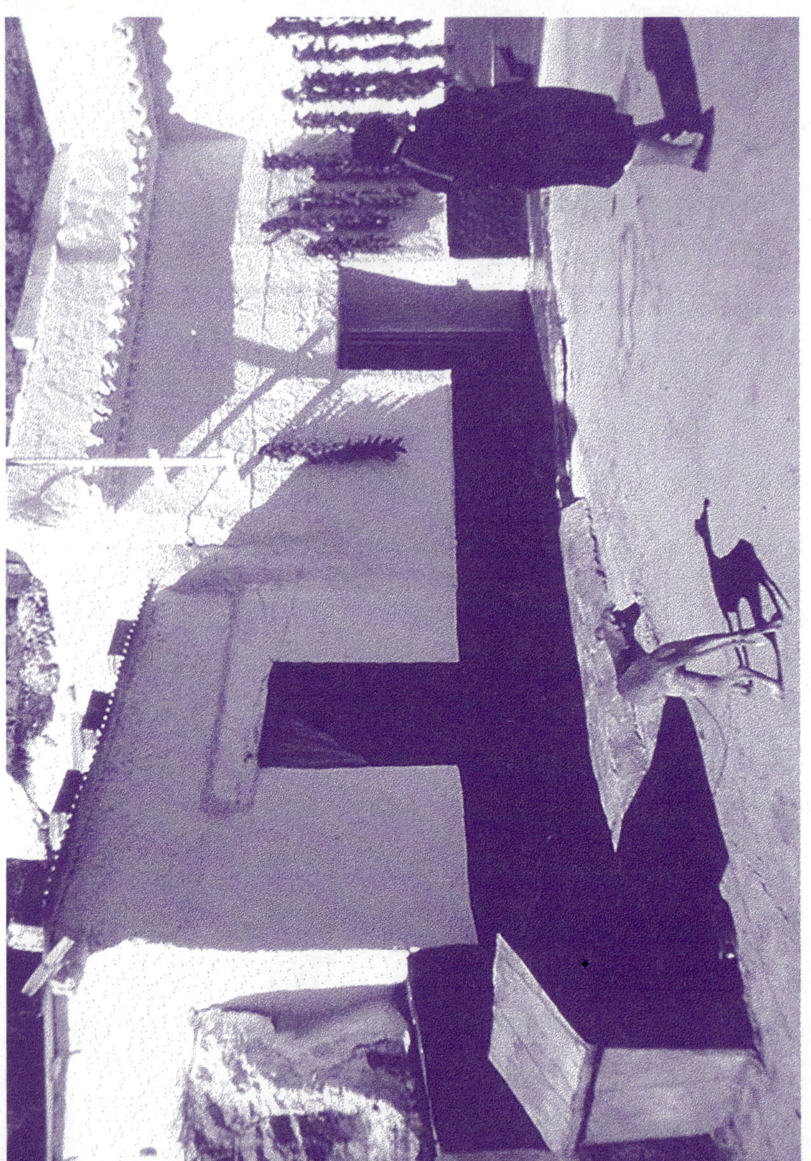

july 4

we don't want work, we want money.
still from *tiempo real* [real time],
(2003), video, 43 min.

we don't want work

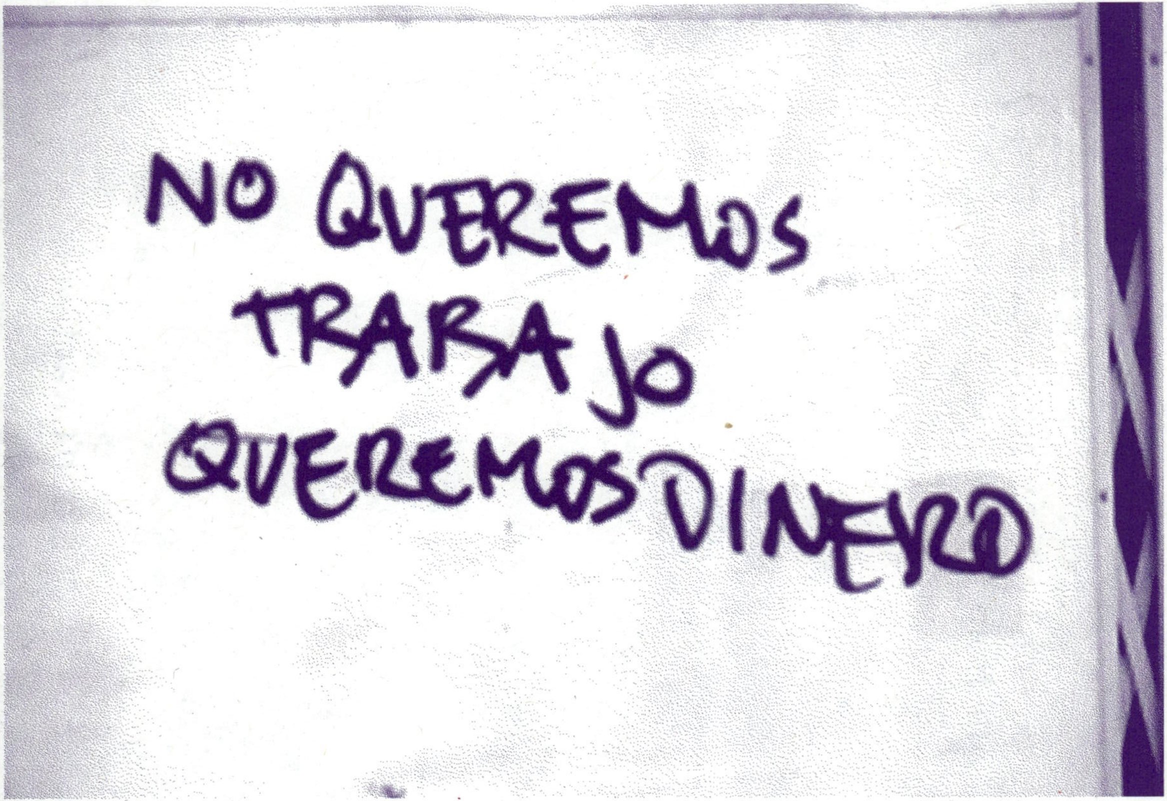

NO QUEREMOS
TRABAJO
QUEREMOS DINERO

july 5

an ironic attempt to mind the
immortal delacroix!

la ménagère guidant le nettoyage…

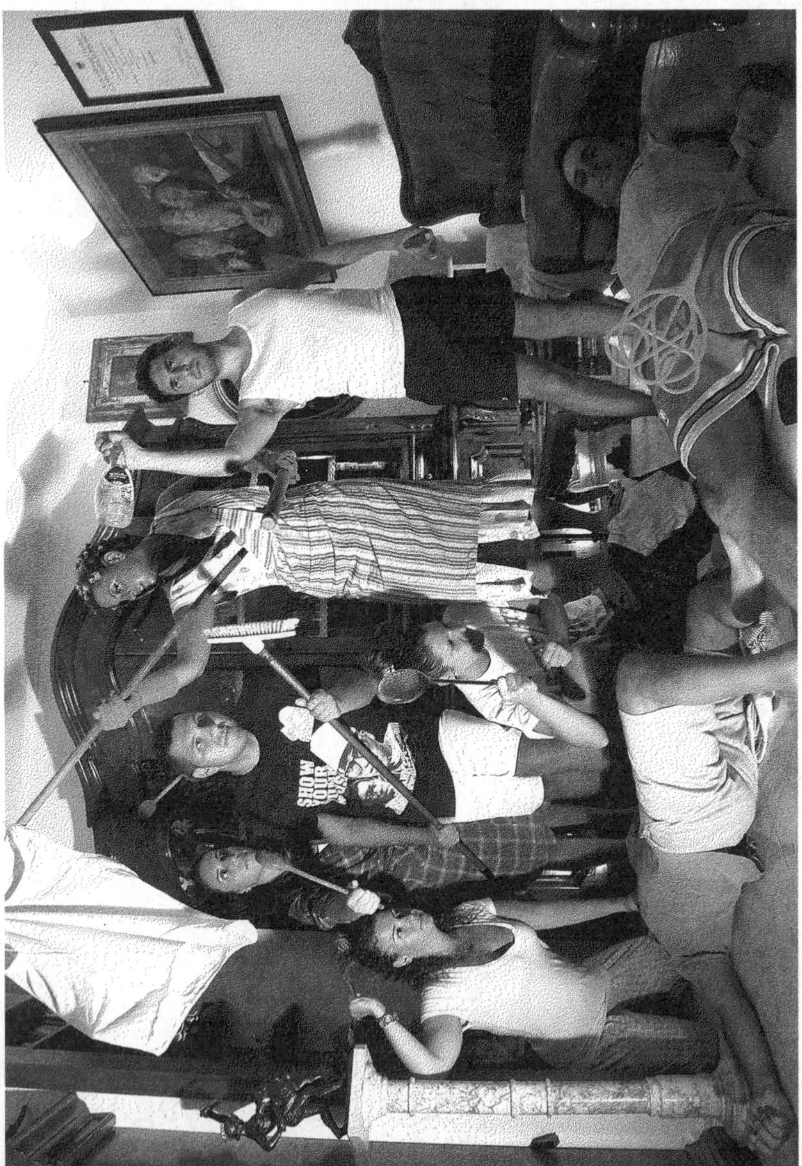

july 6

life is getting better all the time (2011).
photo by thamanta.

creature comforts no. 3

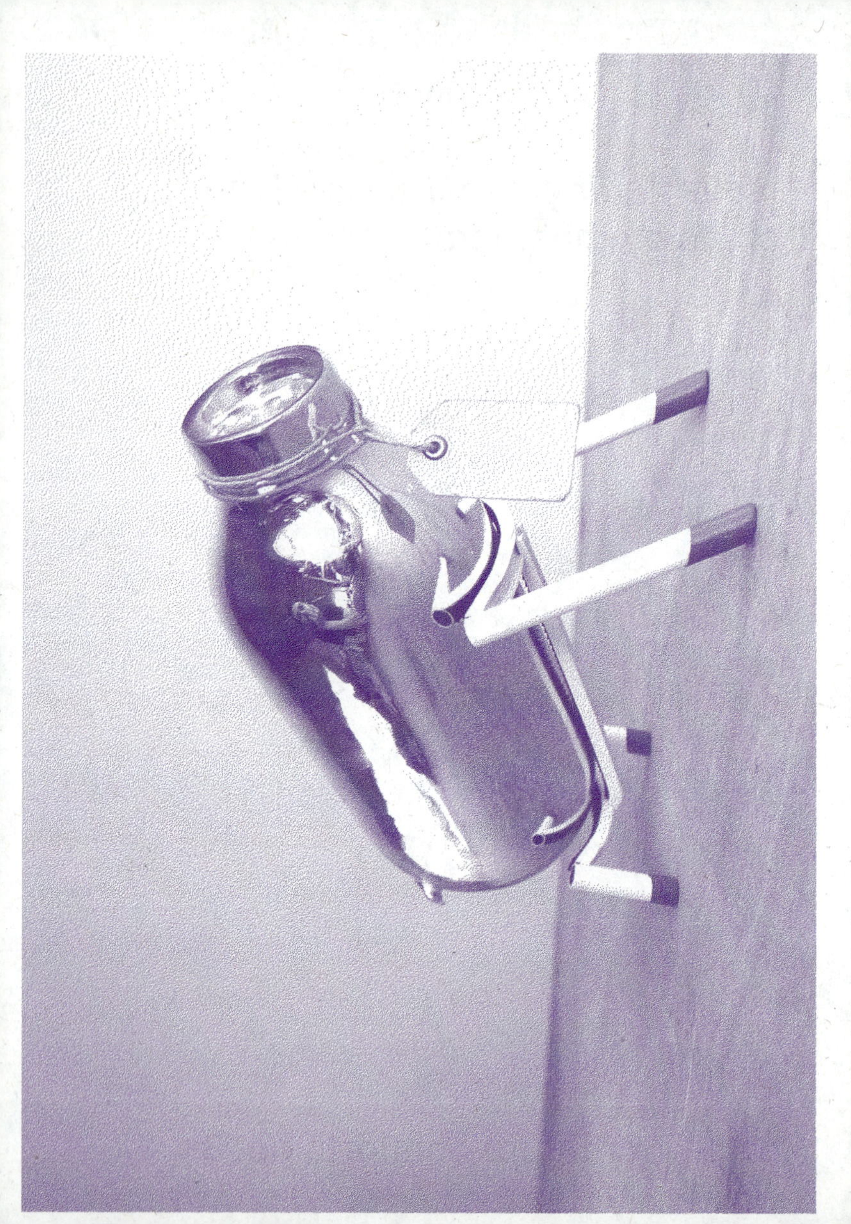

this is my own creation made of
recycled straw and paper. justice for
domestic workers demand recognition
in making domestic work visible in
british society. this is my way of remem-
bering our own filipino tradition and
it also helps me to ease my loneliness
when i'm celebrating christmas away
from my family and home with my
j4dw family in the uk.

christmas lantern

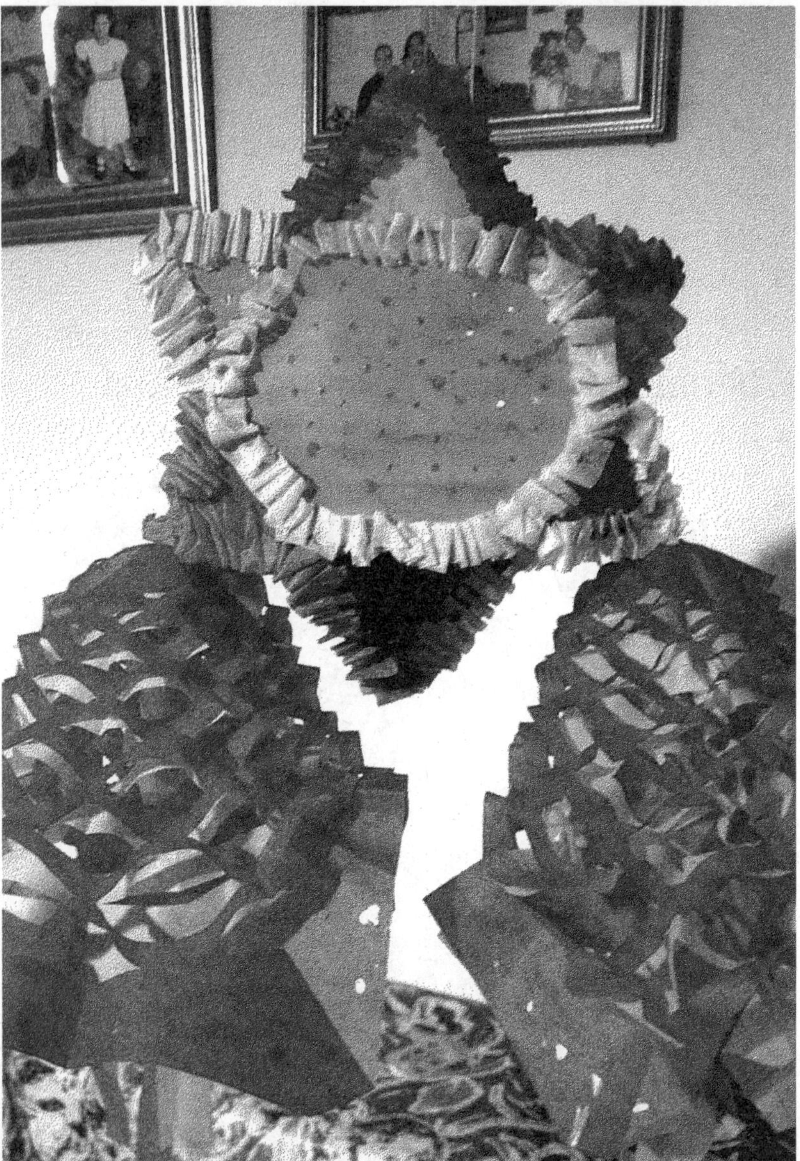

july 8

cleaning lady, cleaning dust.
view from above.

movement no. 4

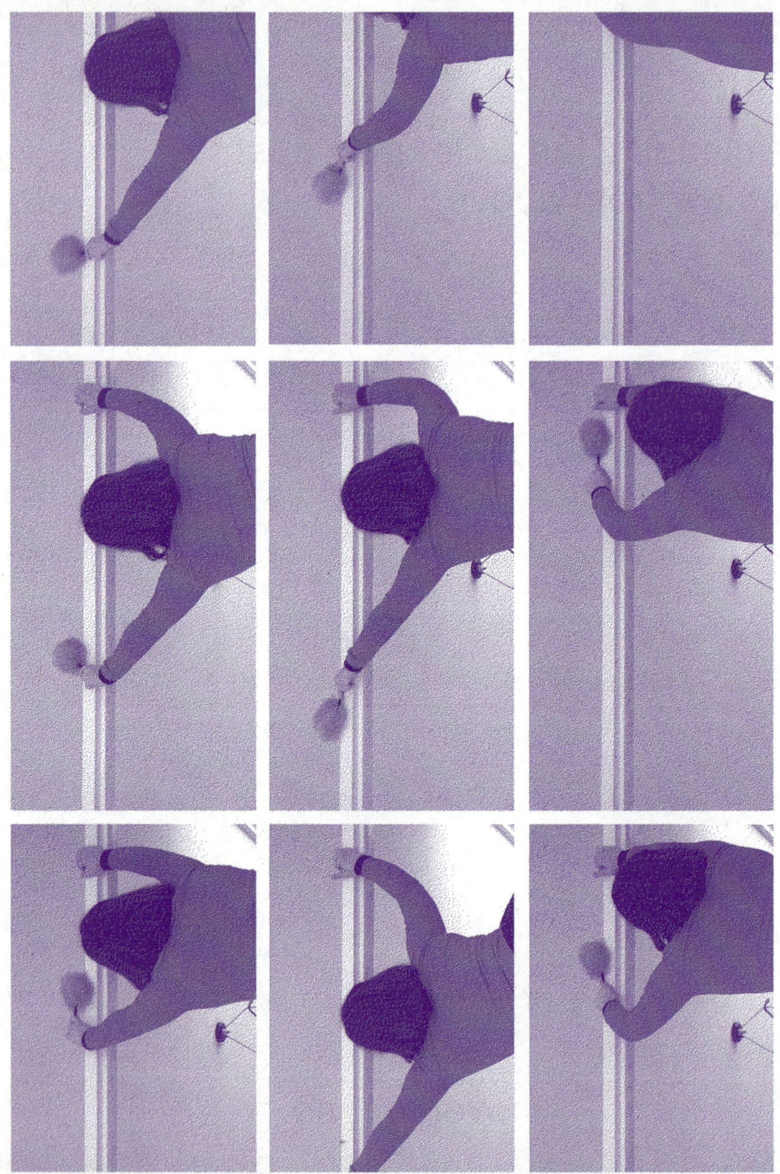

july 9

photograph from the house where
i grew up, taken by my father or
my mother in 1982 or 1983.

gardening

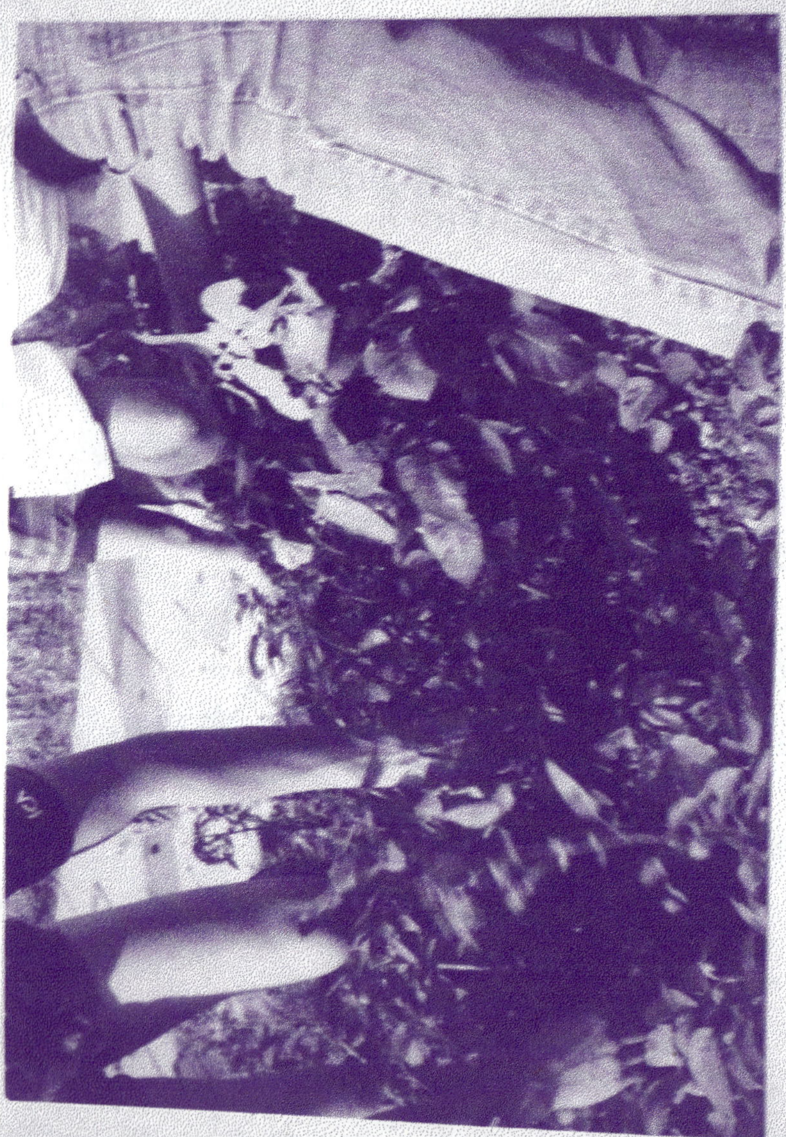

july 10

we are still working.

upward mobility

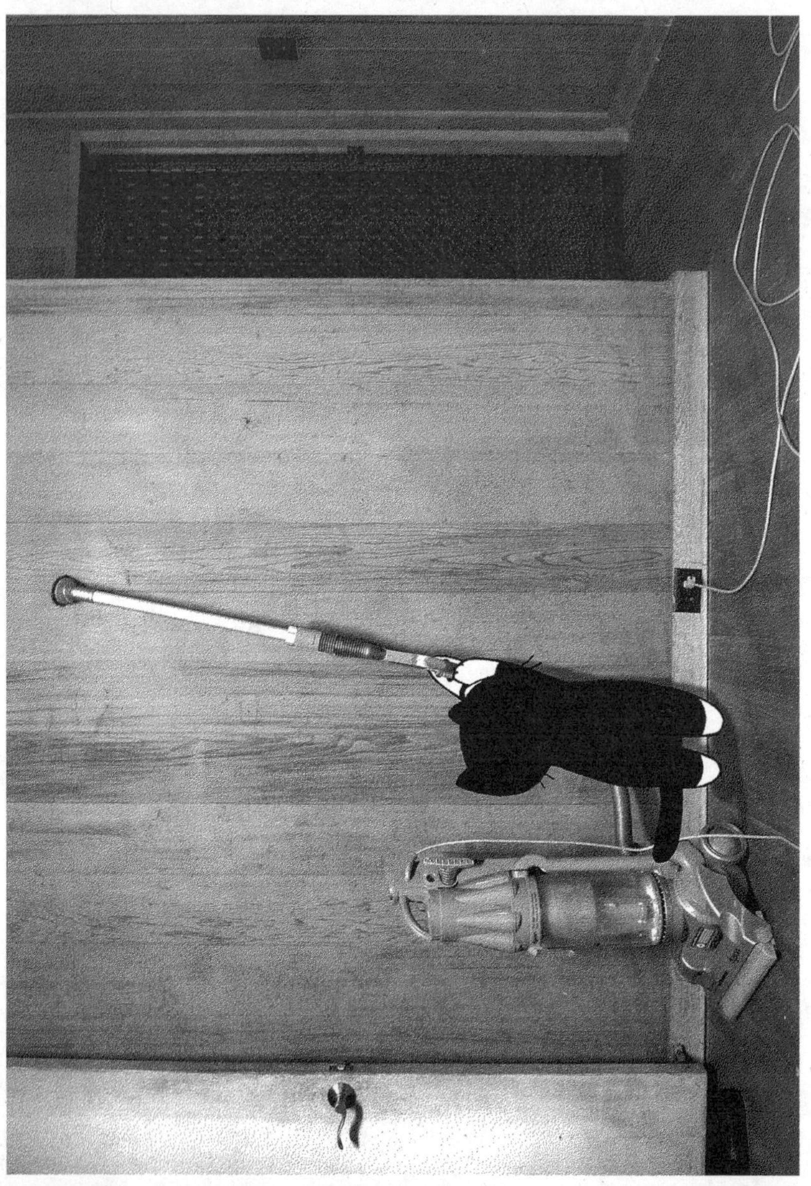

when a domestic worker's sacrifice
is too much to bear and fighting to
survive is the only way. "oh, god!
please let our sister live…" six months
she may survive, one year maybe
or she may even reach five years—
the last stage of cancer she is so
determine to defeat. going home to
the philippines seems hell and bitter
as she found sweet refuge in the uk
as her home. a smiling face greeted me
as i open the door, full of life, with no
trace of fear and sorrows. dying is too
near and yet too far. to embrace her
strength within, i wonder where it
comes from, as i hold her to feel her
warm heart again.

a dedication of life

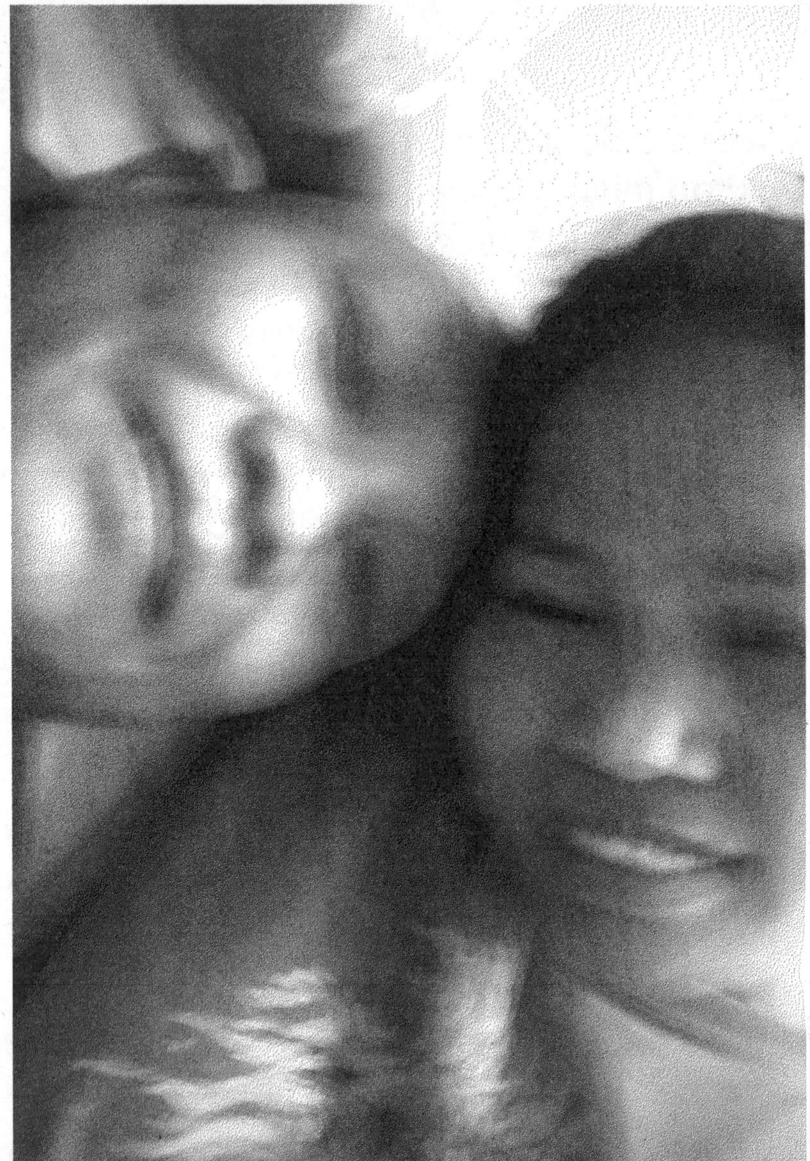

july 12

magazine cut-out.

serving wolf

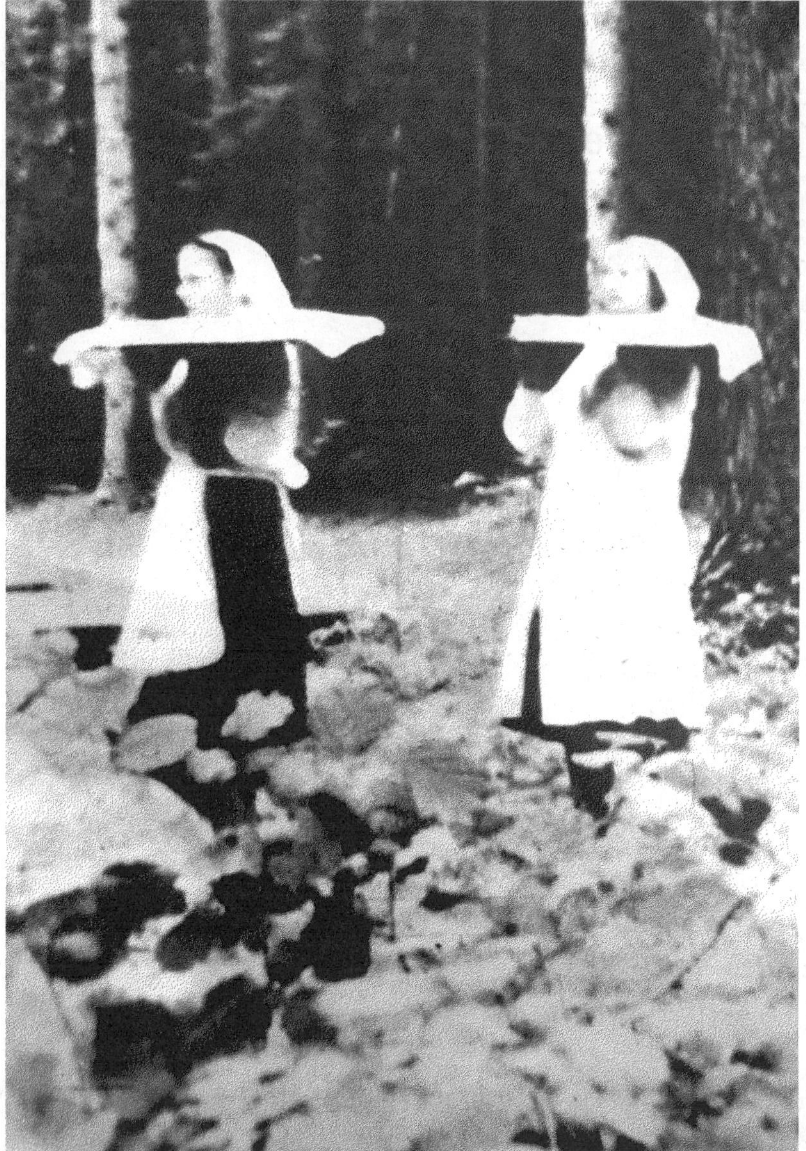

july 13

tool to brush the cat, fluff.

mass production system

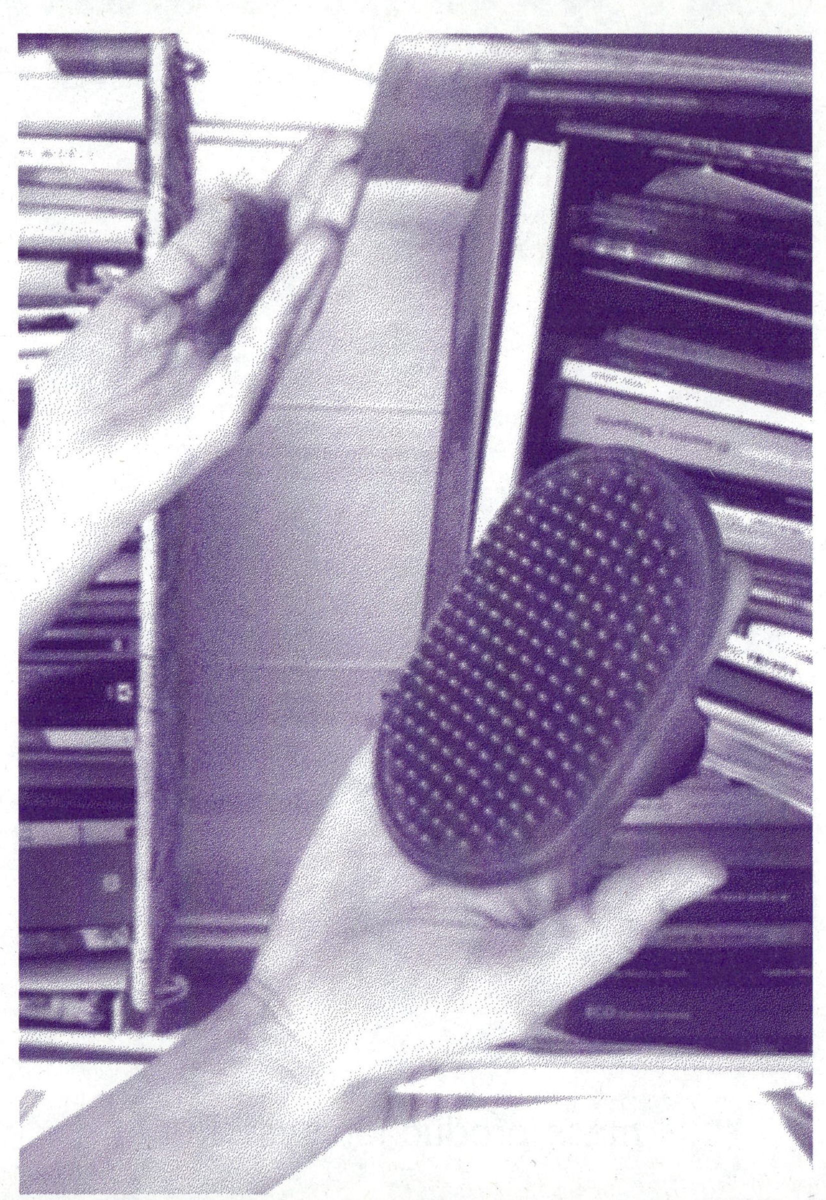

july 14

there is always hope for domestic
workers to have a better life,
for respect and to be recognized
within society.

sunflower

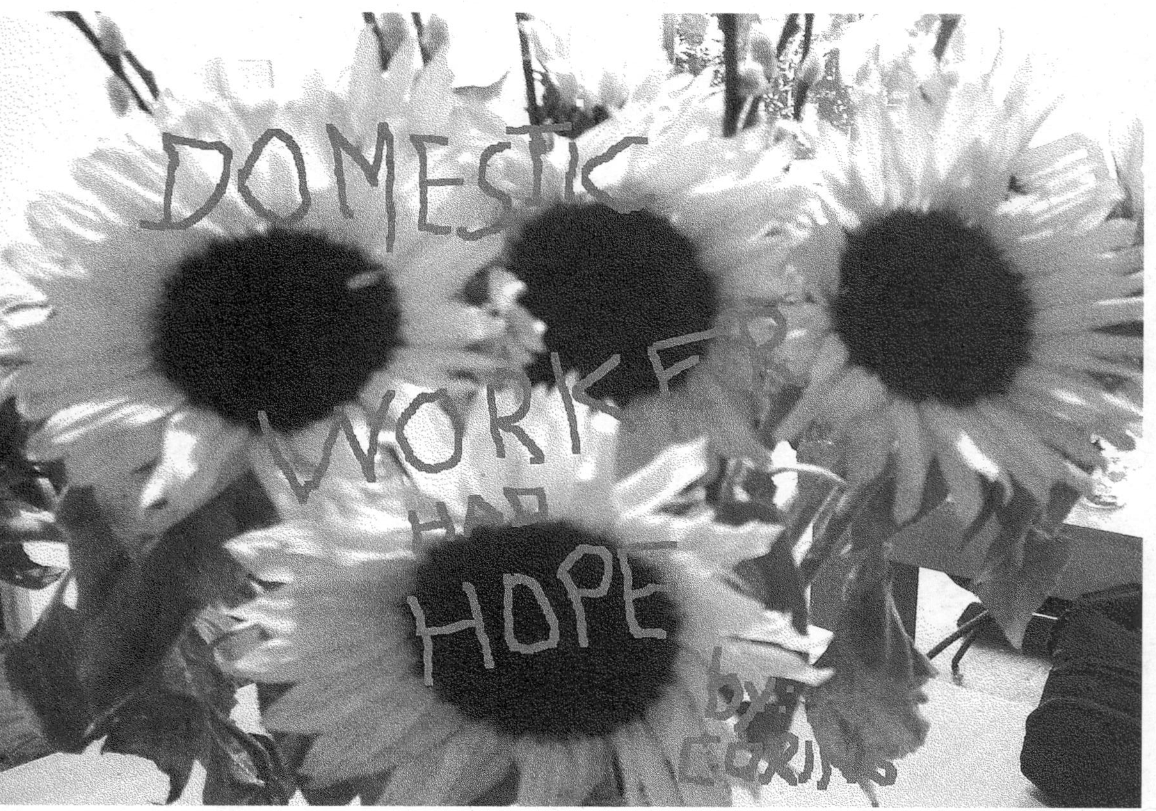

DOMESTIC
WORKERS
HOPE
by CORINS

july 15

i'd like to be remembered as someone who showed up for the job. i consider myself a worker.

milanese worker

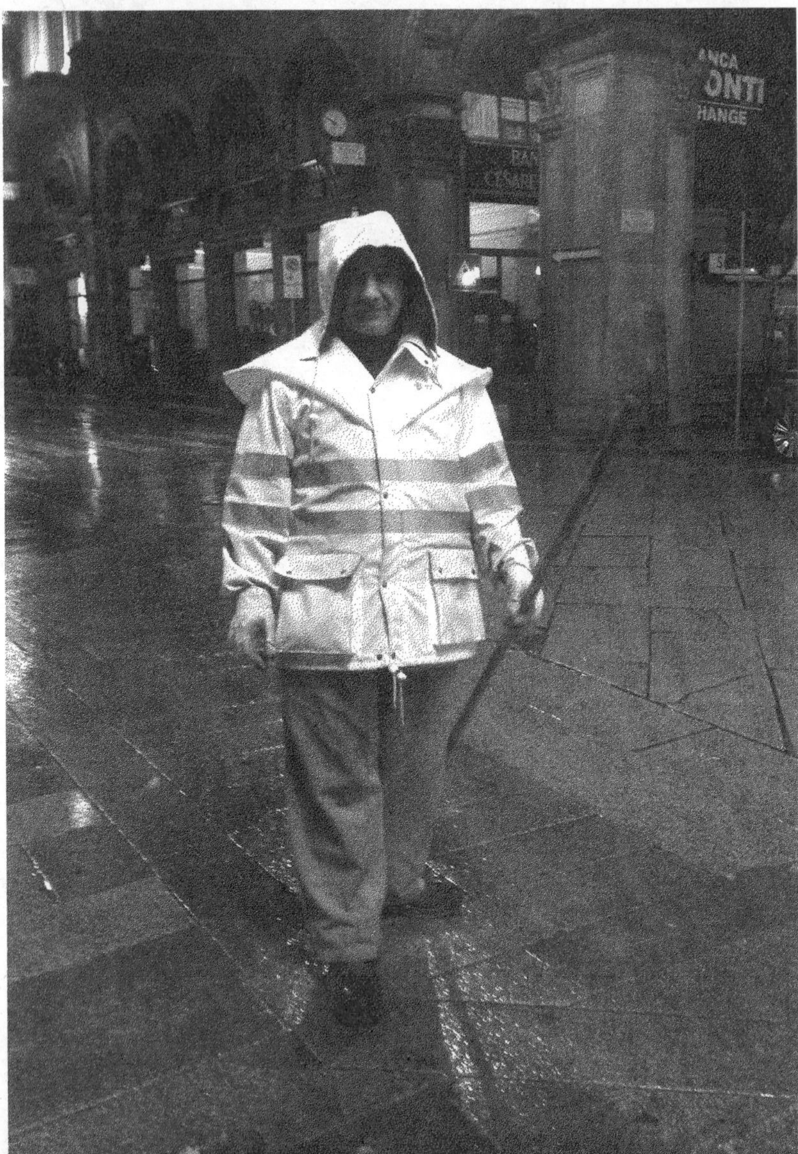
ANCA
ONTI
HANGE

july 16

short distance transport of tools
and materials used to rework a post-
foreclosure house into a machine
for living collaboratively with nature.

improvised tools

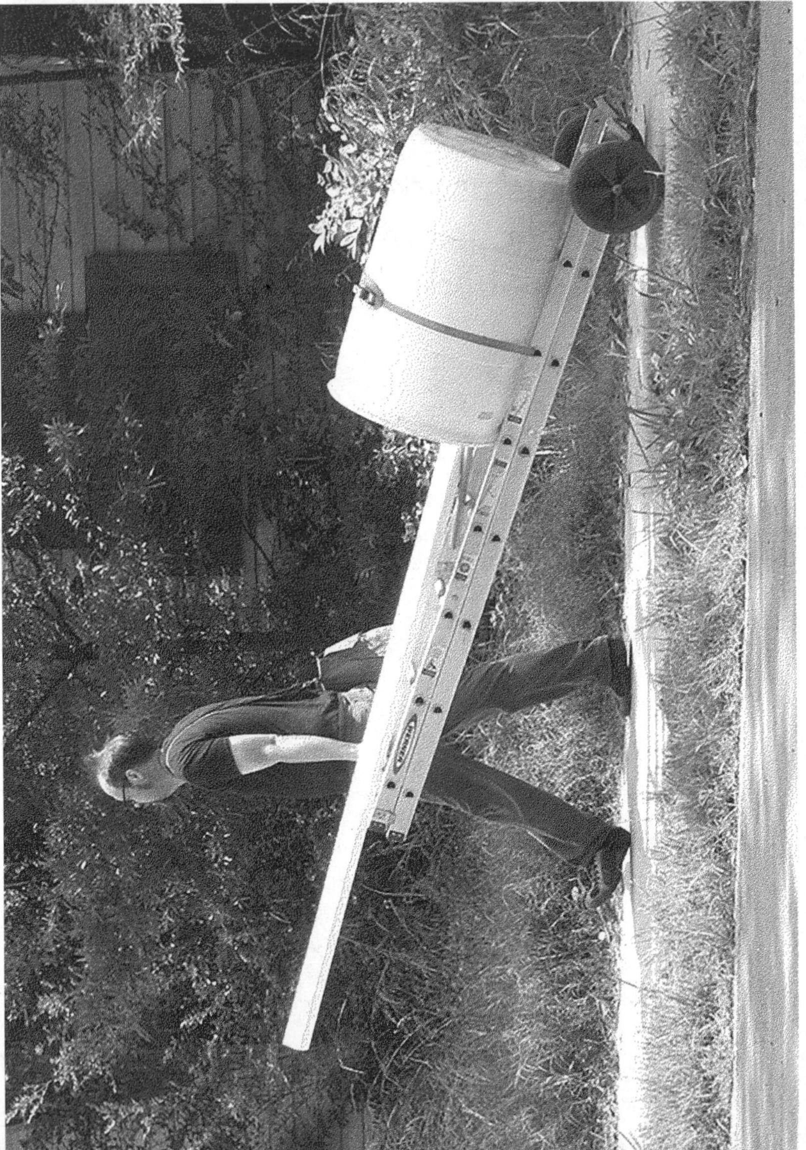

july 17

professional order.

cleaning tool

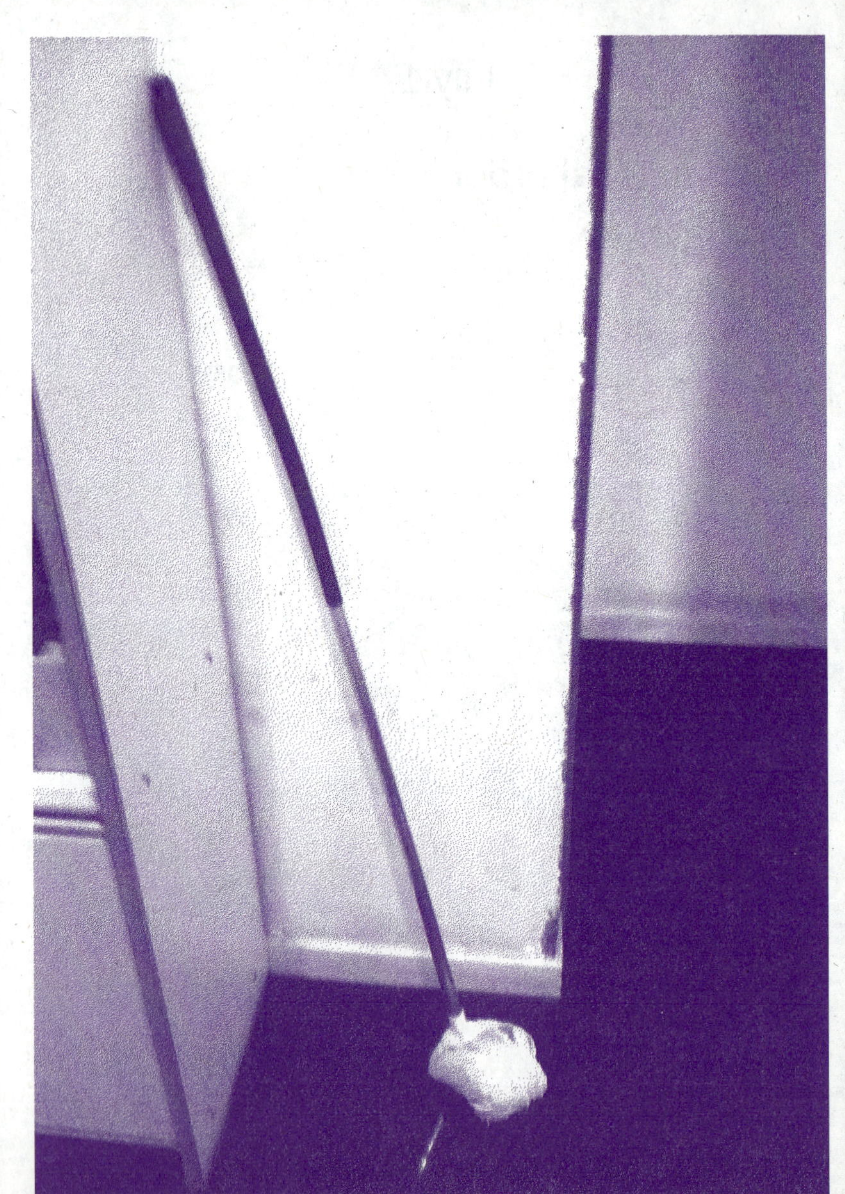

july 18

www.stopdesahucios.es/.

stop evictions

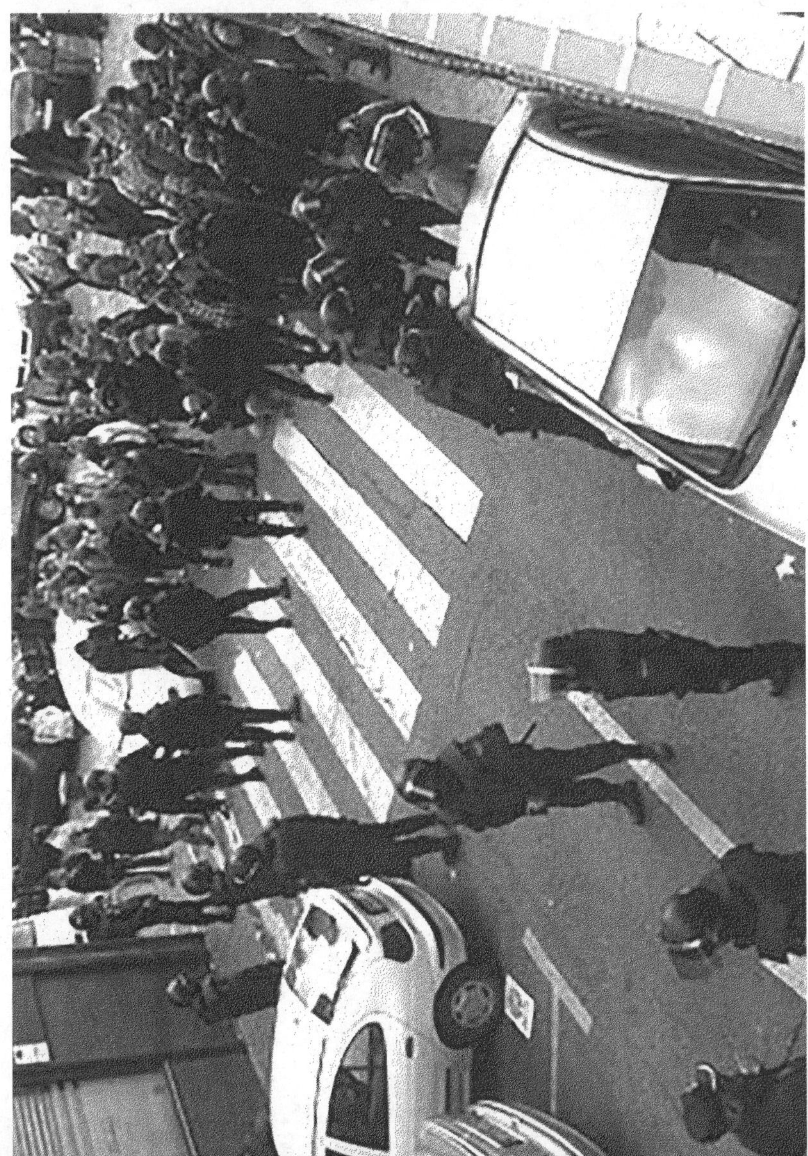

july 19

cultural workers move/migrate for
residencies, exhibitions, appointments,
teaching, internships, etc.

moving

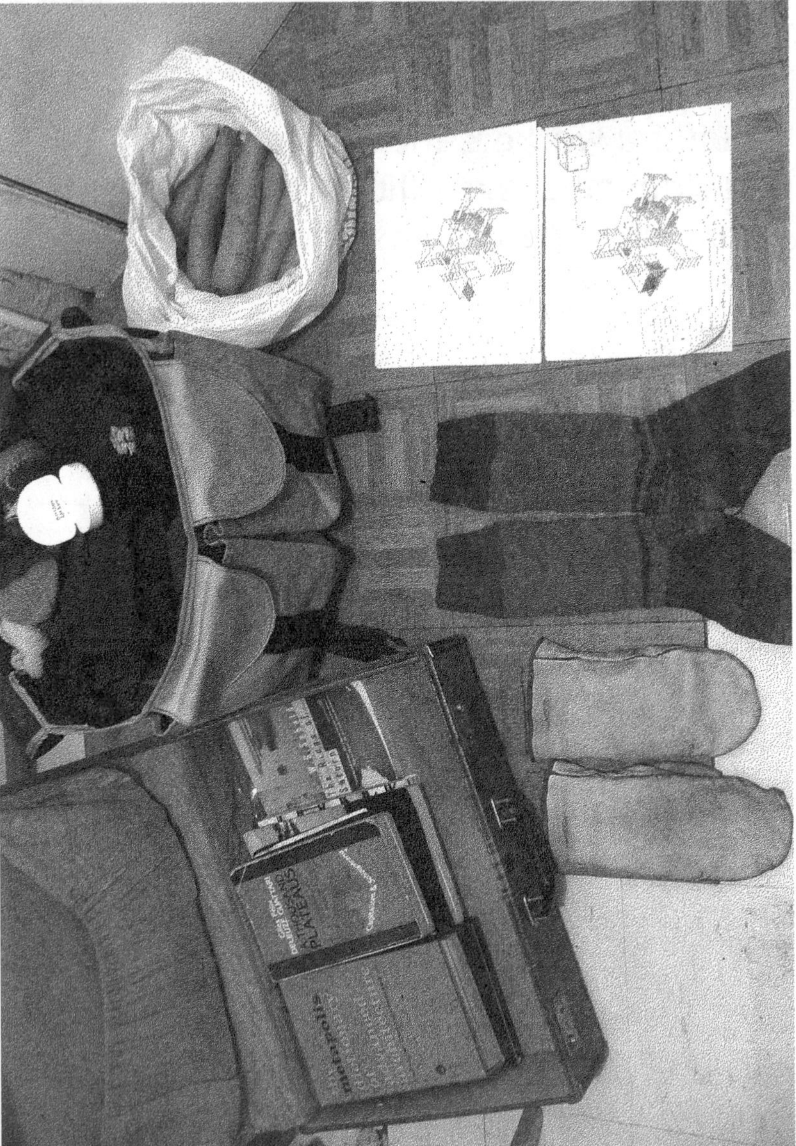

gingerbread. family time, saturday
morning, january 2011. 1 in 3 children
are living in poverty in the uk.

www.endchildpoverty.org.uk

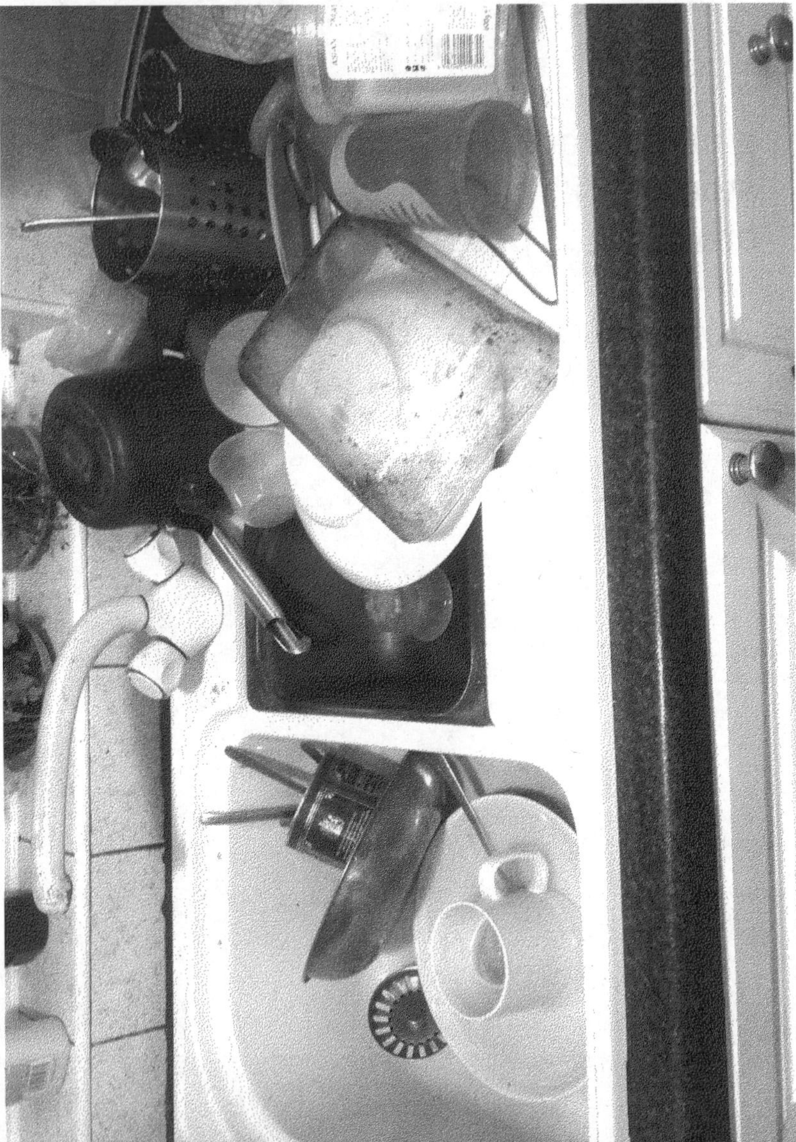

july 21

victory pose.

fucking backyard

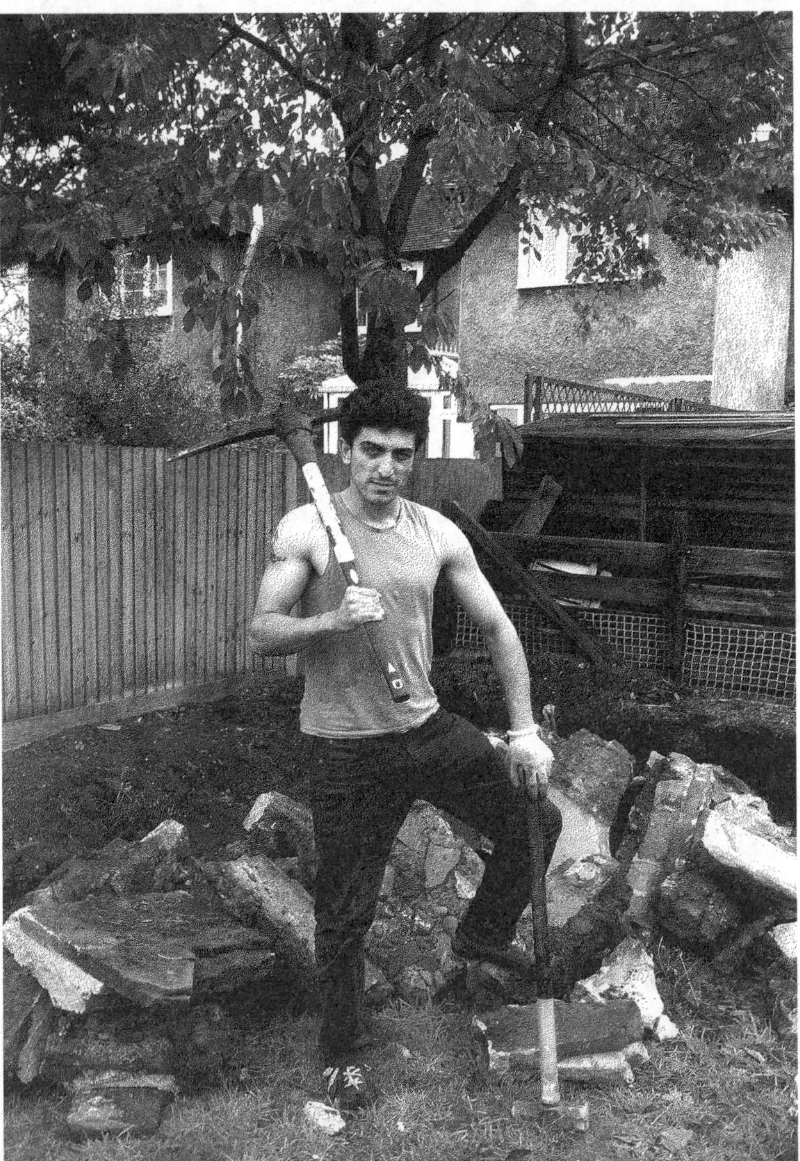

july 22

real economy, real estate, real madrid.

the real

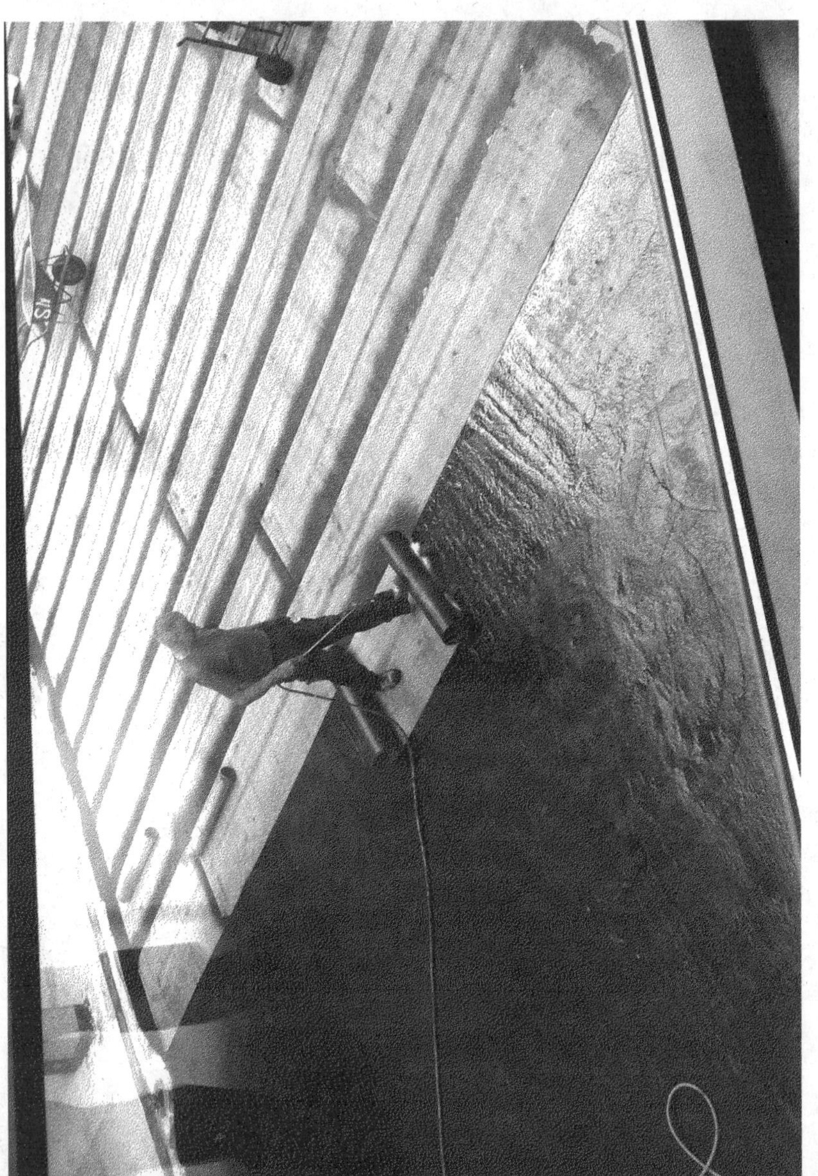

july 23

office

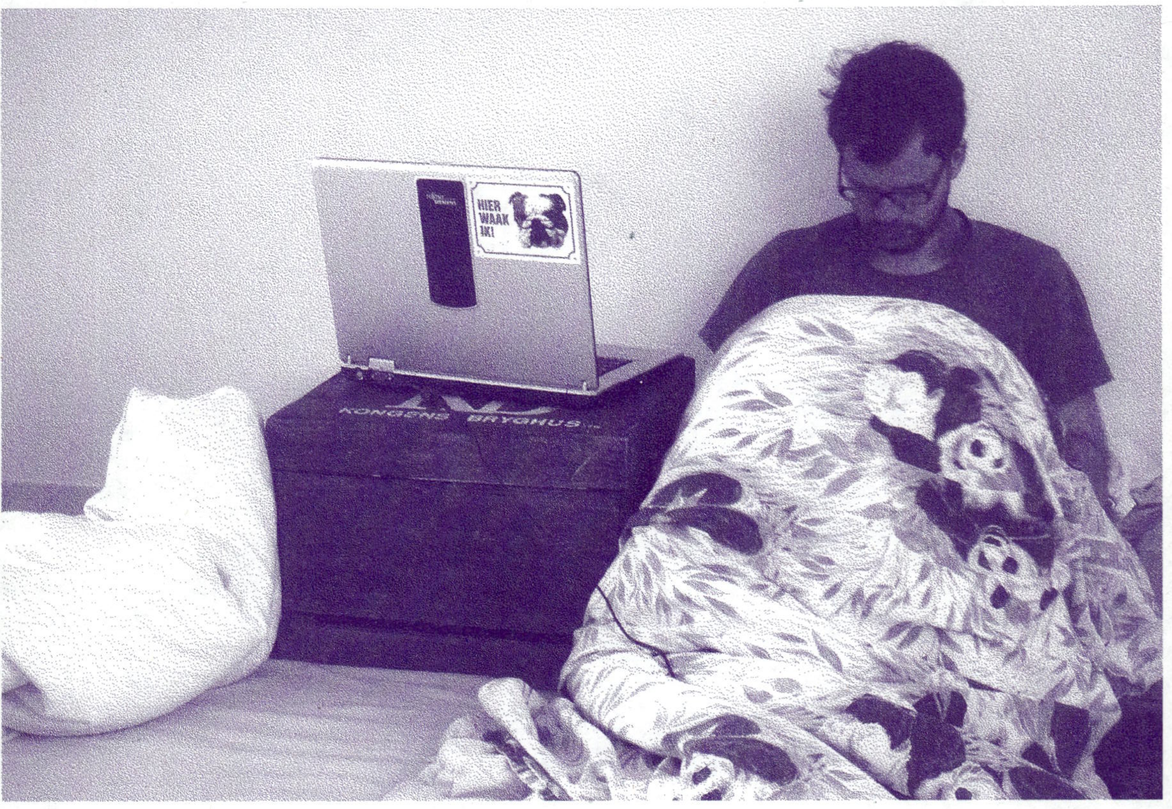
HIER
WAAK
IK!
KONGENS BRYGHUS

july 24

last week is still present on the
kitchen stove.

reminder

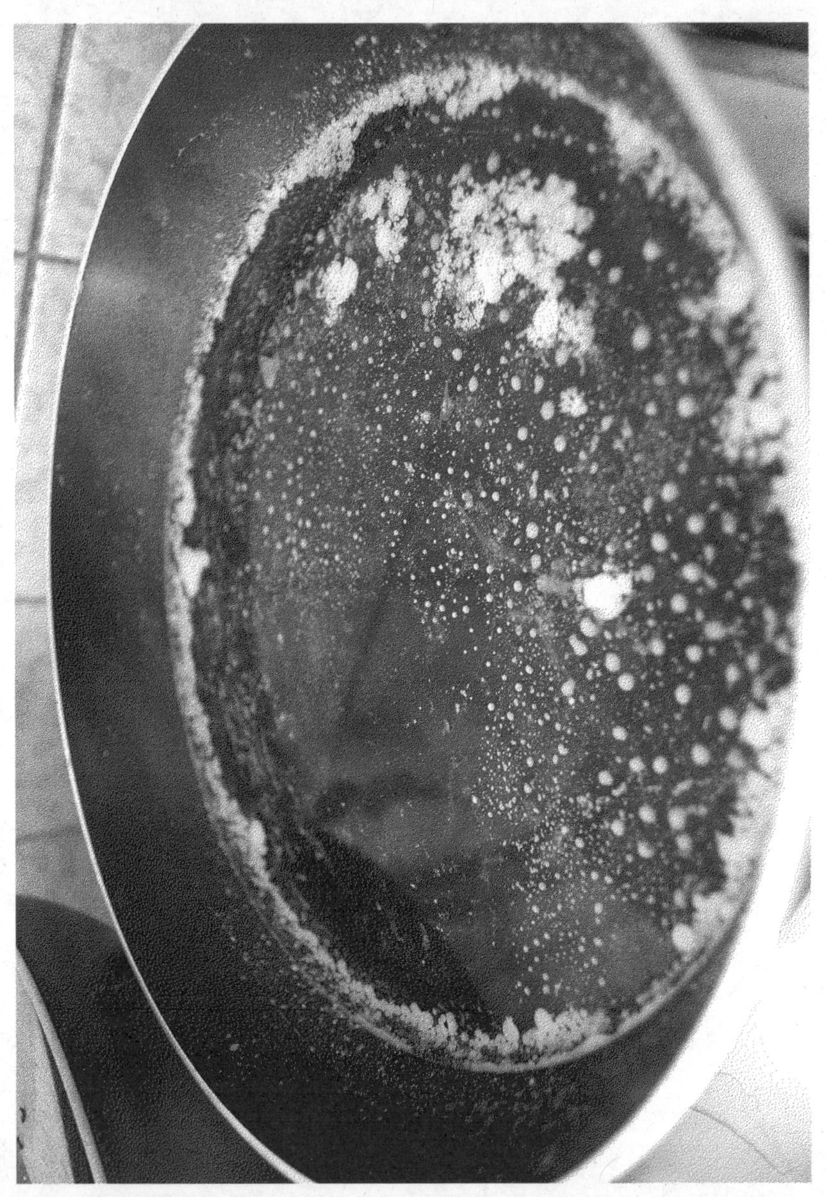

july 25

letto

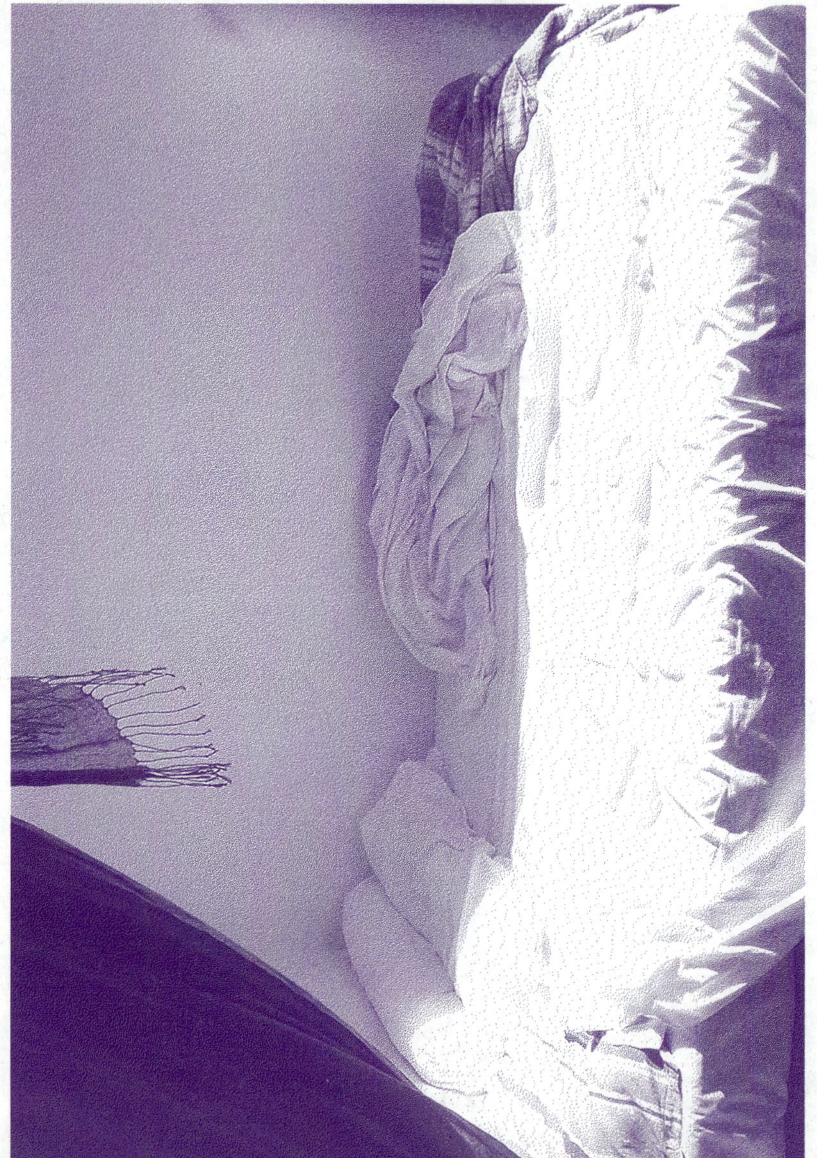

july 26

my friend works for two days at the office and three days at home. often when he works at home he sits slumped on the couch, and sometimes he only wears his bathrobe. they call this the "new work."

new work

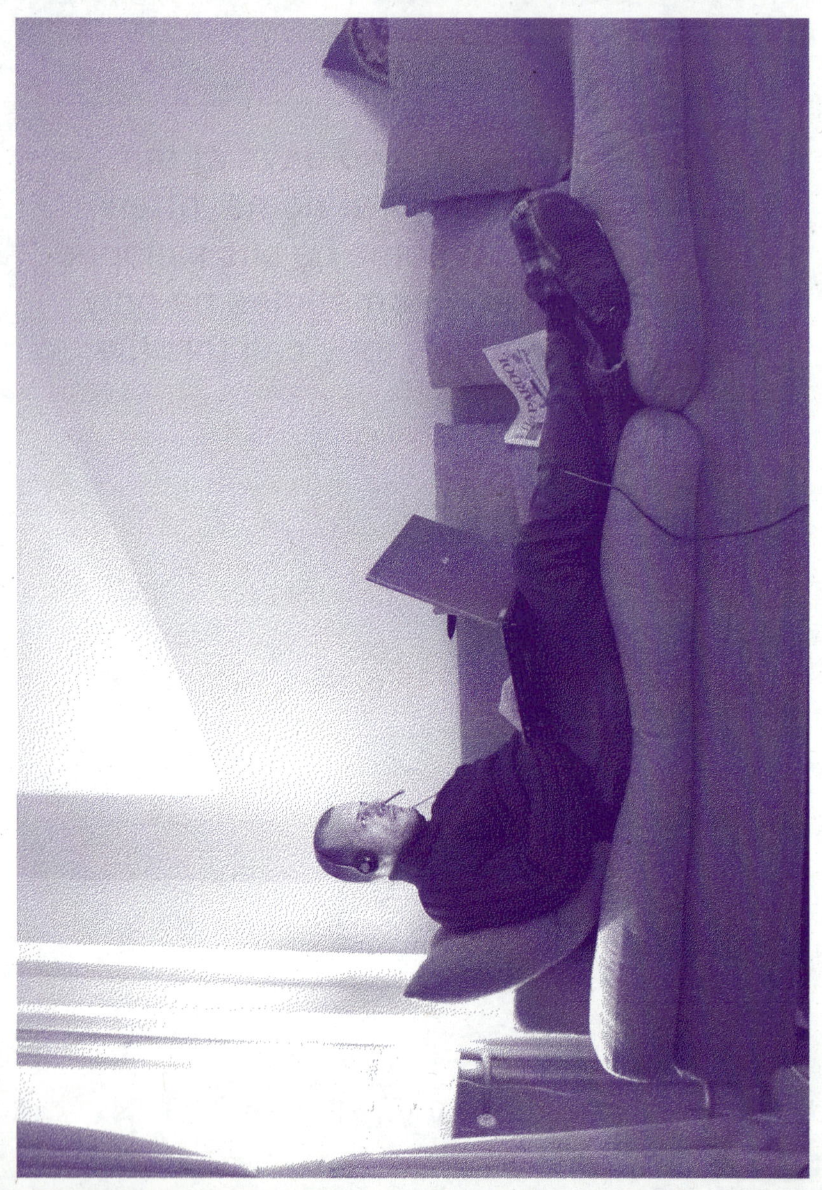

july 27

cosy.

messy but

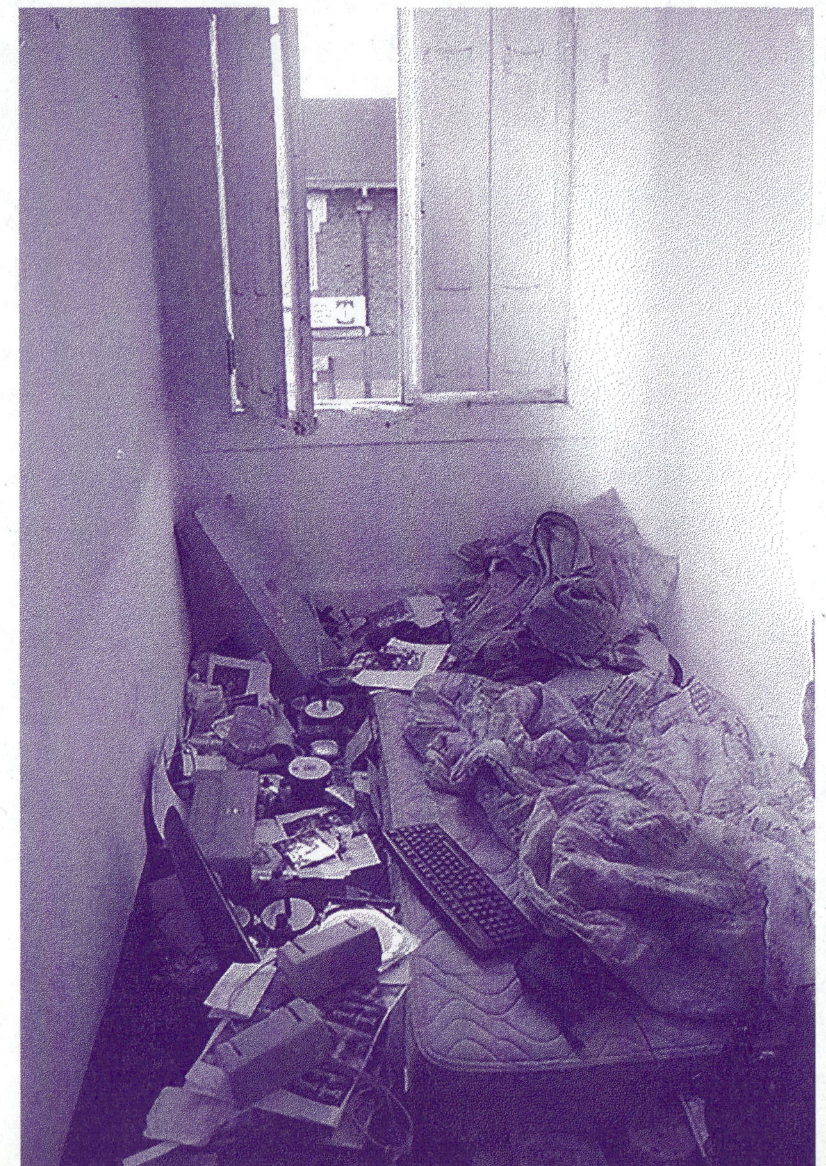

july 28

gardening in green.

what do you want to reach?

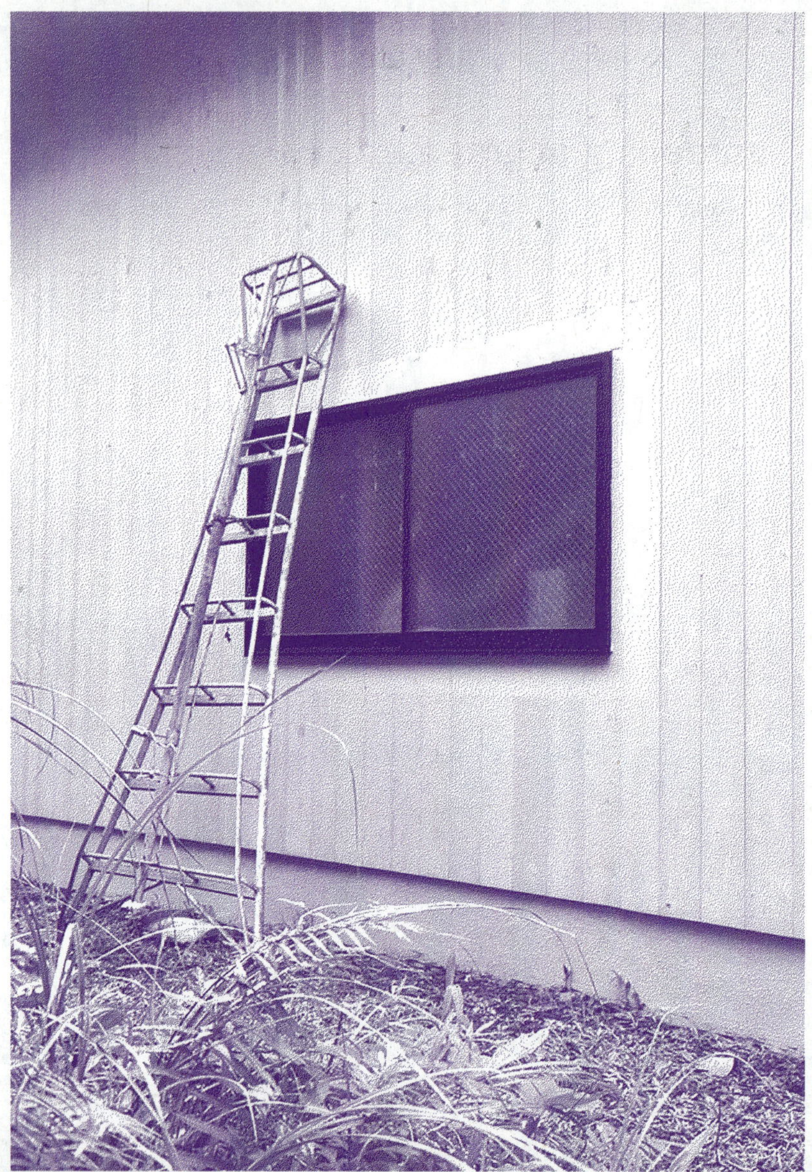

july 29

this is teamwork! a whole week
of intense work. i like the smell
of fresh paint.

my parents painted our house

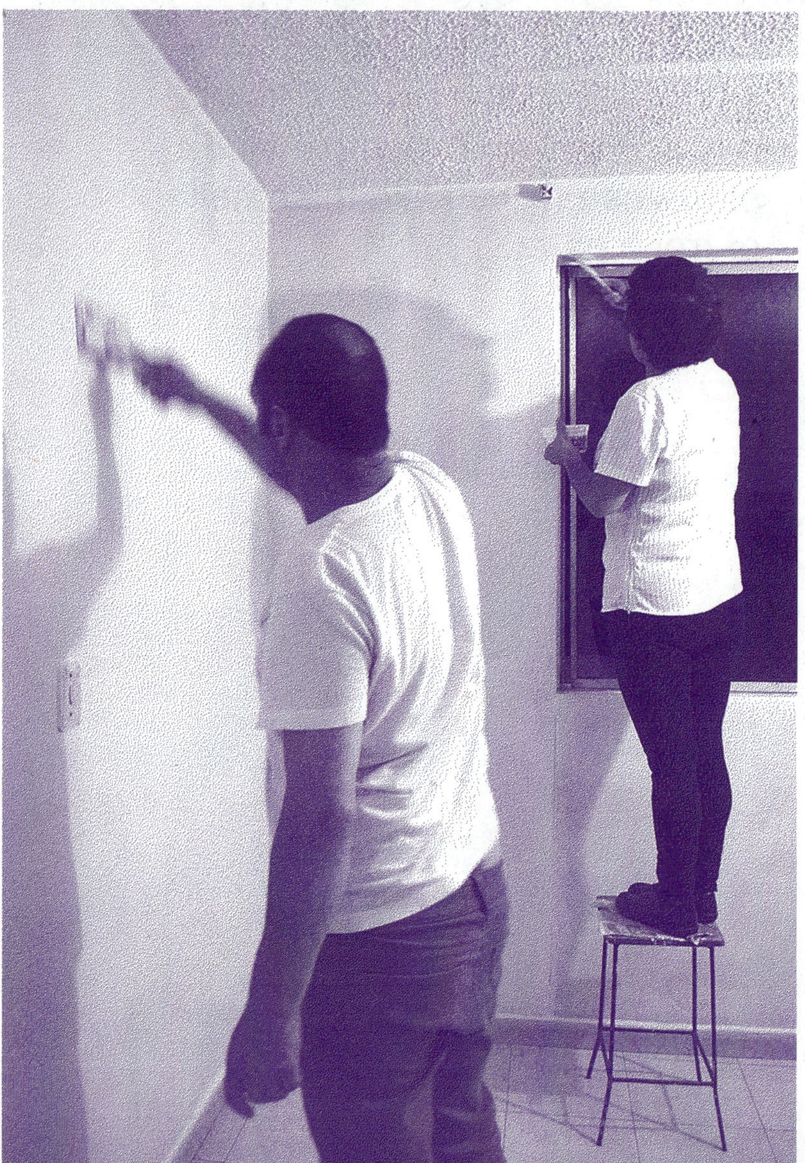

july 30

vanité.

vanity

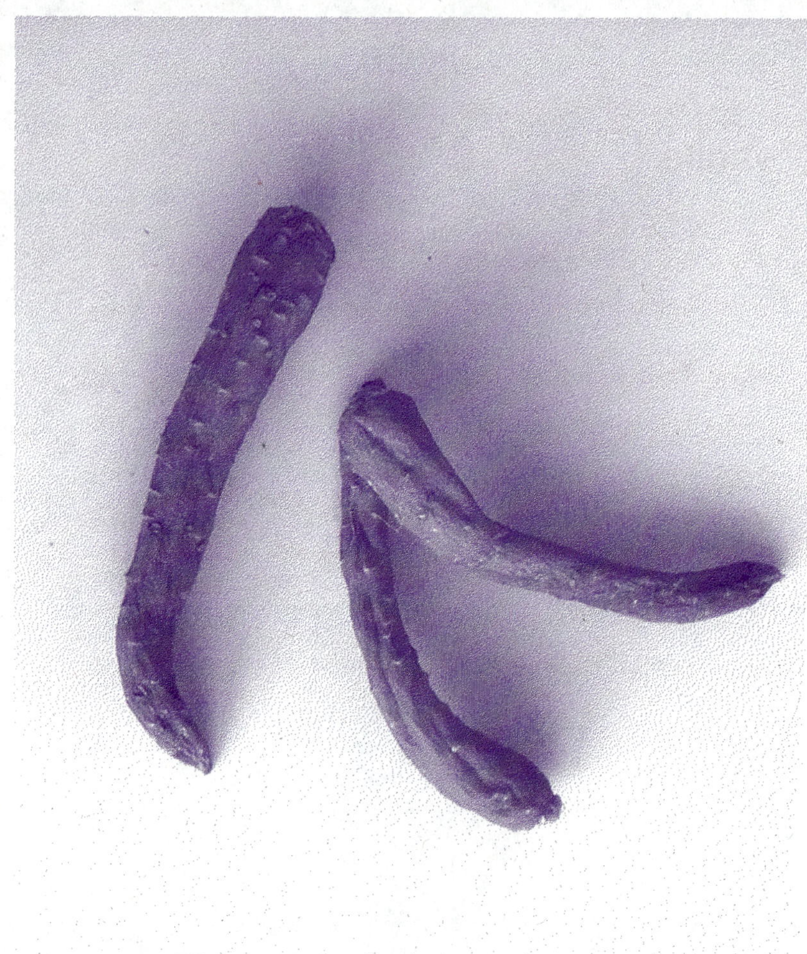

july 31

lunchtime. the weather is sweaty.
easy living and a dishwashing
machine. family of four. coming
of age count: two.

first photograph i ever took

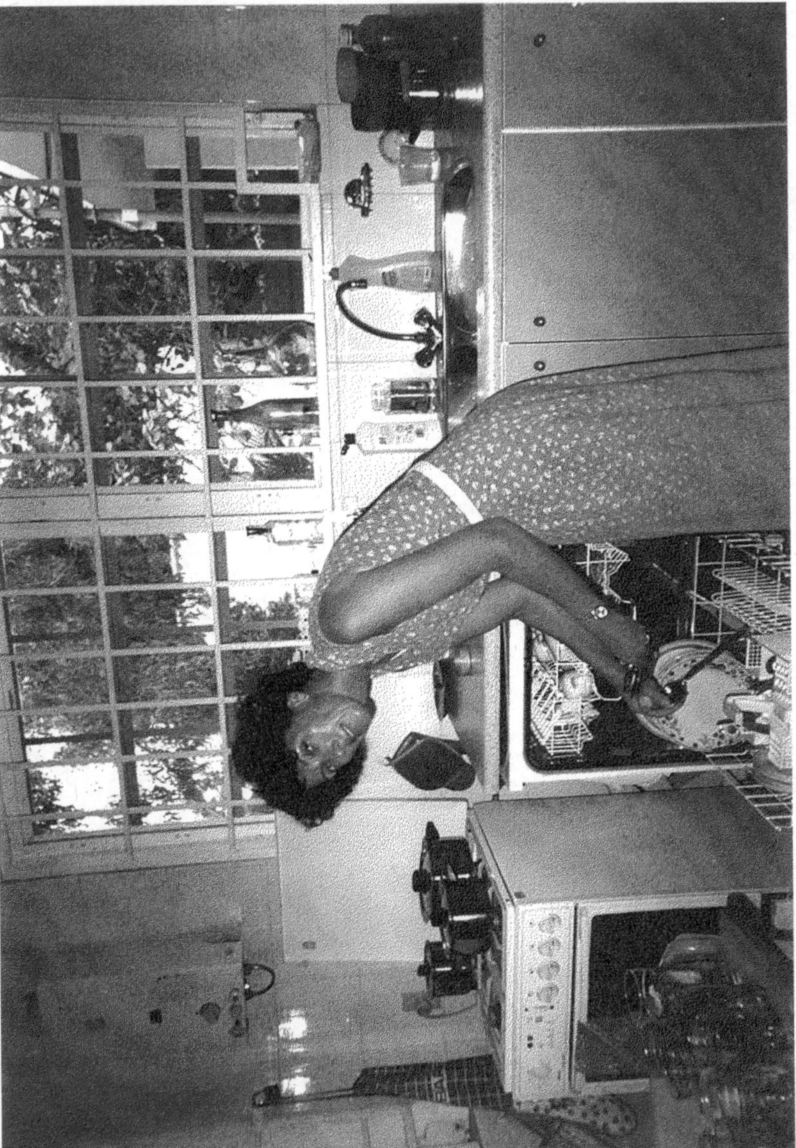

august 1

sunday.

today's mail

Sjoerd Ebberink
Boschdijk 372
5622 PB Eindhoven
522 PB
no. 372
SJOERD EBBERINK
BOSCHDIJK 372
5622 PB EINDHOVEN
POSTFILTER
44

august 2

mother wants to talk about cleaning.

invisibility

CHECK CONTENTS   THROUGH OPENING
WE NEED TO TALK
—MOM
North Atlantic Operating
Company, Inc.
VISIT US AT
www.zigzag.com
ZIG-ZAG

august 3

blue cubes and flowers on the plates.

i wash my bowl of flowers

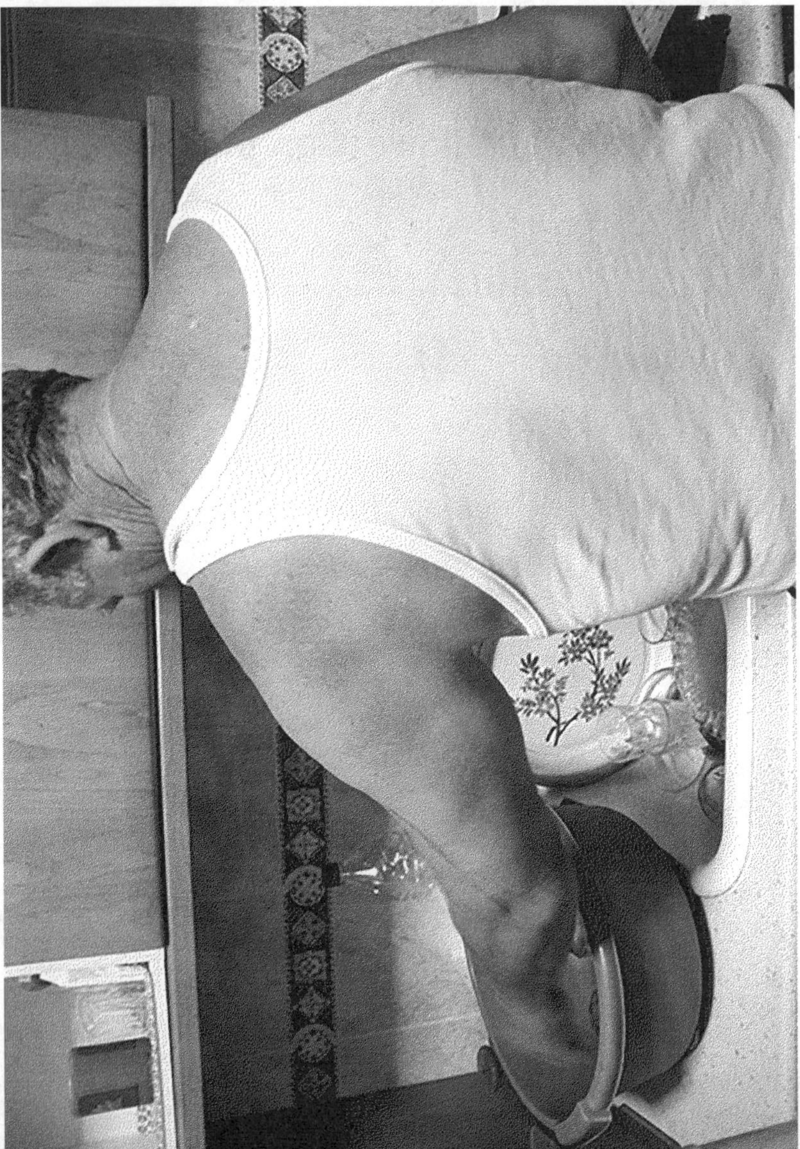

august 4

proyecto de futuro jardín casero.

macetas

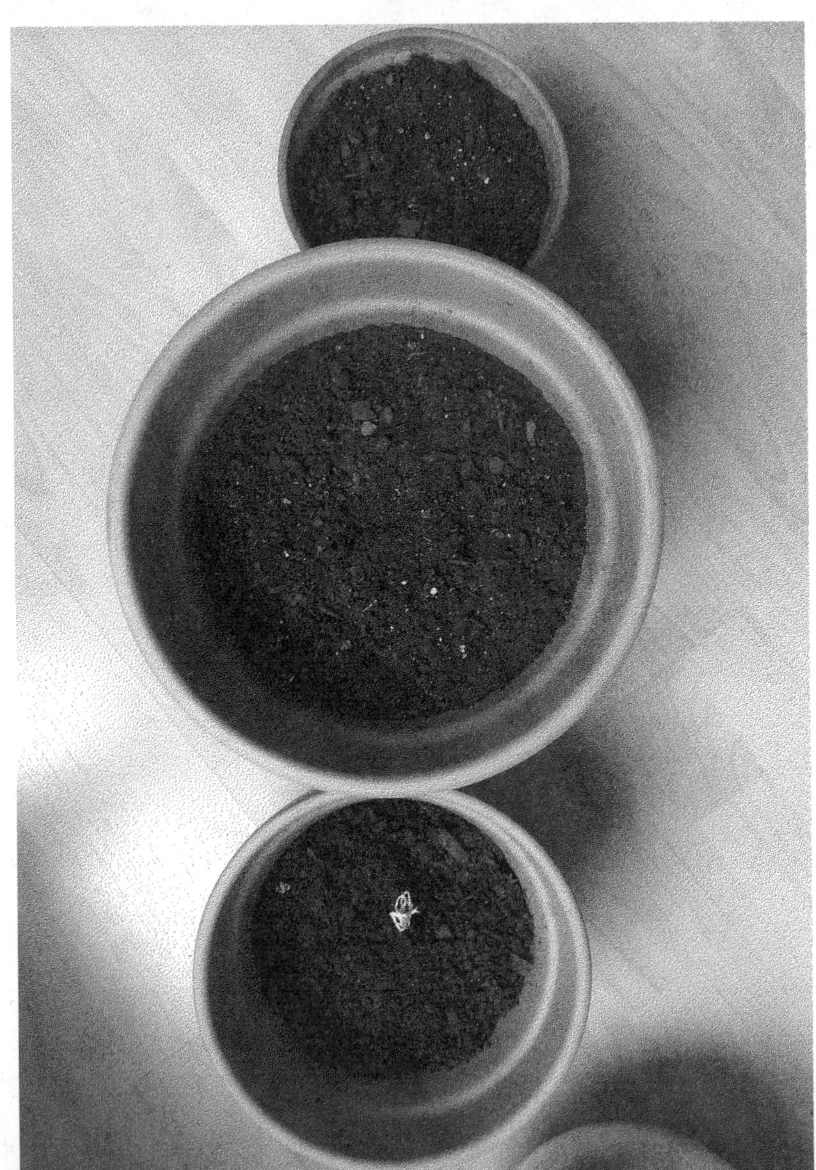

august 5

doing her thing.

august 5

feminism

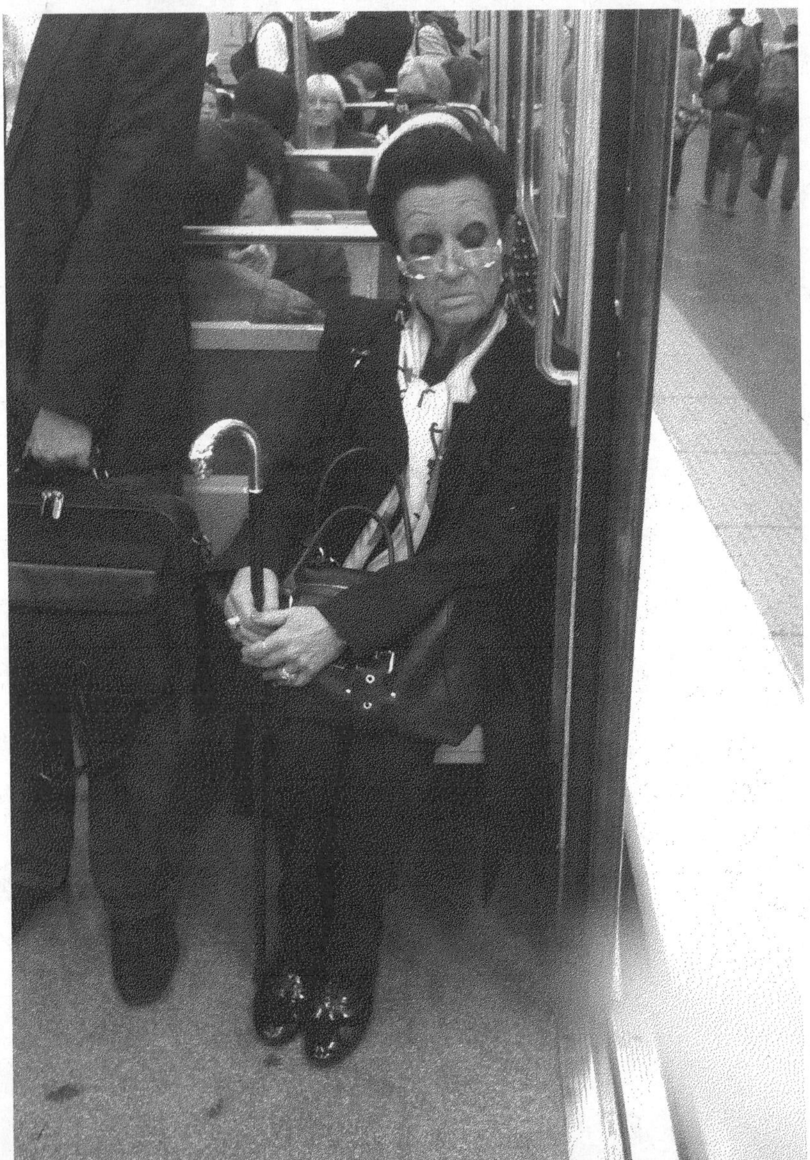

august 6

i have changed houses seven times
in the last years.

moving out and in = life in a box

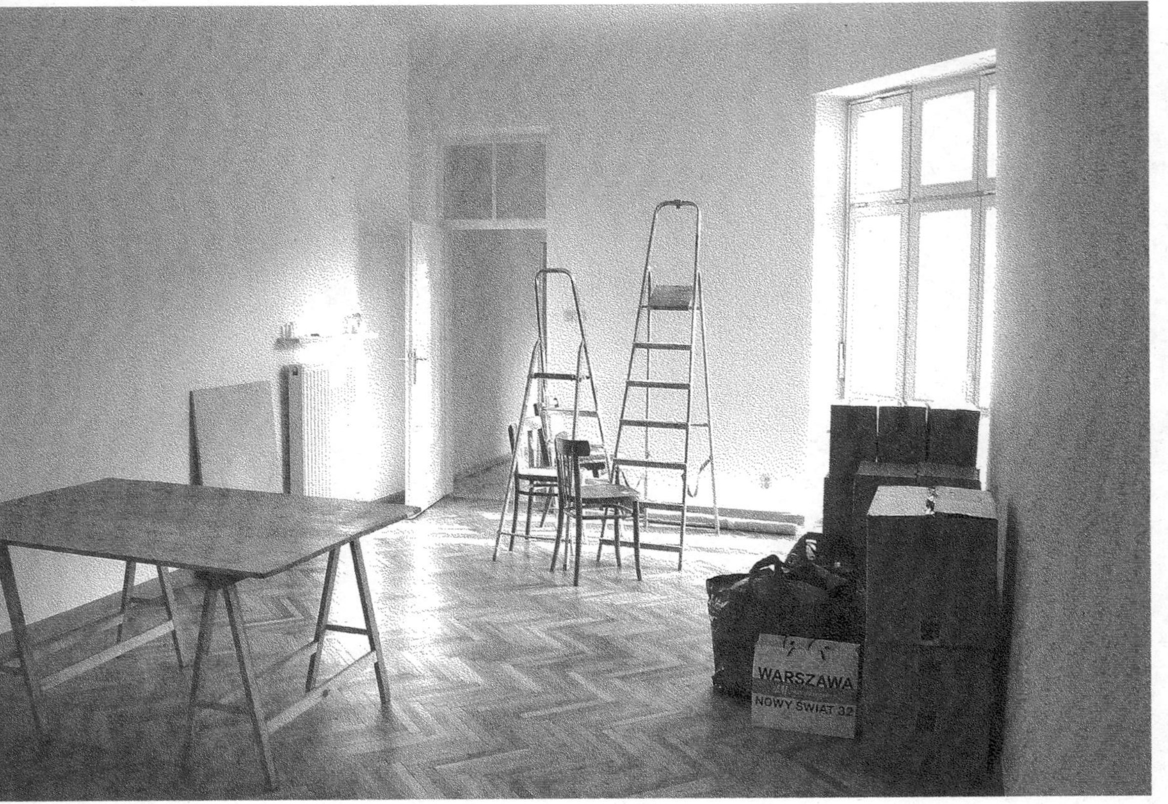

WARSZAWA
NOWY ŚWIAT 32

august 7

laundry

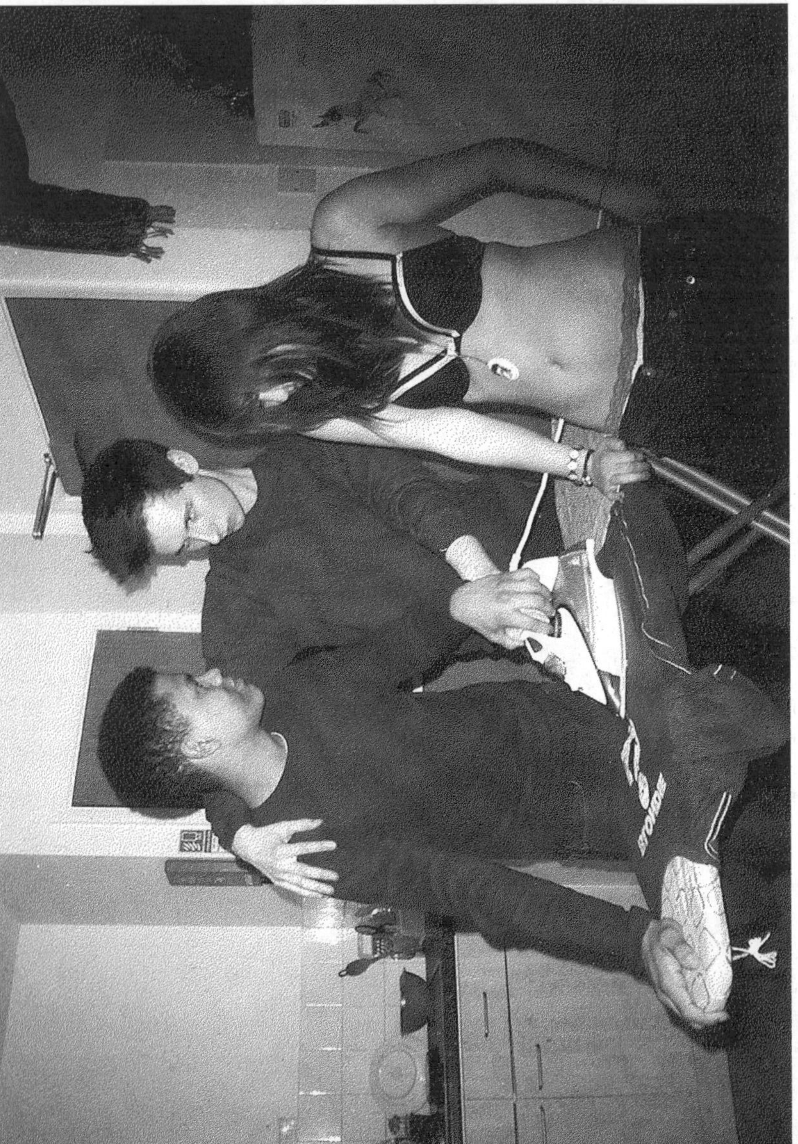

august 8

electricity breakdown at my apartment in barcelona. julio, the owner of the bar downstairs came to have a look and also youness, a friend. i thought i'd have to pay for a new installation in order to fix it and have light again. two days later, pablo, the neighbour from the first floor, knocked at my door to ask if i had light. we called the real estate emergency telephone and surprisingly a man came two hours later to fix the electric box at the entrance of the building. he said that the electric system could burn at any moment. i decided to leave 10 days later. i've also emigrated to the netherlands.

electricity breakdown

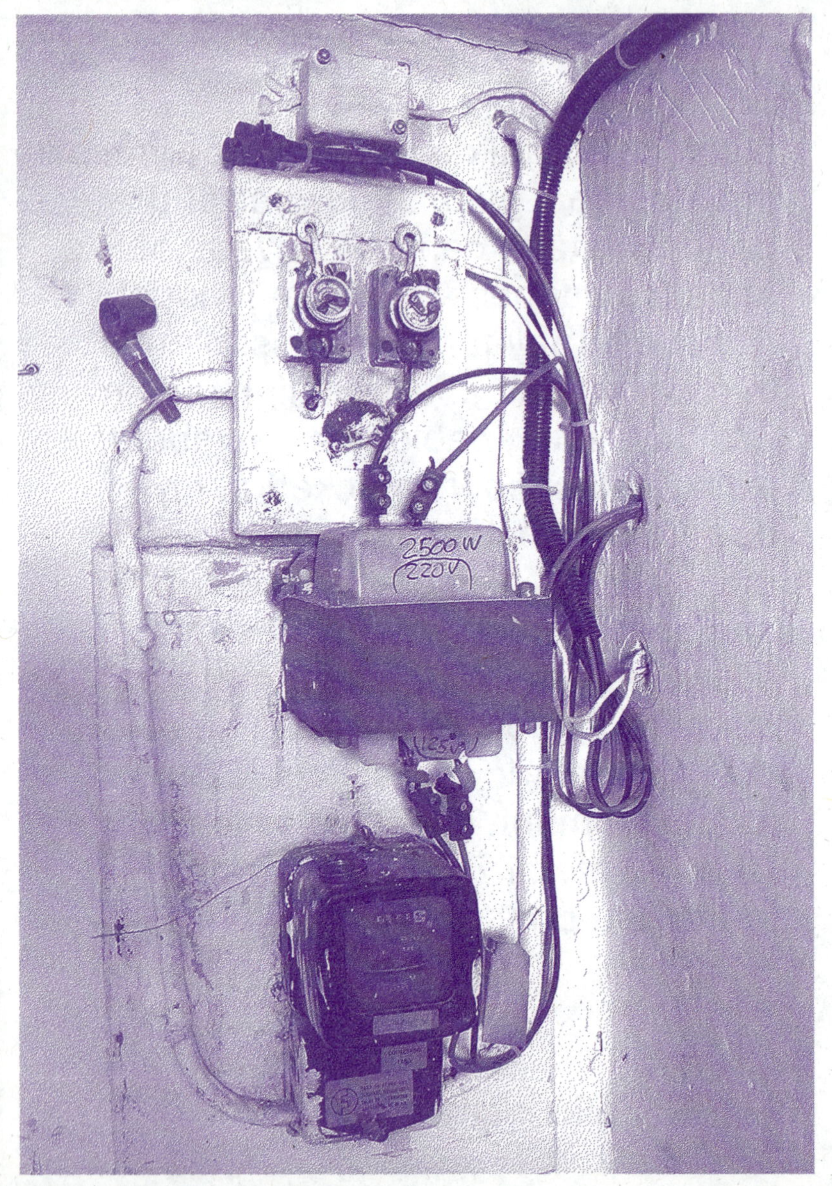
2500 W
220 V
125 V

much like cleaning can really change
the atmosphere in a positive way,
i've also found that frequently changing
the art on the walls of my home has
a very invigorating effect. this might
require making new art, getting your
friends to loan you some, checking
out thrift stores, or buying art within
your budget on the web. buy some
of those cheap pop-out frames
and you can easily exchange printed
matter works with little hassle.
it's easy to get stuck with the same
old stuff on the walls—change it and
you'll see and feel the difference!

picture work

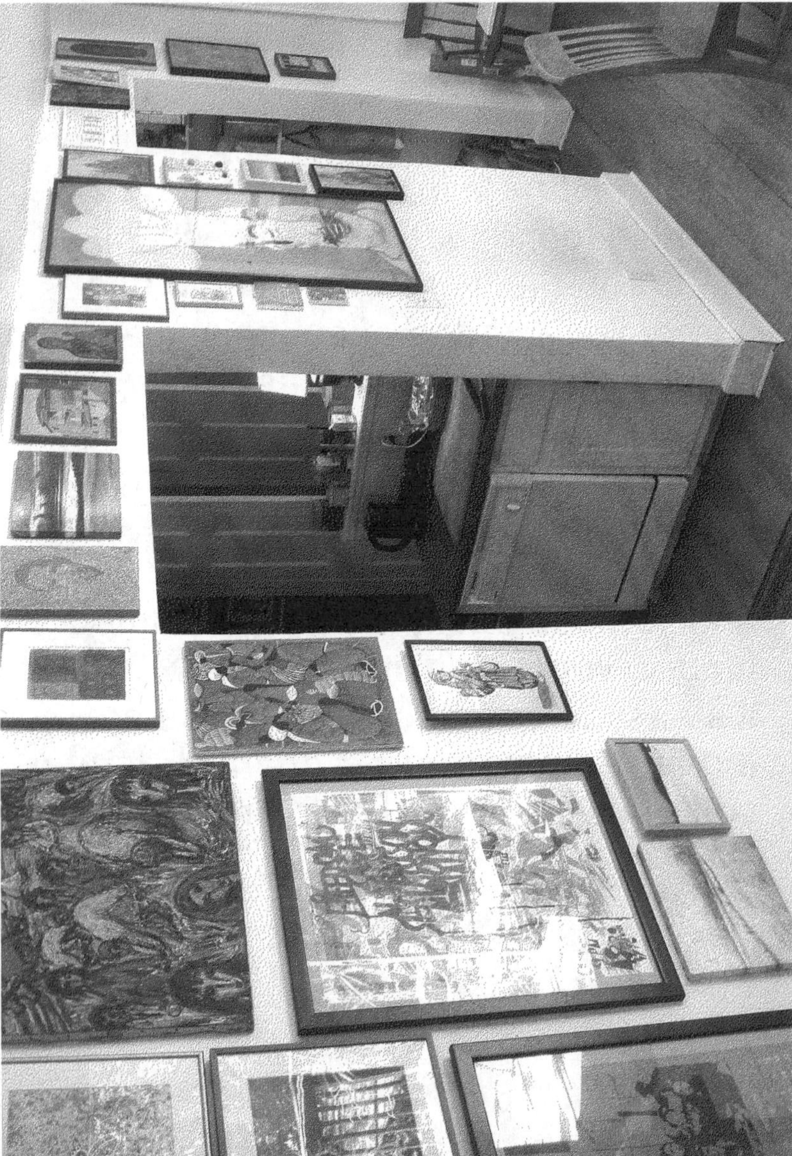

august 10

me working at home (unpaid) with the images from eurovision (visions of europe) song contest on domestic work. the polish contribution.

eurovision (visions of europe)

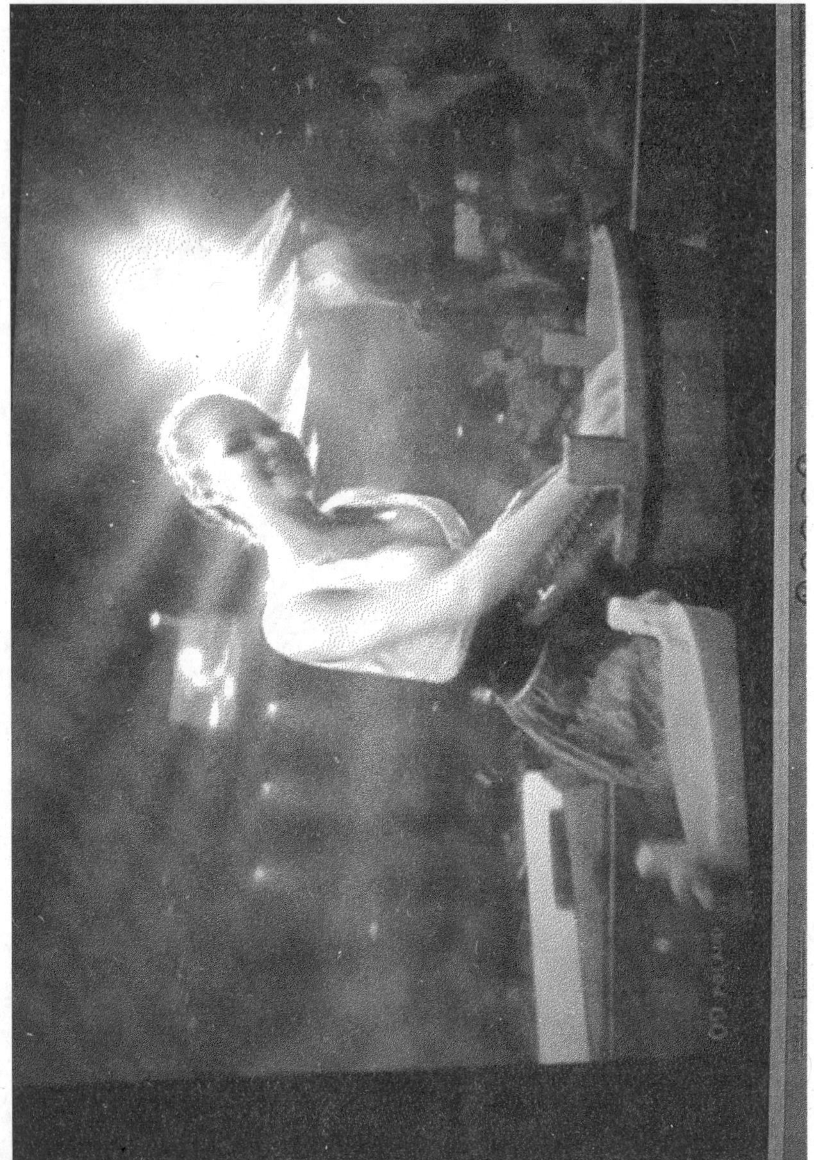

august 11

if you need to buy something, you only have to put the money in this "technology" and send down the rope, shouting someone who will put it in, and up it will go!

lazy way, napoli way

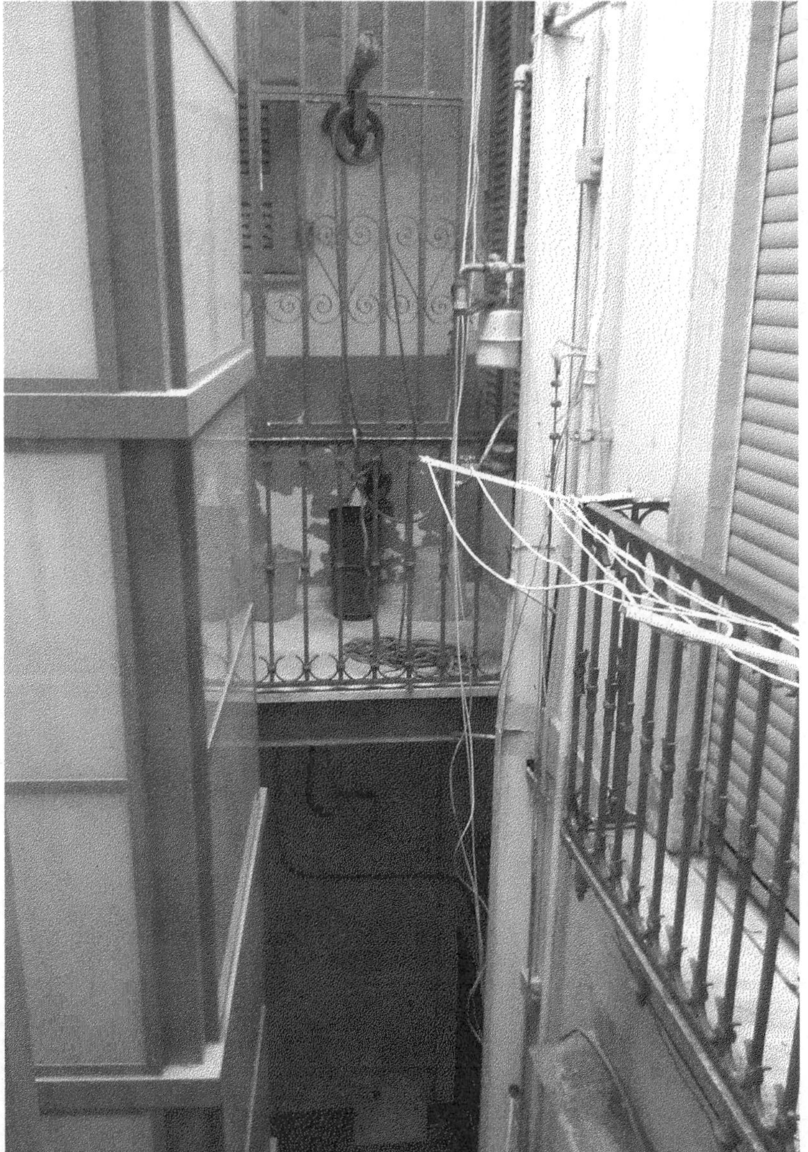

somehow i have more party and
holiday pictures than domestic work
pictures in my albums.

laundry

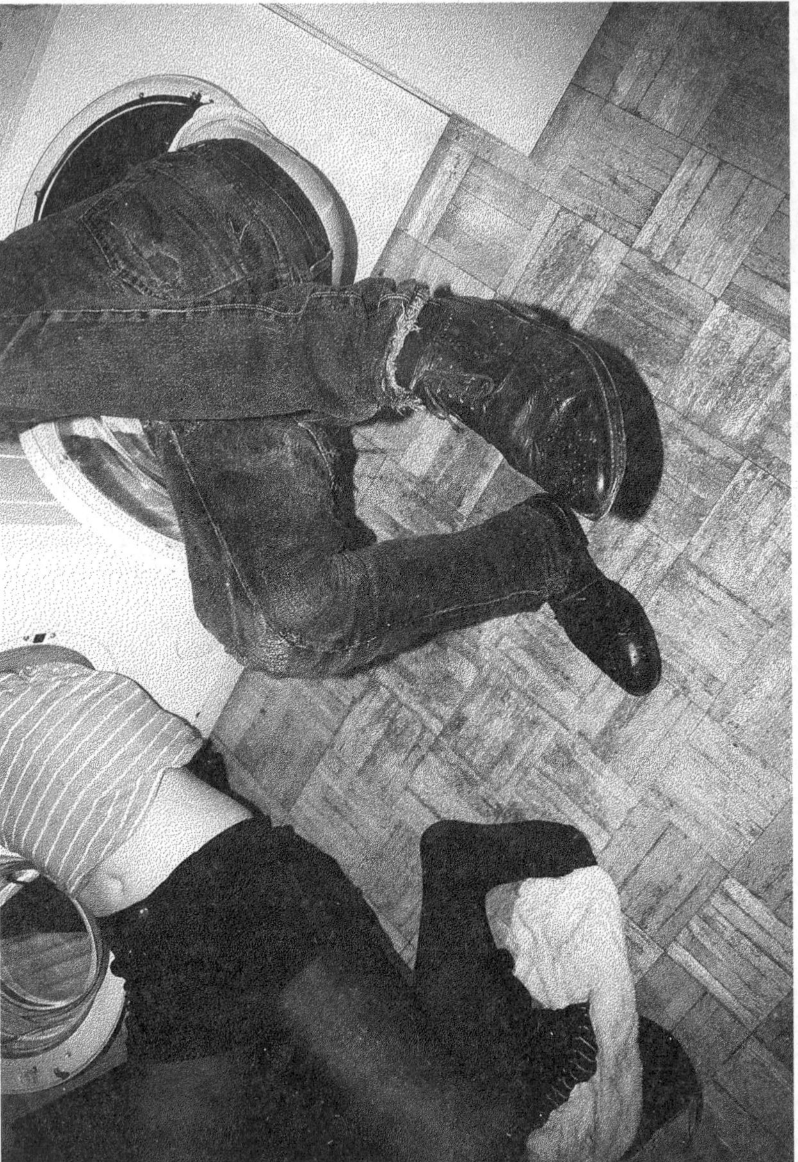

august 13

*(8.30 pm, exhausted): "did you buy some food for dinner?" / ° (still stuck at the laptop): "no, i didn't have time, i had tons of emails to answer" / *(exhausted and a/hu/ngry): "i had many emails, too…" / °: "yes, but you work from home…"

semiotics of the kitchen

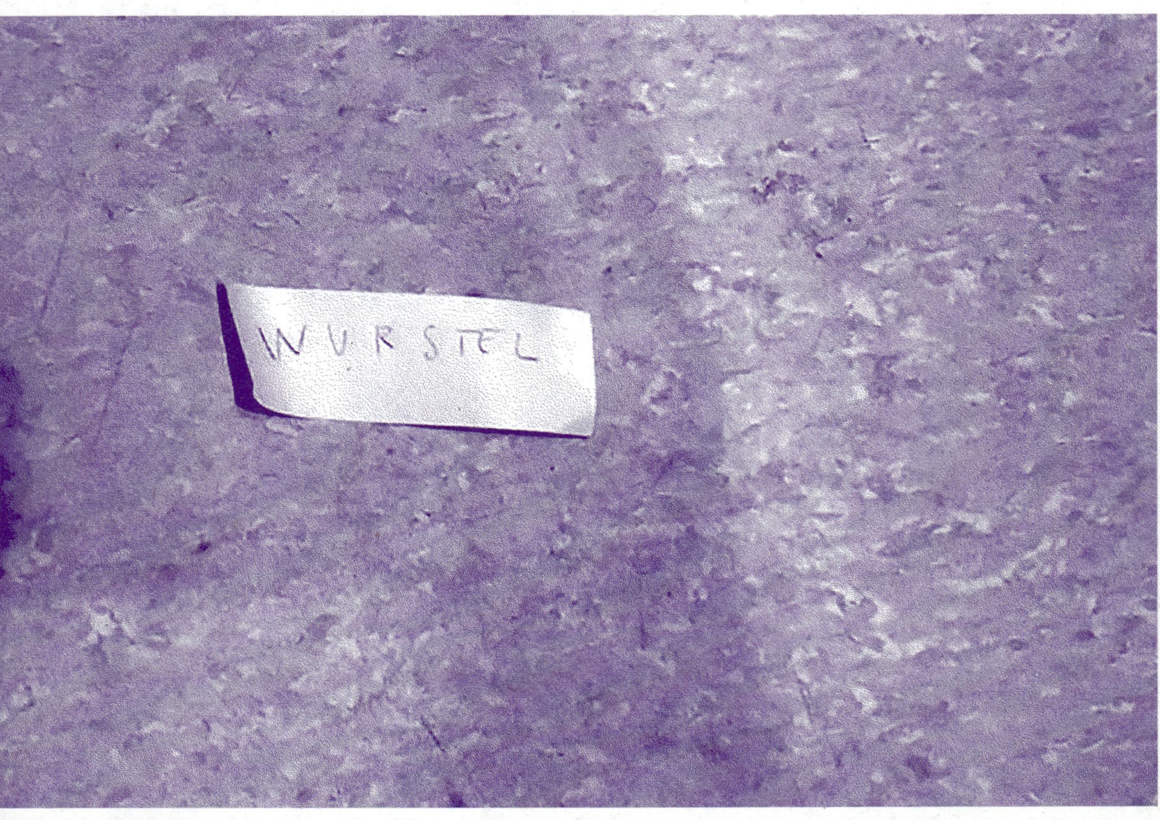
WURSTEL

august 14

domestic safety vs. wanderlust.

commodified zen-ness

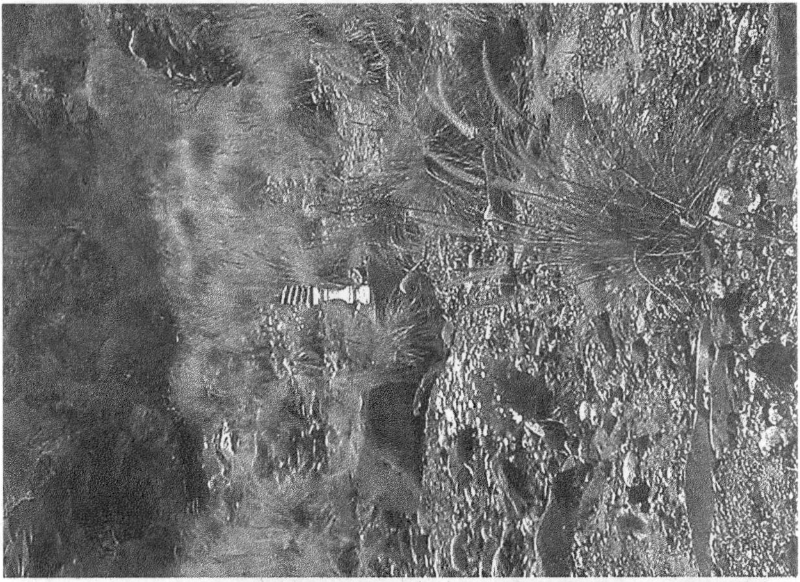

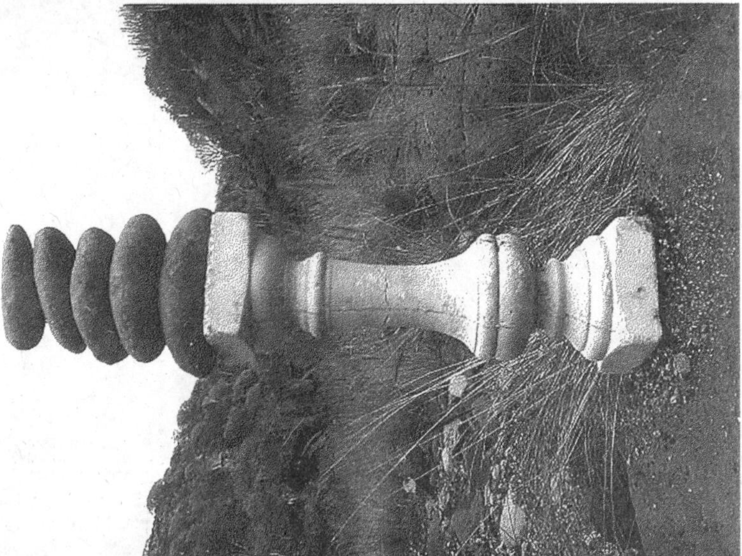

august 15

domestic work as a suspension of
other work at home riddled with anxiety
(over the time spent and therefore less
time for other work) or experiencing
catharsis (getting things done and
making a proper home ground),
it demands its own time and pace.

cleaning dust

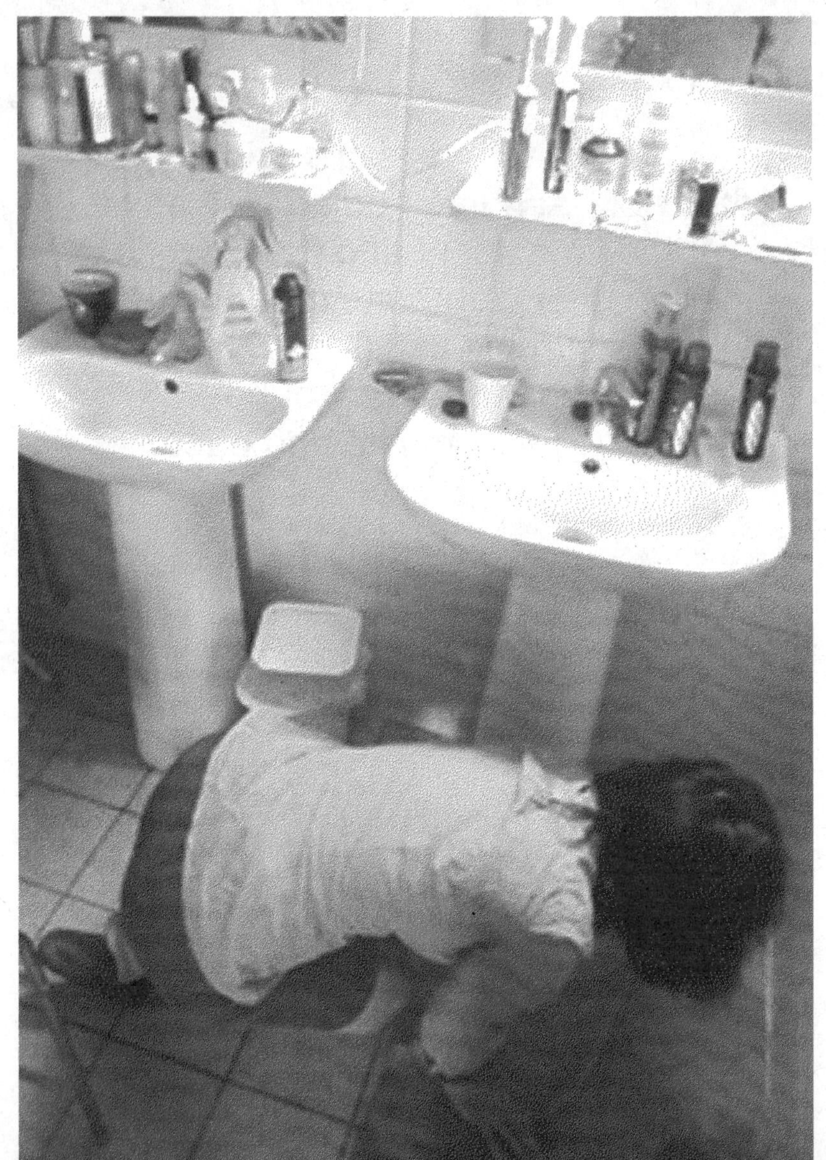

august 16

cleaning at night with christina
in portimão.

at night

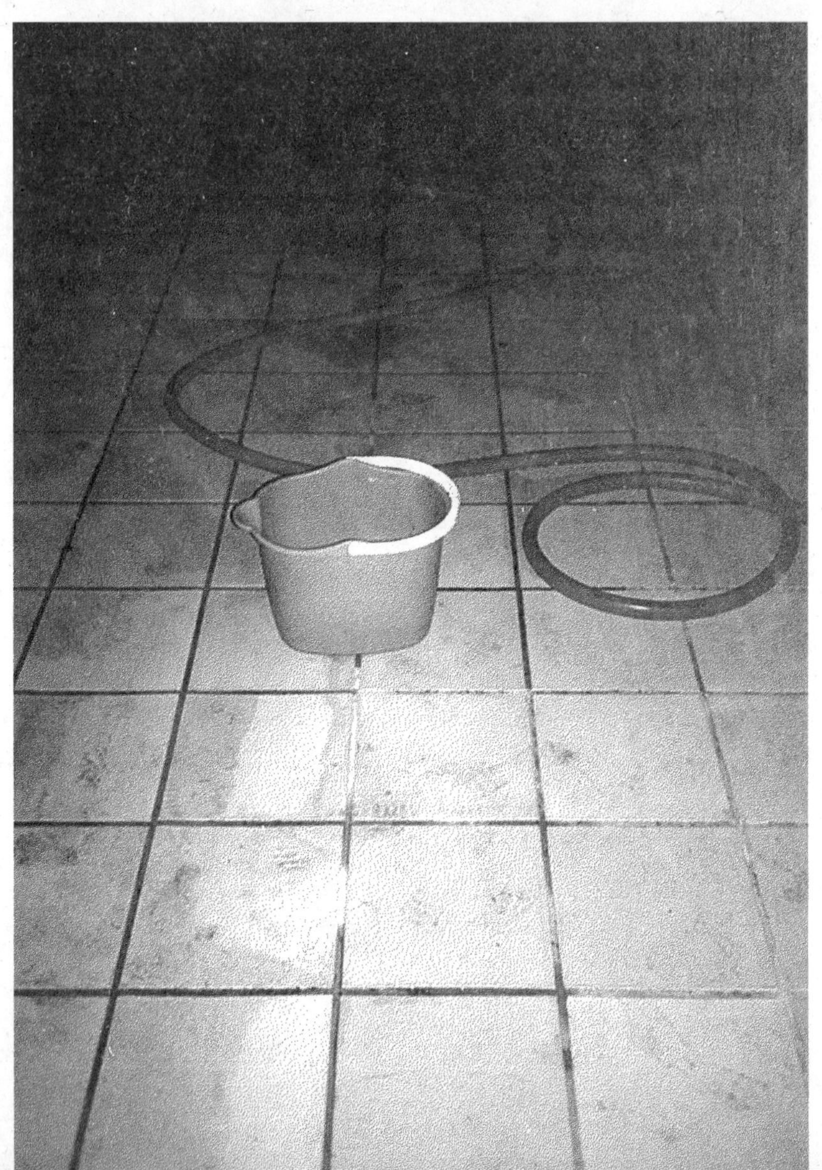

august 17

dustbunny galore—capitalism revisited!
powered by miele.

dustbunny galore

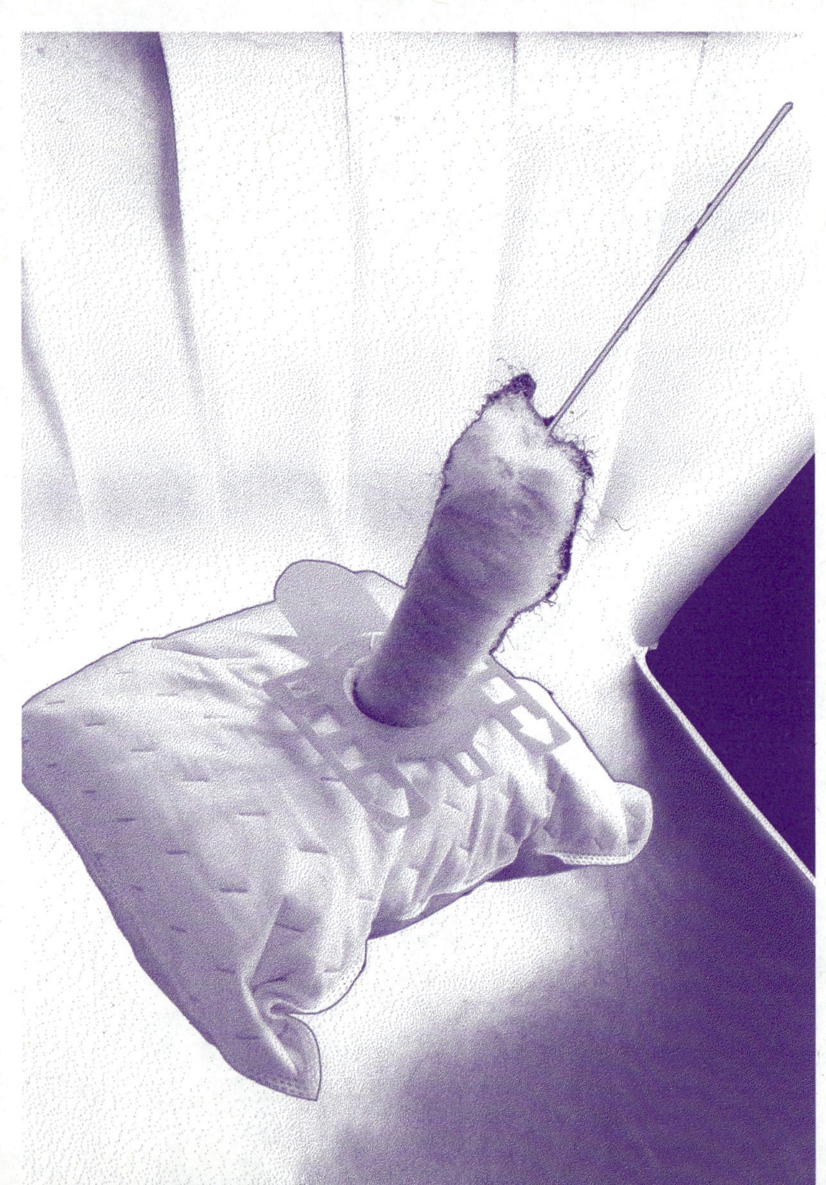

august 18

cleaning and ordering helps me think!

bang! nice and tidy

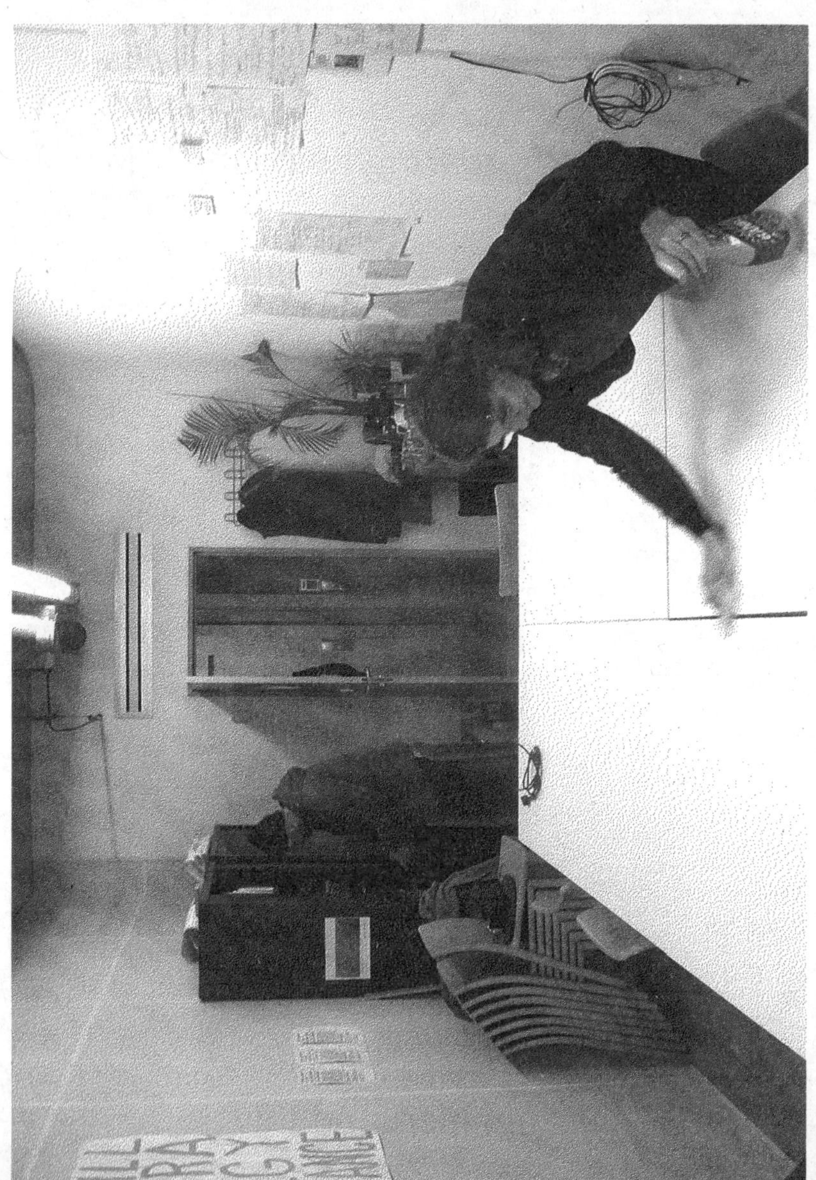

silence. (lat. silentĭum)
1. n. abstention from speaking.
2. n. lack of noise.
3. n. lack or omission of something
in writing.

artificial. (lat. artificialis).
1. adj. by hand or art of man.
2. adj. unnatural, false.
3. adj. produced by human ingenuity.

artificial silence

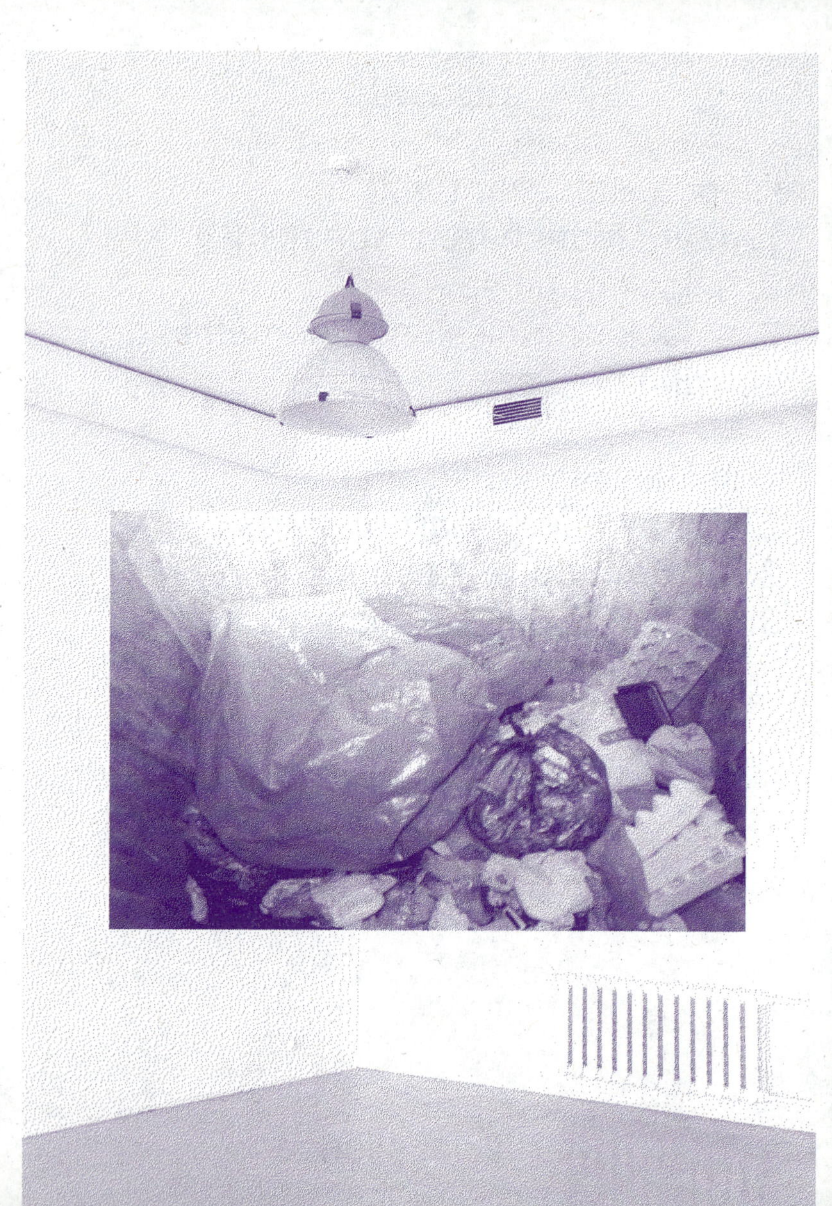

august 20

cleaning windows is part of our work.

cleaning windows

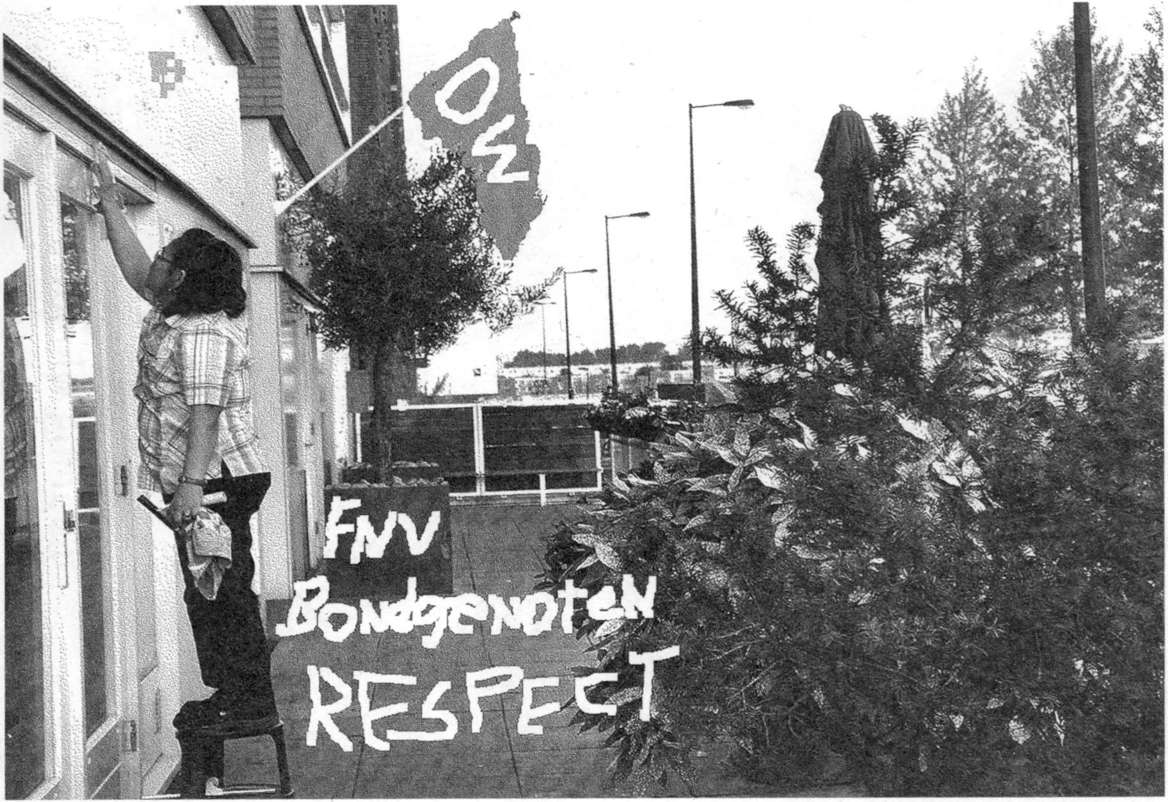

OW
FNV
Bondgenoten
RESPECT

august 21

sky, shadow, tate. millennium bridge.
cold wind. soft breath. a lovely noon.

pipol at tate

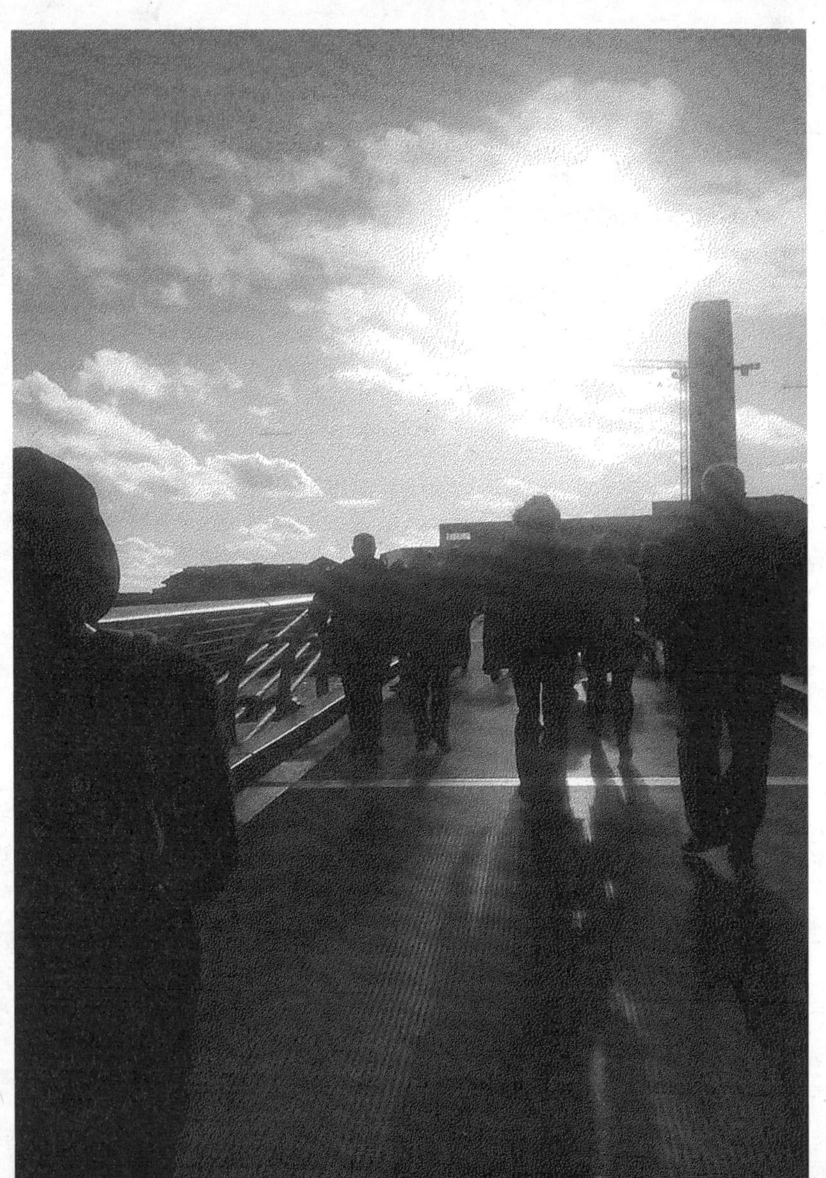

freedom, equality, rentability.
still from *tiempo real* [real time],
(2003), video, 43 min.

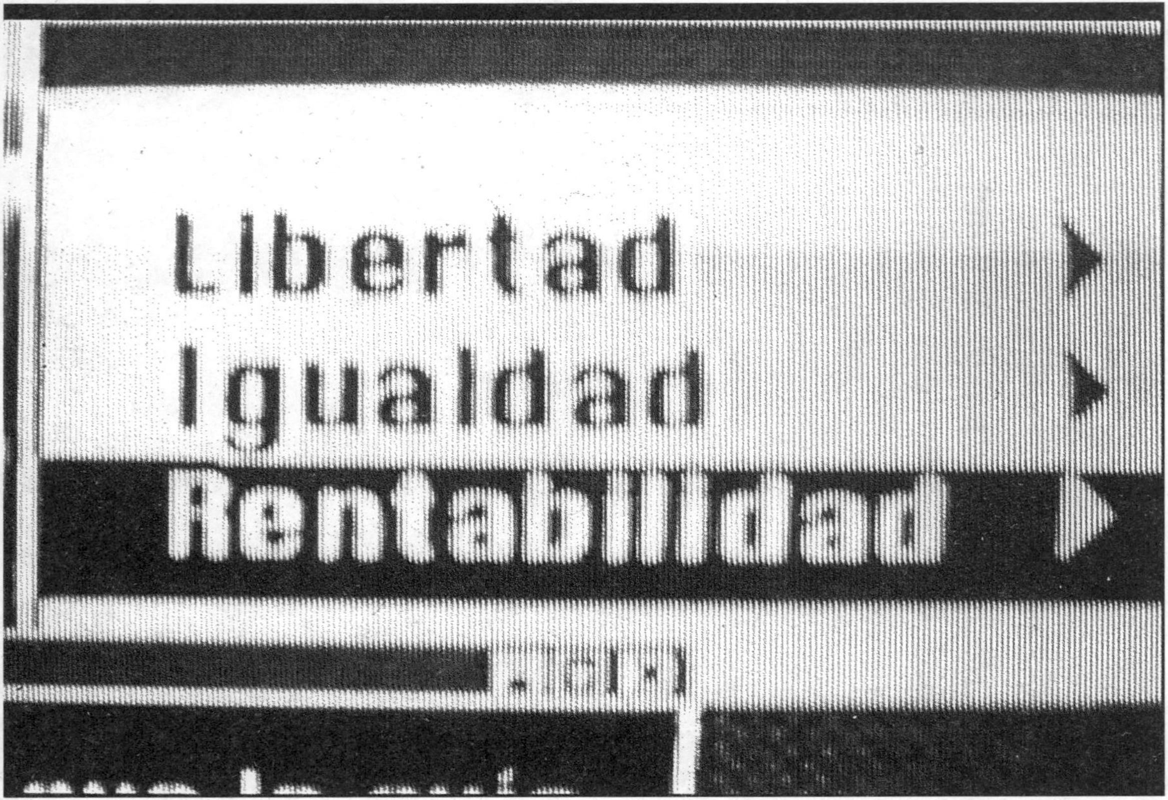

Libertad
Igualdad
Rentabilidad

august 23

ninety-seven selected photographs
showing groups of wealthy peruvian
people in daily domestic situations.
in the background of each image one
can see either a figure or a deletion
of a domestic worker. all images have
been collected from the social network
site facebook.

97 house maids

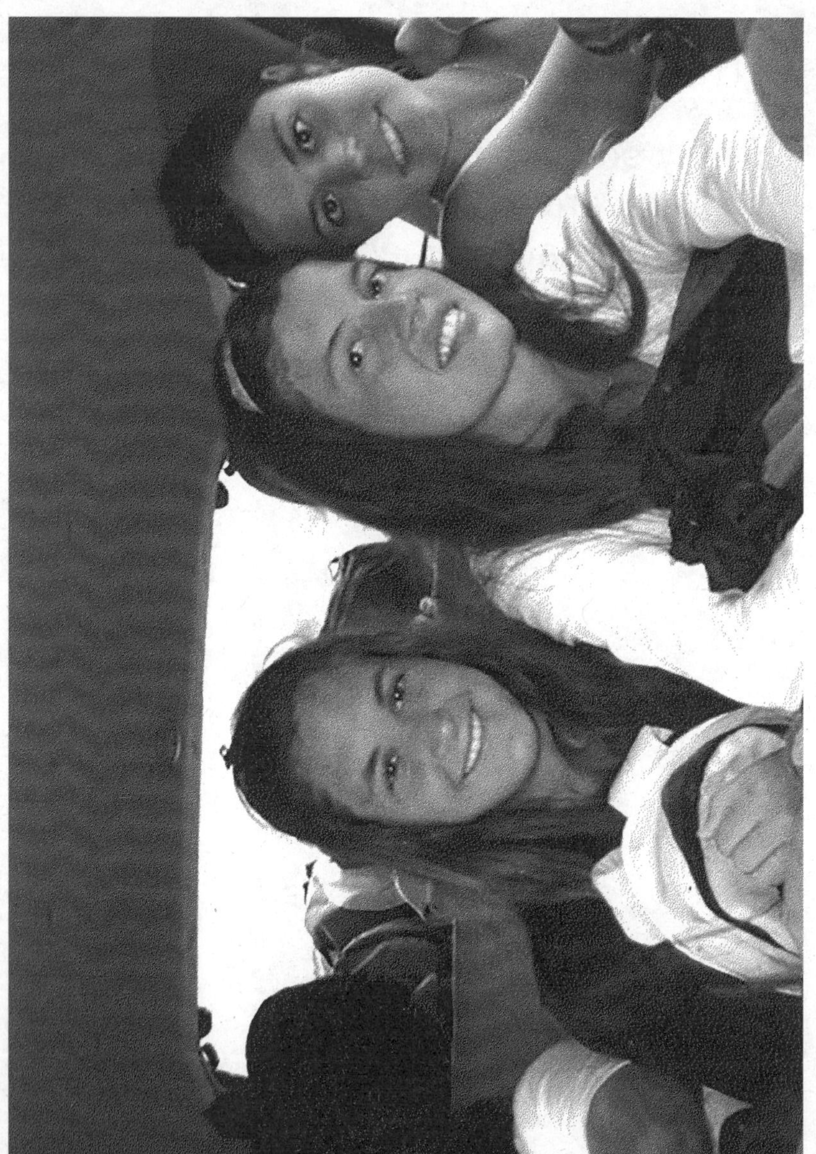

august 24

photo taken after the filming.

christian's studio

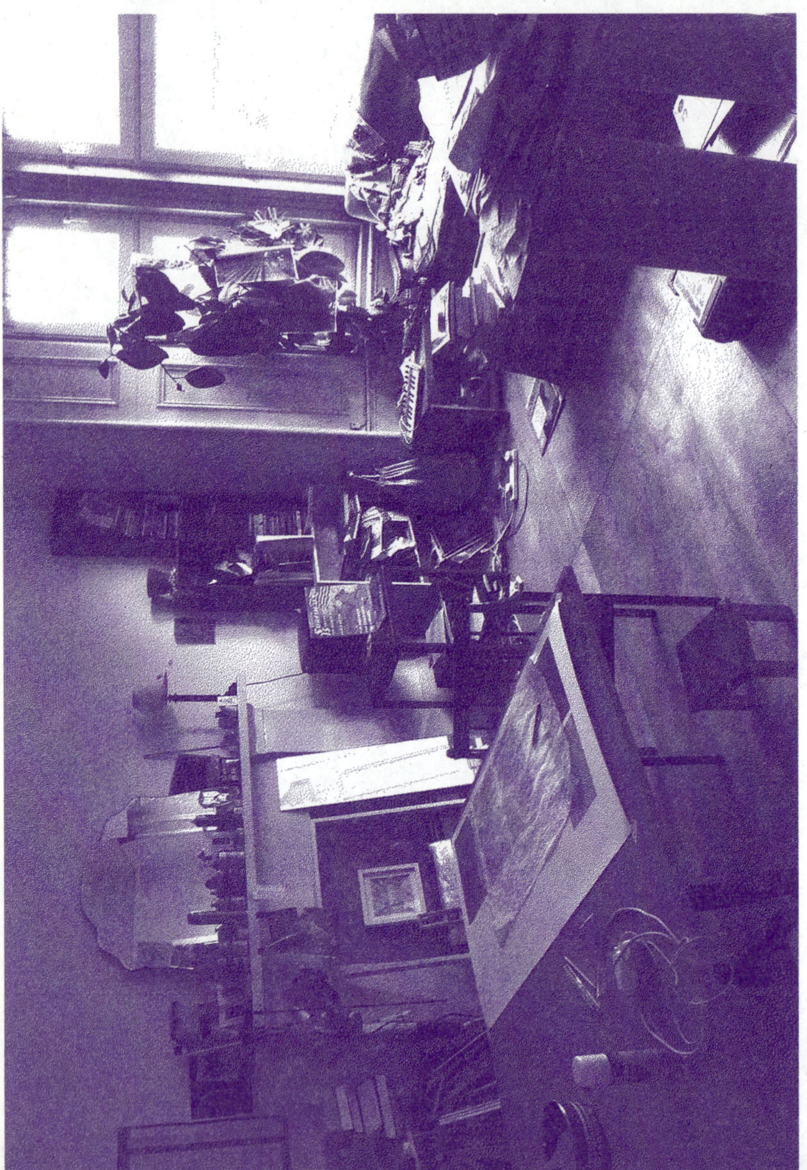

august 25

the walk to school is never boring in autumn… the leaves on the ground would smile and tell me, "oooppss, watch-out!" i would chose among these shapes of wonders and place some in my book to keep them warm and safe. my little girl would greet me with a very sweet smile as we walk home hand in hand. domestic work is work, such responsibility with love and affection for the children and families we love and care for needs recognition. families are the building blocks of every nation. justice for domestic workers demand recognition in making domestic work visible in british society.

walk to school in autumn

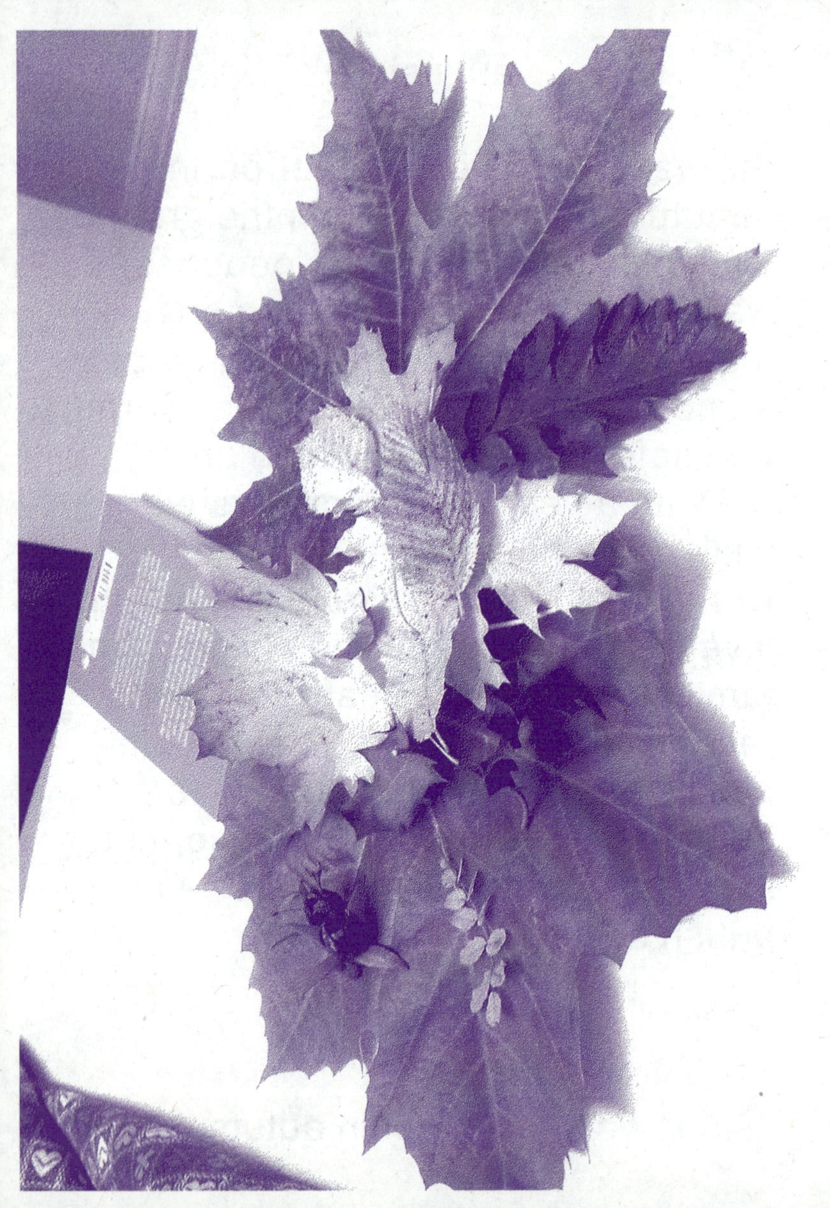

august 26

we are still working.

thinking time

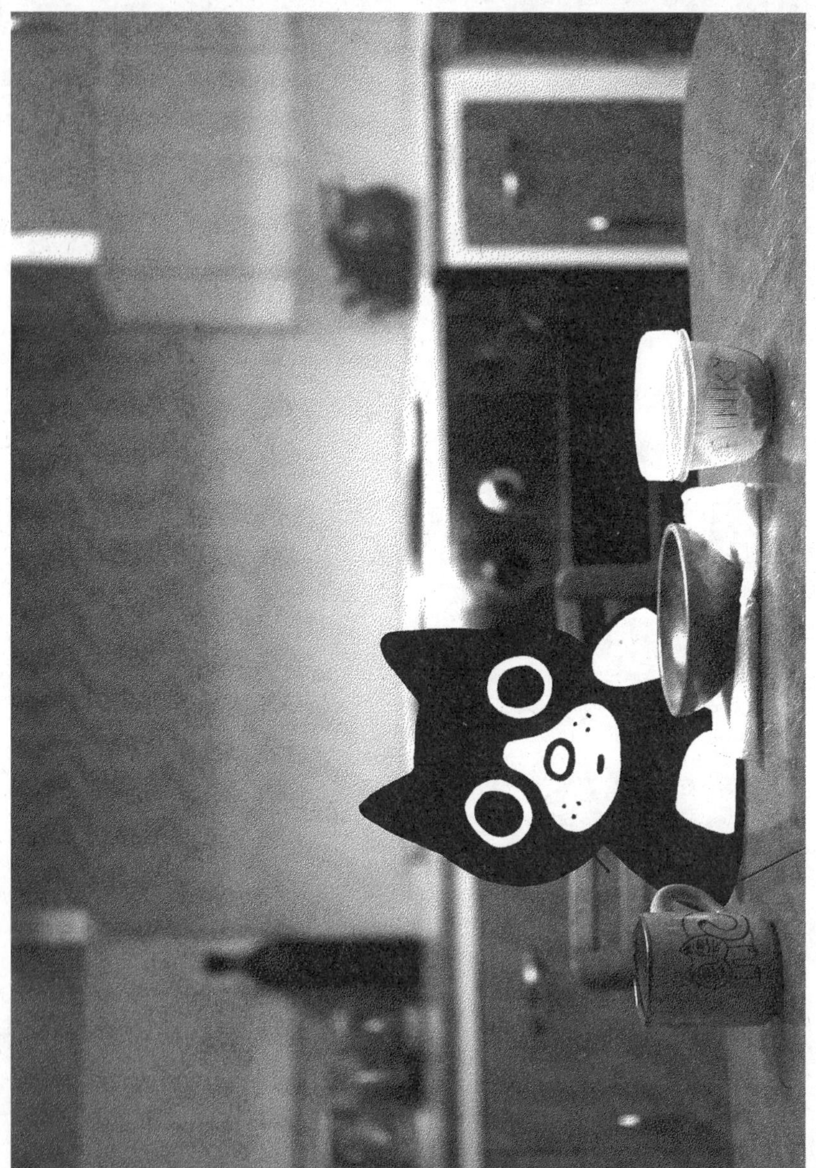

august 27

she is leaving home, but her only hand
luggage is a shopping trolley, so she
will have to go back. another domestic
excuse to occupy the public space.
amsterdam, 1998.

leaving home

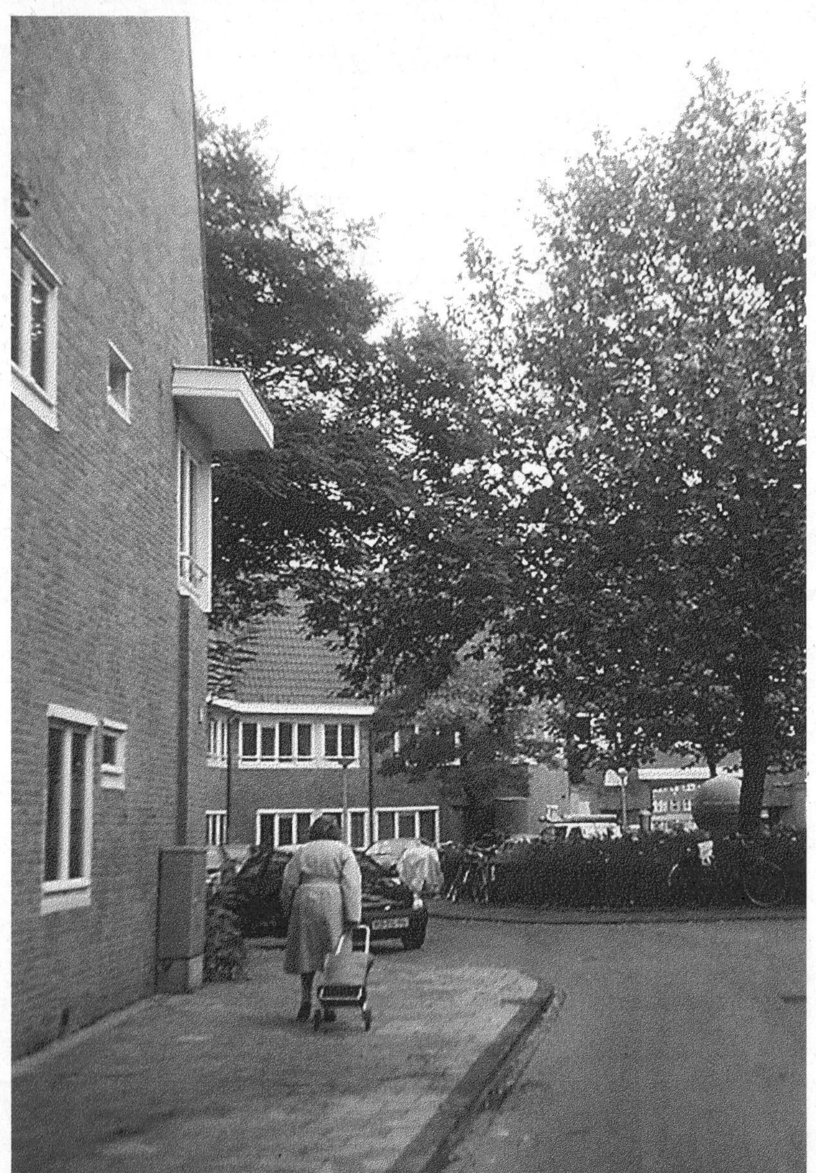

august 28

crouch on floor and cover body except
feet and ankles.

action 3

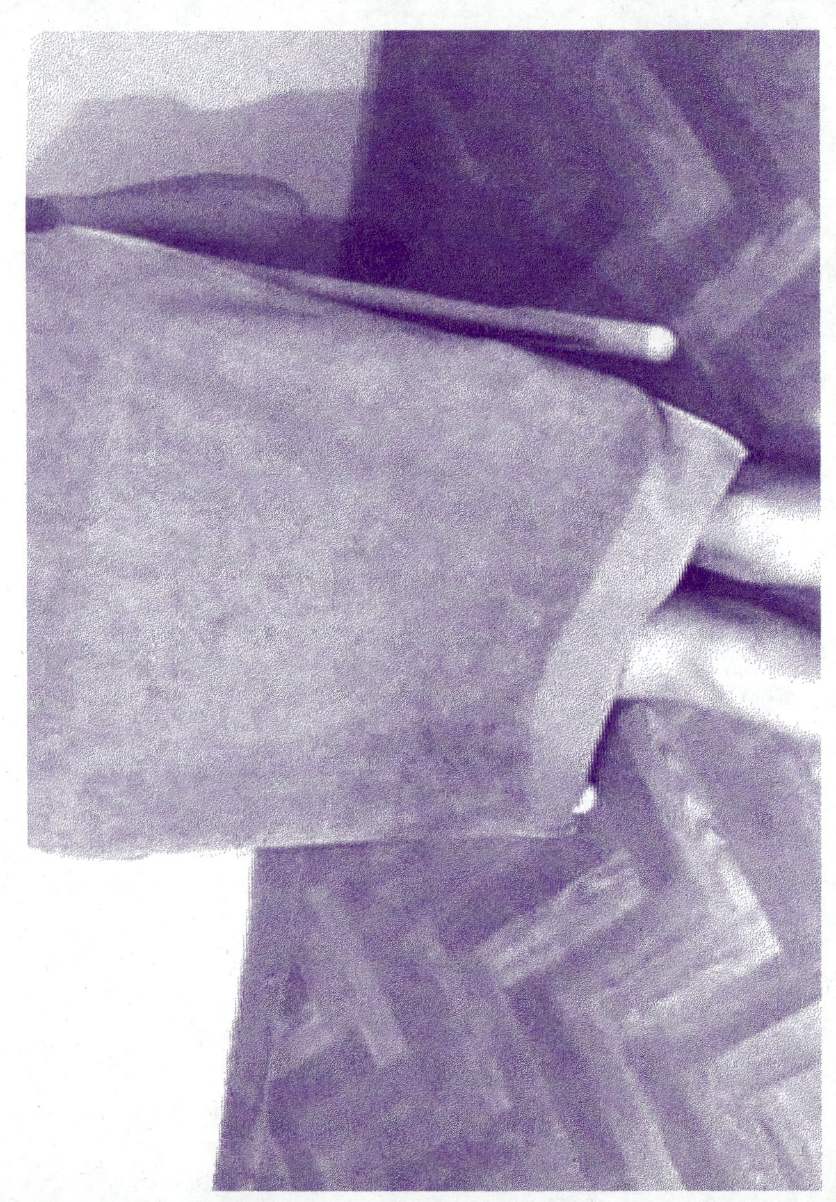

groups of clothes separated by colour
or tones and fabrics. attention, error
means the end of a garment—delicate,
hand wash…

laundry

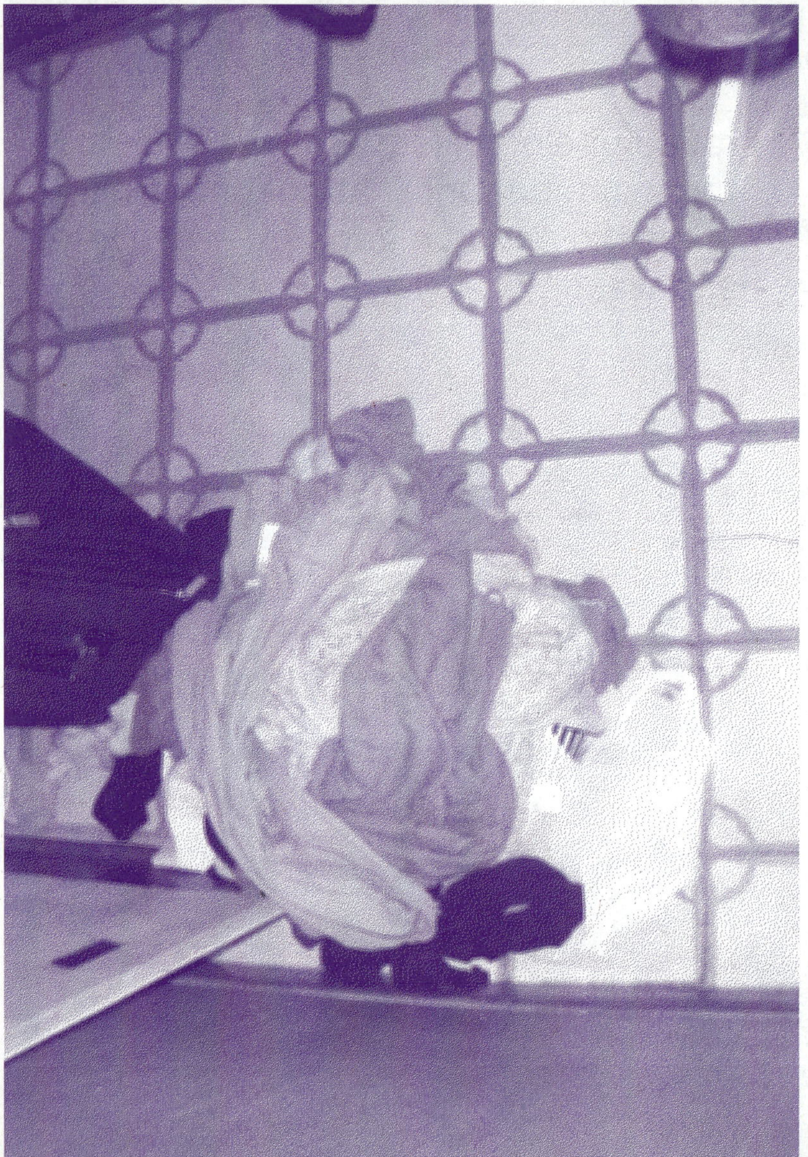

august 30

use a banana to clean your shoes.

shoe cleaner

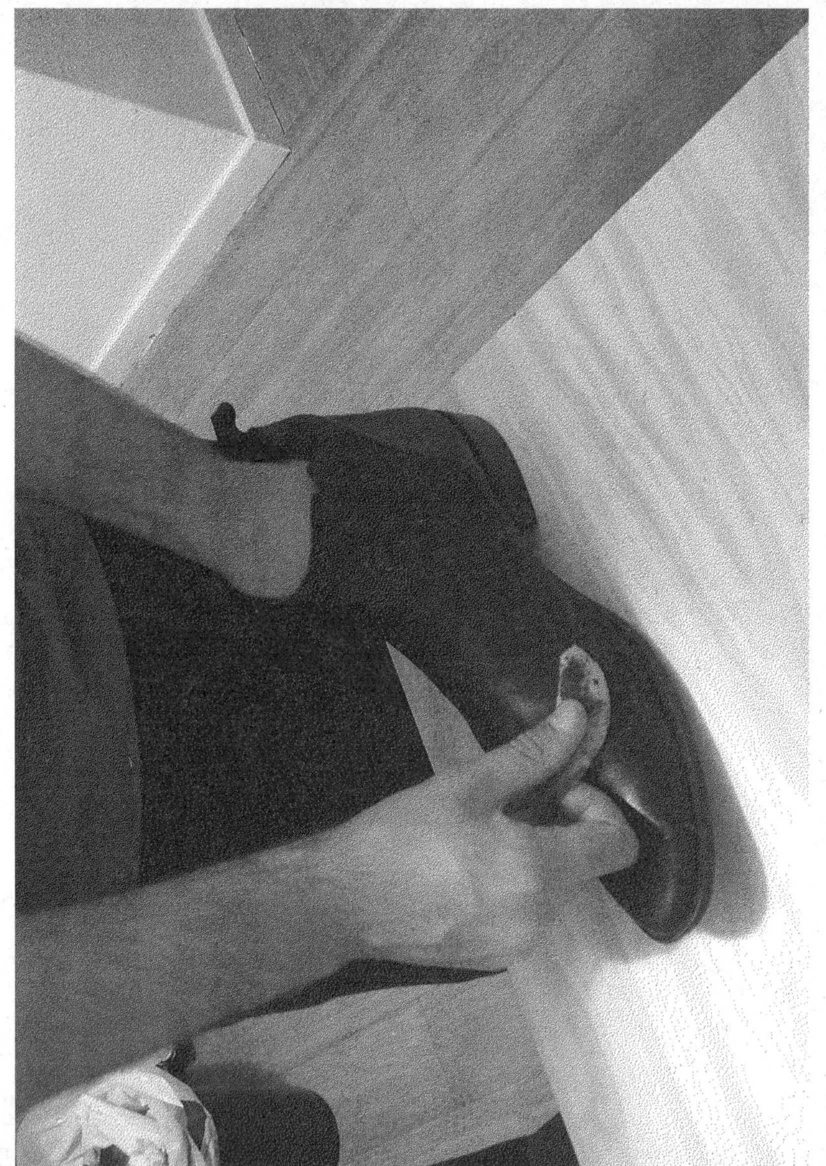

august 31

professional order, invisibility,
silence, working conditions.

tools

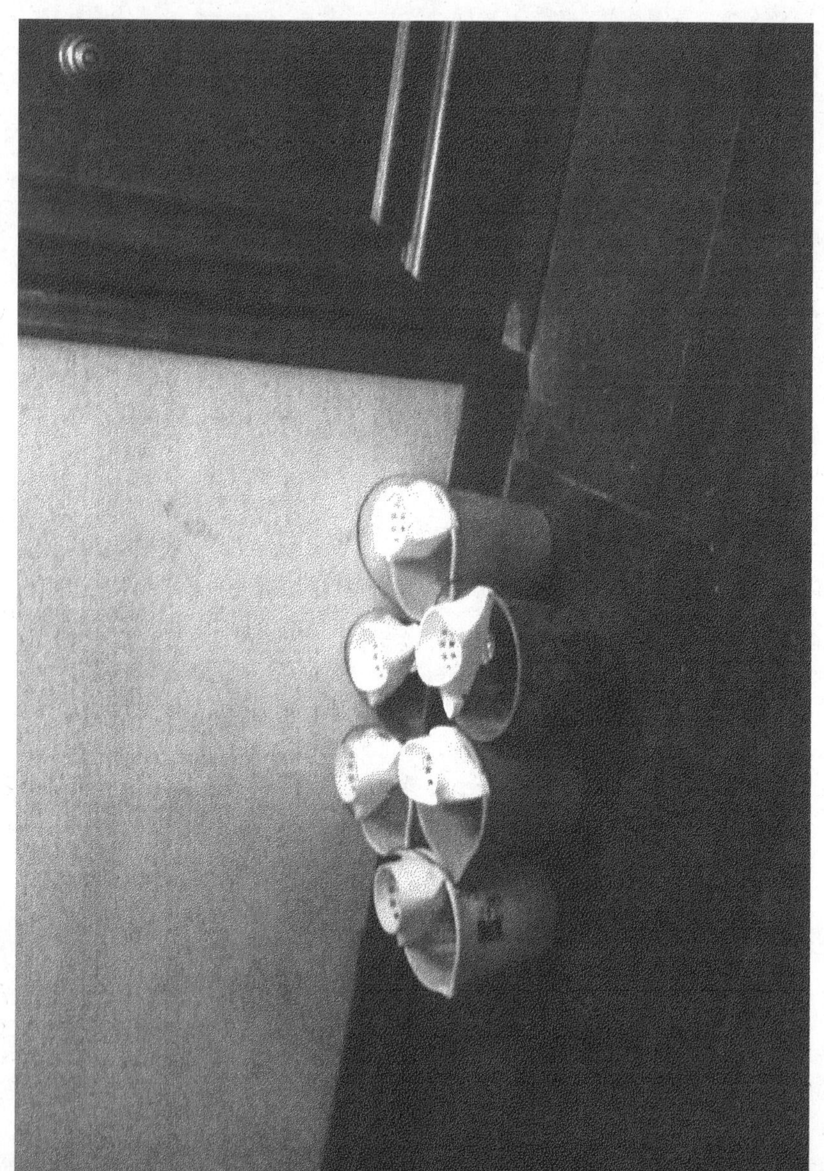

domestic workers play a major role
in keeping the environment clean and
green. this work and contribution is
often unseen when things are done
properly but gets noticed when things
go wrong. justice for domestic workers
demand recognition in making domestic
work visible in british society.

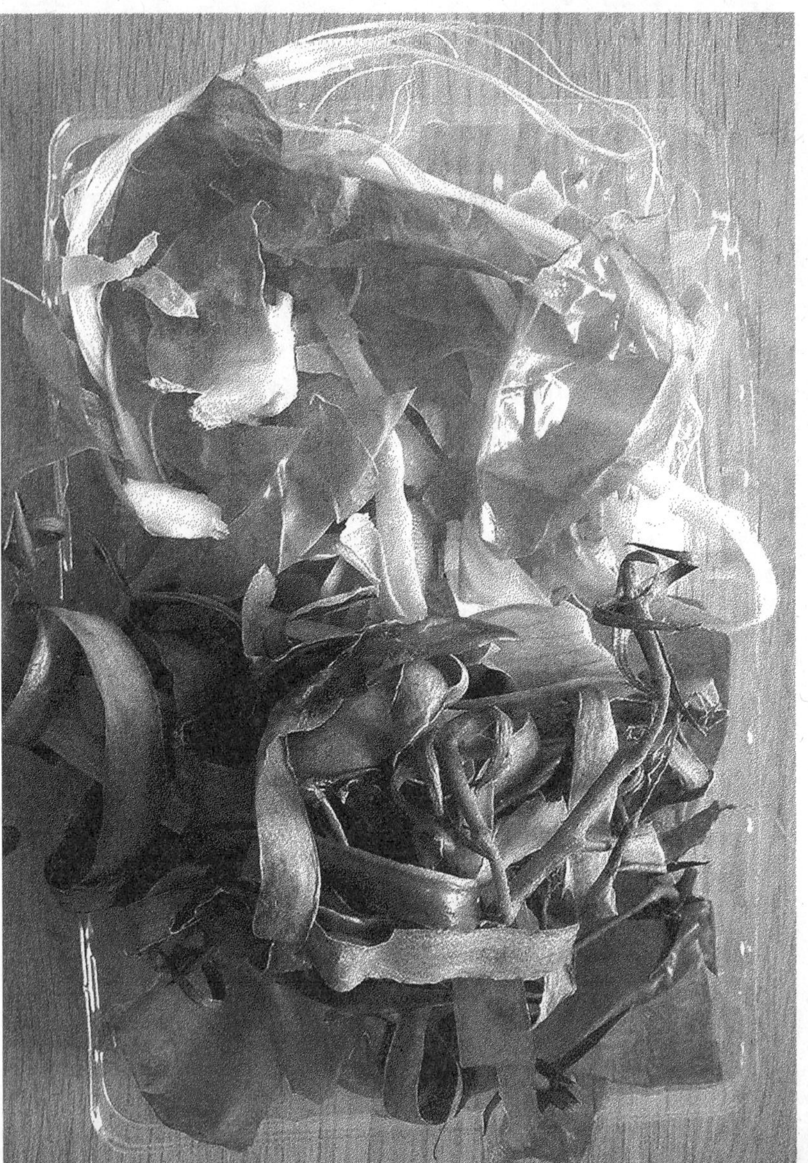

we worked last summer for a prop
design company in brixton. we had
to trim 1000 giant paper roses that
were made in china and then shipped
over to us to style and be painted
because they were the wrong colour.
the roses painted the roses in a room
with no ventilation. we were not
allowed to open the roll up door
because the warehouse backed onto
coldharbour lane, which we were told
was called the murder mile, but every-
where in london has its own murder
mile. it was a horrible job, but it was
also the best paid job i've had since
i graduated with a fine art degree.

being a prop bitch pays,
until the paint fumes kill

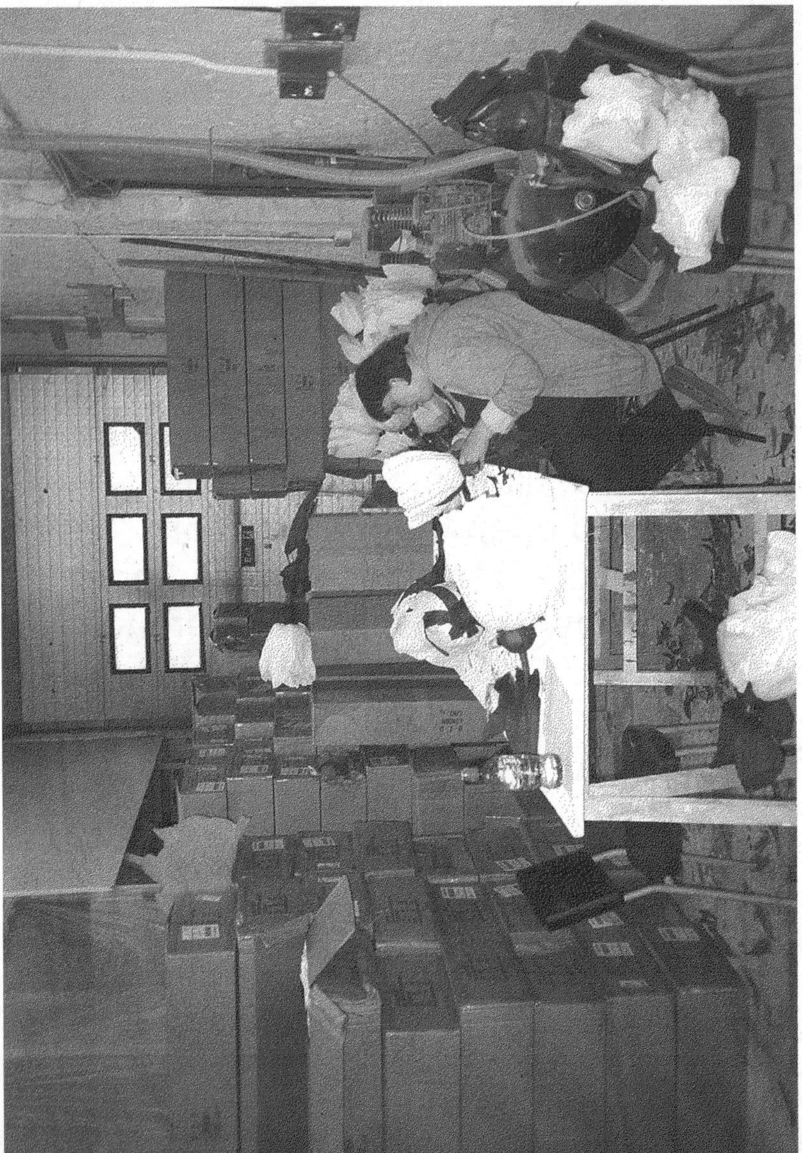

september 3

gingerbread. family time, saturday morning, january 2011. 1 in 3 children are living in poverty in the uk.

www.endchildpoverty.org.uk

cooking—at home

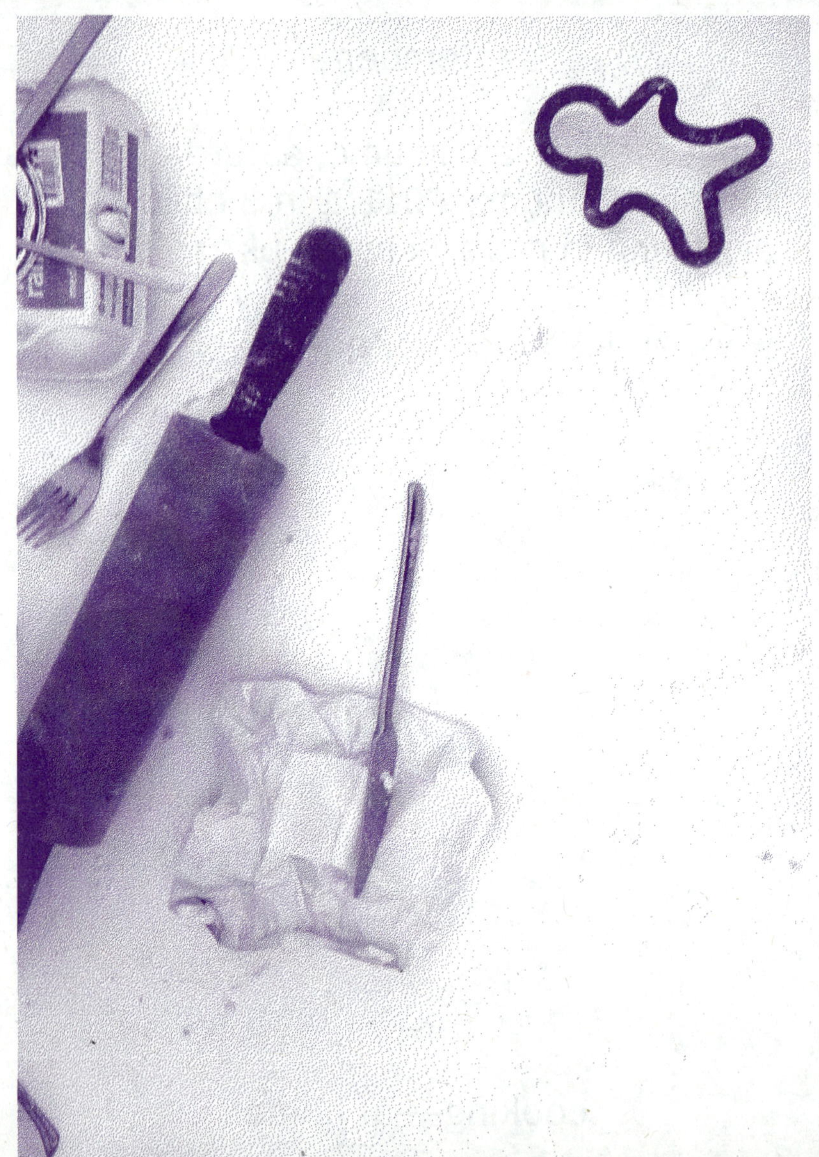

september 4

newspaper cut-out, dagblad trouw.

dishes best by hand

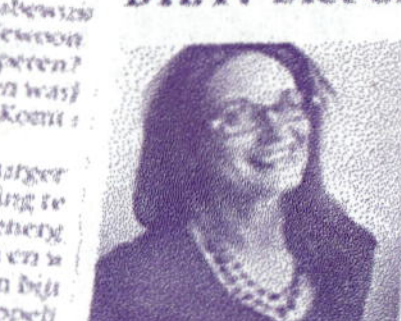

16 juli 2011

Vaatwasser-geheimen

Het lijkt een soort heilig dingetje. De vaatwasser inruimen. Vaak is een iemand verantwoordelijk, gewoonlijk de man. Die neemt zijn taak doorgaans heel serieus. Rek voor rek wordt gevuld als staat er een reis naar Mars op stapel. Iedereen begrijpt meteen dat verder niemand zich aan deze klus dient te wagen omdat dat onherroepelijk tot ongelukken leidt. Niet dat het erg is als paps dit rotklusje op zich neemt. Ik ken leukere karweitjes dan vette afwas stapelen.

Aan de andere kant is daar het uitruimen, uit praktische overwegingen meestal 's morgens vroeg. Uitruimen is bijna zoveel werk als handmatig afwassen. Plus het serviesgoed ruikt niet lekker, zeg maar stinkt. Een heuse halve citroen per wasbeurt erbij leggen en eens per maand op de hoogste stand afwassen om bacteriën te doden schijnt te helpen, al blijven sommige agressieve zwarte schimmels dan zitten en zijn er legio mensen die gek worden van hun stinkende vaatwasser. Zo de dag beginnen is niet mijn idee van een lekkere start, daarom was ik 's avonds met de hand af. Weliswaar is een vaatwasser in de meeste huishoudens niet meer weg te denken, ik ken toch flink wat gezinnen zonder, ook drukke tweeverdieners met kinderen. Goed als de kinderen samen leren afwassen, zeggen sommigen, zo'n ding is water- en energieverspilling, vinden anderen. Er zitten zeker voordelen aan een vaatwasser, vooral met etentjes of feestjes. Dat zijn meteen de enige keren dat hij echt

tijdwinst oplevert. Mensen die denken dat ze dagelijks veel tijd sparen dank zij hun afwasmachine draaien zichzelf, en anderen, een rad voor ogen. Klokt u maar eens handmatig afwassen tegen een vaatwasser in- en uitruimen. Het verschil is zoiets als 100 of 130 rijden op de Afsluitdijk. Verwaarloosbaar.

Mensen die om water- en energiespaarredenen het korte wasprogramma kiezen, eindigen net iets te vaak met een vette vaat. Dan helpt voorspoelen. Alleen verbruik je daarmee weer zoveel tijd en water dat, alweer, handmatig afwassen rendabeler is. Wat dat onschuldig ogende, in plastic verpakte blokje betreft, met een groot zwart kruis erop zodat je het niet per ongeluk in je mond stopt: ben ik nou zo wantrouwig als ik denk dat die dingen niet goed voor de gezondheid zijn? Dat spul komt dag in dag uit op lepels, vorken, borden, mengt zich met ochtendkoffie, versgeperst sinaasappelsap en relaxbiertjes. Het excessieve glansspoelmiddel dat erin zit droogt dan wel in een mum van tijd je vaat en voorkomt druppels op de glazen, maar mij geven die onnatuurlijk glimmende borden en mokken hetzelfde ongemakkelijke gevoel als die vieze glimtomaten van Albert Heijn. Je weet dat het niet zo hoort. Je bent alleen vergeten dat het ook anders kan.

Vaatwasmachine of met de hand? Reacties op gidspost@trouw.nl of via www.twitter.com/DietGroothuis

september 5

ha ha.

not working

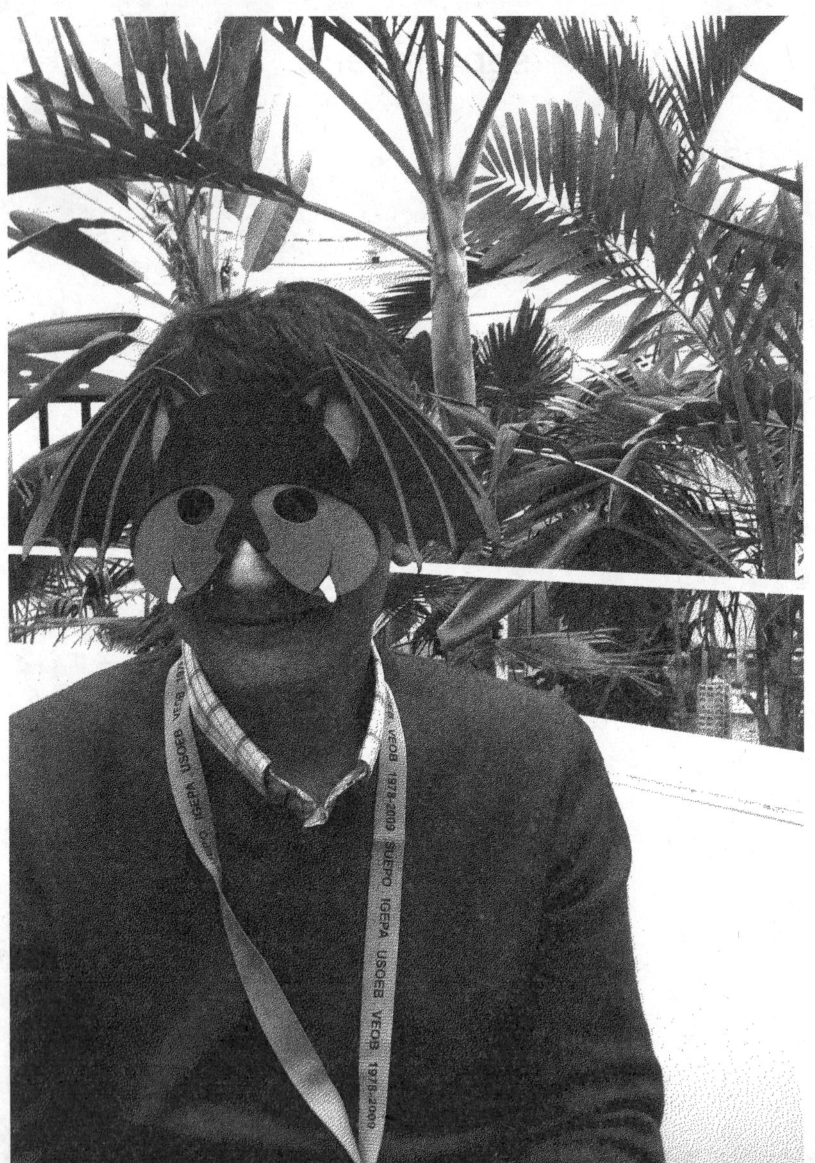
VEOB 1978-2009 SUEPO IGEPA USOEB

september 6

how much a woman can bear.

women's strength

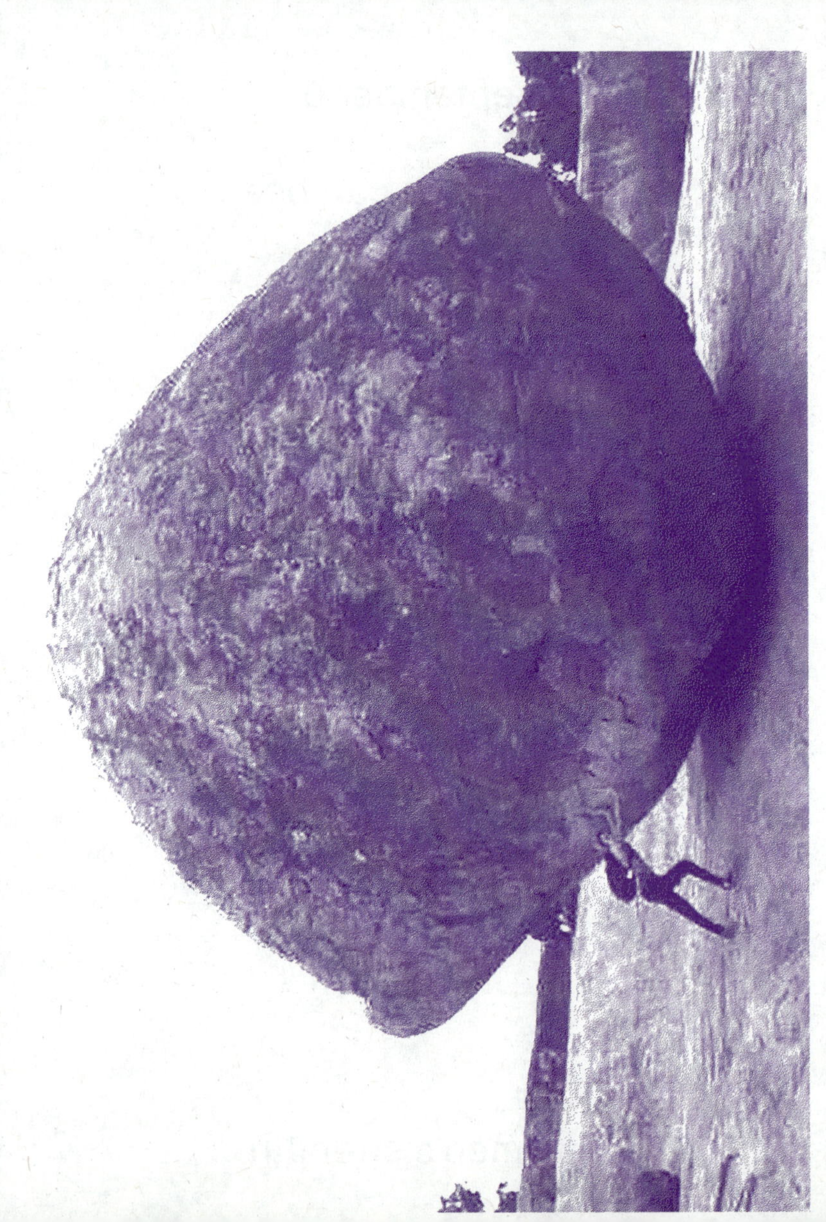

september 7

first steps to a cleaner and more productive life.

multitasking

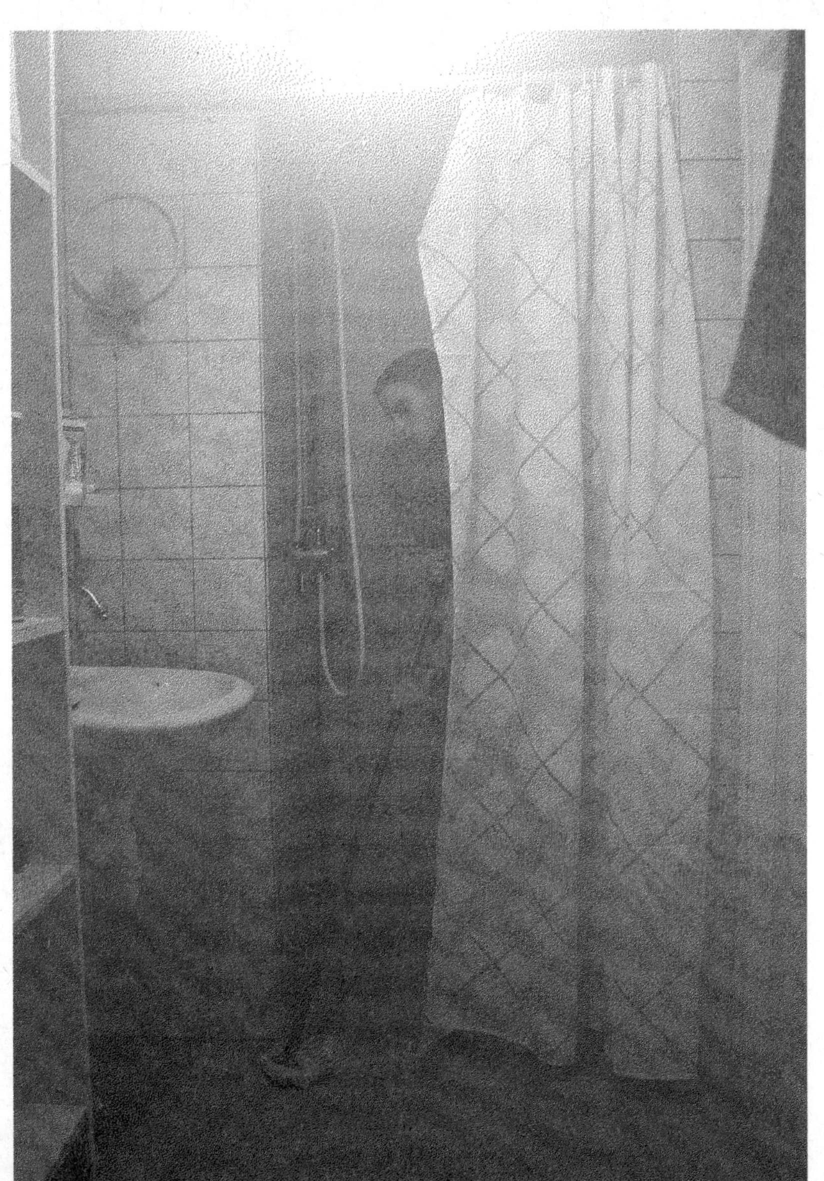

when i was studying grammar, the example they would always use to explain what the word 'synecdoche' meant was the "all hands on deck" saying… where the hands stand in for the 'man' or the 'sailor.' where the person, as a worker, is minimized down to their hands. to the utility of their body. to the utility of a part of their body. class is mapped onto our hands.

synecdoche vs. metonymy

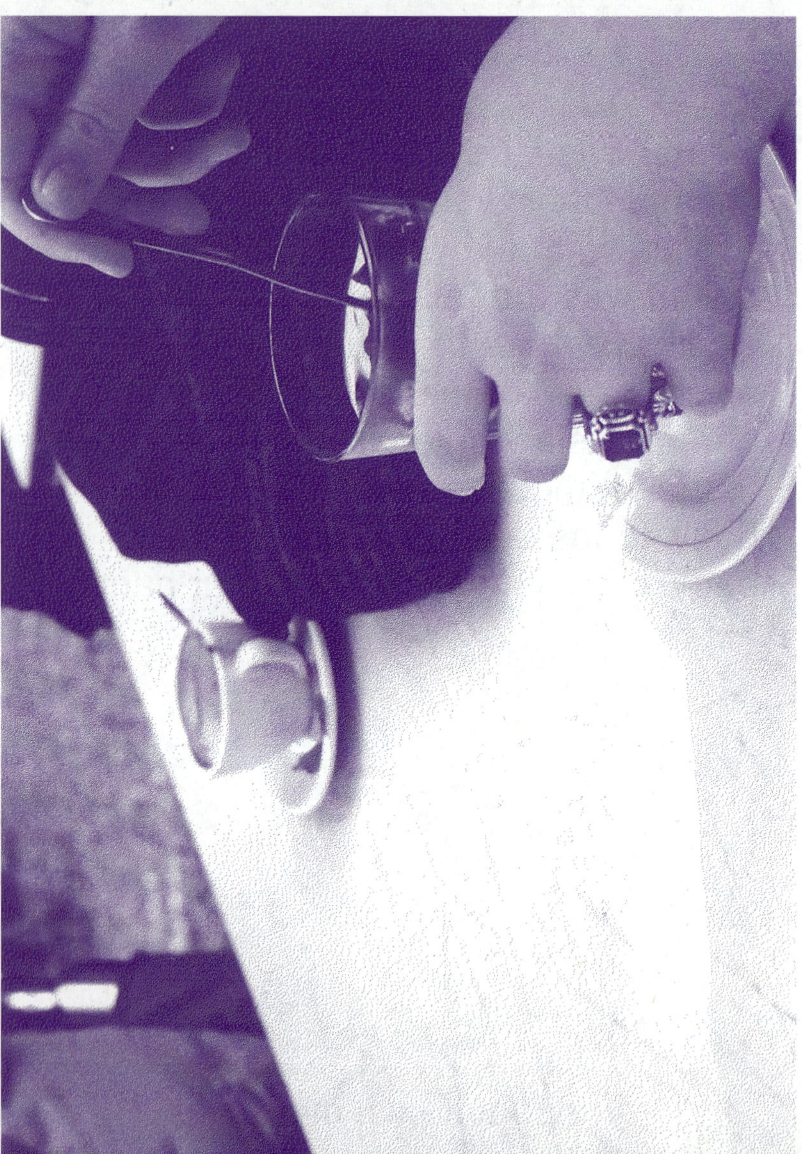

september 9

the new associate.

new project

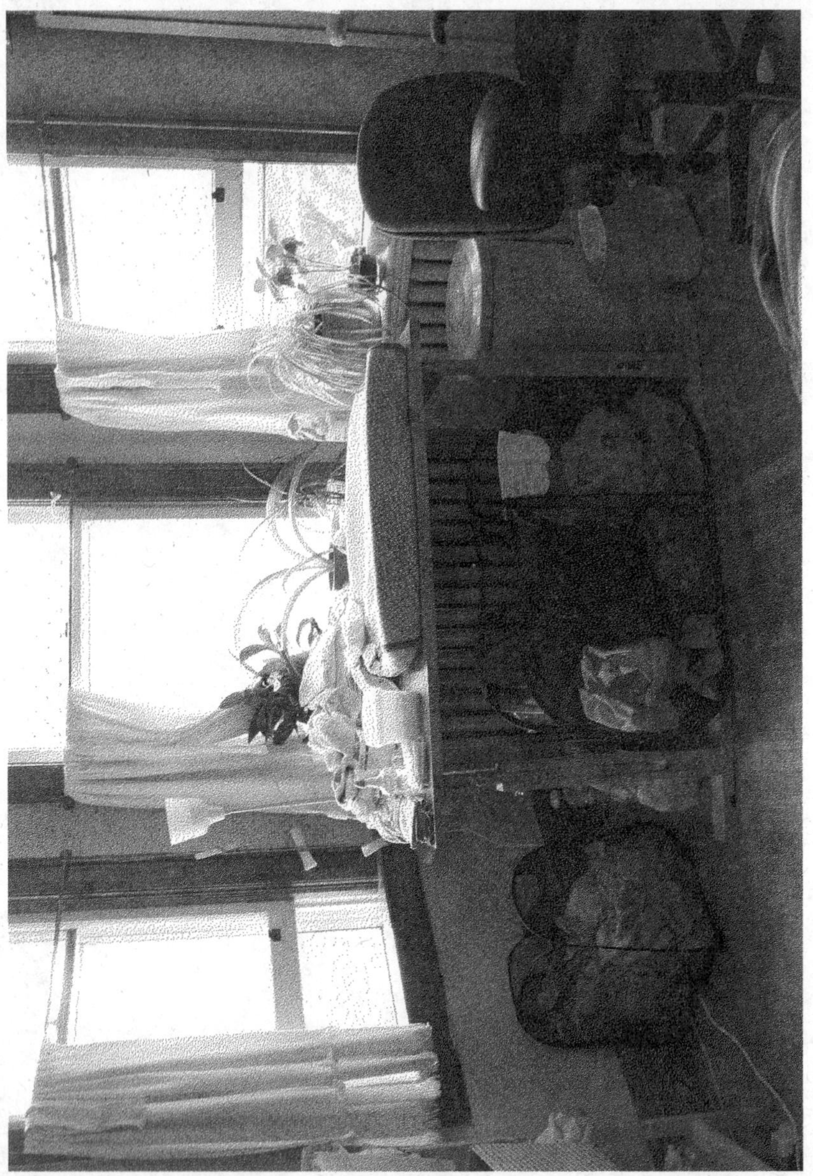

collective cooking. the last sausage
in the pan. was it too short/long/
ugly/perfect?

lonely

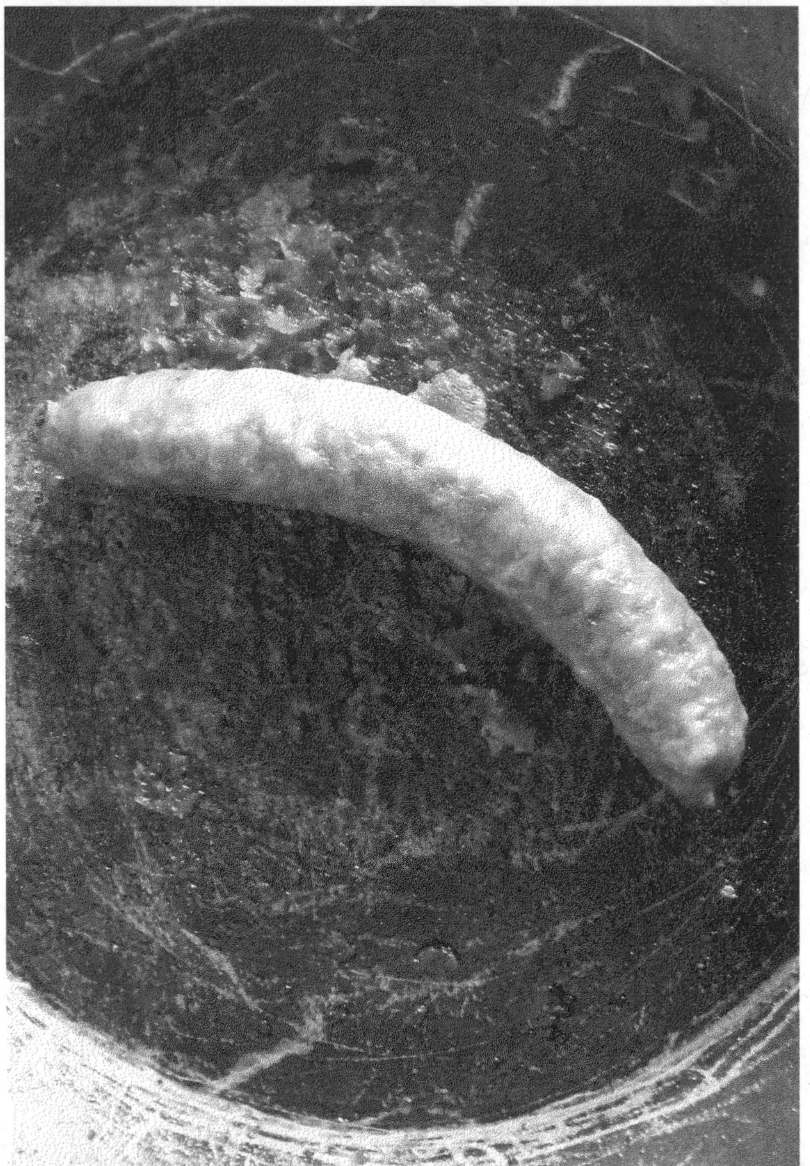

september 11

collecting objects, furniture, and books
from the street.

gold

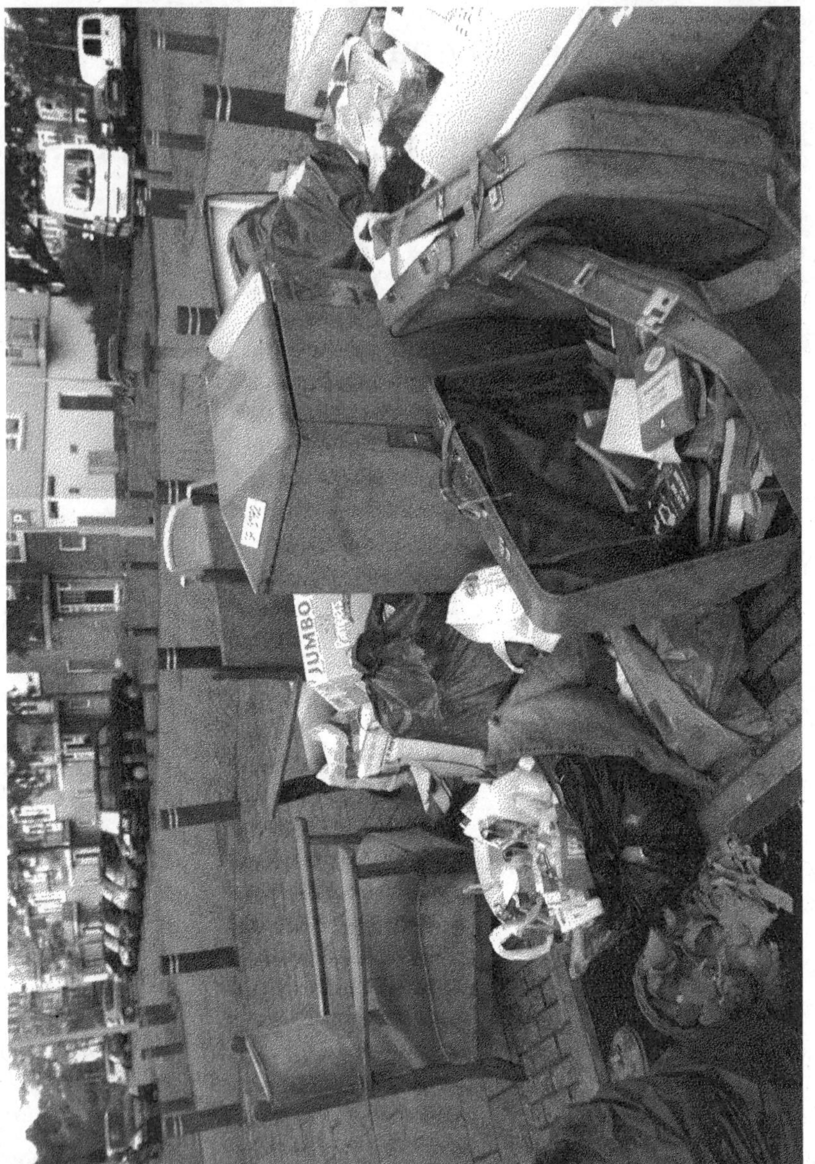

september 12

the knife and the fight.

dirty laundry

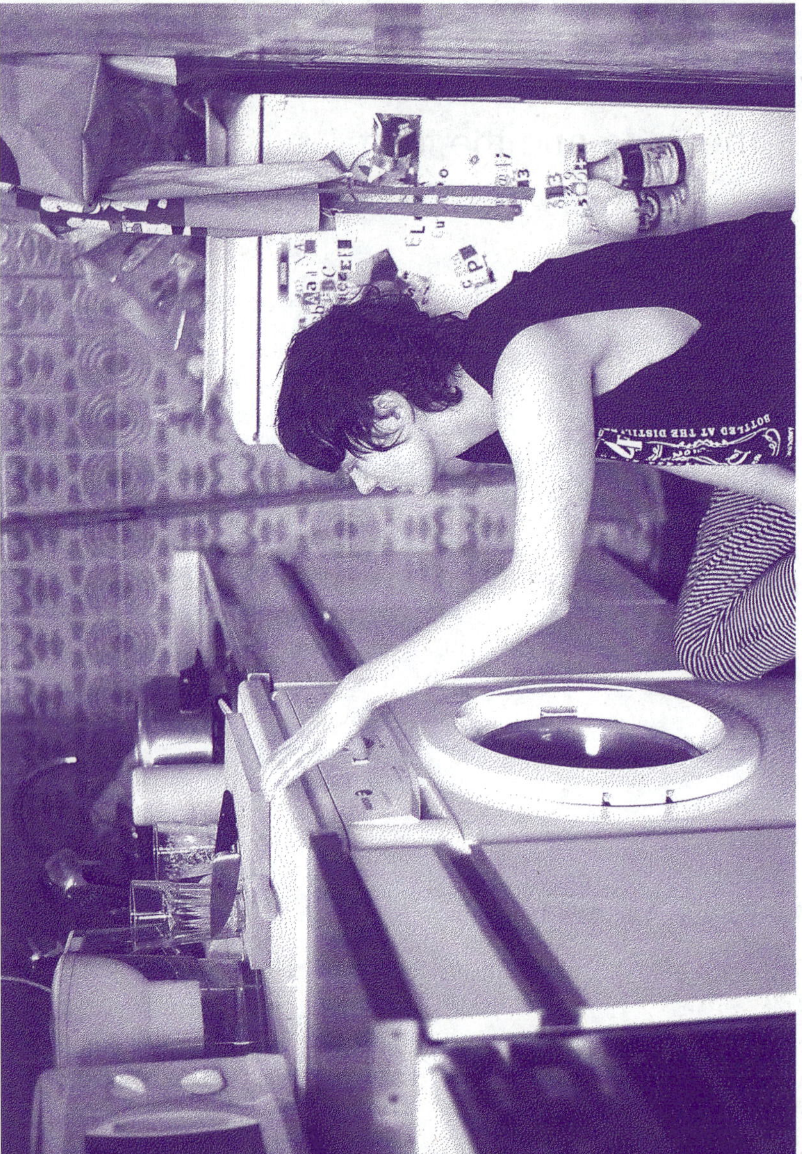

september 13

outside home, my toilet window,
são paulo, brazil, private space,
building, architecture, chaos.

são paulo

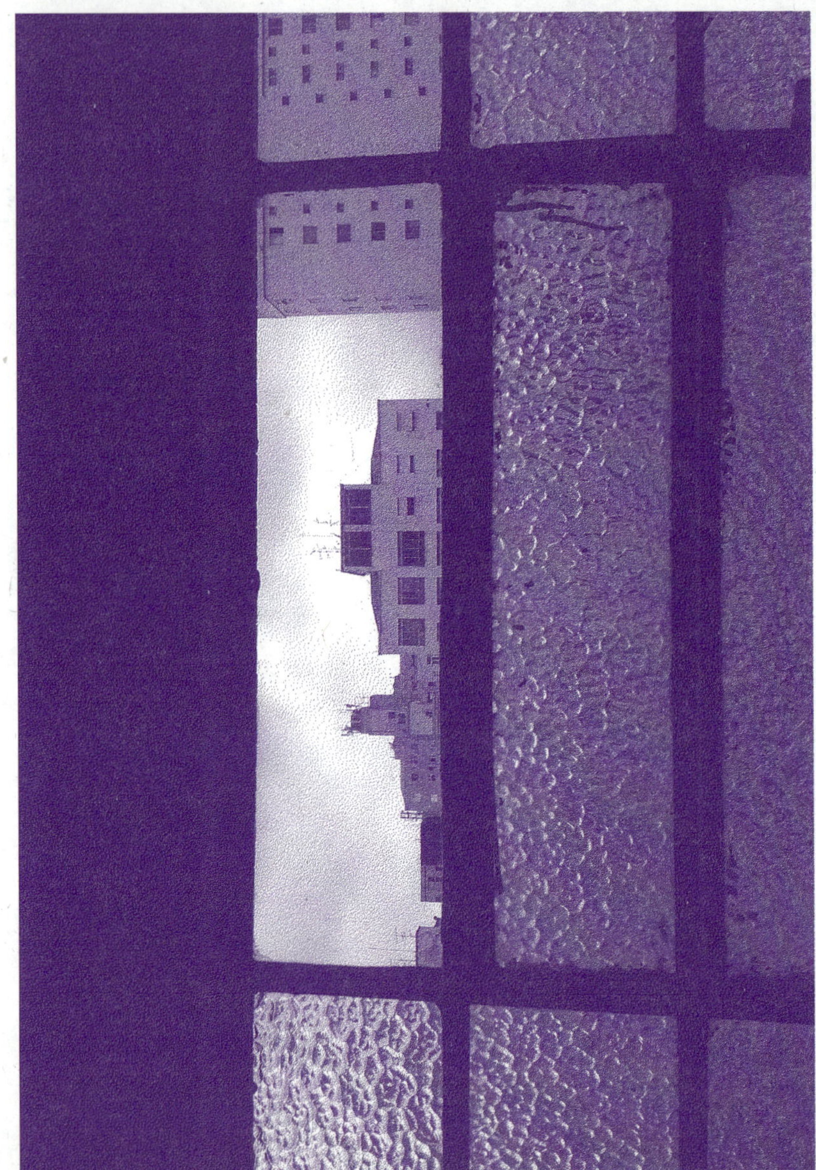

september 14

en mi biblioteca hay un tramo en
el que las cosas dejan de estar
en vertical porque no caben…
¡o necesitan descasar!

unfinished novel

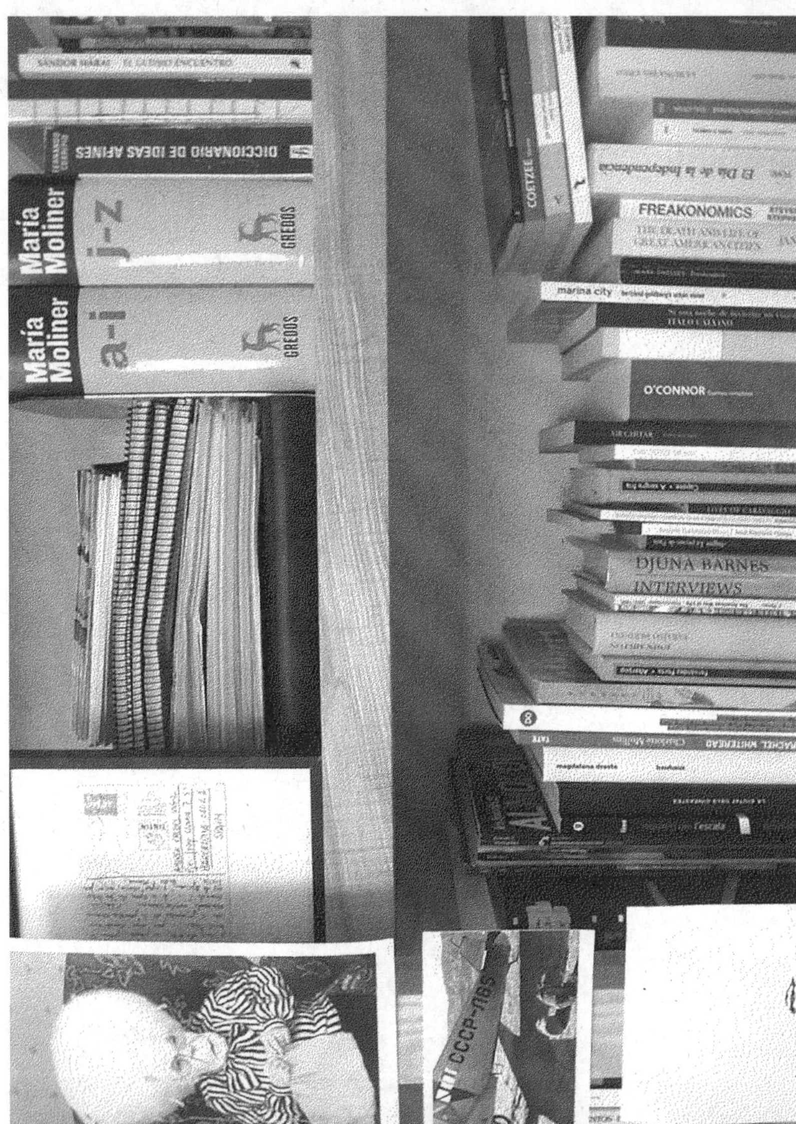

september 15

i love my dog so much. even though
i have lots of work i still find time
to play with her, cos she needs love
and attention.

me and my cute dog

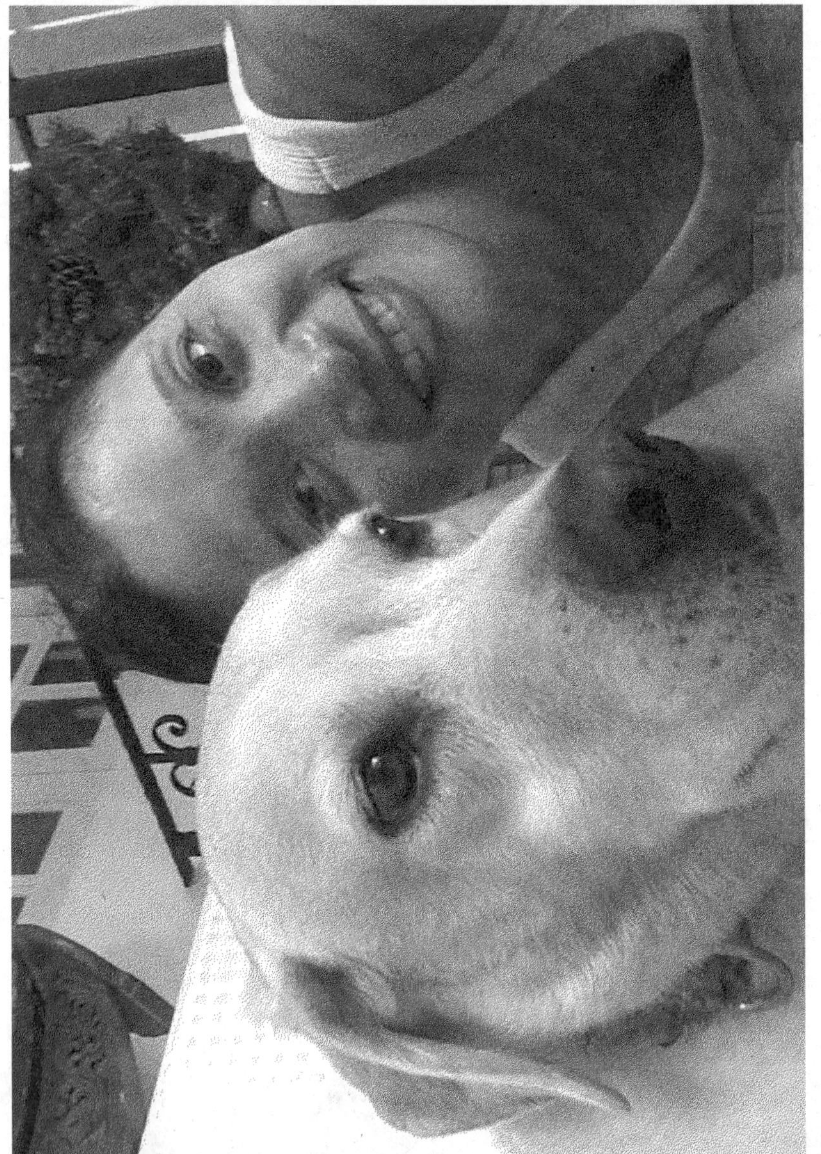

september 16

preparing for graduation.
working overtime.

am/pm

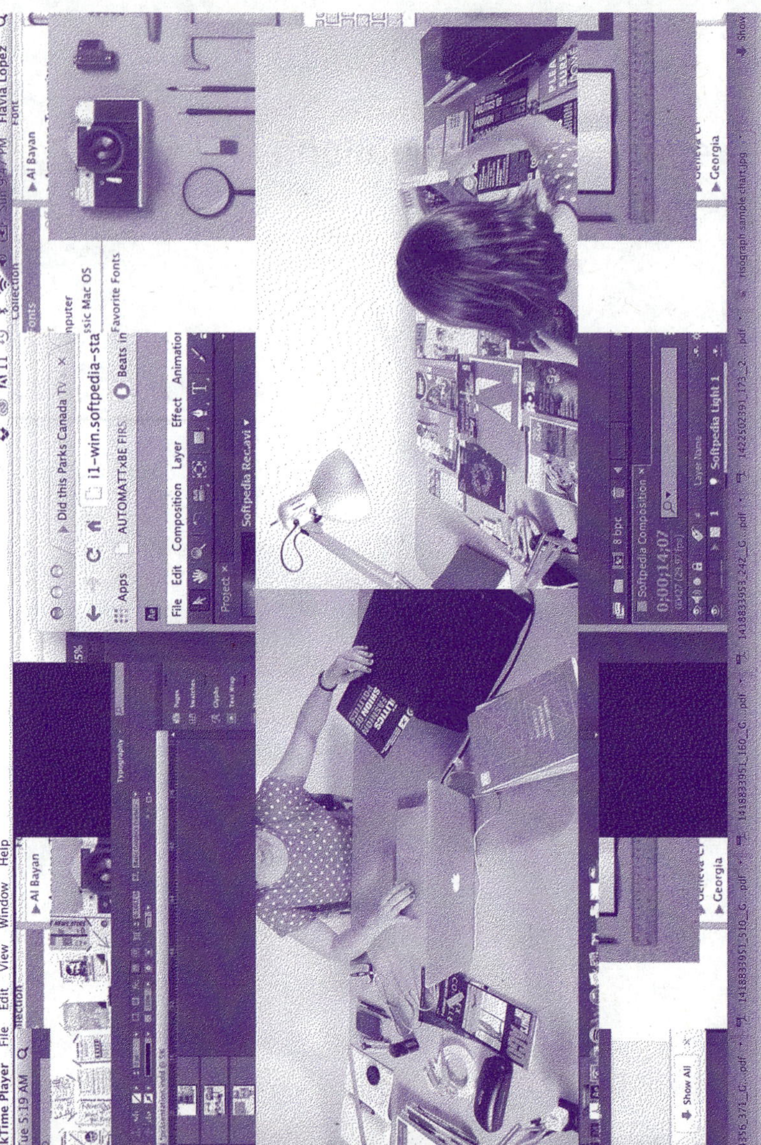

september 17

to share the cake

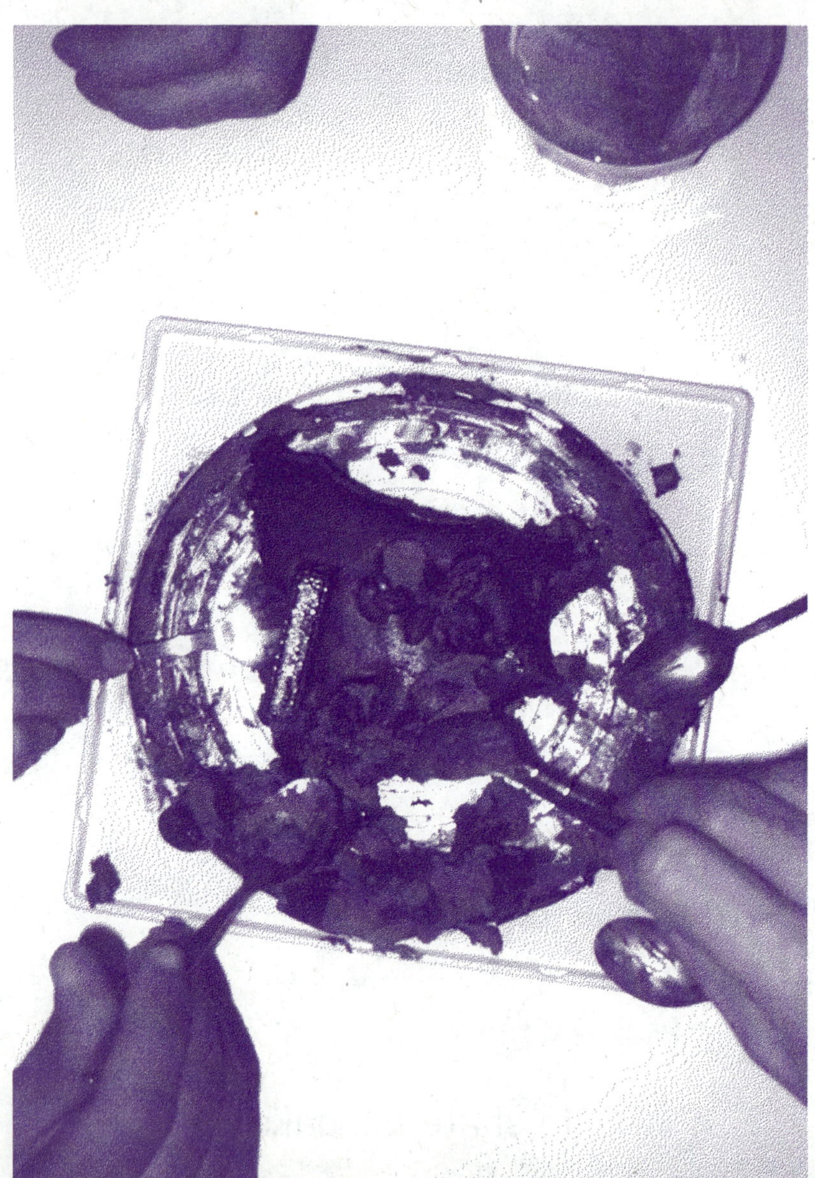

following a shower, before preparing
for work. was i presentable? the mirror
had been cleaned the previous day
and i did not want to leave smudge
marks. but there was no time to wait,
there never is. so i lightly pressed
a scrunched up towel onto its canvas
of condensation.

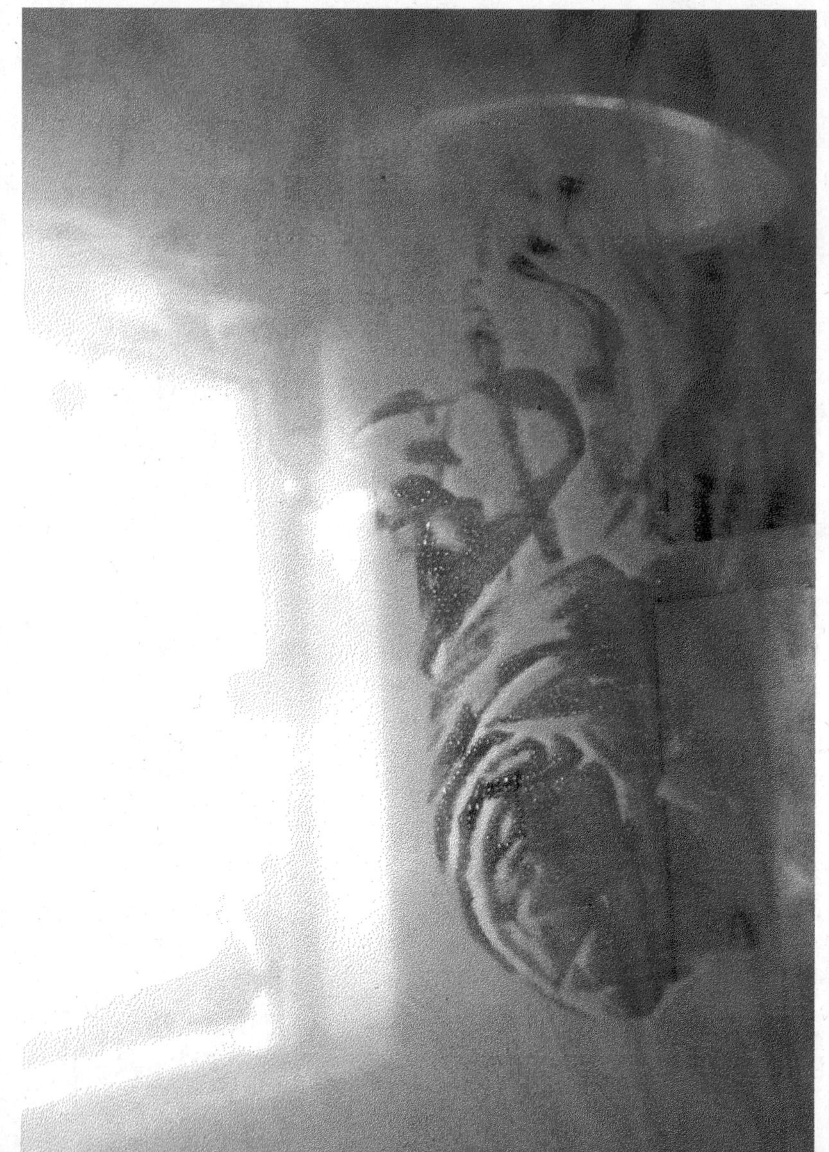

september 19

working class family. gabriel casas,
ca. 1933.

raval

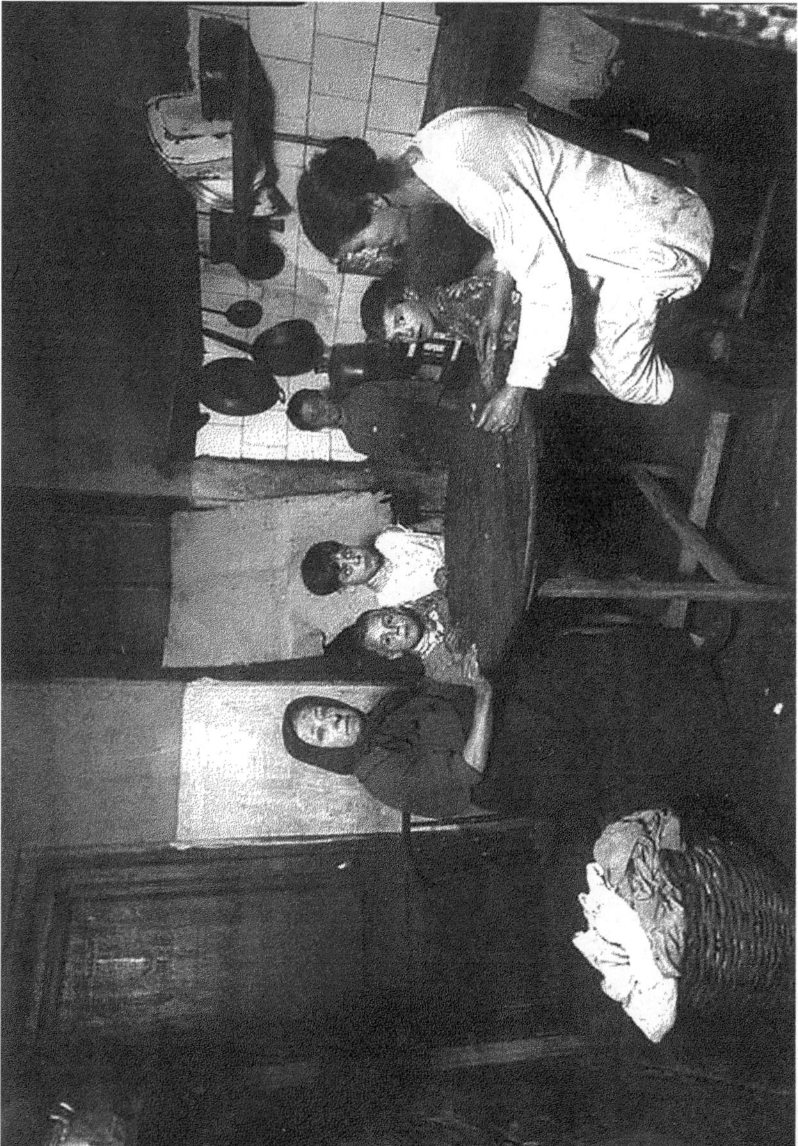

september 20

conceptual artists on the rampage

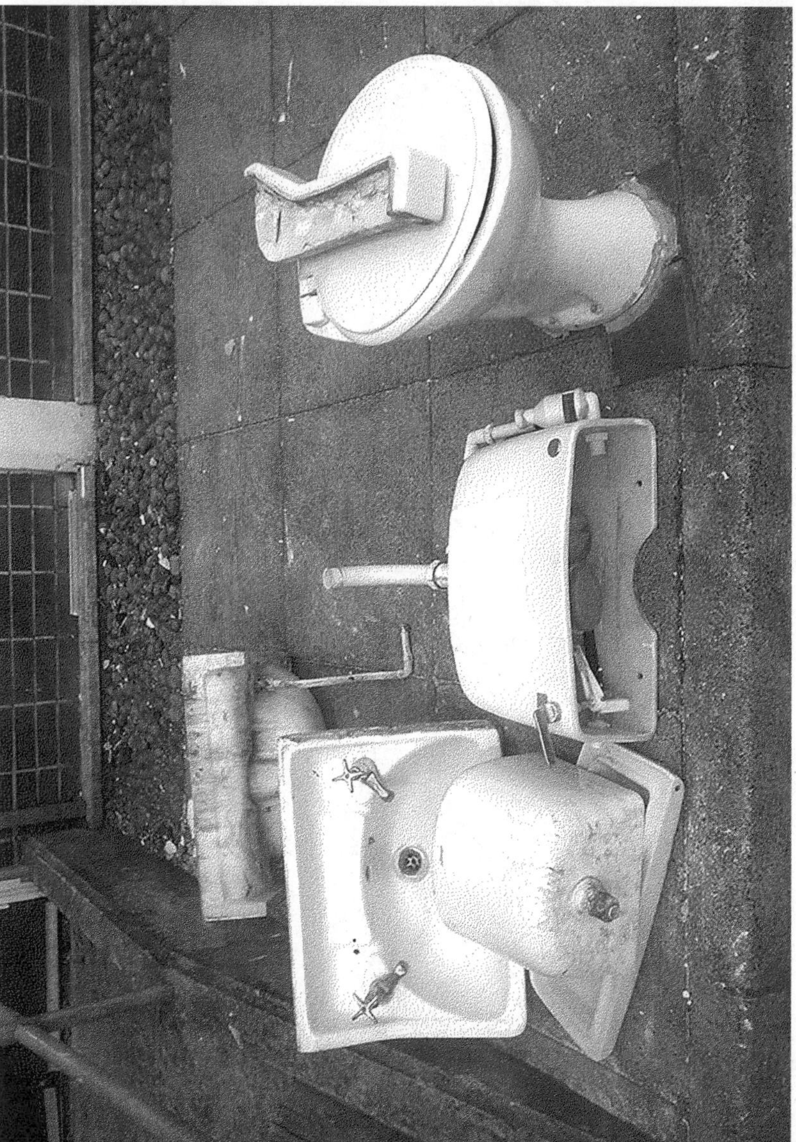

september 21

how to make a garden from
your kitchen.

garden

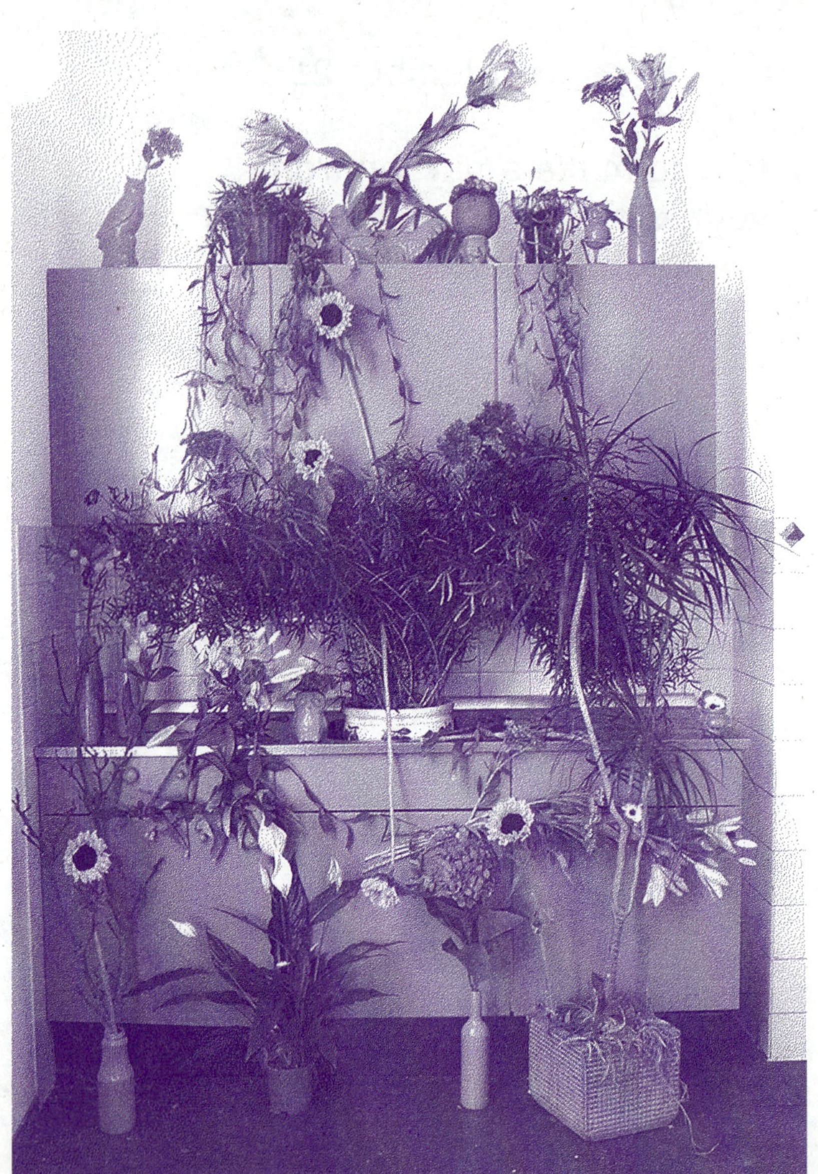

september 22

my friend's place in berlin. finally got
the fire burning after using the
cardboard from the box that the logs
came in as tinder.

heating

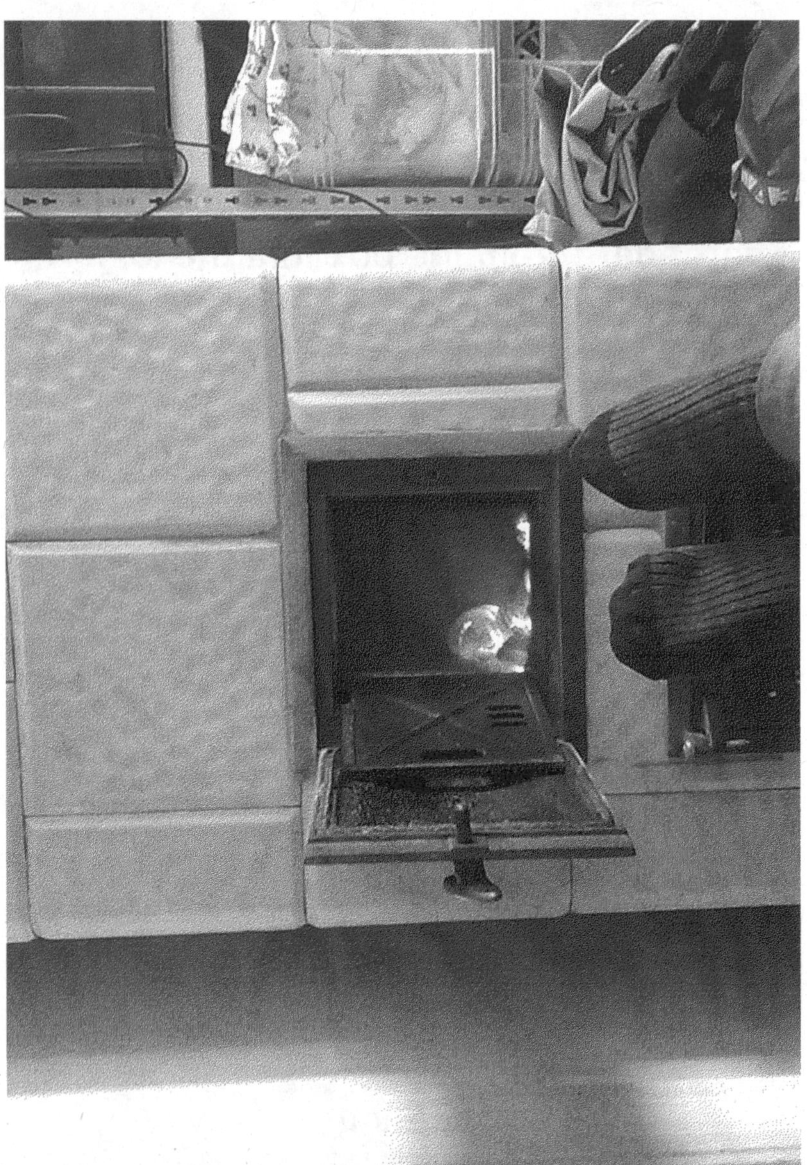

september 23

re-contextualization.

speaker bracket

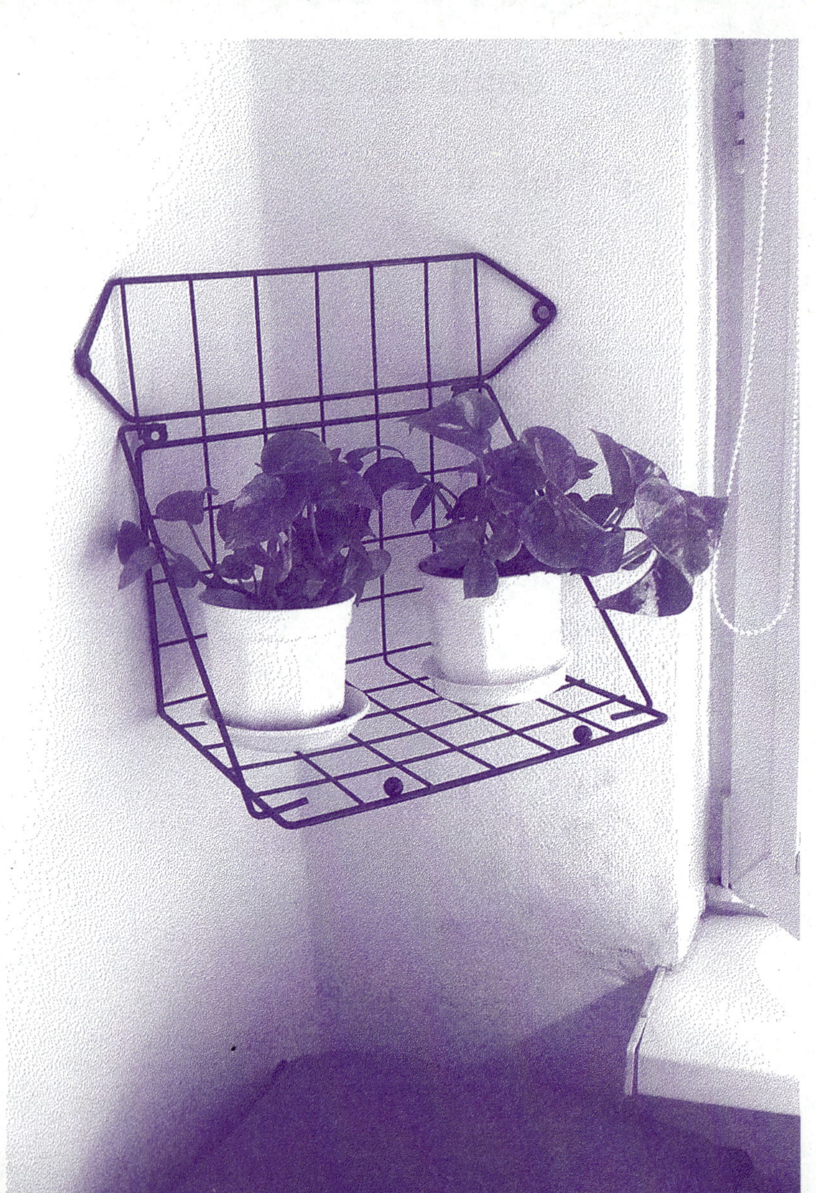

september 24

picture taken in delft.

architecture student house

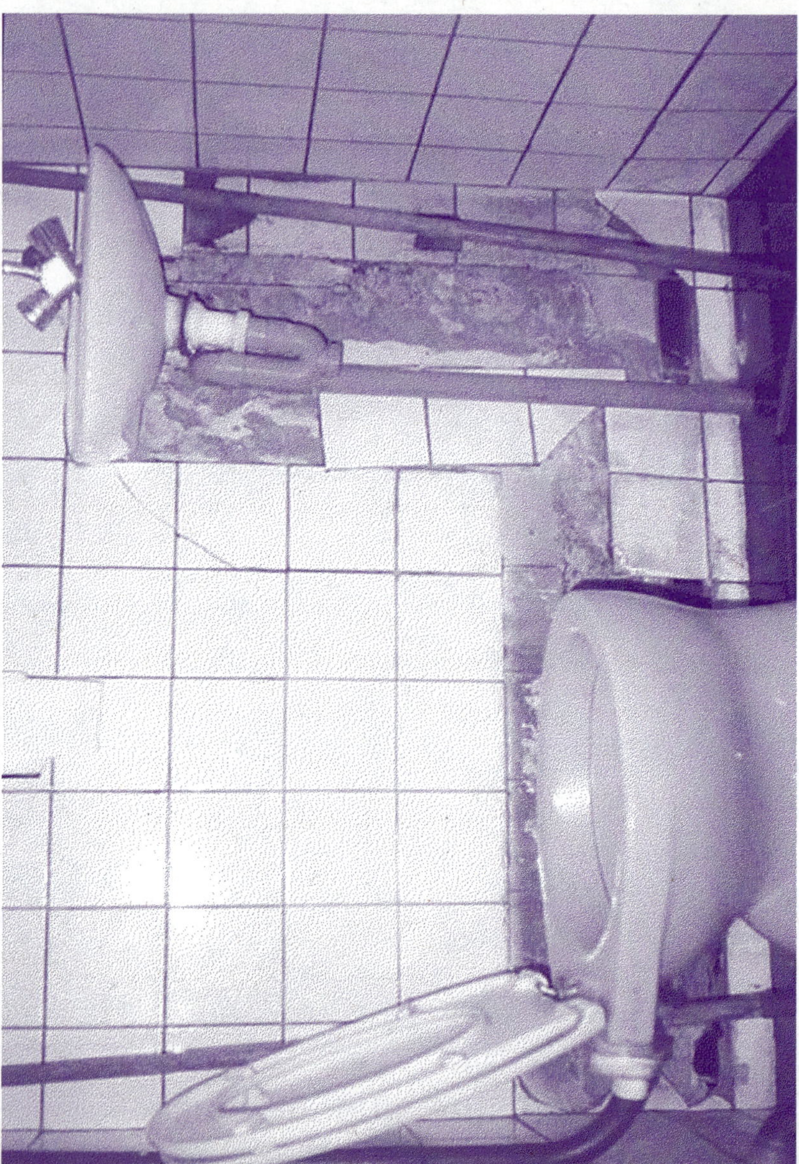

september 25

what you experience in daily life
is never freedom.

sleep

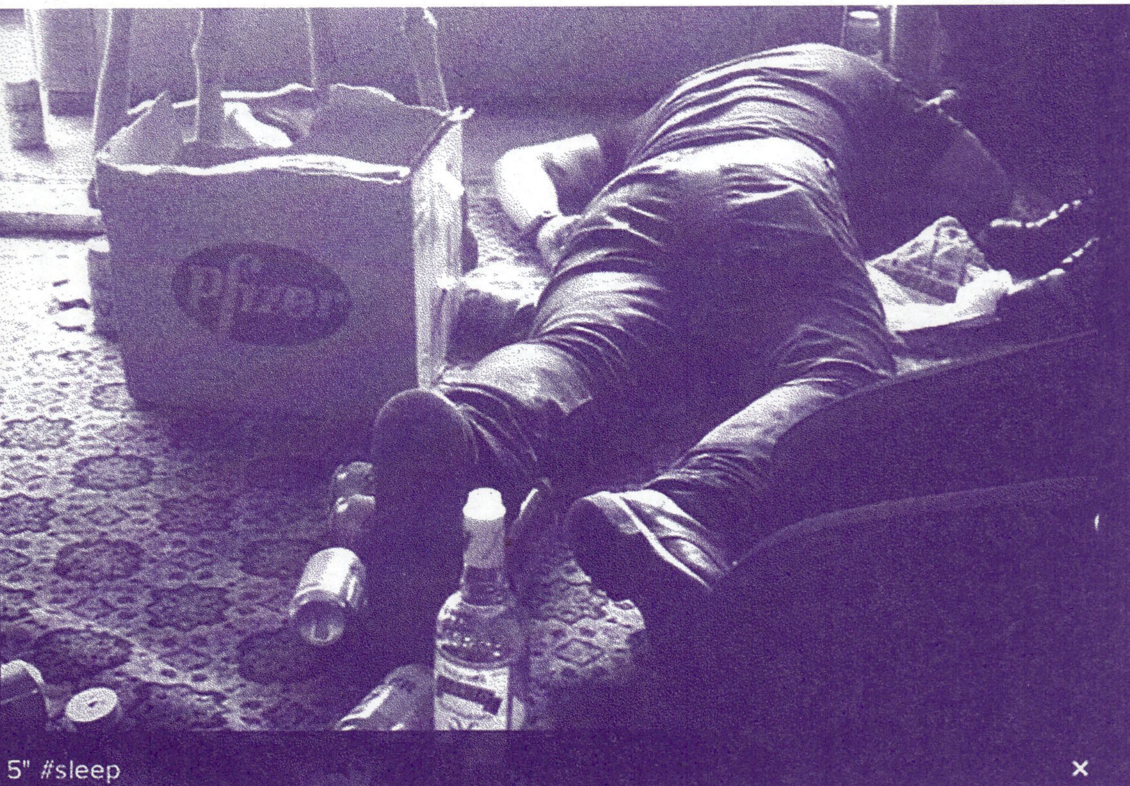

Pfizer
5" #sleep
x

september 26

the afternoon work: café com leite.

café com leite

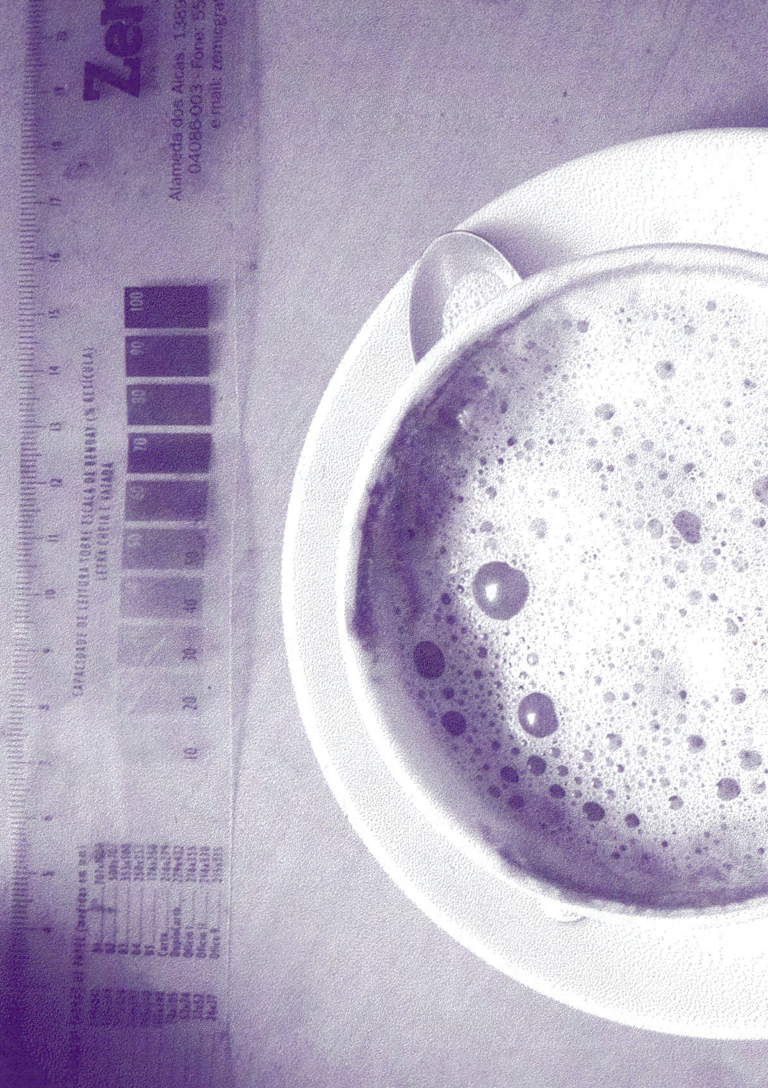

september 27

yo pongo la mesa.

javi preparando la comida

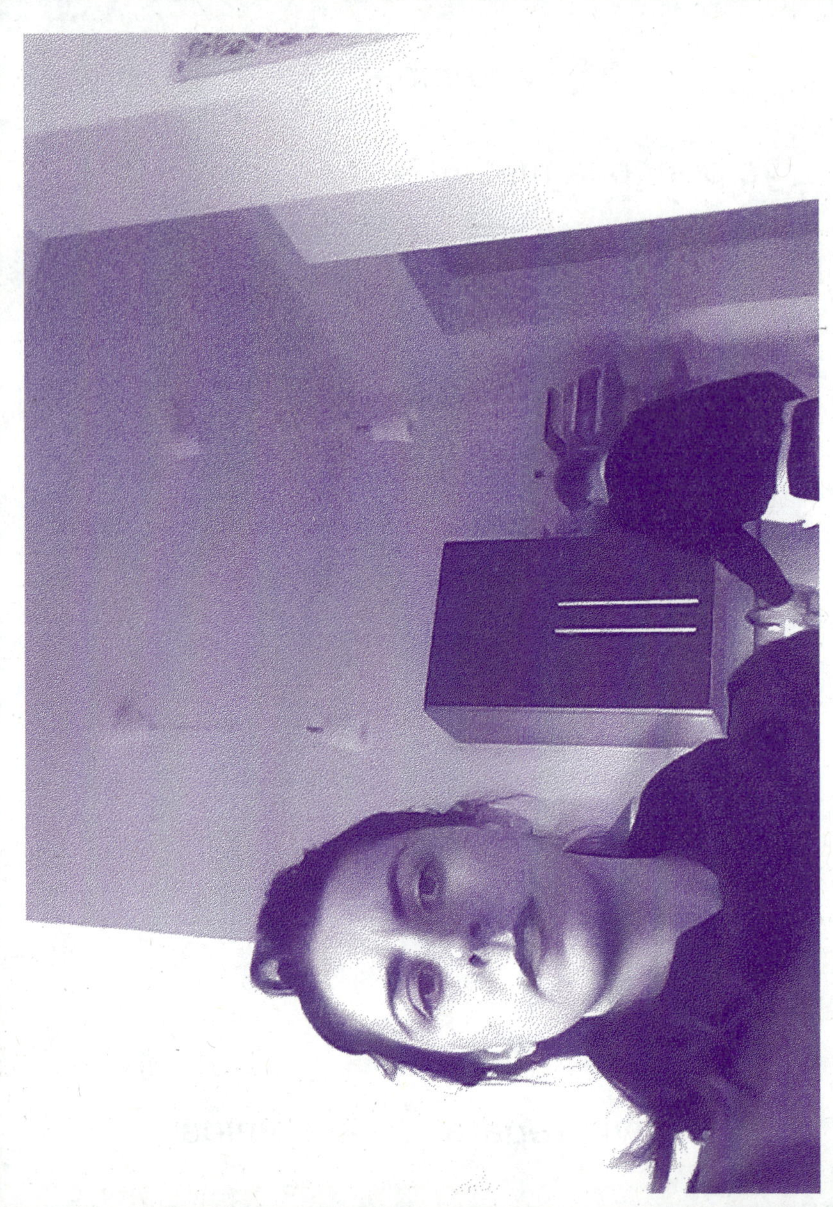

september 28

for extra mental padding.

sheepish in my studio

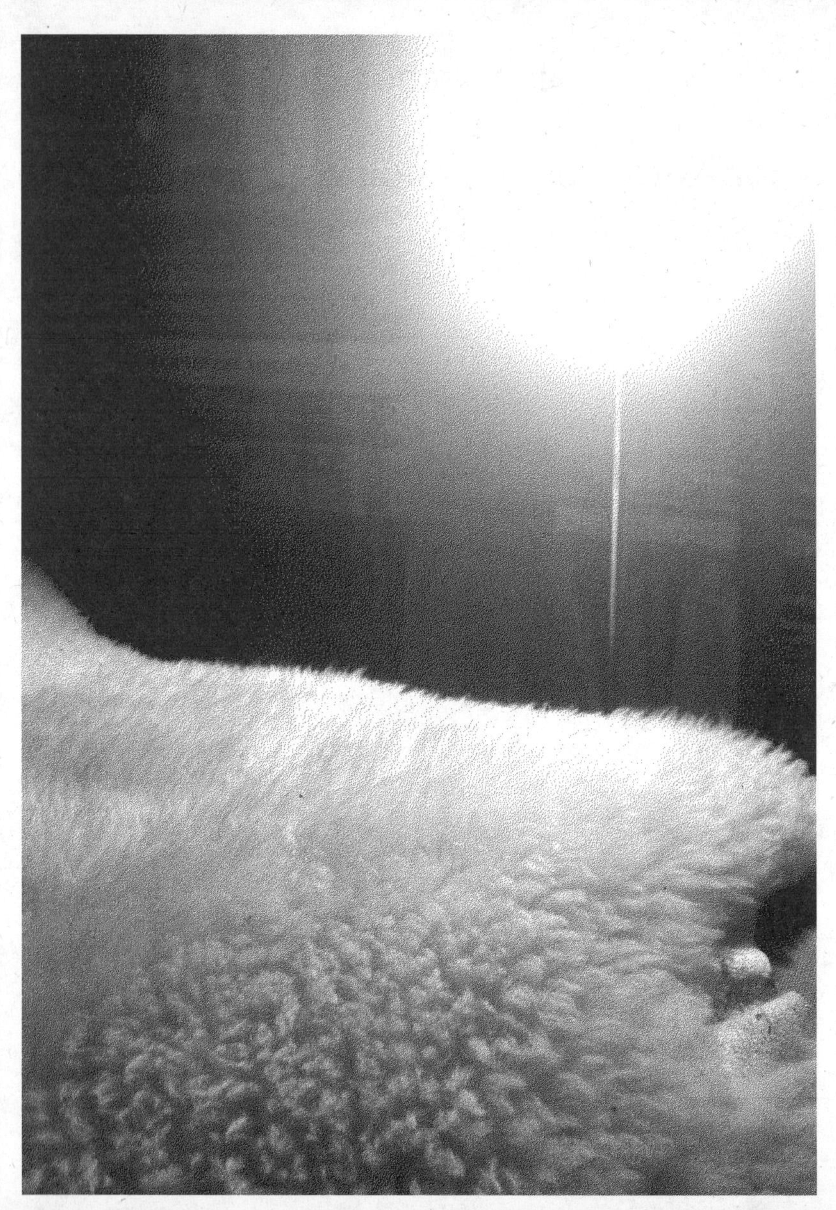

september 29

i normally cook the beans, mixed with
any other vegetable as soup base for
her pasta dinner ready to serve with
grilled/oven-cooked fresh steak, chicken
fillet, or fish fillet. when becky is back
from school, the moment we enter the
house she will say, "i'm hungry!" so i
make sure i have food ready to serve
because i know she is a starving hungry
beautiful creature. domestic work is
invisible and ignored—indeed the
better they are at their work the more
invisible it is. domestic work is support
work, unnoticed if it is done well,
but noticed if it isn't done. justice for
domestic workers demand recognition
in making domestic work visible
in british society.

happy face

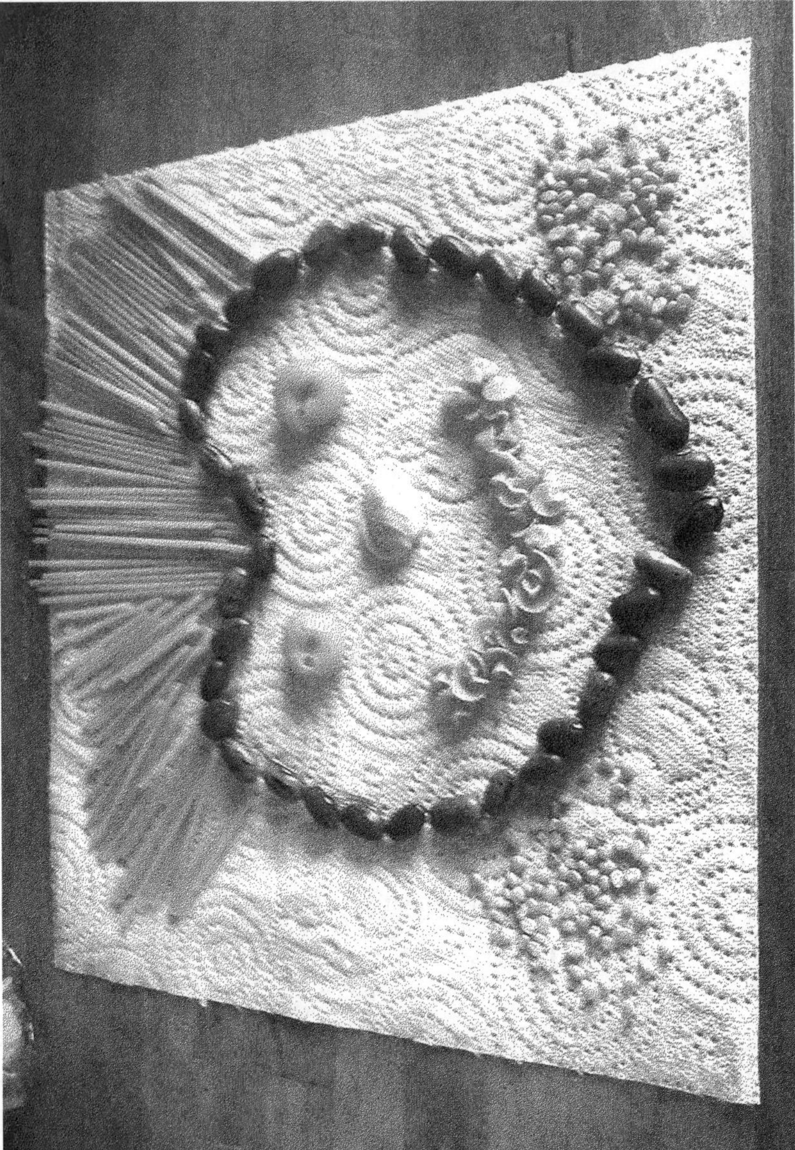

thoreau's intention during his time
at walden pond was "to conduct an
experiment: could he survive, possibly
even thrive, by stripping away all
superfluous luxuries, living a plain,
simple life in radically reduced conditions?" he thought of it as an experiment in "home economics." although
thoreau went to walden to escape
what he considered, "over-civilization,"
and in search of the "raw" and
"savage delight" of the wilderness,
he also spent considerable amounts
of his time reading and writing.

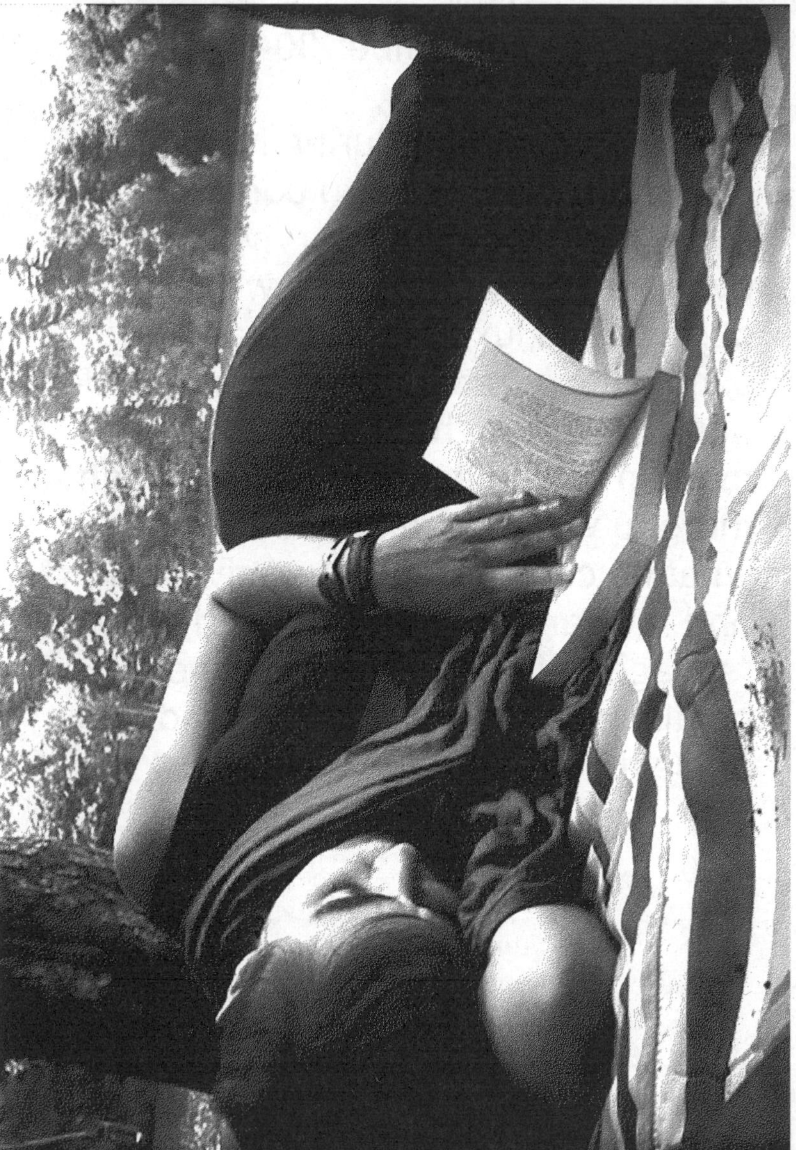

october 1

athiraman kannan jumped to his death
from the 147th floor of the world's
tallest building, the burj khalifa. from
india, he came to dubai to work as
a cleaner in the newly opened building.
in an attempt to honour his courageous
call for attention to be given to the
lives of migrant workers, i photographed
what i describe as a 'pop out city.'
these are spaces that are an attempt
at permanency and comfort in an
always vulnerable life as a migrant
worker. unlike the families they work
for, whose life exists behind walls,
their lives exist on the street, forging
new notions of 'the public.'
al naeem, 2011.

in memory of athiraman kannan

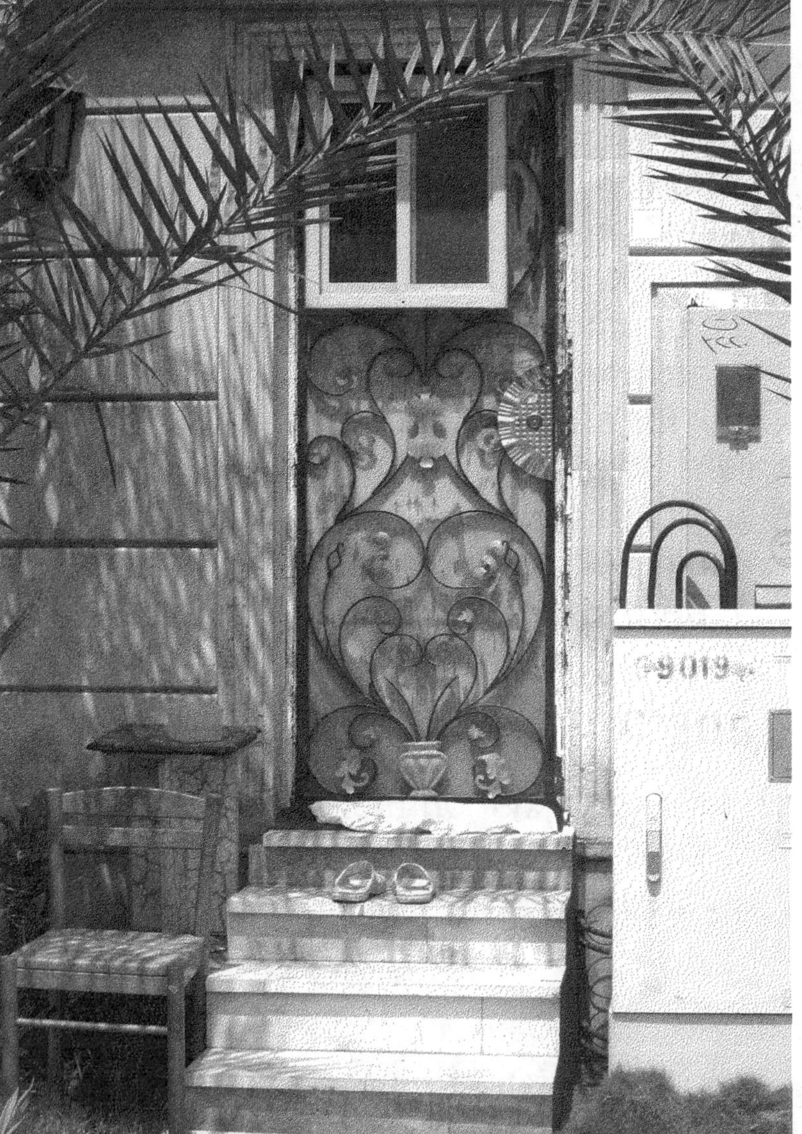

october 2

justice for domestic workers, uk.
protect, support, understand,
and campaign for the rights and
welfare of all migrant domestic
workers in the uk.

circle of human race

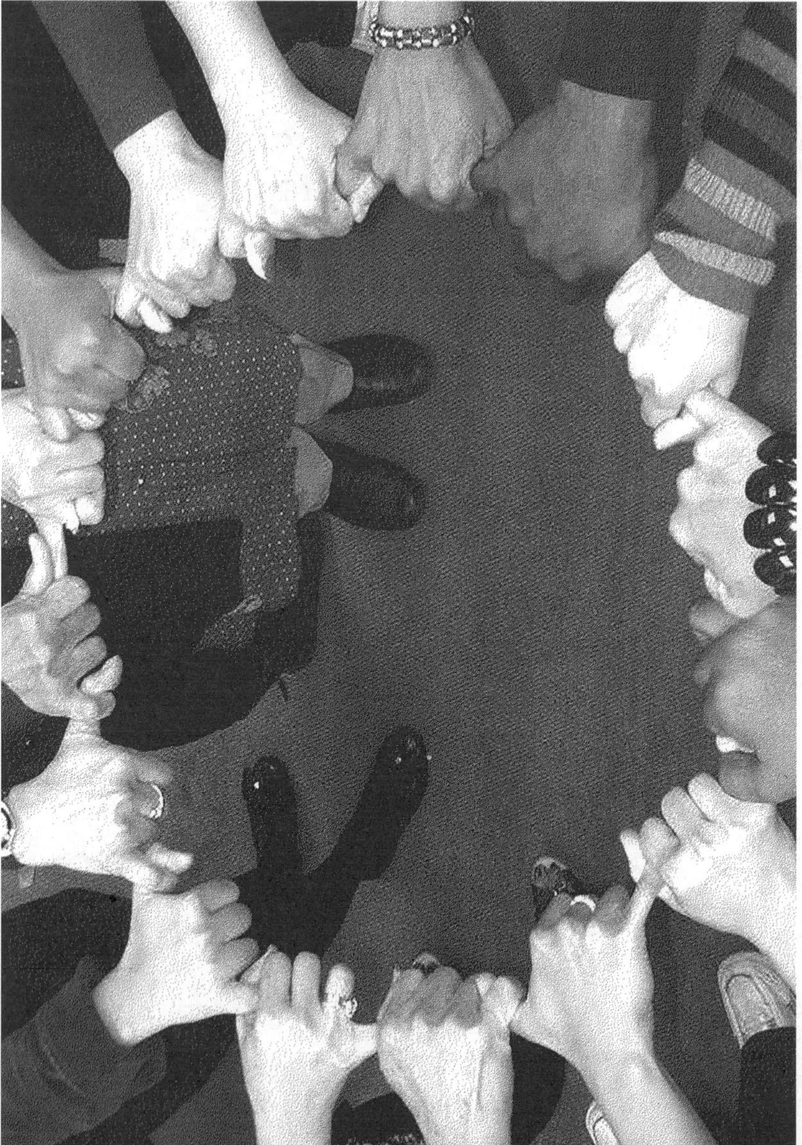

october 3

we are still working.

disappearing work into living

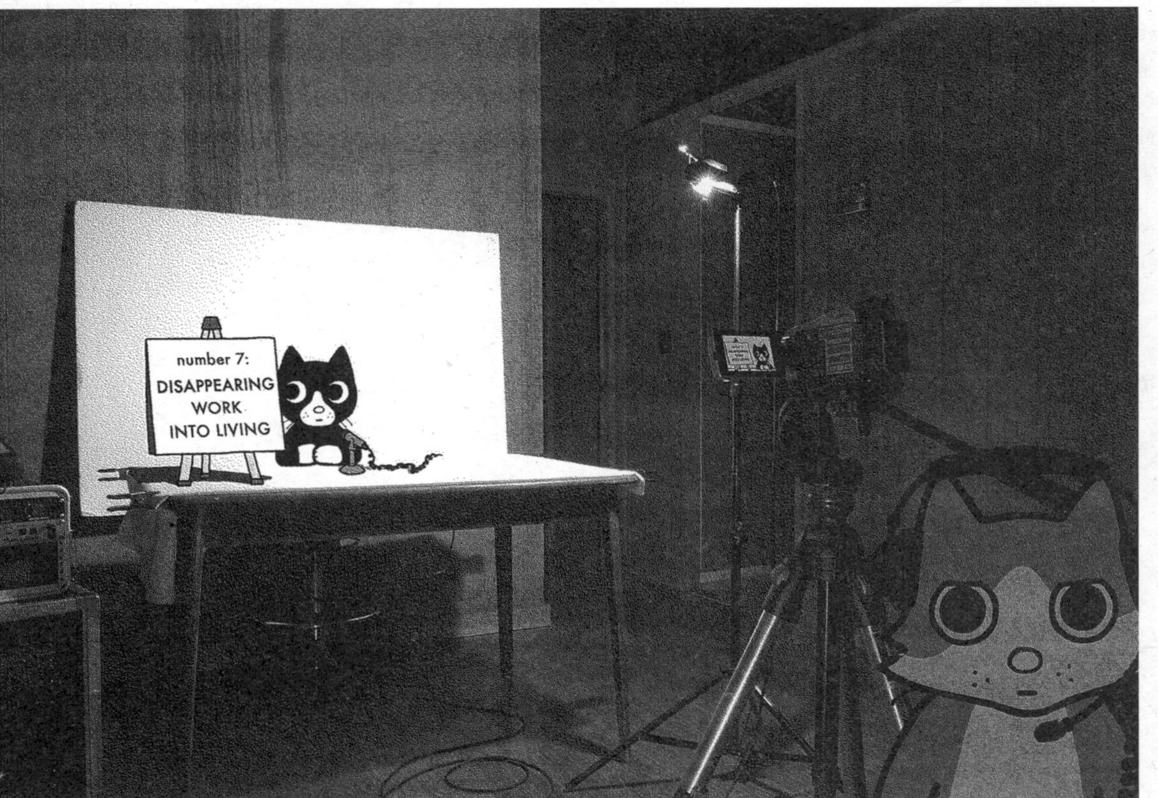

number 7:
DISAPPEARING
WORK.
INTO LIVING

october 4

ninety-seven selected photographs
showing groups of wealthy peruvian
people in daily domestic situations.
in the background of each image one
can see either a figure or a deletion
of a domestic worker. all images have
been collected from the social network
site facebook.

97 house maids

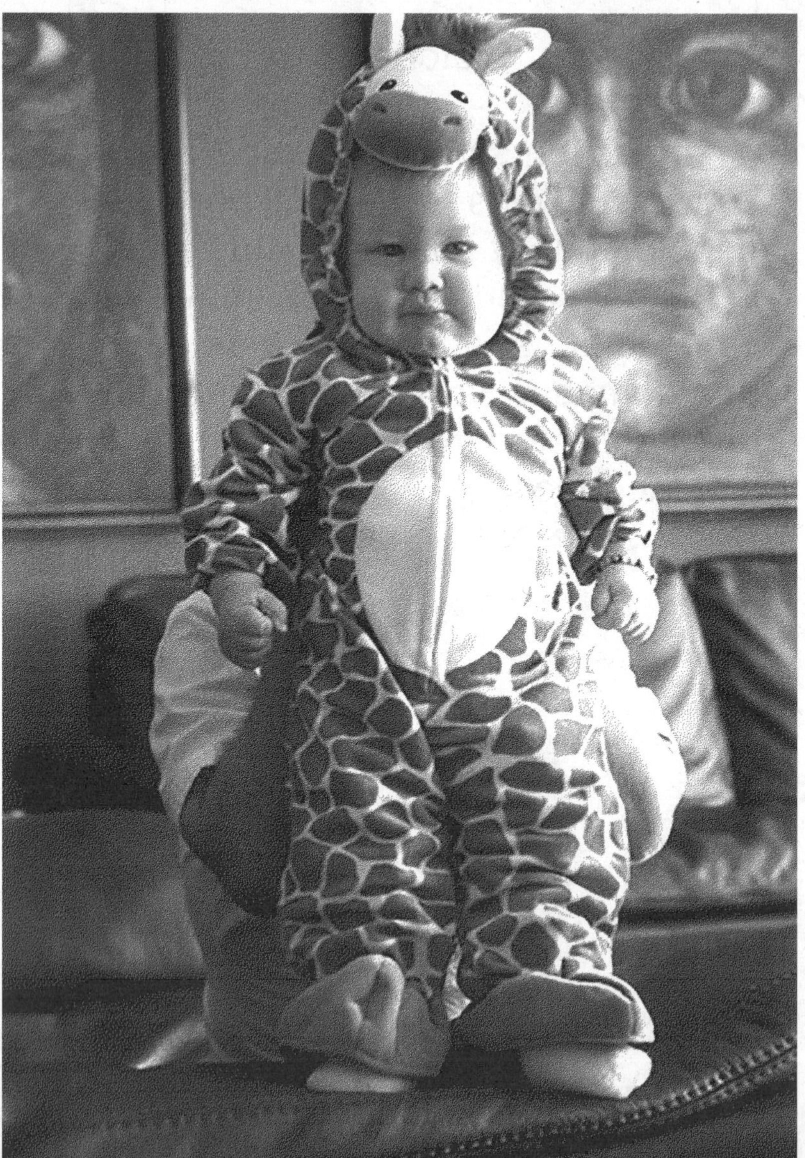

october 5

dew point

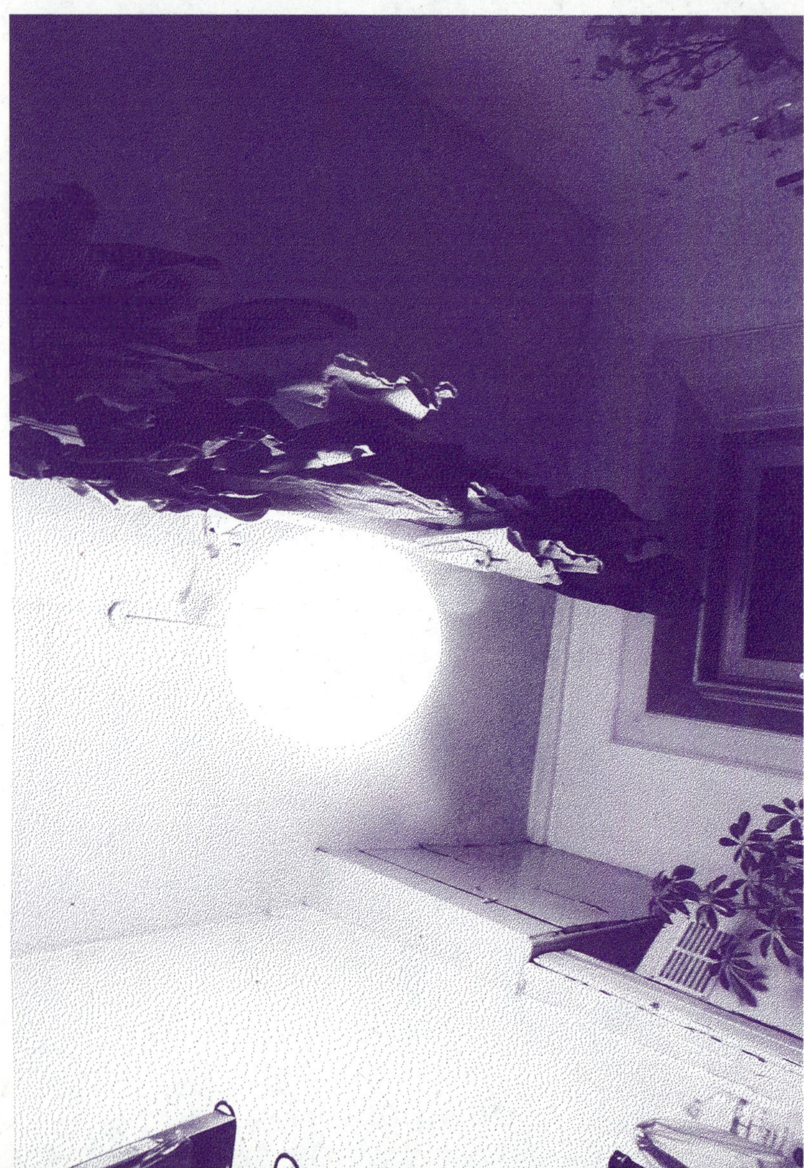

finally, i have decided to open my
kitchen, my prison. using the hammer,
i felt my freedom was beginning.
photo taken in castellón, 1993.

breaking walls

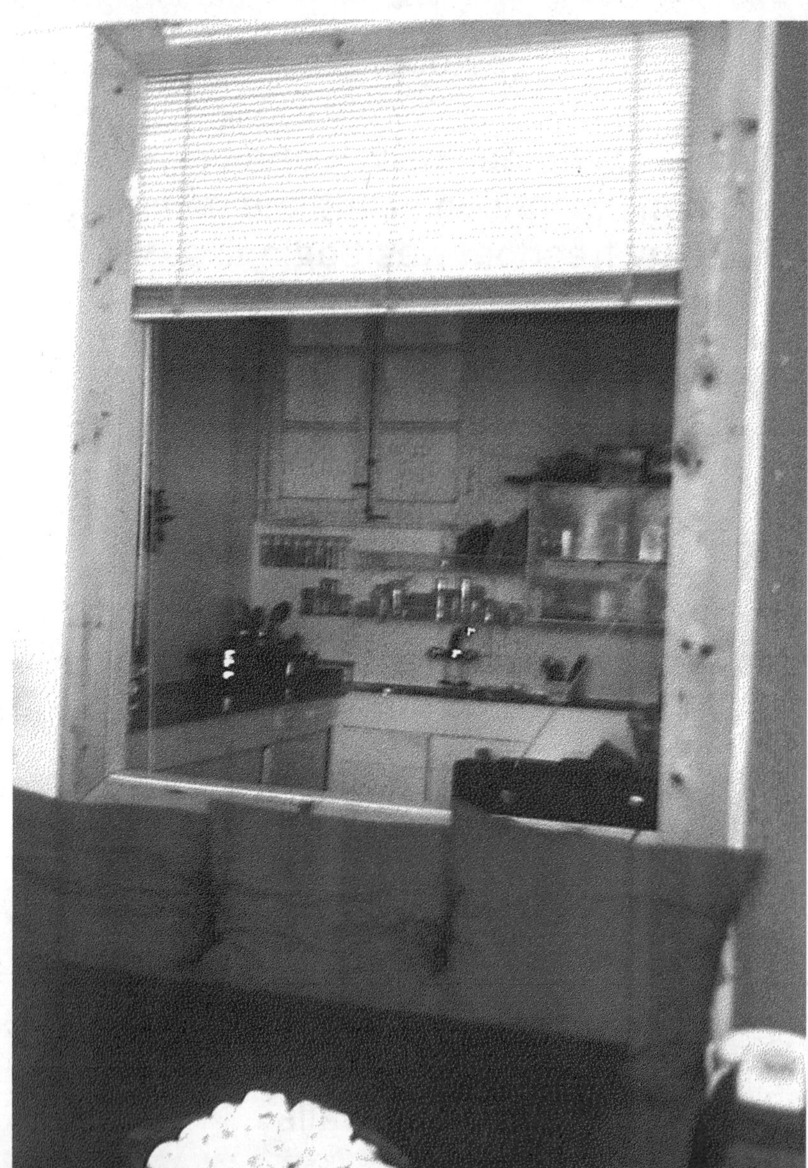

"i perceive that the work we raise is
not unique, nor isolated, that the air
around it constitutes other surfaces,
other grounds, other ceilings [...]
the work is not made only of itself:
the outside exists. the outside shuts
me in its whole which is like a room."

le corbusier, *precisions*,
([1930] 1991) p.78.

invisible domestic labour:
the dusting frenetically series

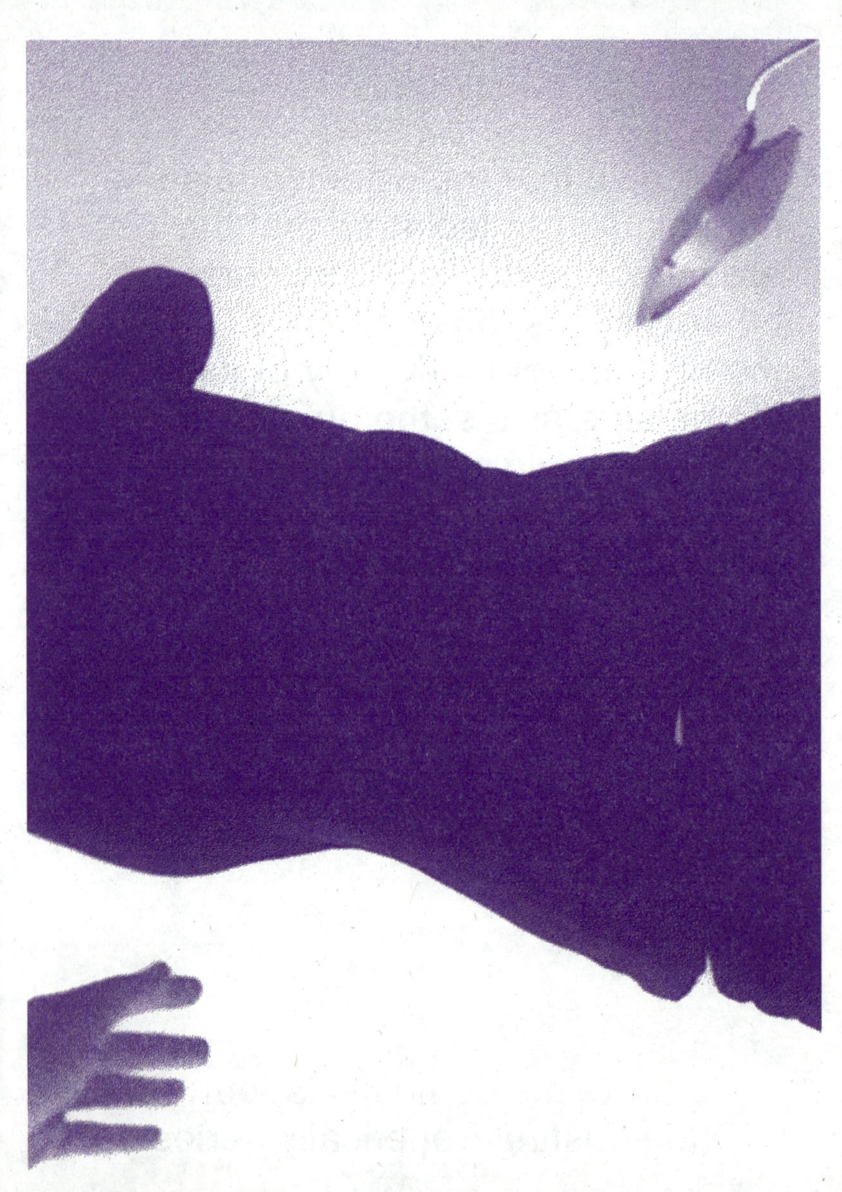

october 8

use a crate on your bike.

october 8

go work

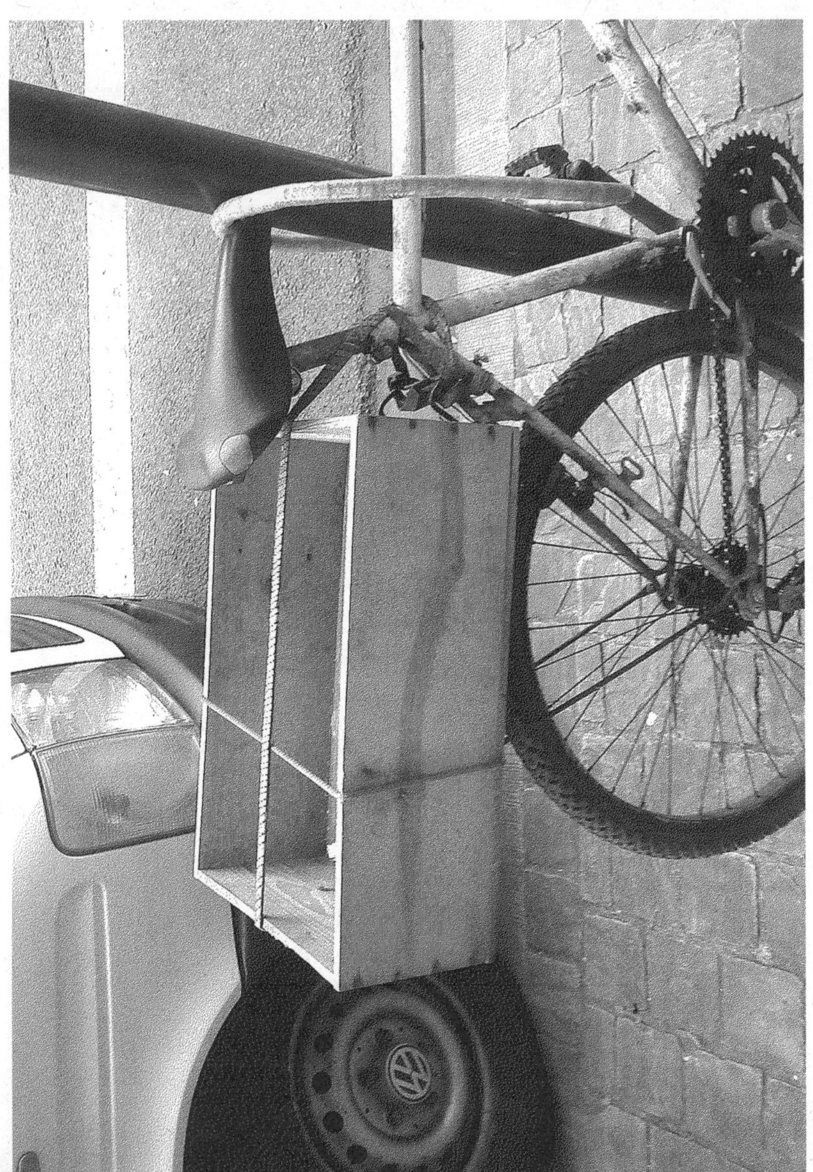

october 9

discarded sign found during the demo-
lition of one of the last remaining
grocery stores in the neighbourhood.

urban food desert

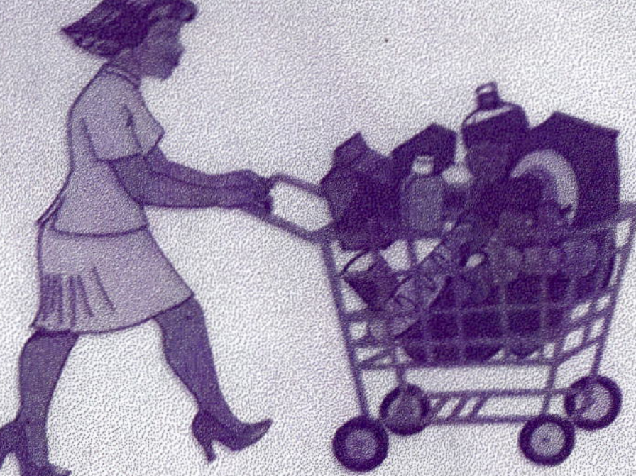
NO. 1
SUPER
MARKET

october 10

hawaiian party held in zeeland in
summer 2011 with friends from
our community.

time for happiness

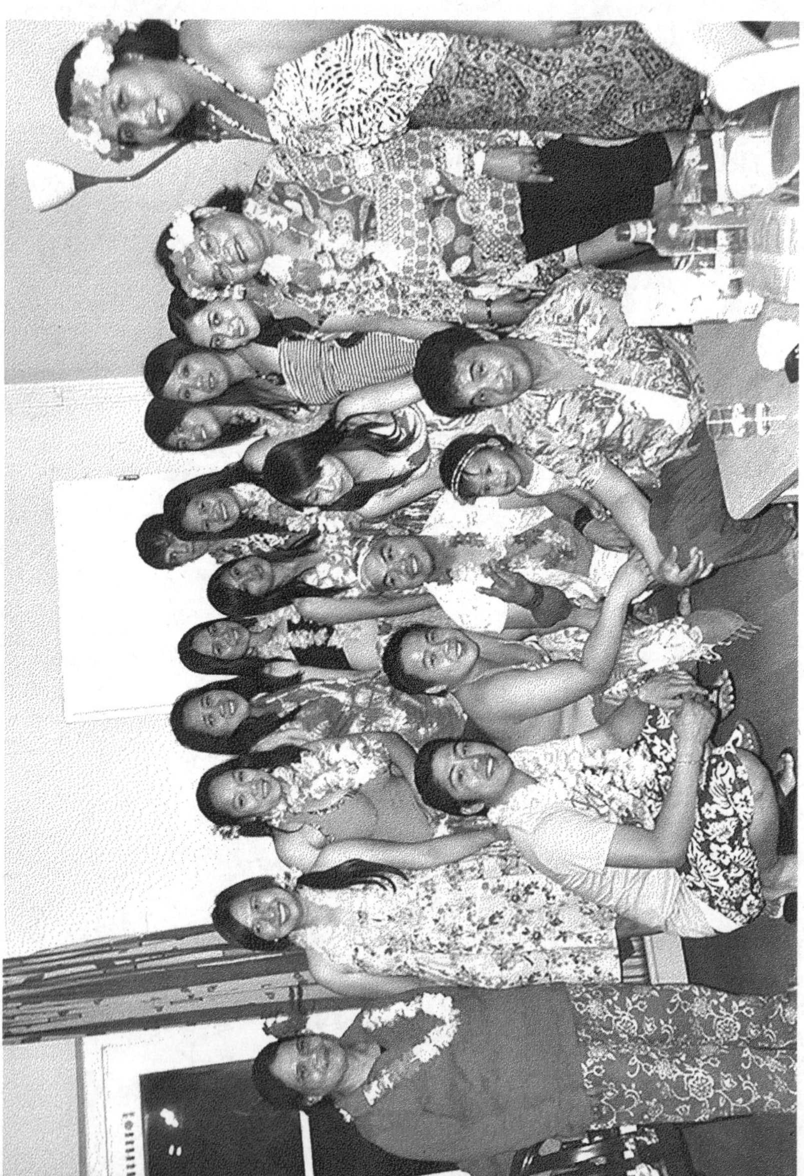

the frequency of reports increased
during the early 20th century, when
westerners began making determined
attempts to scale the many mountains
in the area and occasionally reported
seeing odd creatures or strange tracks.

laundry

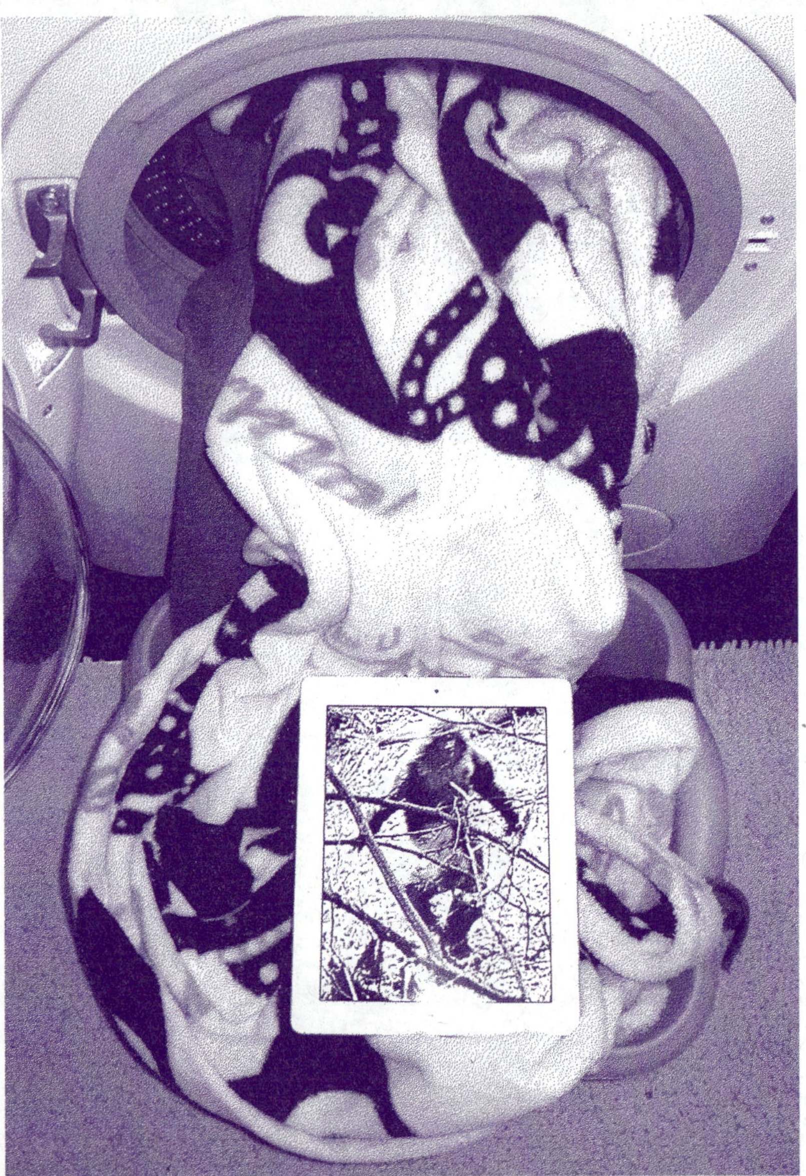

"set in a mansion, the film starts with the guests arriving twice. shot slightly differently, the beginning seems to set the tone for a seemingly non-sensical experience. if you can have breakfast twice in one day, why can't you enter the same room twice?" read full text at: https://m-est.org/2011/08/12/onfor-production/.

e-flux

e-flux

Generally speaking, art is an expression of man's need for an harmonious and complete life, that is to say, his need for those major benefits of which a society of classes has deprived him. That is why a protest against reality, either conscious or unconscious, active or passive, optimistic or pessimistic, always forms part of a really creative piece of work. Every new tendency in art has begun with rebellion.

–Leon Trotsky

6 hours ago · 💬 1 👍 44 · Like · Comment

october 13

rubber bands, ordered by size
and by age/rigidity.

15 min

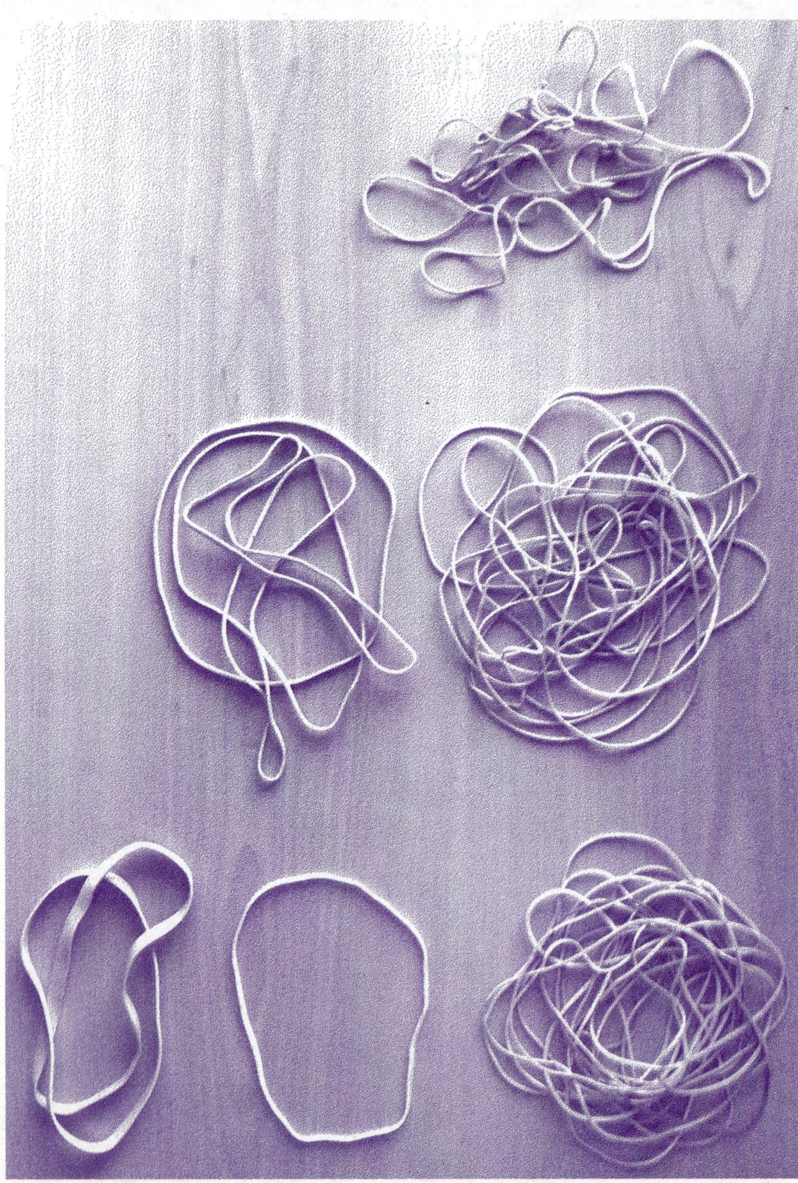

october 14

neema preparing ugali and calling.

ugali

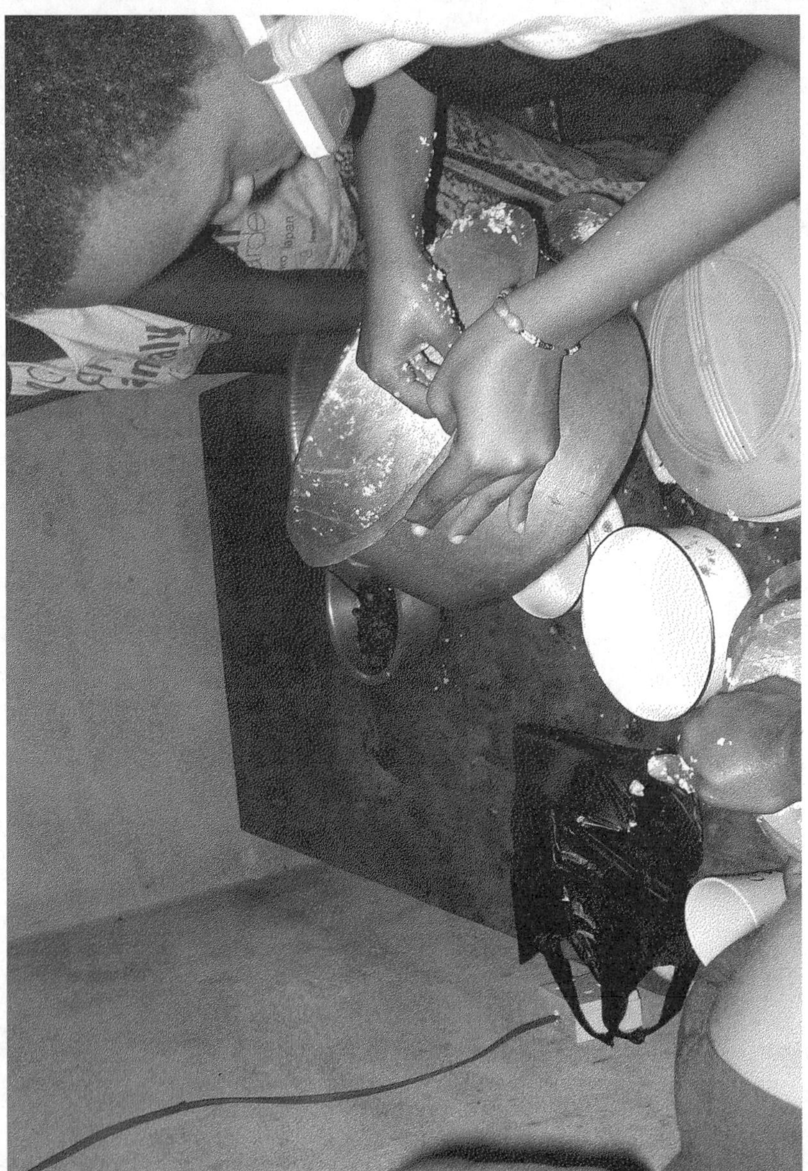

october 15

street view in casco viejo.

drying in panamá

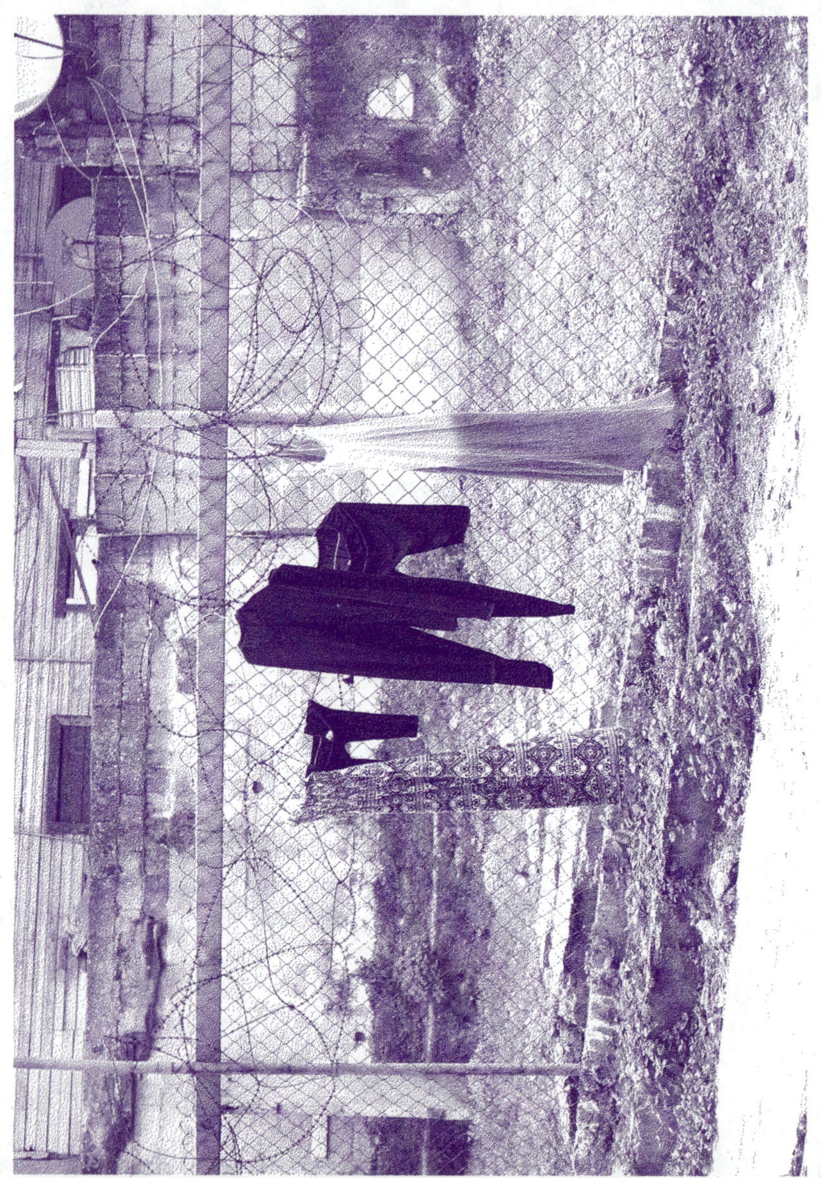

october 16

combining principles.

dishes

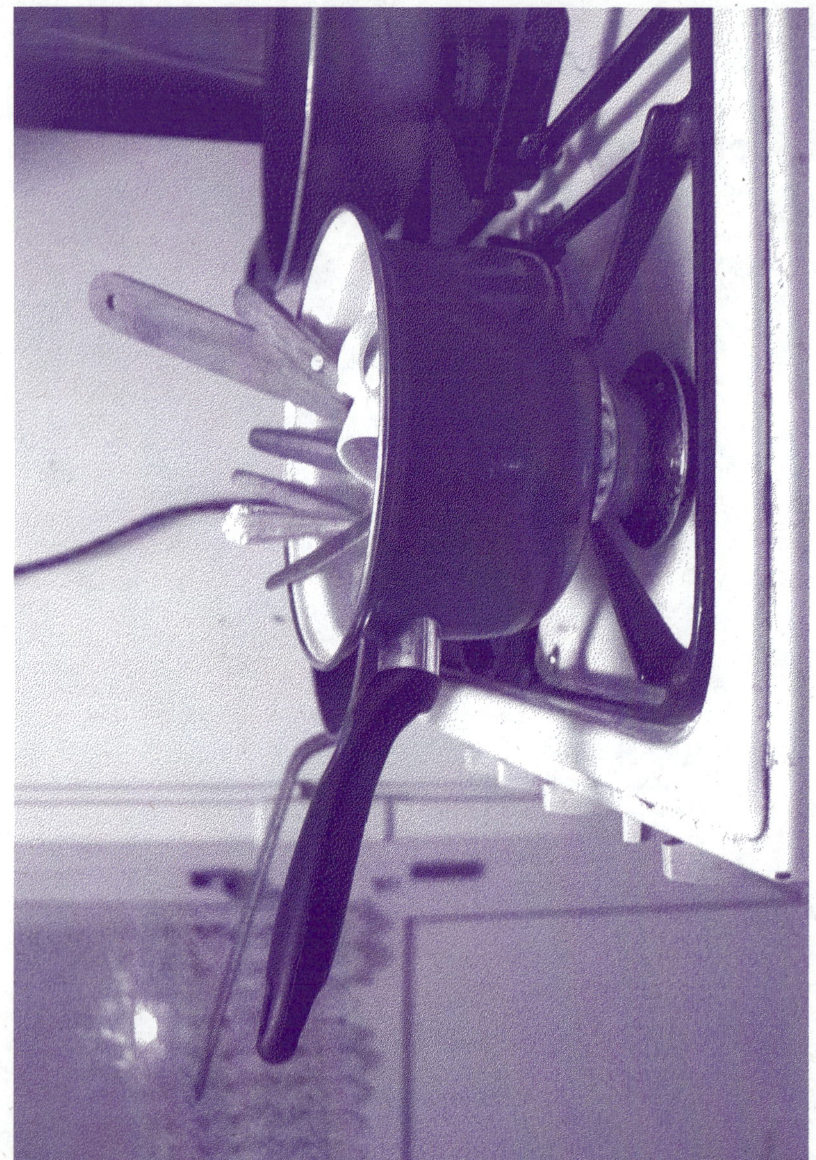

october 17

when our hands are not working our
hands are always working.

hands at work

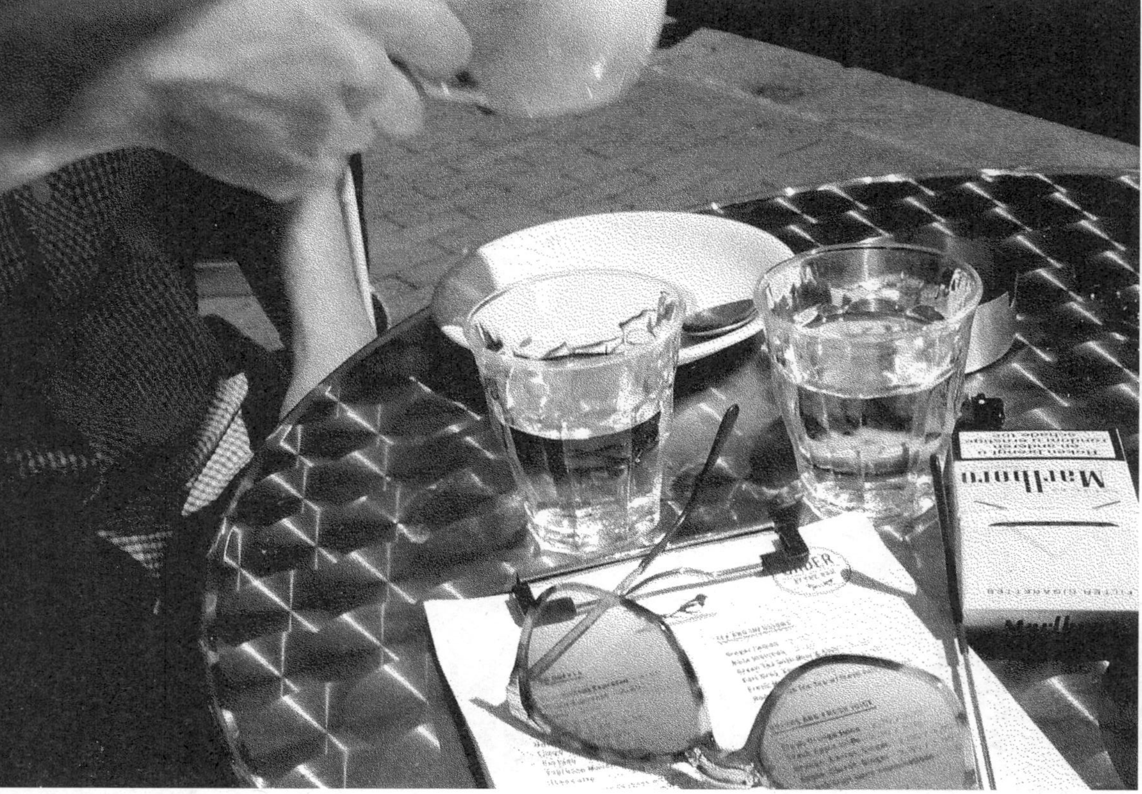
Marlboro
FILTER CIGARETTES

october 18

first time being a nanny, she's super cute but also hyperactive.

first time being a nanny

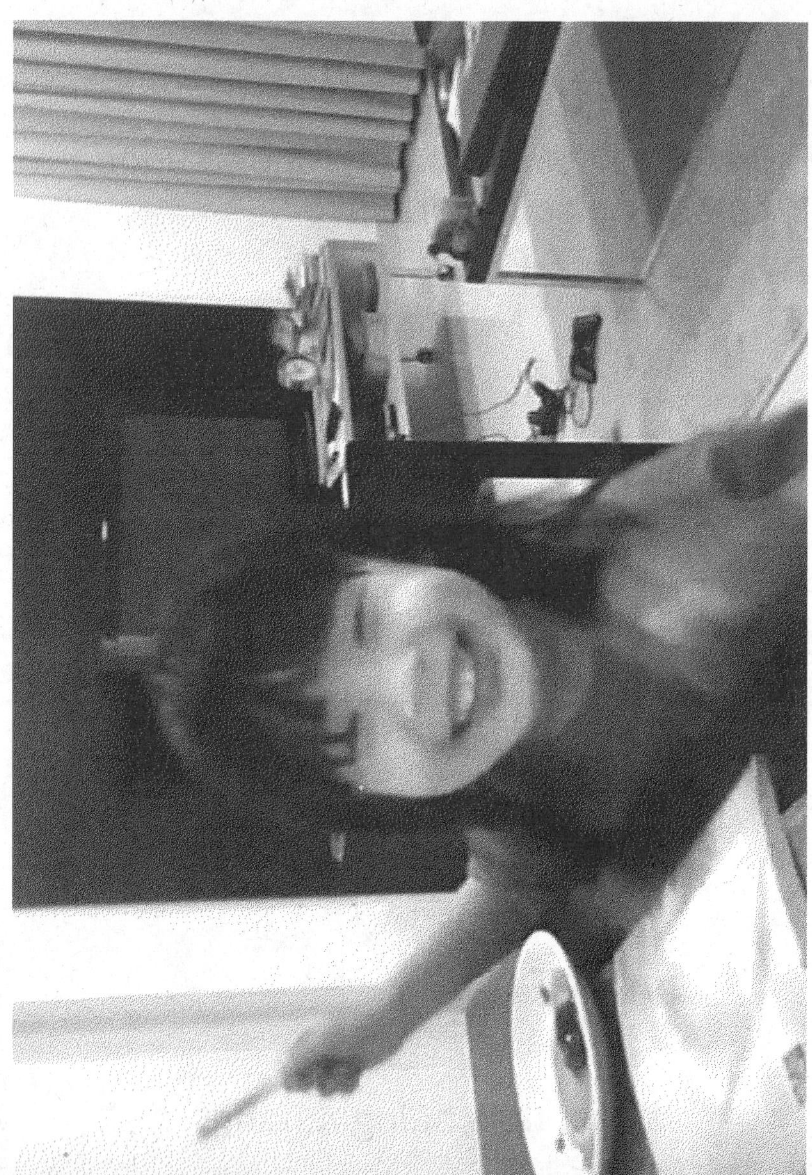

october 19

my aunt wakes up every morning
at 4:30 am to feed the pigs in her
farm, while her husband will probably
get up around nine to do "manly" work.

good morning!

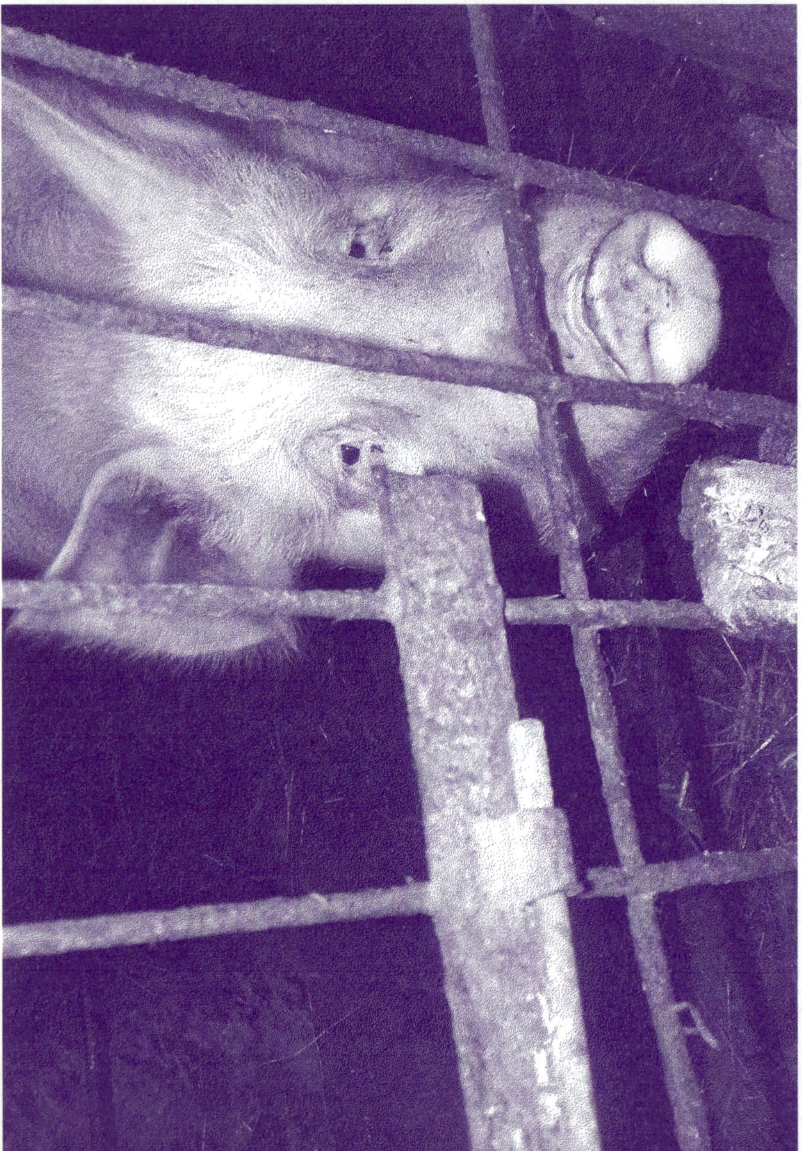

october 20

house upside down. working hard
to circulate a positive energy. i believe
when you organize things, you get
good results.

cleaning

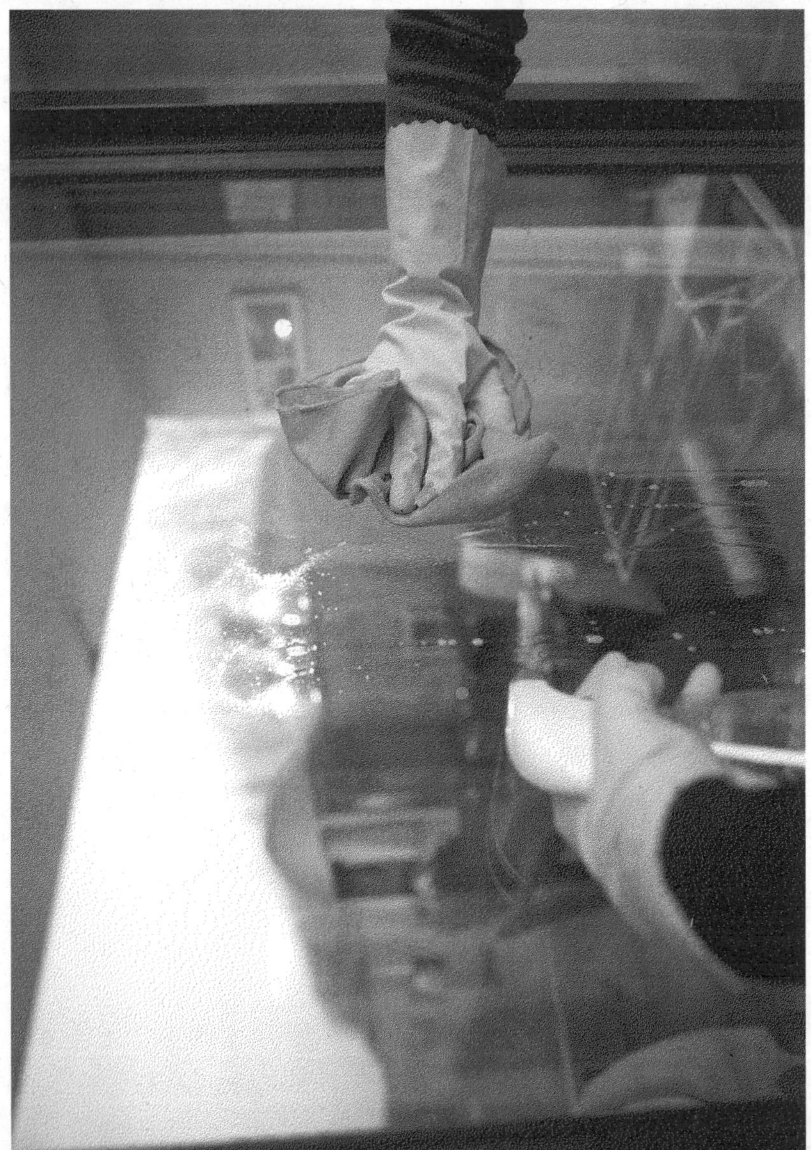

repetitive strain injury (rsi). anybody
who regularly makes continuous
repetitive motions for a length of time
runs the risk of contracting rsi.
the initial stage of rsi is characterized
by tingling and tired arms, neck or
shoulders. these symptoms can
develop into persistent pain and
loss of strength in arms and hands.
in this phase treatment is often
no longer successful.

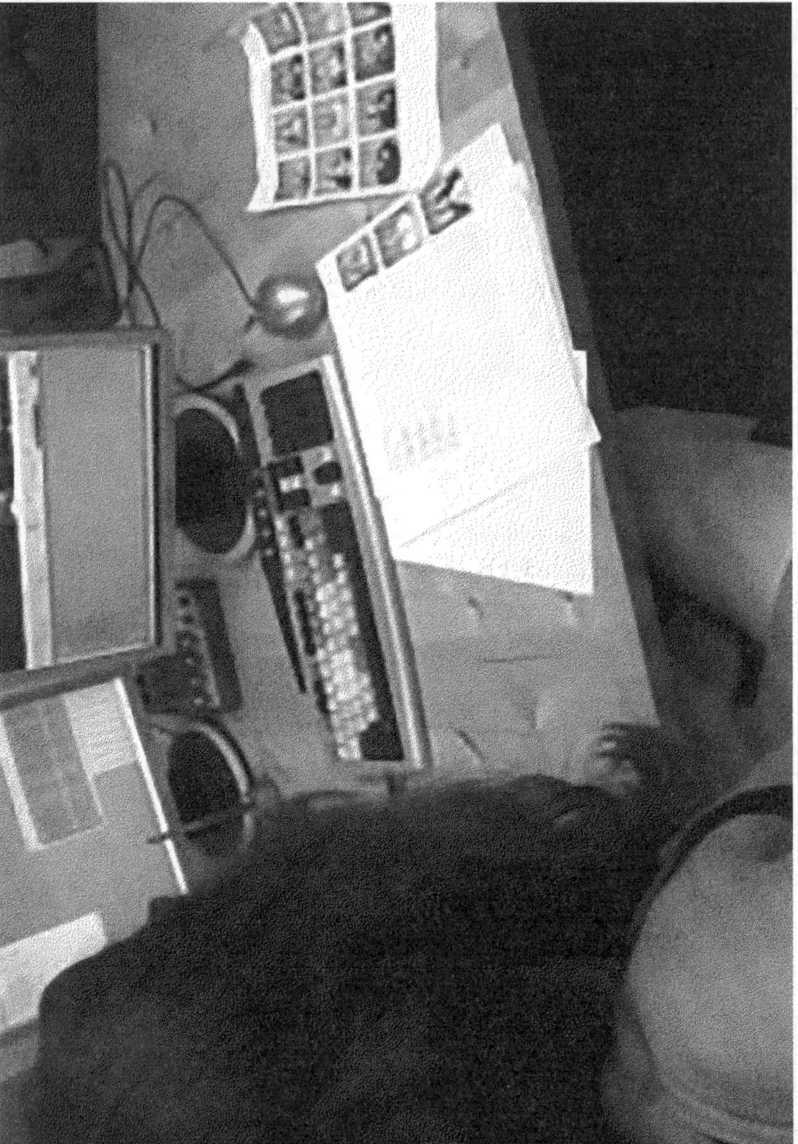

october 22

this is how they leave the doors
of a house after an eviction: sealed.

eviction

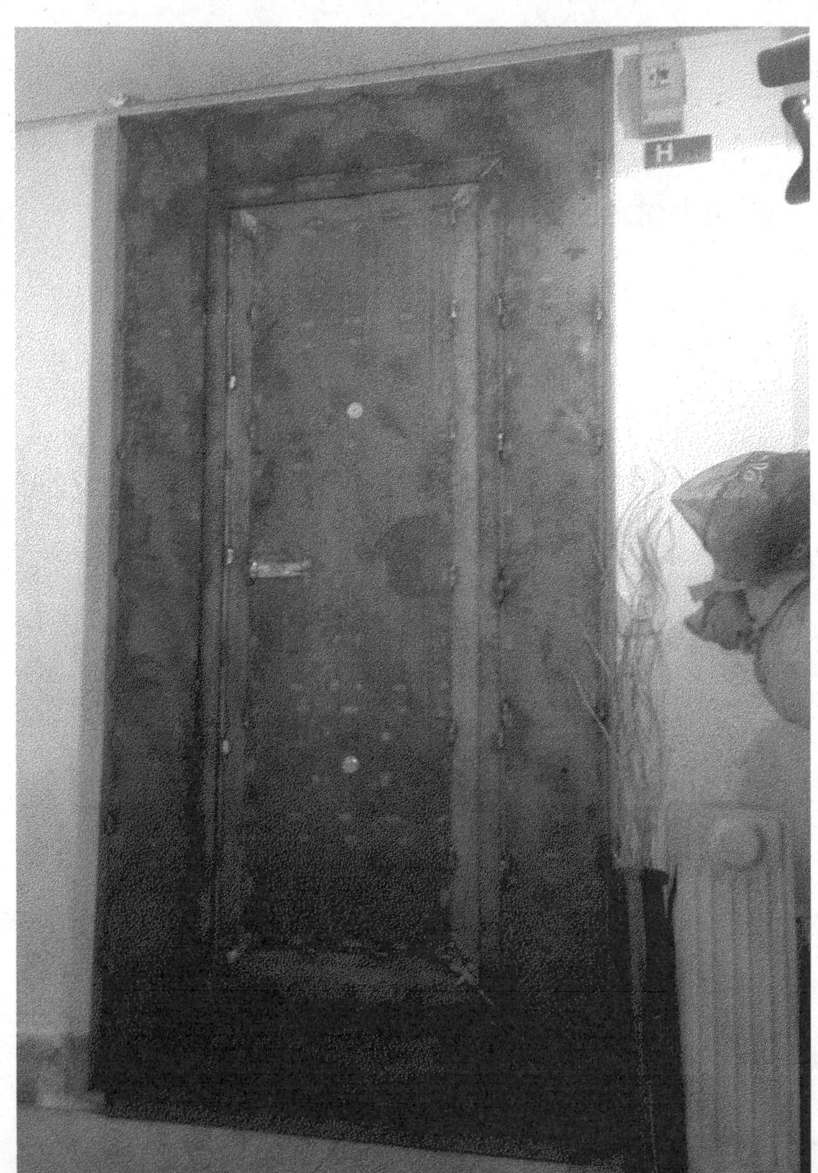
H

october 23

unsafe housing because of our
neglectful landlord.

unsafe

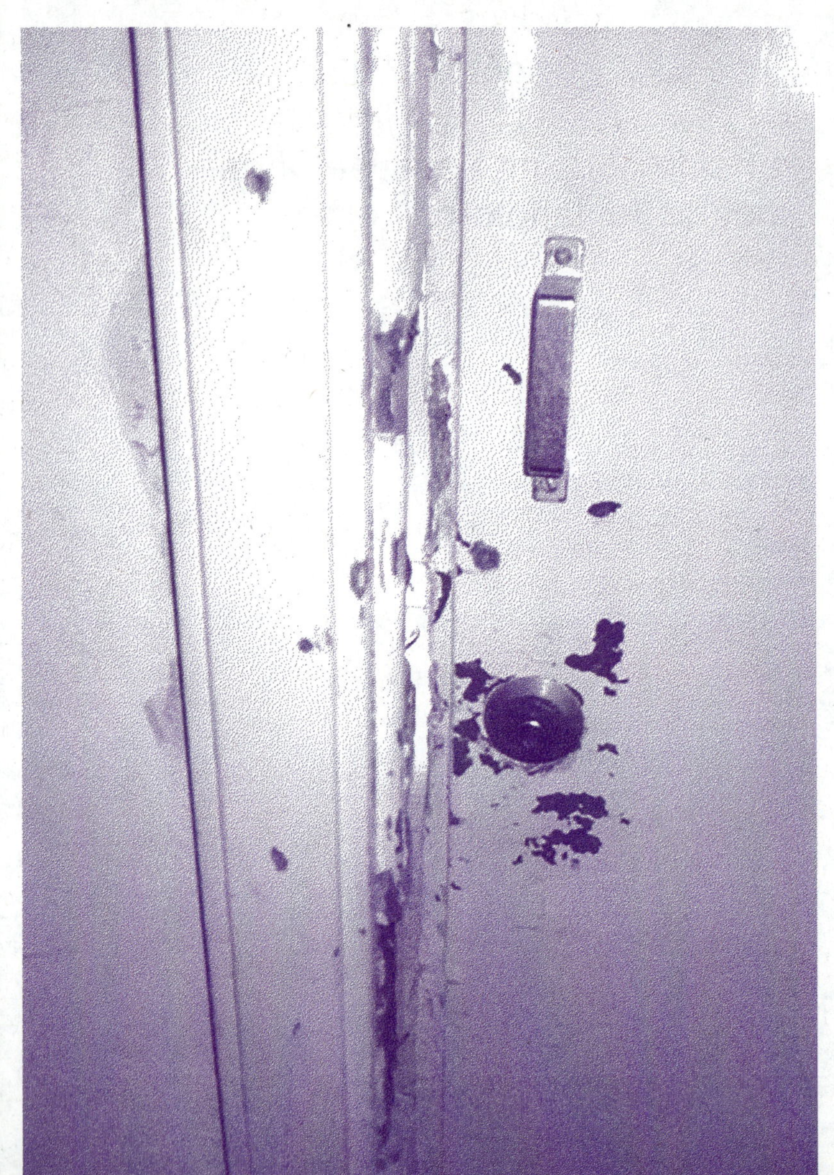

we, domestic workers play a big role in moulding children inside the household, yet we are denied recognition and acknowledgement. we are the beginning and end of all labours, but we are deprived from being called workers. we are like shadows of the economy and education.

shadow

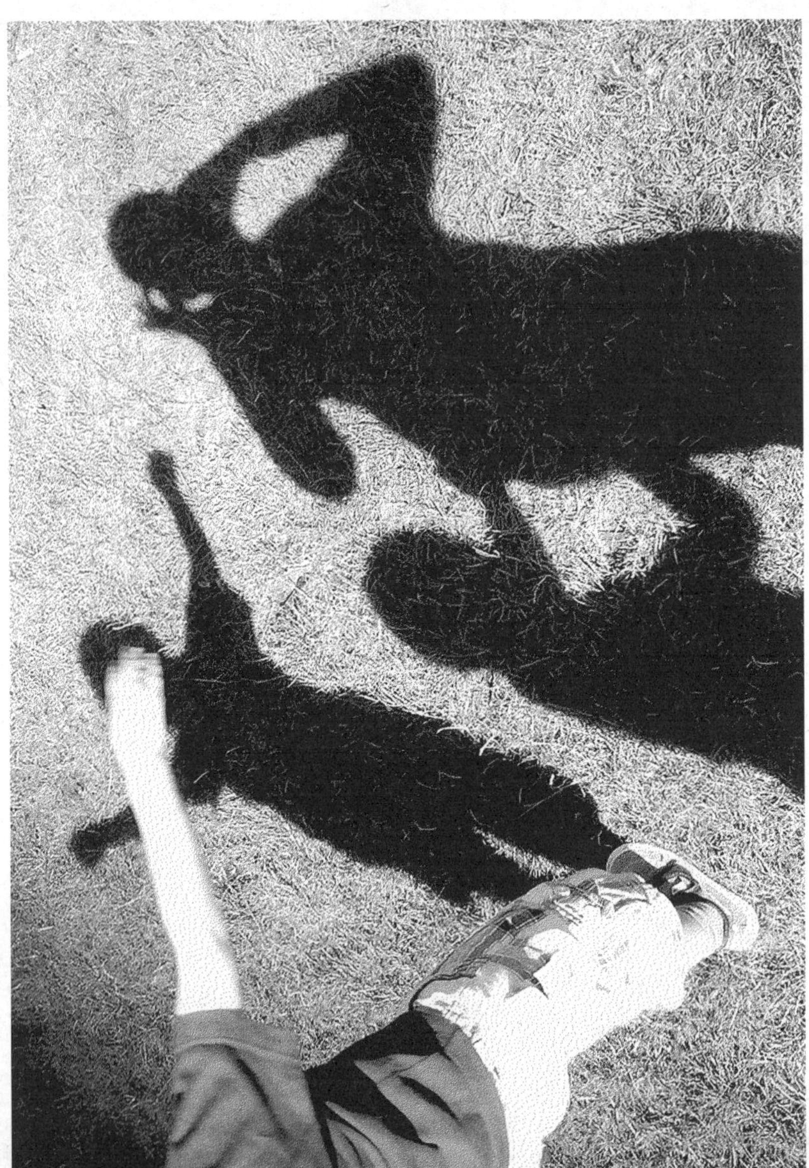

ladislav hudec was shanghai's most important art deco architect. in china i slipped into his house, opened drawers, looked through the dusty windows and took this picture. next to its door, there is a plaque: "residence of hudec. designed by ladislav hudec. built in 1930. masonry structure. english country house style." according to my guide, now it's a museum.

the house museum
is a western concept

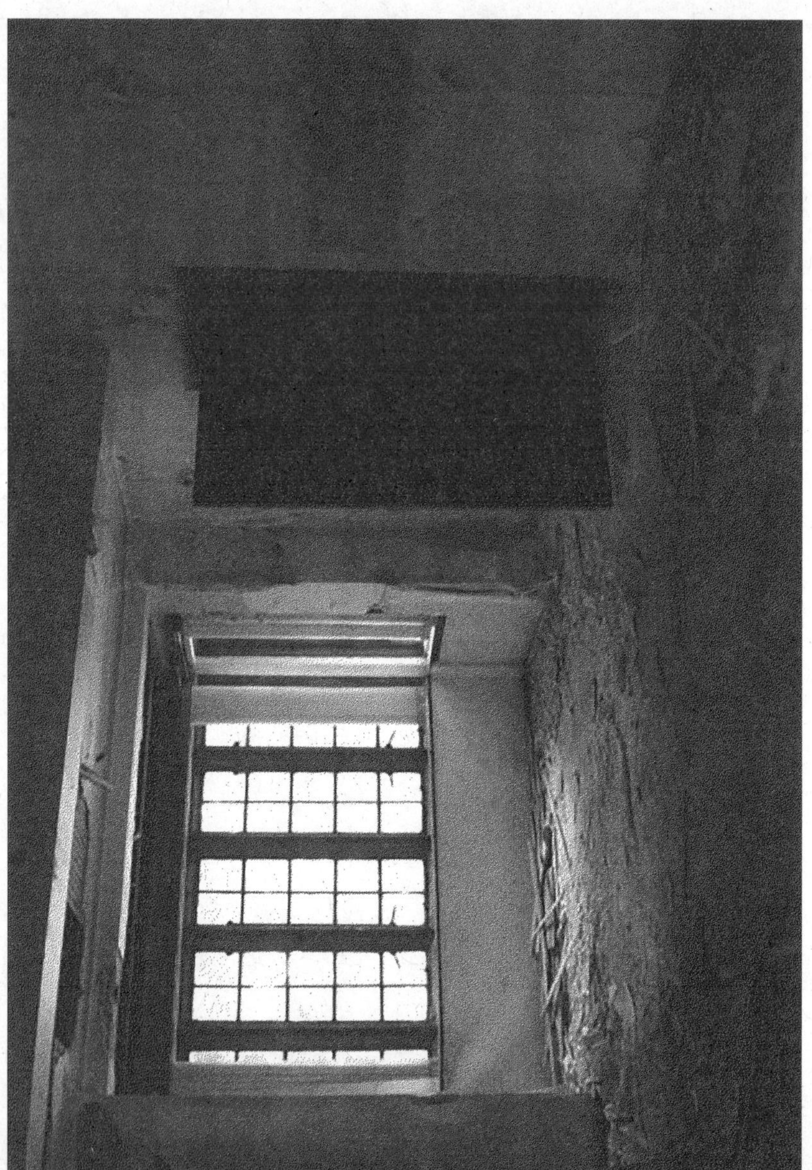

october 26

in order to get new clothes i sell
or trade my old ones on facebook.
buy here and renew your wardrobe.

l'armari

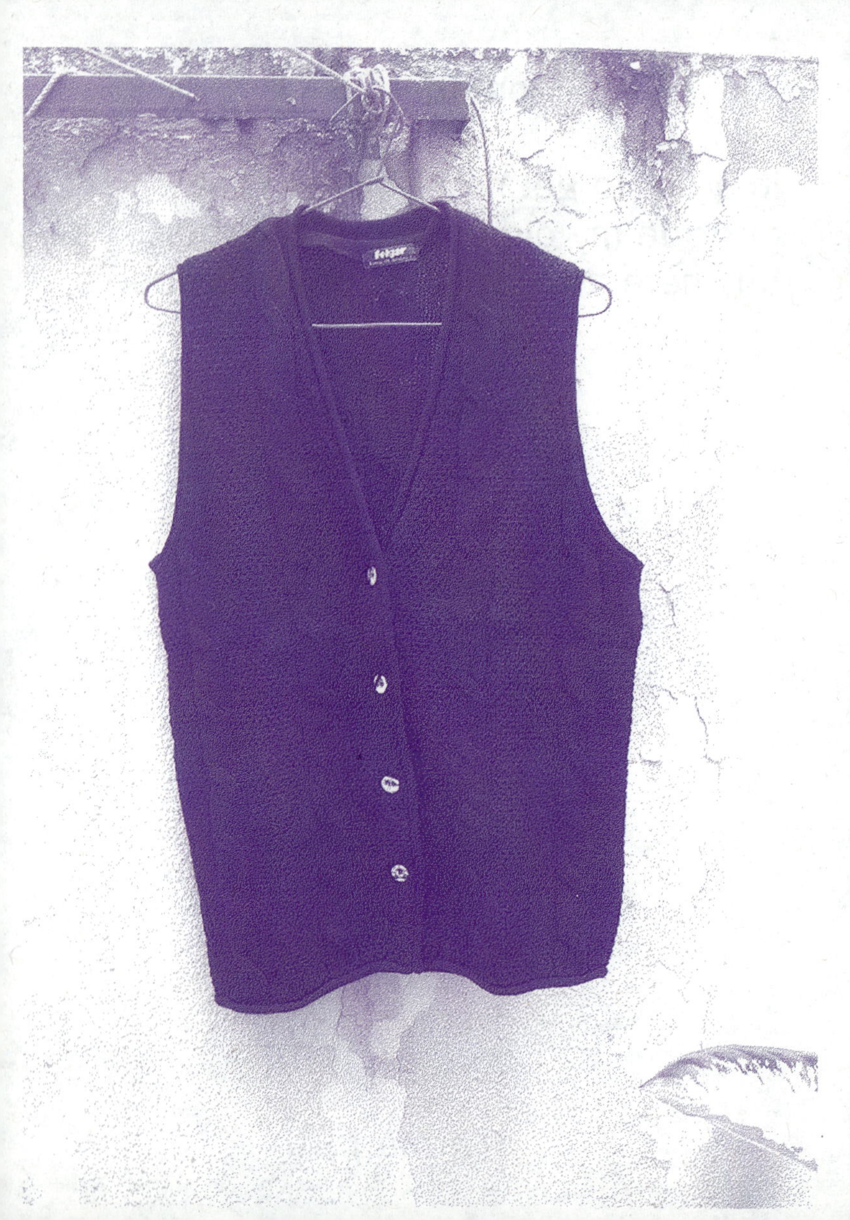

october 27

old postcard.

paul l'avait aussi

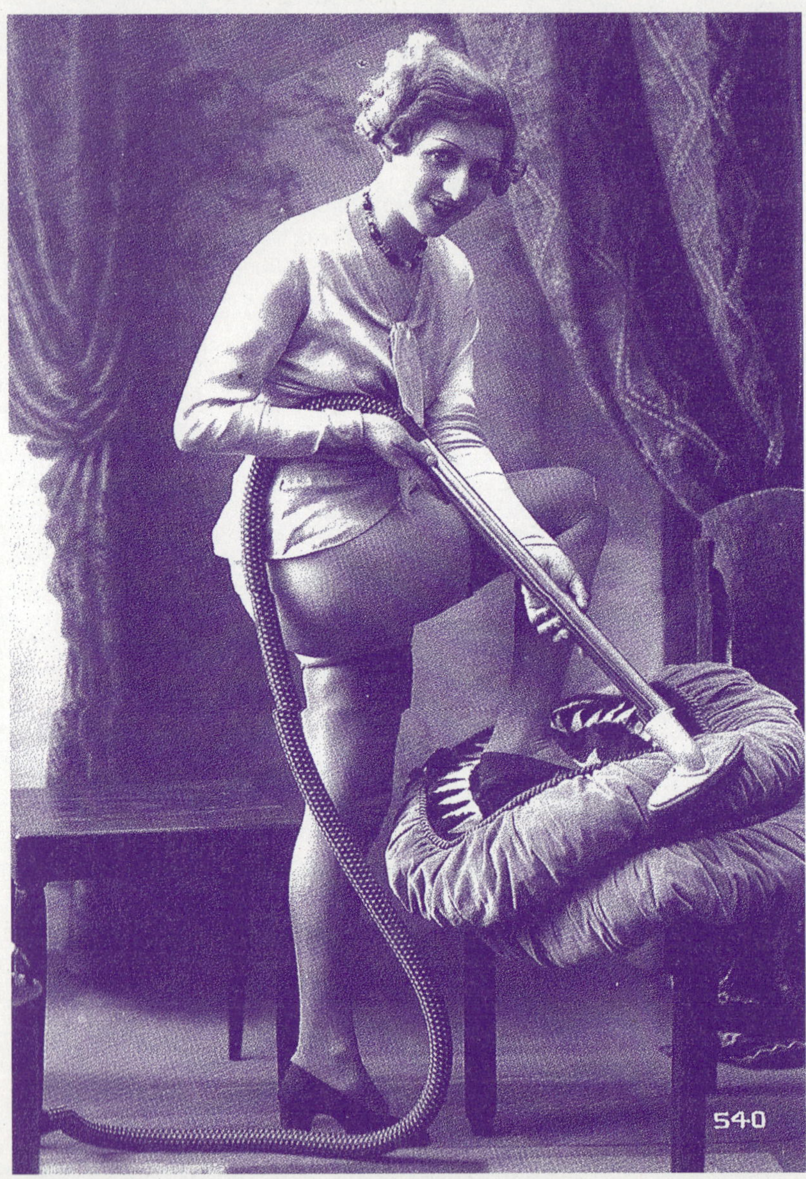
540

october 28

image by henning von berg.

astroboi

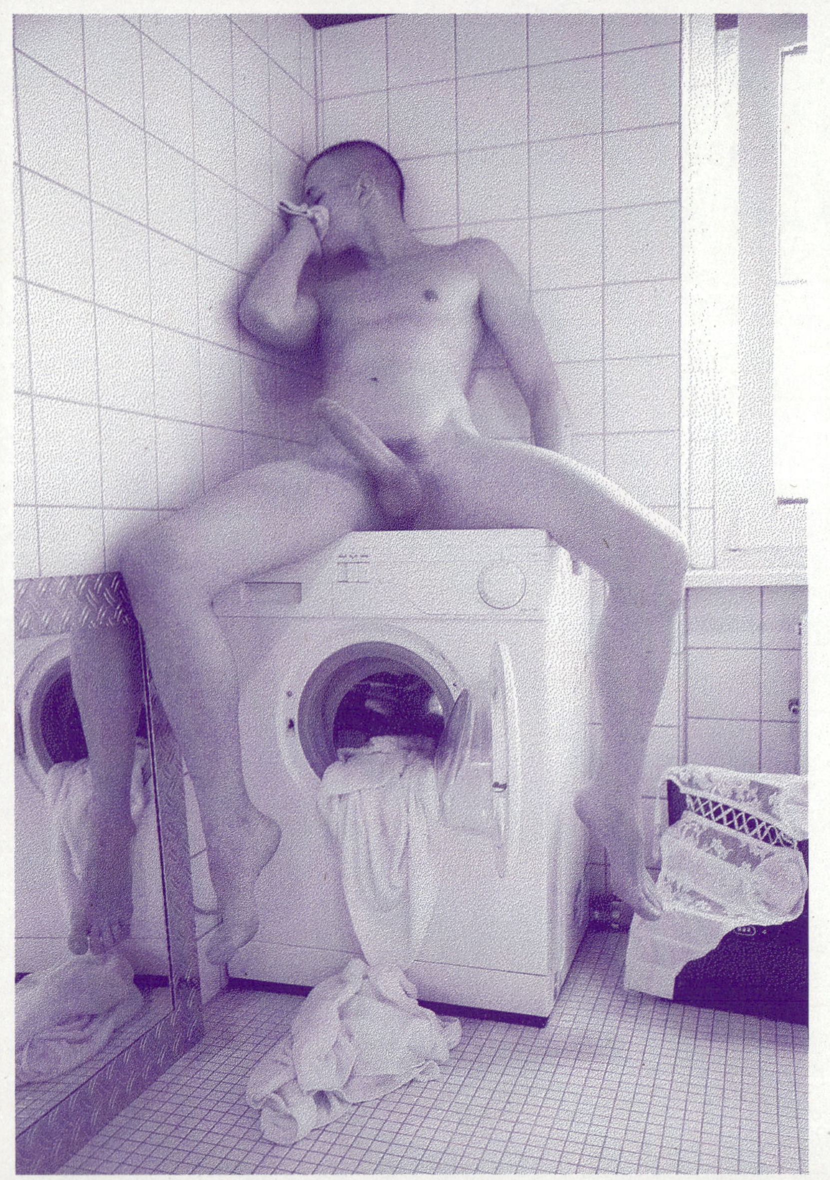

october 29

the iron and the bitch

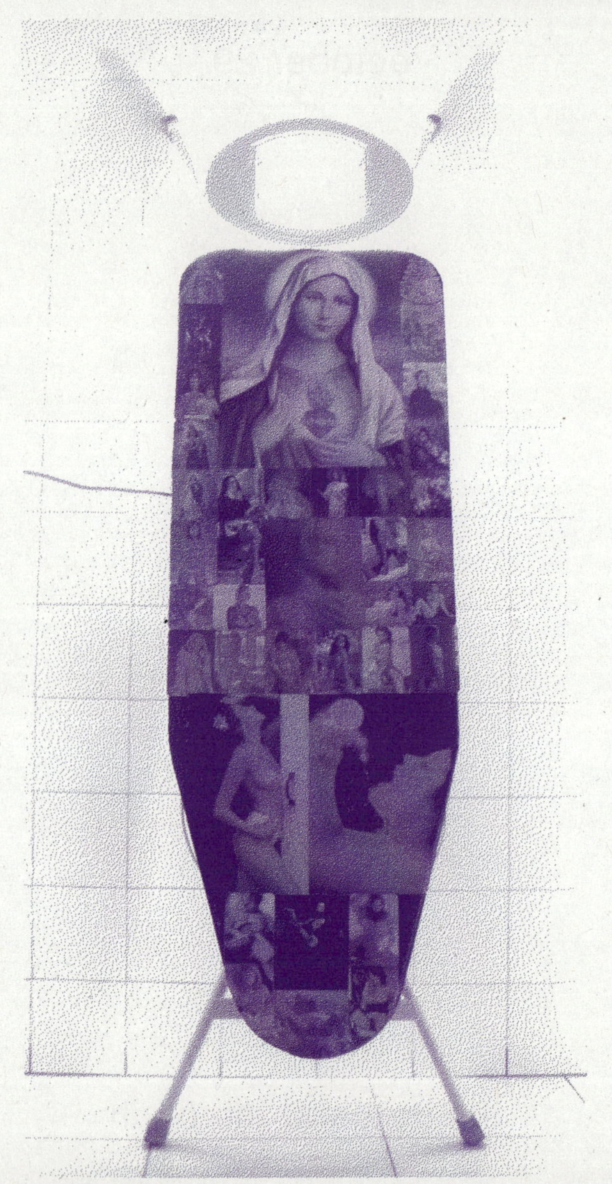

dartington hall school (1926–1987)
offered progressive education
and a coeducational boarding life.
as a first to do so it was notorious
for mixed sleeping.

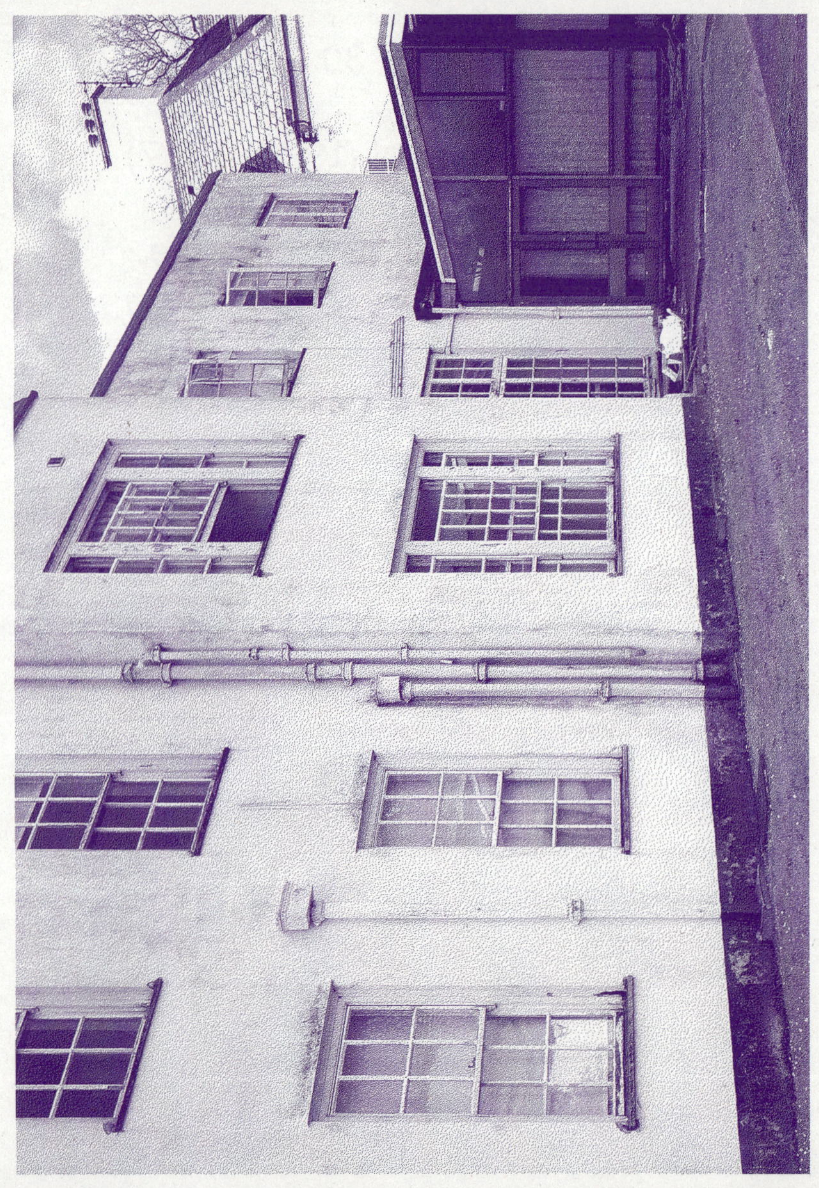

informing other domestic workers
about the importance of being
together, fighting for workers rights.

organizing

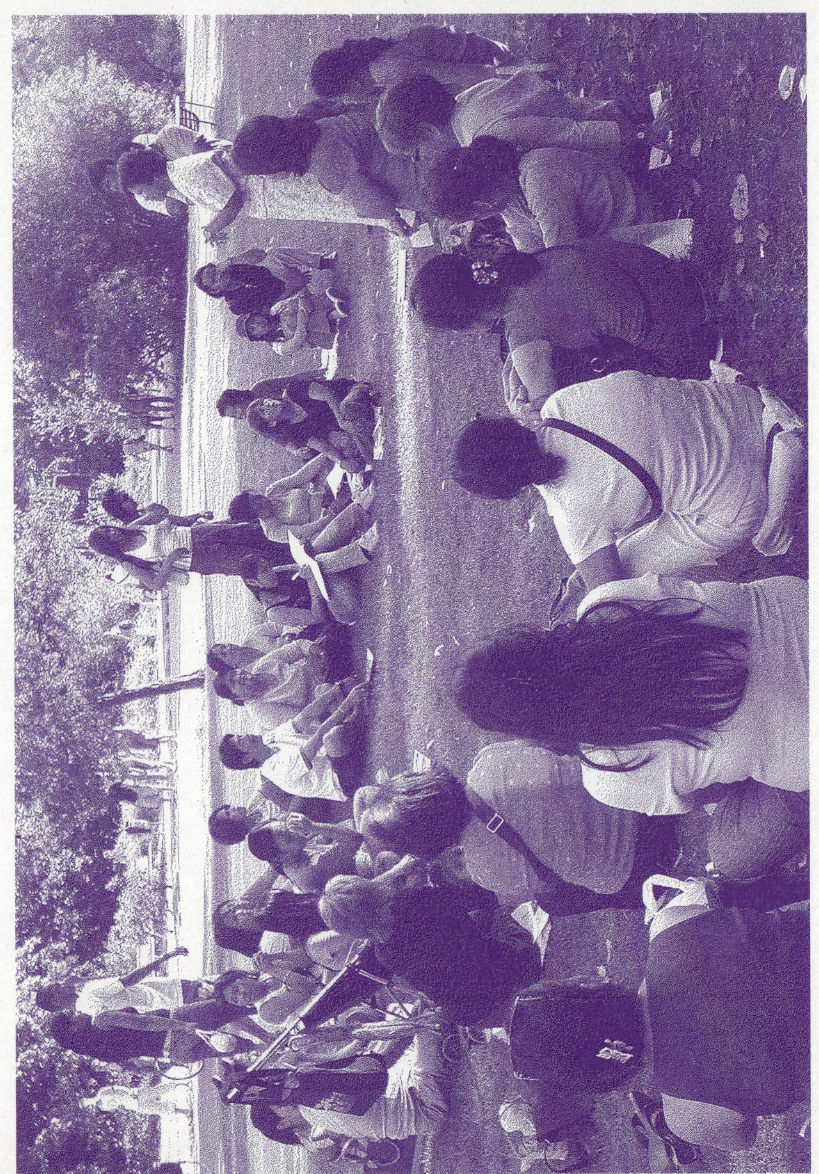

november 1

"subjectivity as a material to trade,"
white ink on $1 bank notes.

making of "subjectivity
as a material to trade"

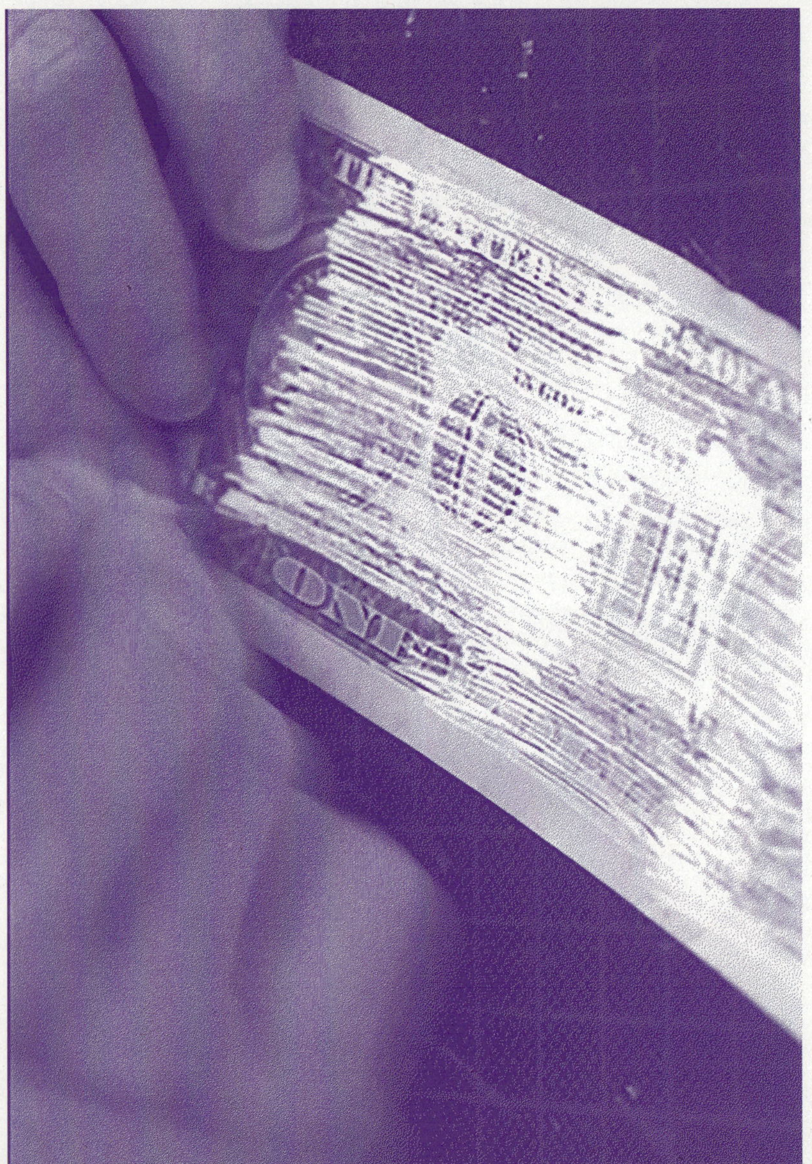

this "ich" mirror is part of an installation of glass pieces in the beautiful garden of a good friend. visiting him and his family in the country is like going to an island… with time for reflecting about myself, sitting there… dazzled by little reflections dancing on the plants.

mirroring my morning

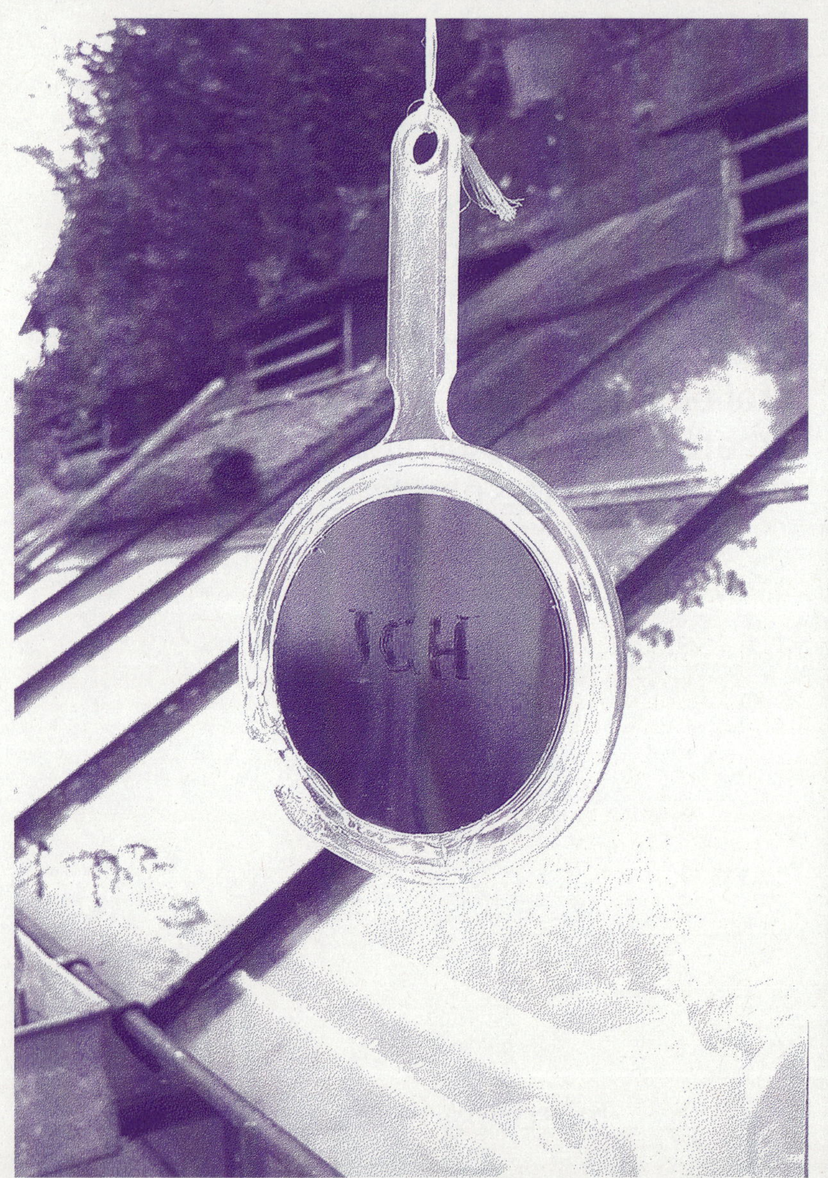

ICH

november 3

sleeping at the atelier like a real artist.

breaking up

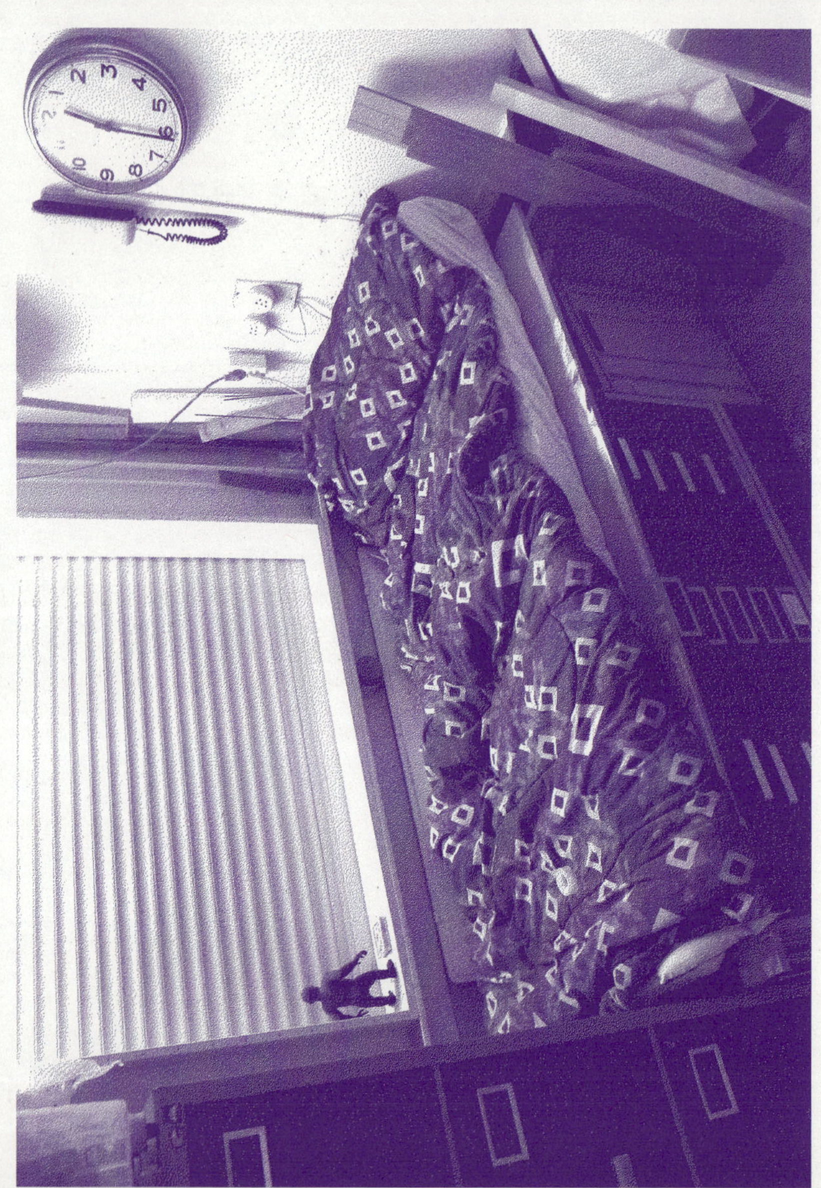

november 4

self-portrait in a home office.

drawing diary

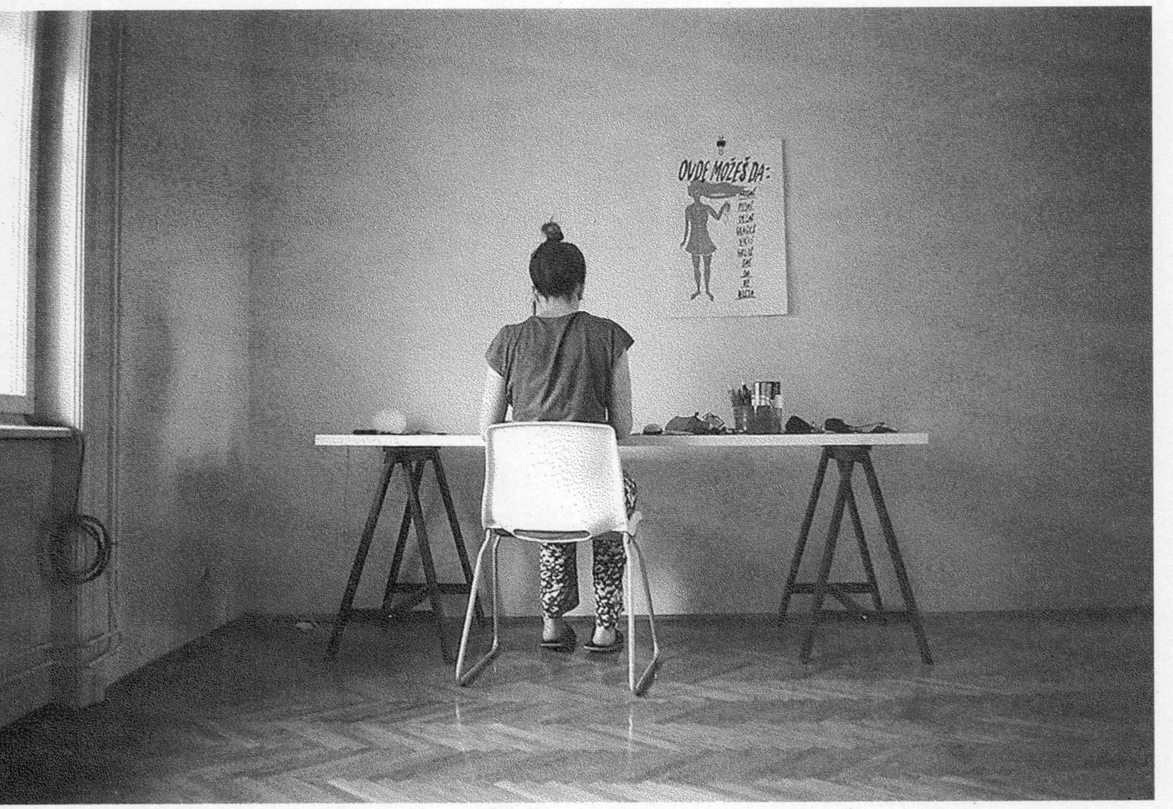

OVDE MOŽEŠ DA:

november 5

i have come to enjoy doing the
dishes by hand.

a start

iMessage
Yesterday 8:33 pm

Hi ▮▮▮, sorry to disturb your winter evening here in Amsterdam, but would you mind helping me to remove the dishwasher down the stairs? I know it's a heck of a job, but then at least we have a start. Pls let me know. Thx.

▮▮▮

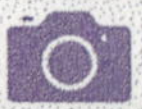 iMessage Send

november 6

domestic workers have no social life.
we work very long hours, from 16–24
hours a day. with the busy schedules
of justice for domestic workers we
make sure that in a calendar year,
the four months with 5 sundays, j4dw
members get out for some fresh air
to relax and enjoy: on the beach,
the farm, or to museums and other
historic places. we use this as one way
to raise funds and encourage other
fellow domestic workers to join us
in upholding the rights, values,
and contribution of migrant domestic
workers justice for domestic workers
demand recognition in making
domestic work visible in british society.

the precious 5th sunday of the month

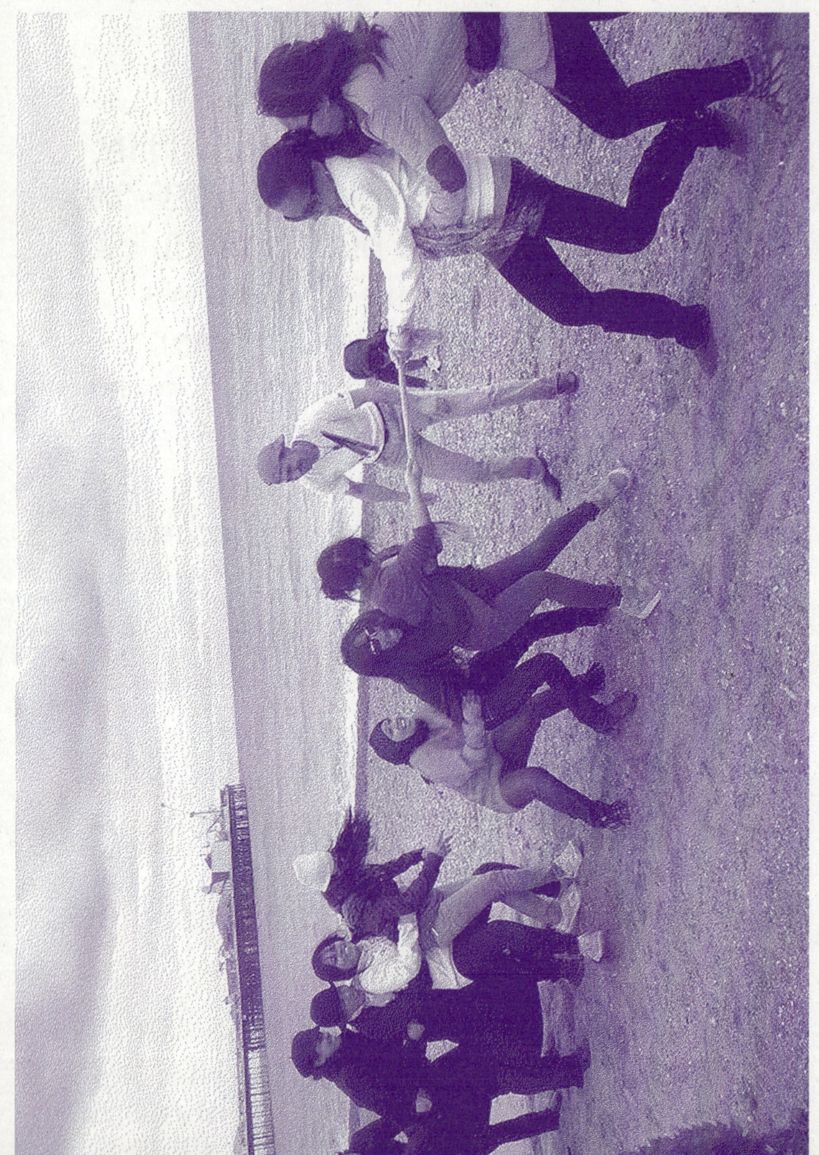

the lady justice was ripped off, beaten, exploited, harassed, humiliated, enslaved, abused, cursed, and worst... that lady justice is for sale.

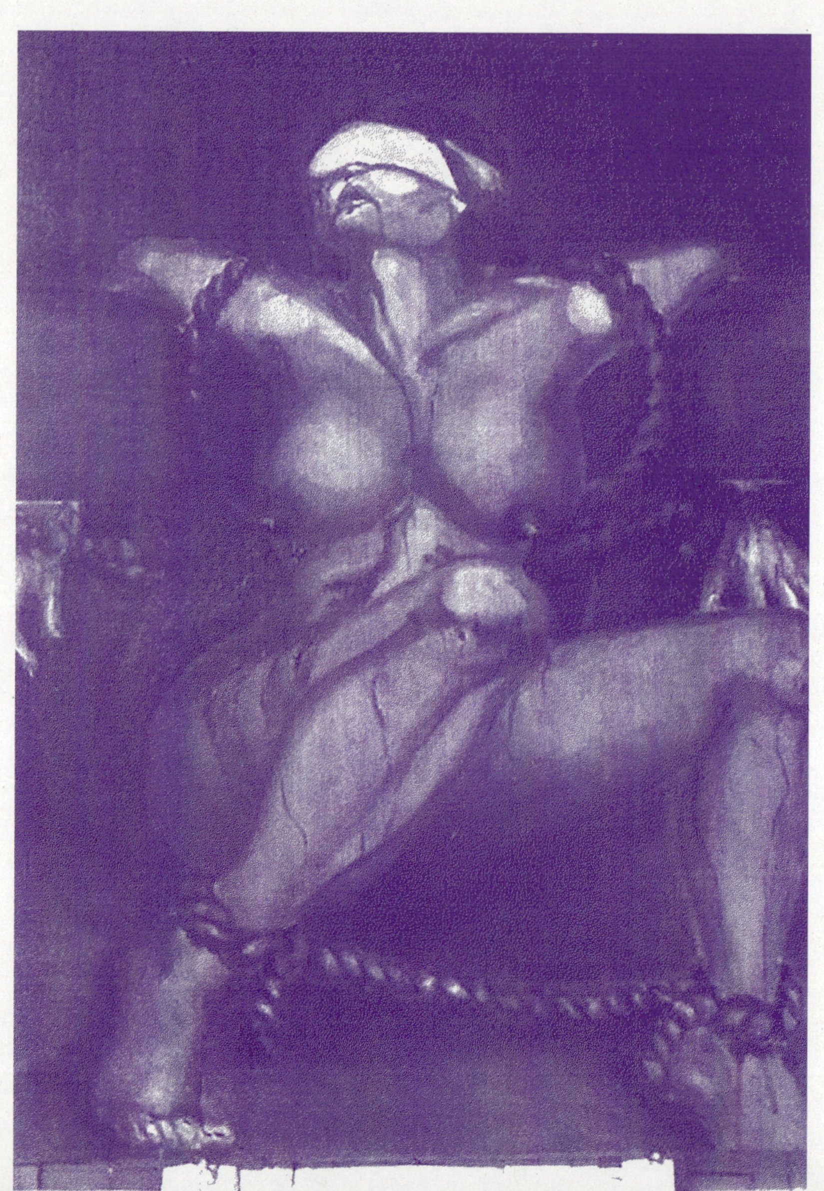

november 8

we are still working.

home security

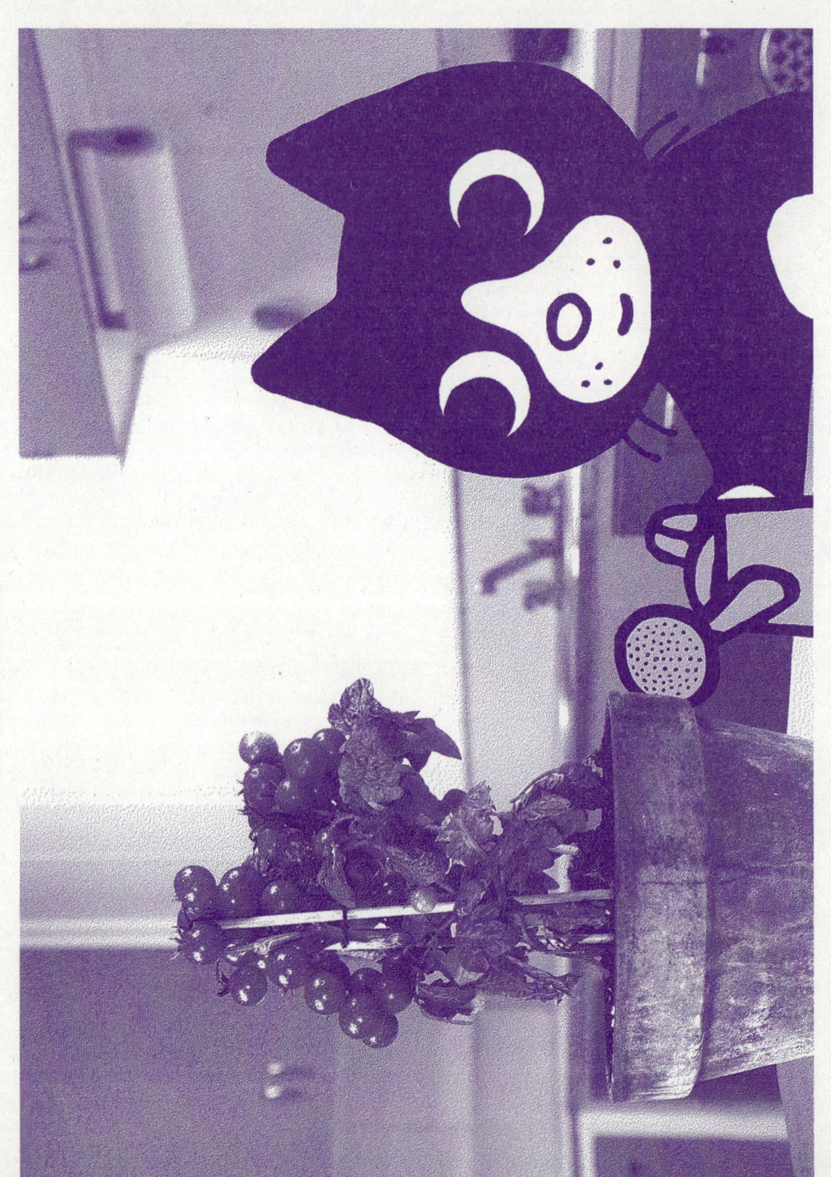

november 9

ninety-seven selected photographs
showing groups of wealthy peruvian
people in daily domestic situations.
in the background of each image one
can see either a figure or a deletion
of a domestic worker. all images have
been collected from the social network
site facebook.

97 house maids

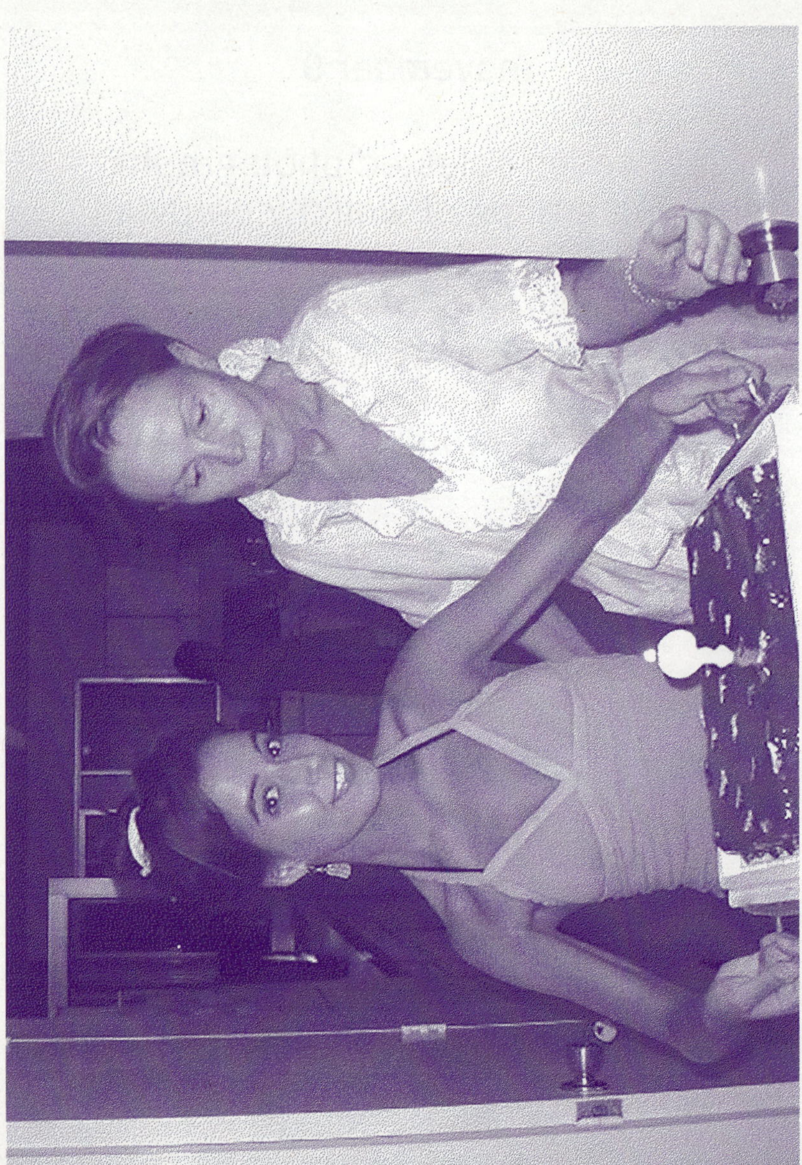

november 10

sindihogar taking part in the assembly
in plaça catalunya, barcelona.

asambleas del 15m

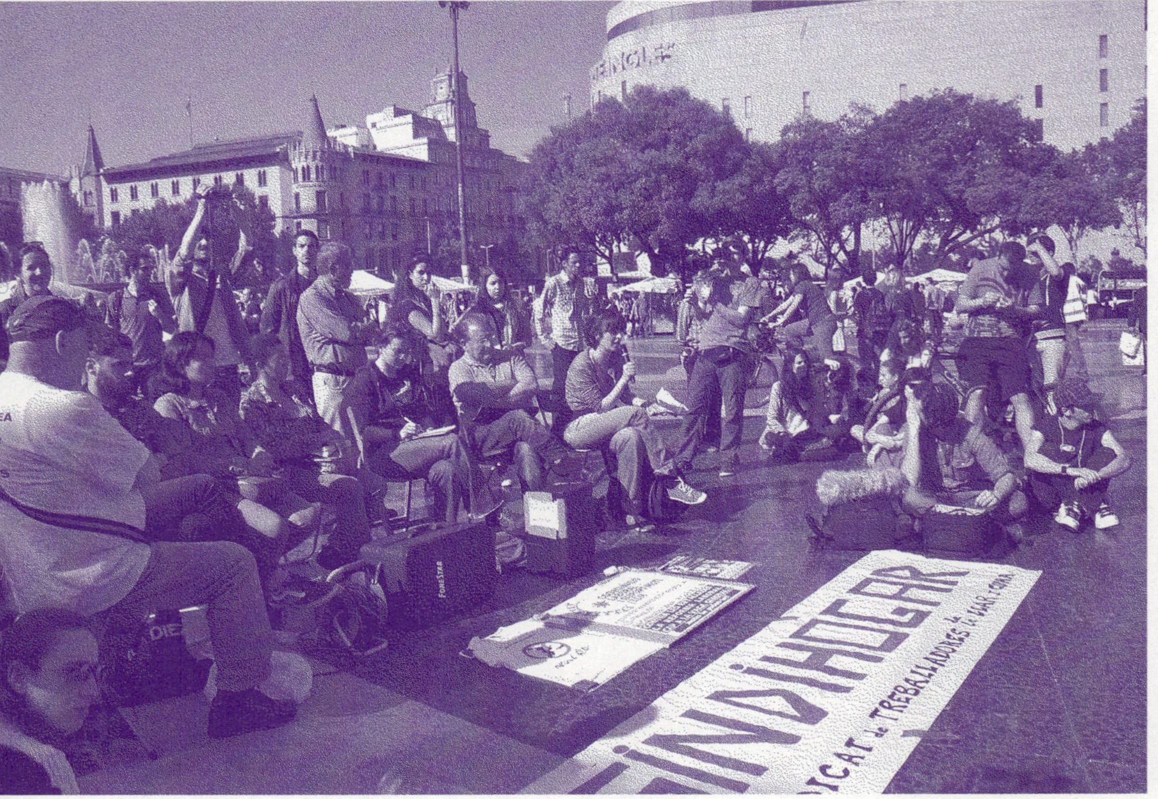
SINDIHOGAR
SINDICAT DE TREBALLADORES DE BARCELONA
FONESTAR

november 11

something that could be a juicer
from the 70's but its not (2011).
photo by thamanta.

creature comforts no. 2

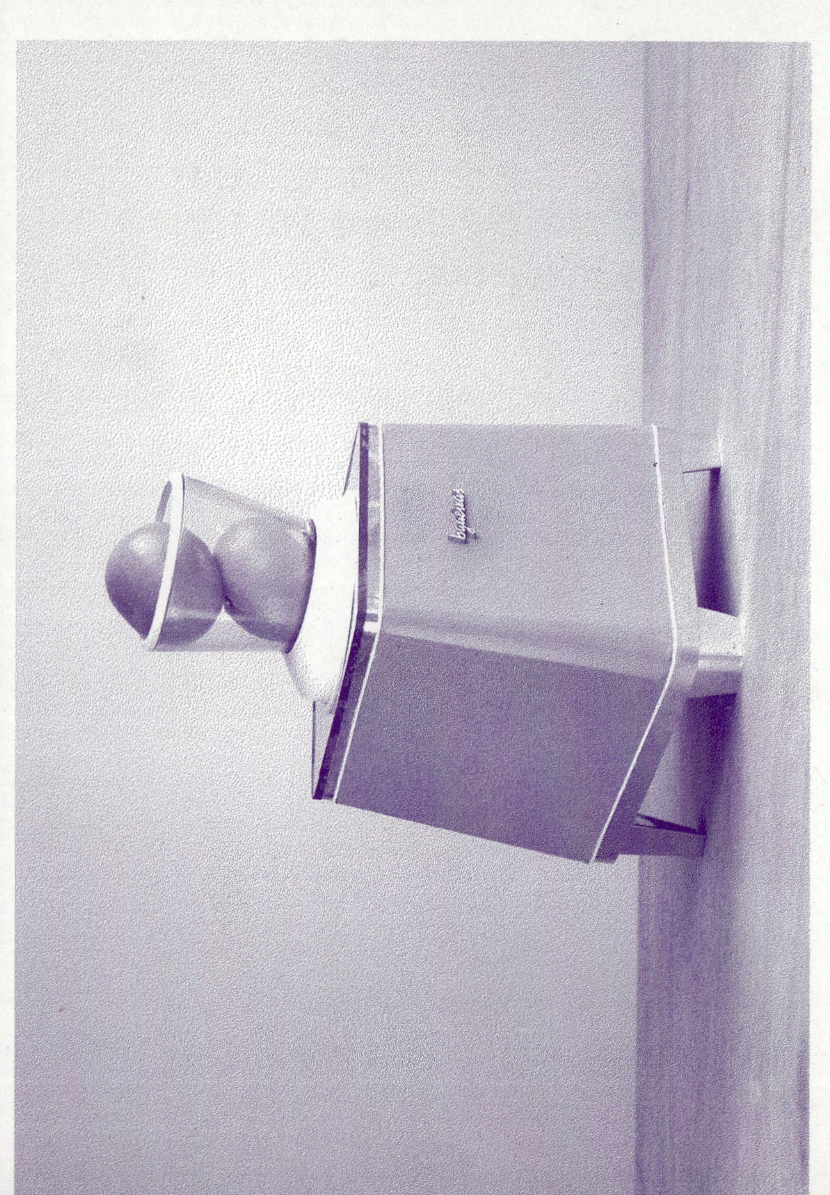

november 12

storm. collect clothes and drop
them indoors.

laundry

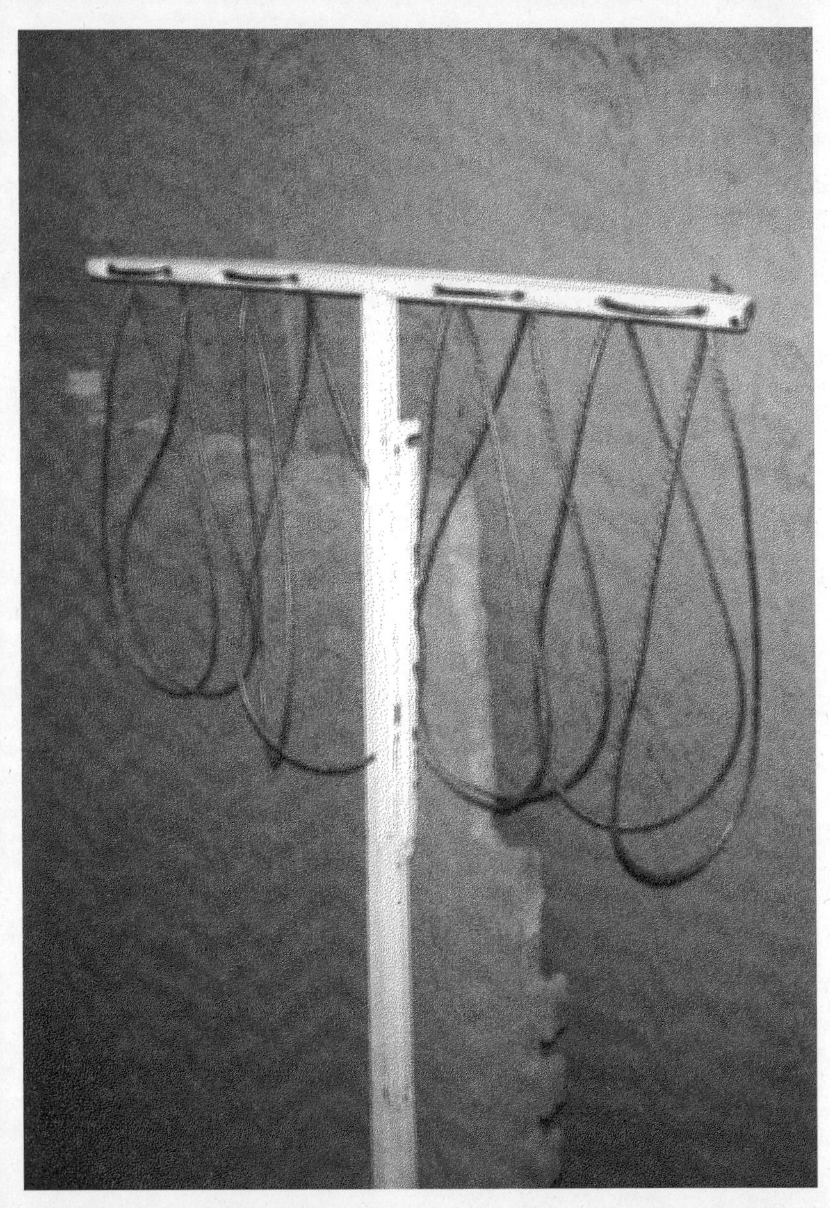

november 13

guerrilla garden planted behind the
trash dumpster of an ohio motel by the
maids who live and work there.

guerrilla garden

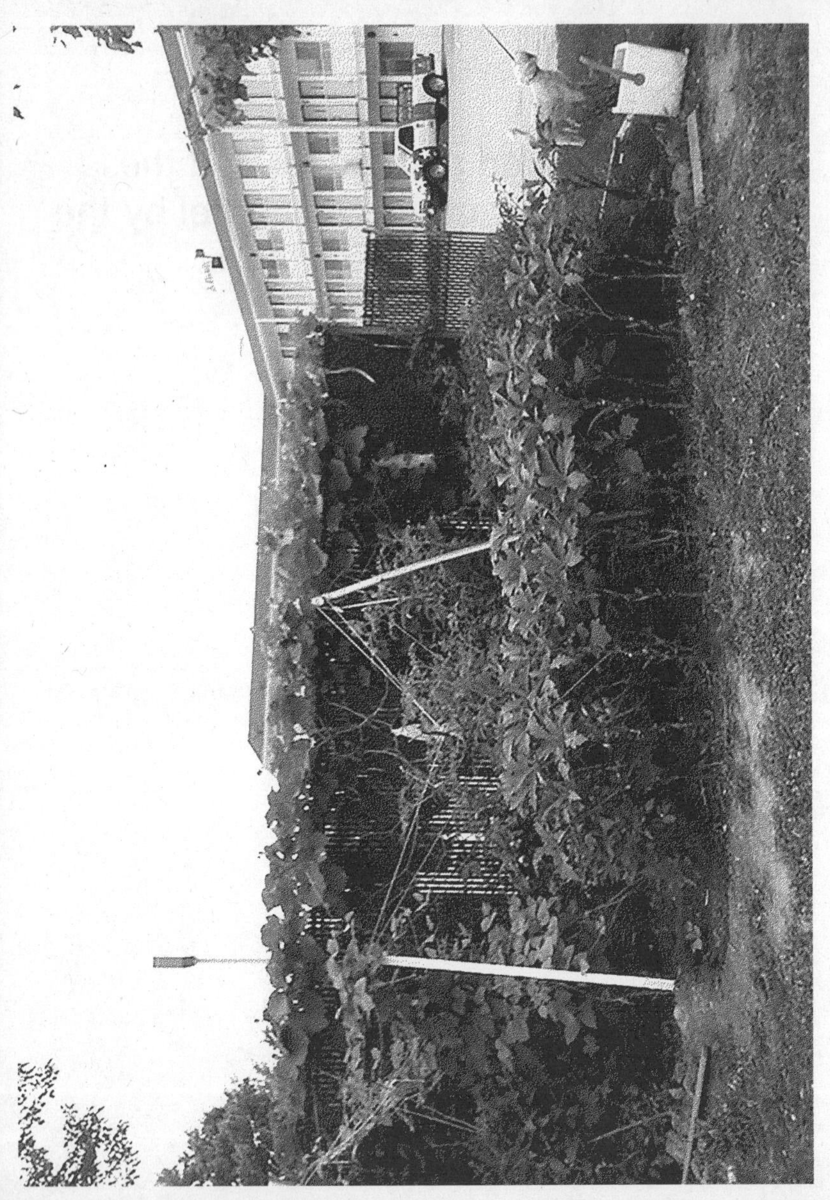

november 14

youngest sister looking into a
cookbook for the working woman.

cookbook

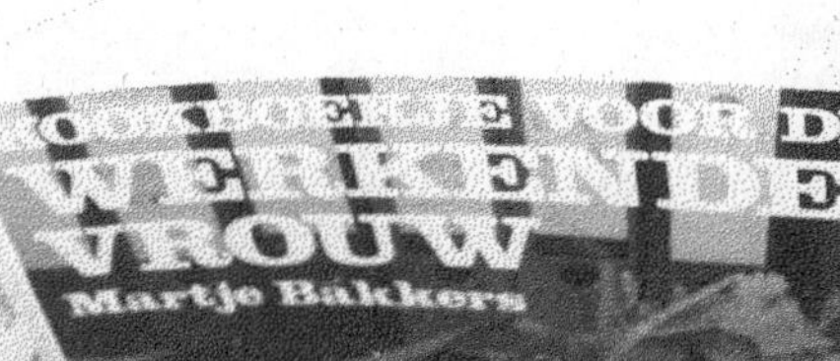
VOORBOEKJE VOOR DE
WERKENDE
VROUW
Martje Bakkers

november 15

and here comes sunday's slave.

sunday

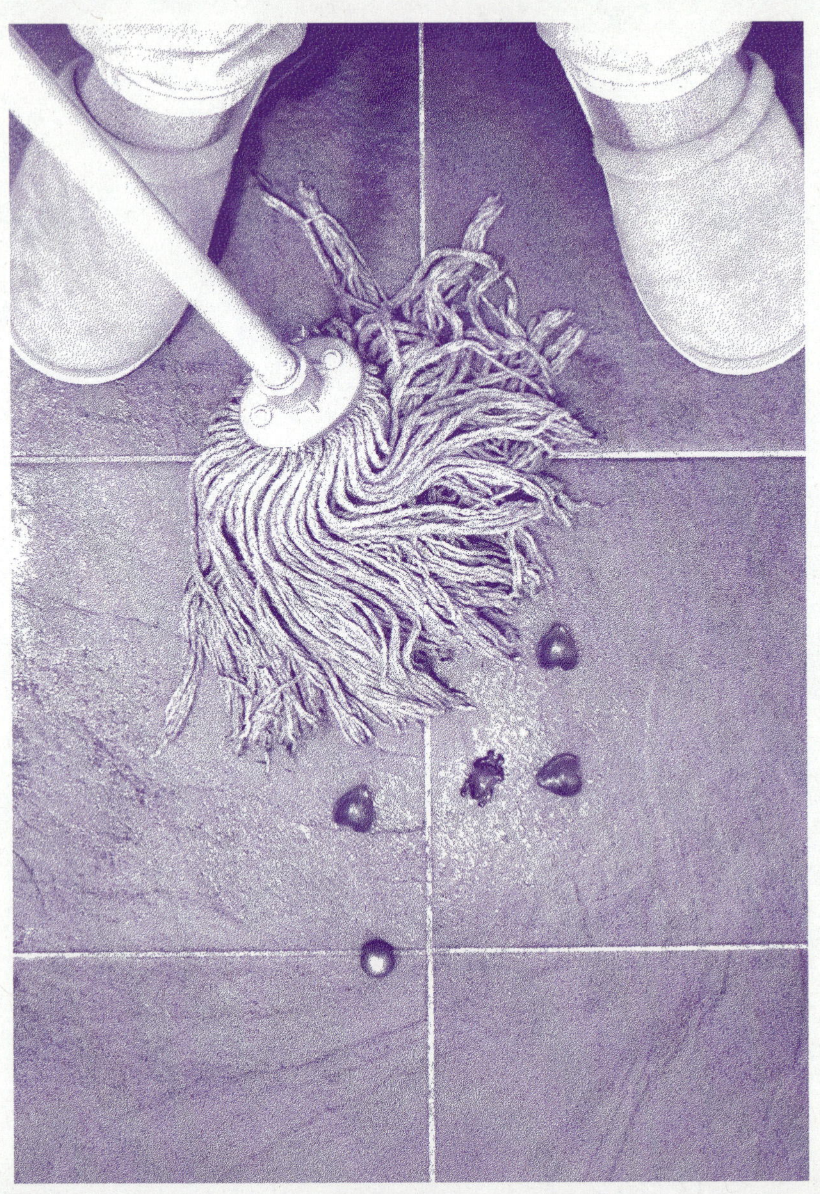

november 16

earth.

work as usual

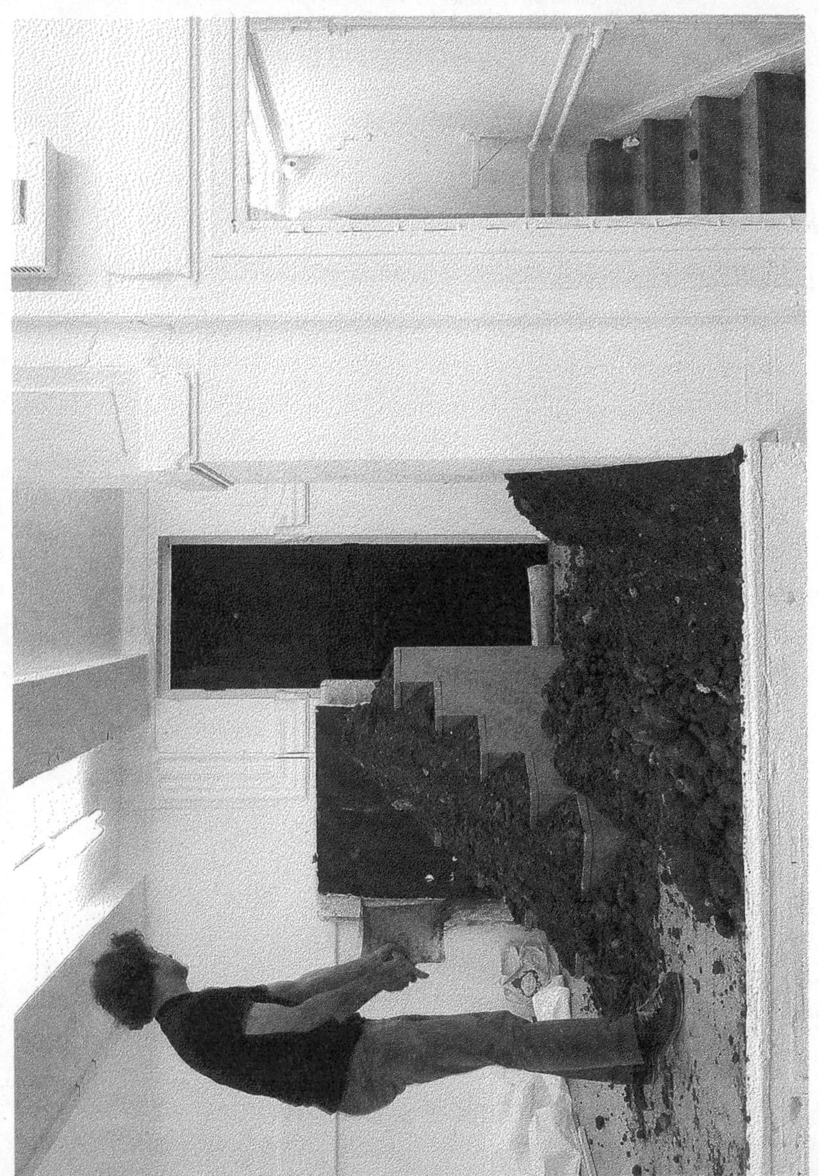

modern slavery advertisement.

invisibility

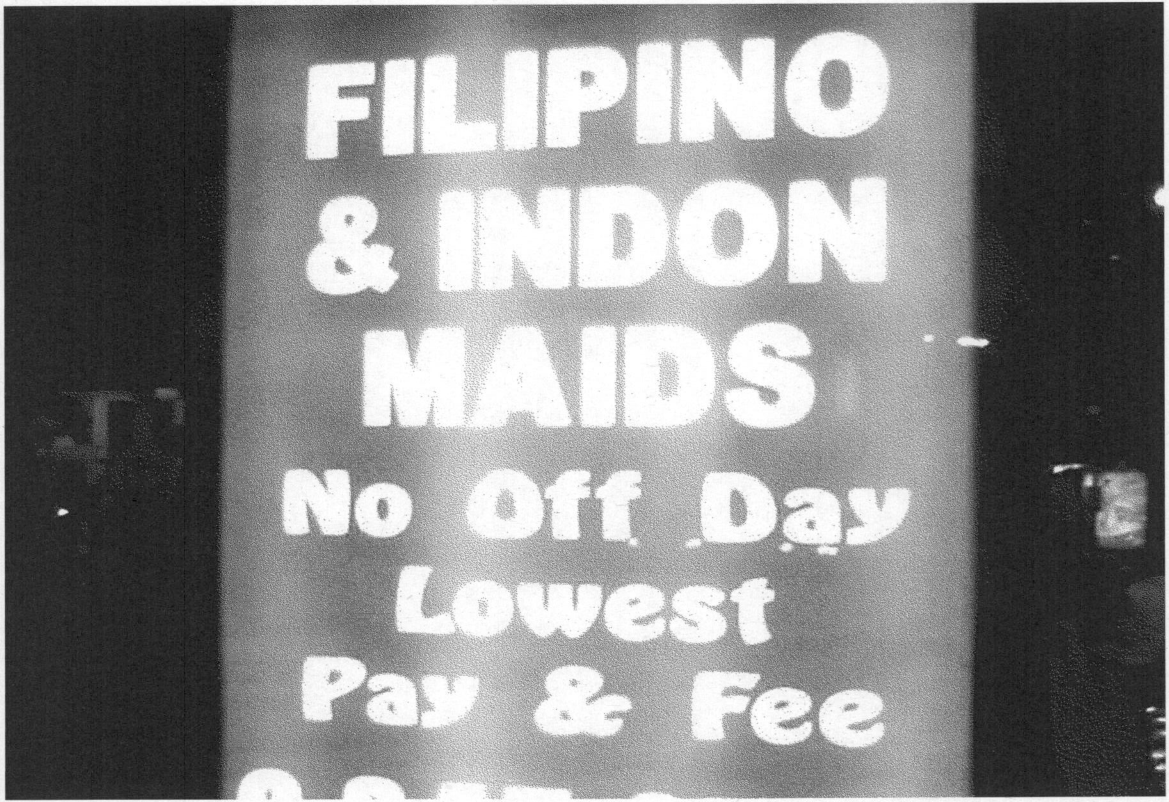

FILIPINO
& INDON
MAIDS
No Off Day
Lowest
Pay & Fee

november 18

invisible pet, named gary. i feed him
every day, in return he shits on my
kitchen stove. have only seen him
twice. one fine friend.

pet

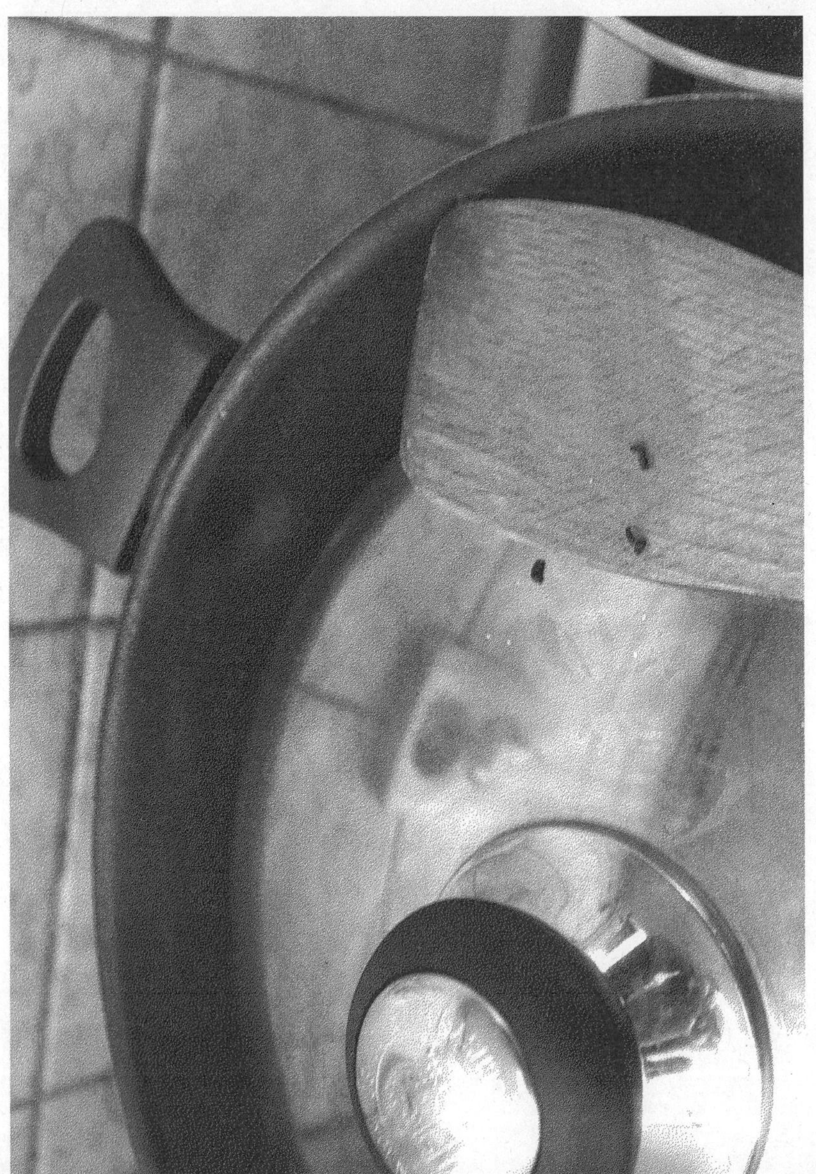

everything before and after this breakfast table is domestic work. gathering,
preparing, setting… then, gathering,
cleaning, putting away. it is always
bookended by these tasks, so you
draw out the inbetween for as long
as you can. (photograph of my grand-
father and our daily breakfast ritual).

the inbetweens

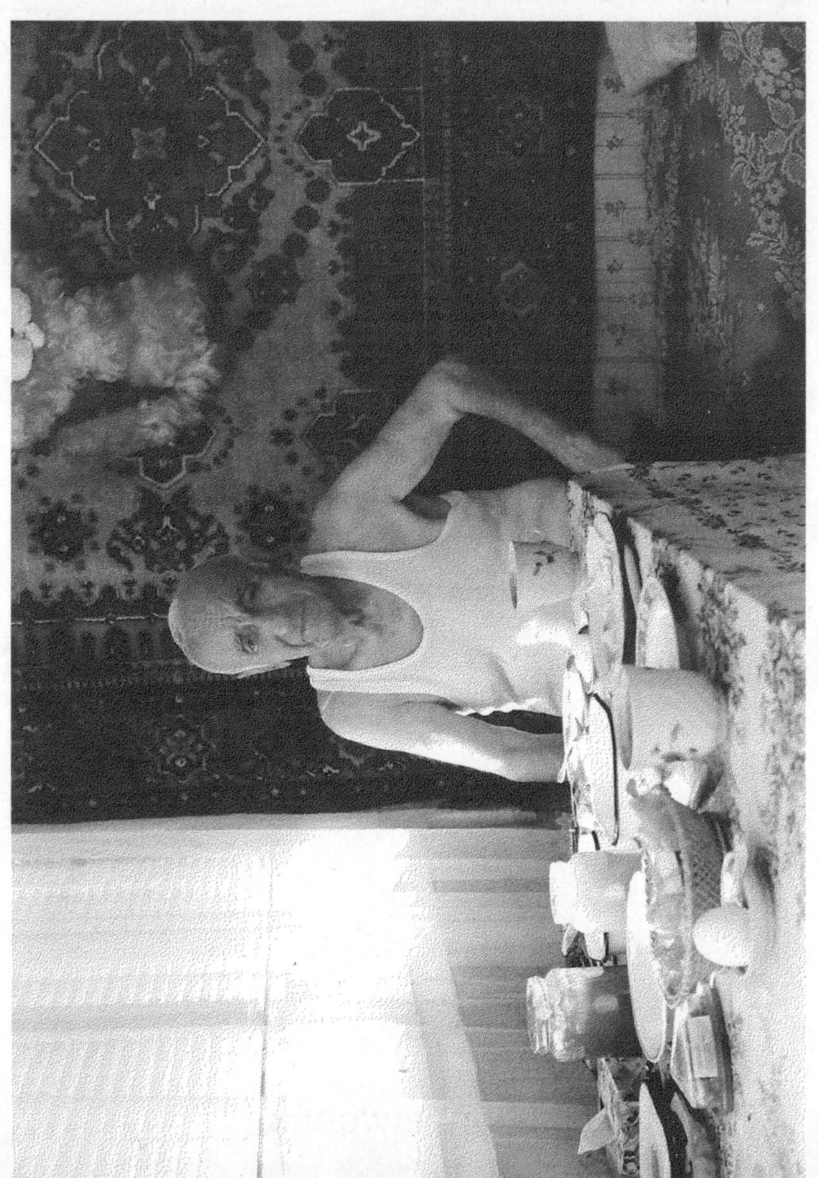

november 20

big tub, little tub

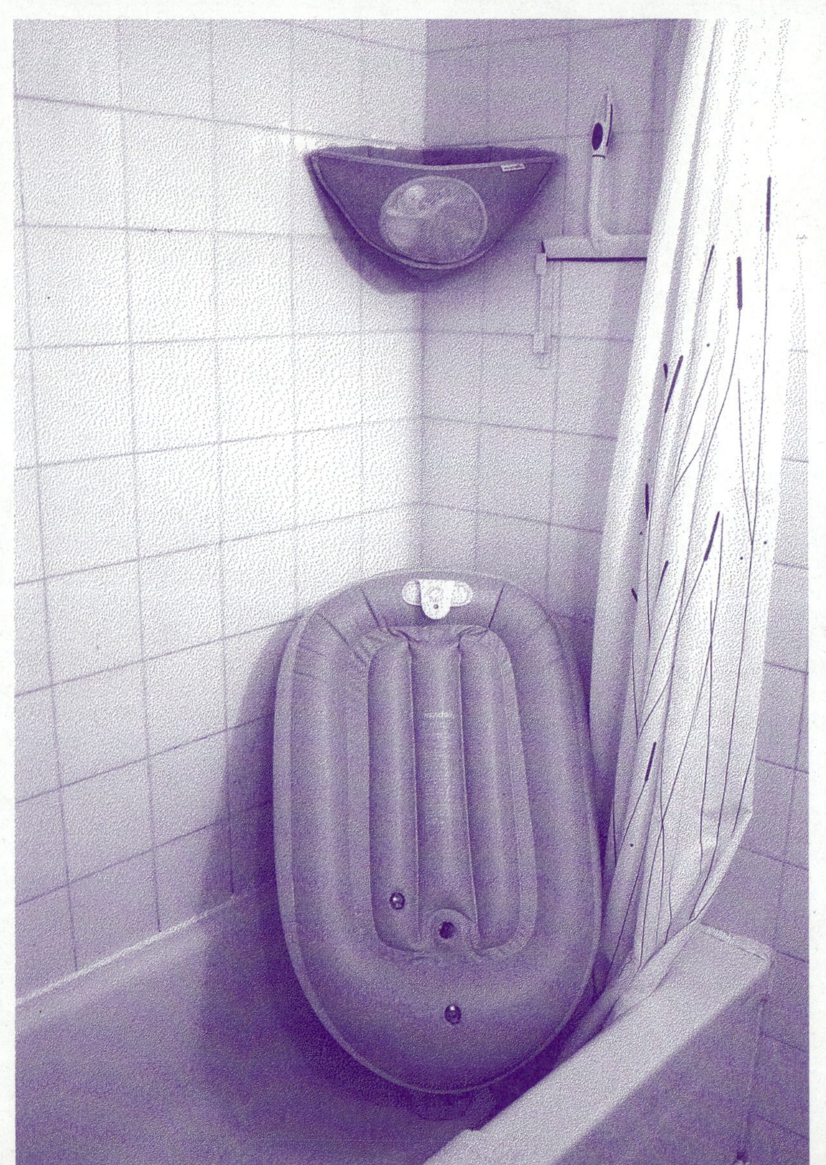

november 21

still from *the pine-tree, the bonsai
and the sequoia* (2011), video.

cleaning structures (pine-tree)

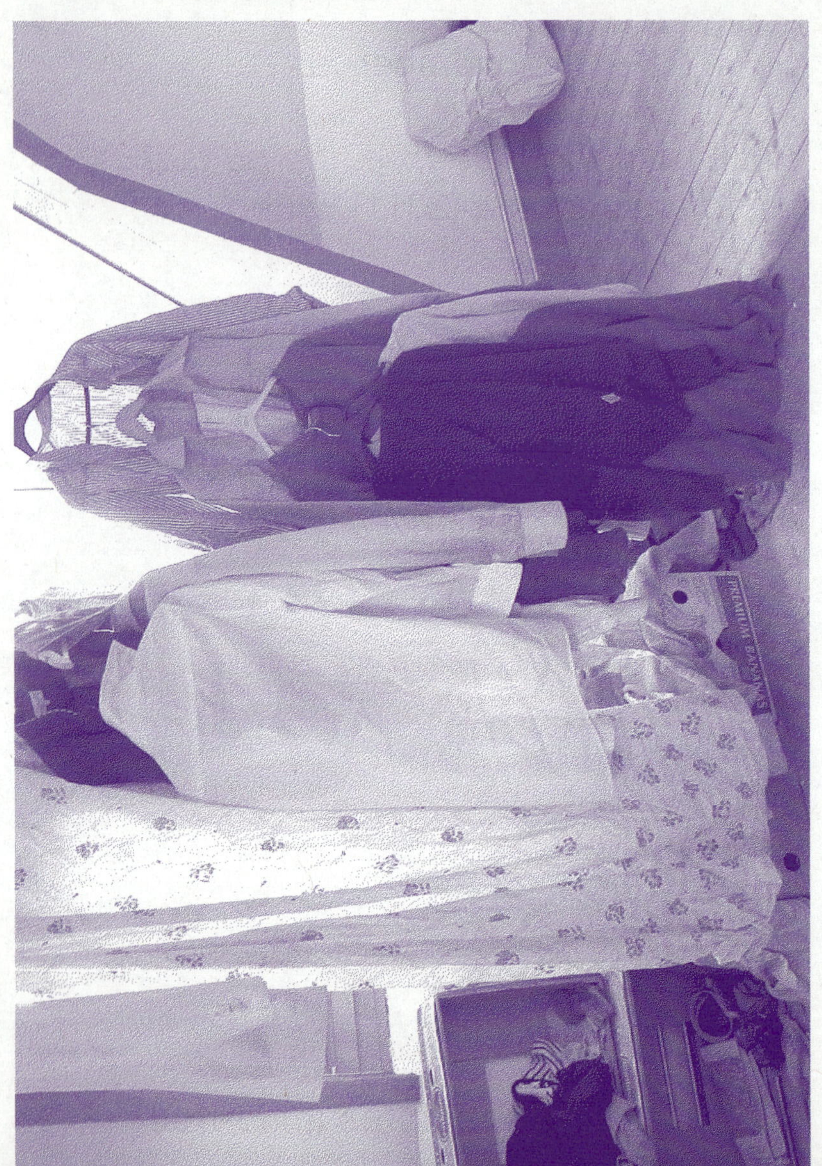

november 22

café in berlin. taking a moment to
eat my salad after frantically catching
up on emails (no internet where
i was staying).

free wifi

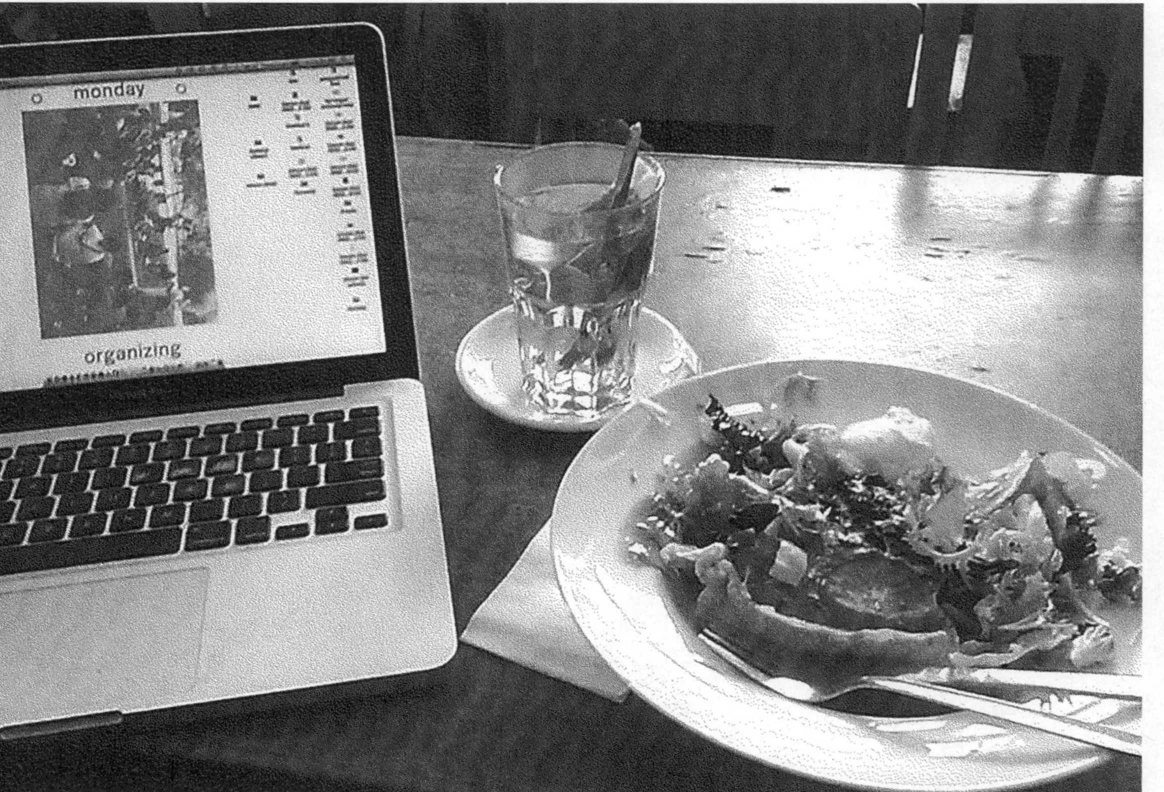

monday
organizing

november 23

a woman who has just been evicted
from her house.

eviction

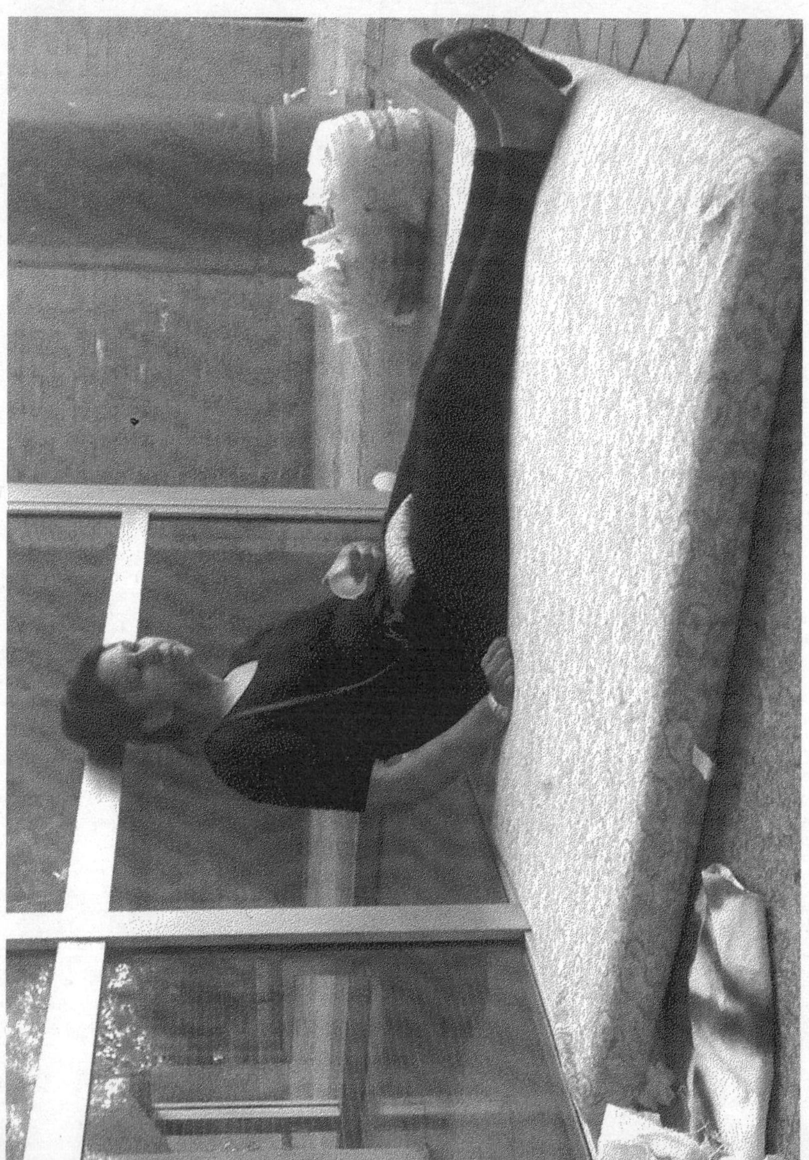

november 24

how visible is the work of an art worker?

art workers won't kiss ass. art workers
coalition (1969)

invisibility

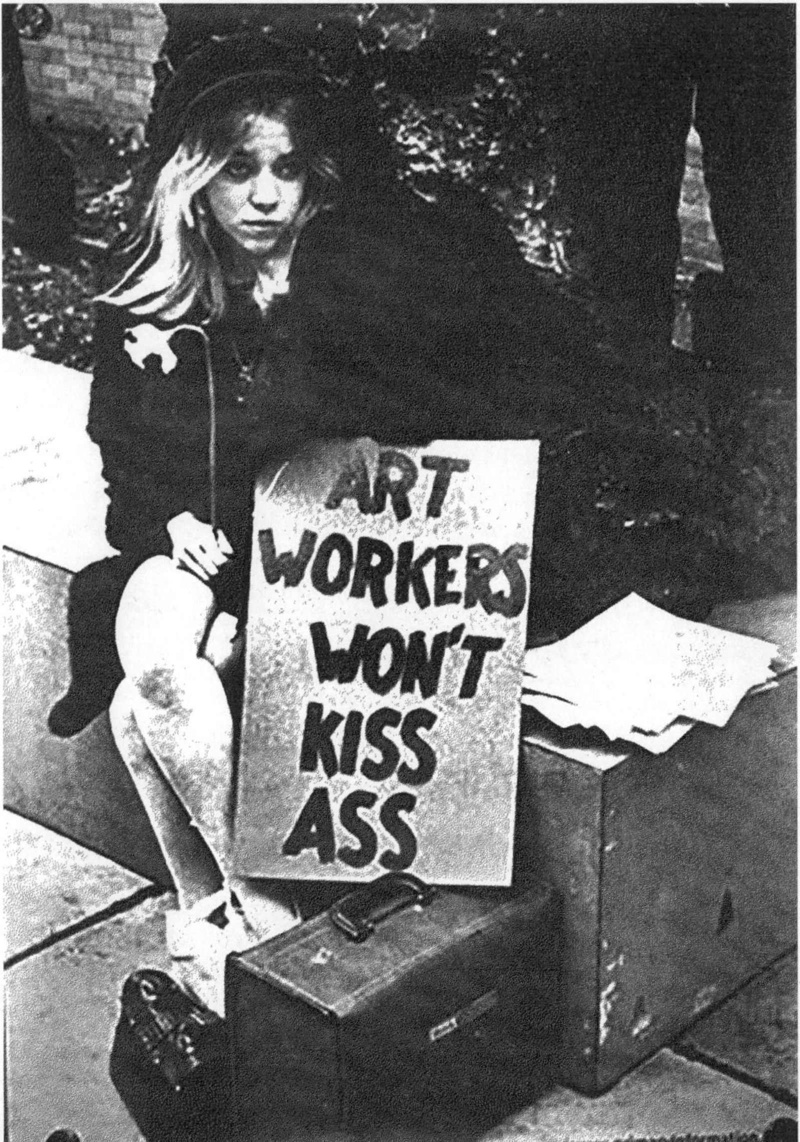

ART
WORKERS
WON'T
KISS
ASS

november 25

waiting for the clothes to be dried
at home, you don't want to lose thirty
minutes and €3.50 in the laundry.

site-specific

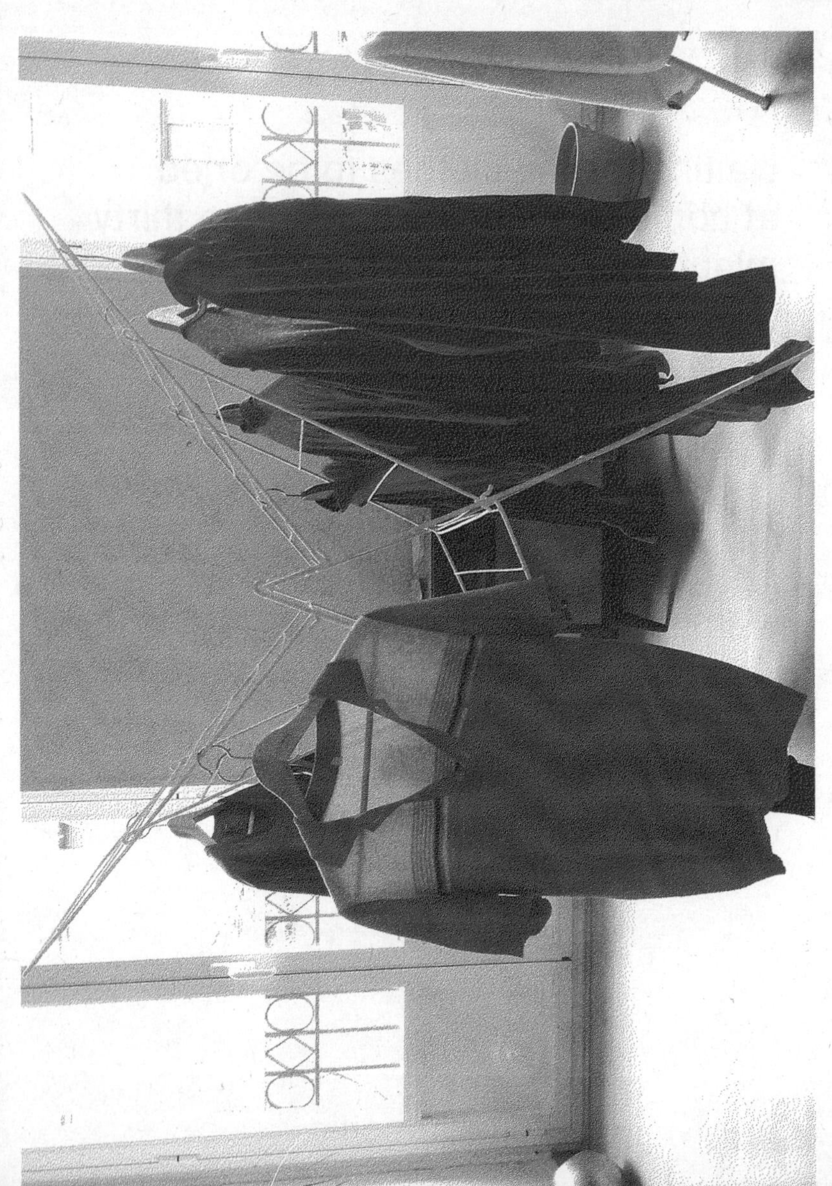

robot vacuum cleaner and raw blue
pigment on tiling.

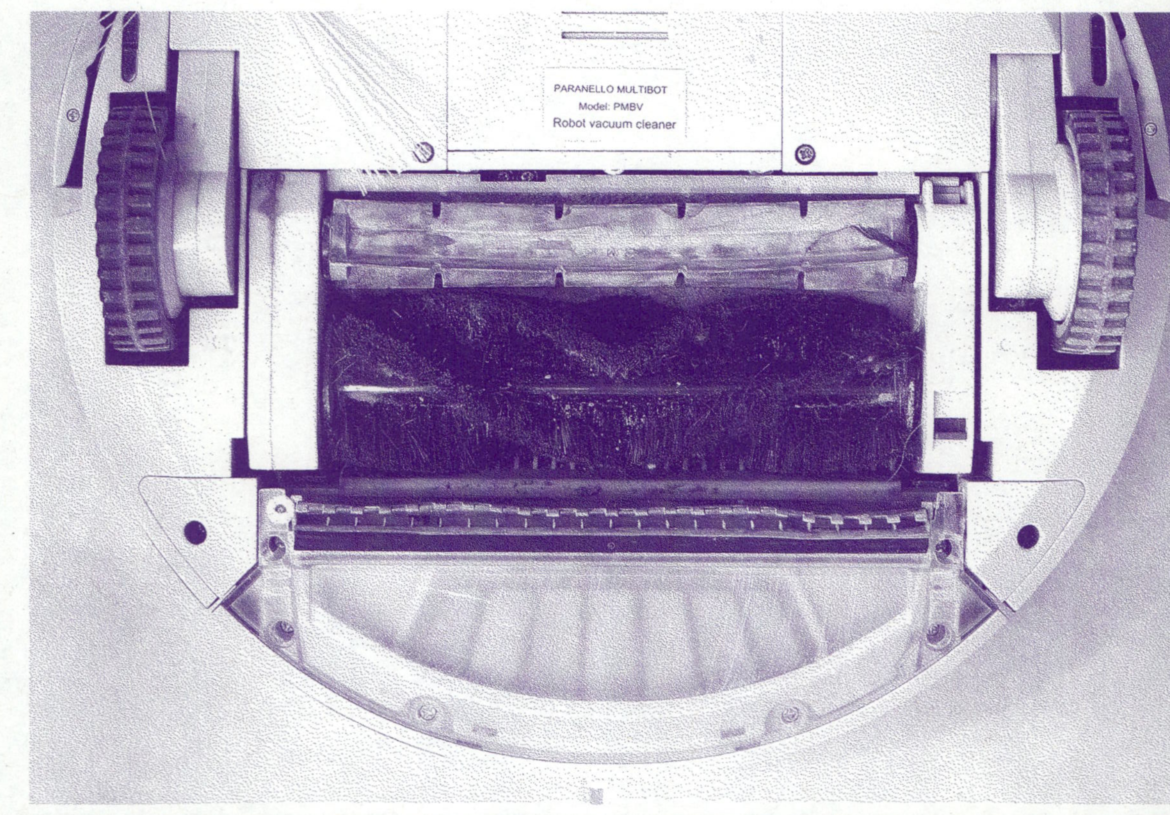

PARANELLO MULTIBOT
Model: PMBV
Robot vacuum cleaner

november 27

oh tannenbaum

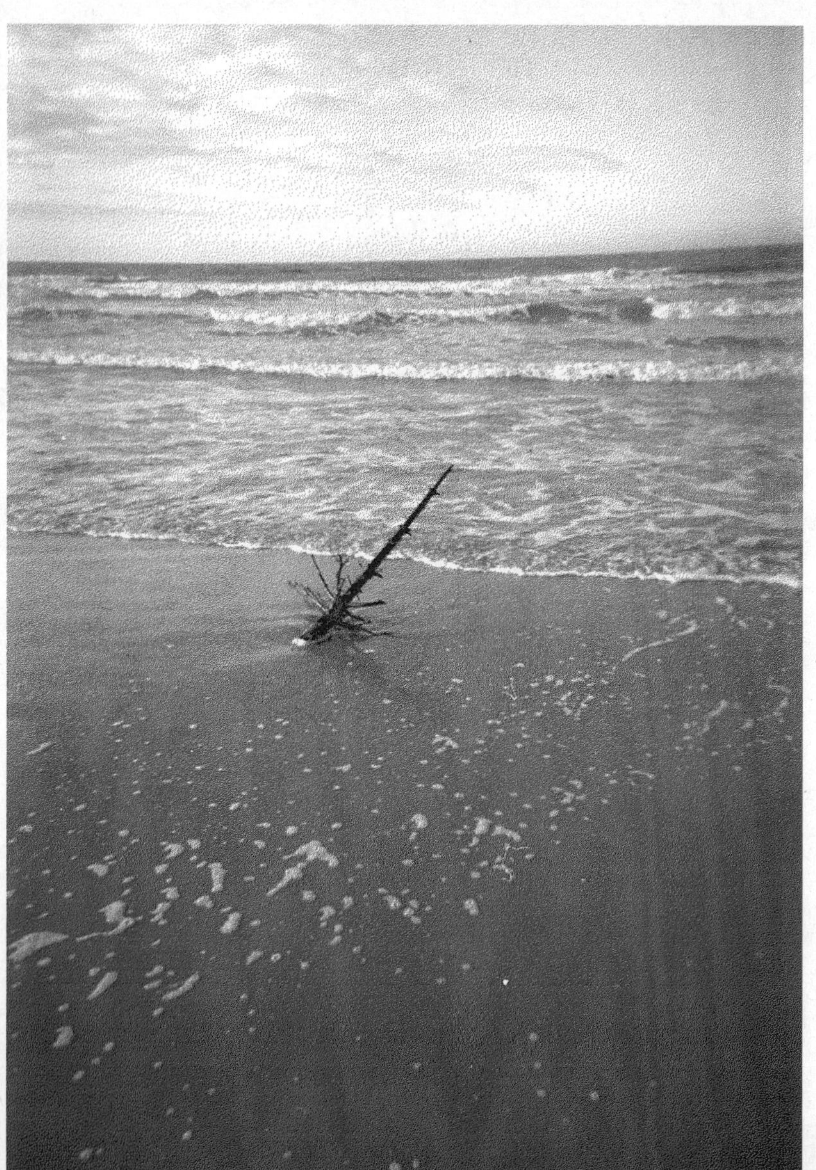

in the biography of the artist, what is
important to know as far as this
artwork is concerned?

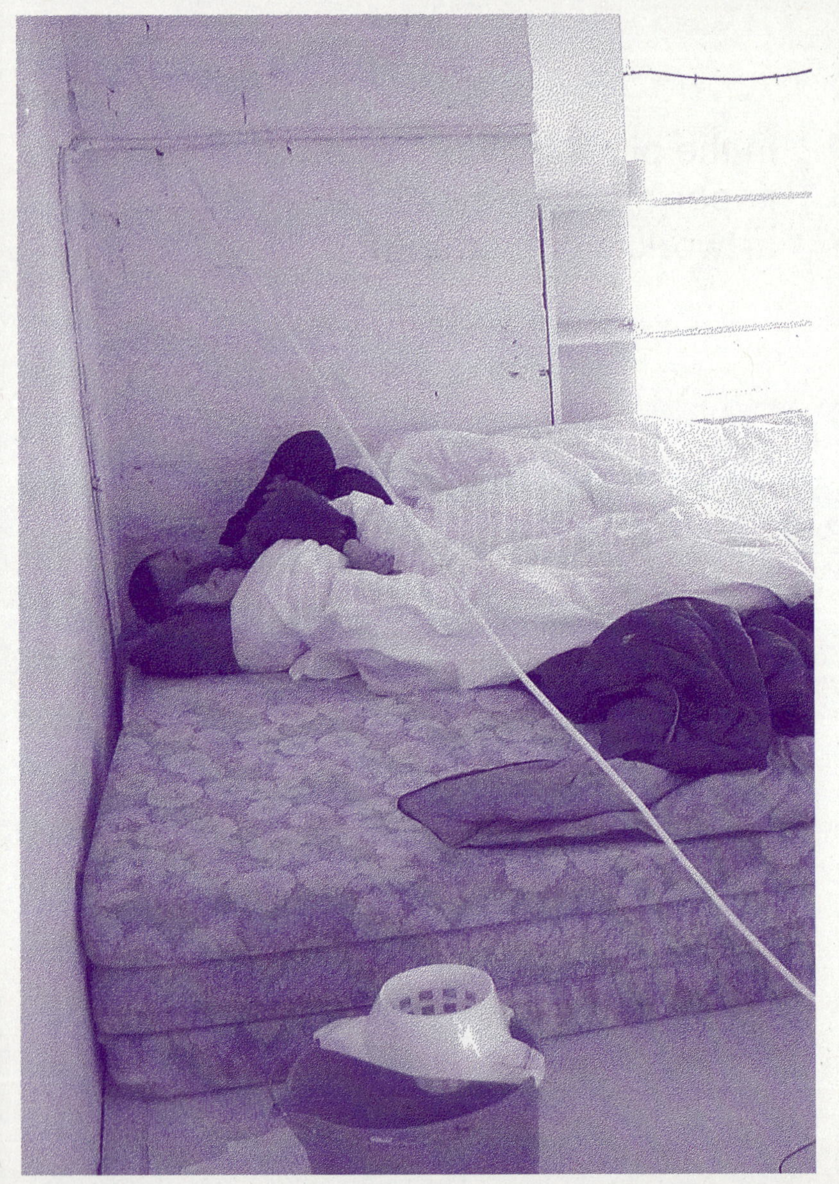

november 29

washing up done, recycling to go!

mr

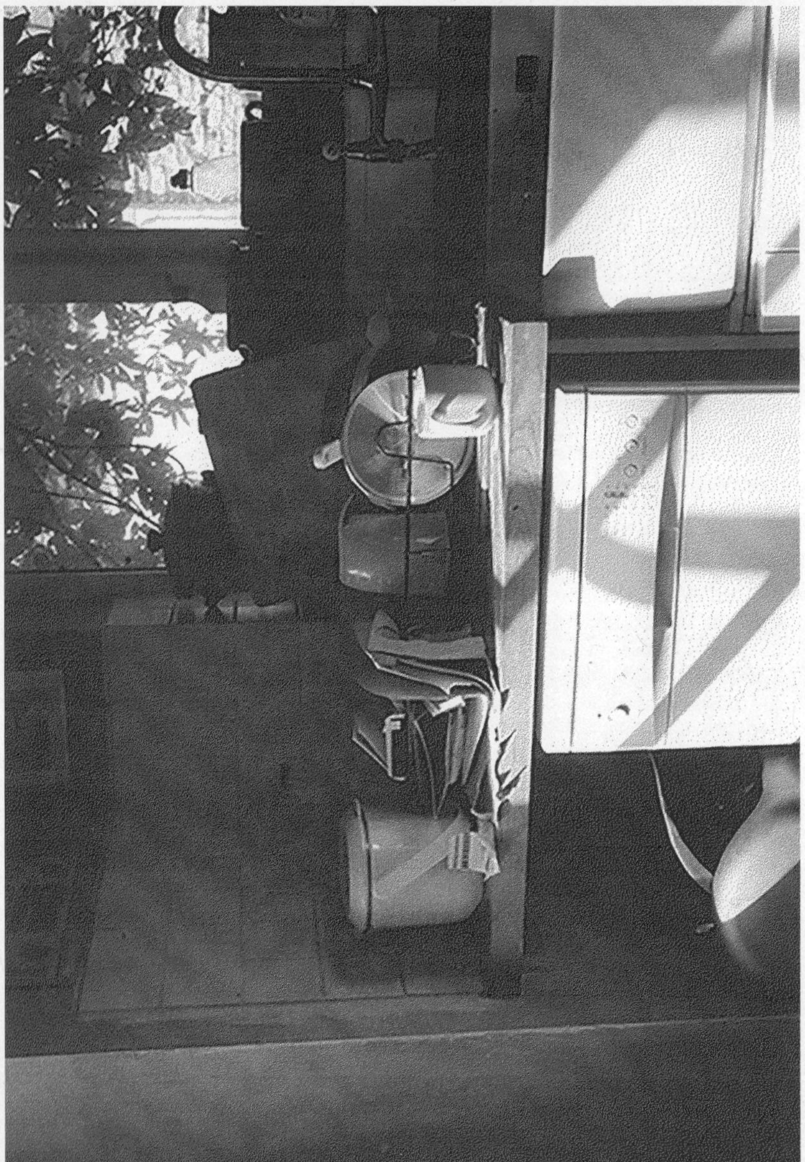

november 30

napkins

december 1

hard work curating.

cleaning curator

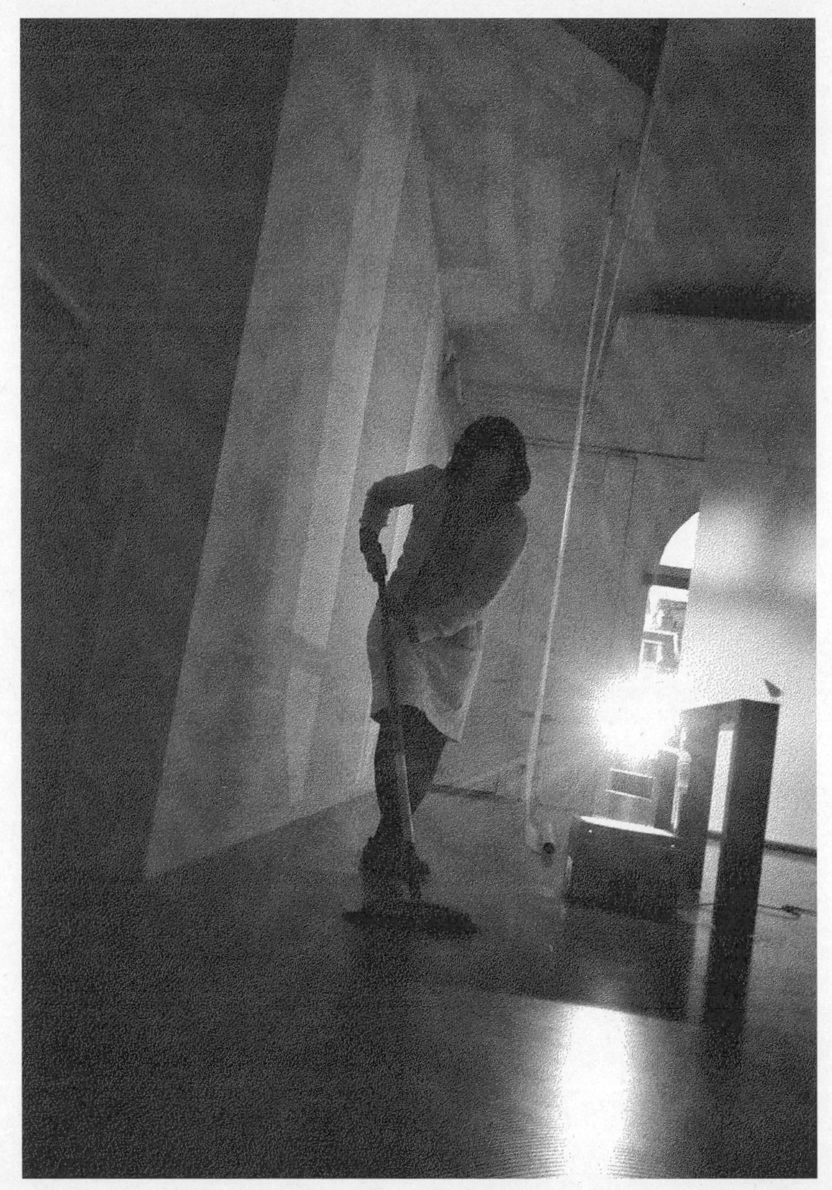

office toilet changed into bathroom
but please don't use this shower,
it's leaking too much water.

leaking water

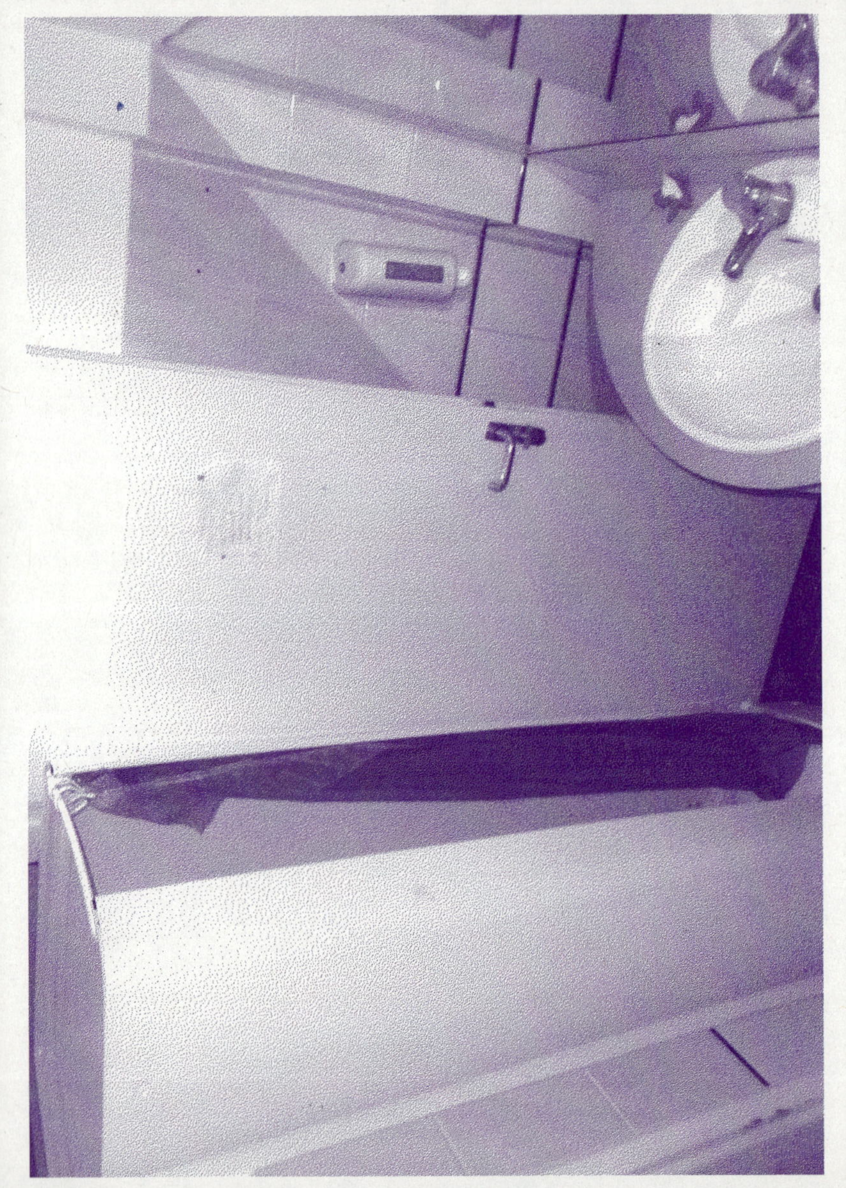

december 3

self-representation, voluntary work with friends in slaughterhouse. impossible to enter in the rooms of killing. try to understand, meat. the work is easy but the place is cold and strange.

slaughterhouse

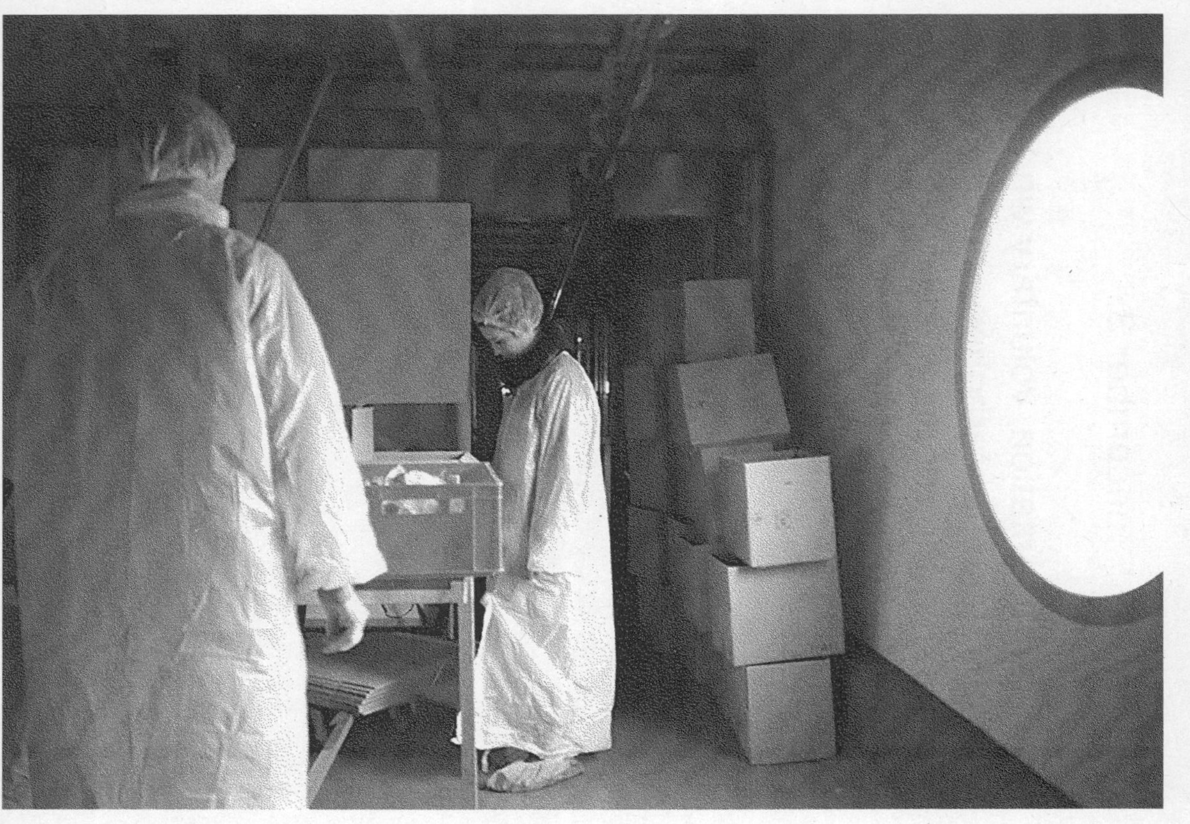

tate modern has introduced to justice
for domestic workers the wonders of
unwanted things. the arts doesn't have
to be expensive. out of nothing there
is actually something valuable that
is often ignored. since then, it stayed
in my mind that before throwing things
in the bin and recycle, made me think
of what other things i could do. i have
now loads of arts collections for our
own exhibit in tate modern with theme
of making domestic work visible in
british society.

wanted, the unwanted

ORIGINAL
POMBEAR
The T...
A Potato Sna...

...is month, 2 mil...
...f you v...
...pen fro...

december 5

athiraman kannan jumped to his death
from the 147th floor of the world's
tallest building, the burj khalifa. from
india, he came to dubai to work as
a cleaner in the newly opened building.
in an attempt to honour his courageous
call for attention to be given to the
lives of migrant workers, i photographed
what i describe as a 'pop out city.'
these are spaces that are an attempt
at permanency and comfort in an
always vulnerable life as a migrant
worker. unlike the families they work
for, whose life exists behind walls,
their lives exist on the street, forging
new notions of 'the public.'
al naeem, 2011.

in memory of athiraman kannan

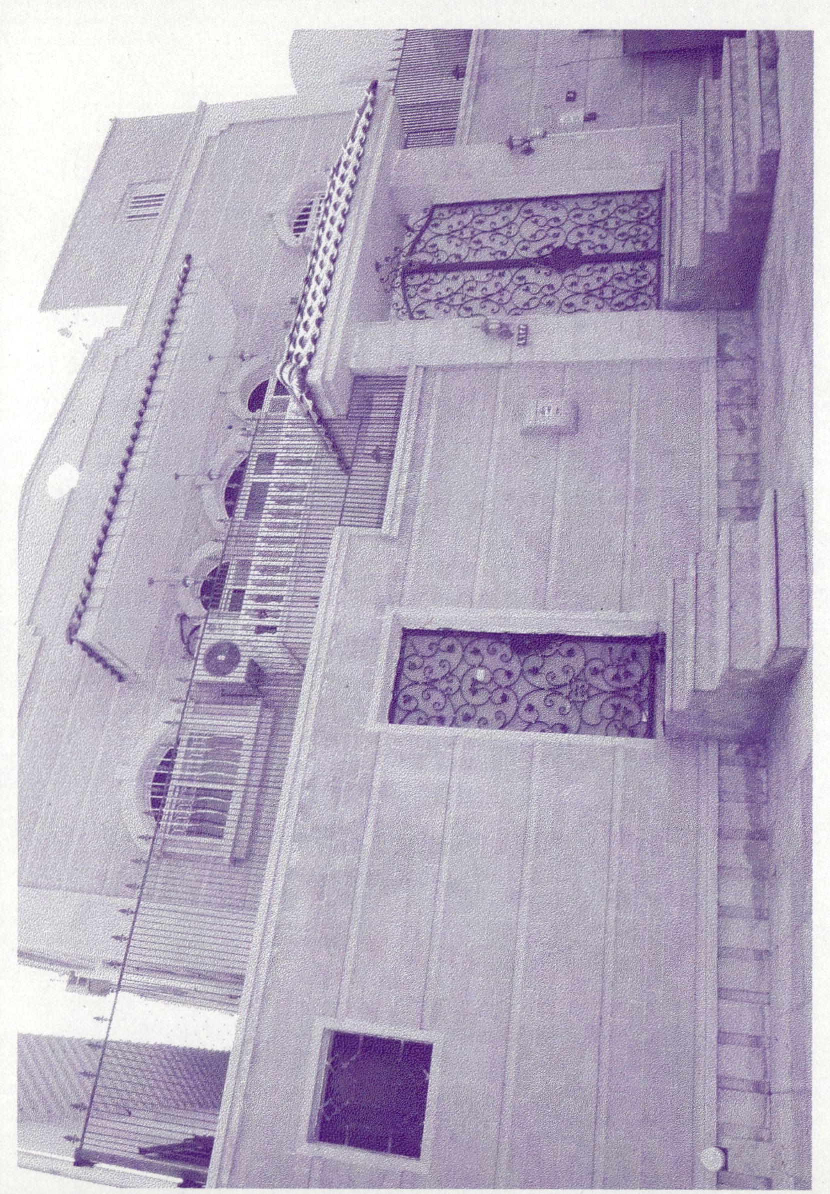

december 6

still from *tiempo real* [real time],
(2003), video, 43 min .

la culture

LA CULTURE ?

MAIS C'EST LA MARCHAN-
DISE IDÉALE, CELLE QUI
FAIT PAYER TOUTES LES
AUTRES. PAS ETONNANT
QUE VOUS VOULIEZ L
OFFRIR A TOUS...

december 7

office/study/futon/bed

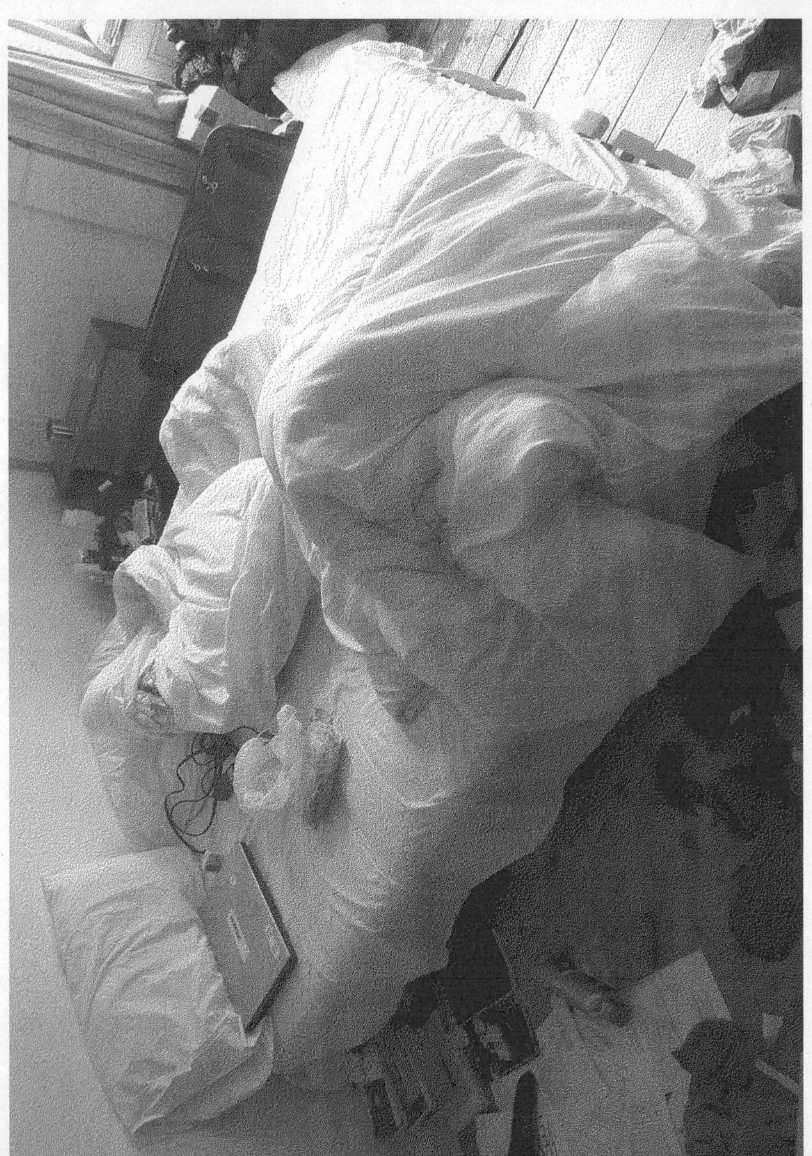

december 8

place towel over head and pose.

action 1

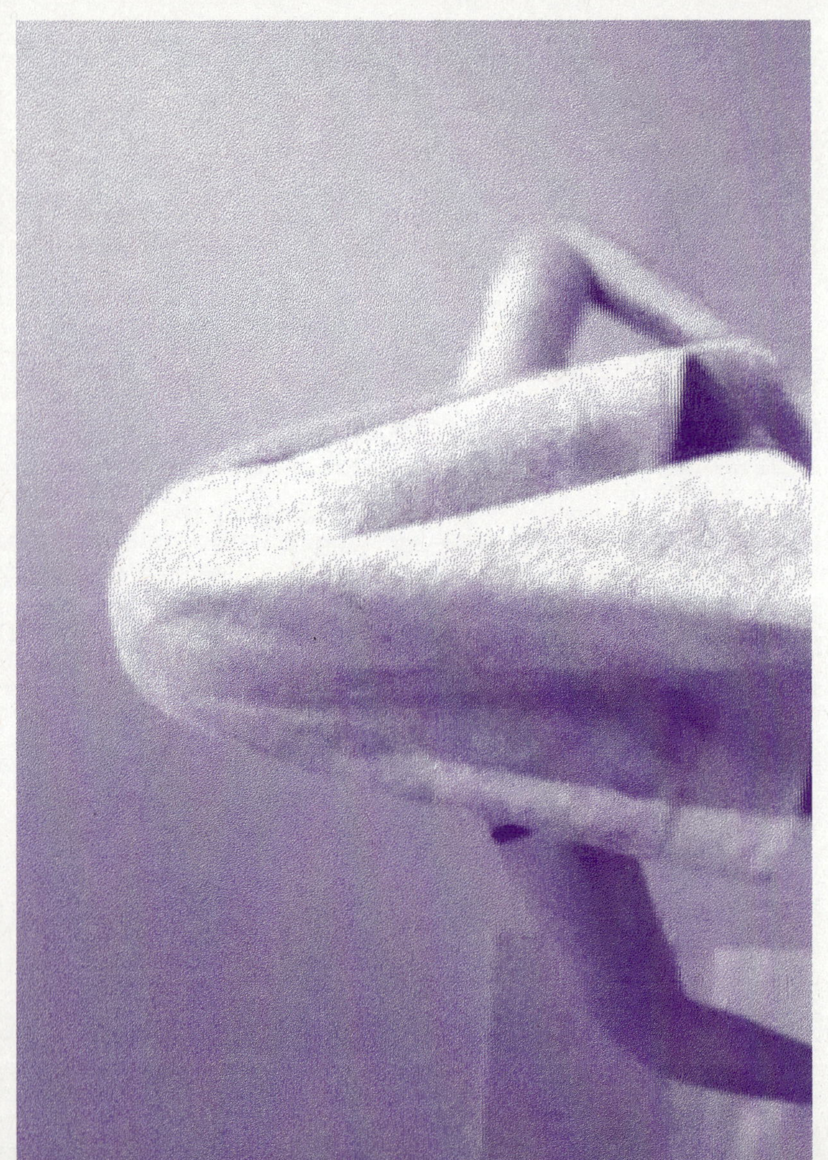

december 9

megaphone with traffic cone. speaking
in the narrowest part, cast your voice
in the desired direction.

resist

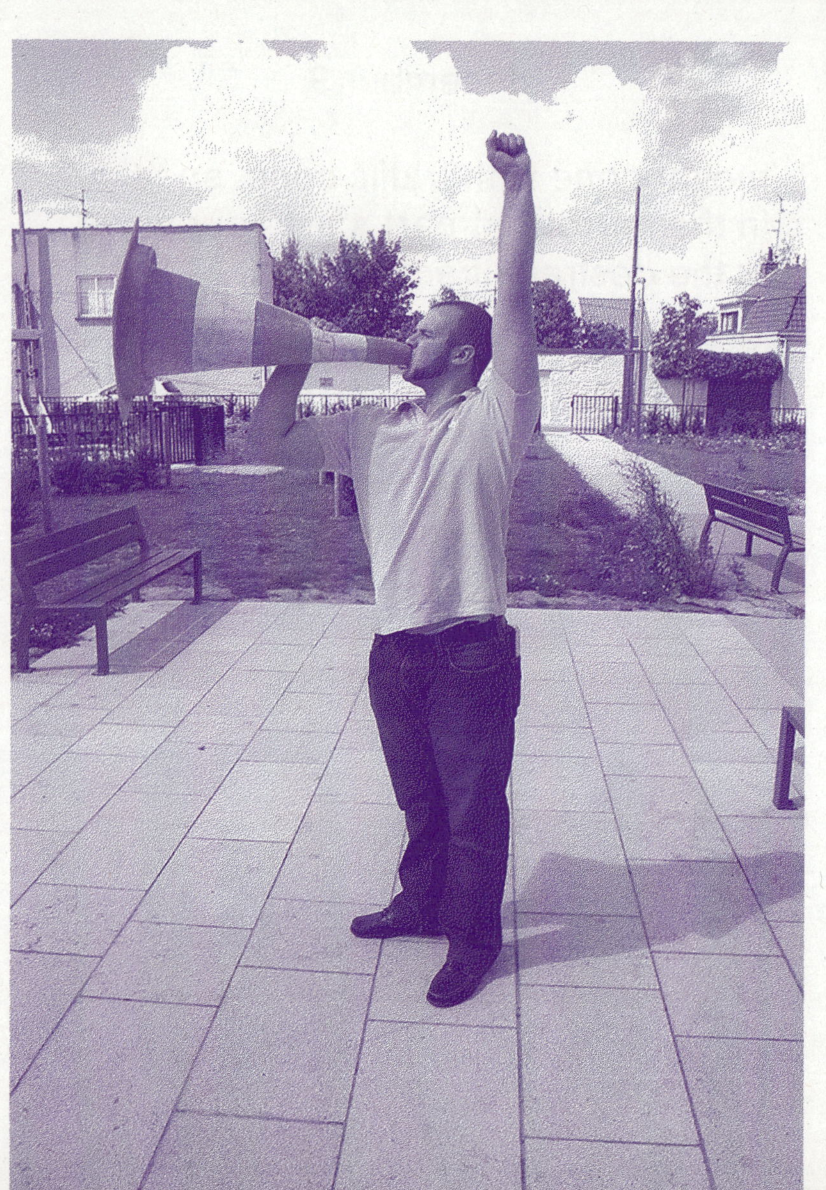

december 10

is there real work in home jobs?
yes there is some, but, it is not nearly
as plentiful as you would think consid-
ering the amount of interest there is
in working from home.

home office

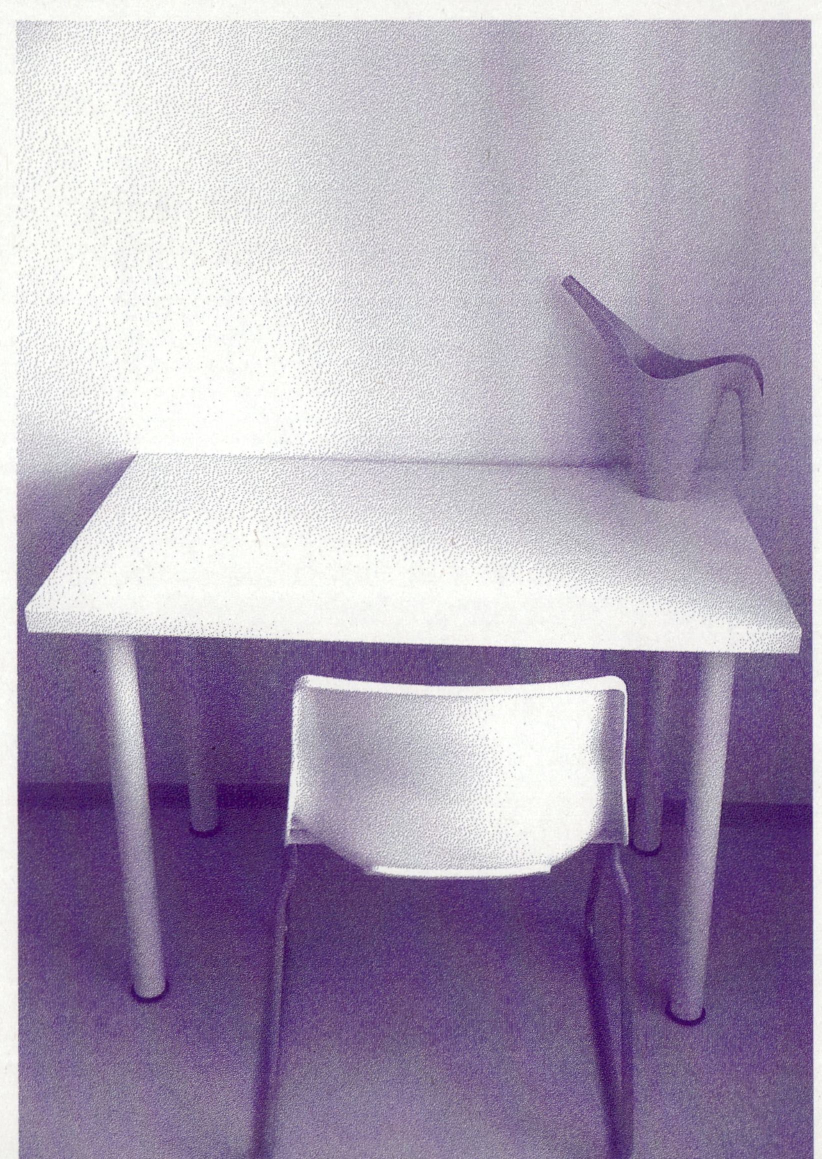

december 11

cleaning gloves

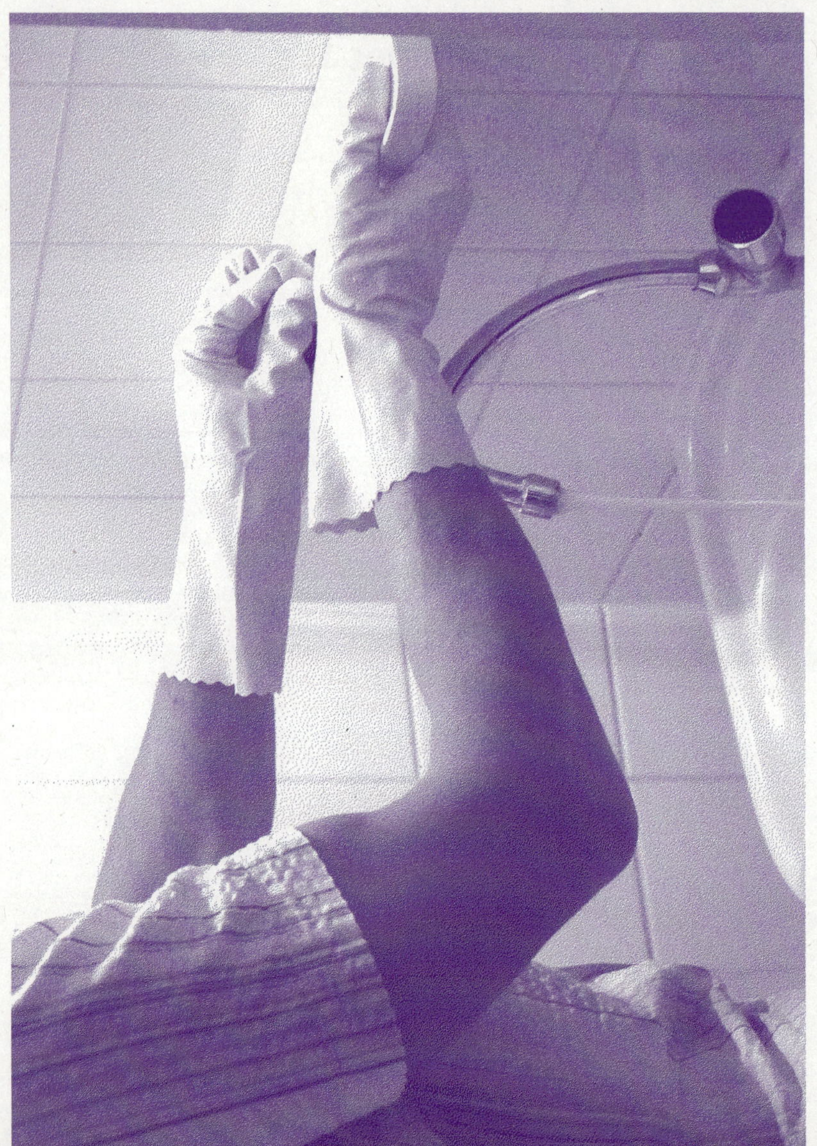

december 12

jungle

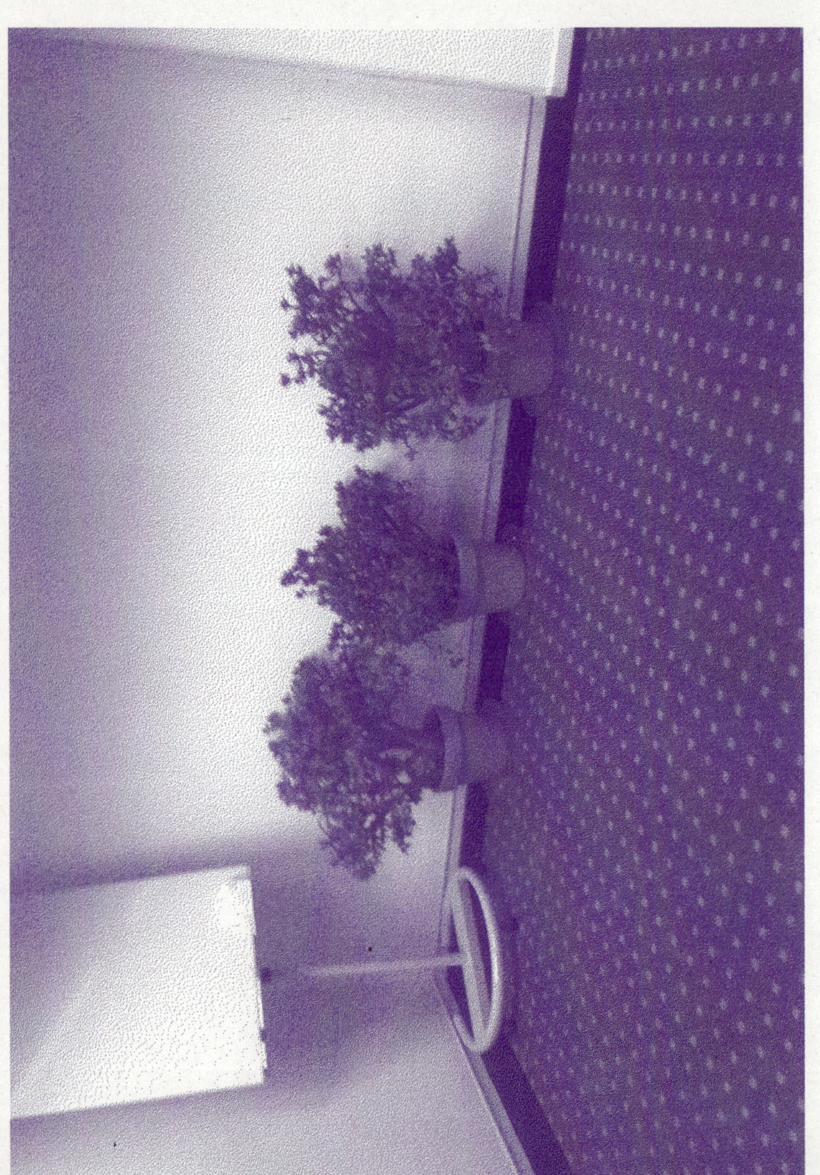

december 13

grandma on her way to the supermarket. this daily routine is keeping
her life busy.

food journey no. 2

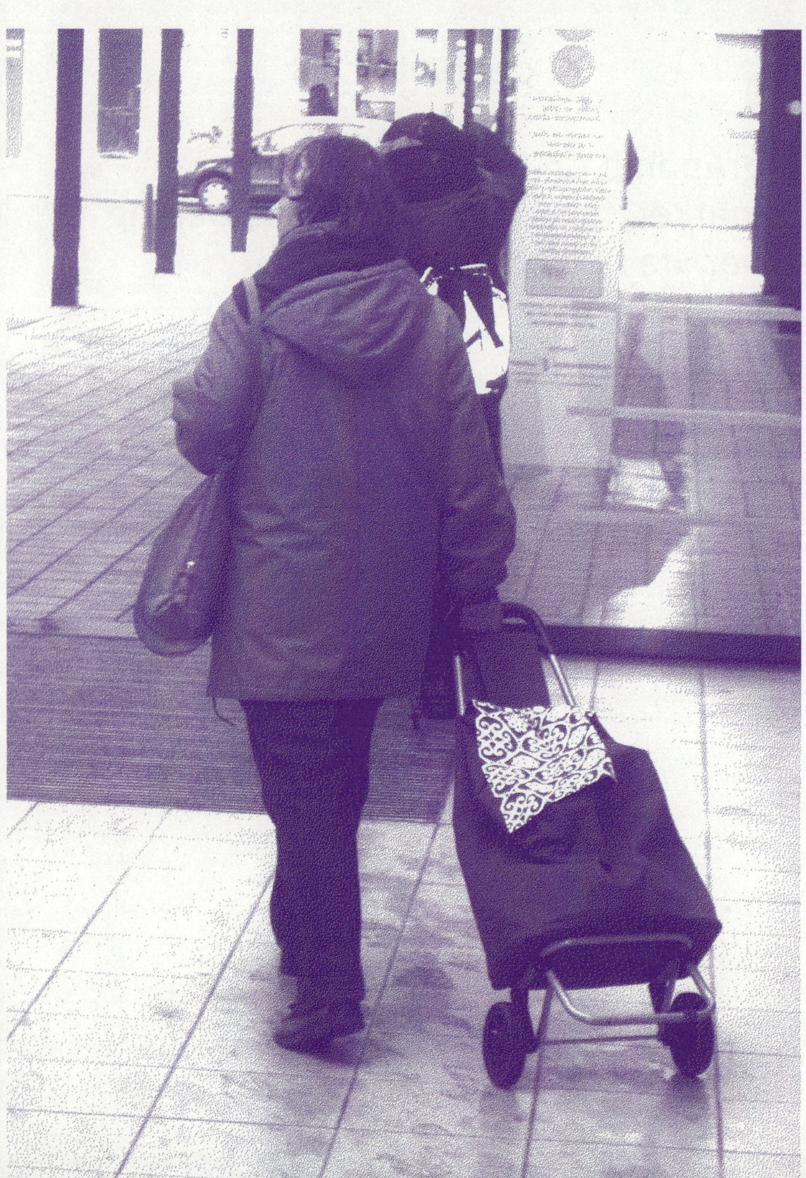

our neighbourhood is going through
an accelerated gentrification process,
the local supermarket offers all kinds
of expensive organic fresh foods for
it's new inhabitants.

shopping for healthy food

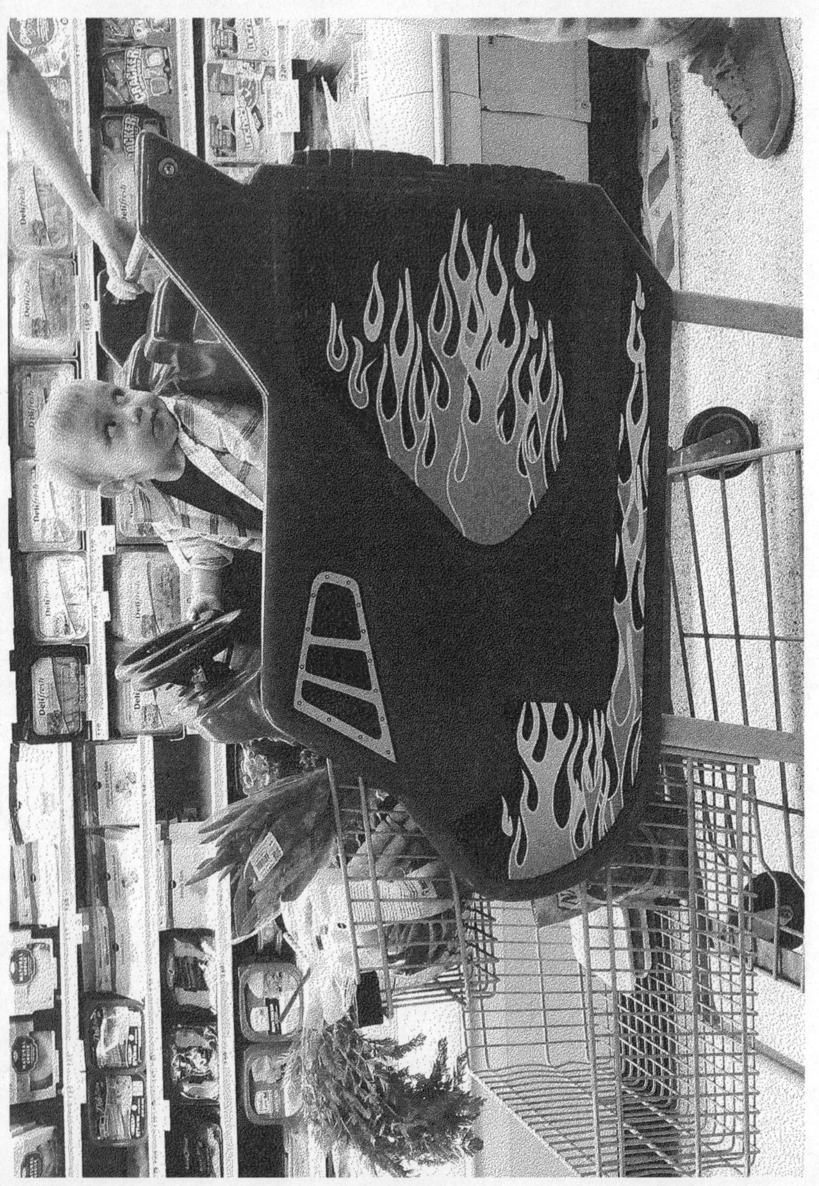

december 15

from an article from internet.
"she has already great comment
on this. my worst enemy, my arch rival,
my most infamous nemesis, worse
than superman's kryptonite, more
daunting than a dark, bleak wintery
day, my least favourite domestic
chore: the laundry pile!"

my least favourite domestic chore

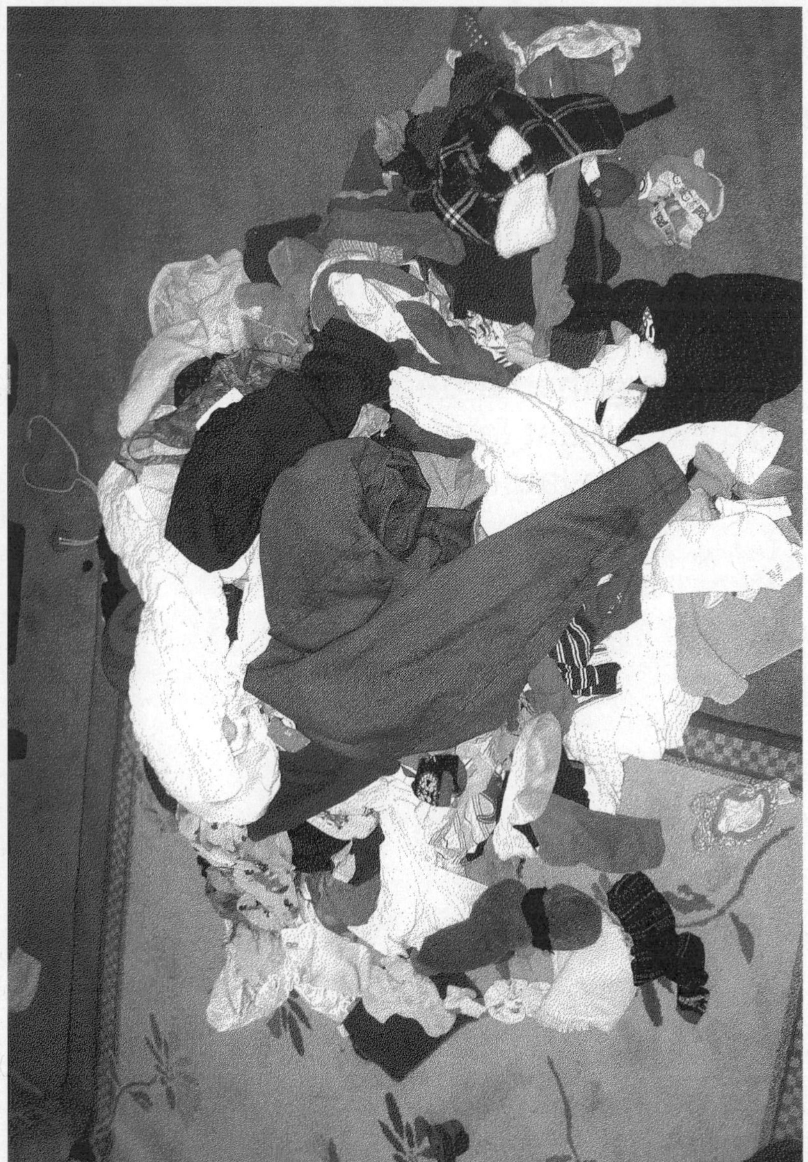

december 16

still from *the pine-tree, the bonsai and the sequoia* (2011), video.

cleaning structures (bonsai)

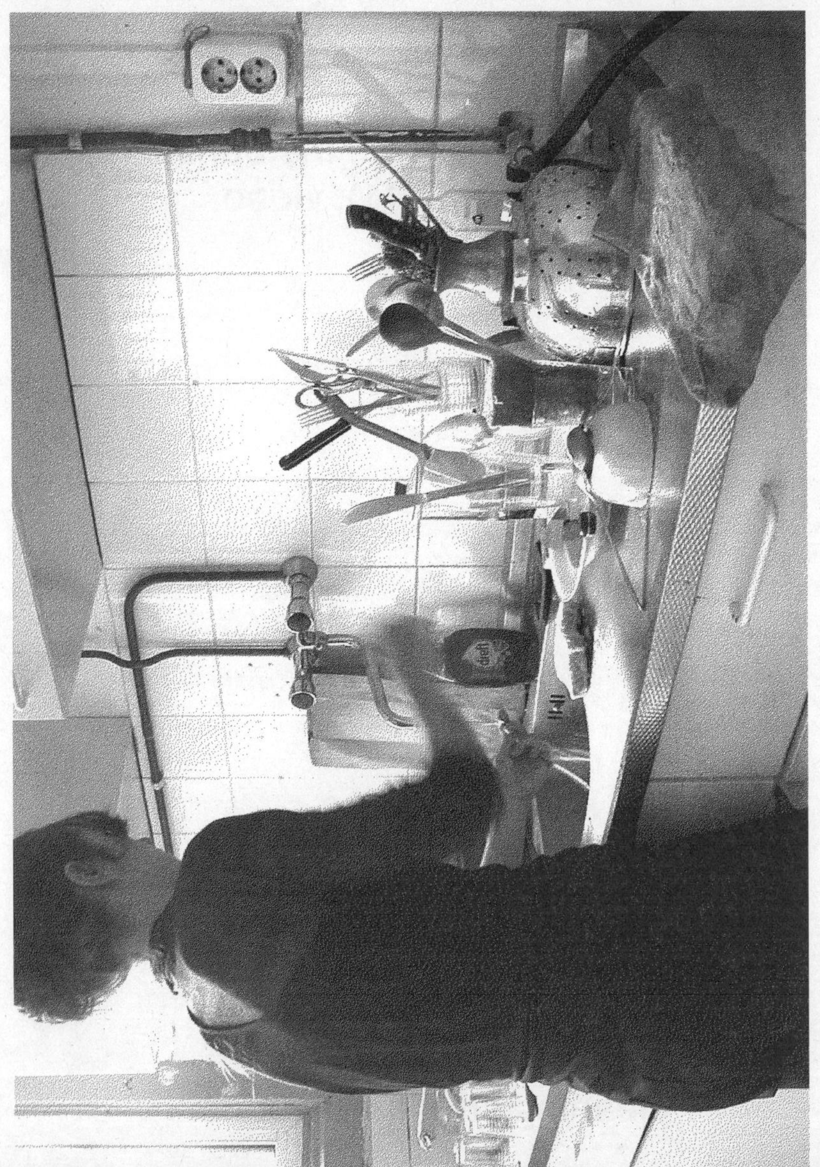

december 17

my small kitchen is sweet.

my kitchen window makes me sigh

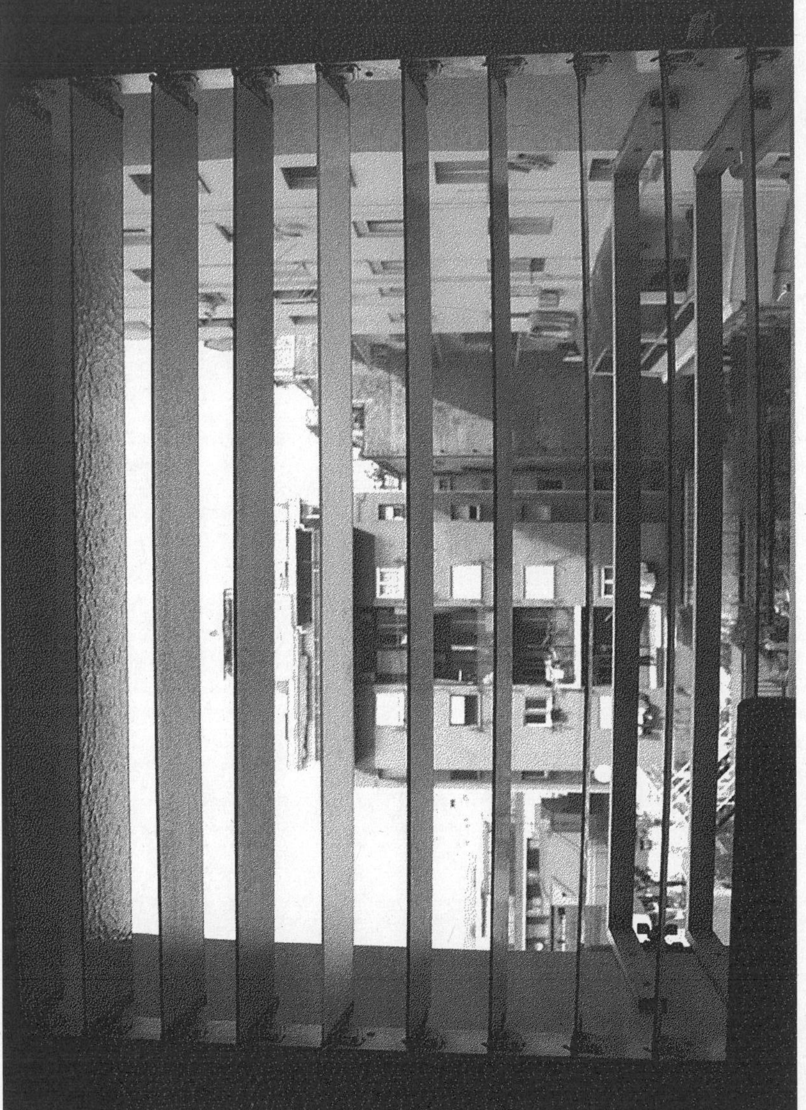

december 18

new arrival sitting in my bookshelf
(polaroid hello kitty, from takaido-
higashi, suginami-ku, tokyo, 1997)

hello kitty

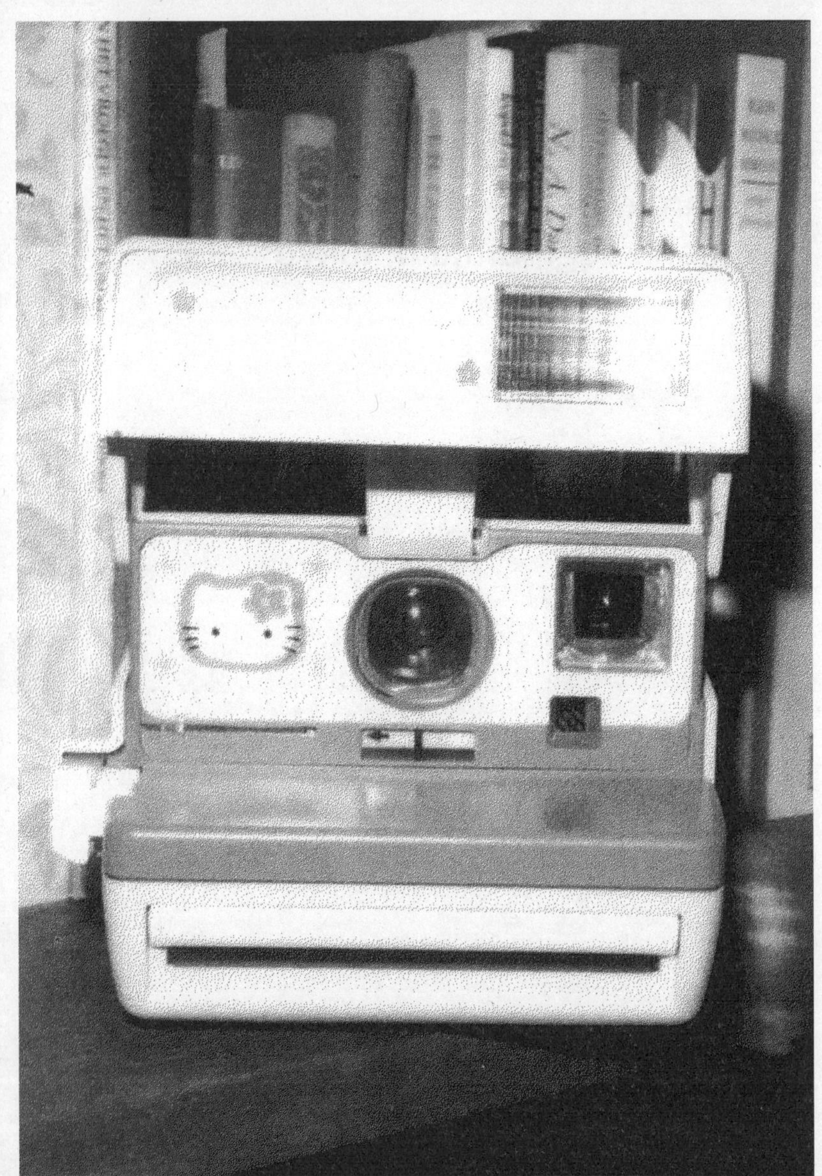

december 19

mannequins protesting at work.

anytime, anywhere, anyhow

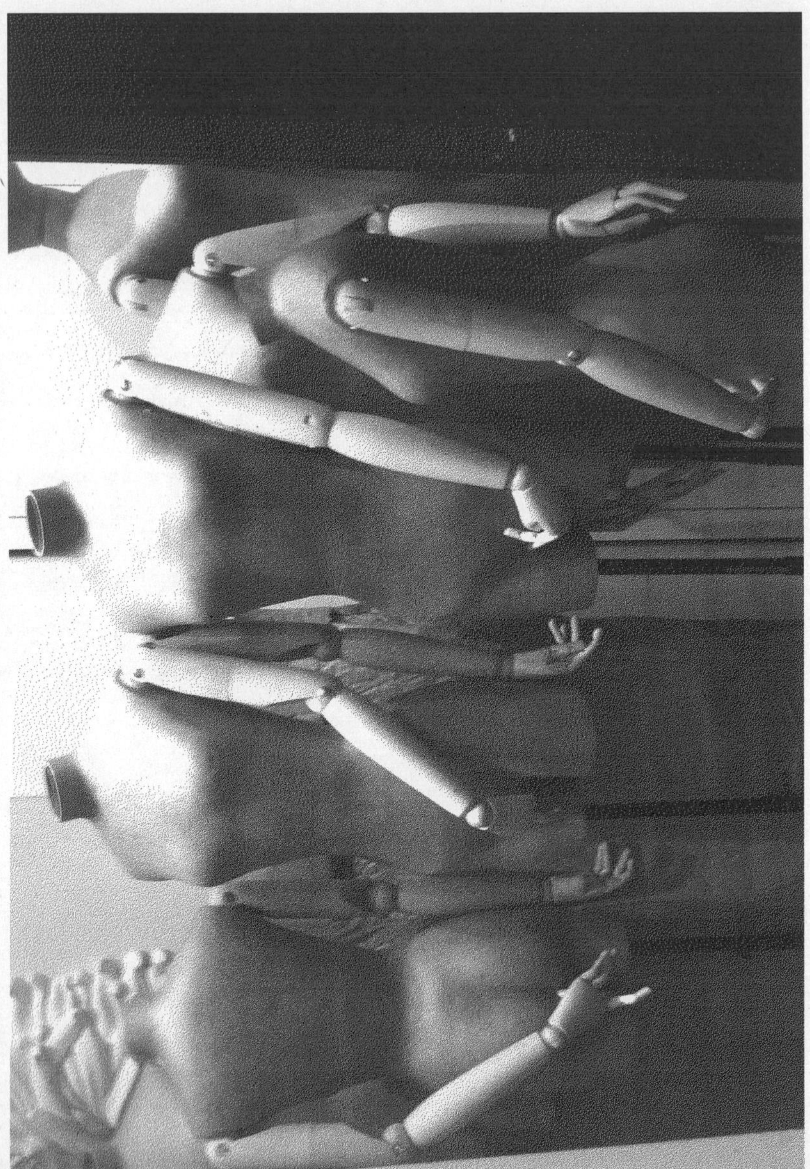

december 20

self-portrait.

home office

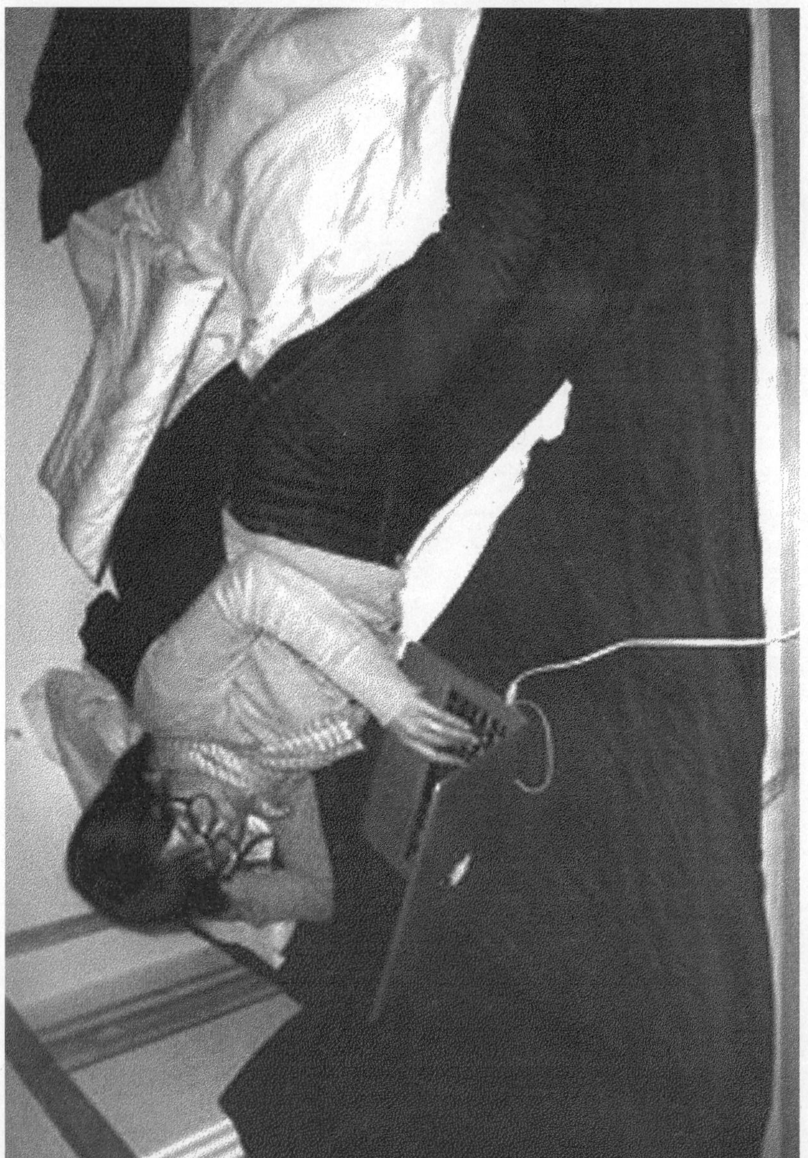

december 21

gustave caillebotte, *les raboteurs
de parquet*, 1875.

post-impression

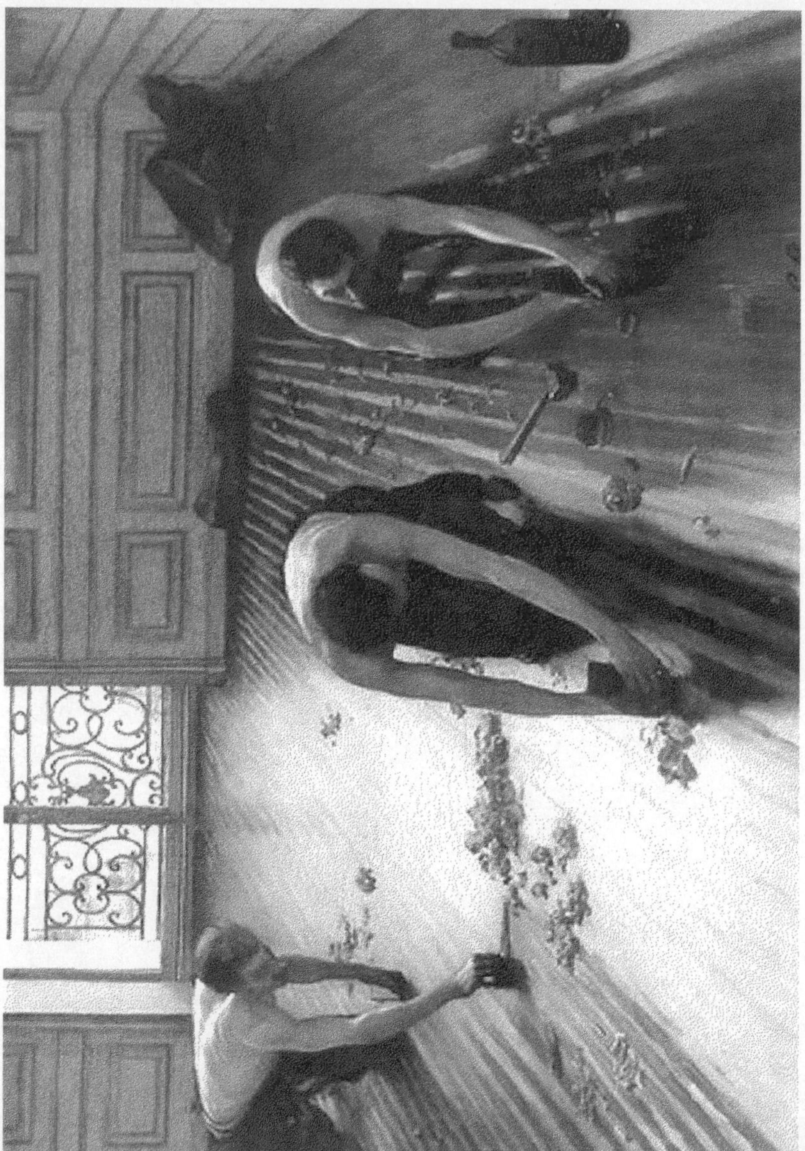

december 22

a room of her own with a door.
an advice by helen escobedo, shared
here: www.loccasionecon.tumblr.com/.

opening

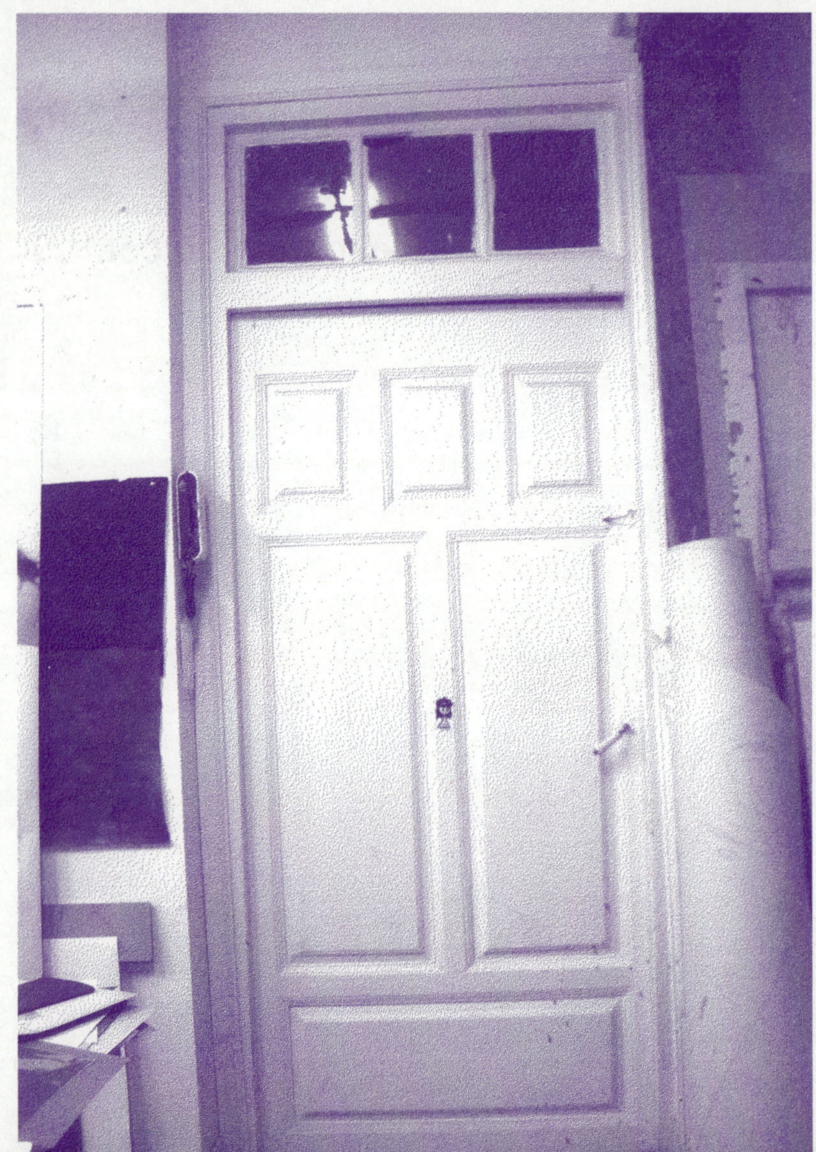

december 23

tirei casas de aranhas,
limpei o pó pra danar.
lavei louça de montanhas,
logo tive que secar.

washing dishes

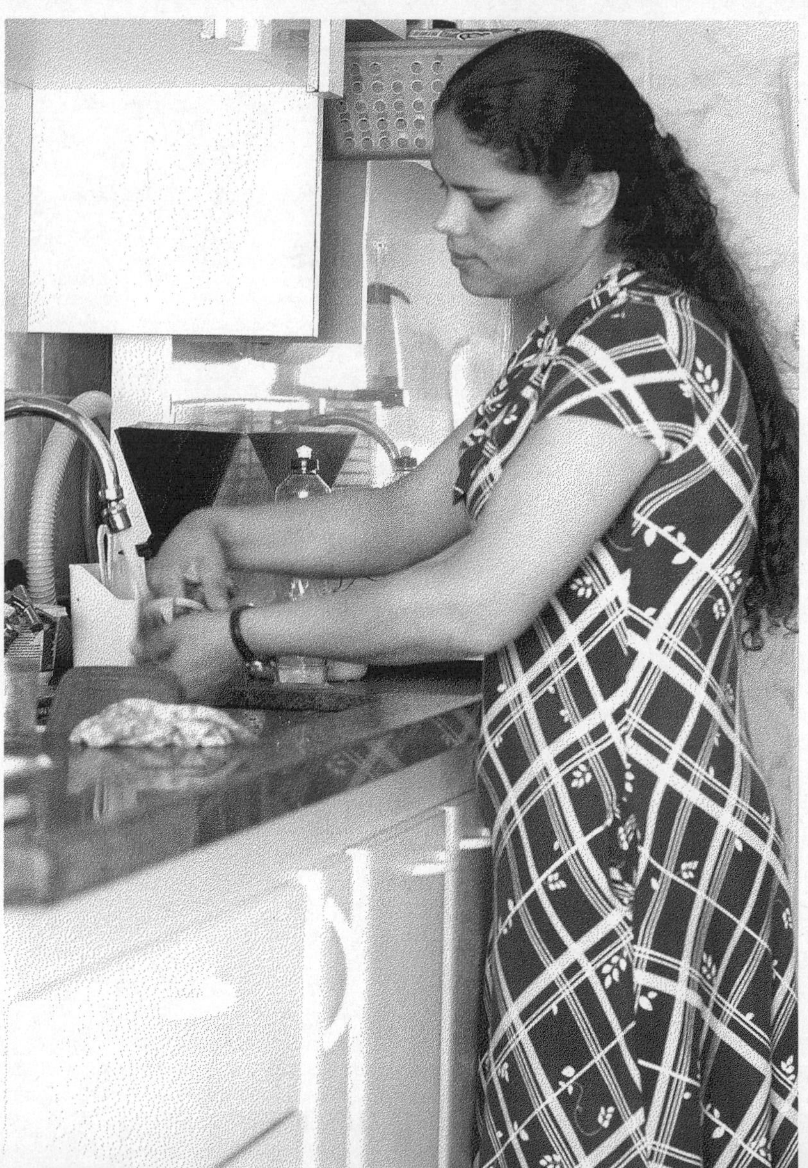

december 24

having a break from my work. from
time to time, i go to the toilet/bathroom.
it's the only time my employer won't
bother me.

work break

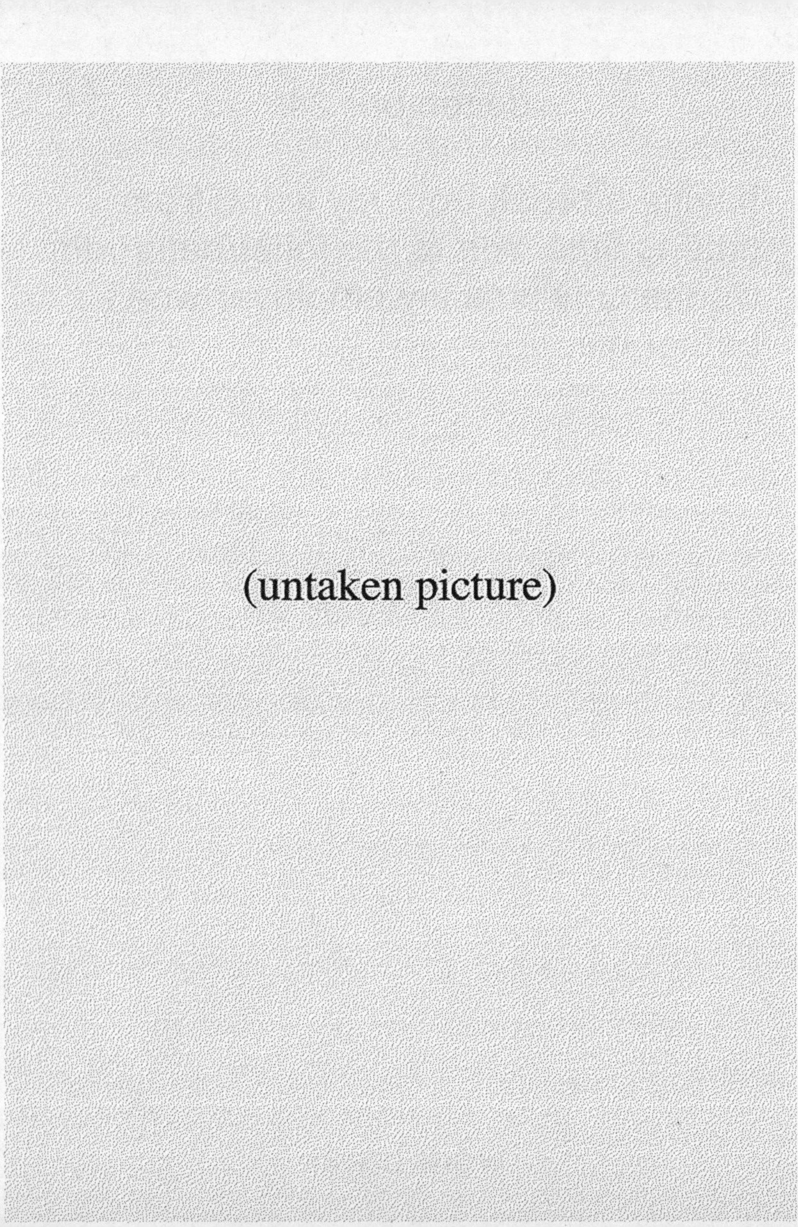

(untaken picture)

aisd stands for "auto imposed sensorial deprivation." this is the view from my home-office. i get no sunlight except for 40 minutes around 3 pm. the rest of the time i don't know what time it is, if is it cold, hot, or raining.

aisd

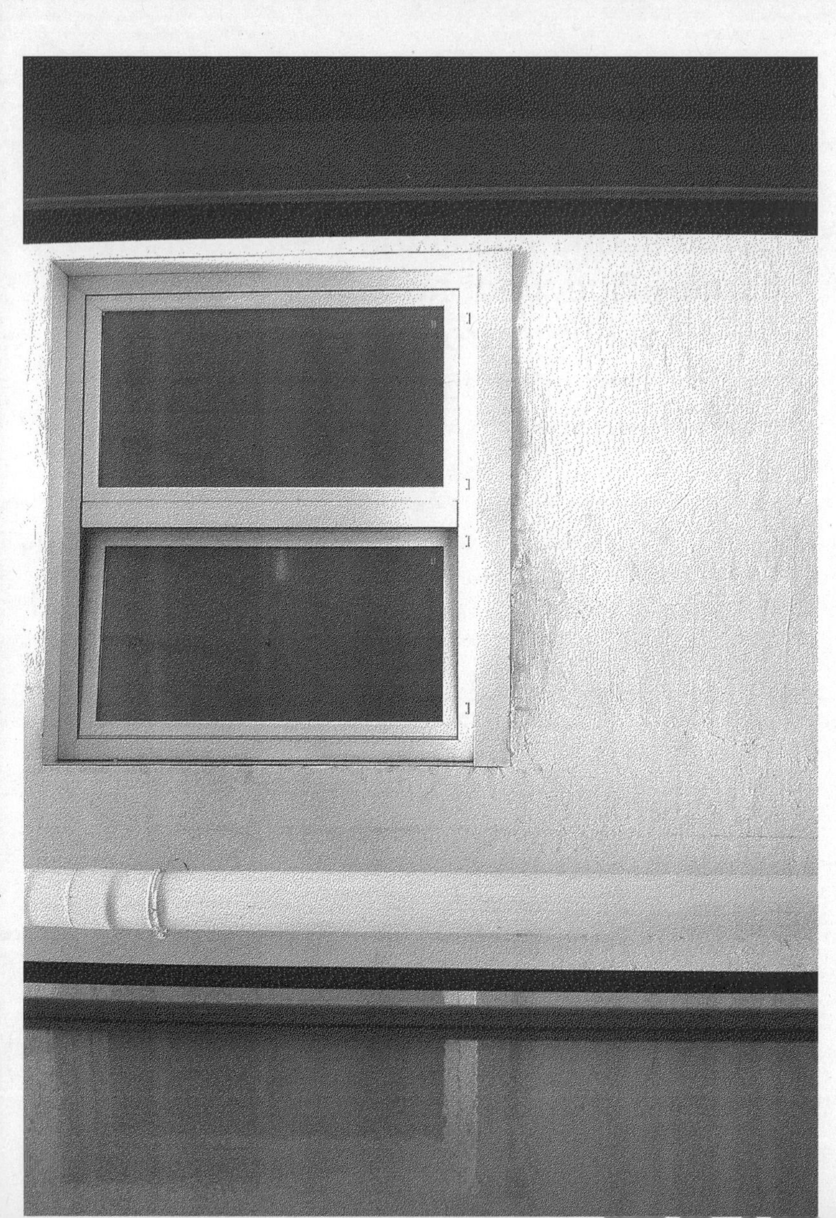

december 26

of, or related to missing the boat.

oops

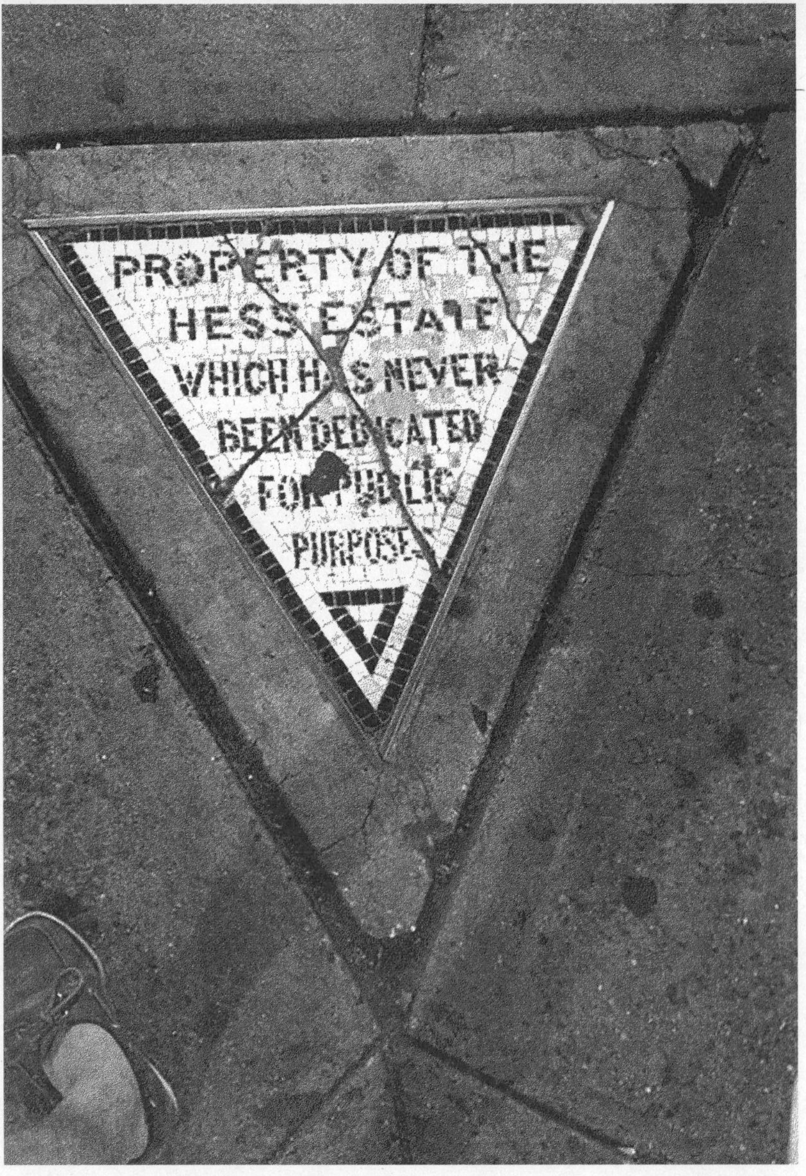

PROPERTY OF THE
HESS ESTATE
WHICH HAS NEVER
BEEN DEDICATED
FOR PUBLIC
PURPOSES

december 27

a fungal encounter by chance.
cleaning day. domestic networks.

mouldy jar

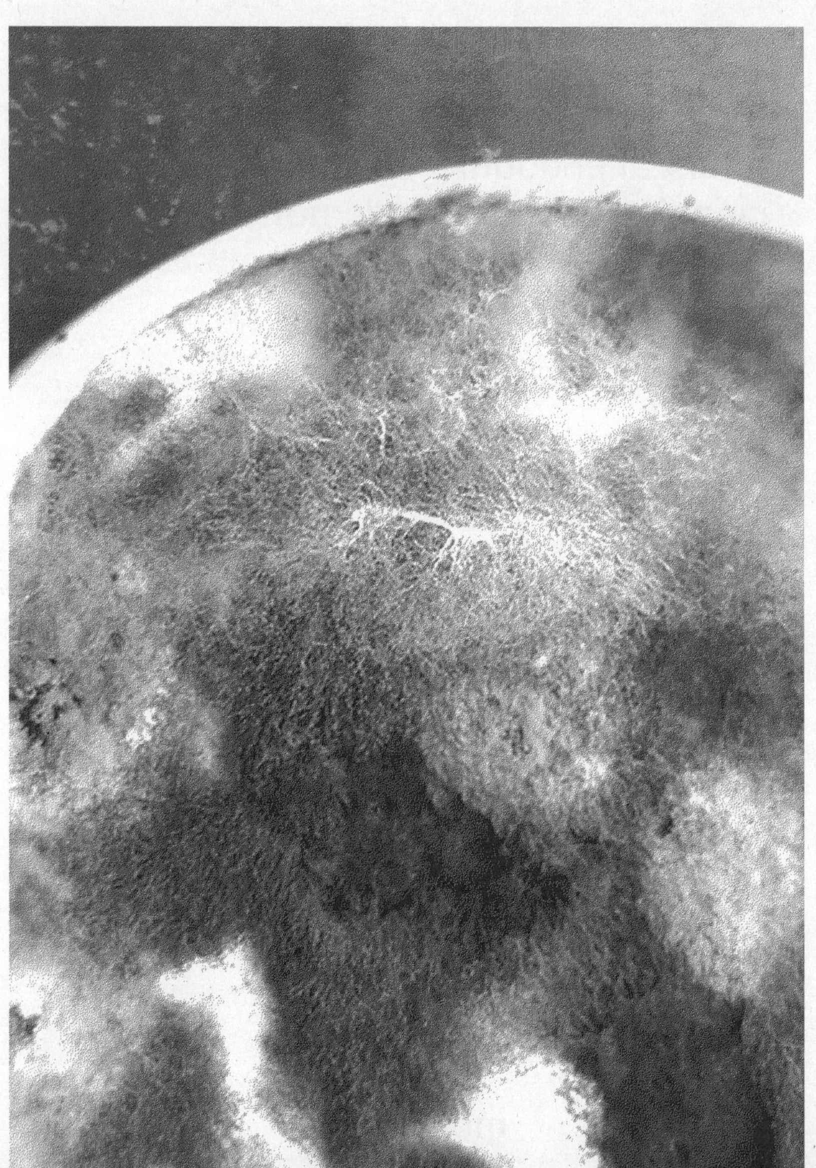

december 28

domestic workers play a big role
in raising children in the uk.
photo taken by me at the rainbow
park, southbank, london.

raise

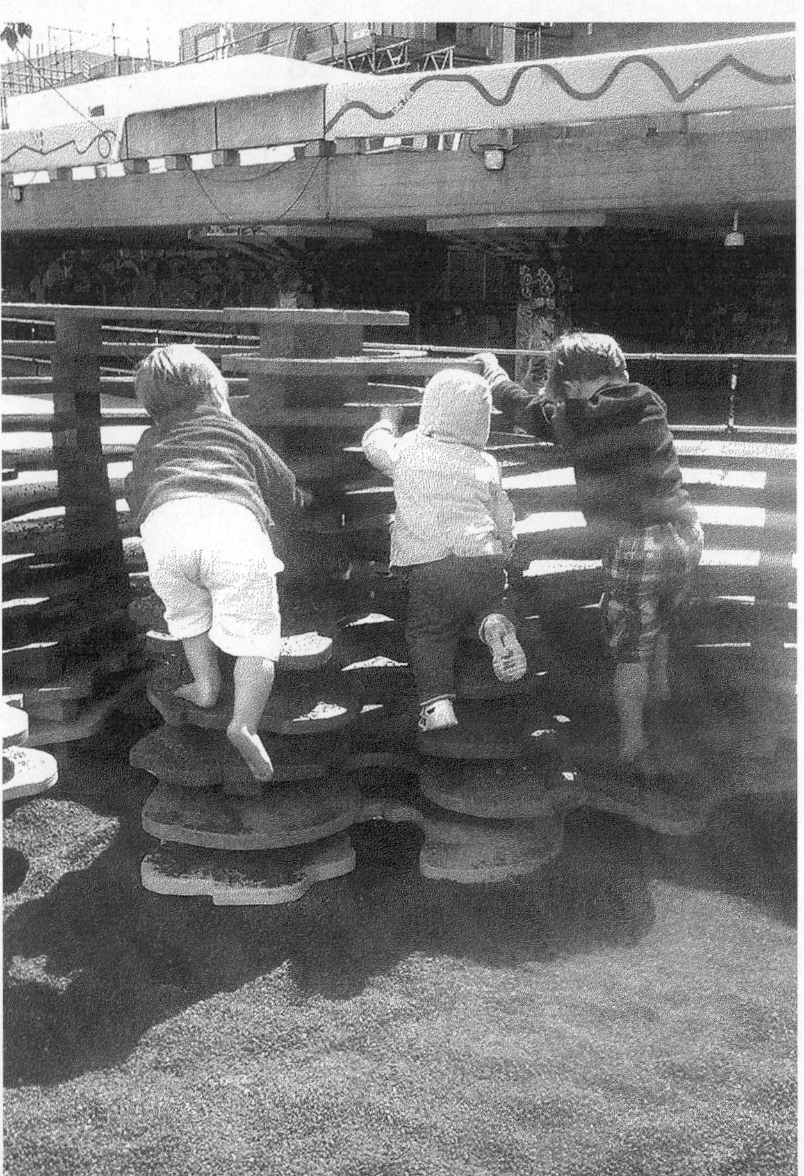

december 29

we are still working.

the undesirables

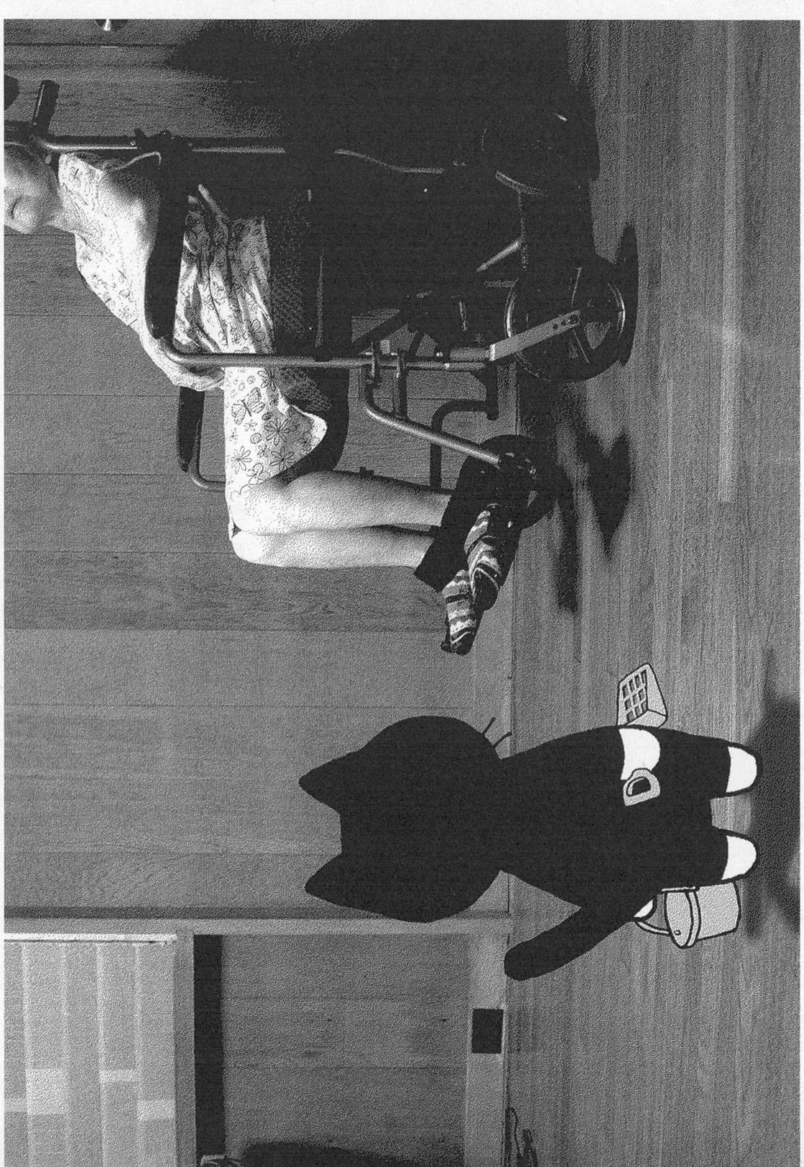

after lunch, i hate staying alone in
my dark little kitchen, making coffee
and doing the washing up. everybody
is laughing in the dining room. three
metre long corridor, my unhappiness.
castellón, 1995.

alone in the kitchen

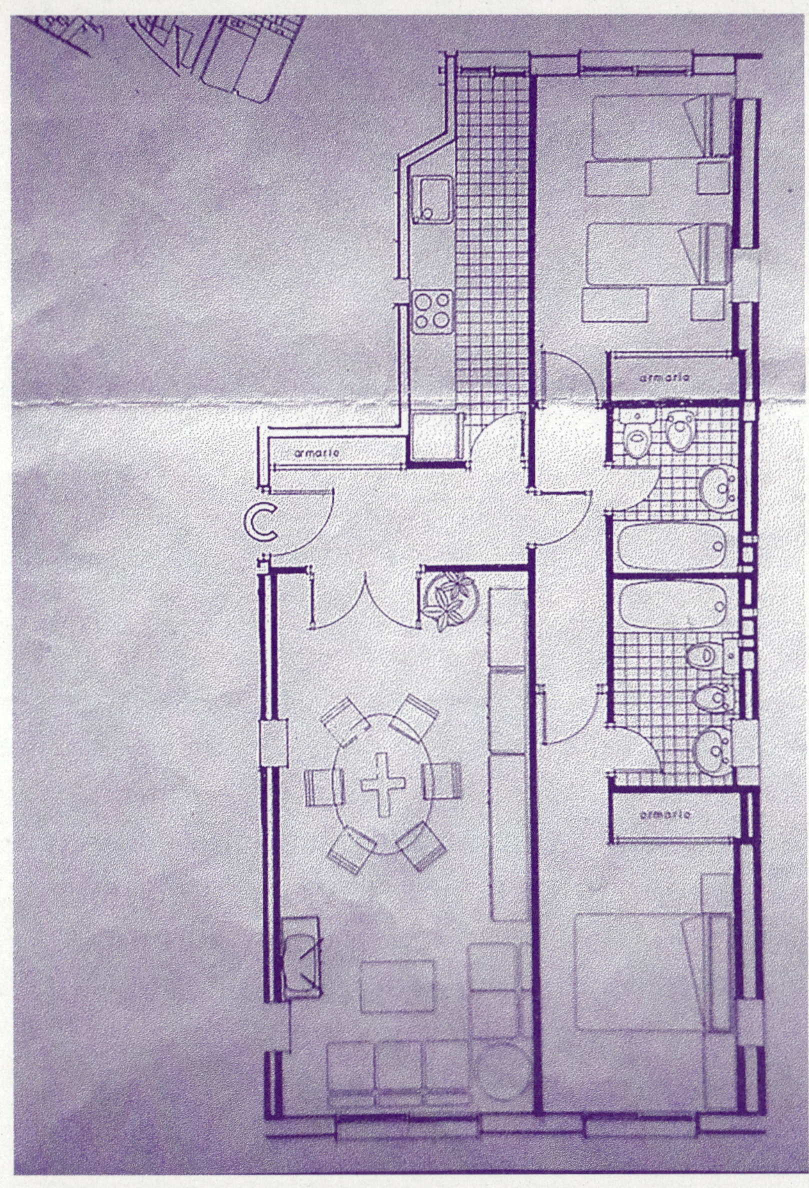

armario
armario
armario
armario

december 31

photograph from the house where
i grew up, taken by my father or
my mother in 1982 or 1983.

looking after a kid

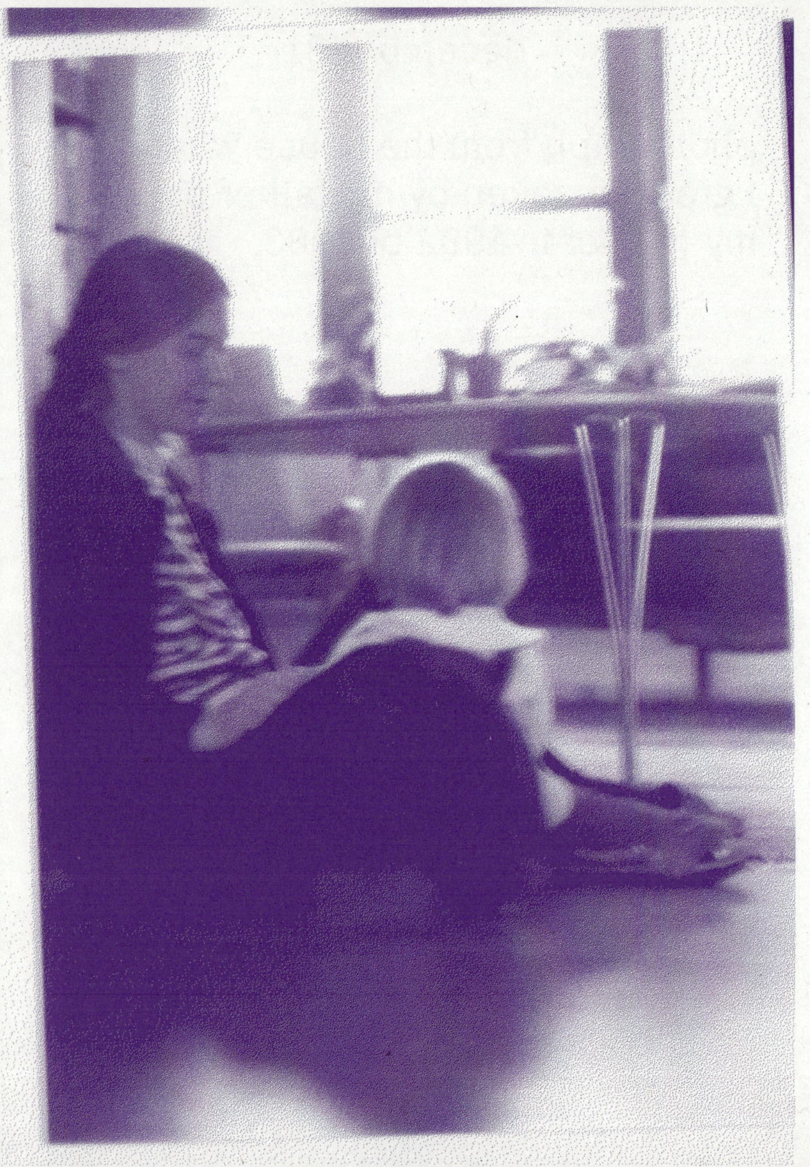

january 1

should eat something...
getting inspiration.

post-fordism

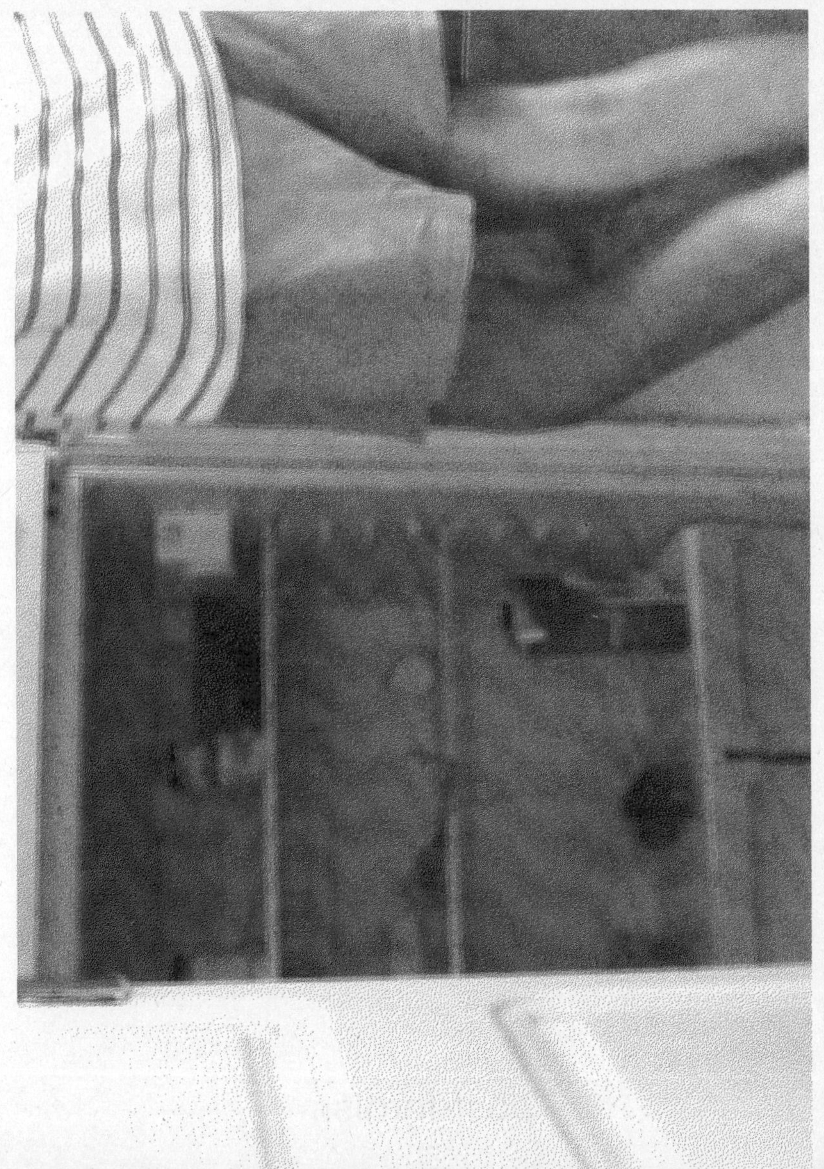

january 2

ironing

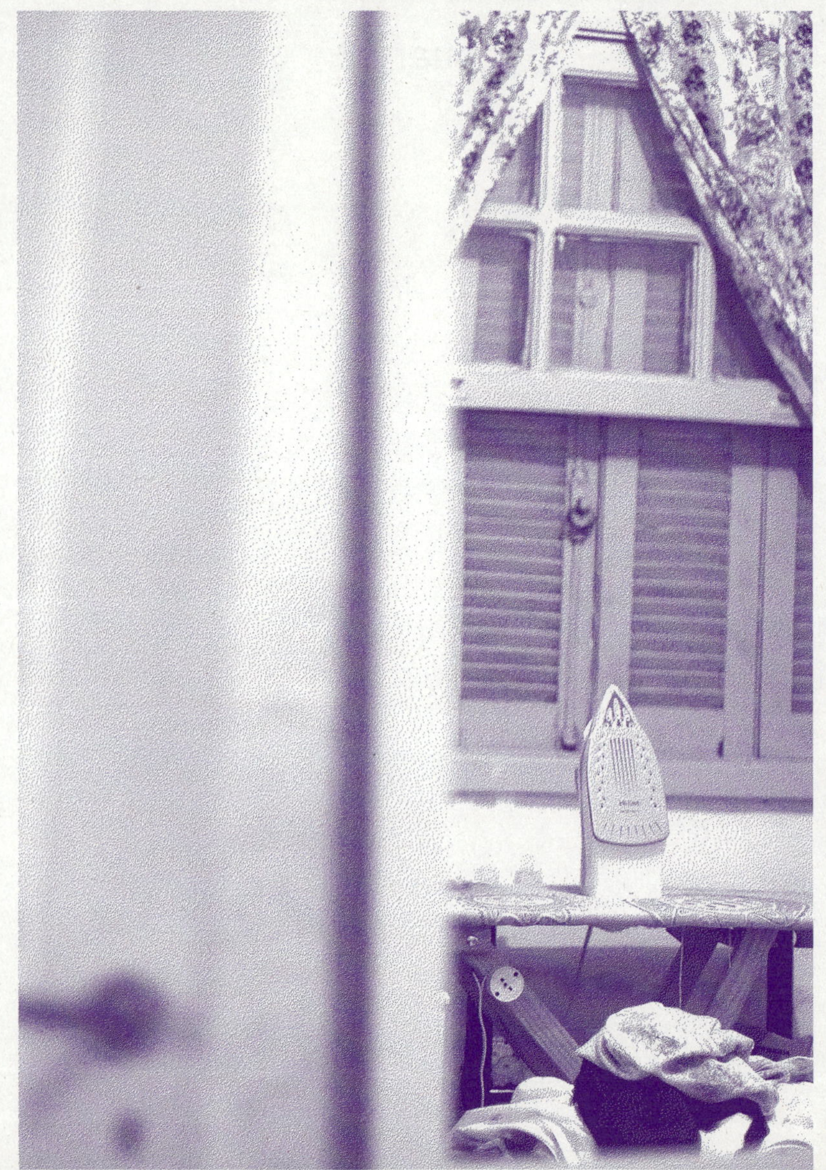

january 3

when a woman can do everything!

se questa è una donna…

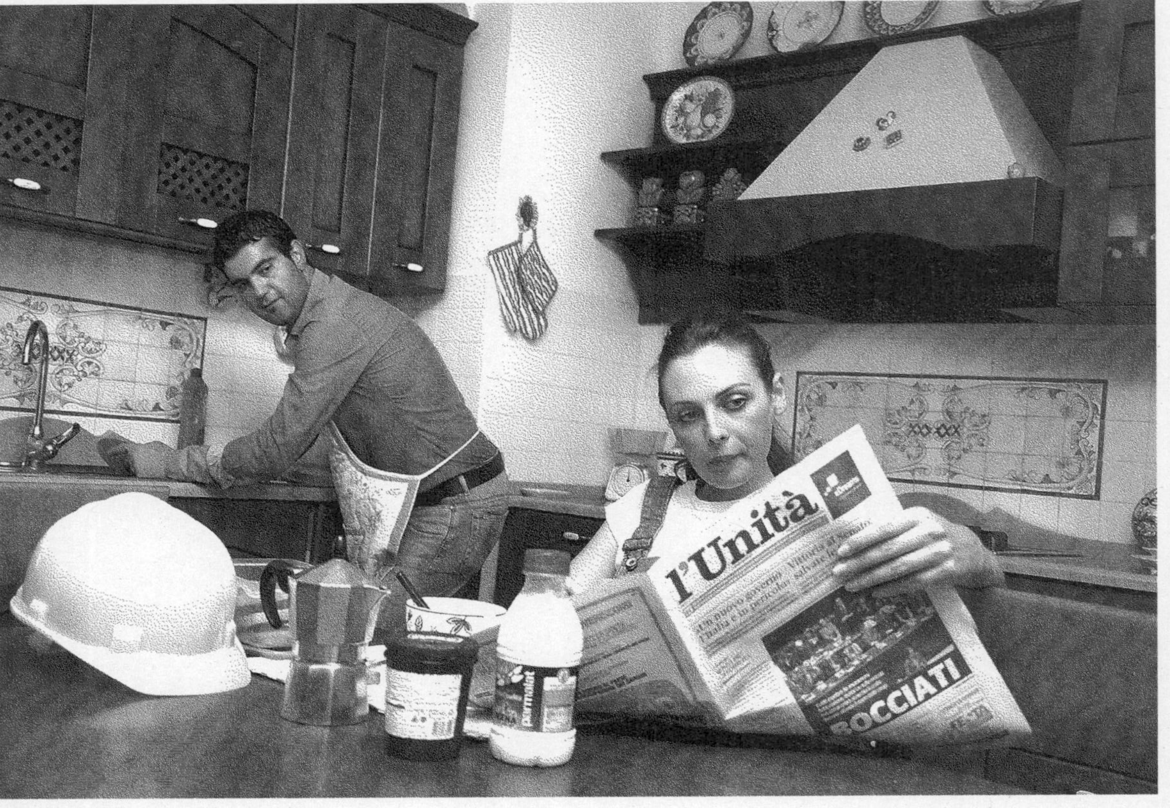

l'Unità
BOCCIATI

january 4

australian feminism

Australian
Feminist
Arts Journal
1984

lip

LANA E
INDUMENTI
DELICATI IN
LAVATRICE

january 5

goodbye bouquet for our office cleaner
yuki, who is going back to singapore
and will be dearly missed.

still life with flowers and
cleaning accessories

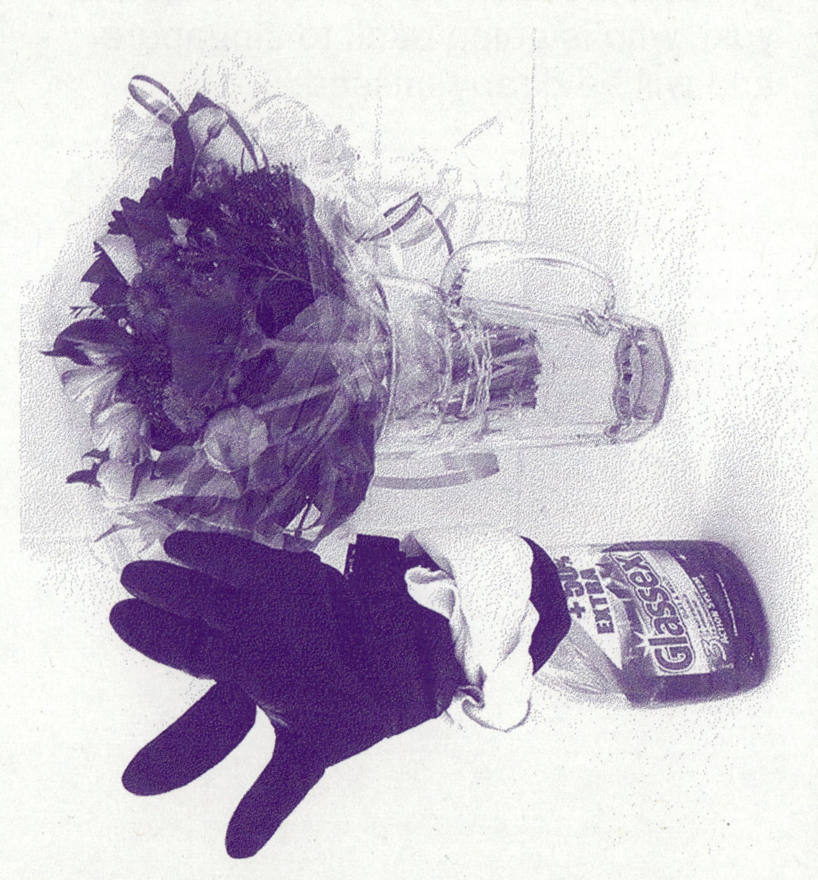

january 6

better use twice, clothes
become washcloths.

second life

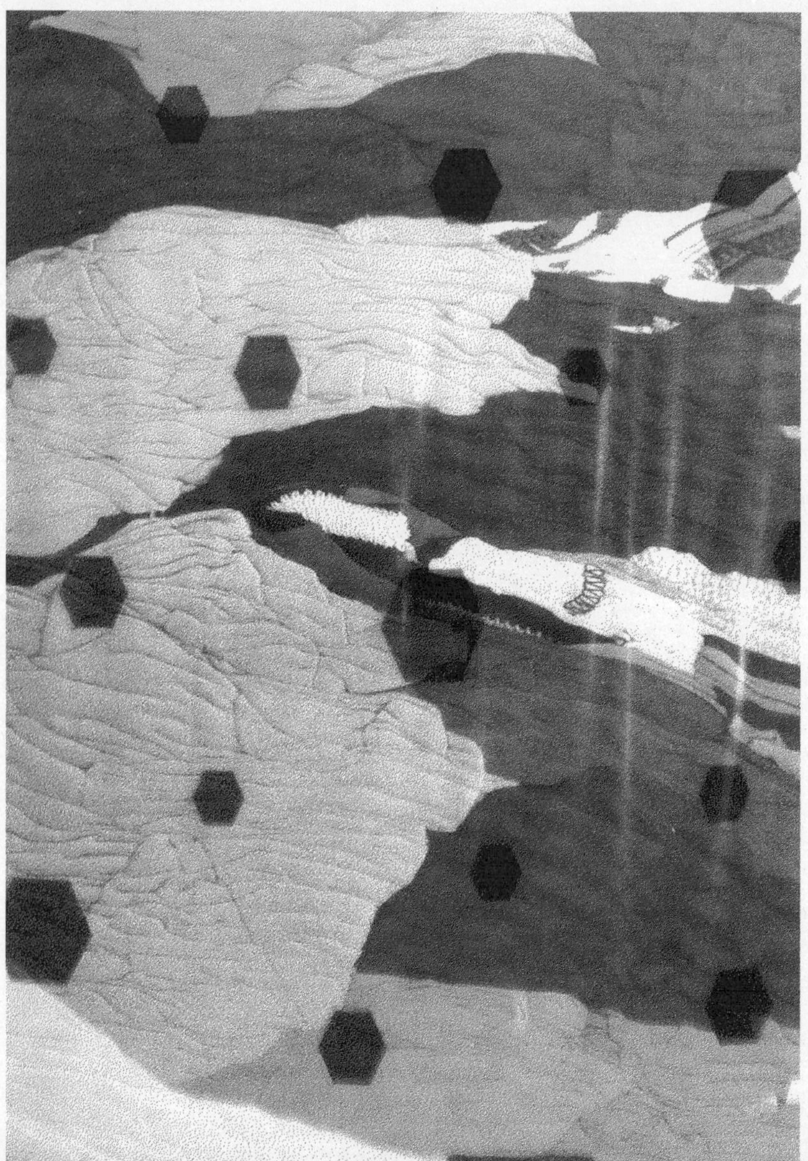

january 7

heed the day of wodan.

january 7

standing by

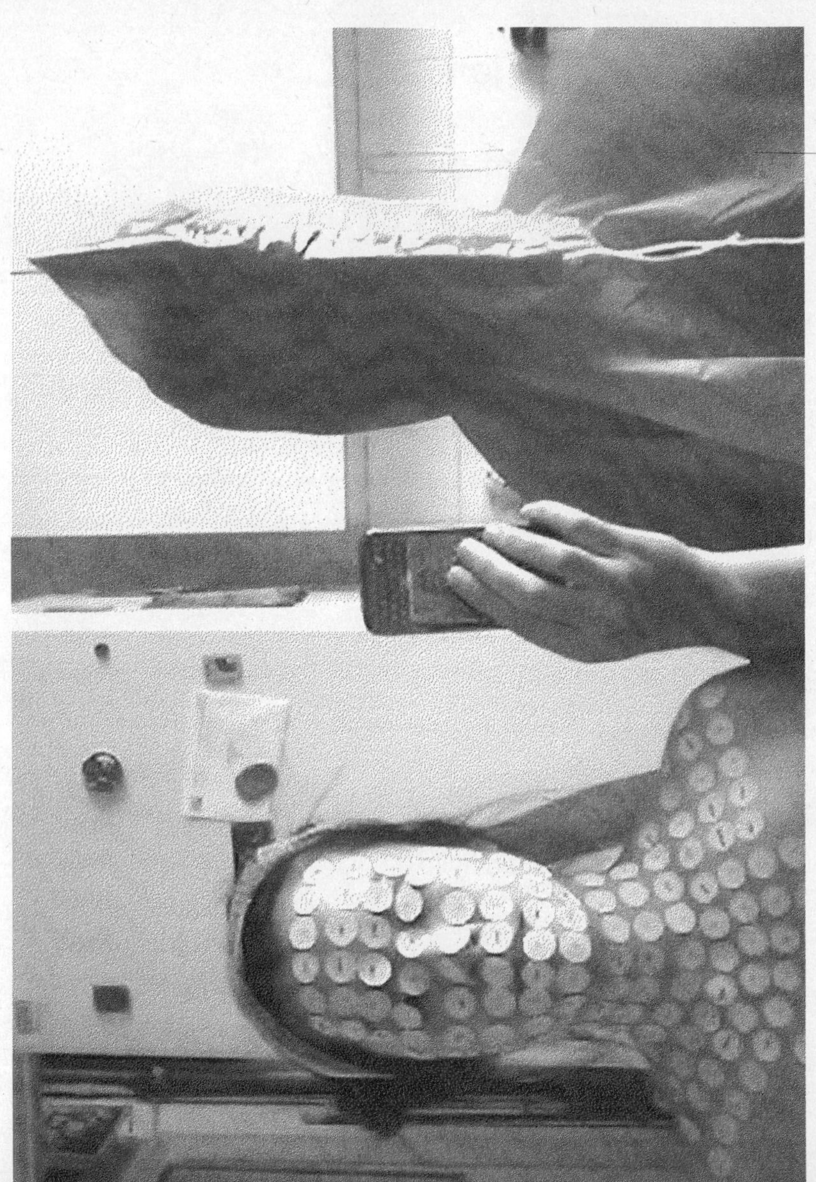

january 8

first four frames from vintage found
film strip.

small business film strip

SMALL BUSINESS PROVIDES
58% OF THE TOTAL
US BUSINESS EMPLOYMENT

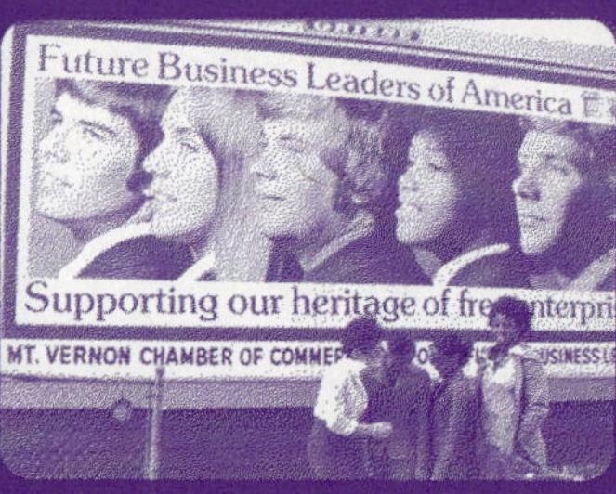

Future Business Leaders of America
Supporting our heritage of free enterpri
MT. VERNON CHAMBER OF COMMER

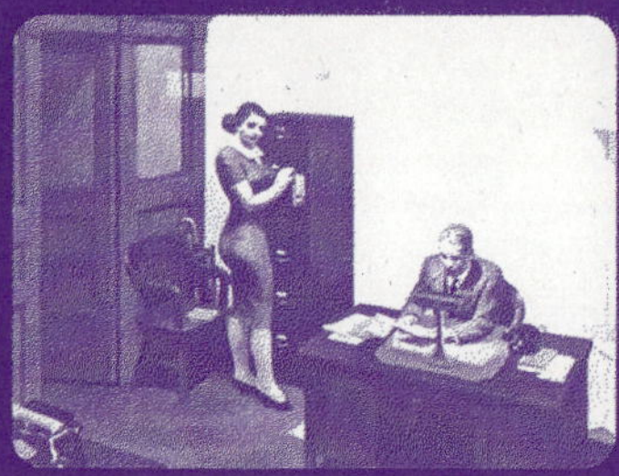

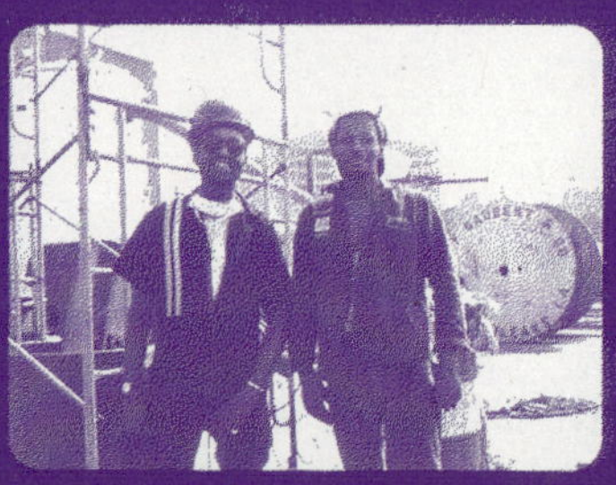

january 9

while working as a domestic worker,
i also think of my future and family,
even with my little salary. i always
make sure that i save every month.
so far i now have farmland with fruits
and rice fields. i also managed to build
my own house bit by bit. i am looking
forward to settle back home with my
two children and husband who are
waiting for me. i am one of only a few
among my fellow domestic workers
whose family is not torn apart.
domestic workers have to leave family
back home in the hope of better life
and future for our children and families.

the fruit of my labour

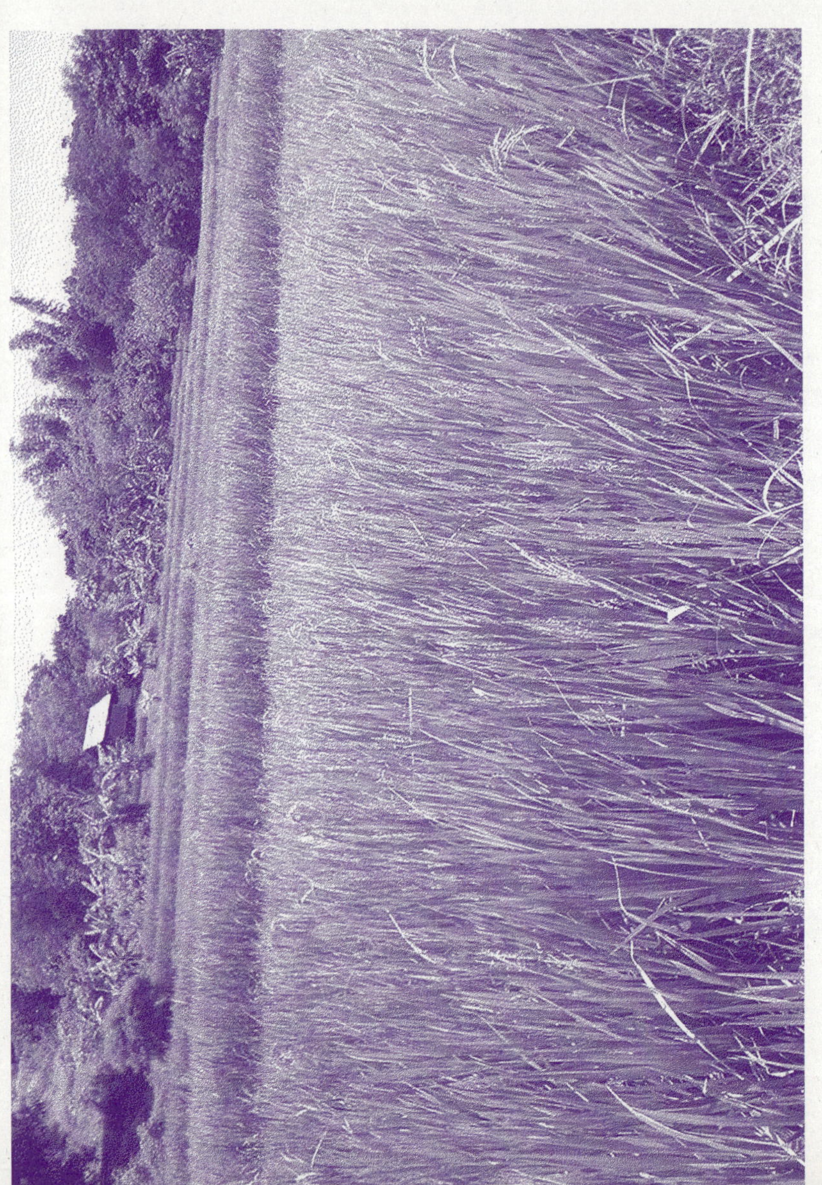

january 10

during my walking around the city centre i found a second hand camera shop in são paulo.

saldão

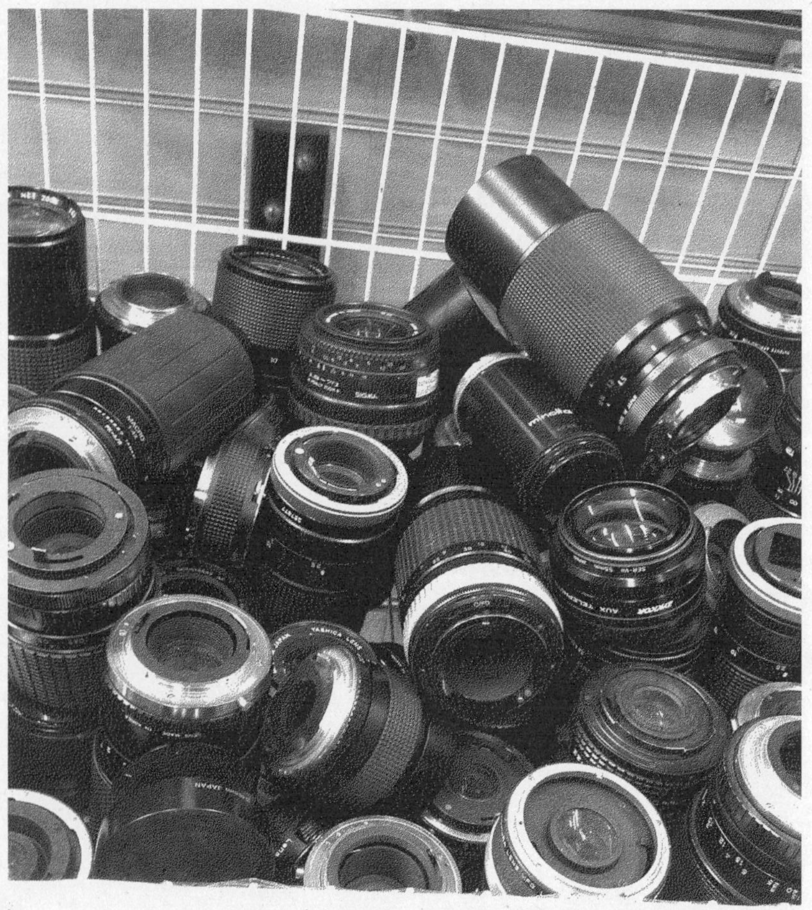

SALDÃO

january 11

i live in a farm outside bogotá. i have breakfast and lunch outdoors.

lunch

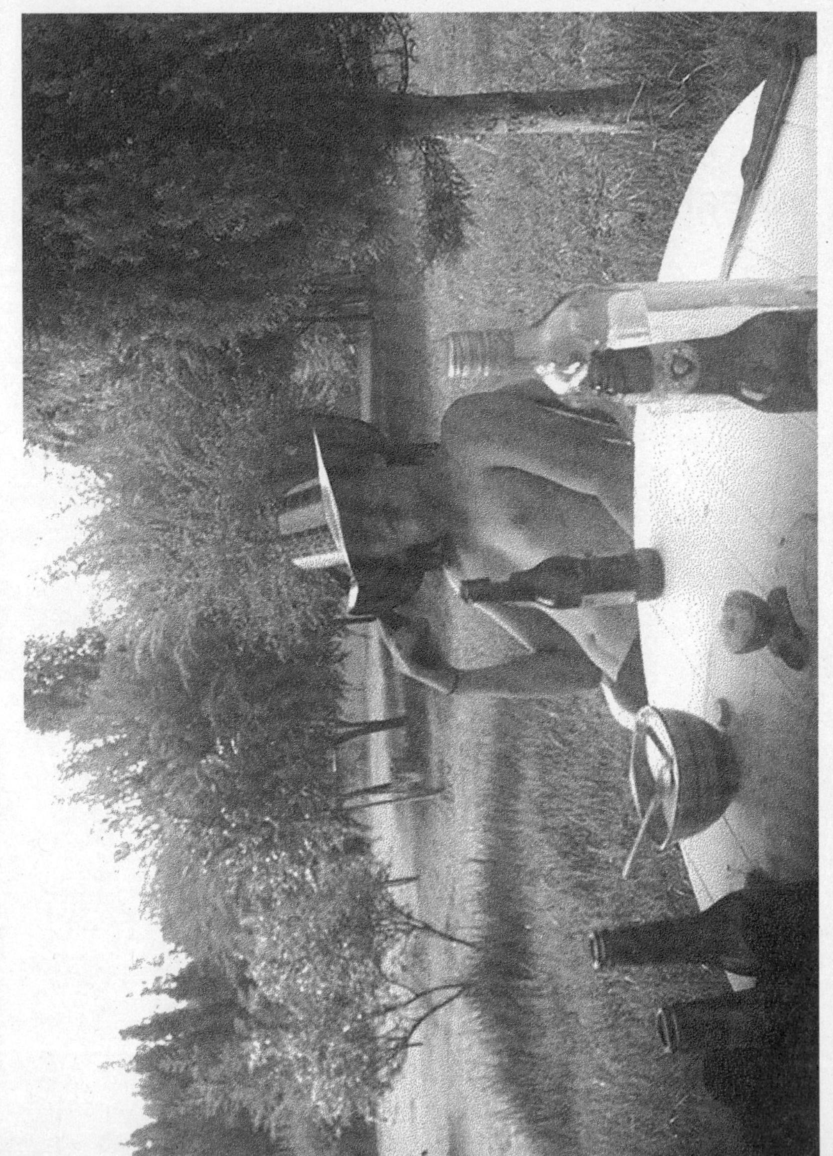

january 12

sunday night in front of the tv reorgan-
izing the desktop of my computer.
rename finished projects with a clear
title for finding it back easier. cleaning
'never used' files by using the trash
can. 'empty trash can'—thinking did
i loose an important software or
something?

trash can

- Rpm 08.30
- Geld 28,60 op de bank zetten
✓ email Esther, (offertes gedaan)
-
- Berm Roos uitnodiging juist maken
  klaar om te drukken

- Berm Dorte A4 uitnodiging proberen, namen!

- boekje toneelmakerij, volgorde, tekst juist

- ~~Gosco 15.00 daar~~
- Factuur maken voor Berm ₹

- afwas
- was opruimen
- ~~Computer opruimen!~~
- ~~kijken of de Hema al naast en~~

Oma Sonja bellen → koffer
~~10 okt~~ ~~20.30~~

tekst kant
beeld kant A   A3 } op één vel??
beeld kant B   A3 {

Rijnja   08.00 → 17.00   open
                    n/a → VR

talenten dag
absolute topper

january 13

cleaning

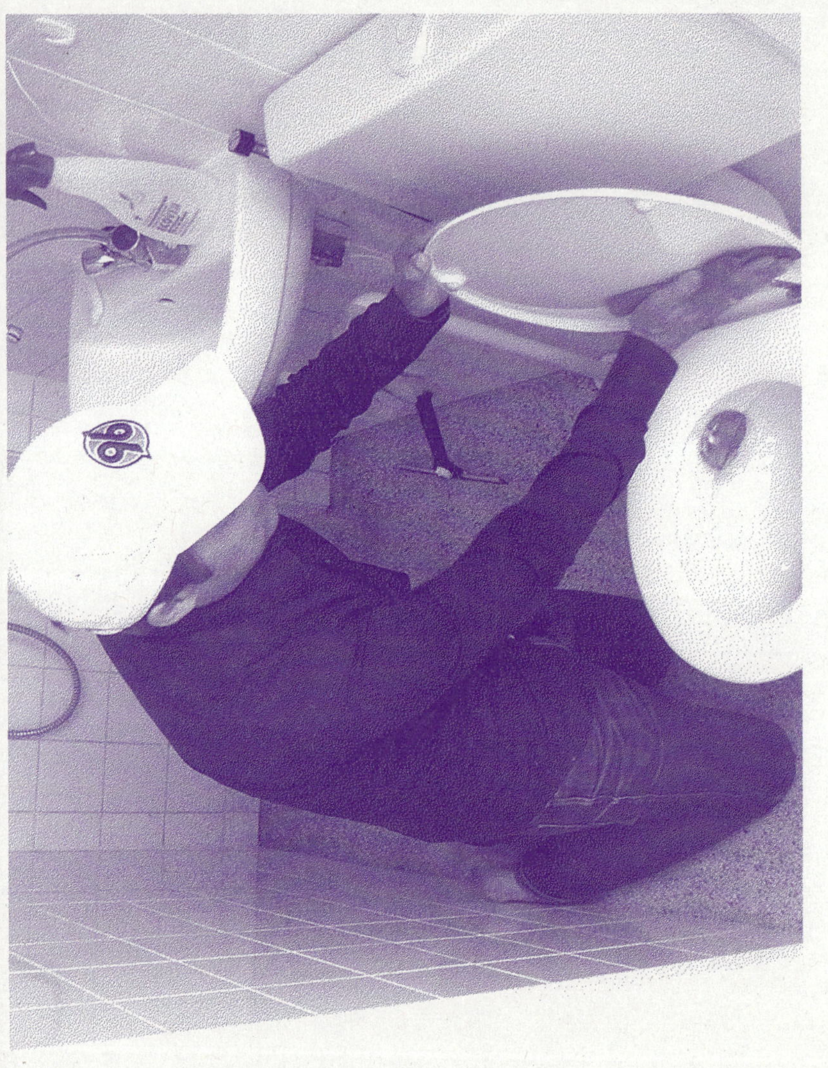

january 14

in order to cover the whole rent of the
studio i live in, me and my landlord—
who often comes to work here—
decided to rent my bedroom on airbnb
to tourists for some 10 days a month.
in this way, we can continue to use
this space, but we have to take care
of changing bed sheets and towels,
fixing the windows for the winter,
warming up the space before they
arrive, cleaning after they left, and
having our stuff always randomly
displaced across the studio. be the
boss of yourself taken one step further.

mi casa es tu casa

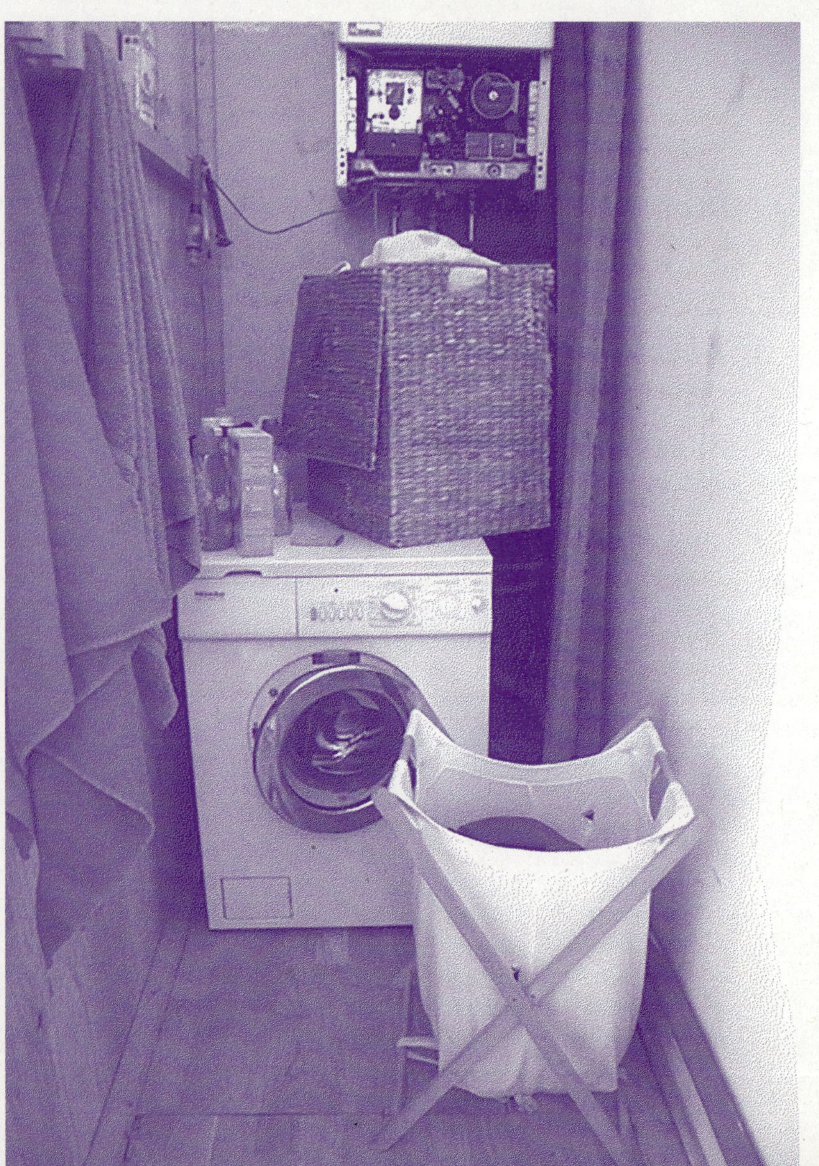

january 15

self-portrait. facing the mess in the
early morning, starting to clean after
a last cigarette…

sweet sunday

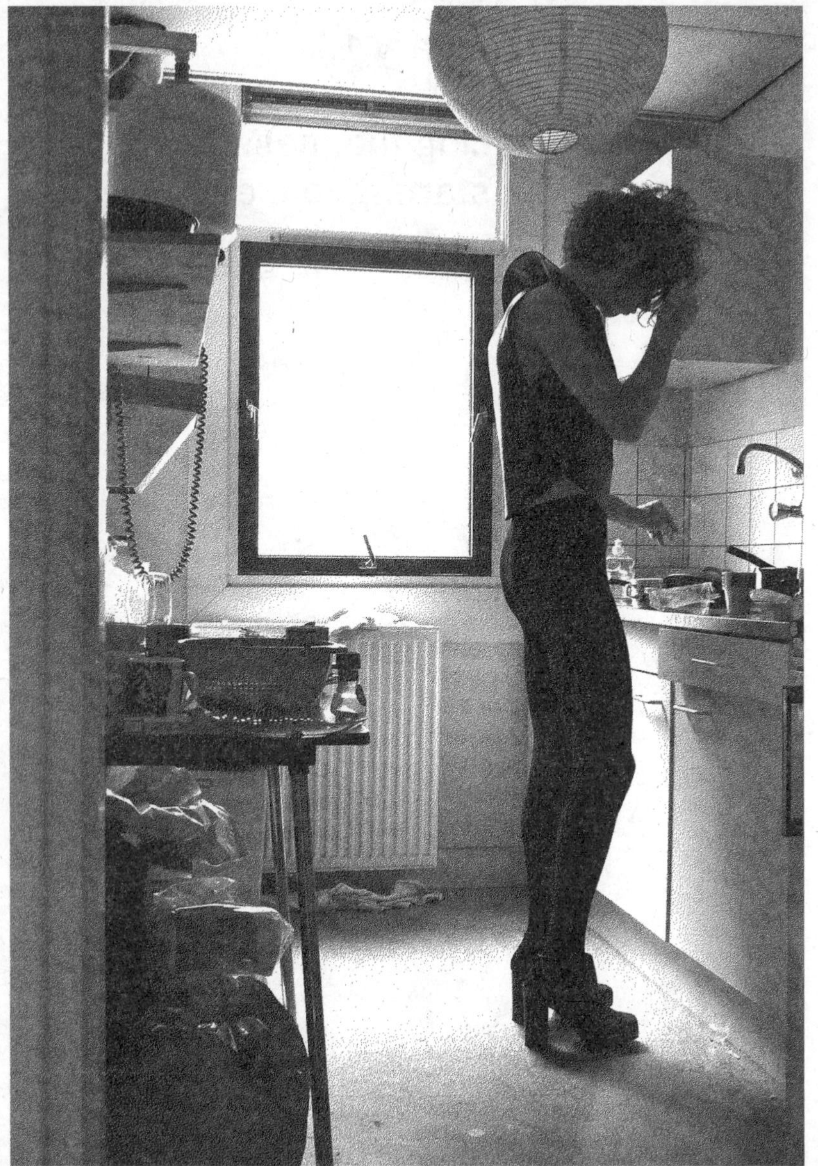

free reign, open ended, do what
you want, take over.

in charge

NO
MASTERS

january 17

tying migrant domestic workers to
employers equals slavery and trafficking. justice for domestic workers
fights back to restore rights to the
domestic worker visa.

domestic workers in the uk
are caged, set us free!!!

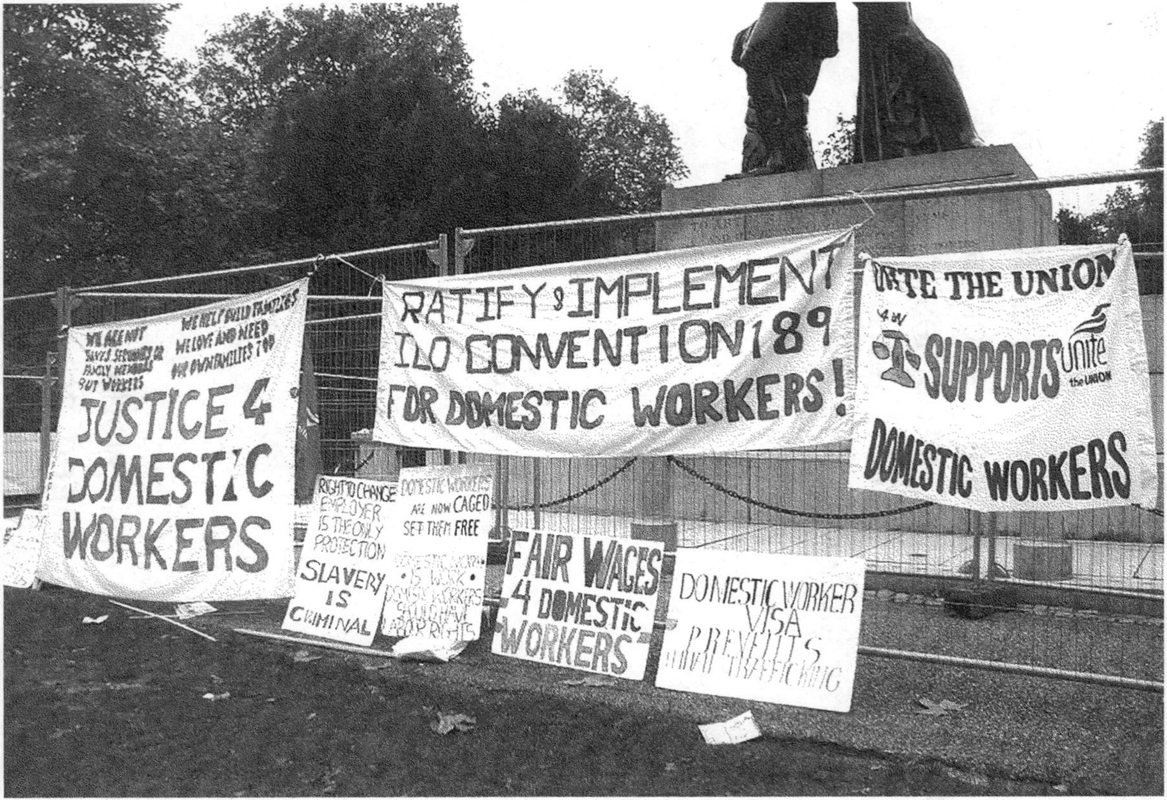

WE ARE NOT
JUST SECURITY OR
FAMILY MEMBERS
BUT WORKERS
WE HELP BUILD FAMILIES
WE LOVE AND NEED
OUR OWN FAMILIES TOO
JUSTICE 4
DOMESTIC
WORKERS
RATIFY & IMPLEMENT
ILO CONVENTION 189
FOR DOMESTIC WORKERS!
UNITE THE UNION
4 IN
I SUPPORTS unite the UNION
DOMESTIC WORKERS
RIGHT TO CHANGE
EMPLOYER
IS THE ONLY
PROTECTION
SLAVERY
IS
CRIMINAL
DOMESTIC WORKERS
ARE NOW CAGED
SET THEM FREE
DOMESTIC WORK
IS WORK
DOMESTIC WORKERS
SHOULD HAVE
LABOR RIGHTS
FAIR WAGES
4 DOMESTIC
WORKERS
DOMESTIC WORKER
VISA
PREVENTS
HUMAN TRAFFICKING

athiraman kannan jumped to his death
from the 147th floor of the world's
tallest building, the burj khalifa. from
india, he came to dubai to work as
a cleaner in the newly opened building.
in an attempt to honour his courageous
call for attention to be given to the
lives of migrant workers, i photographed
what i describe as a 'pop out city.'
these are spaces that are an attempt
at permanency and comfort in an
always vulnerable life as a migrant
worker. unlike the families they work
for, whose life exists behind walls,
their lives exist on the street, forging
new notions of 'the public.'
al naeem, 2011.

in memory of athiraman kannan

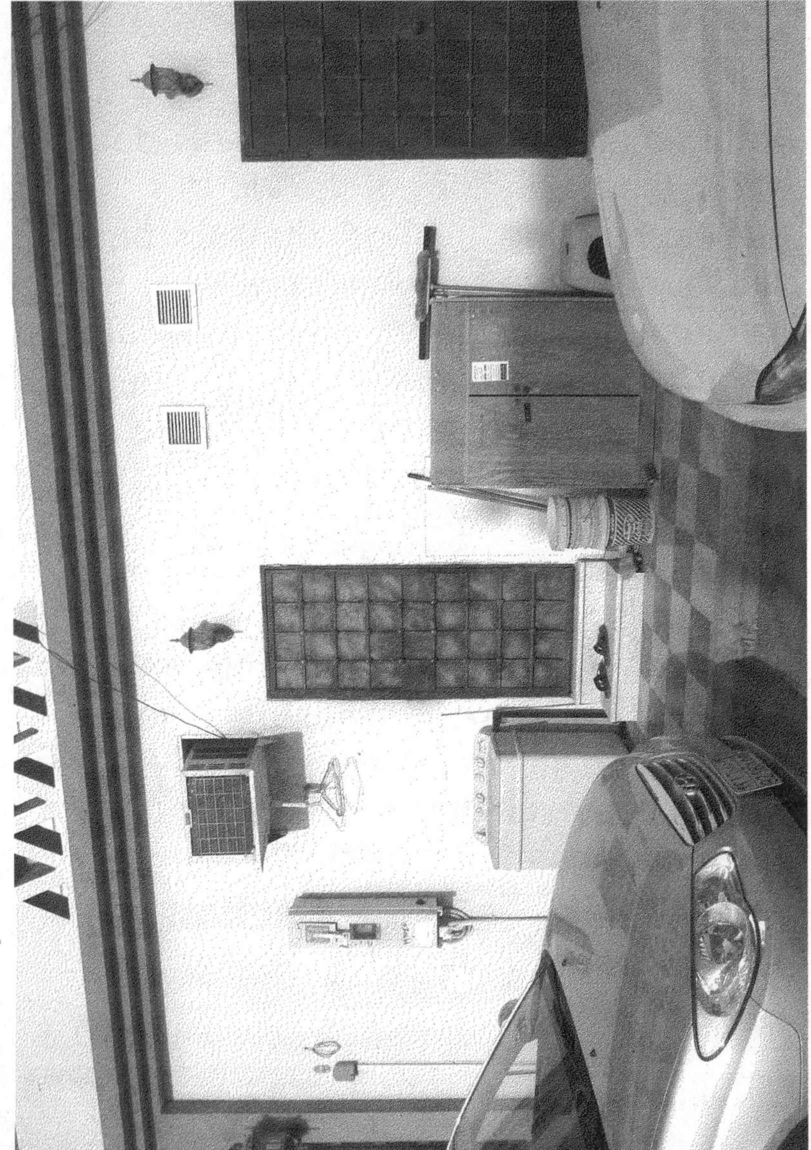

january 19

photograph from the house where
i grew up, taken by my father or
my mother in 1982 or 1983.

sewing

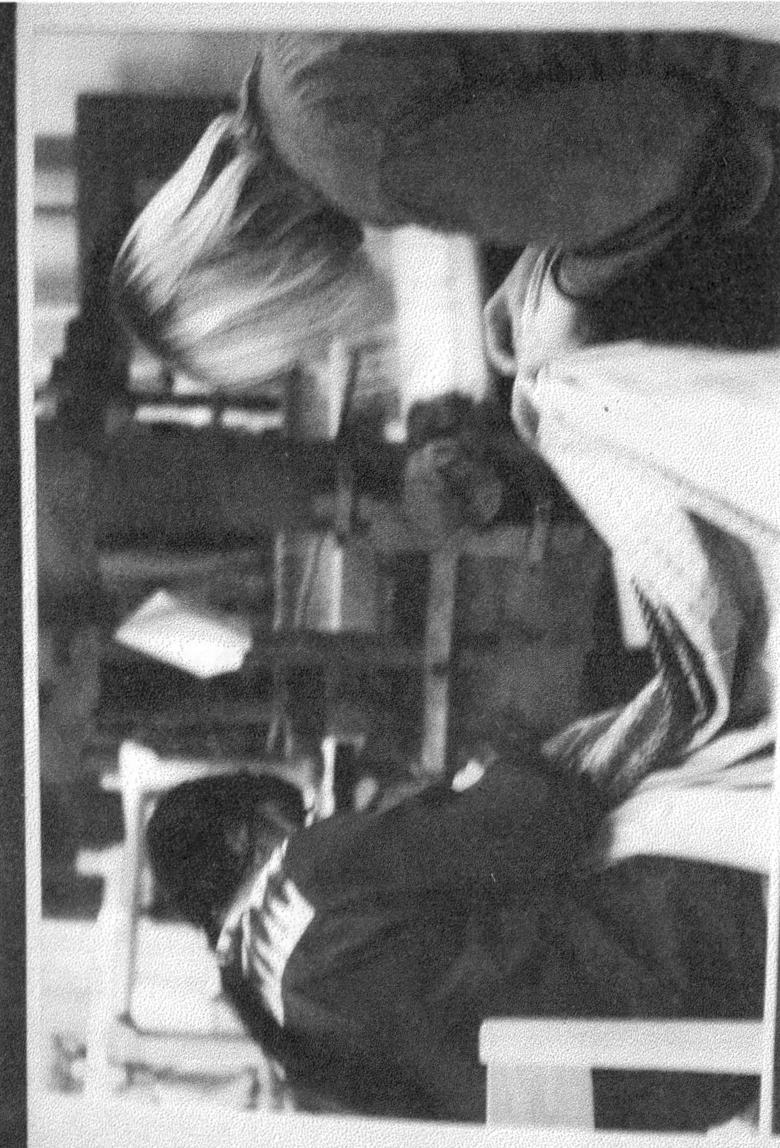

january 20

hold towel up to head
and obscure face.

action 2

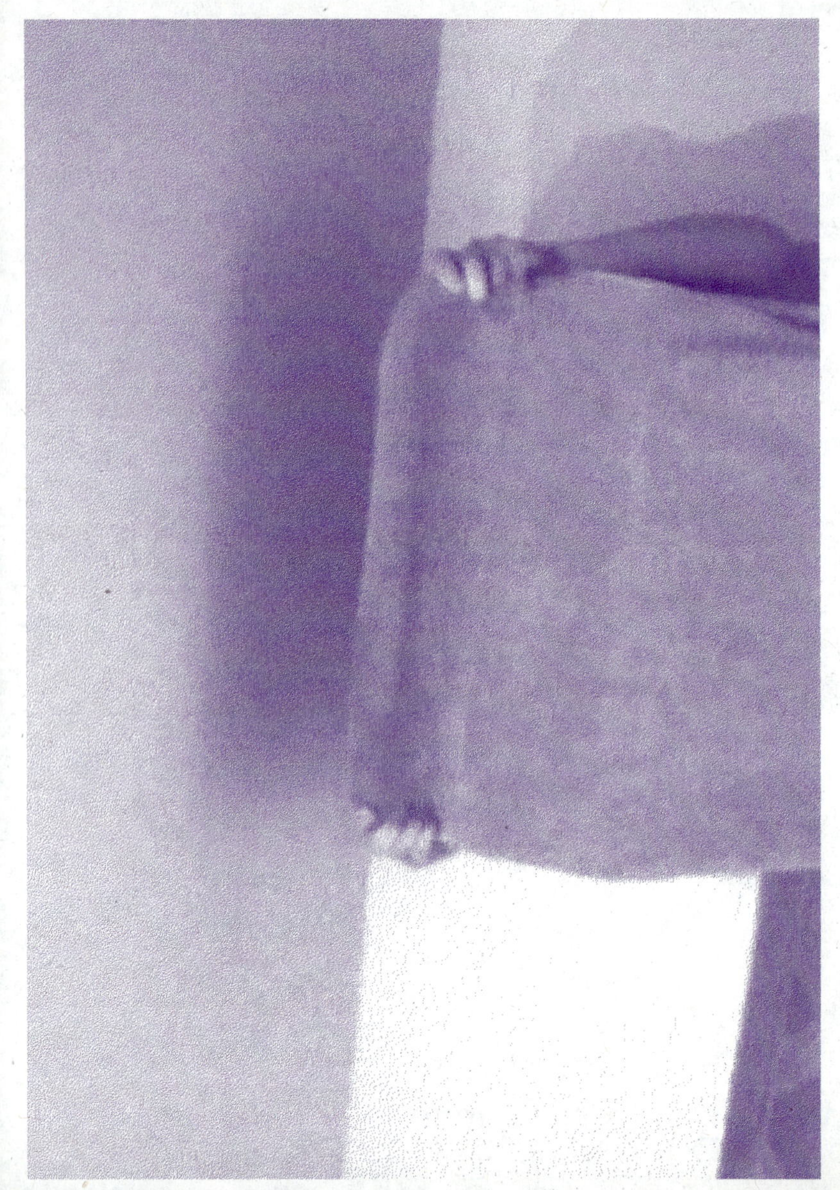

january 21

gravity drained water tank destined for attic level of autonomous household water system.

autonomous water supply

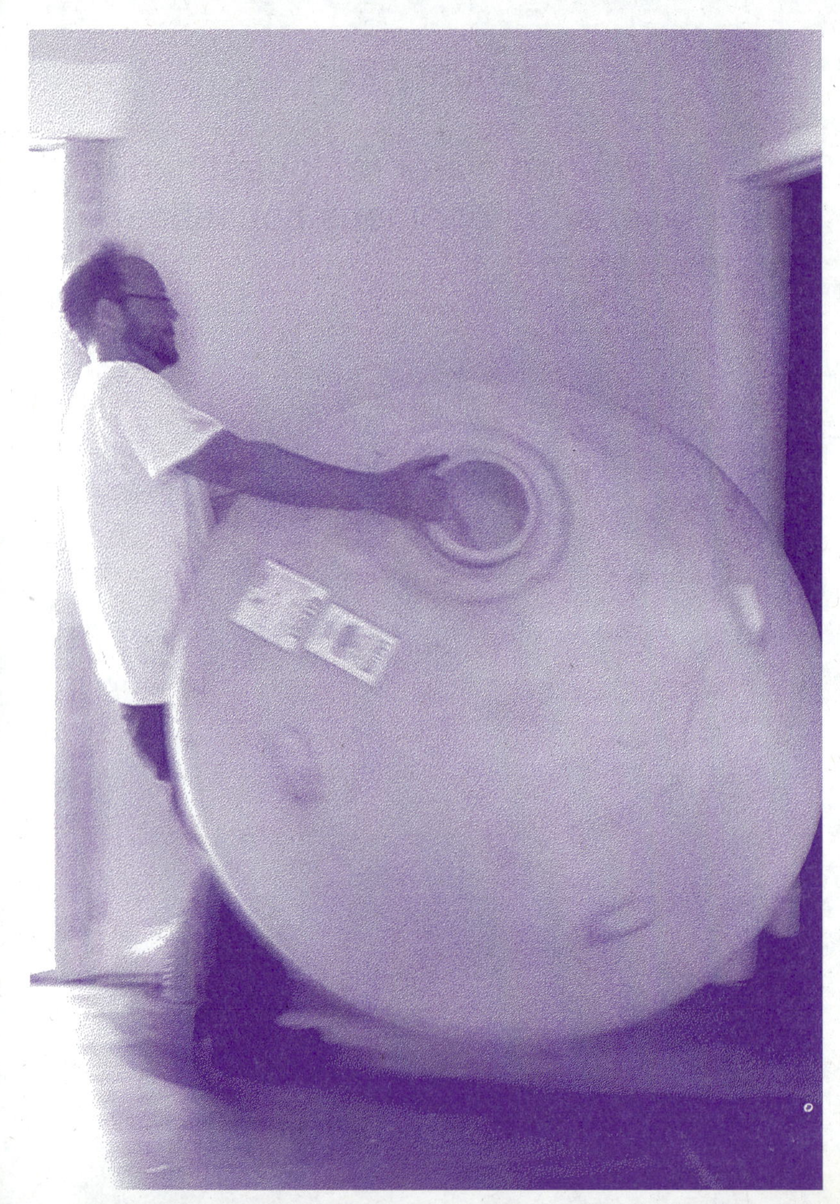

january 22

cultural workers move/migrate for
residencies, exhibitions, appointments,
teaching, internships, etc.

moving

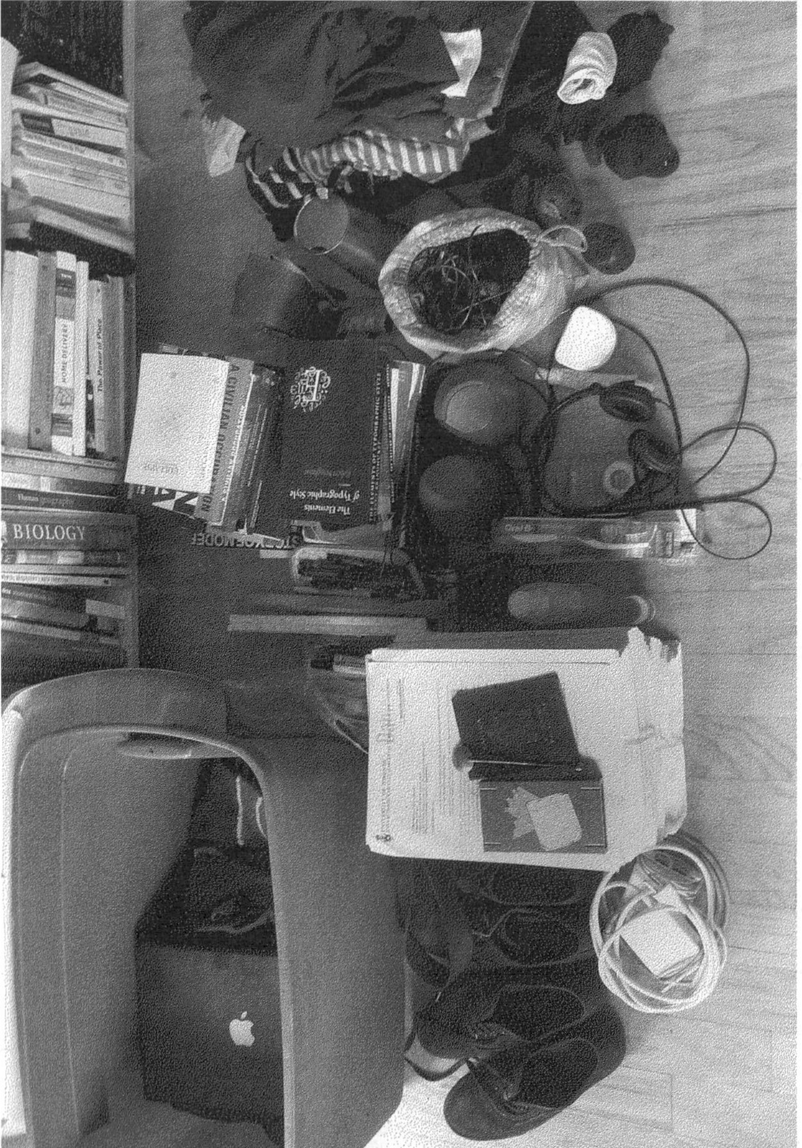

january 23

camp home—domestic exercise
and rehearsal.

stunts

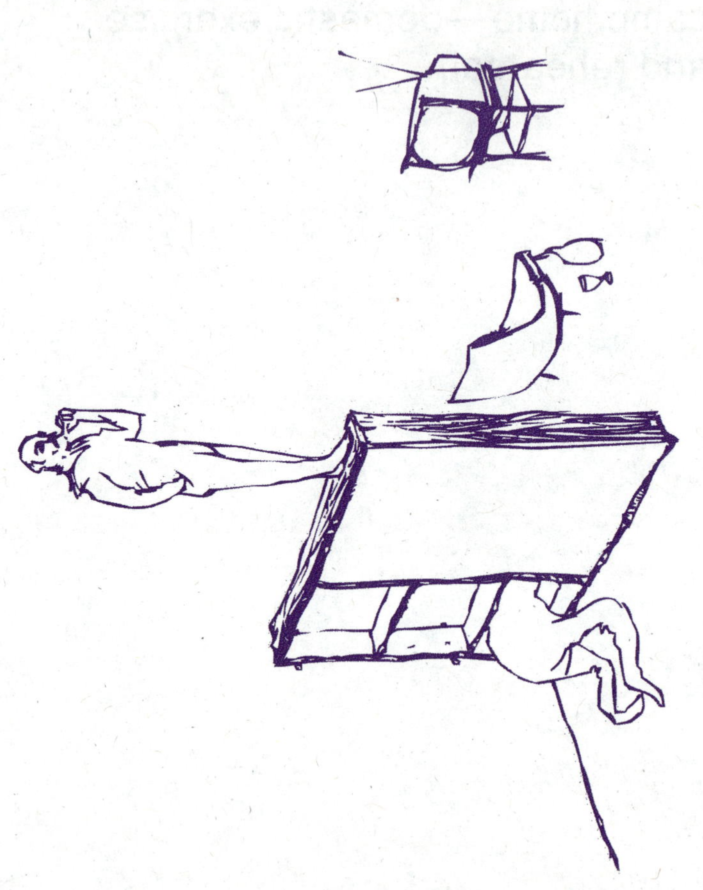

january 24

sometimes you need to connect
with earth to get inspired.

feeling inspired in portugal

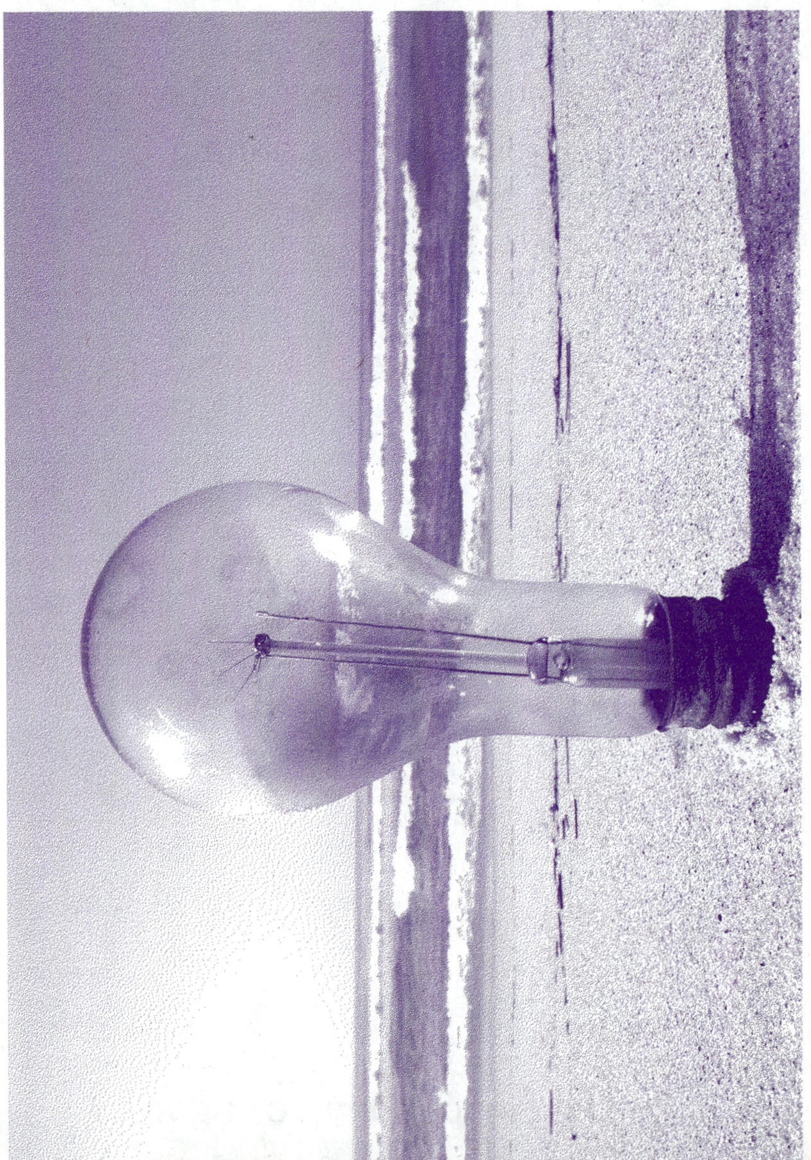

this is my father rowing a group of
children around, somewhere at a
dacha near minsk (belarus). when
i showed him this picture he said that
this was one of the things he liked
about living in a communist (socialist?)
country… that when the weekend
came you had complete freedom from
work… you weren't thinking about
it seven days a week, there were
moments to just let go.

boating for beginners

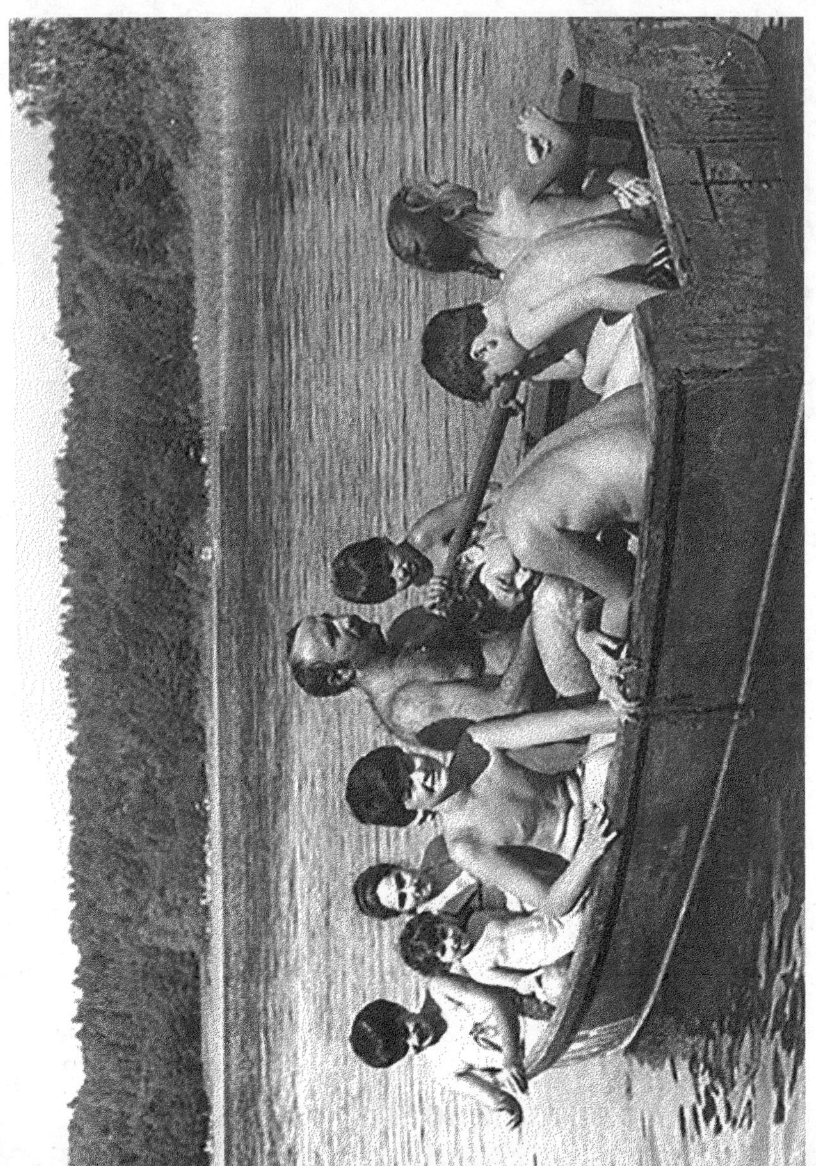

january 26

the freedom to be a slave

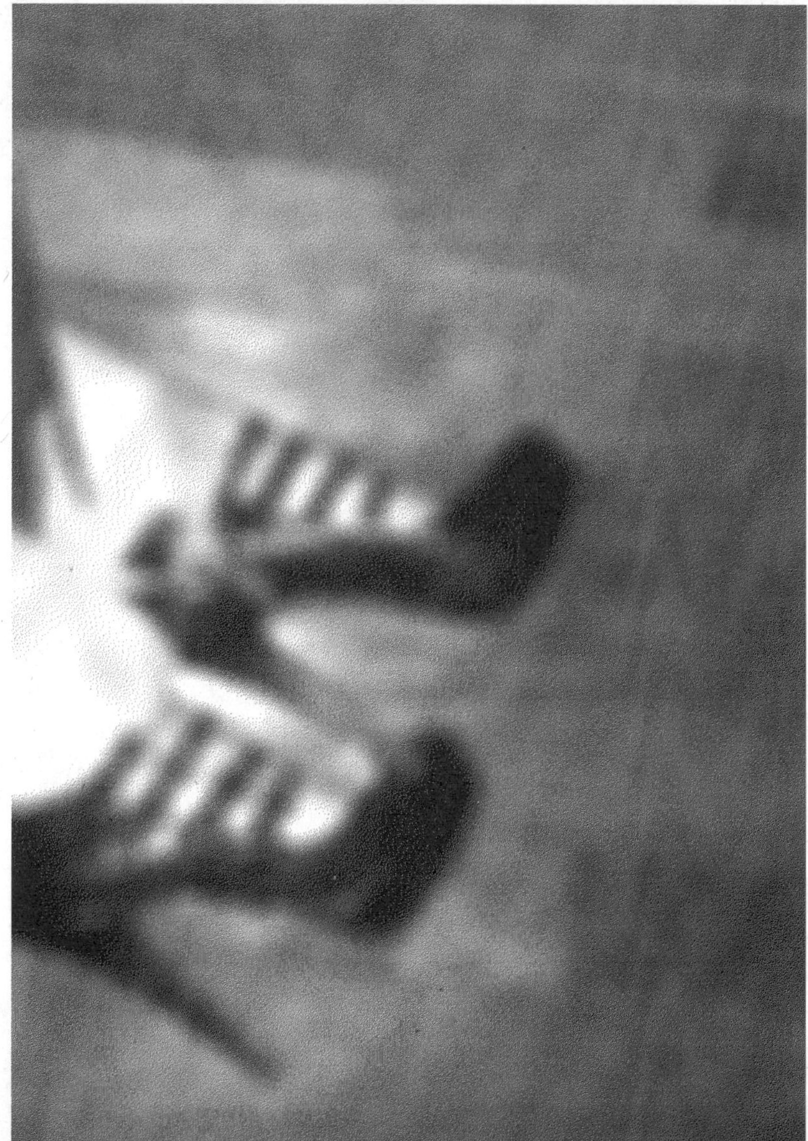

january 27

we bring in aid to save the lives of our
fellow domestic workers in destitution.
domestic workers in singapore are
still very vulnerable with no rights or
protection. we would like to highlight
the need to improve the working and
living conditions of migrant domestic
workers in singapore. domestic workers
are workers. they are not slaves.

domestic worker
can make a change

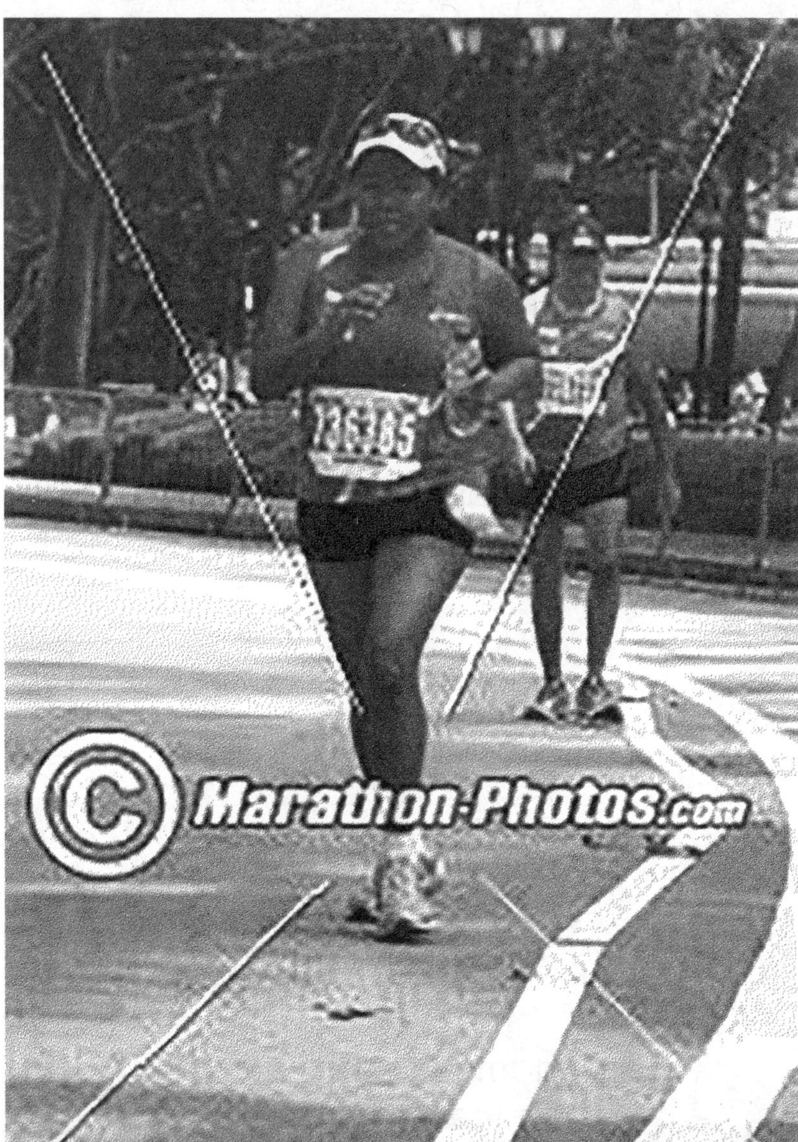

©Marathon-Photos.com

january 28

domestic labour in my mailbox.

looking for work

Hallo mijn naam is Valentina.
Ik ben op zoek naar 3 à 4 uur schoonmaakwerk per week.
Ik heb jarenlange ervaring en referenties (06-12355973) in deze buurt.
Ben jij serieus op zoek naar hulp in de huishouding?
Bel me dan na 18.00 uur op: 06-36304020

january 29

my mummy can do everything.

carme maria

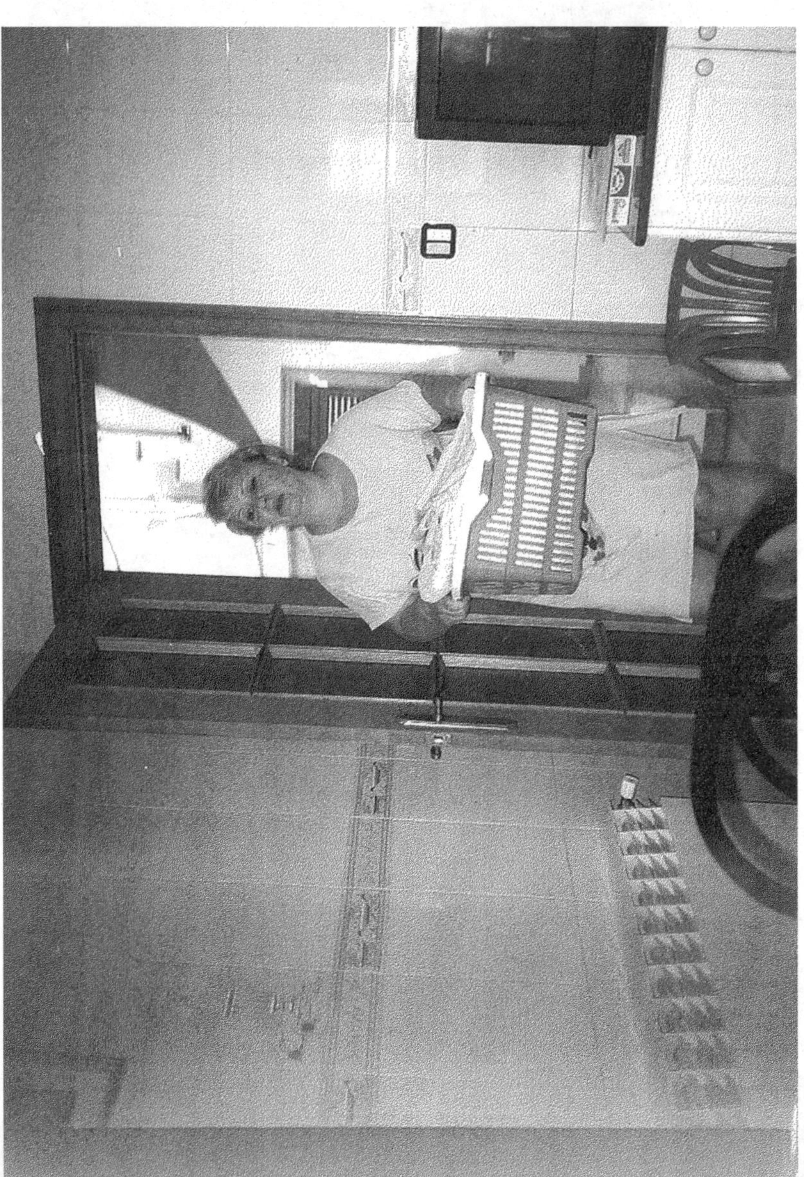

january 30

mixed storage management system.

inventory management

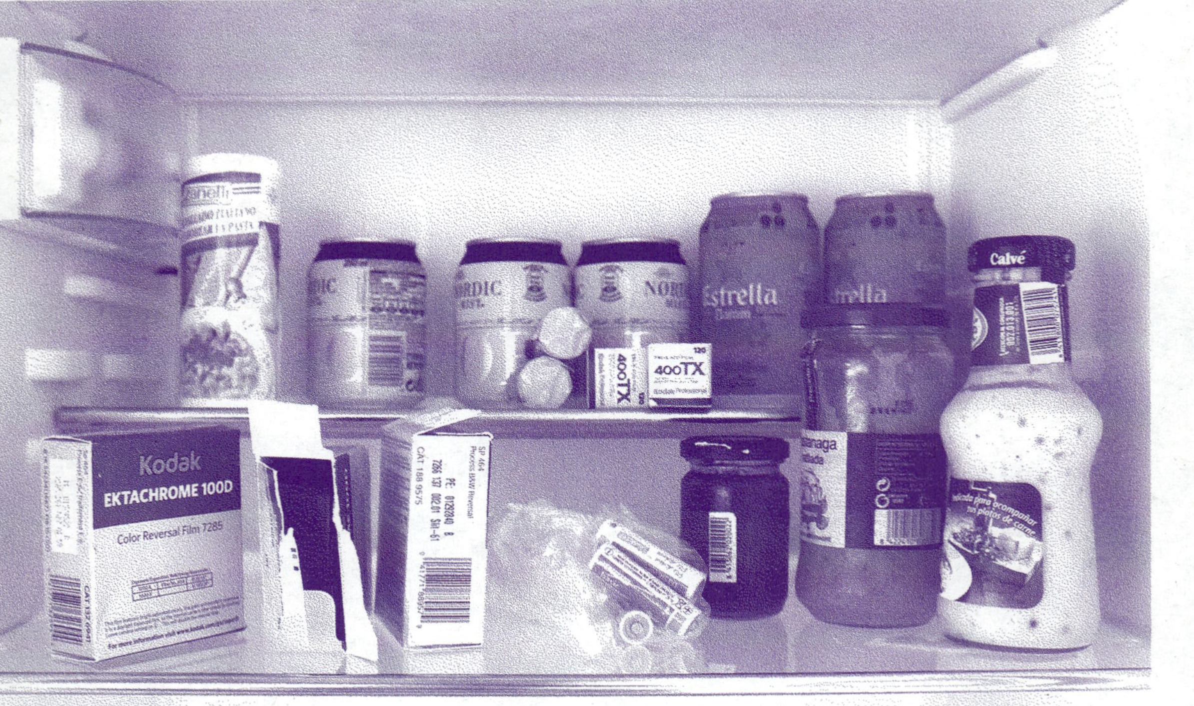

nanetti
NORDIC
NORDIC
NORDIC
estrella
estrella
Calvé
400TX
400TX
Kodak
EKTACHROME 100D
Color Reversal Film 7285
SP 464
Process B&W Reversal
PE: 01292840 B
7286 137 002.01 SM-61
CAT 188 9575
salida para acompañar
sus platos de carne

january 31

(home) work

office

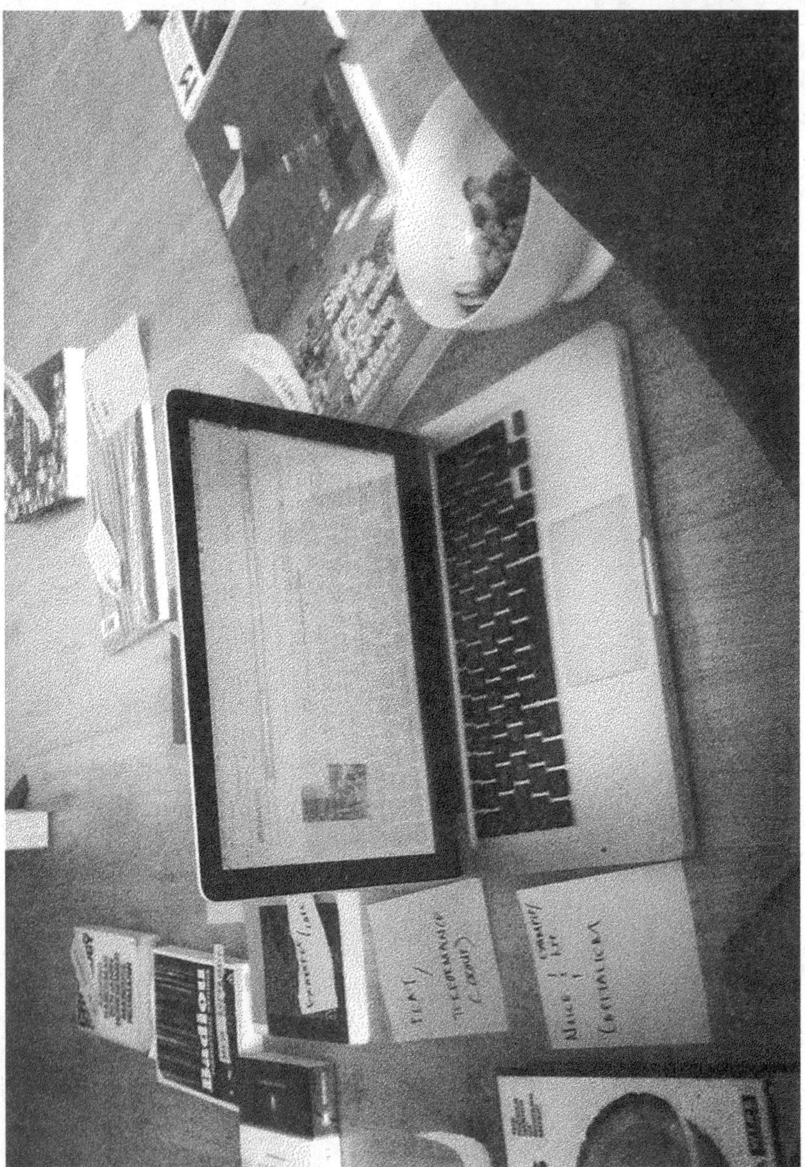

february 1

after party, delicious breakfast.

breakfast

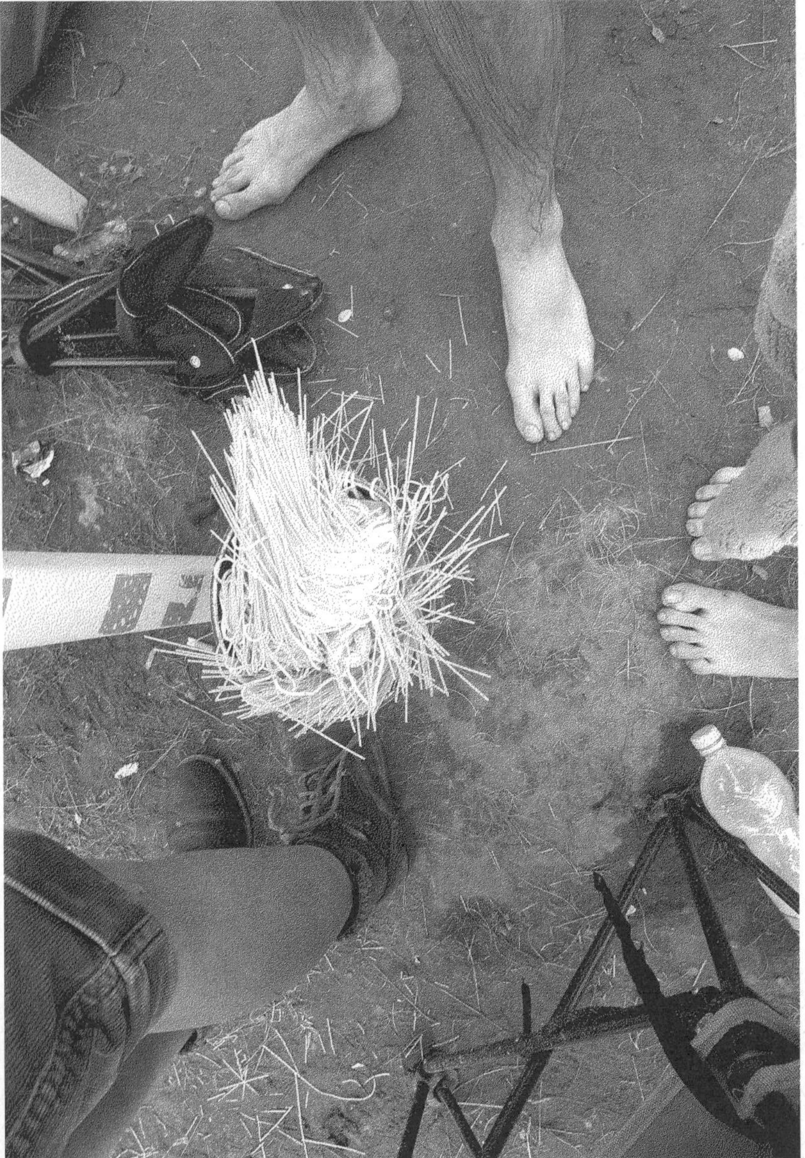

february 2

the studio sink, a filthy creature shared
by many, it cleans but never gets
cleaned.

dirty creature

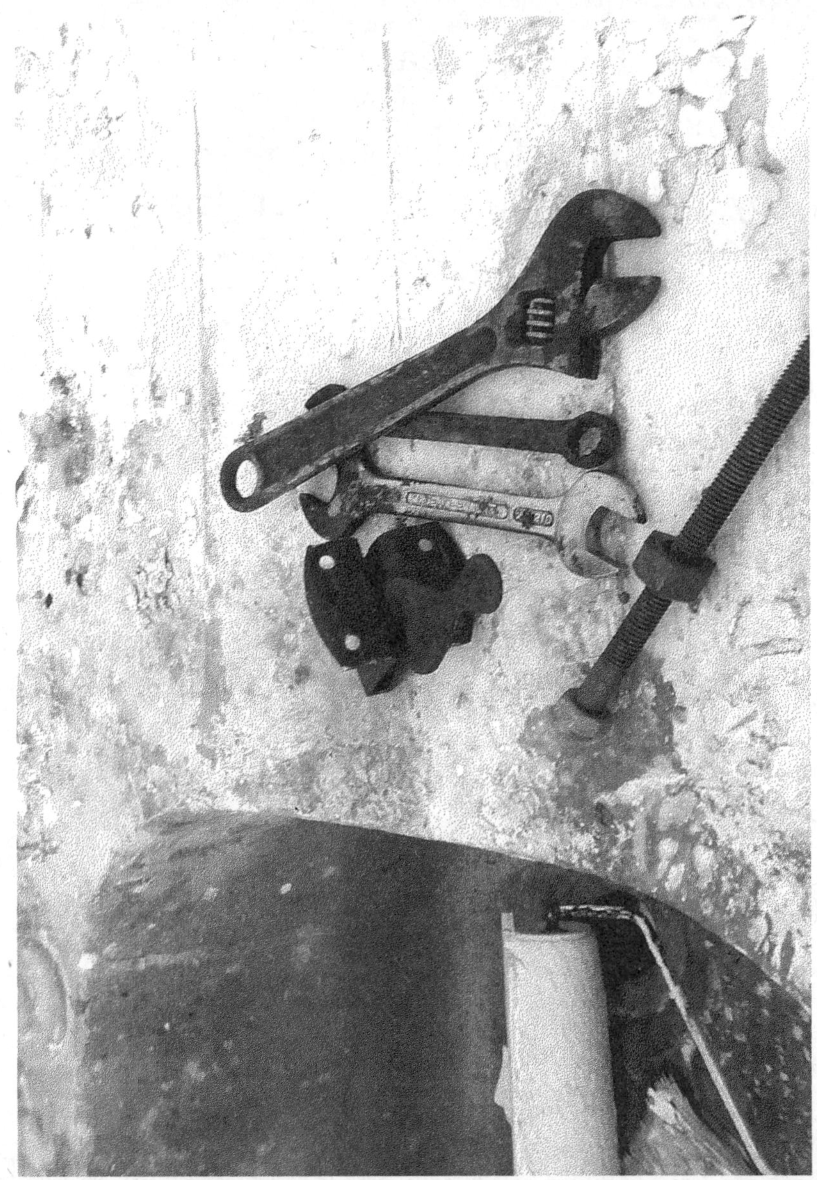

february 3

saturday night is my bedtime story
night with the big boys i'm taking care
of. photo taken in singapore.

big foot

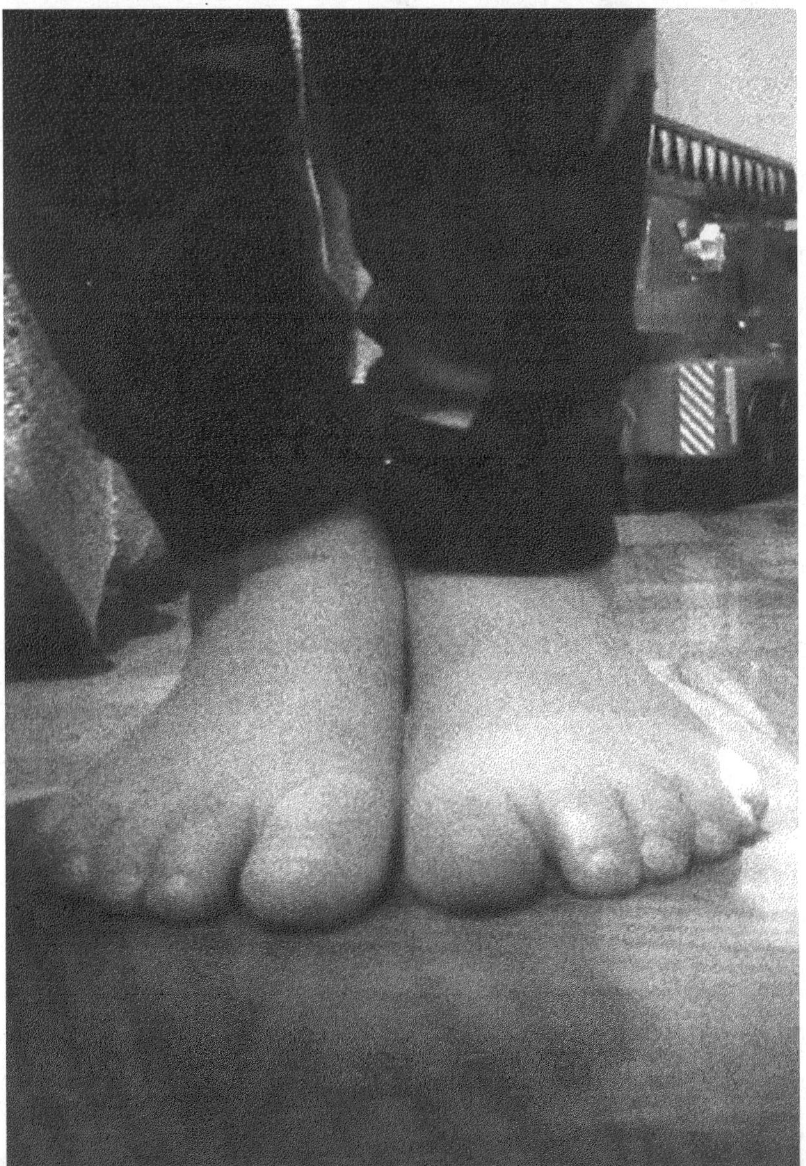

february 4

still from *tiempo real* [real time],
(2003), video, 43 min.

no experience required

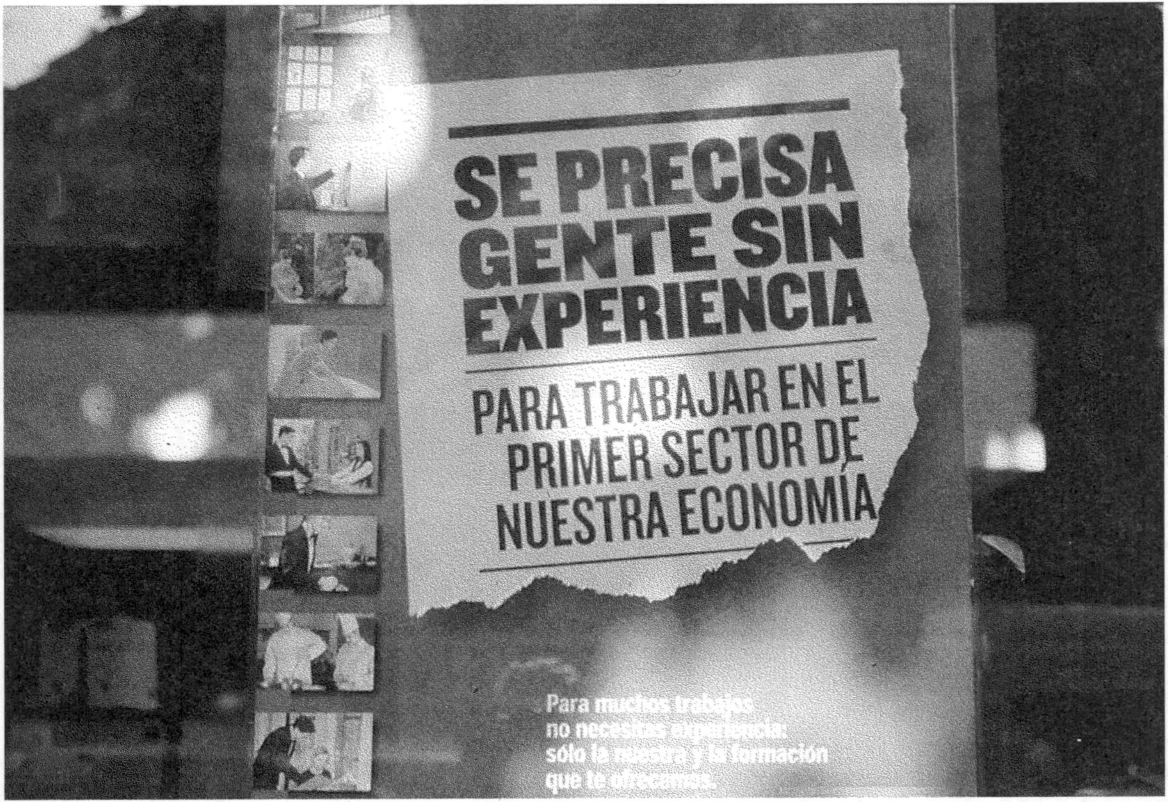

SE PRECISA GENTE SIN EXPERIENCIA
PARA TRABAJAR EN EL PRIMER SECTOR DE NUESTRA ECONOMÍA

february 5

during corpus christi procession,
women hang the best bedspread or
tablecloth from their balconies, clean
and perfectly ironed. photo taken
in castellón, 1993.

clean bedspreads

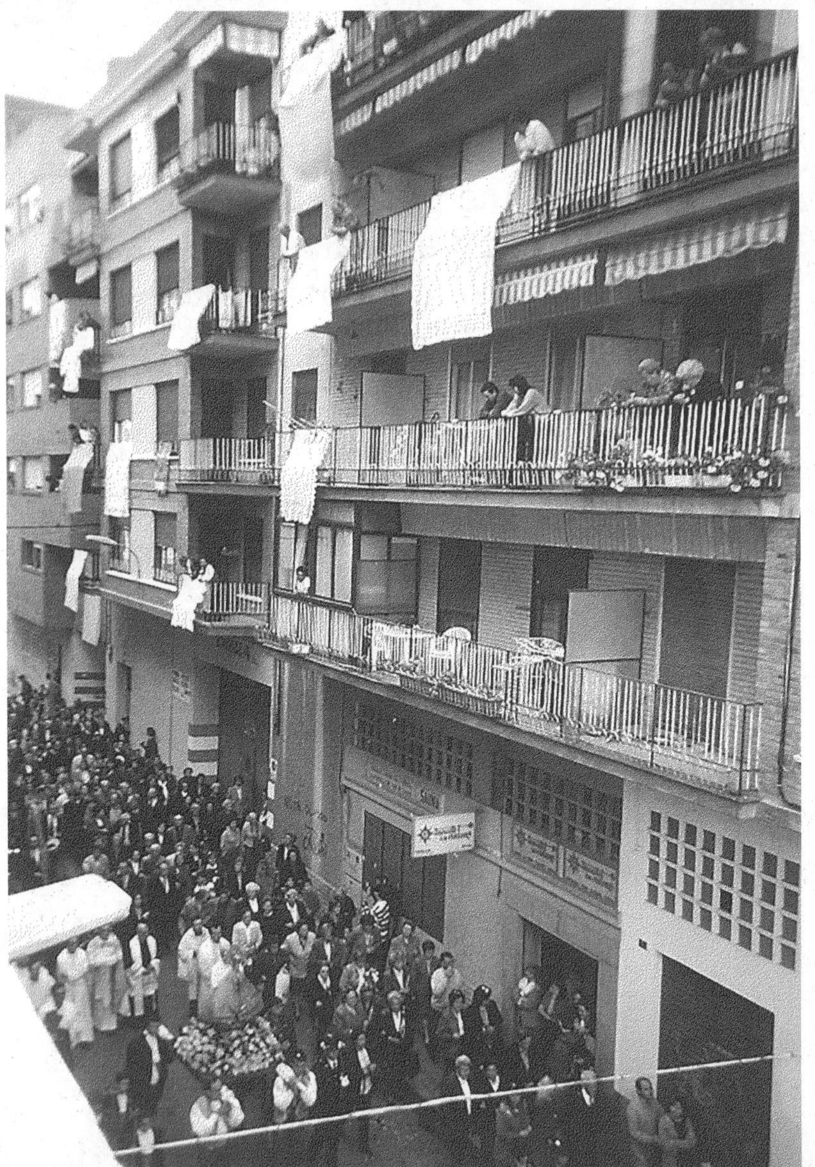

discarded tires used to grow potatoes vertically. each planting is a response to a situation of precarity for our friends, family, and community.

tire potato planters

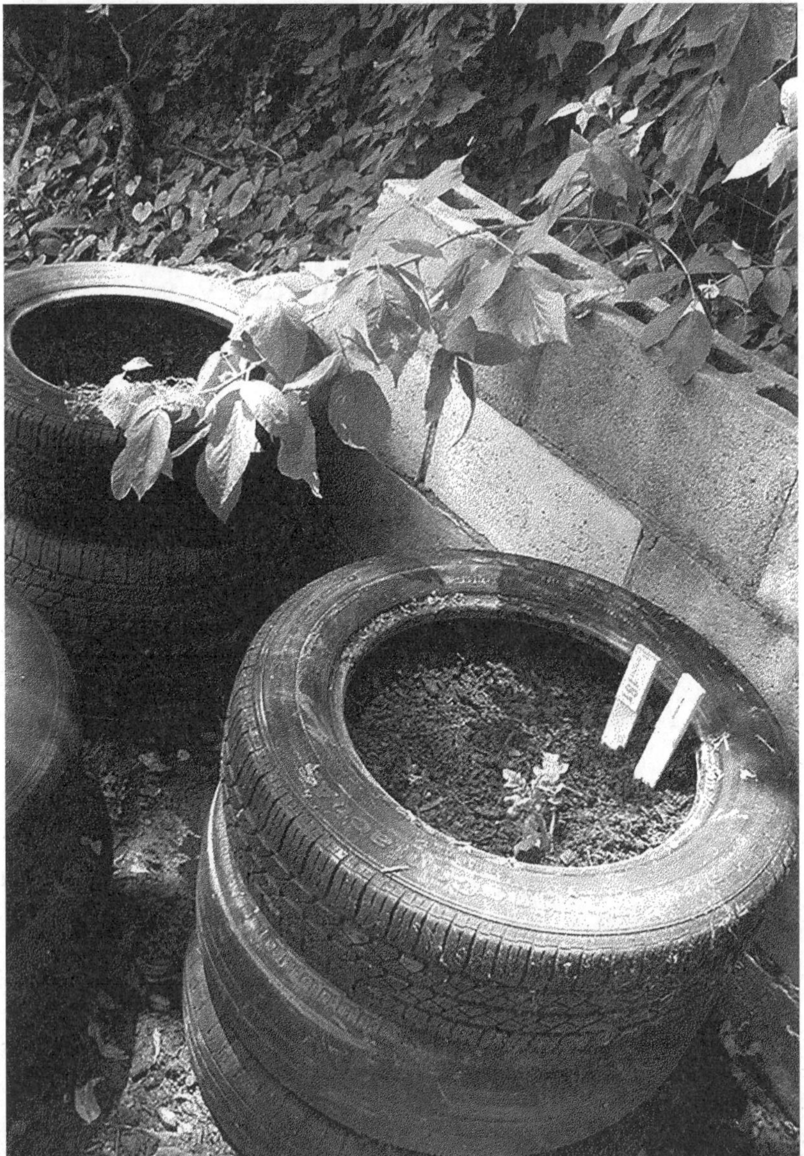

february 7

fisheye

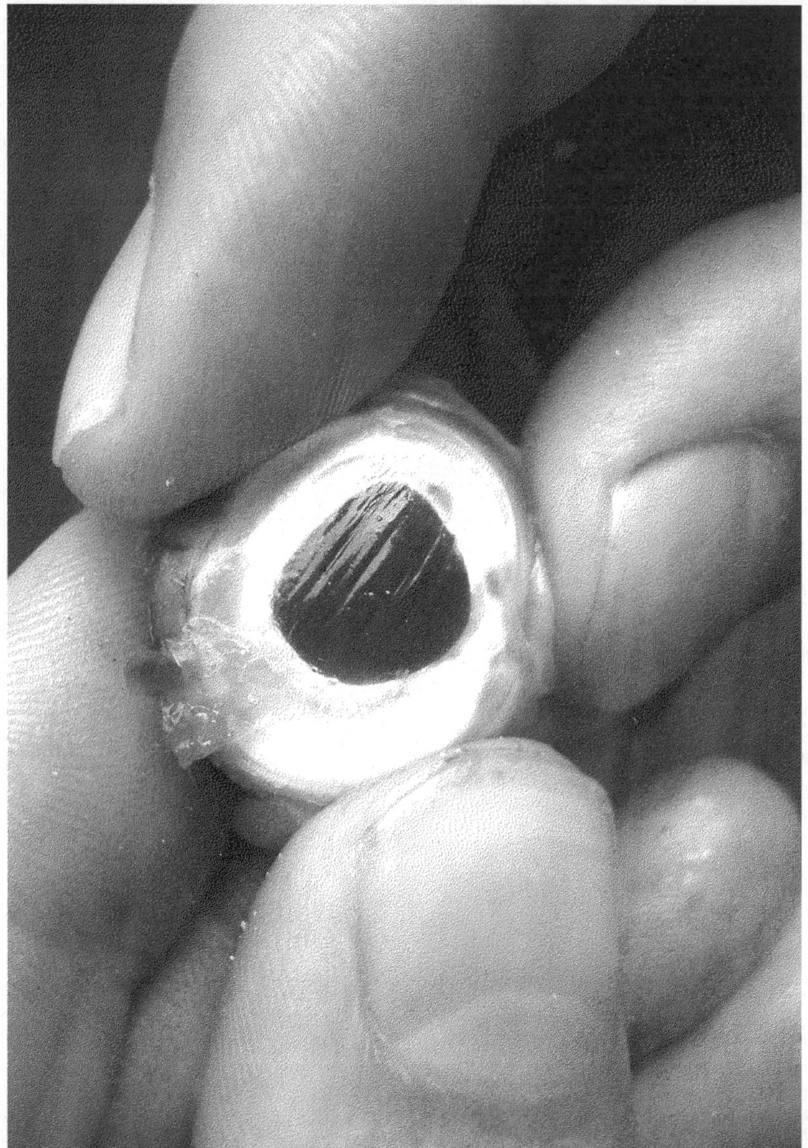

this woman in kabul sells magazines
in the street to make a bit of extra
money for their household. selling
these magazines is regarded as just
slightly more worthy than begging
or prostitution.

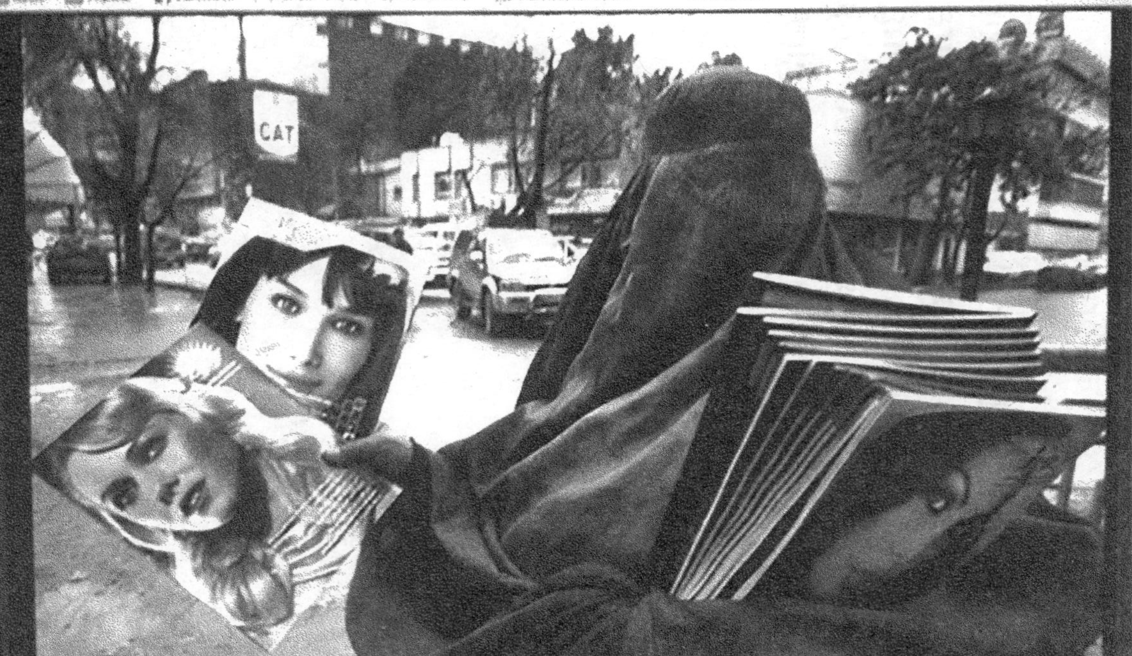
Chrome   File   Edit   View   History   Bookmarks   Window   Help
News   Popular   Facebook   Gmail   Yahoo Mail   Blackboard
CAT

february 9

pre-wash

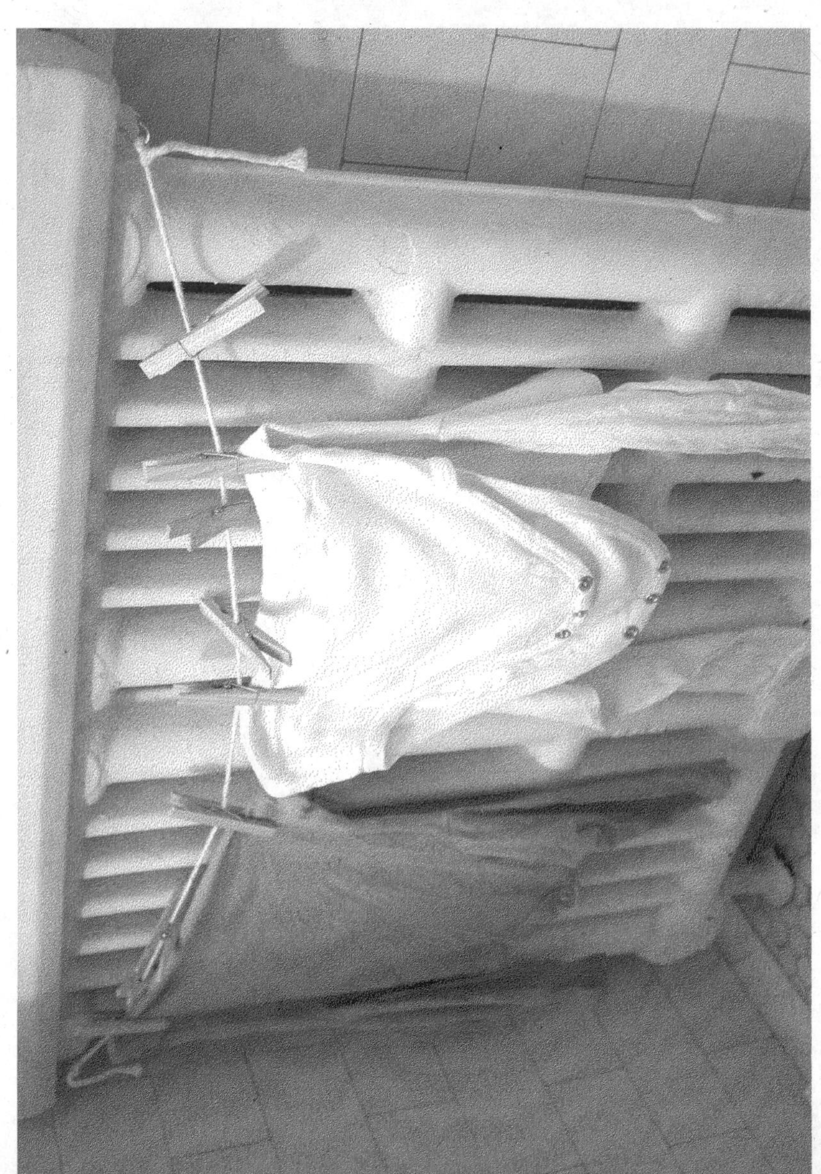

february 10

wall street needs a real clean up.

clean up wall street!

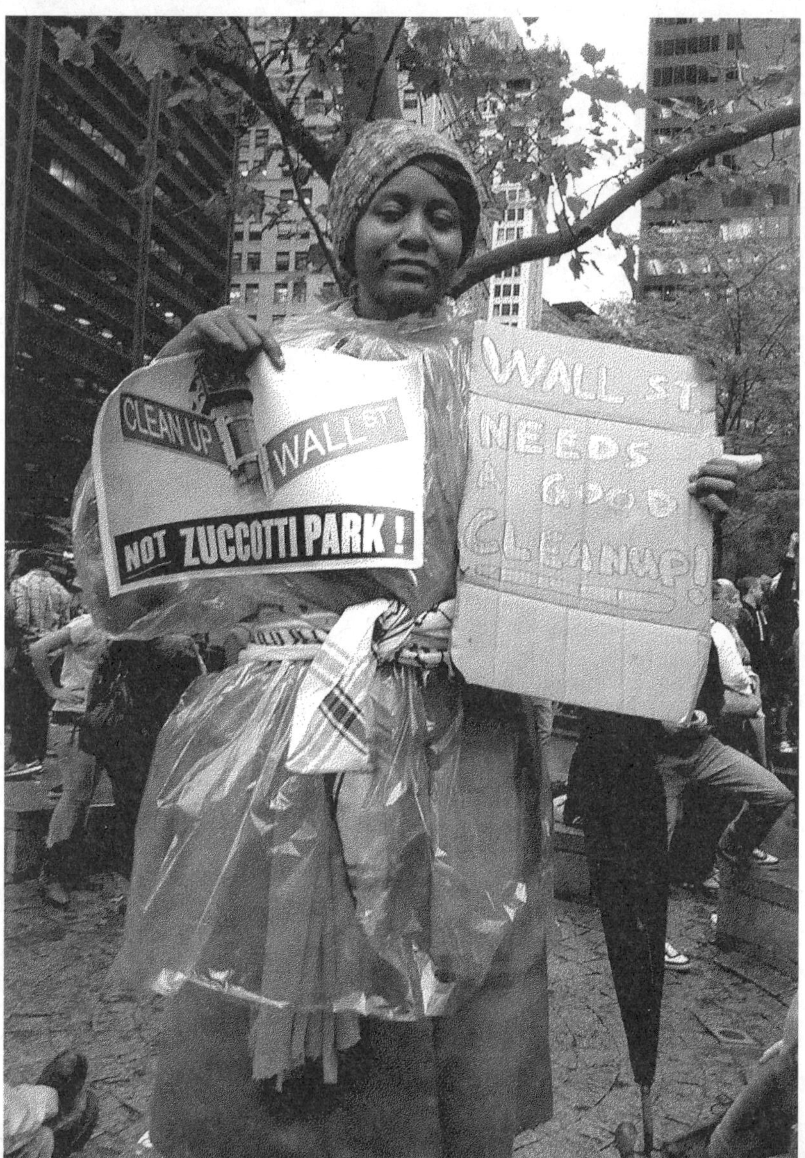

CLEAN UP WALL ST NOT ZUCCOTTI PARK !
WALL ST NEEDS A GOOD CLEANUP

february 11

my friend's place in berlin. to take
a bath you need to pull out the tub
from underneath the kitchen sink.

bath-time

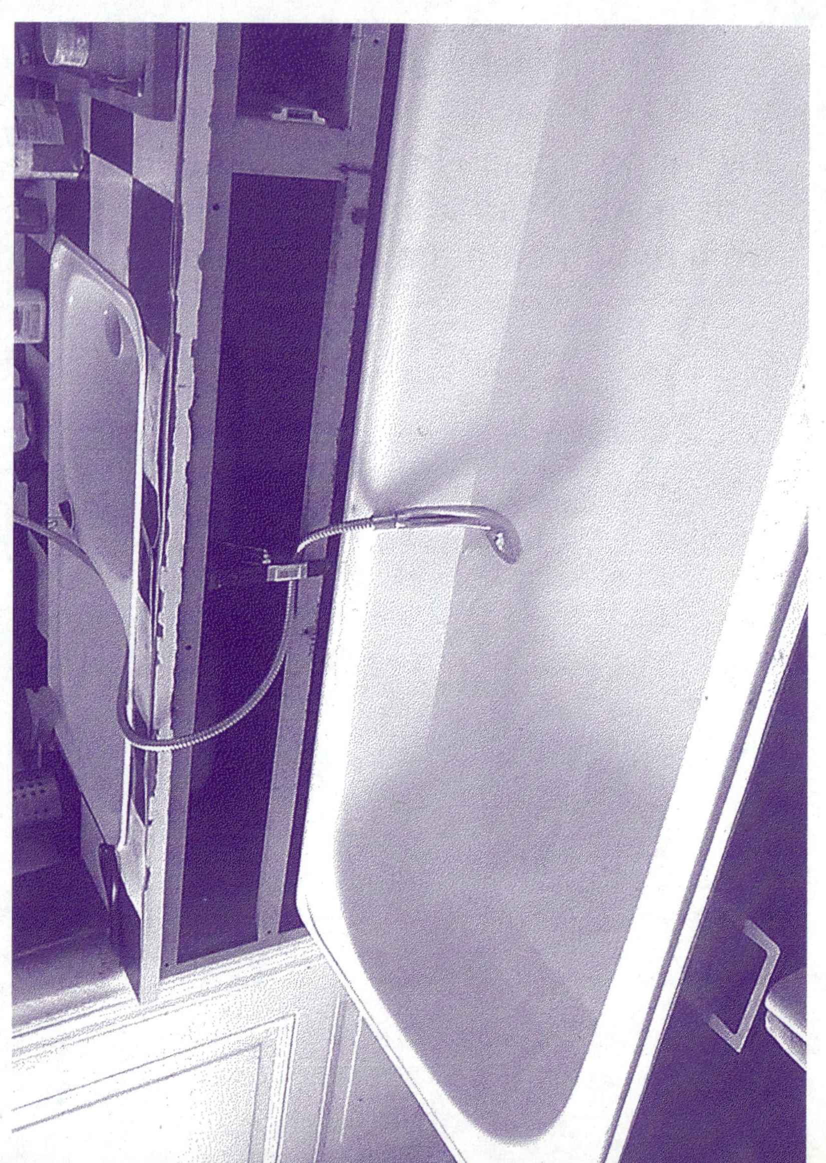

february 12

washing adventures.

priscilla queen of the desert

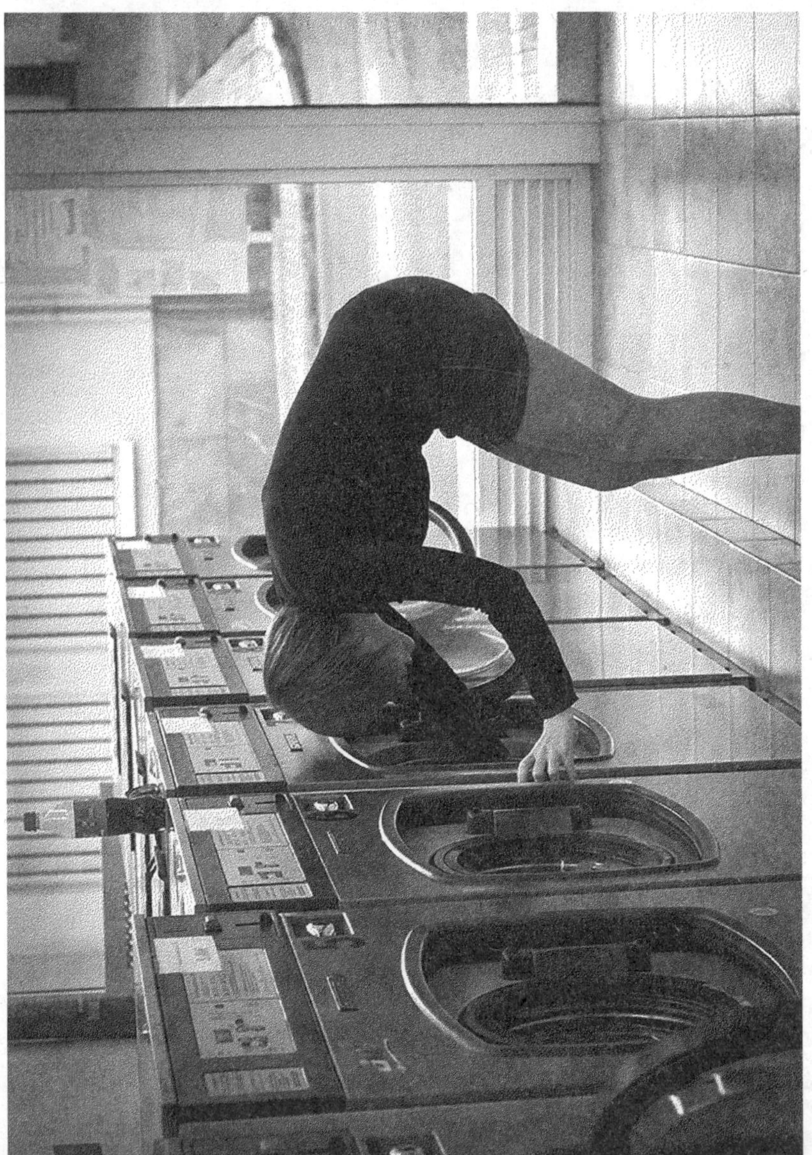

february 13

book found about domestic workers.

a stranger in the house

A

Stranger in The House

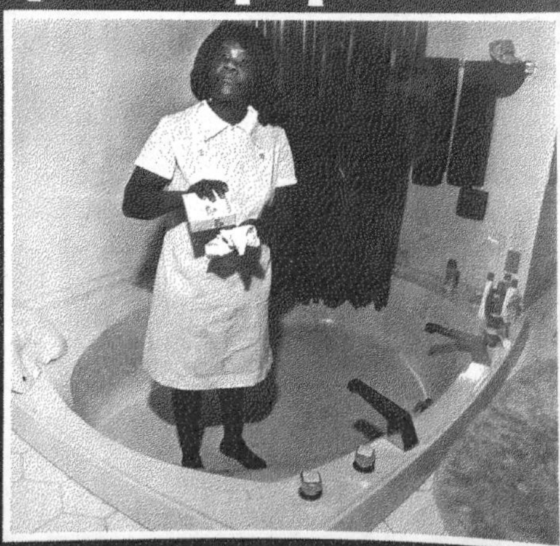

Robert Hamburger/Susan Fowler-Gallagher

february 14

i don't know who you are but your
words made me stop. i hope you'll find
what you need.

i need

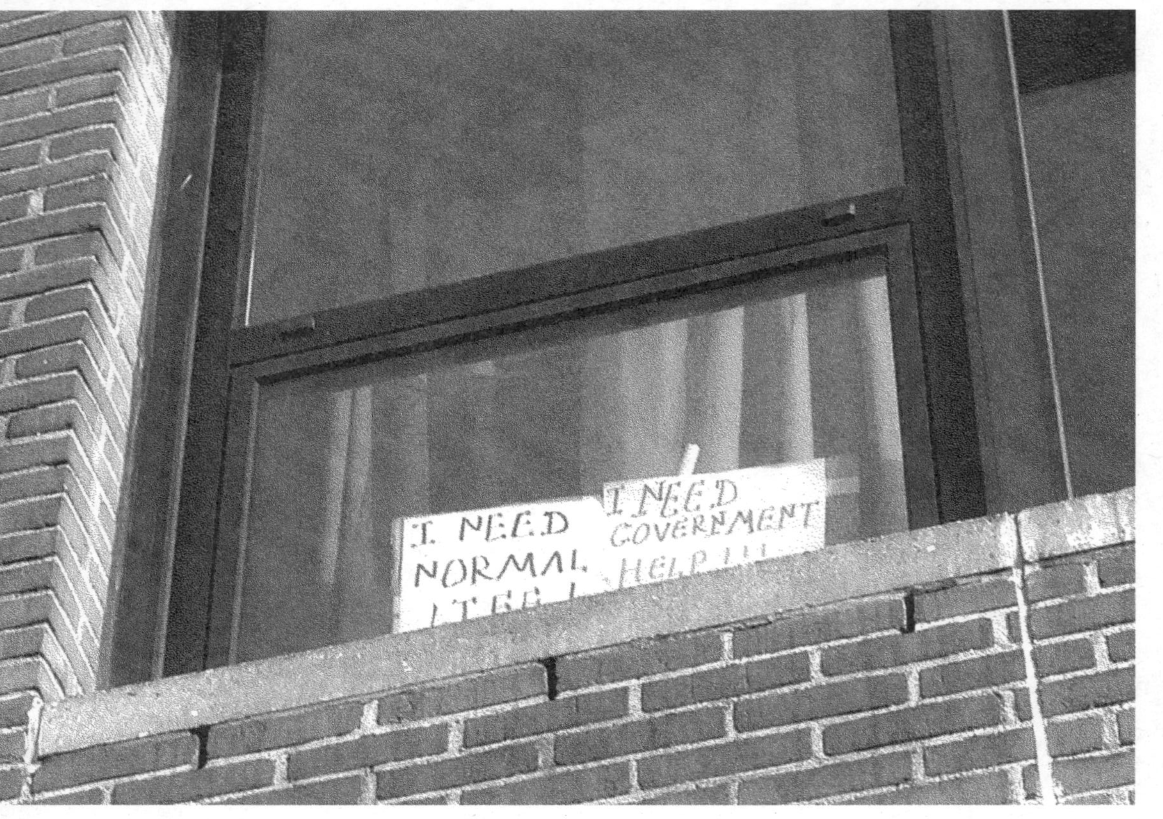
I NEED
NORMAL
I FEEL

I NEED
GOVERNMENT
HELP!!!

february 15

every morning my dolphin calf gets
me my newspaper. i give her hugs
in return.

i want to be your dog

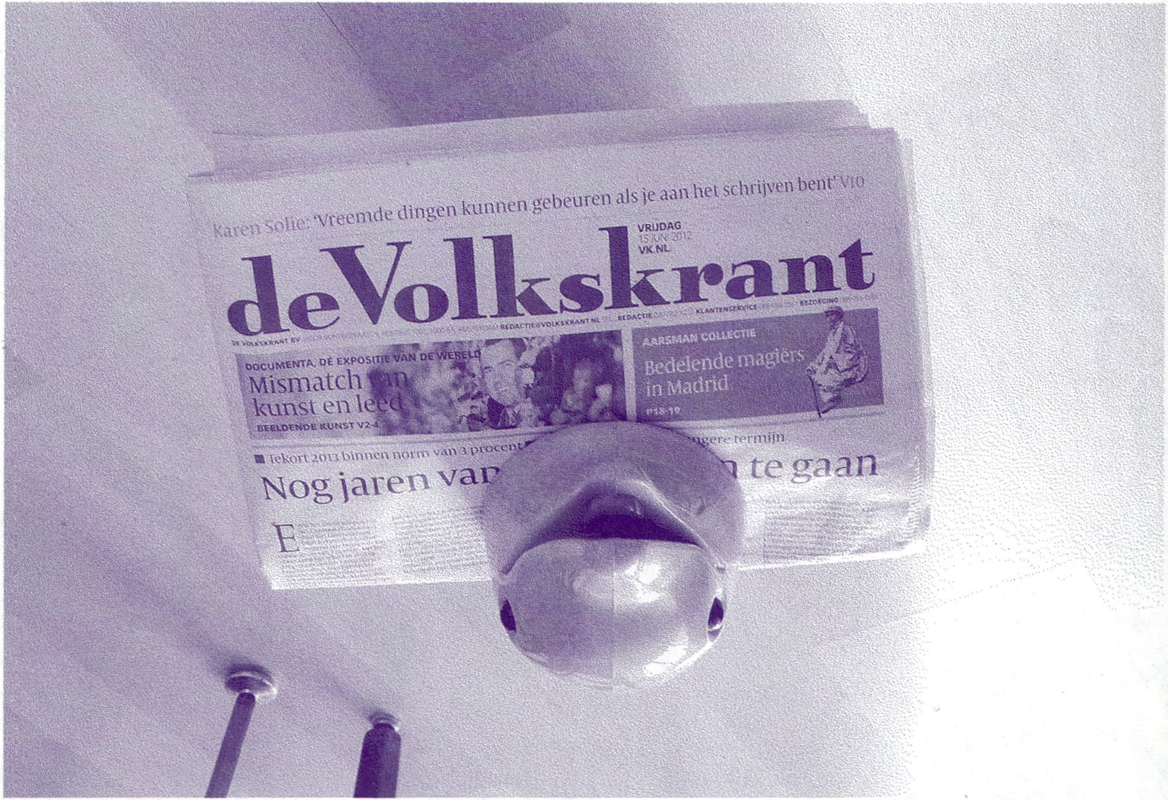

Karen Solie: 'Vreemde dingen kunnen gebeuren als je aan het schrijven bent' V10

deVolkskrant

VRIJDAG
15 JUNI 2012
VK.NL

DOCUMENTA, DE EXPOSITIE VAN DE WERELD

Mismatch van kunst en leed

BEELDENDE KUNST V2-4

AARSMAN COLLECTIE

Bedelende magiërs in Madrid

V18-19

■ Tekort 2013 binnen norm van 3 procent

Nog jaren van ... te gaan

E

february 16

last hour in gouesnou.

bad tactic

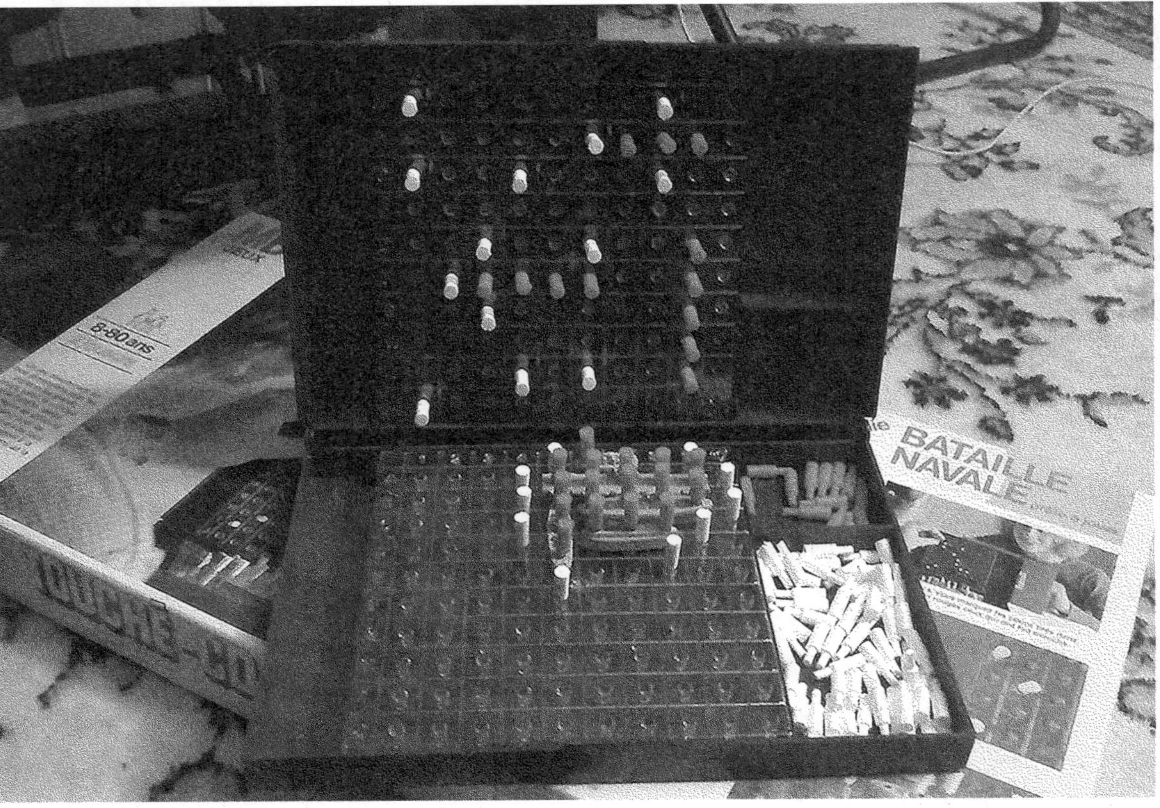

BATAILLE
NAVALE
8-80 ans

february 17

sending things home for our family
in philippines.

sending box home

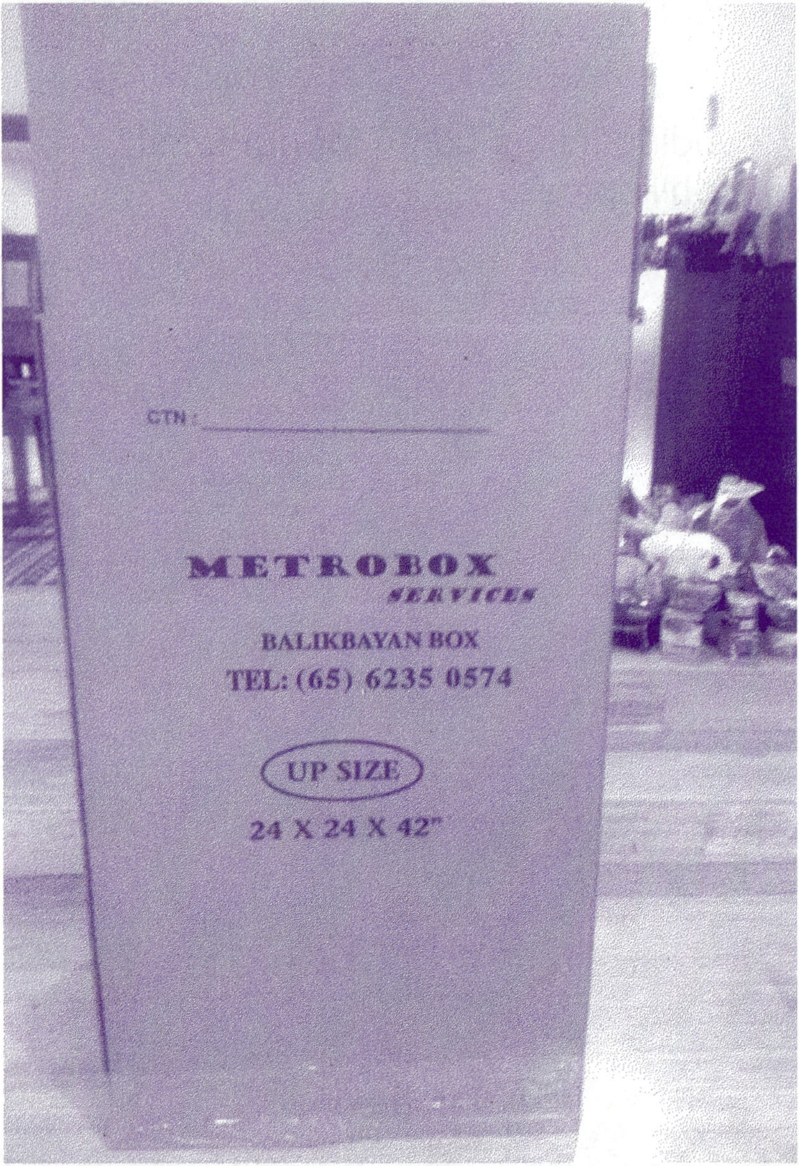

CTN :
METROBOX
SERVICES
BALIKBAYAN BOX
TEL: (65) 6235 0574
UP SIZE
24 X 24 X 42"

february 18

"bears are kept and memories are framed." as we leave our own children and our own country in exchange for money and job and a greener pasture, we missed the many many moments we shared with them. this is the high cost of migration.

frames and bears

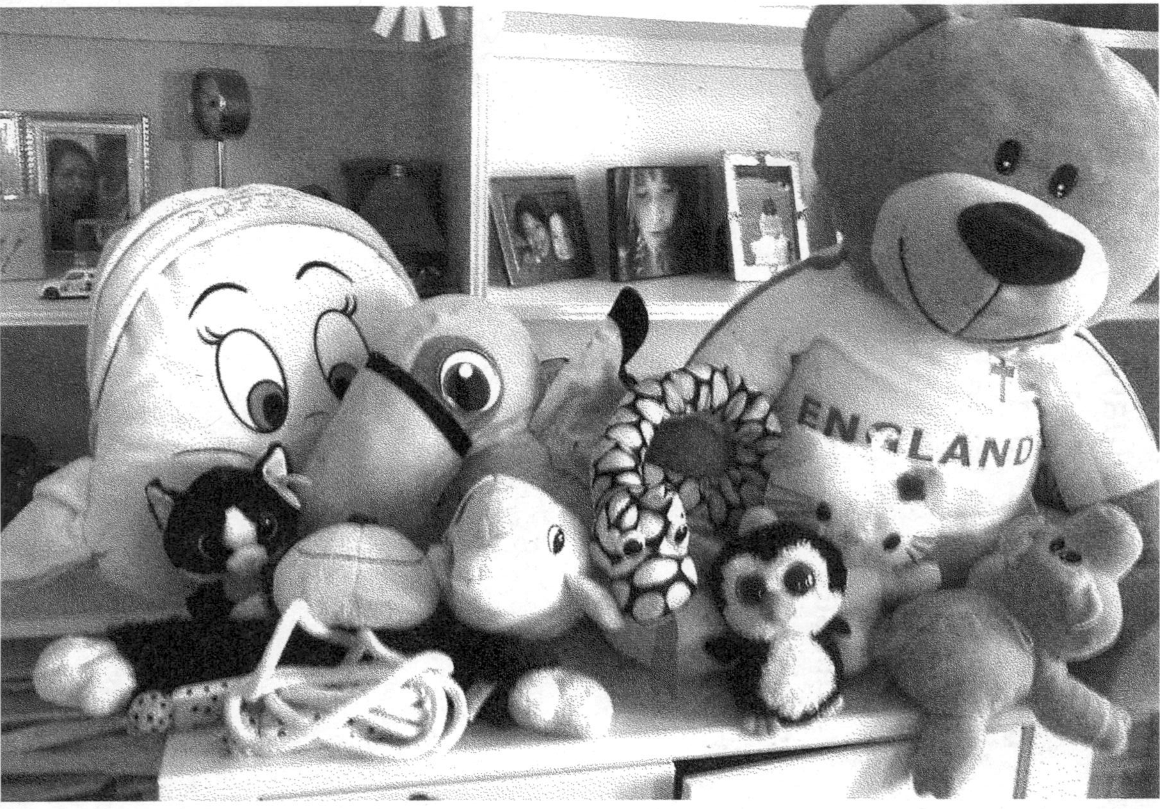
ENGLAND

still from *tiempo real* [real time],
(2003), video, 43 min.

masculine/feminine

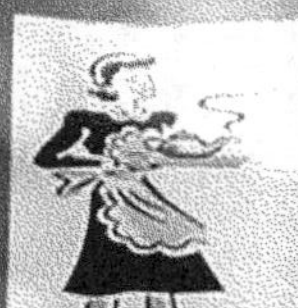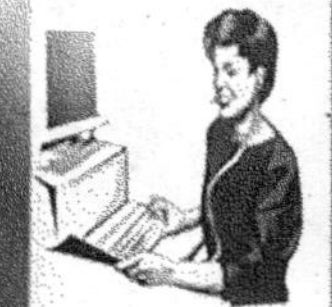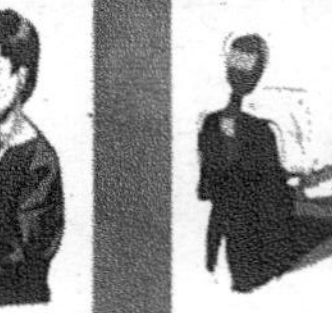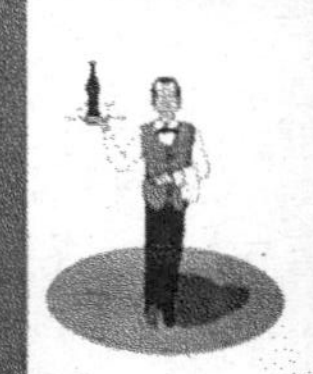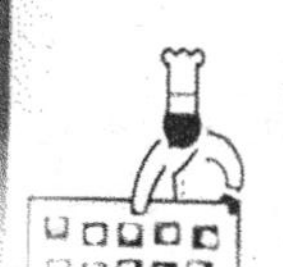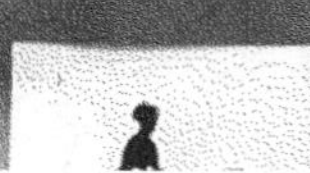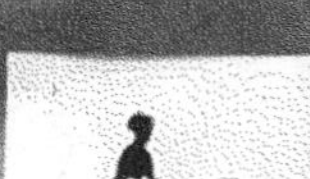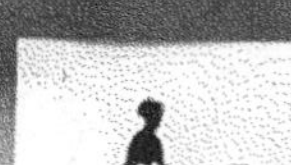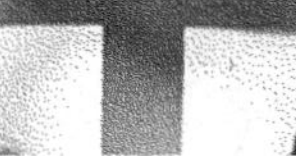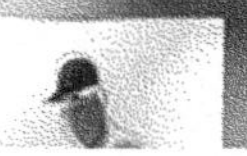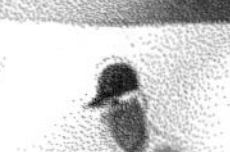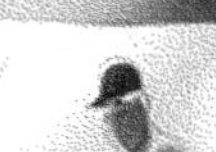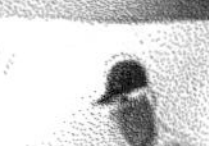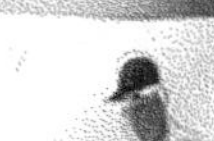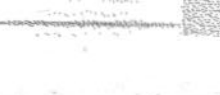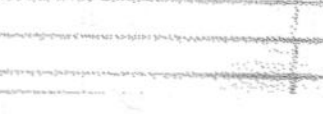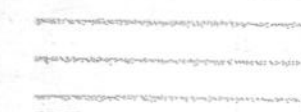

Ofertas de empleo

february 20

photo taken in vilafamés, 1974.

washing place

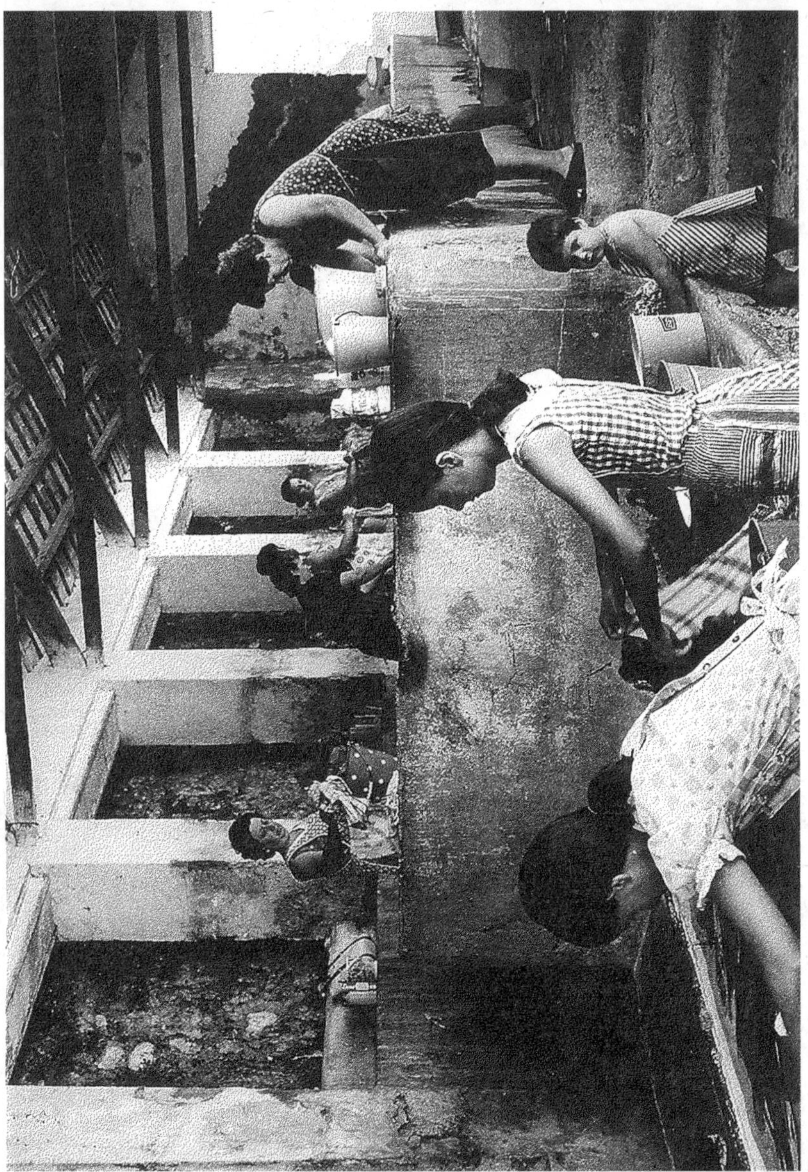

february 21

thursday, 23:53, calculating the value
of your month.

domestic finance

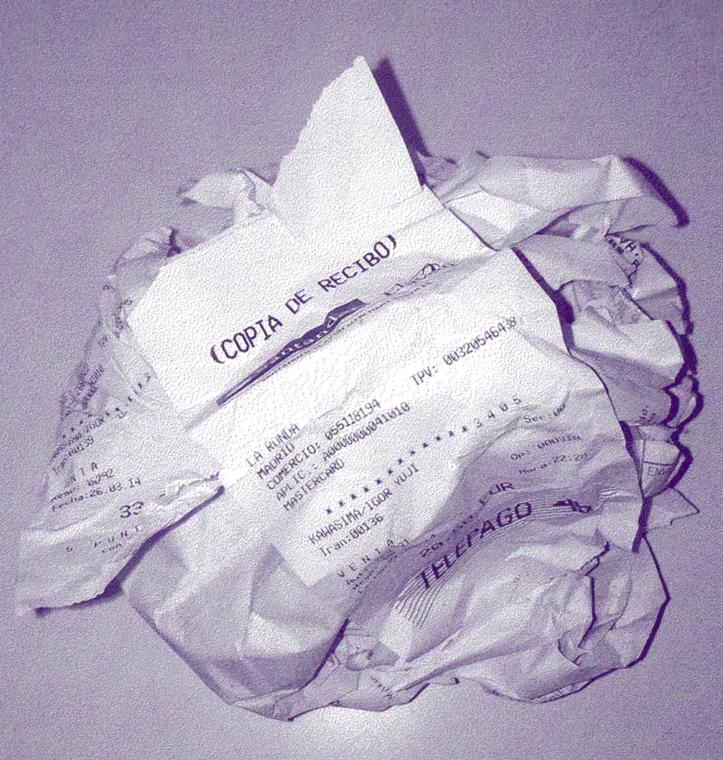
(COPIA DE RECIBO)
TPV: 00320546438
LA RUNIA
MADRID
COMERCIO: 0551/8194
APLIC.: A0000000041010
MASTERCARD
KAWASIMA/IGOR YUJI
Tran:00136
TELEPAGO
Fecha:26.03.14

february 22

**post-fordism, post-industrial, global
tour, institutionalized.**

quietly and too politely

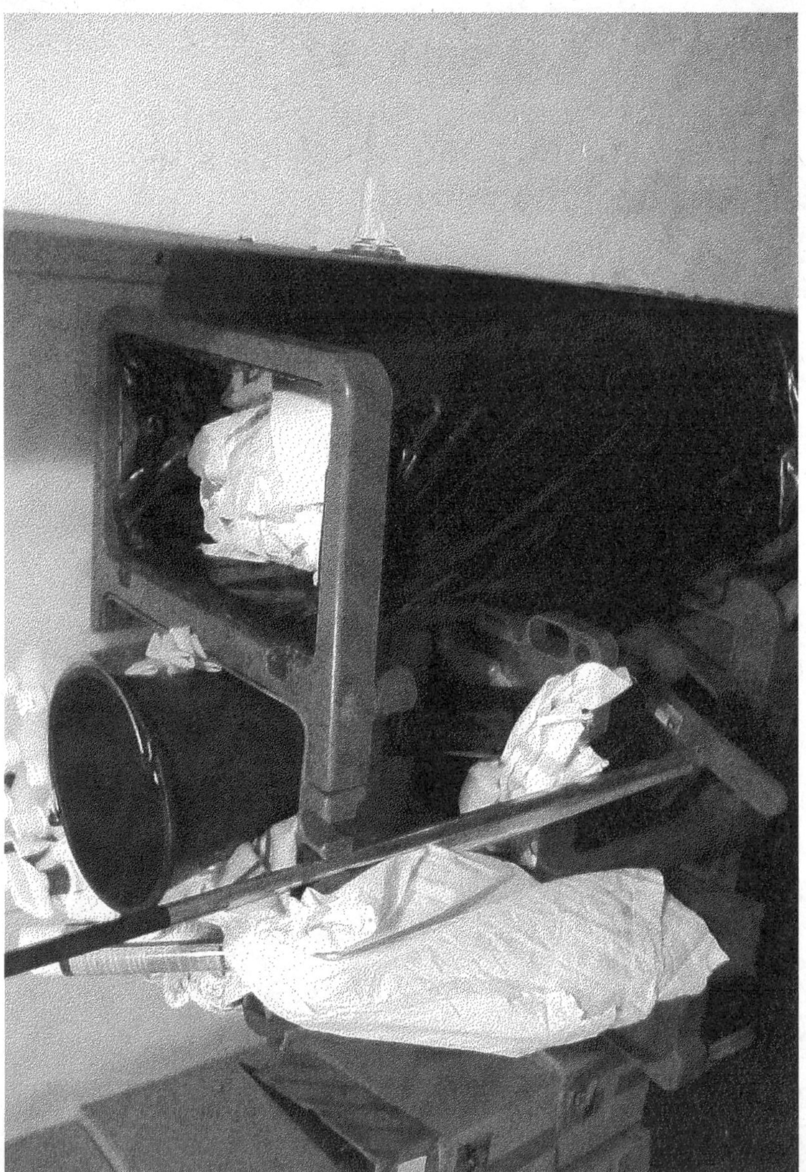

grandma on her way to the supermarket. this daily routine is keeping
her life busy.

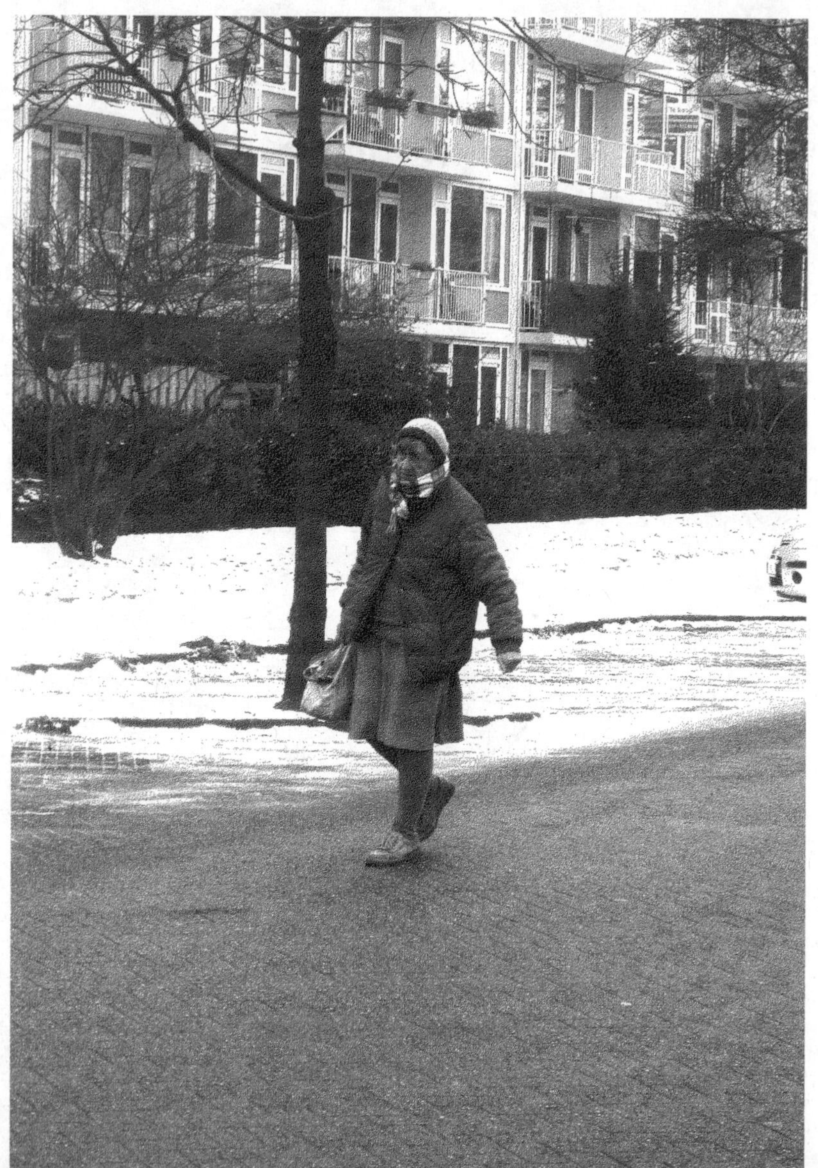

february 24

working at 00:00.

00:00

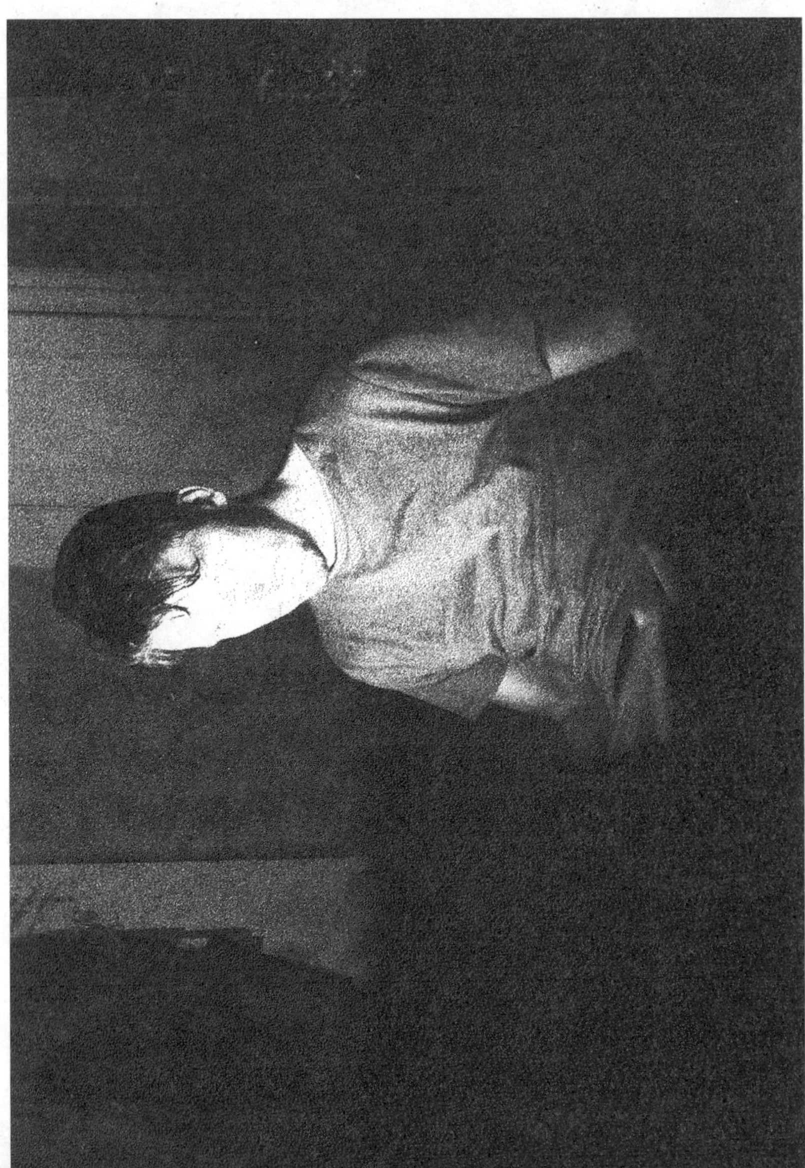

february 25

unexpected situations

LiFF
Rooseindsestraat 37B
5705 BP Helmond
Nederland

Sabine Ruitenbeek
Rijnstraat 51-2
1078PZ Amsterdam

22 november 2010, Amsterdam

Onderwerp: Safe room.

Geachte Mevrouw/Mijnheer,

Op uw website heb ik gelezen dat LIFF is gespecialiseerd in het vinden van hulpmiddelen voor allerlei
(on)verwachte ongewenste situaties. Dit spreekt mij zeer aan.

Ik ben mij op dit moment aan het oriënteren op een Safe room en wil u graag wat vragen stellen.
Uit de informatie op uw website begrijp ik dat een Safe room beschikbaar is in allerlei maten en uitvoeringen,
inpasbaar in bestaande- en nieuwbouw. Mijn 3 kamer appartement bevindt zich op de 2e verdieping en heeft een
balkon. Het oppervlakte van de totale woning is 55 m2. Zou u mij kunnen adviseren op welke plekken en
mogelijkheden ik heb in mijn woning om een Safe room te laten plaatsen? Ook las ik dat het risicoprofiel
bepalend is voor de uitlopende veiligheidsvoorzieningen die in de Safe room kunnen worden geplaatst. Kunt u mij
vertellen hoe ik mijn risicoprofiel kan meten of testen? Misschien zou u mij een checklist of iets dergelijks kunnen
sturen? Zou u een schatting kunnen maken wat een Safe room (verschillende begrotingen van basis tot uiterst
luxueus) voor mijn situatie zou kosten? De mogelijkheid om de ruimte multifunctioneel te maken zodat er
dagelijks gebruik van kan worden gemaakt lijkt mij ook heel handig, aangezien mijn woning een relatief klein
oppervlakte beslaat. Ik vroeg mij af welke multifuncties vaak worden toegepast in Safe rooms?

Ik heb begrepen dat het van belang is dat ik bij interesse voor een Safe room vanaf het eerste moment aan
niemand communiceer over mijn plannen betreffende de Safe room. Ik kijk dan ook erg uit naar uw antwoorden,
adviezen en informatie aangezien ik voor de bekende veiligheidsredenen nog met niemand anders over dit plan
heb kunnen praten.

Met vriendelijke groet,

Sabine Ruitenbeek

february 26

it is the truth, i live in a school canteen.

cantinette

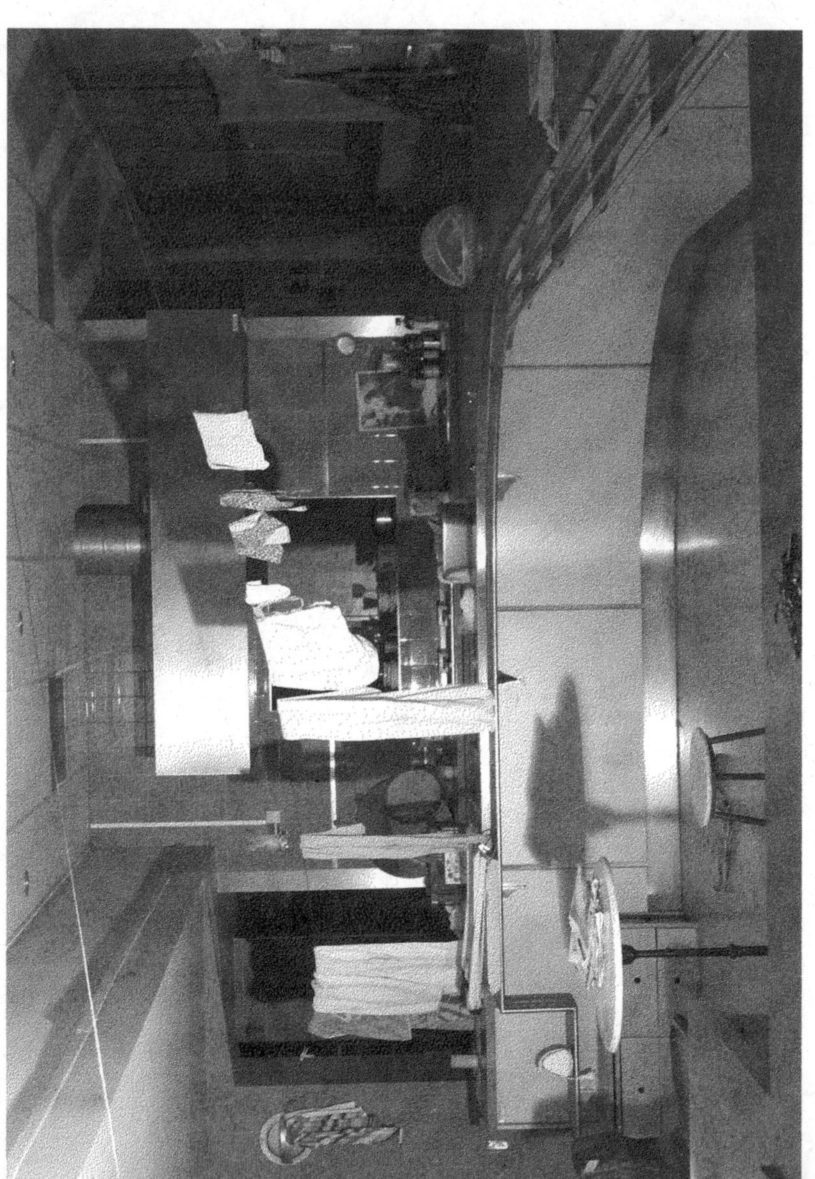

february 27

#171113

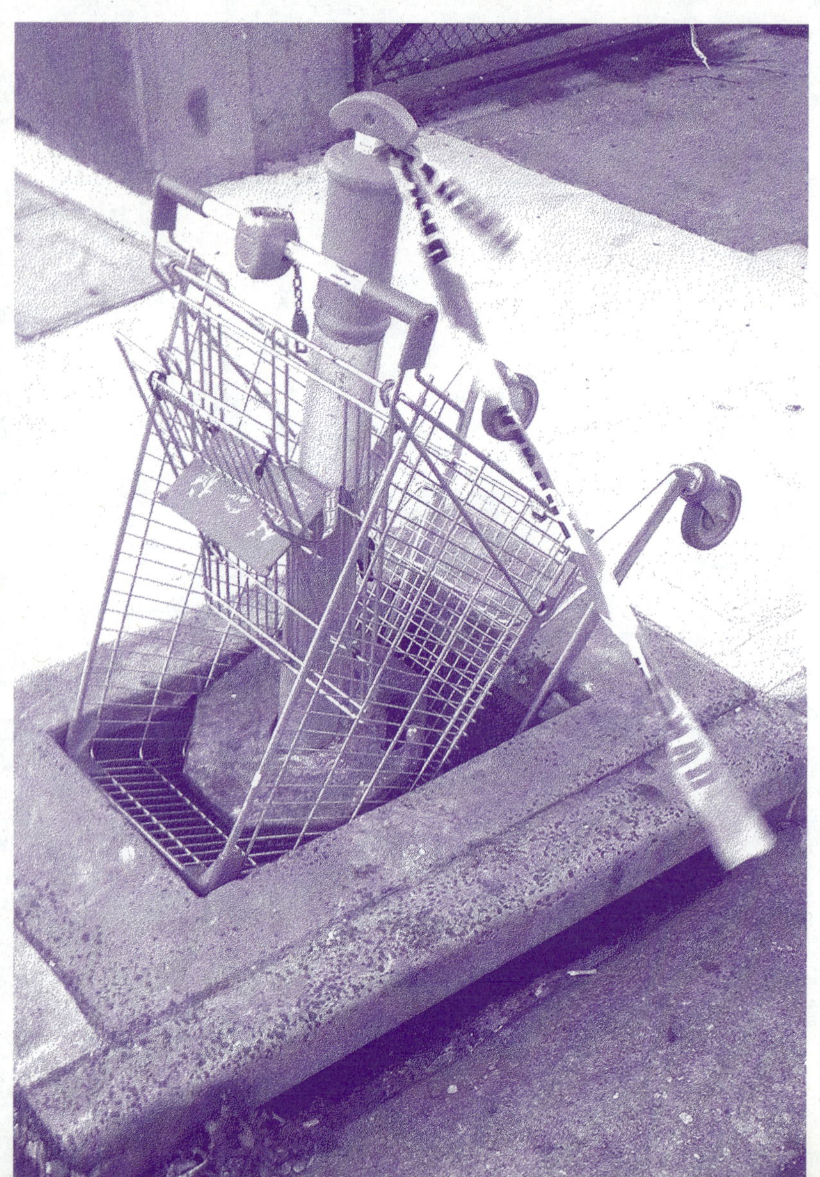

our employers work in the city and often travel for work around the globe leaving their most precious children and home to a domestic worker.
this contribution has been isolated and always treated as something exceptional and unimportant. domestic work is the beginning and end of all labour. justice for domestic workers demand recognition in making domestic work visible in british society.

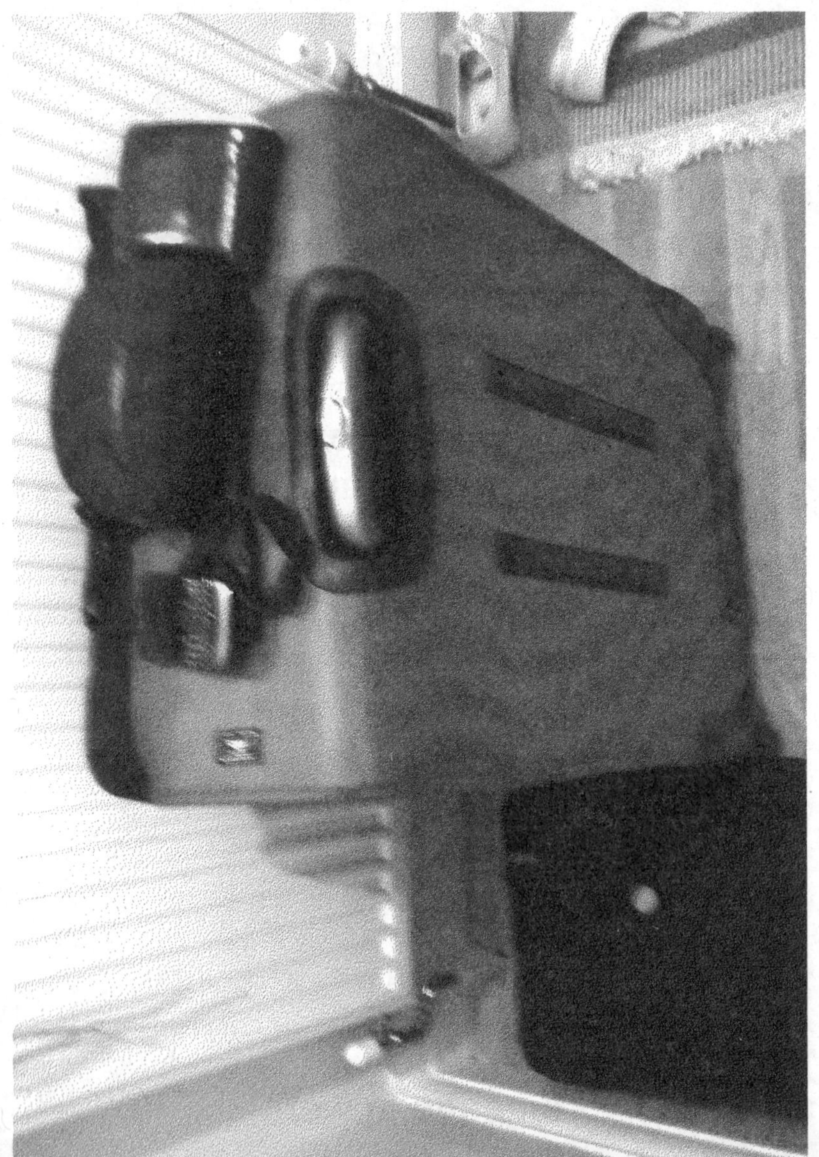

march 1

ninety-seven selected photographs
showing groups of wealthy peruvian
people in daily domestic situations.
in the background of each image one
can see either a figure or a deletion
of a domestic worker. all images have
been collected from the social network
site facebook.

97 house maids

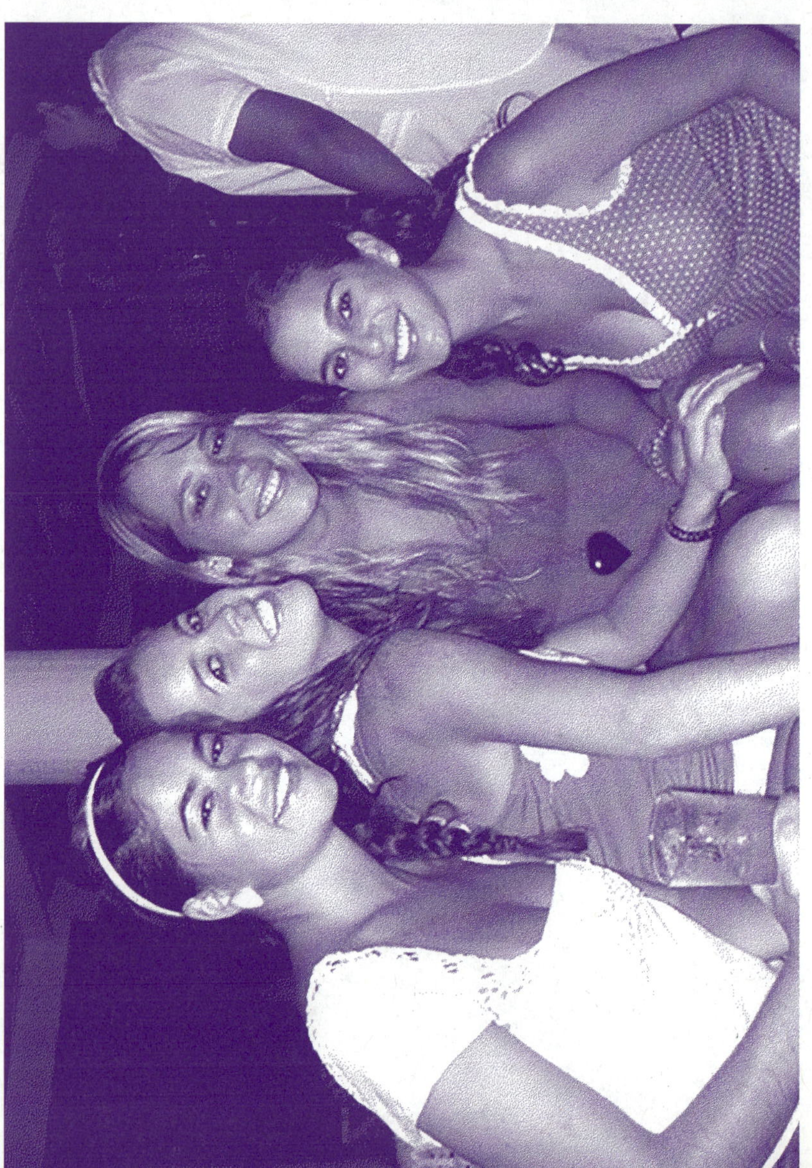

march 2

home tools

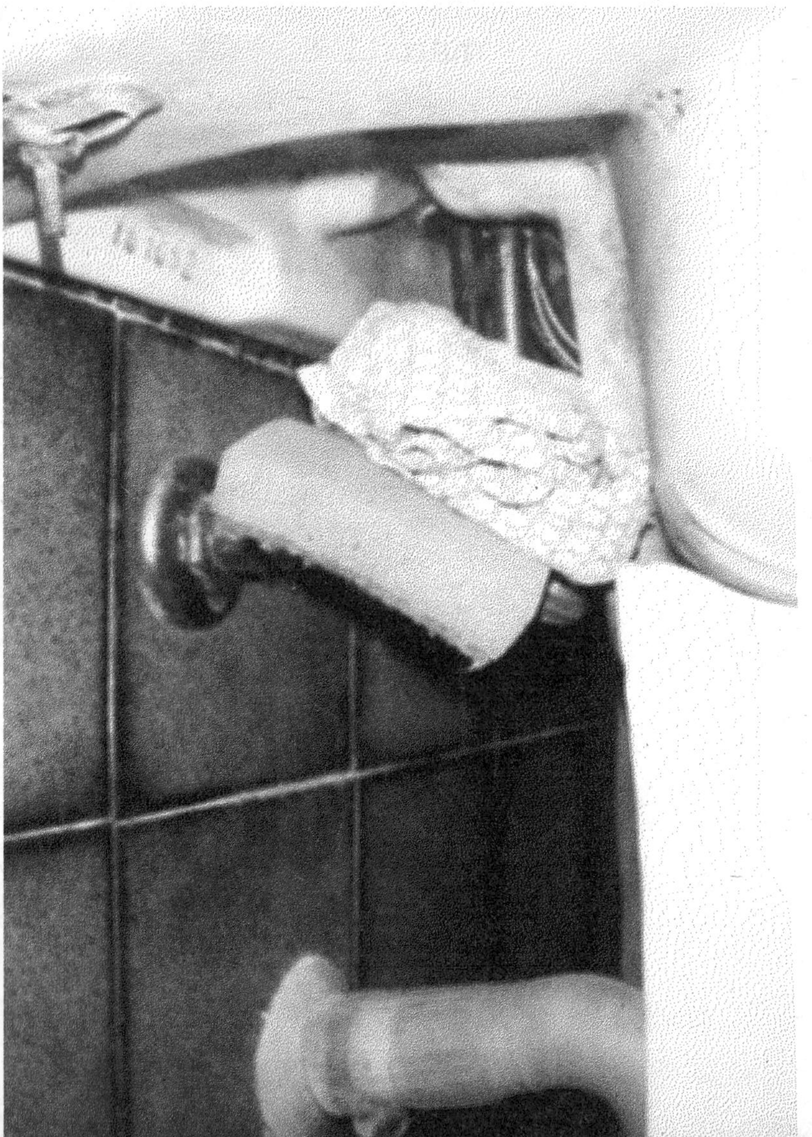

march 3

the "good wife's guide," *housekeeping monthly*, 13 may 1955.

sweet girls

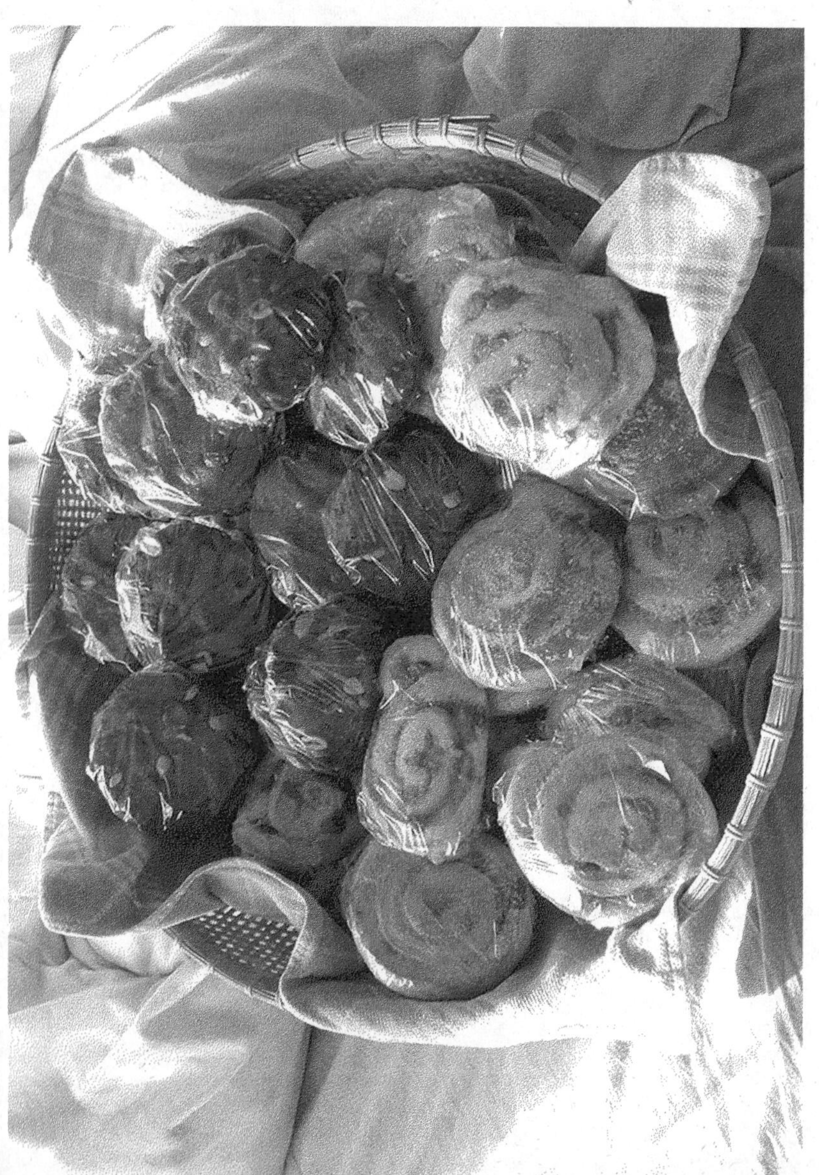

march 4

cleaning lady, shaking cloth. side view.

movement no. 3

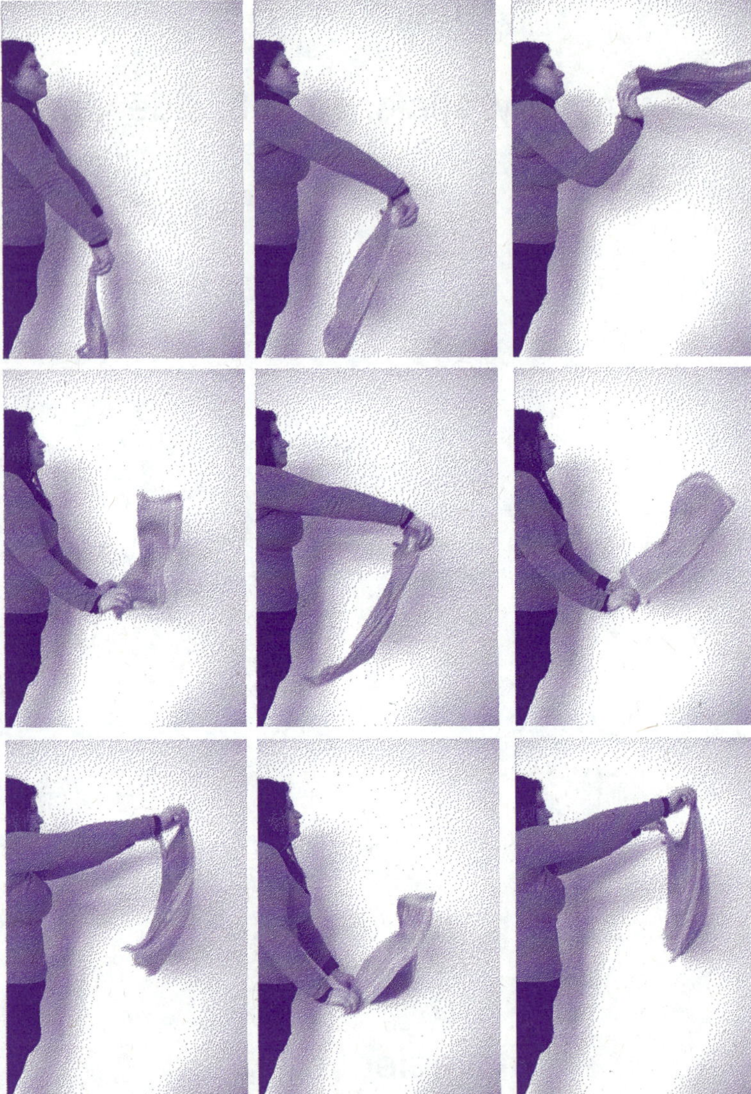

marcel duchamp, *sink stopper*, 1964.
he made it unintentionally, filling in
the leaking section of his shower head
with lead. it eventually became
unusable and he had it cast.

bouche-évier

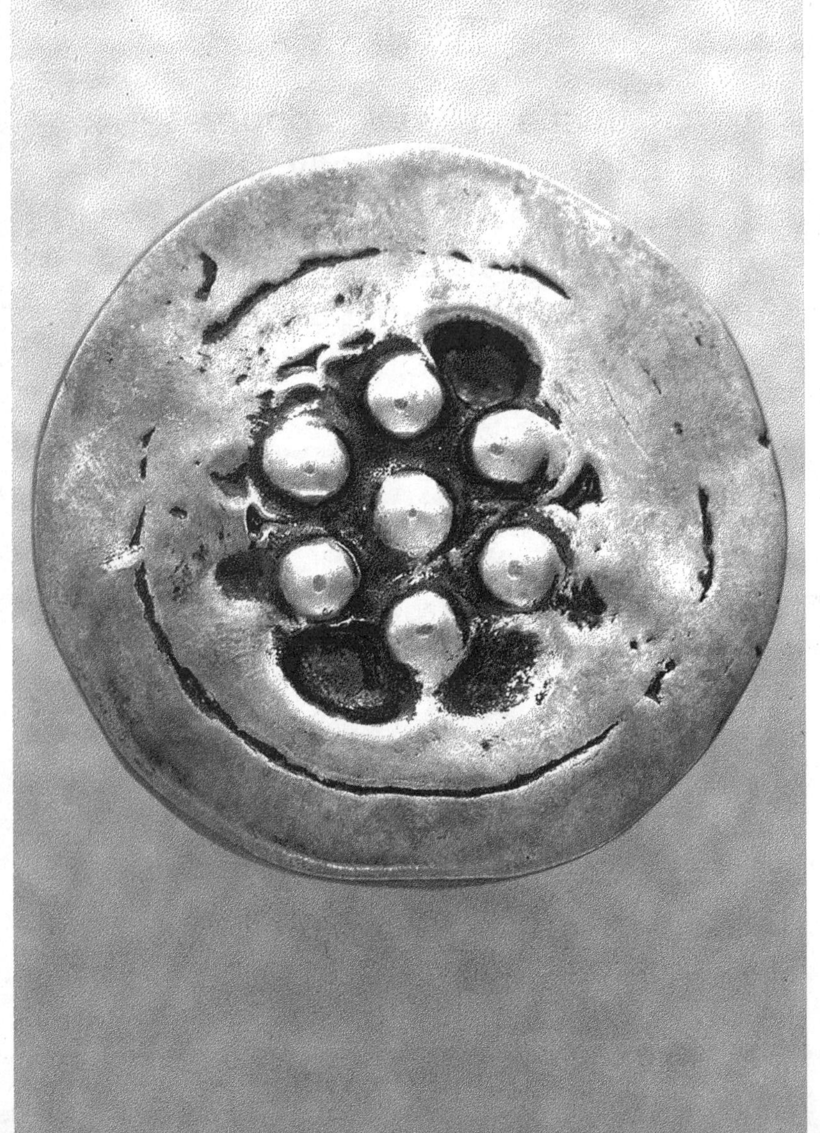

march 6

boiling bottles

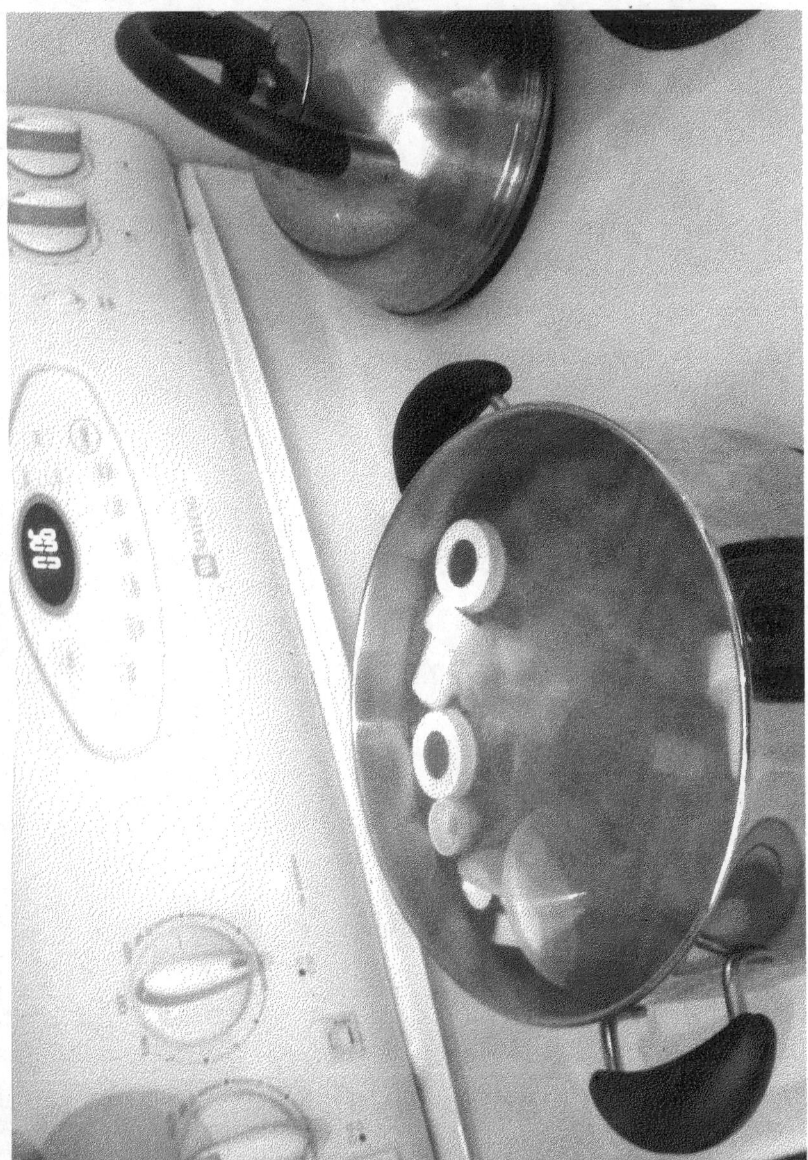

march 7

cleaning the front yard.

yellow gloves

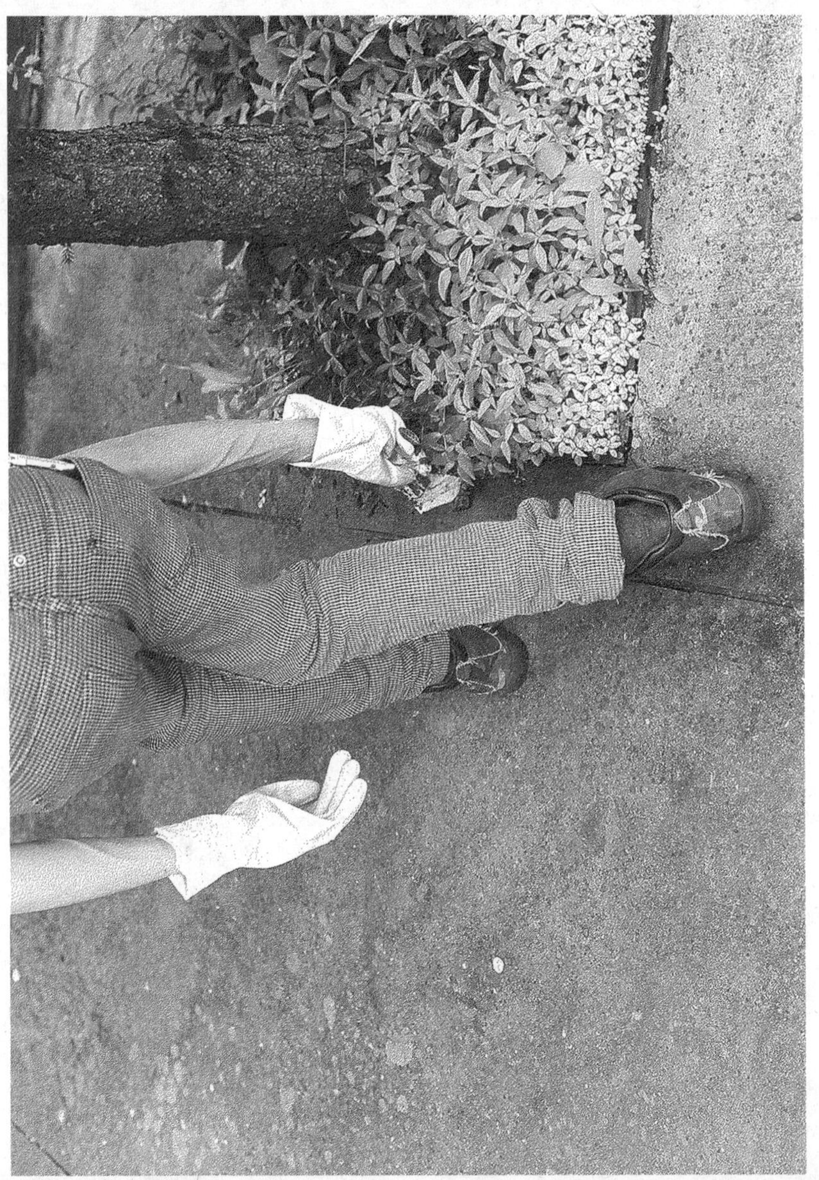

mi compañero trabajando en su
escritorio en compañia de nuestro
gato 'cuco,' algo que jamás podríamos
hacer trabajando para un estudio.

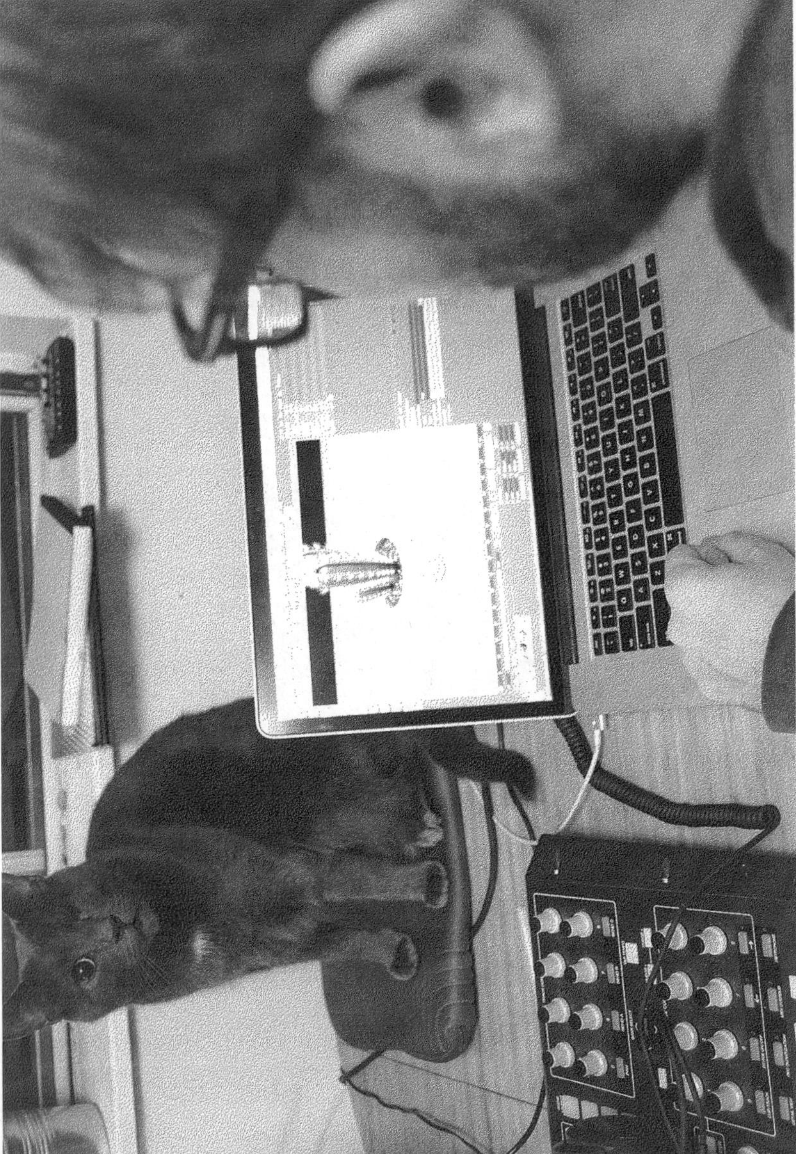

march 9

the home haircuts come soon after
the monthly spending cuts.

haircut day

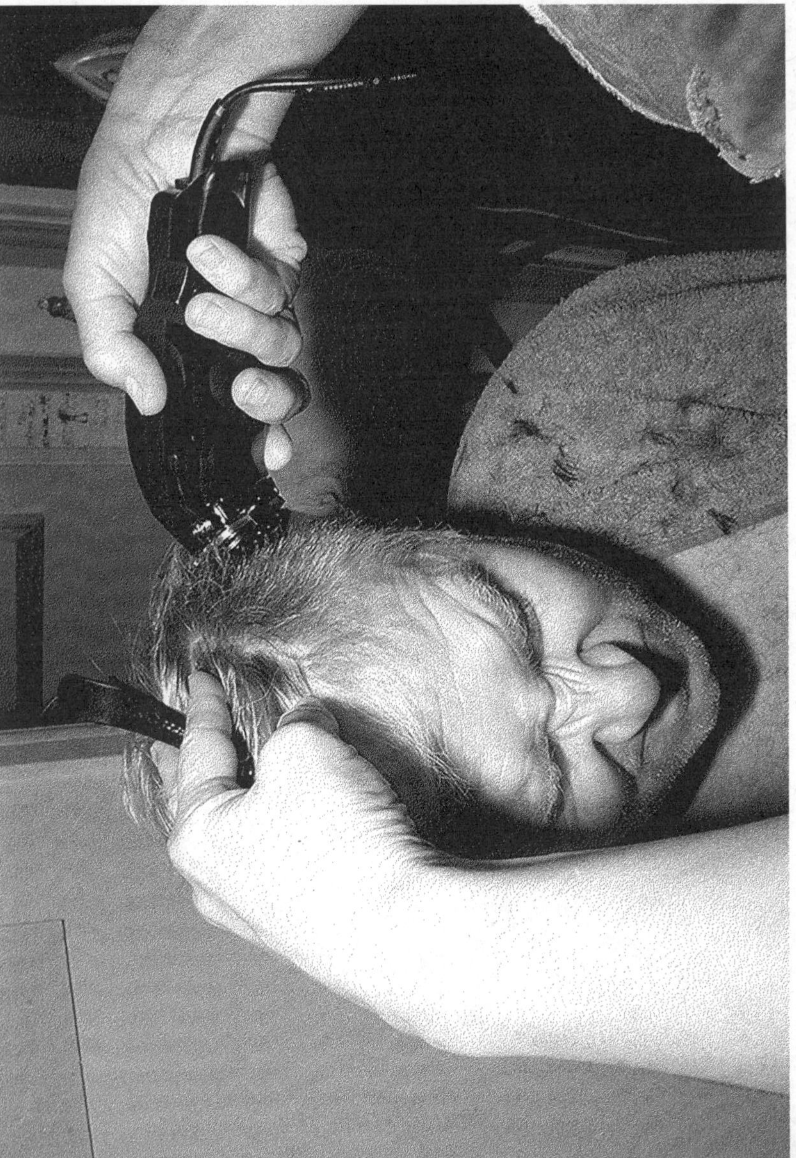

this is what i call the domestic domino
effect. clean at home, work at work,
clean at work, work at home, sleep
at home, clean at home… image
captured in chinatown, new york city,
6 august at 10:11 pm.

late night foot rub

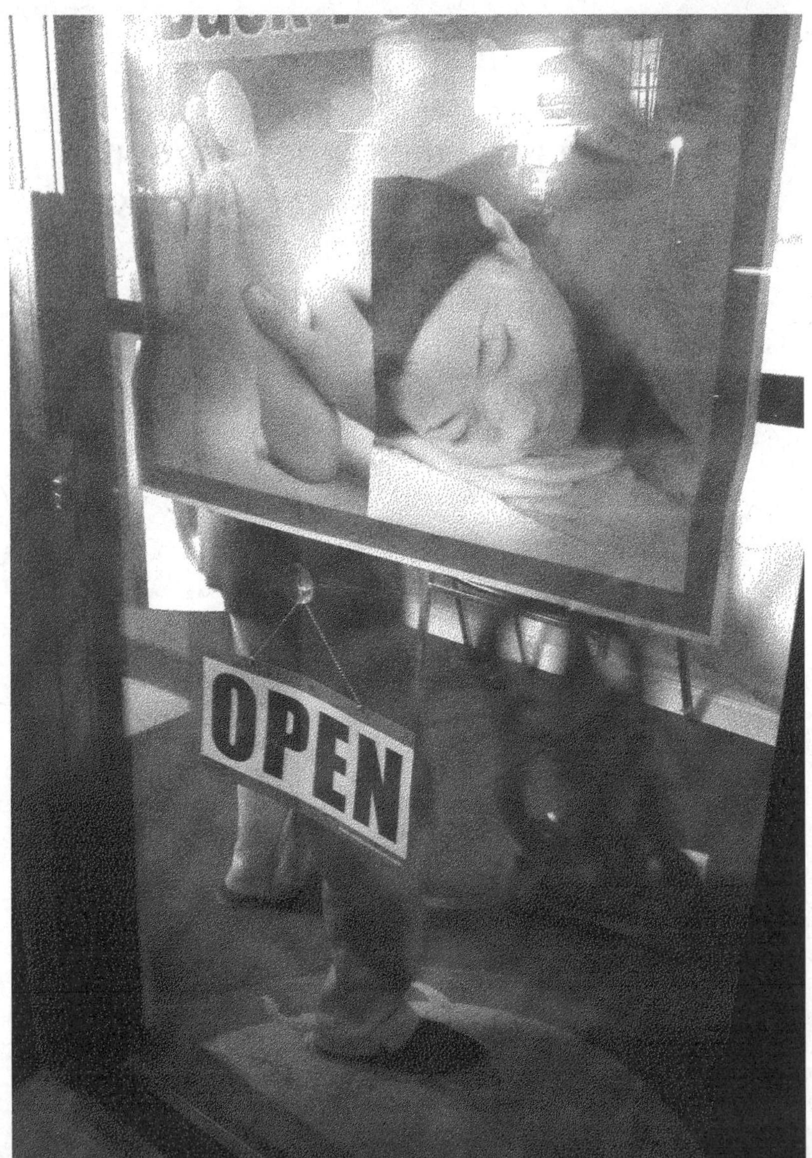

OPEN

march 11

st. petersburg.

doing groceries

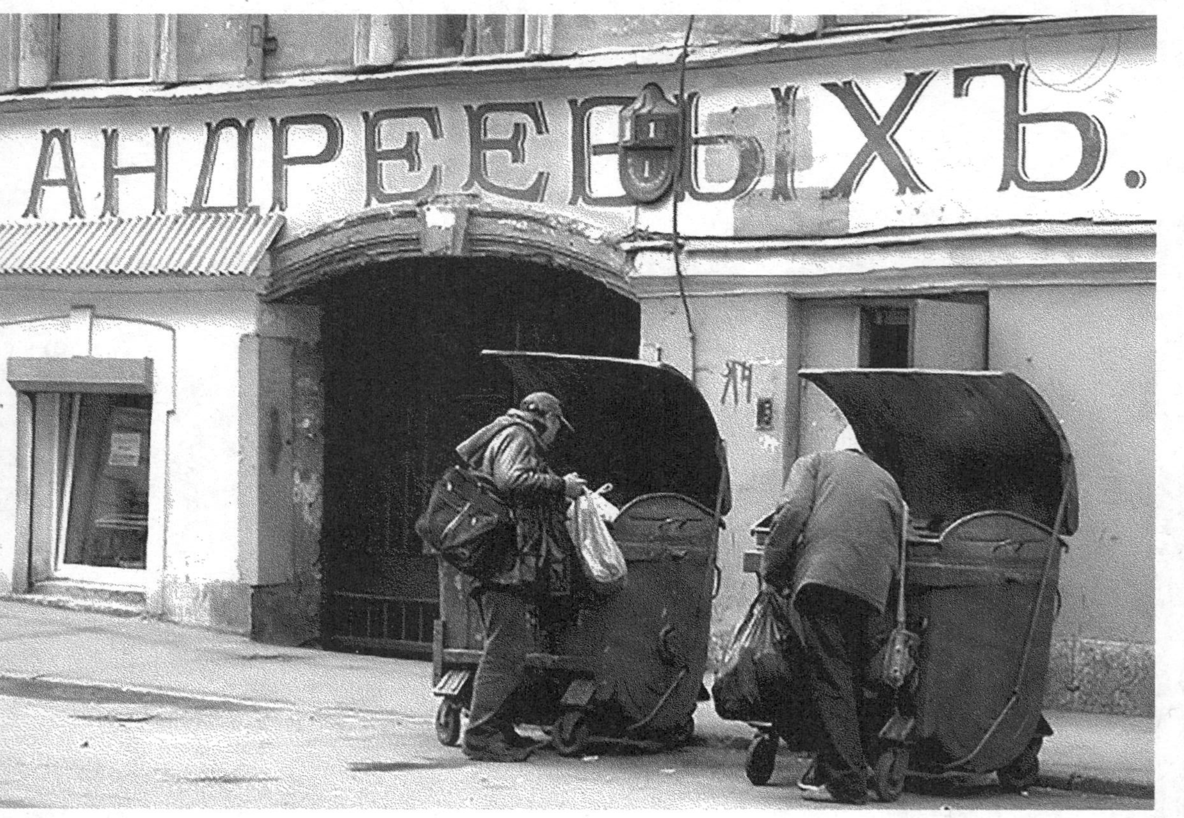

АНДРЕЕВЫХЪ.

march 12

athiraman kannan jumped to his death
from the 147th floor of the world's
tallest building, the burj khalifa. from
india, he came to dubai to work as
a cleaner in the newly opened building.
in an attempt to honour his courageous
call for attention to be given to the
lives of migrant workers, i photographed
what i describe as a 'pop out city.'
these are spaces that are an attempt
at permanency and comfort in an
always vulnerable life as a migrant
worker. unlike the families they work
for, whose life exists behind walls,
their lives exist on the street, forging
new notions of 'the public.'
al naeem, 2011.

in memory of athiraman kannan

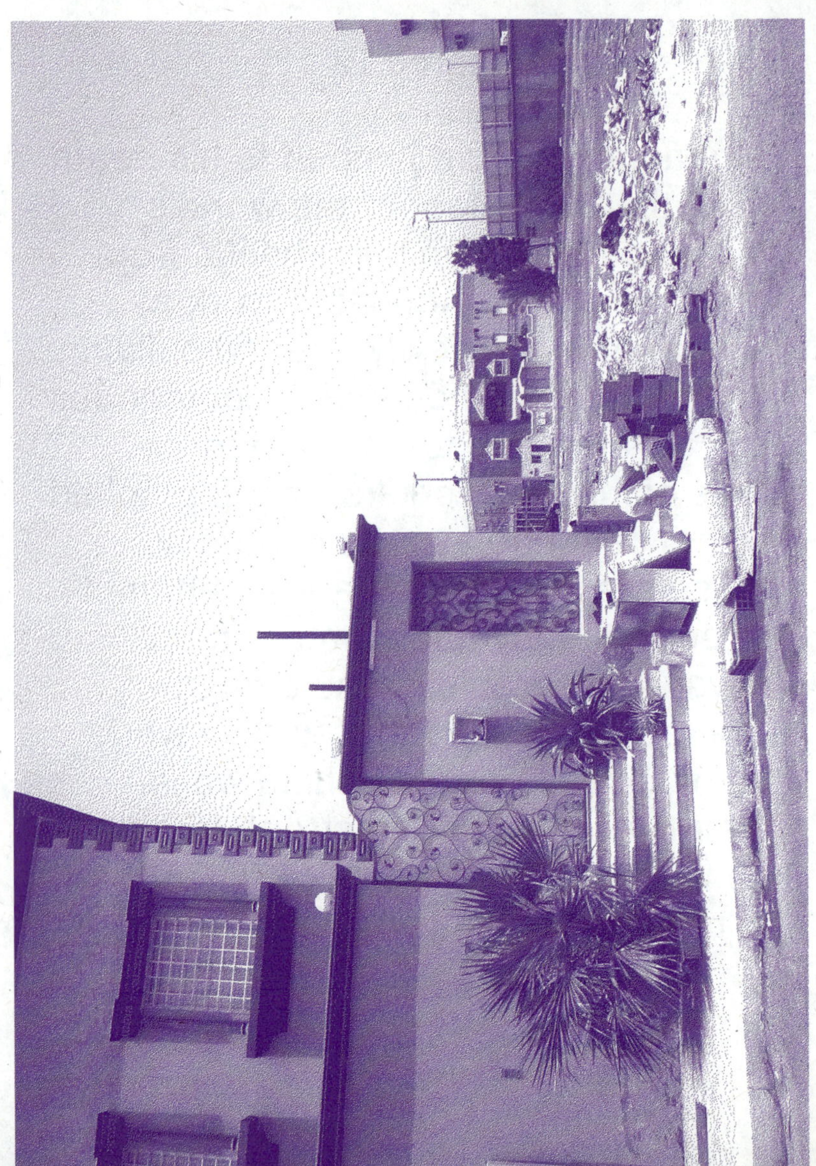

march 13

luce irigaray, "how can we live together
in a lasting way," *key writings*, 2004.

arguing

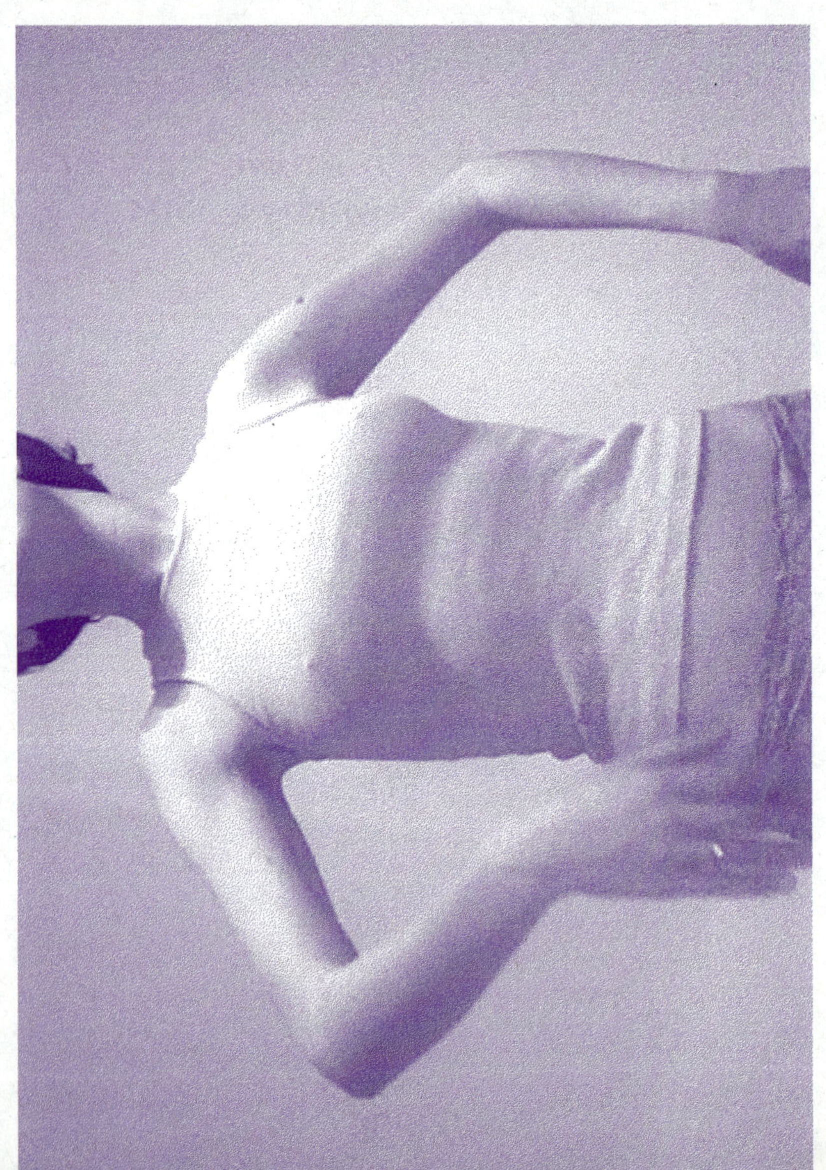

march 14

my family back home missing them
too much. long years of sacrifice.

x-mas

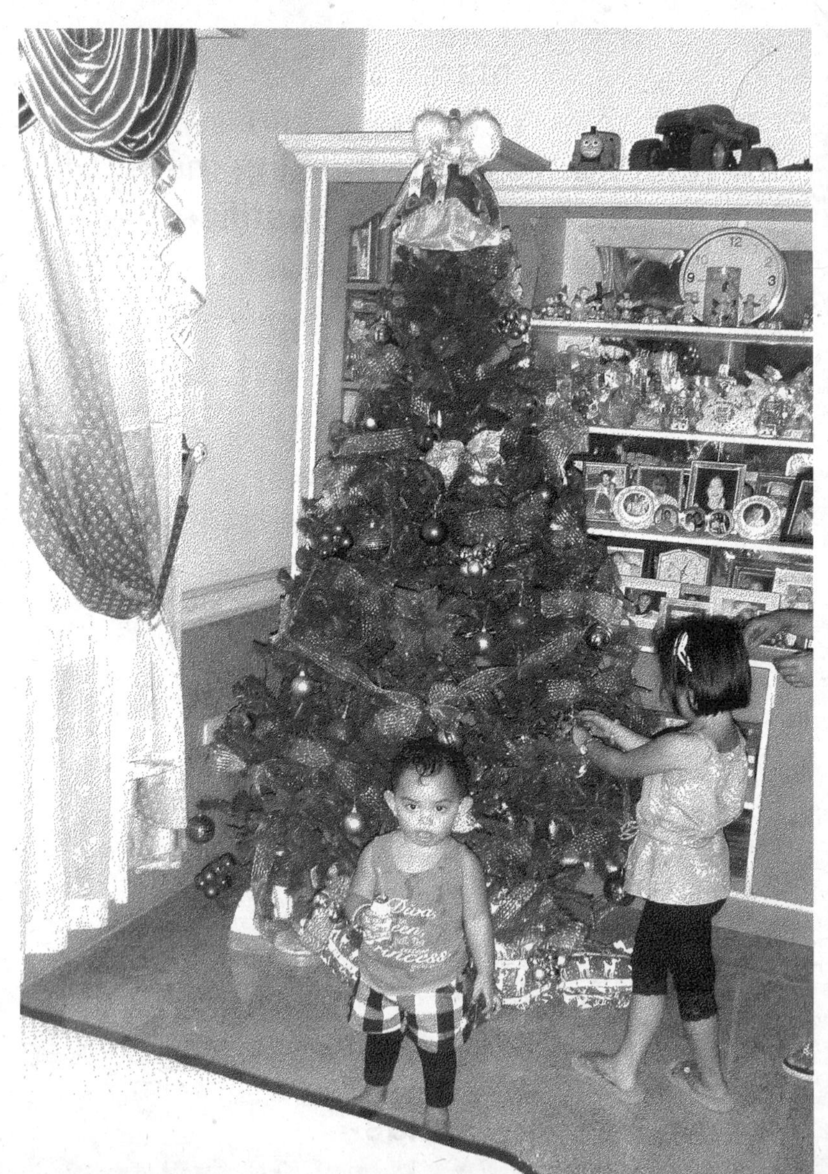

my mum is outside the tent cleaning
the inside and outside of the tent.
inside the light is like an orange
sunset that surrounds you. the smell
is a basement.

cleaning

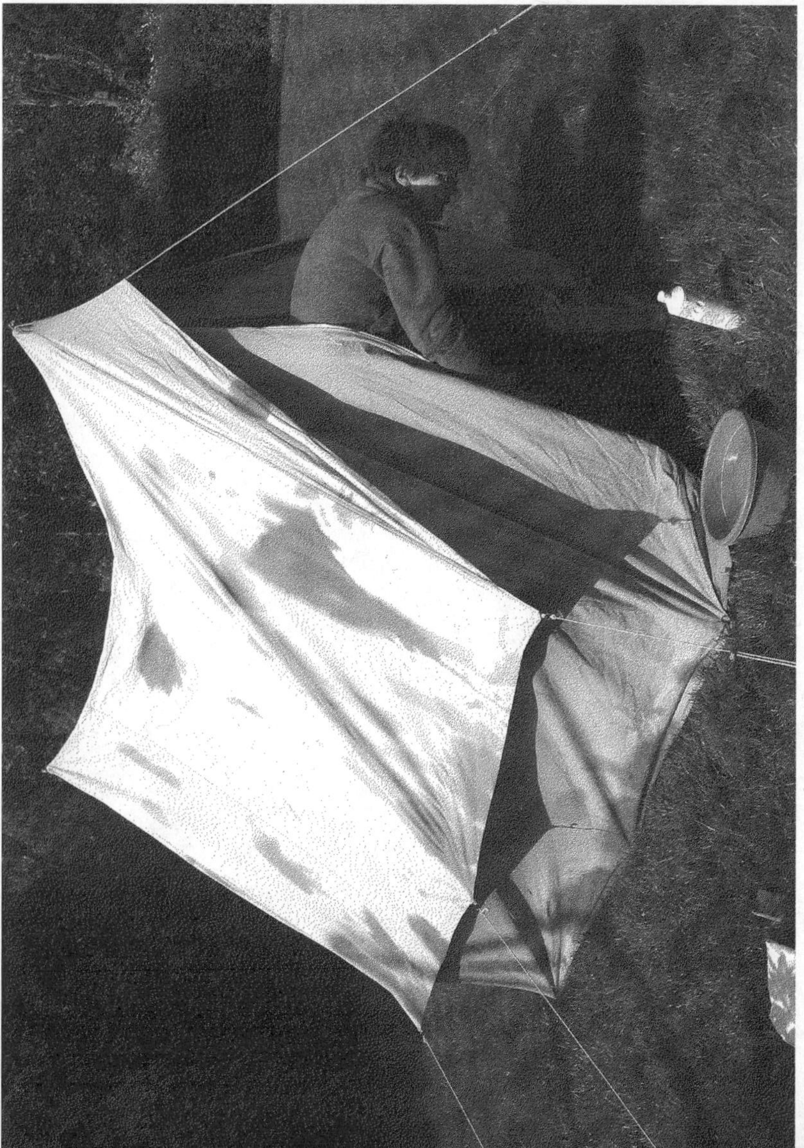

march 16

this is my mother at the same age
i am now (23) hanging the laundry
out to dry.

mom's laundry

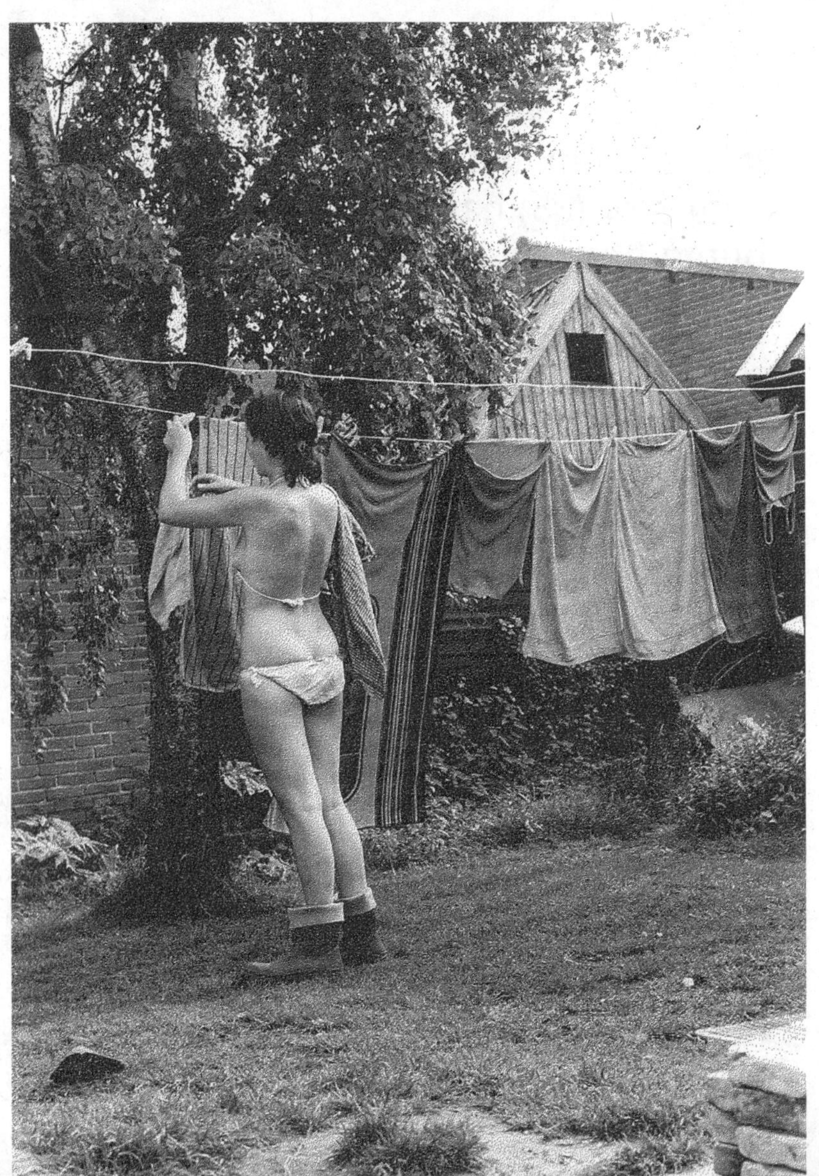

tengo una habitación extra con las cosas de mi amiga alex que vive fuera. a cambio de acogerla en casa durante su último proyecto 'te oímos beber' me ha regalado una tomatera y una pieza.

informal residence

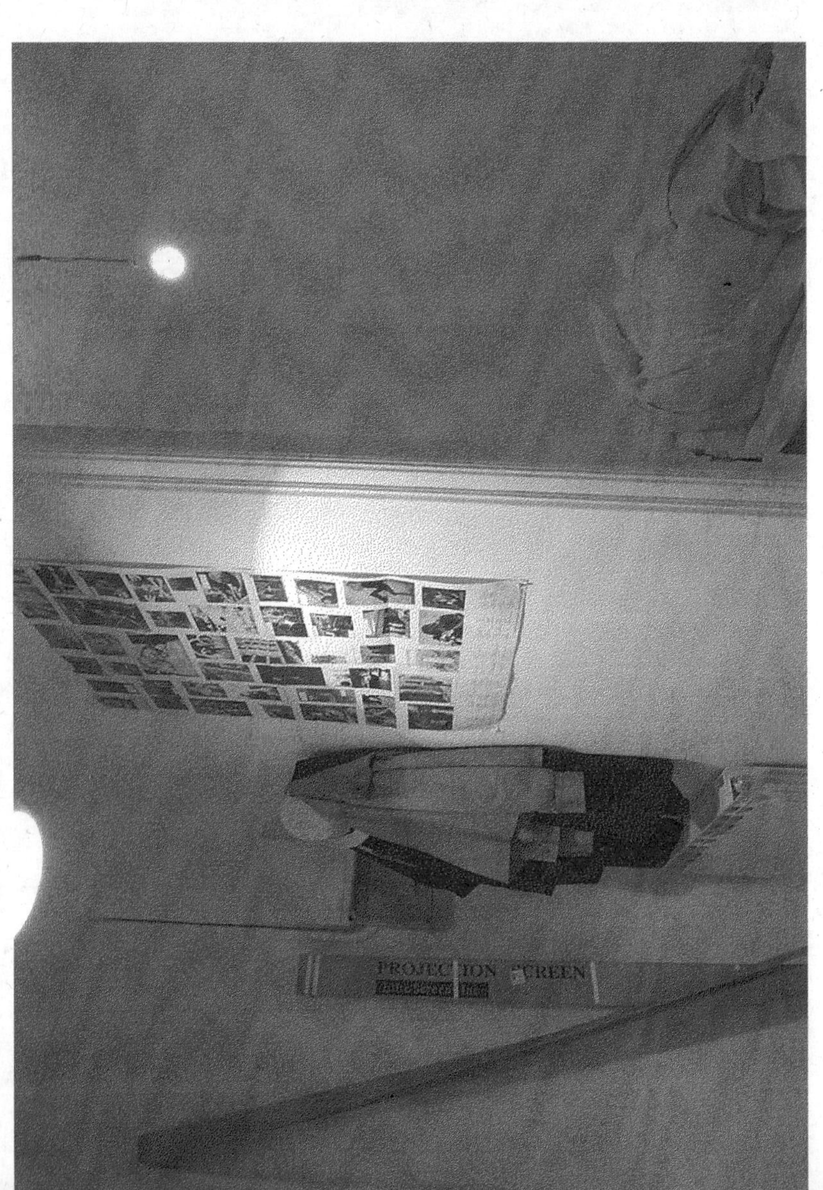

PROJECTION SCREEN

march 18

bedroom—in order to crease
domestic wildness...

primary structures gone wild

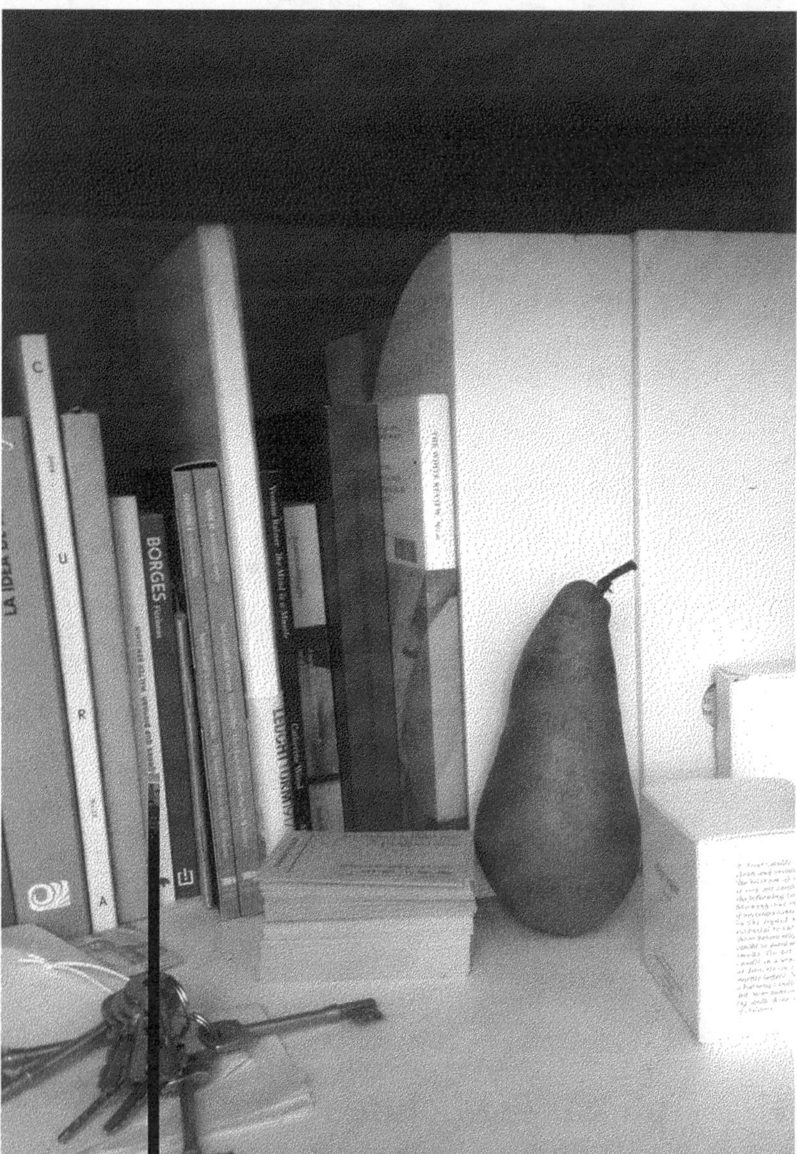

march 19

moving to the countryside escaping
high rent.

speculation strike

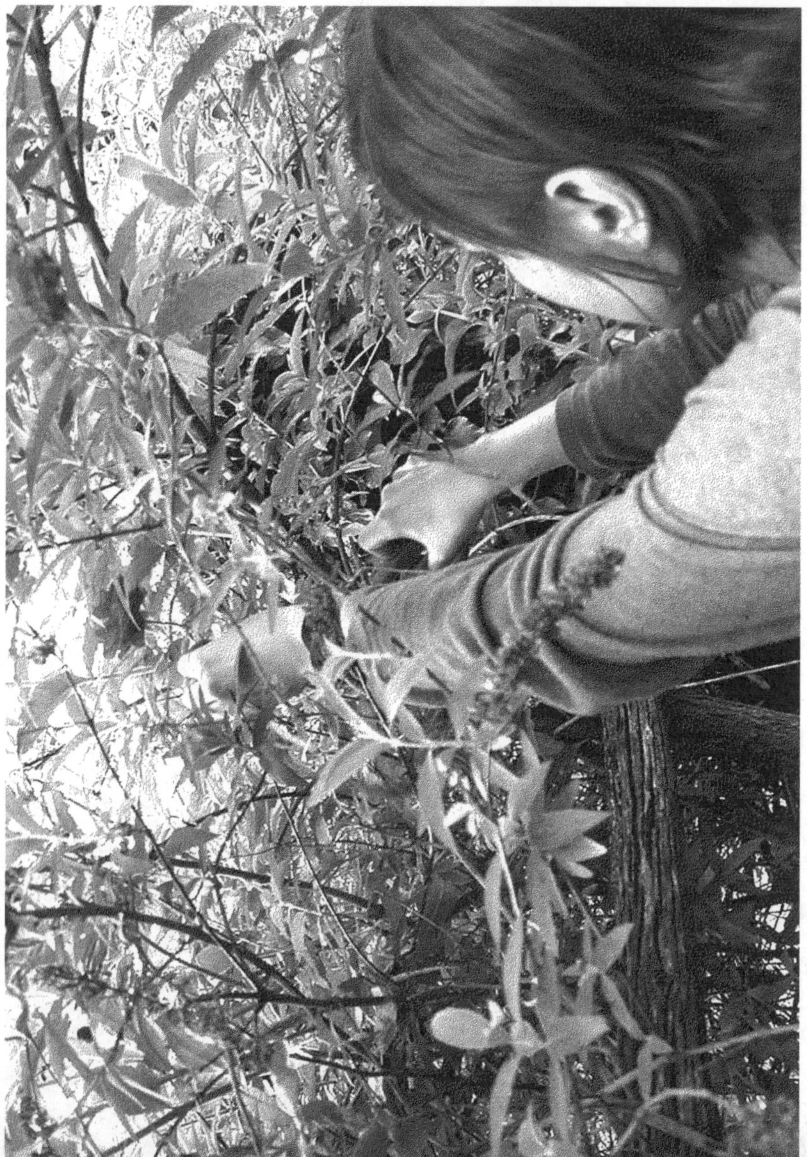

march 20

sometimes table, sometimes bed…

tablebed/bedtable

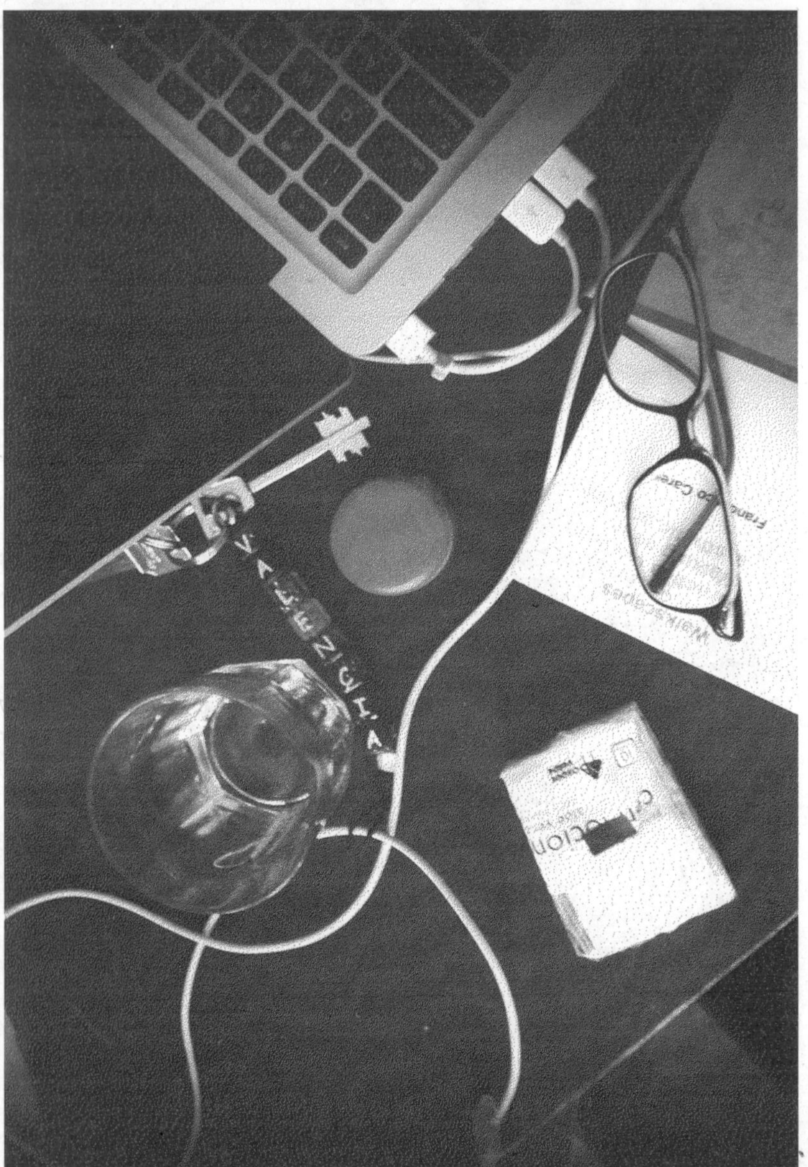

march 21

in the middle of the city, there was
the glimpse of the olympic ring.

olympic glimpse

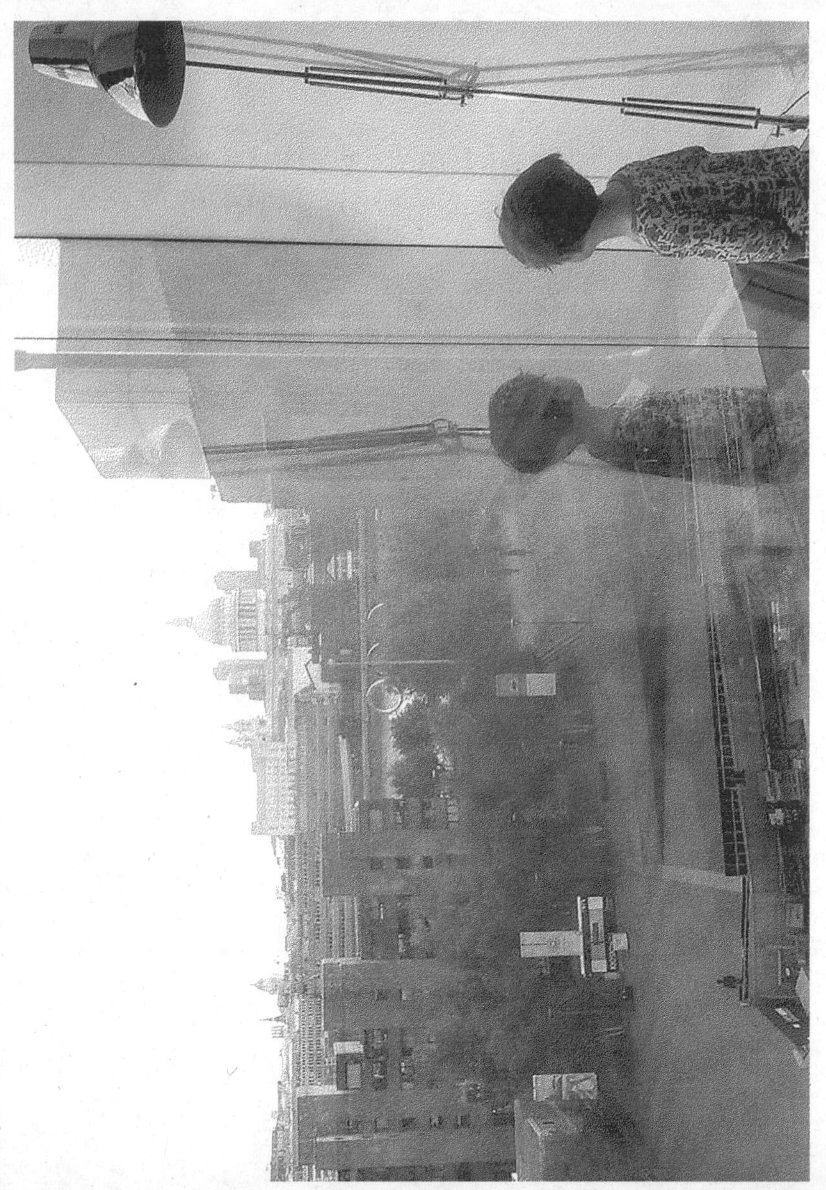

march 22

rights for all women!

derechos para todas!

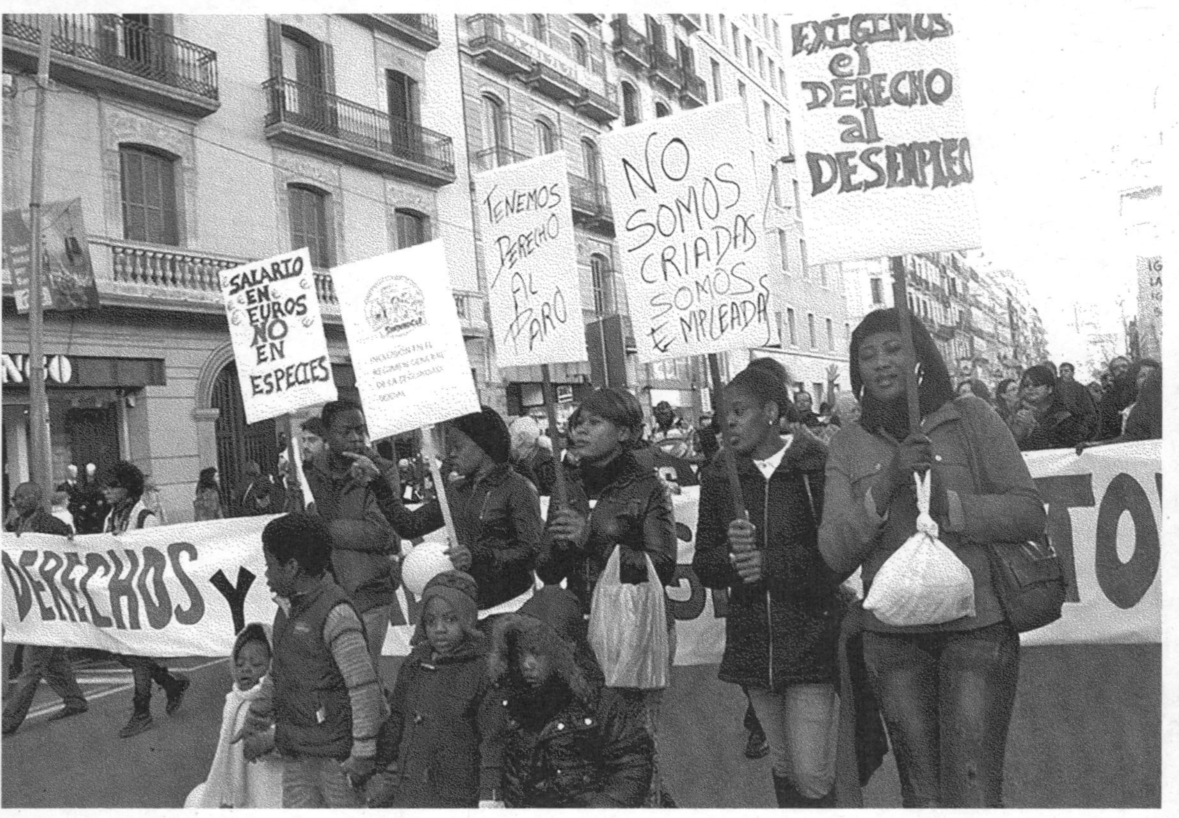
SALARIO EN EUROS NO EN ESPECIES
TENEMOS DERECHO AL PARO
NO SOMOS CRIADAS SOMOS EMPLEADA
EXIGIMOS el DERECHO al DESEMPLEO
DERECHOS Y

march 23

débordé toute la semaine.

busy all the week

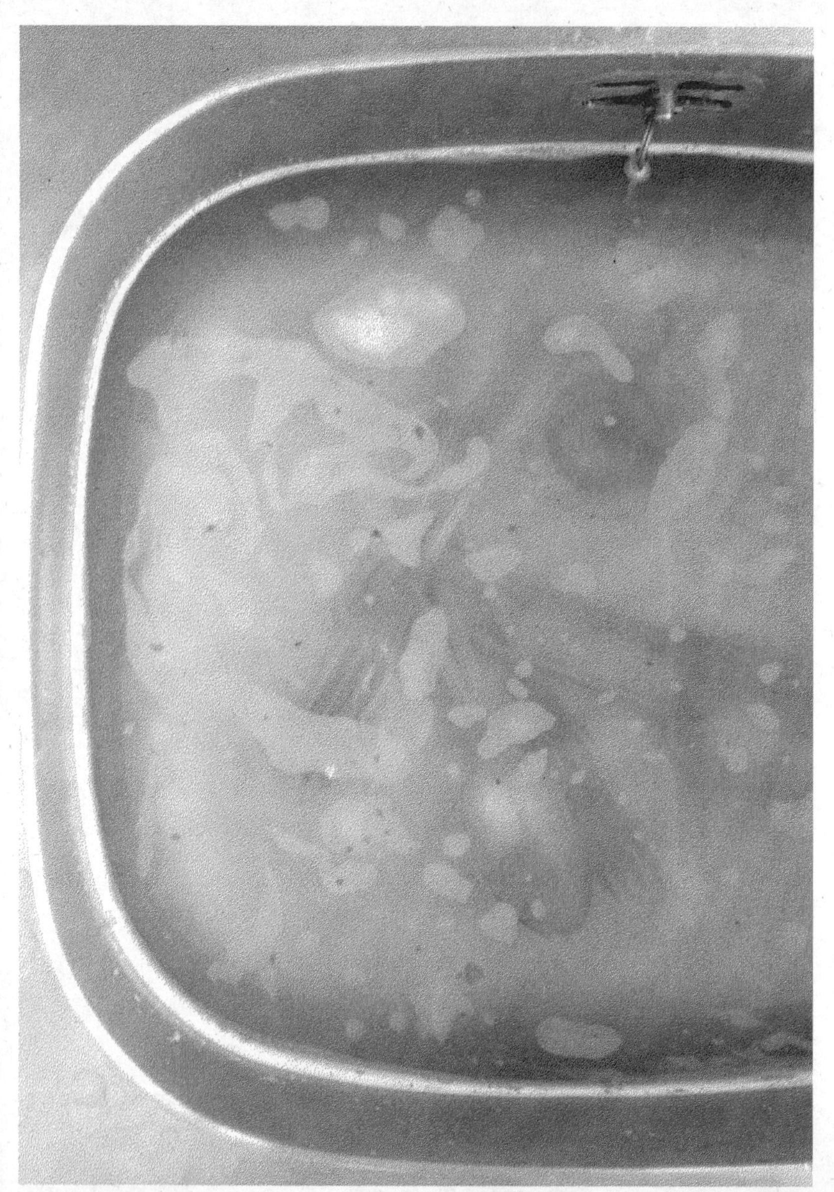

march 24

cleaning lady, cleaning window.
outside view.

movement no. 1

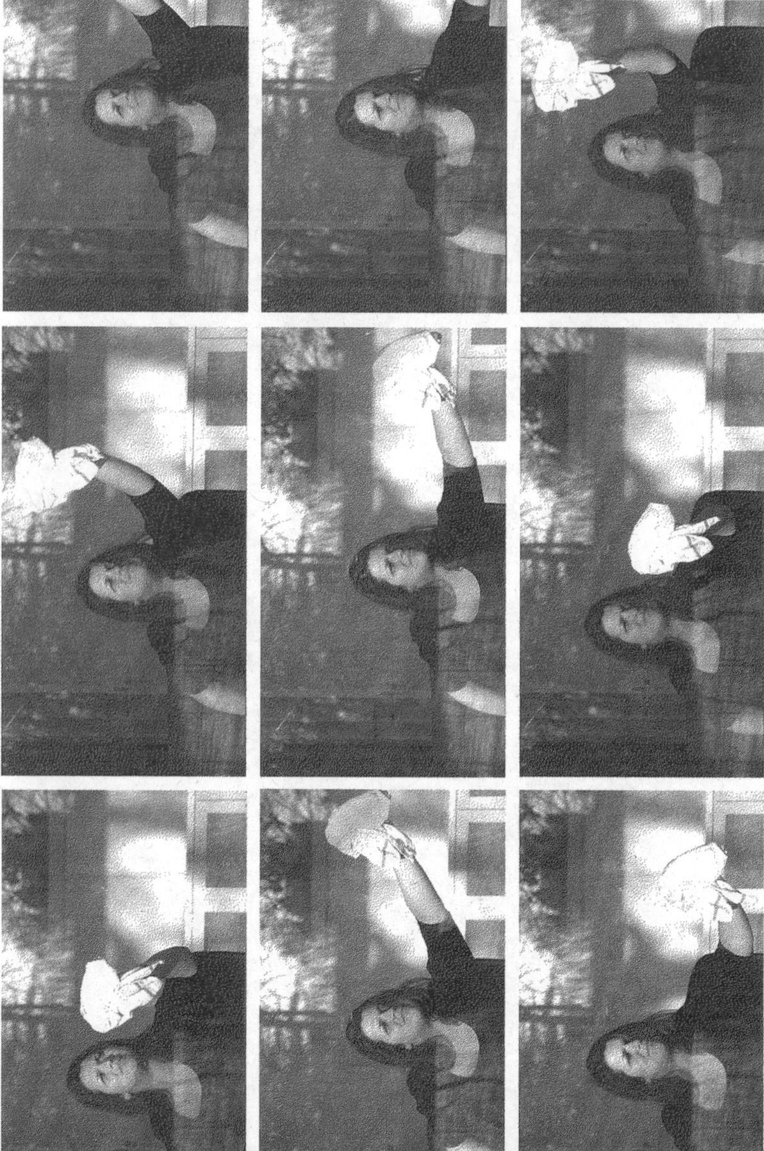

this picture is part of a series about
work and studying at home as an
action and a sort of protest related
to the constant making of art products
that artist are somehow lured into by
the capitalist art making machine.
la boheme is at home, she reminds
of any modernist model, of a male
painter of the times past, but she is
in fact in control and working, as the
portrait is taken with a self timer
camera on a tripod. she is luxe, calm
and volupté, but her mind is very busy.
she can't help to work to move to act
on that supposed stillness of her
coquetish pose.

bohemian odalisca studying

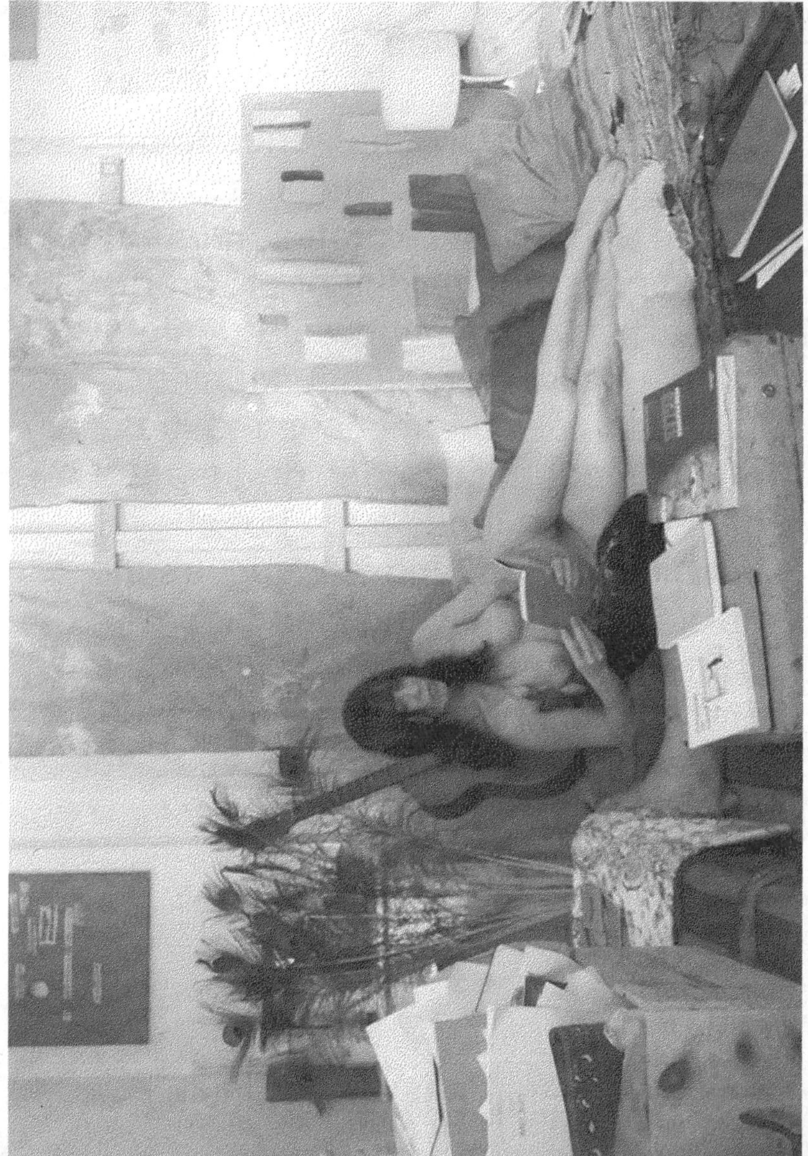

go, little booke, god send thee good
passage, and especially let this be
thy prayer, unto them all that thee will
read or hear, where thou art wrong,
after their help to call, thee to correct
in any part or all. from our dear
home dictionary.

dictionary day

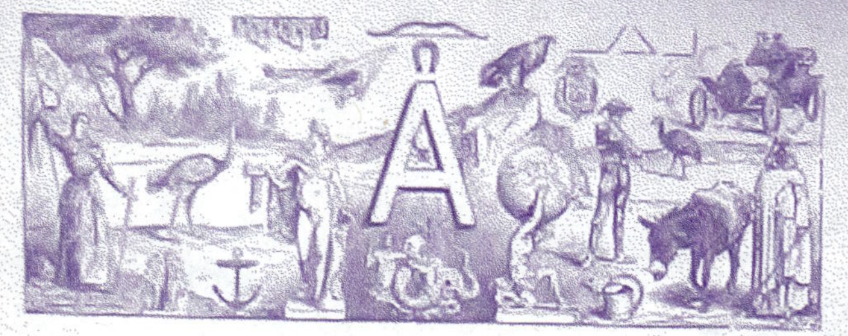

NOUVEAU
DICTIONNAIRE ENCYCLOPÉDIQUE

one of the domestic worker's job is
to teach children inside the household
the good values of cleanliness and
orderliness as they will bring these
as they grow.

cleaning windows

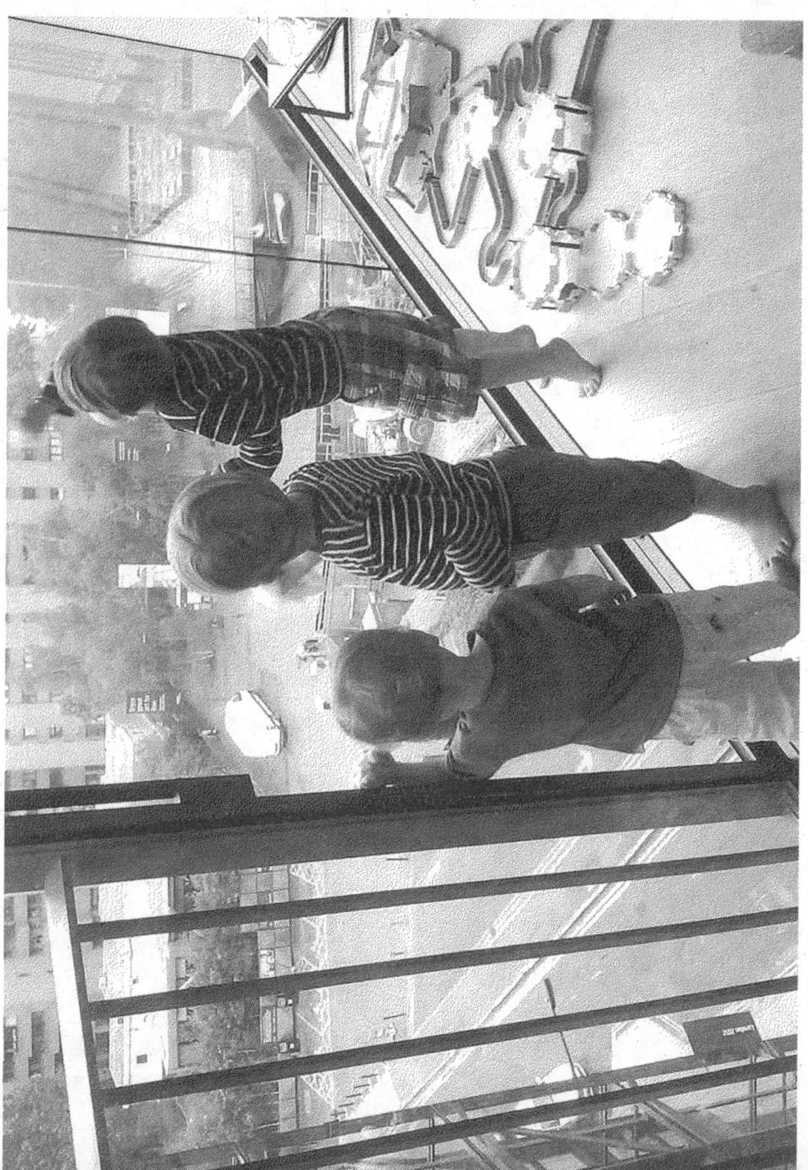

march 28

blue bathroom mop. red mop for
the rest of the house. floor tools

home tools

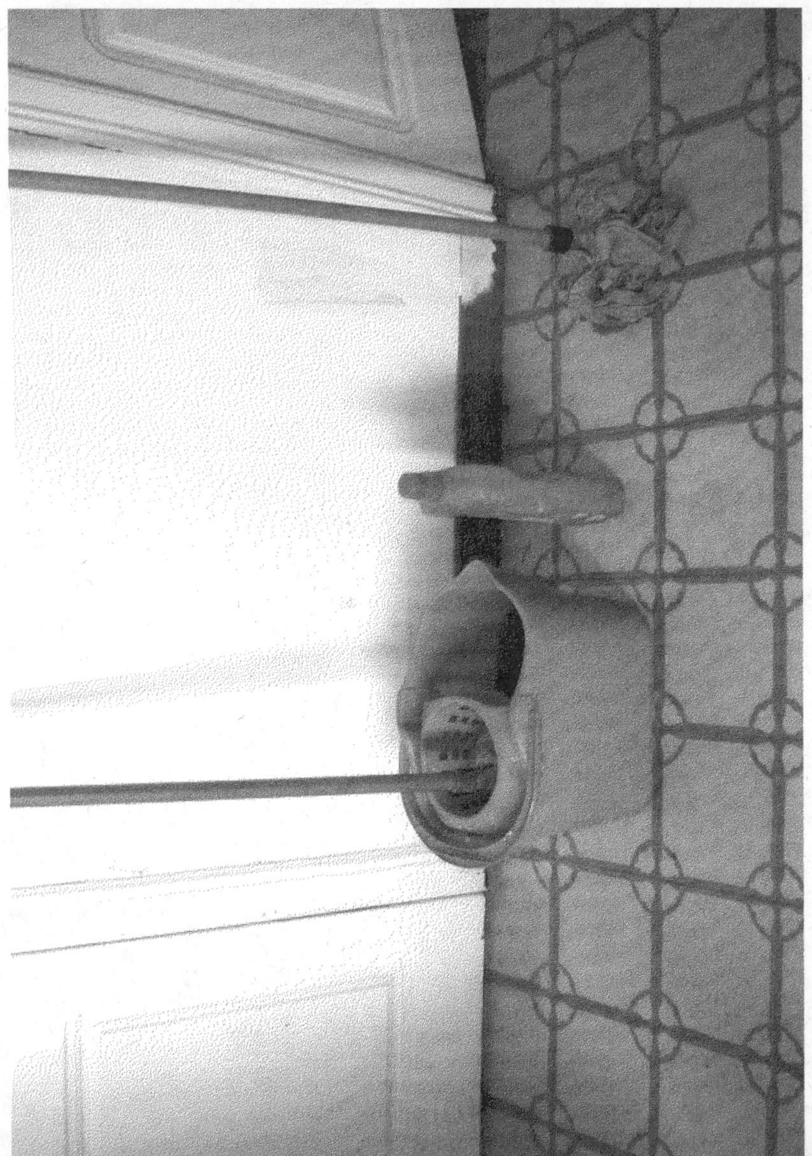

"after the guests move in to the music
room, it becomes apparent that no
one can leave. they move towards
to the hallway, nothing seems to stop
them and yet they cannot leave. this
condition is never stated clearly.
they accept their situation and settle
into the sofas…" read full text at:
https://m-est.org/2011/08/12/
onfor-production/.

e-flux

e-flux
http://art-leaks.org/

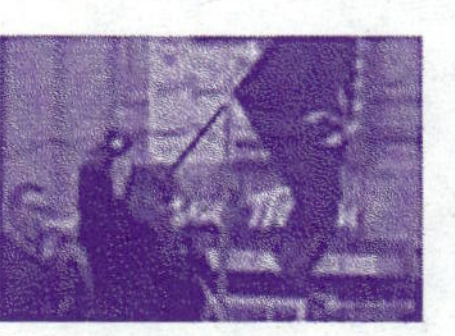

http://art-leaks.org/
art-leaks.org

This protest letter begins with the particular set of circumstances which brought together an international group of art workers from different positions in the field. Through these exchanges, they decided work collectively to make visible the conditions of inequality and exploitation that they want...

Thursday at 7:04am · Unlike · Comment · Share

You and 11 others like this.

Write a comment...

march 30

everyday in lisbon they build their houses from cardboard boxes. every day in different location. at different time. with different neighbours… never the same view through the window.

endless story

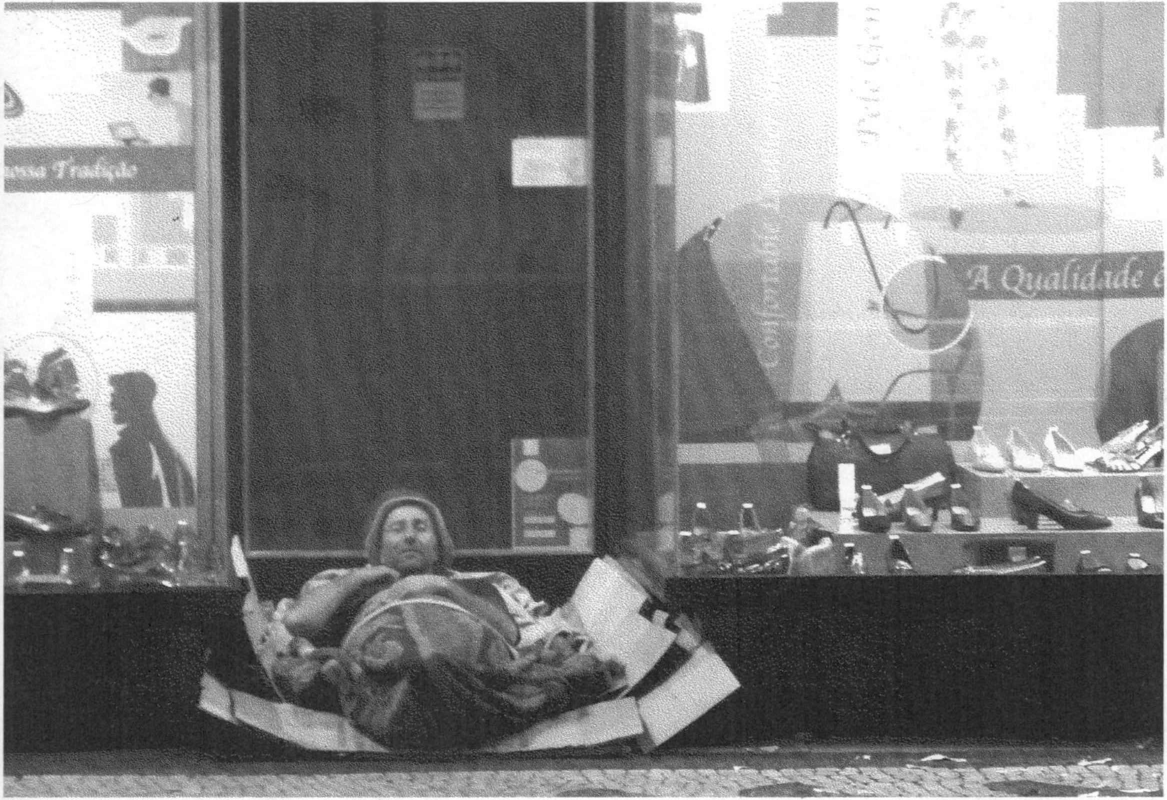

march 31

todo en esta vida es reversible.

luminaria

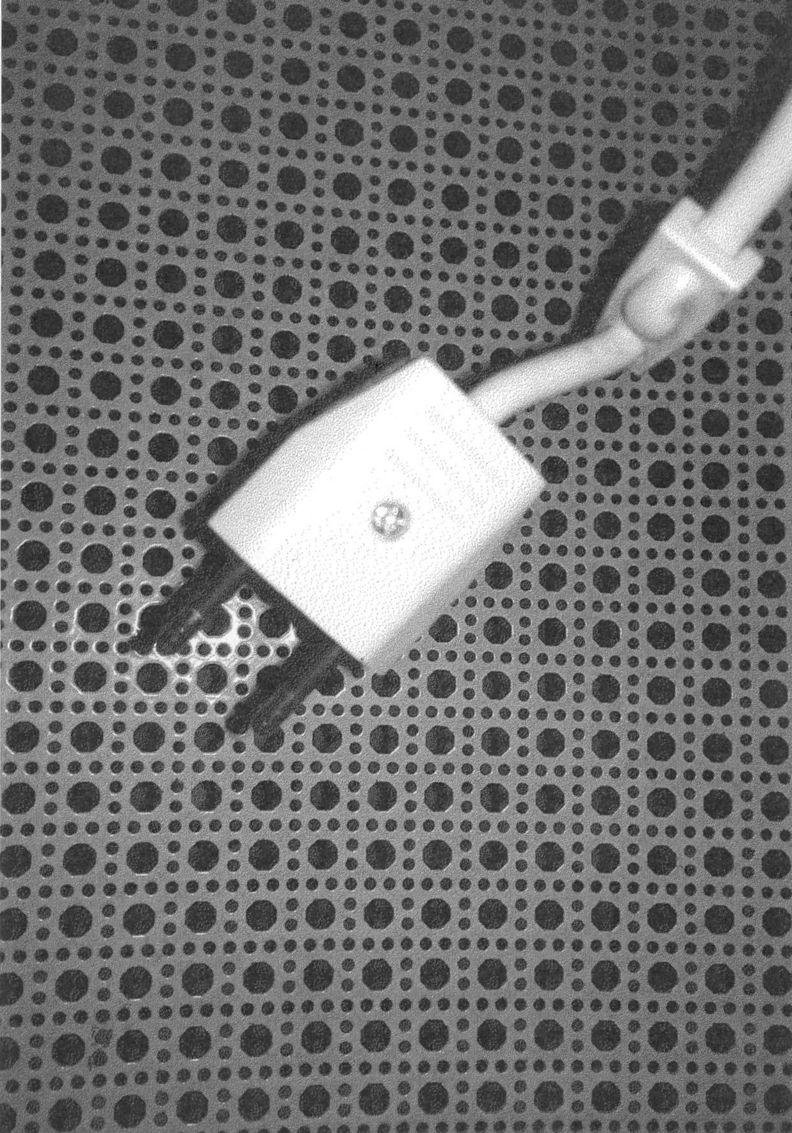

april 1

we see each other quite often,
but it was only after this picture
that we exchanged some words.

glass sharpening

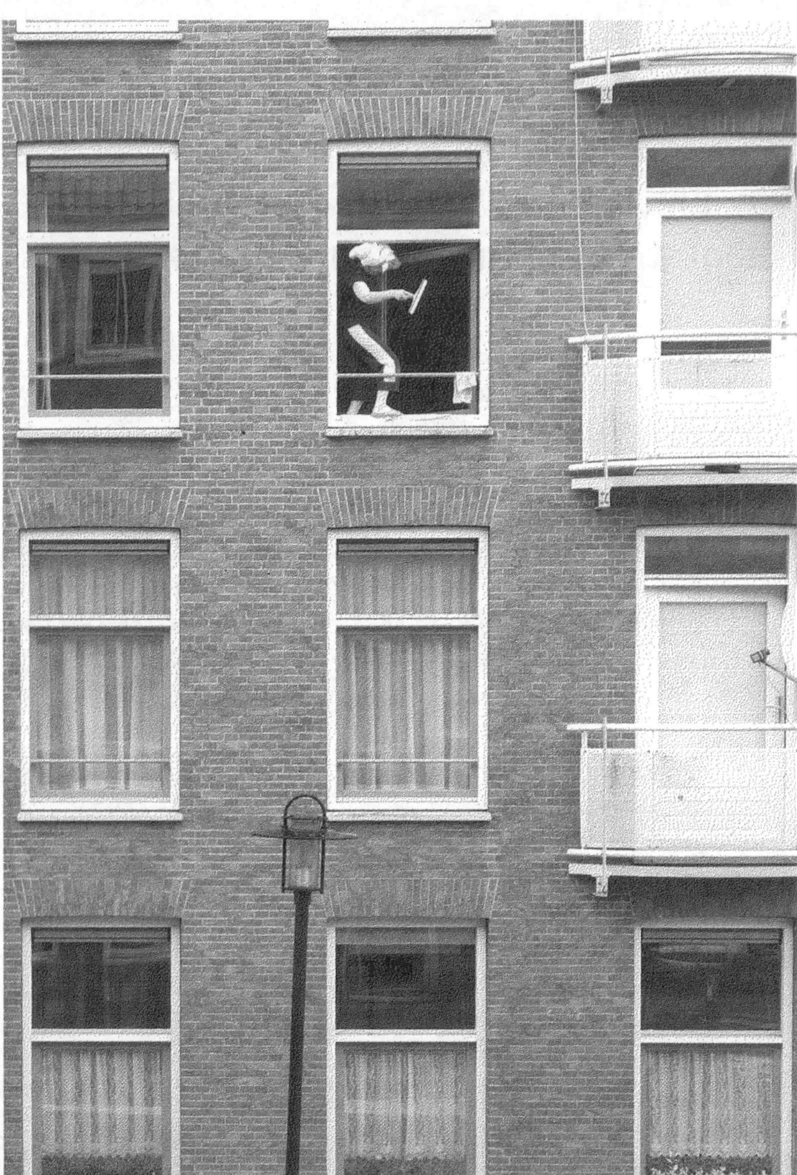

april 2

refreshing art in my bathroom.

tree bath

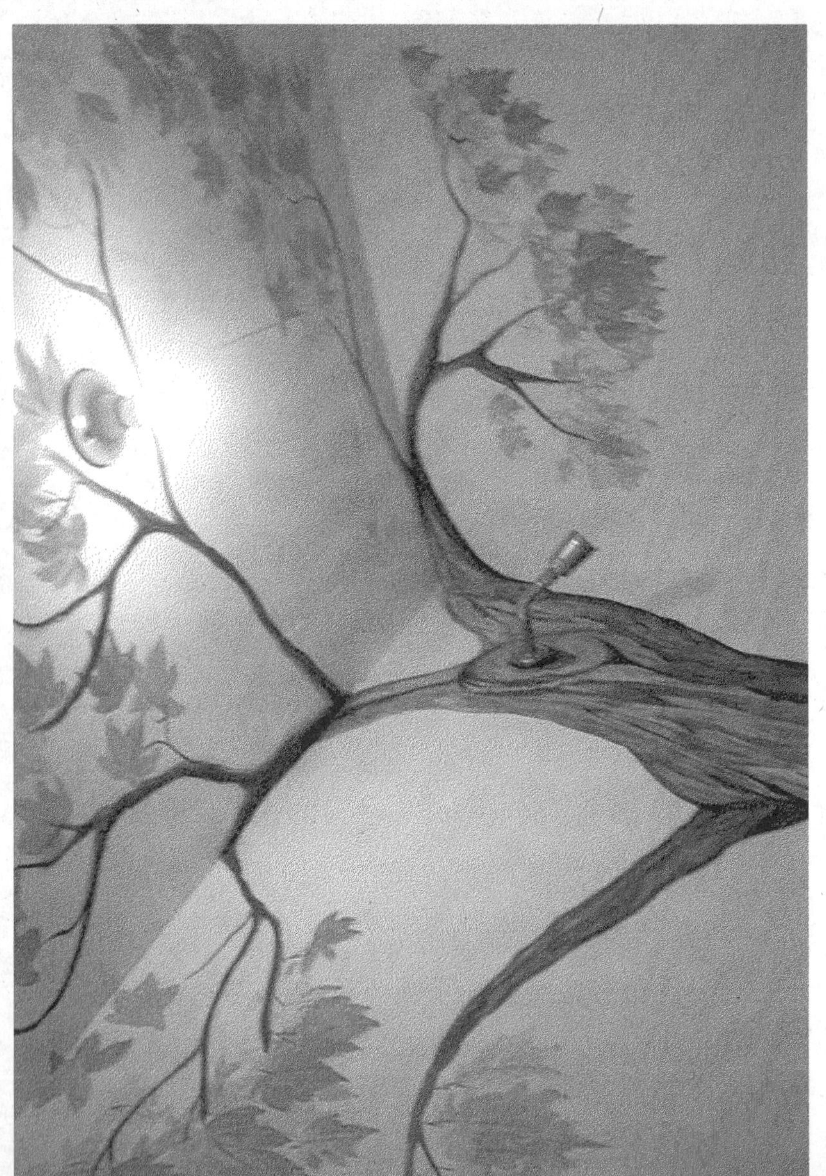

april 3

hidden storage space discovered
during renovations.

concealed storage

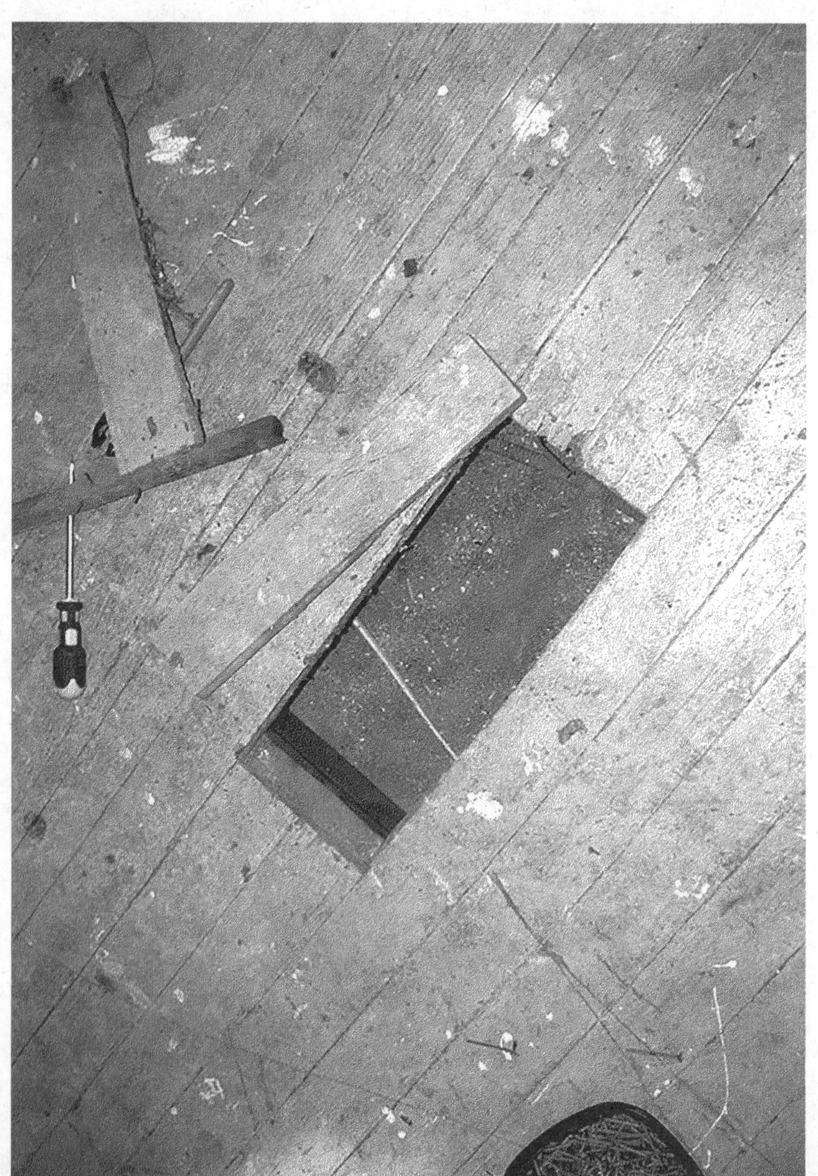

april 4

at home training with my hula hoop.

home olympics

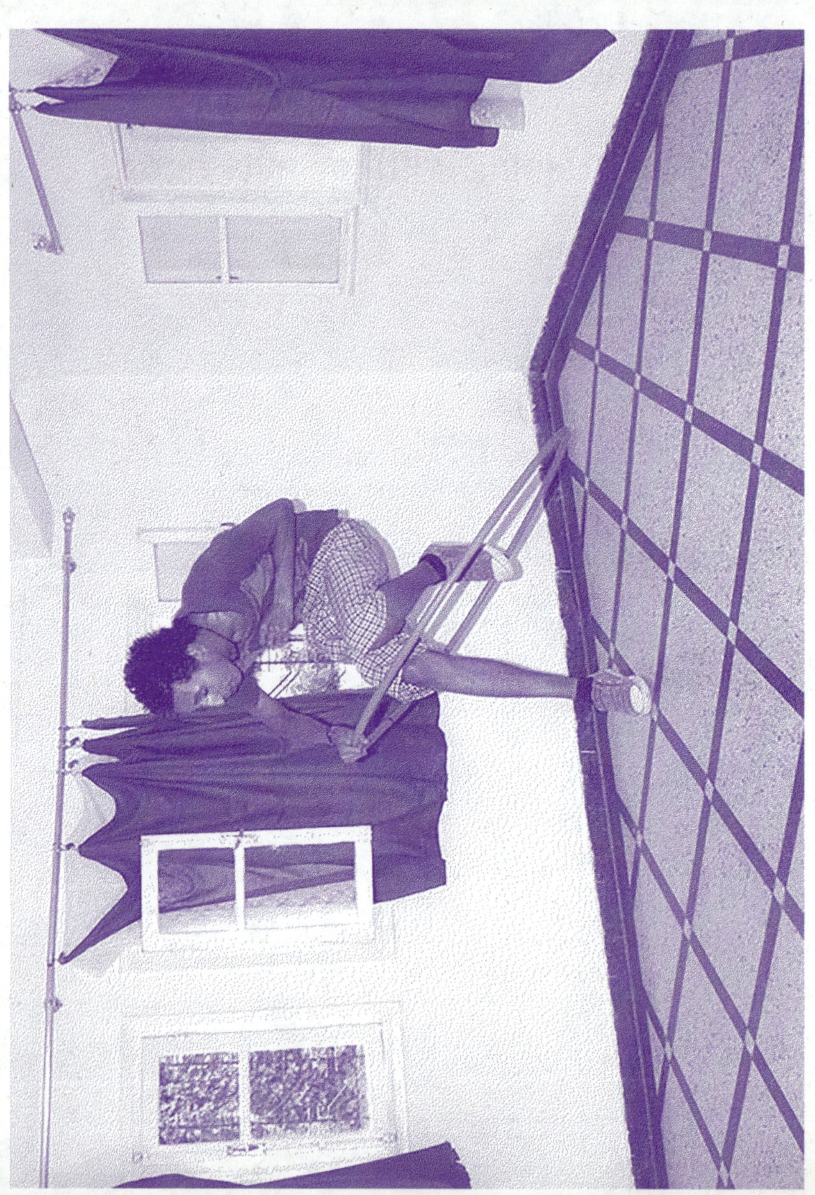

still from *beau travail* (1999) by claire
denis, 90 min. with denis lavant,
michel subor, grégoire colin, richard
courcet. this film focuses on an ex-
foreign legion officer as he recalls
his once glorious life, leading troops
in the gulf of djibouti.

beau travail

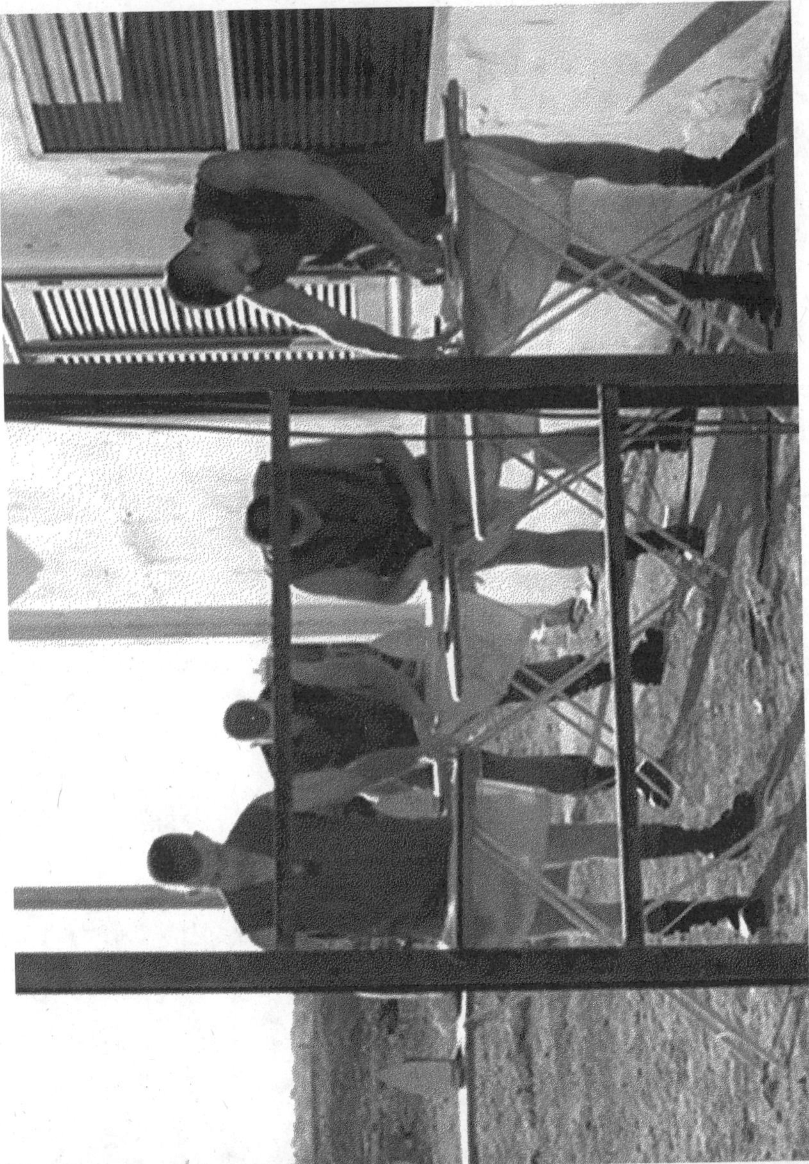

april 6

obsession for food. sunday is
meal day.

sitophilia

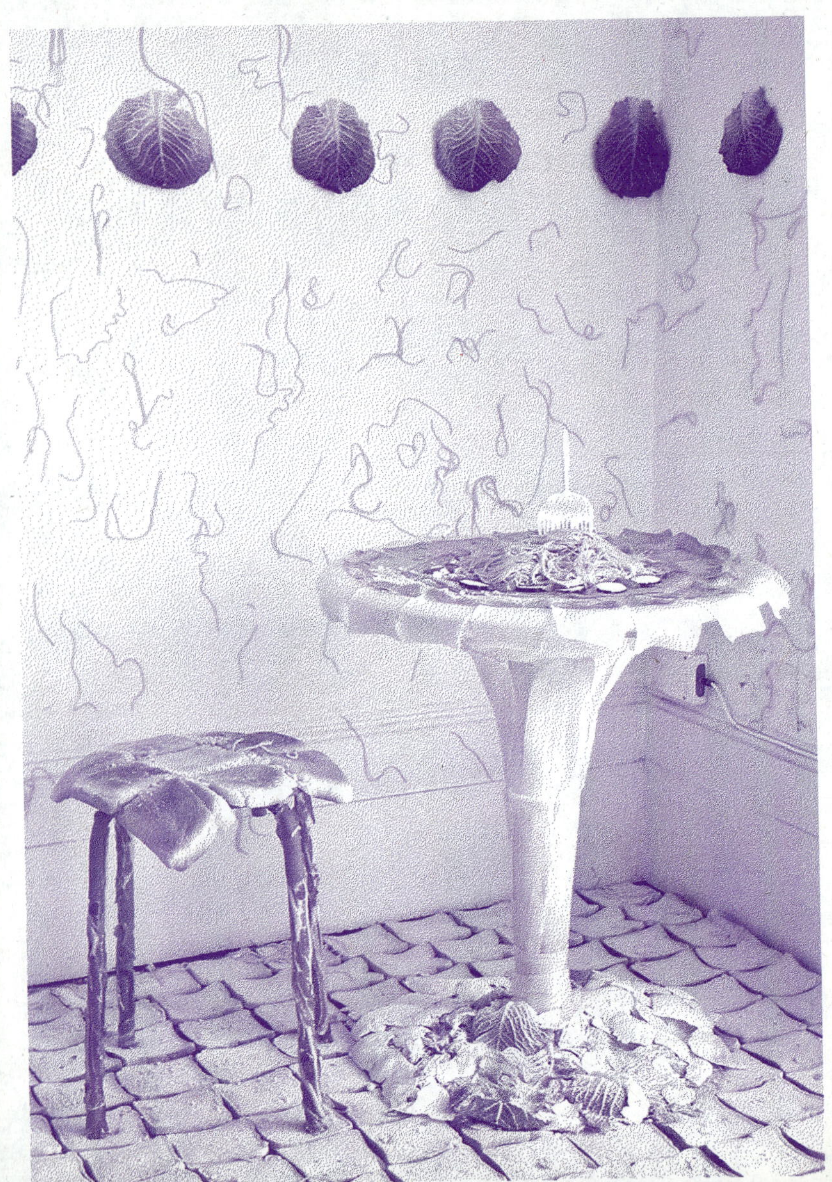

april 7

danger of deportation. still from
tiempo real [real time], (2003),
video, 43 min.

deportation

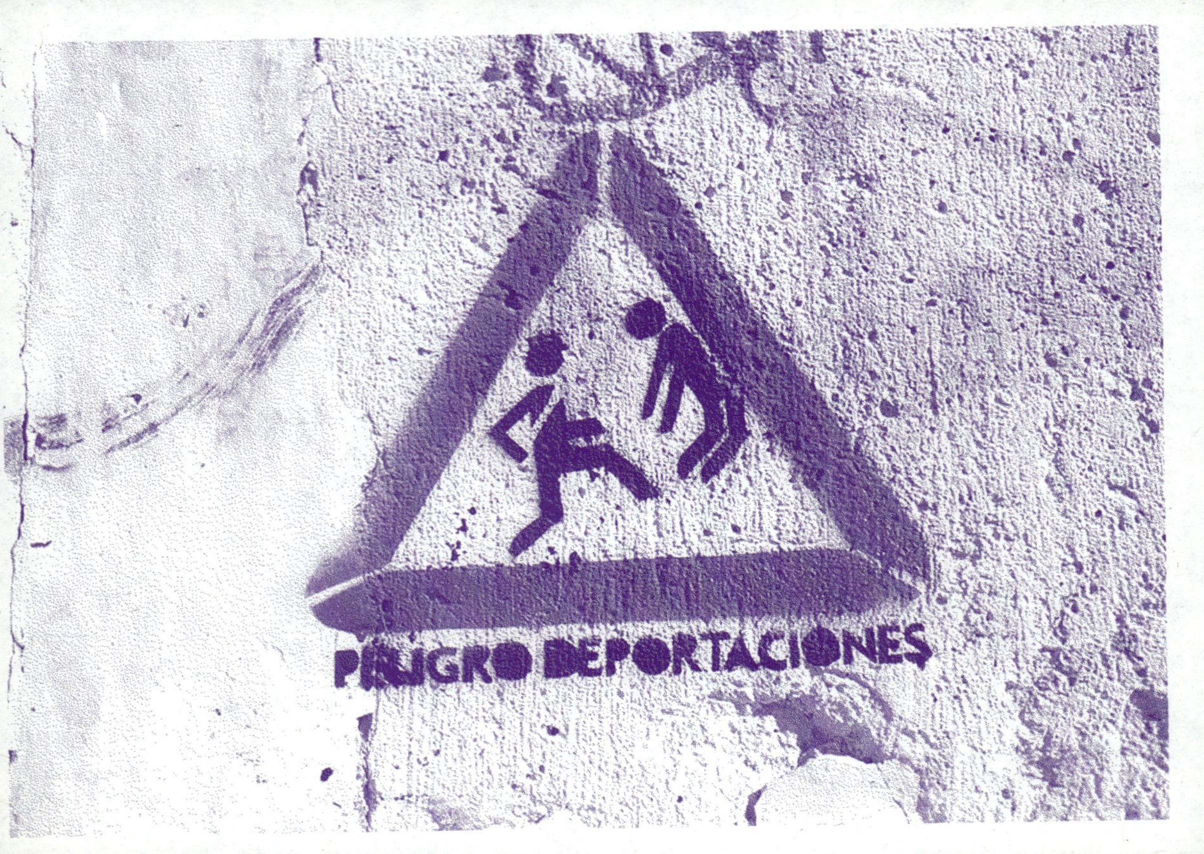
PELIGRO DEPORTACIONES

april 8

gingerbread. family time, saturday
morning, city centre, january 2011.
1 in 3 children are living in poverty
in the uk.

www.endchildpoverty.org.uk

**gingerbread exchanged in
conversation about child poverty**

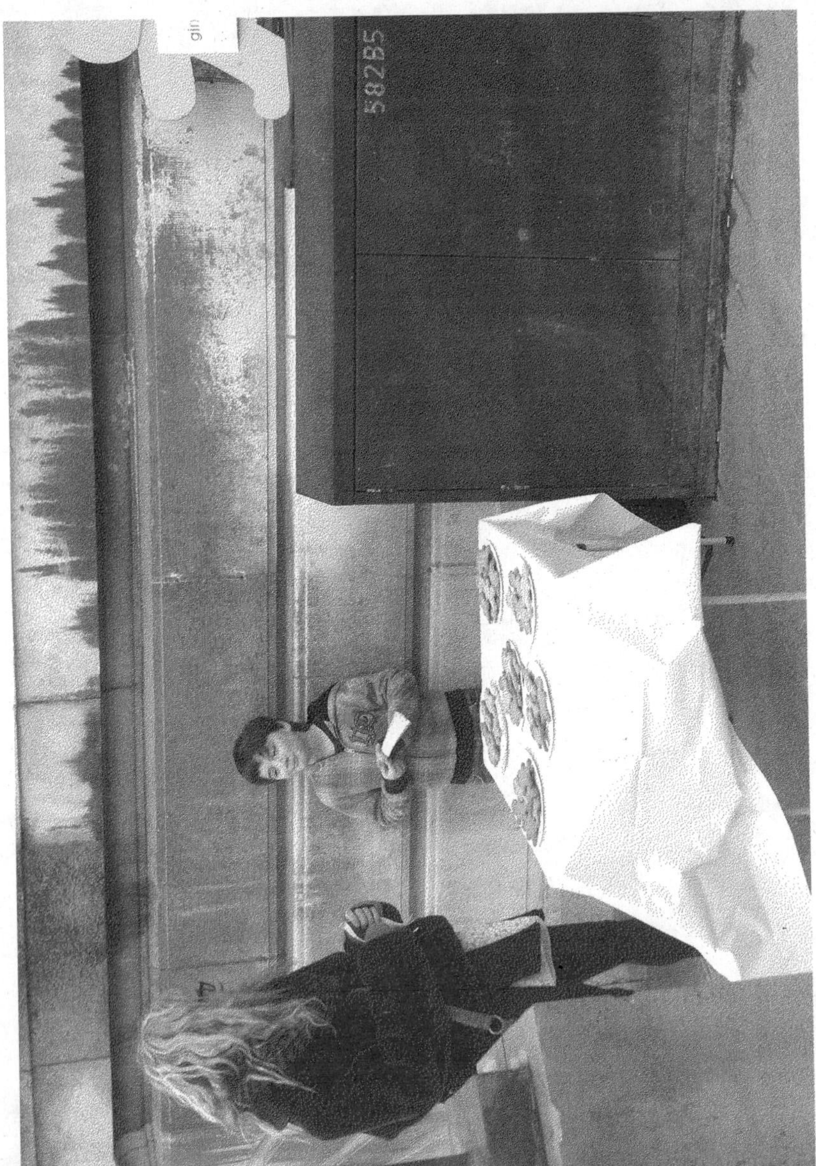

april 9

my flatmate pimping up the ceiling.

paintage moment

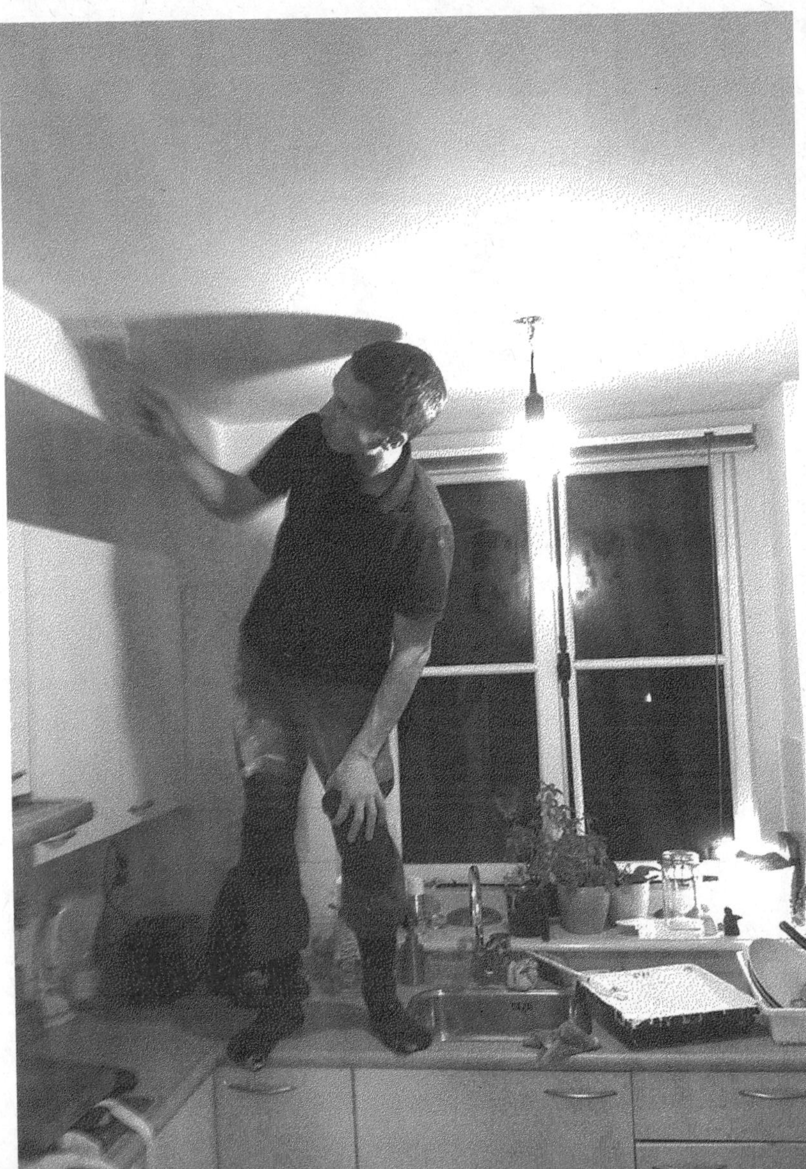

april 10

scrap paper and scissors.

searching for a new apartment

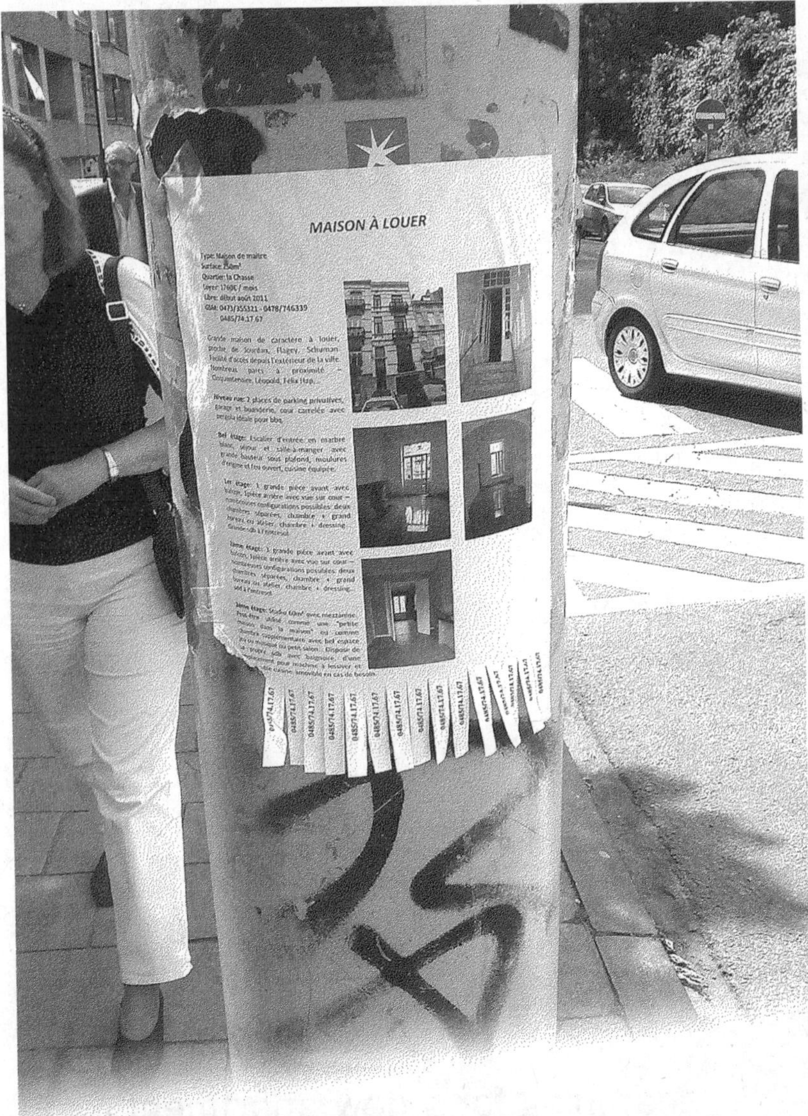

MAISON À LOUER
Type: Maison de maître
Surface: 250m²
Quartier: la Chasse
Loyer: 1760€ / mois
Libre: début août 2011
GSM: 0473/355321 - 0478/746339
0485/74.17.67
Grande maison de caractère à louer,
proche de Jourdan, Flagey, Schuman.
Facilité d'accès depuis l'extérieur de la ville.
Nombreux parcs à proximité —
Cinquantenaire, Léopold, Félix Hap.
Niveau rue: 2 places de parking privatives,
garage et buanderie, cour carrelée avec
pergola idéale pour bbq.
Bel étage: Escalier d'entrée en marbre
blanc, séjour et salle à manger avec
grande hauteur sous plafond, moulures
d'origine et feu ouvert, cuisine équipée.
1er étage: 1 grande pièce avant avec
balcon, 1 pièce arrière avec vue sur cour —
nombreuses configurations possibles: deux
chambres séparées, chambre + grand
bureau ou atelier, chambre + dressing.
2ème étage: 1 grande pièce avant avec
balcon, 1 pièce arrière avec vue sur cour —
nombreuses configurations possibles: deux
chambres séparées, chambre + grand
bureau ou atelier, chambre + dressing.
3ème étage: Studio 60m² avec mezzanine.
Peut être utilisé comme une "petite
maison dans la maison" ou comme
chambre supplémentaire avec bel espace.
0485/74.17.67

april 11

artists do need a clean house. if not
they might get asthma and might not
be able to perform on their 'level' or
to be in that 'zone.'

artists need a clean house too

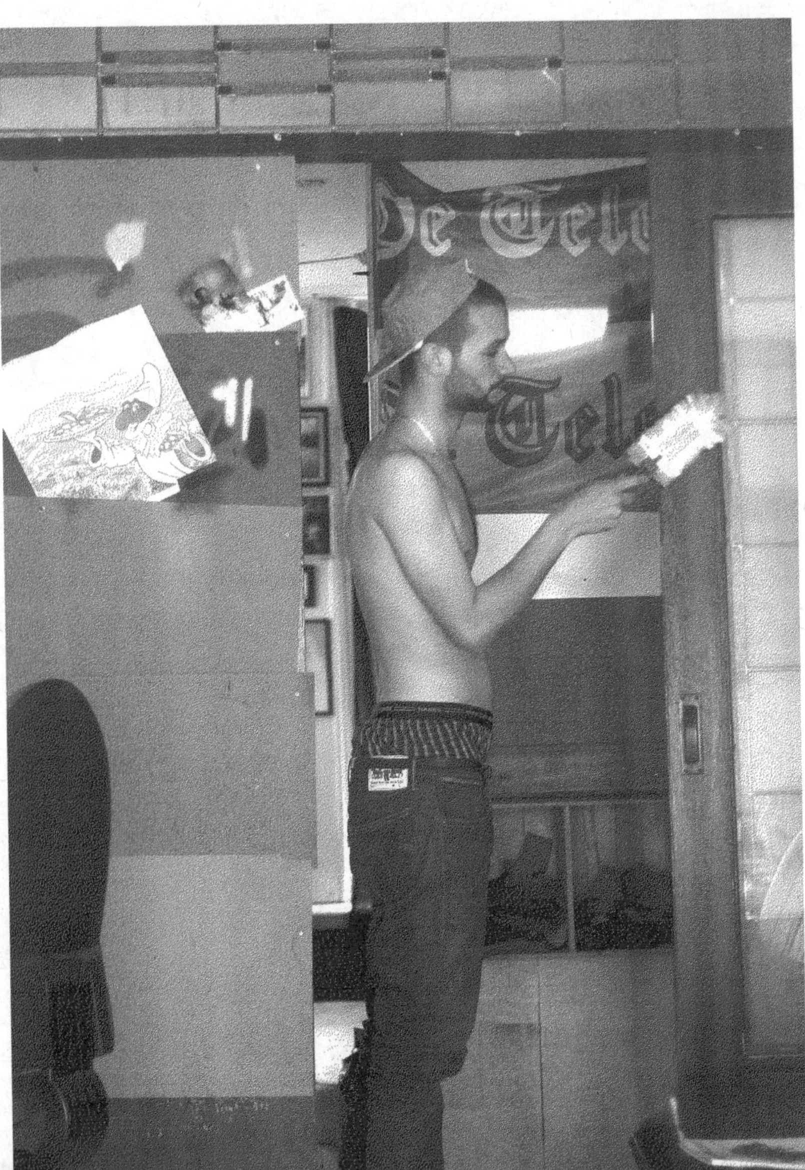

april 12

we are still working.

information gathering

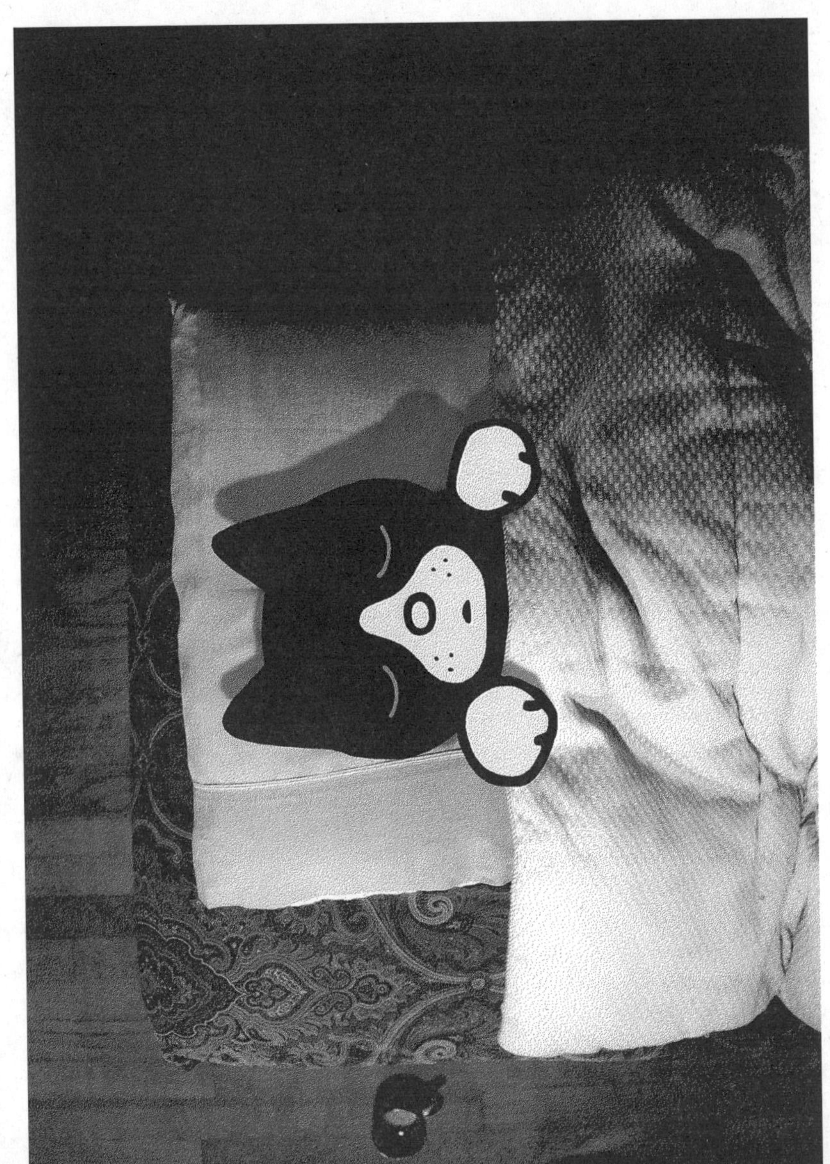

april 13

in the global movement that occupied
central squares all over the world
in 2011, cleaning and caring for public
space became part of protesters
actions. plaça catalunya, barcelona.

cleaning for the revolution

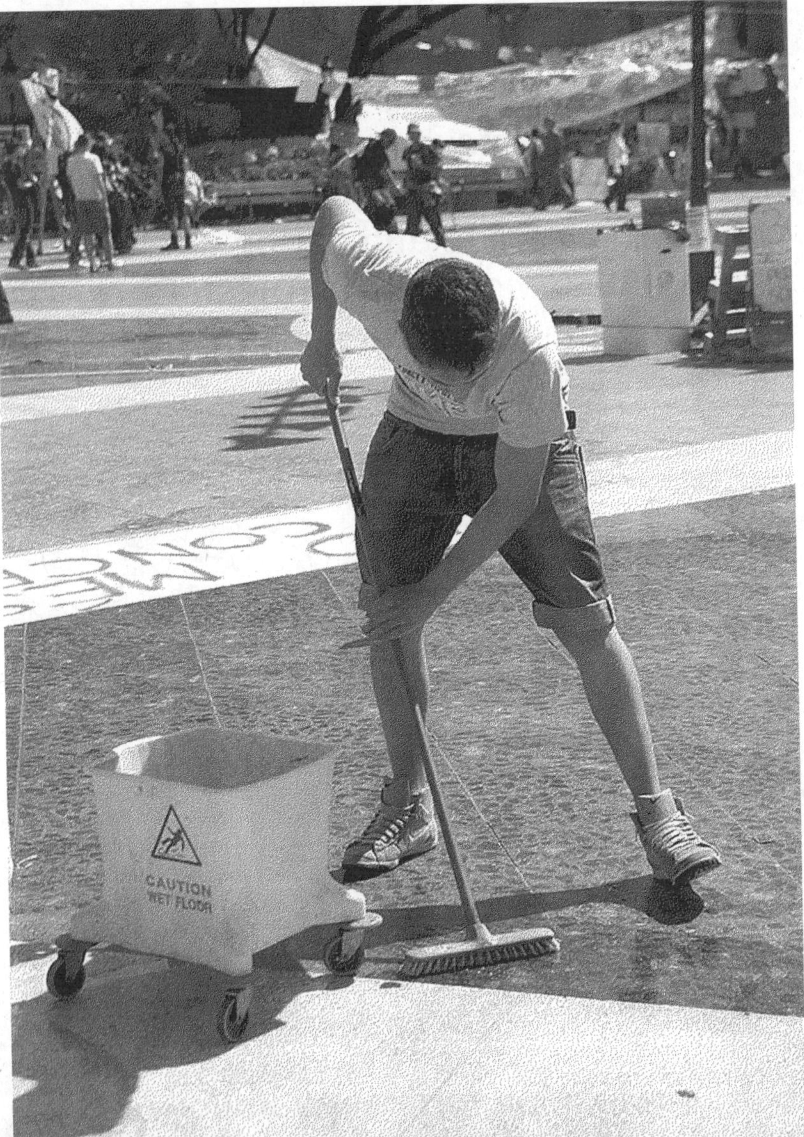
CAUTION
WET FLOOR

april 14

the politics of/on everyday.
sustainable tasks. feet.

remains unsolved

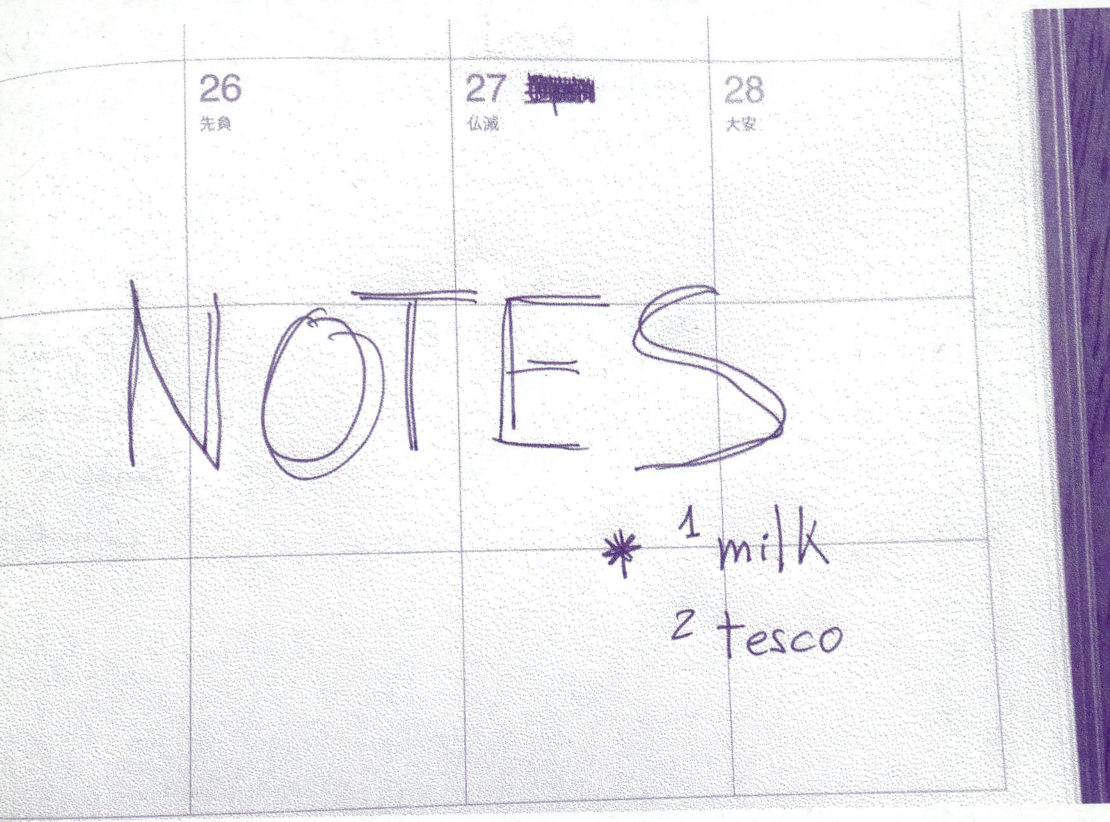

25
先負
26
先負
27
仏滅
28
大安
NOTES
* 1 milk
2 tesco

april 15

a picnic with other domestic workers.
sharing, togetherness, and being
united as one voice.

picnic, 2011

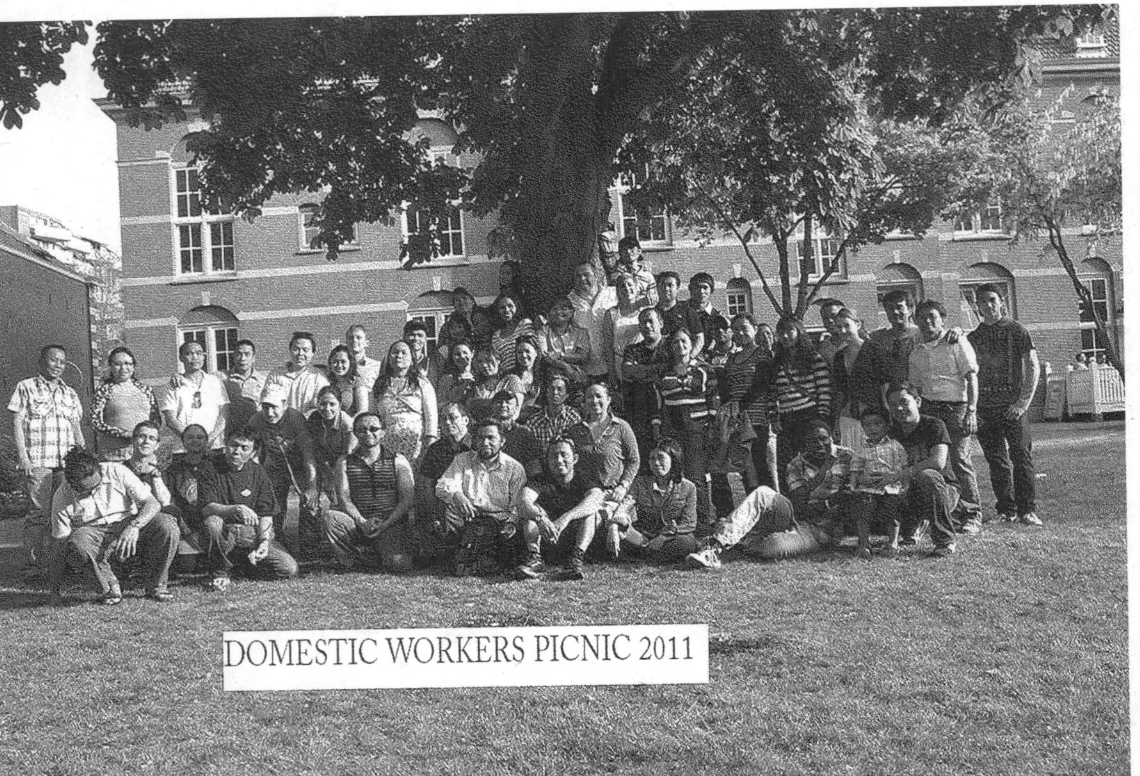

DOMESTIC WORKERS PICNIC 2011

self-portrait (1987). at home, this is my only painting that hangs on the wall, the other ones are just leaning against it.

today i don't feel like ironing

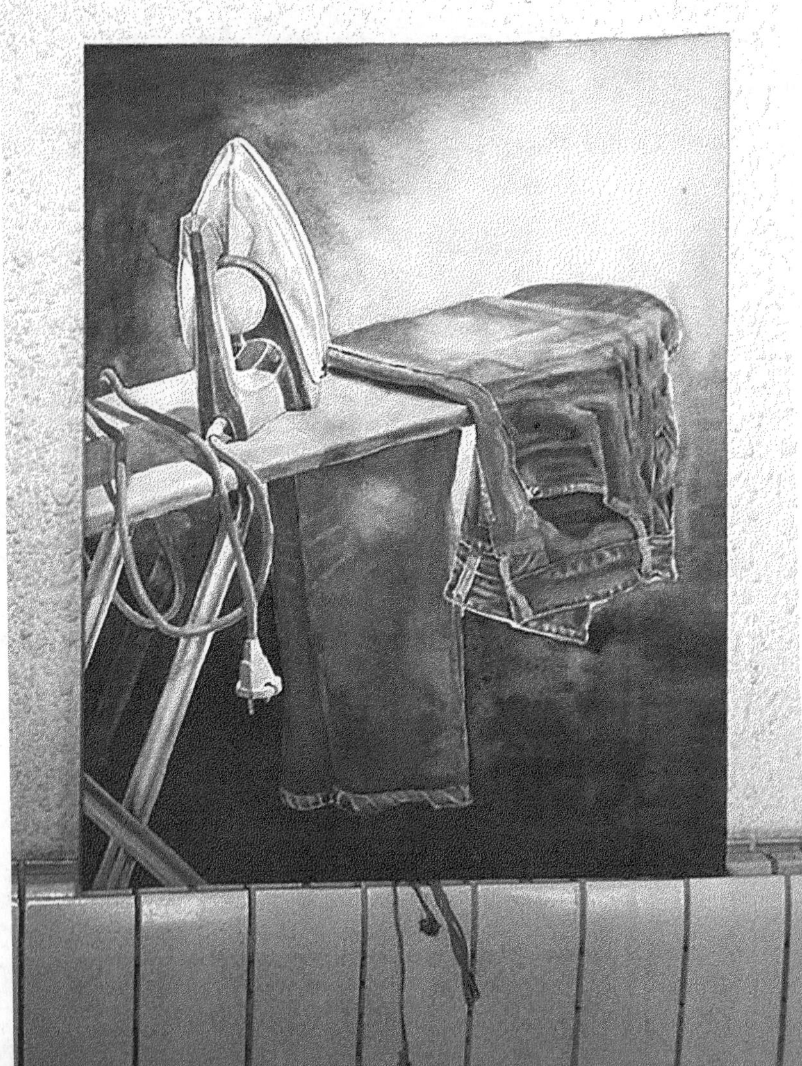

april 17

radio pakita. radio workshop at
centro cultural francesca bonne-
maison. barcelona.

mujeres activistas construyendo

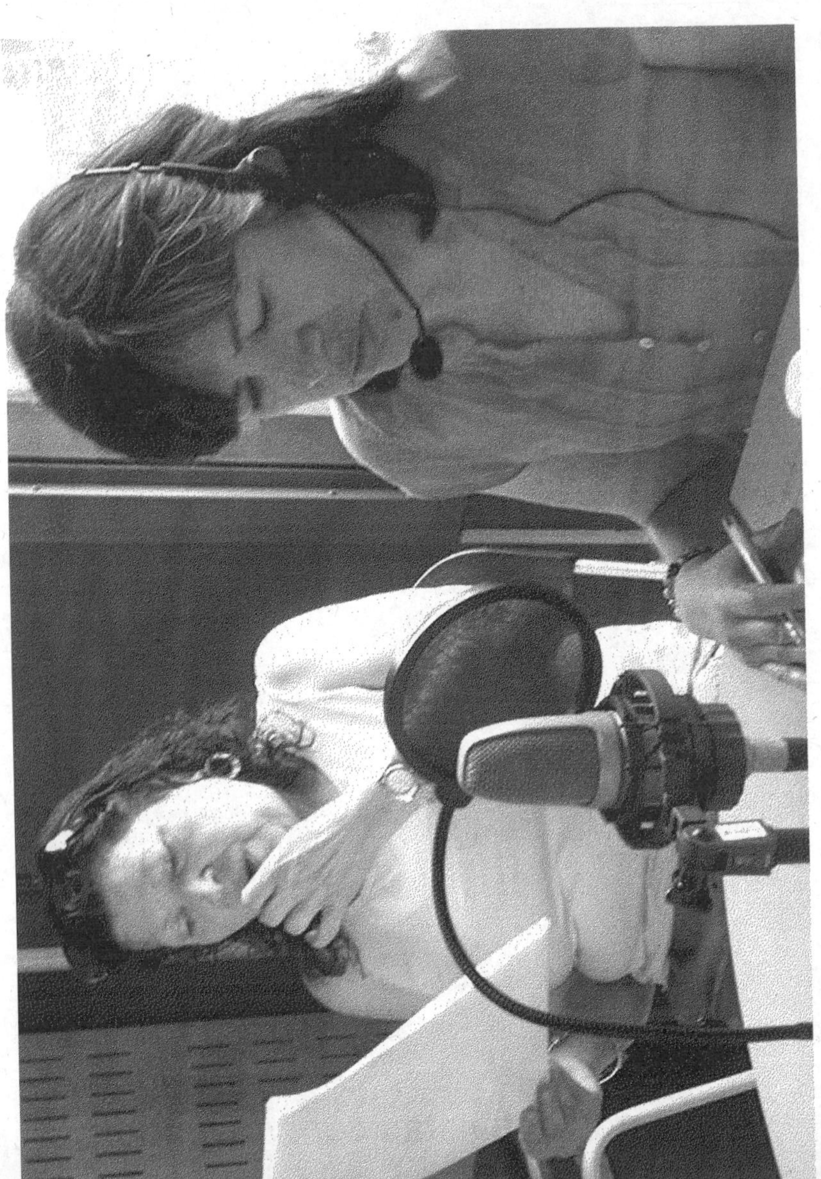

april 18

menu para cuatro.

menu diario

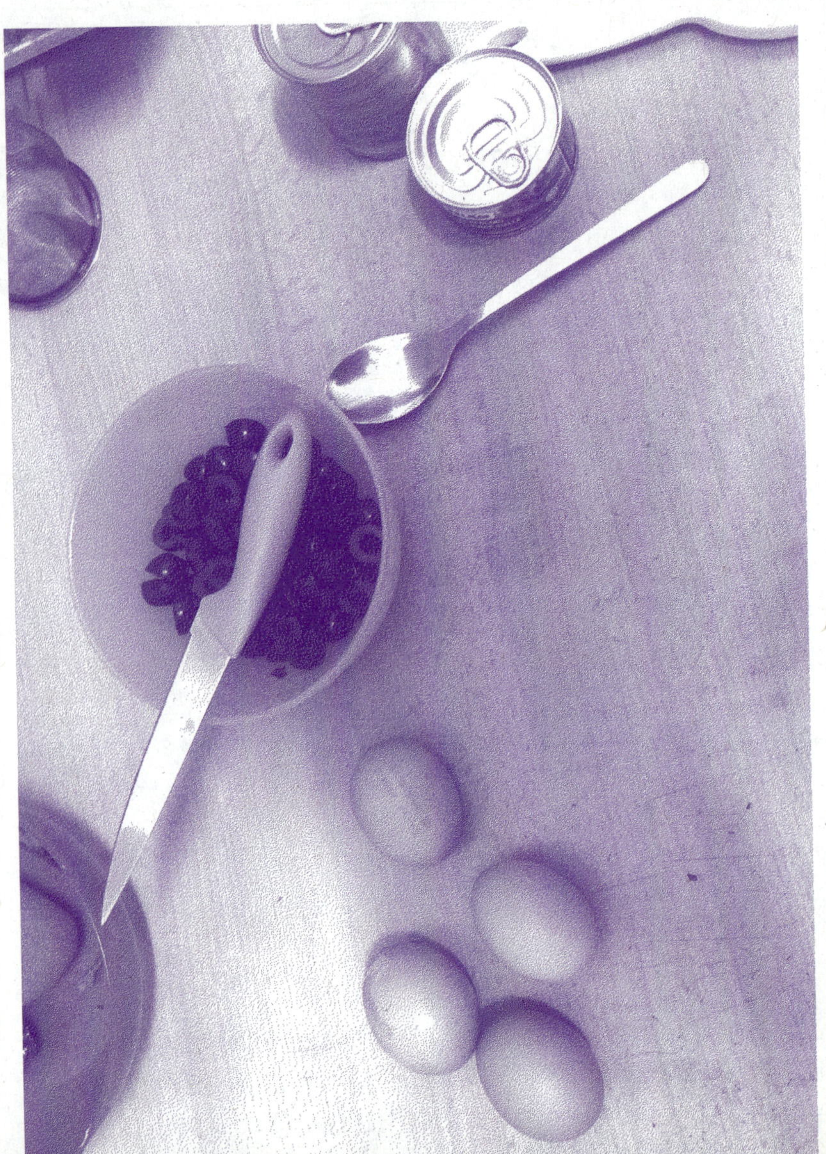

photograph from the house where
i grew up, taken by my father or
my mother in 1982 or 1983.

making music

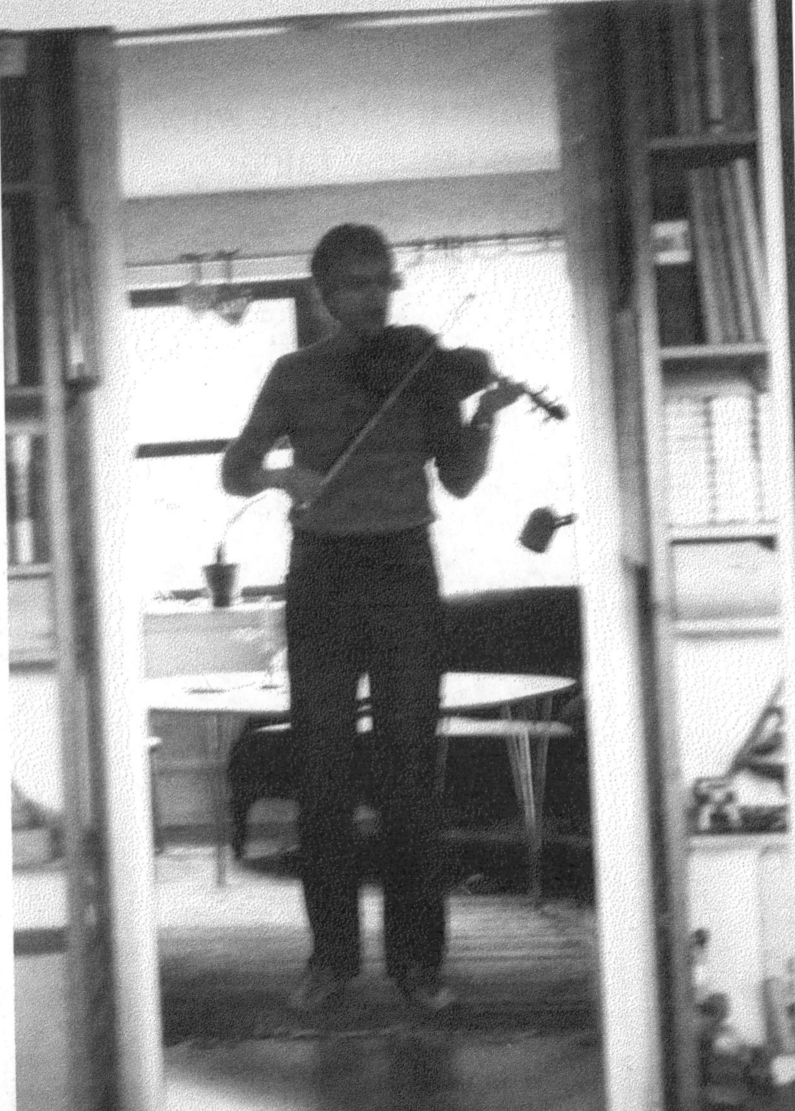

april 20

good breakfast.

orange juice

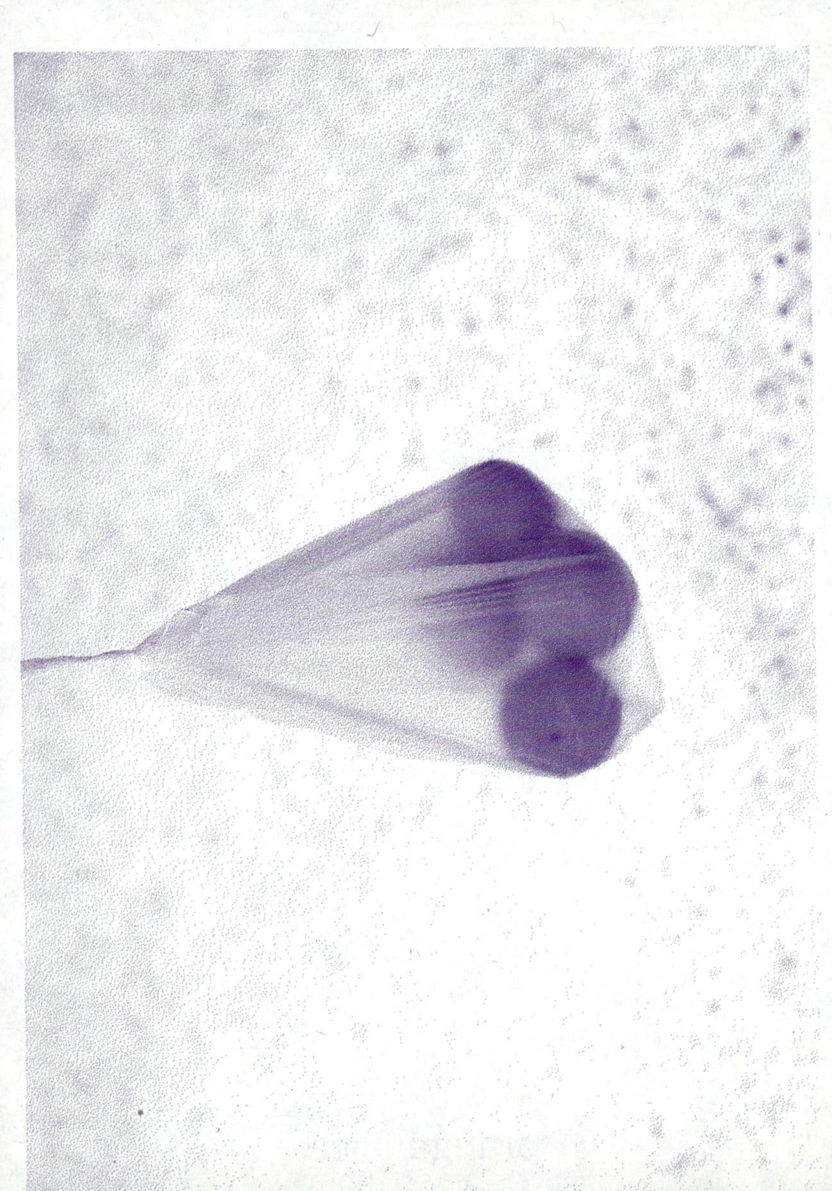

april 21

bathroom washing

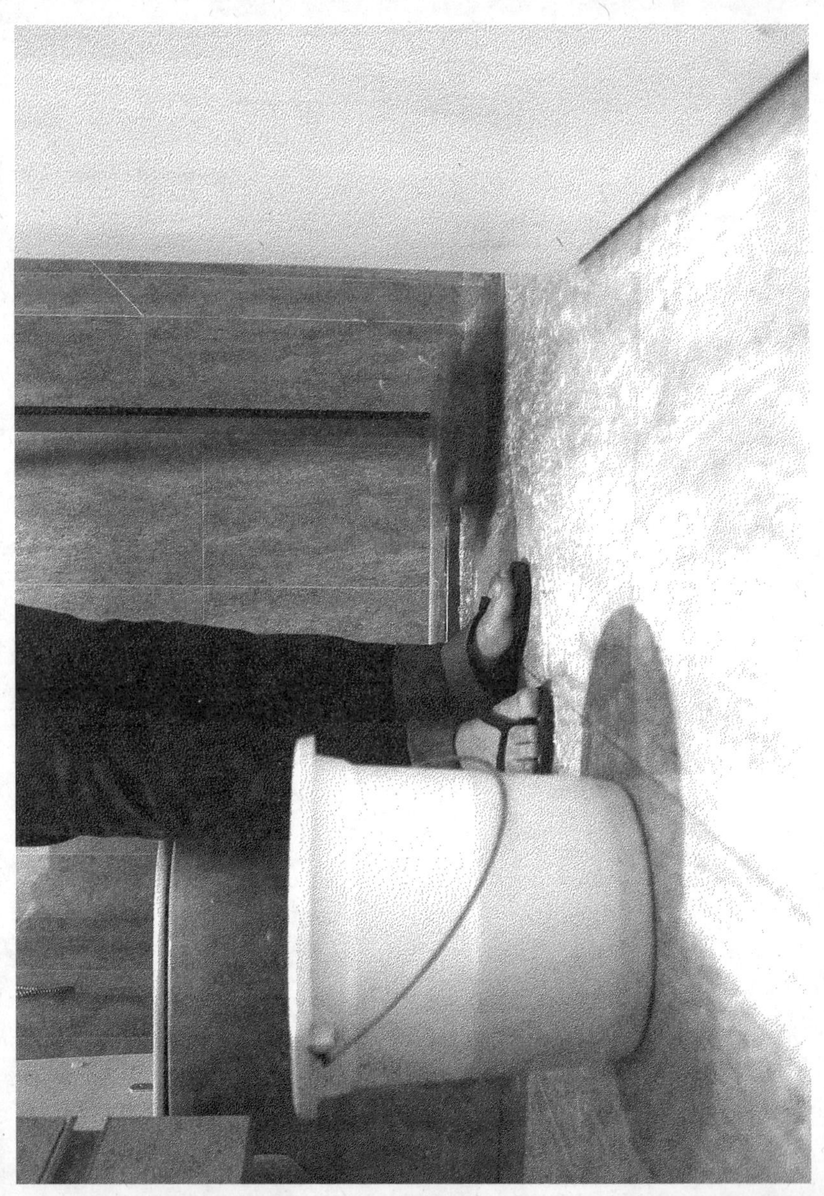

april 22

learning to make empanadas.

empanadas

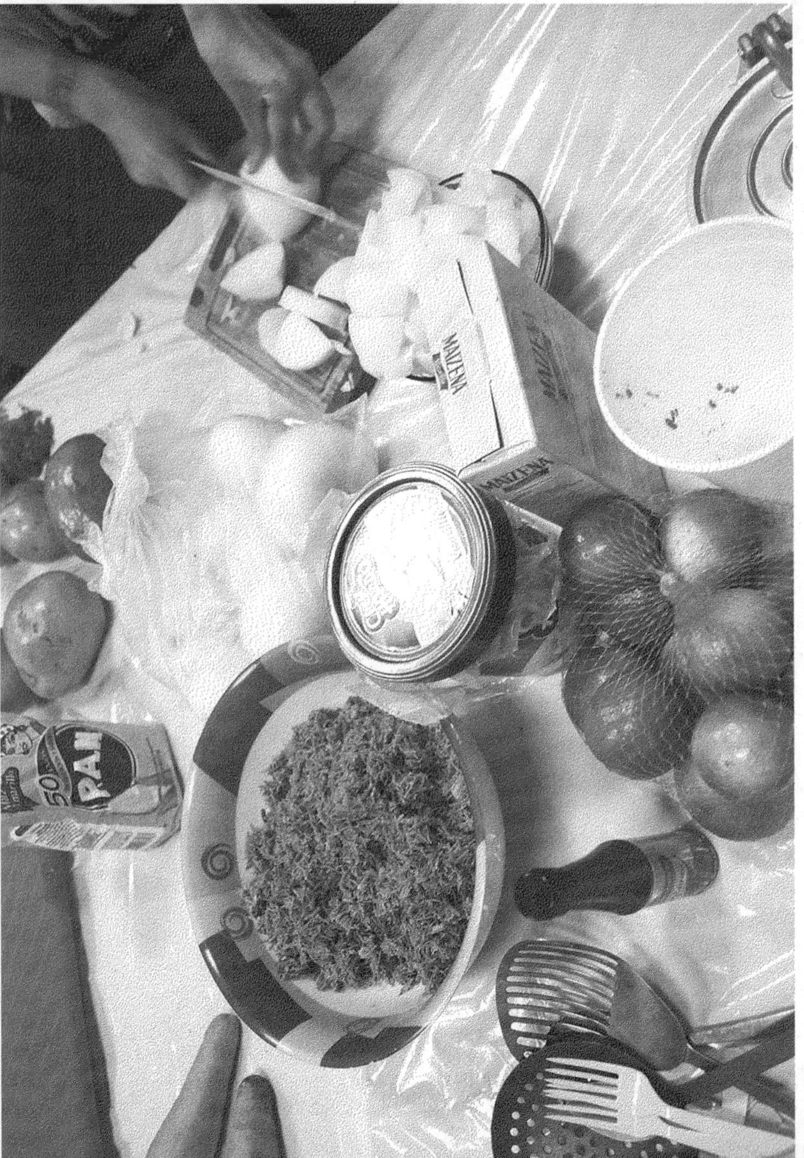

april 23

recycle the function of the household,
not only plastic.

recycle

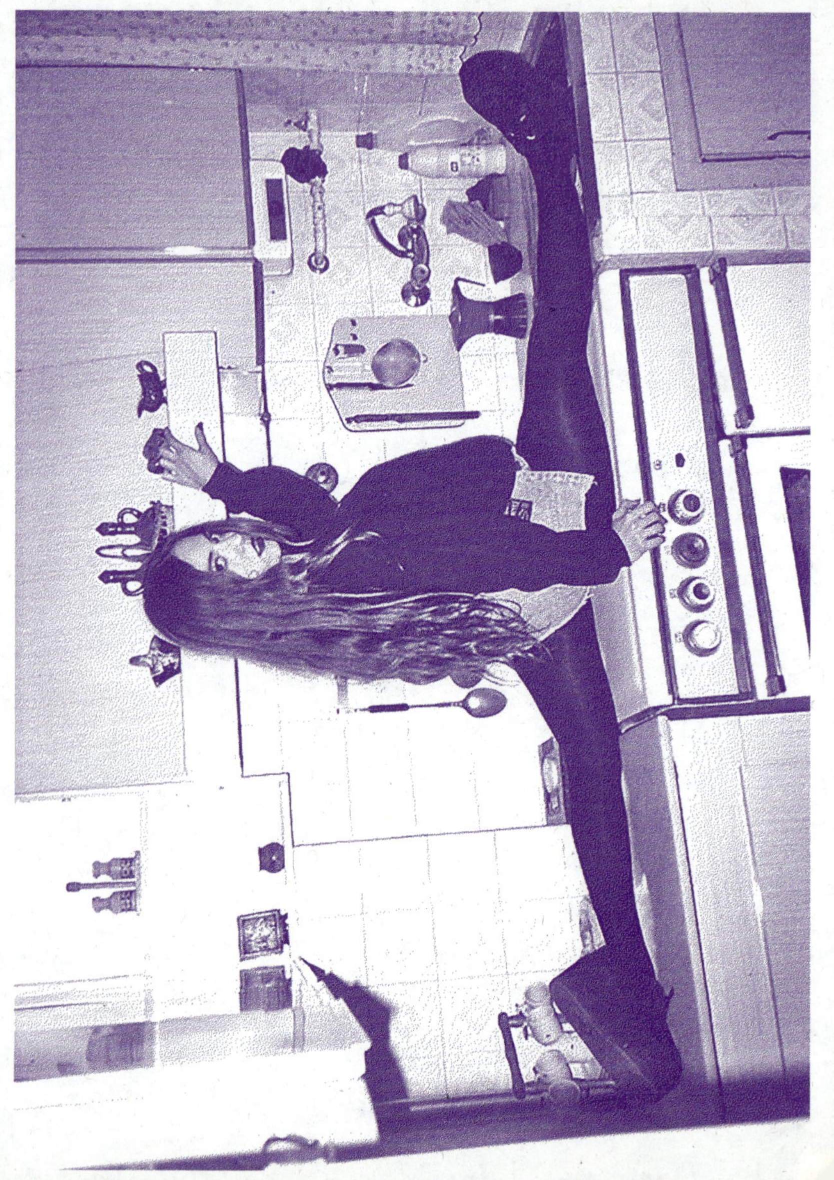

april 24

someone left these two conceptual
monochromes in my office.

white/blue

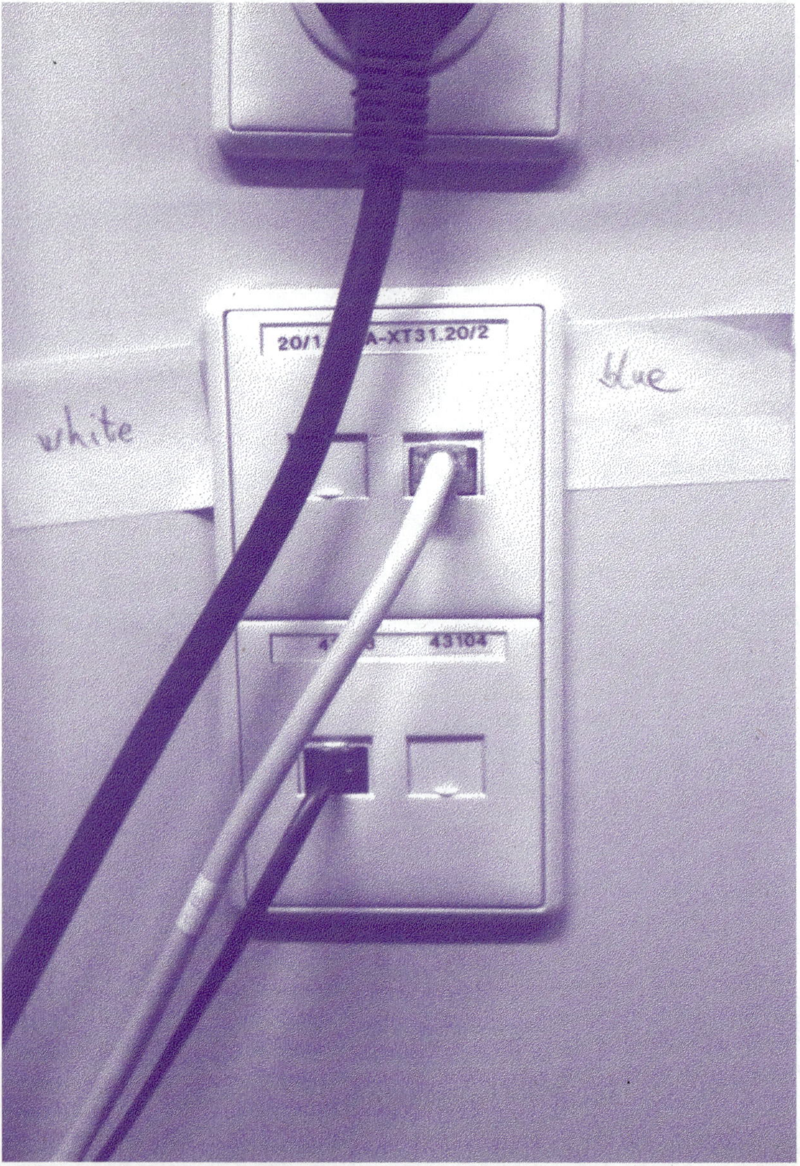

white
blue
20/1   A-XT31.20/2
43104

april 25

is this domestic? is this labour?
(photograph taken by someone in the
family of my father and his friends).

young workers

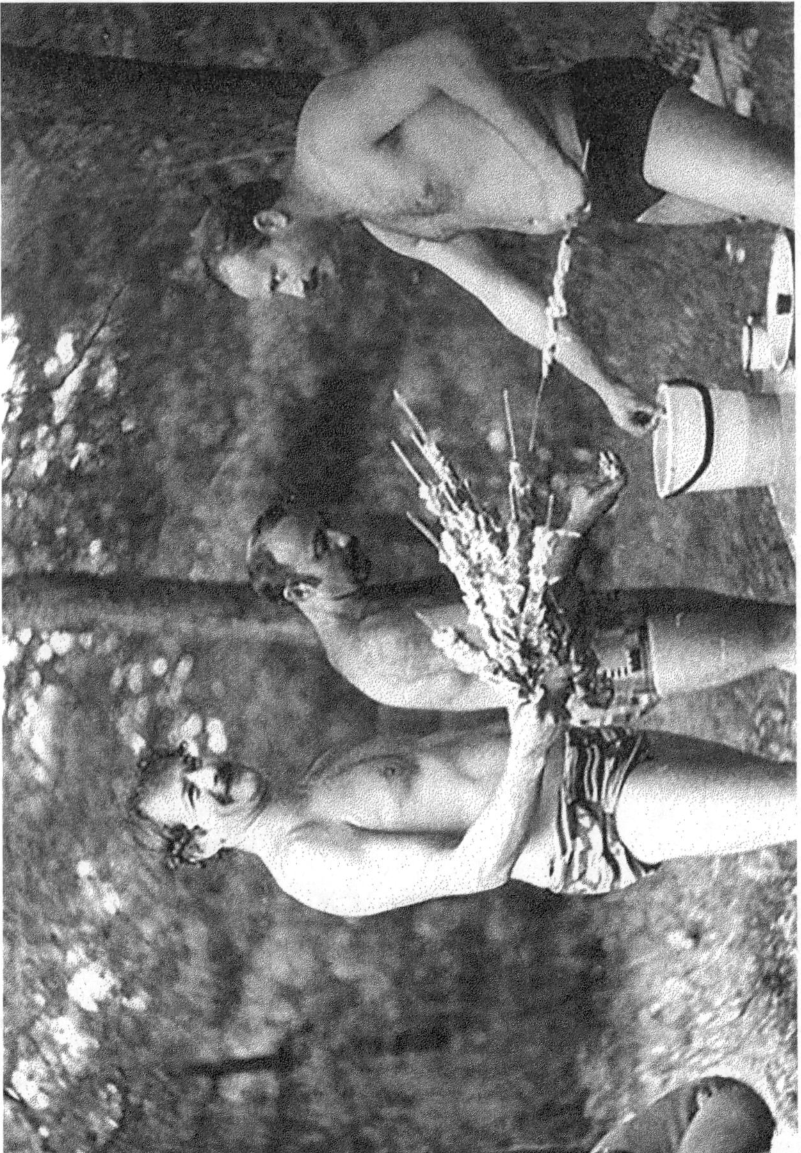

april 26

haircut in exchange for help
on web-coding.

domestic haircut

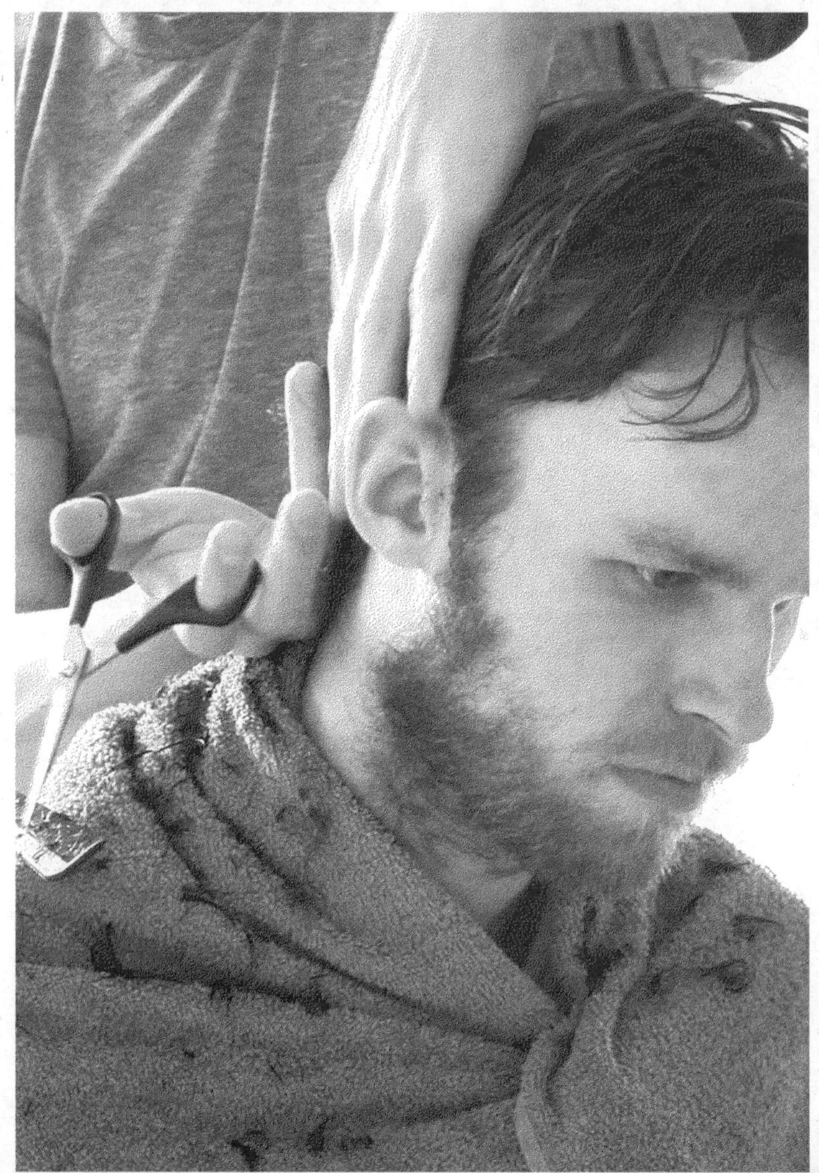

april 27

suicide is not for you.

man with architecture

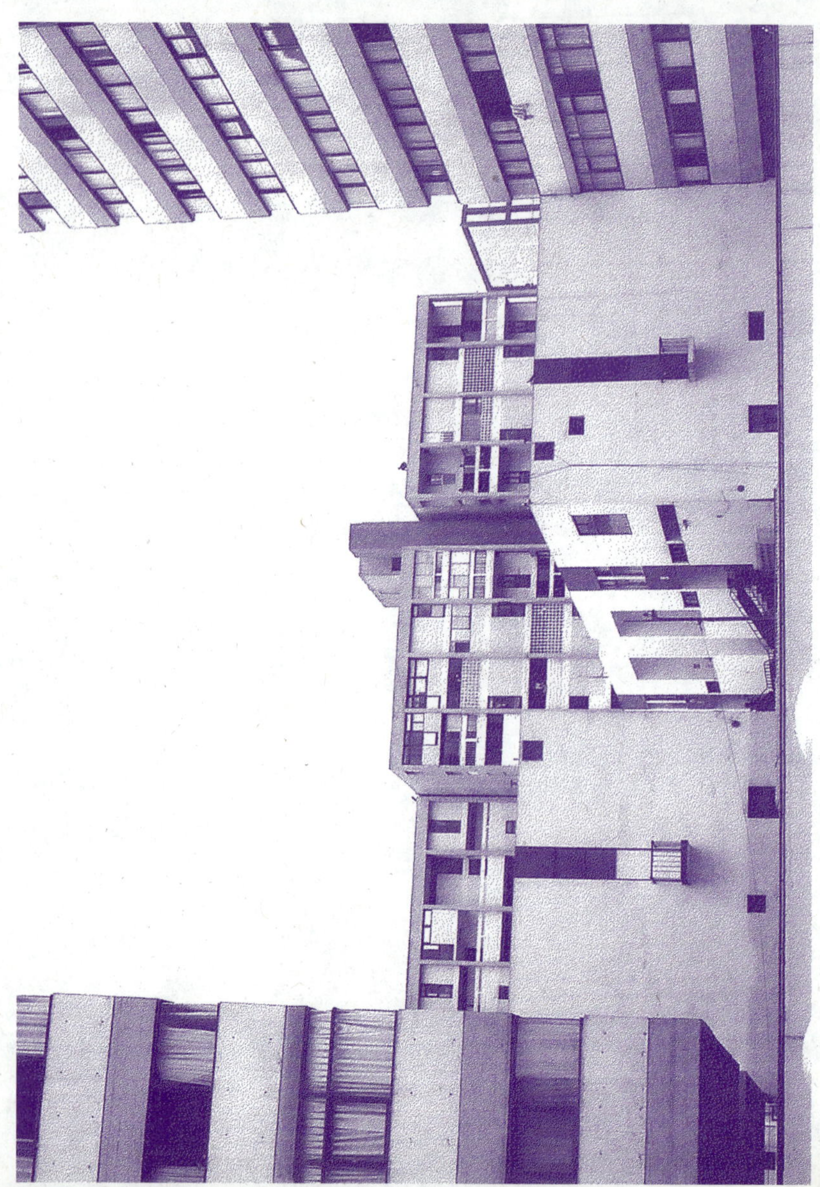

april 28

by cezary bodzianowski. seen at the
exhibition *cartografías contem-
poráneas* at caixaforum, barcelona.

rainbow, bathroom, lodz.

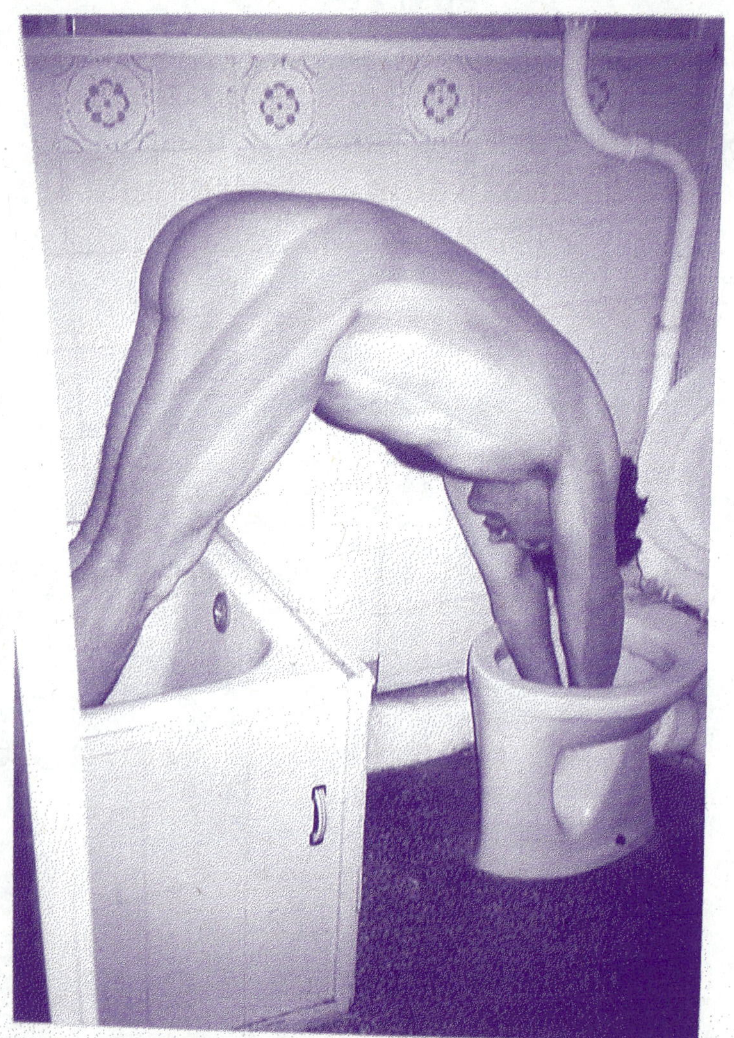

image of our office-house in the '80s.
as it is still now, our headquarters,
this house has a long tradition of more
than a residential space, being a space
of work.

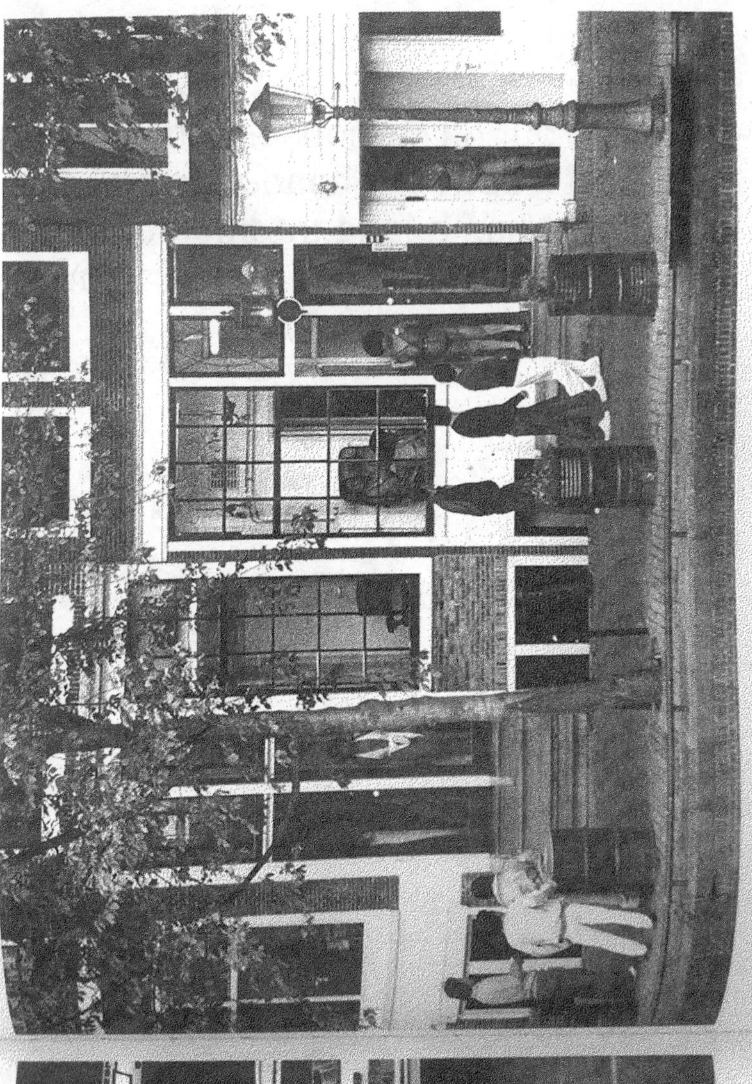

april 30

picking up shells and stones one
thursday afternoon down by the queen
elizabeth walk with the children. picture
shows various elements of arts.

elements

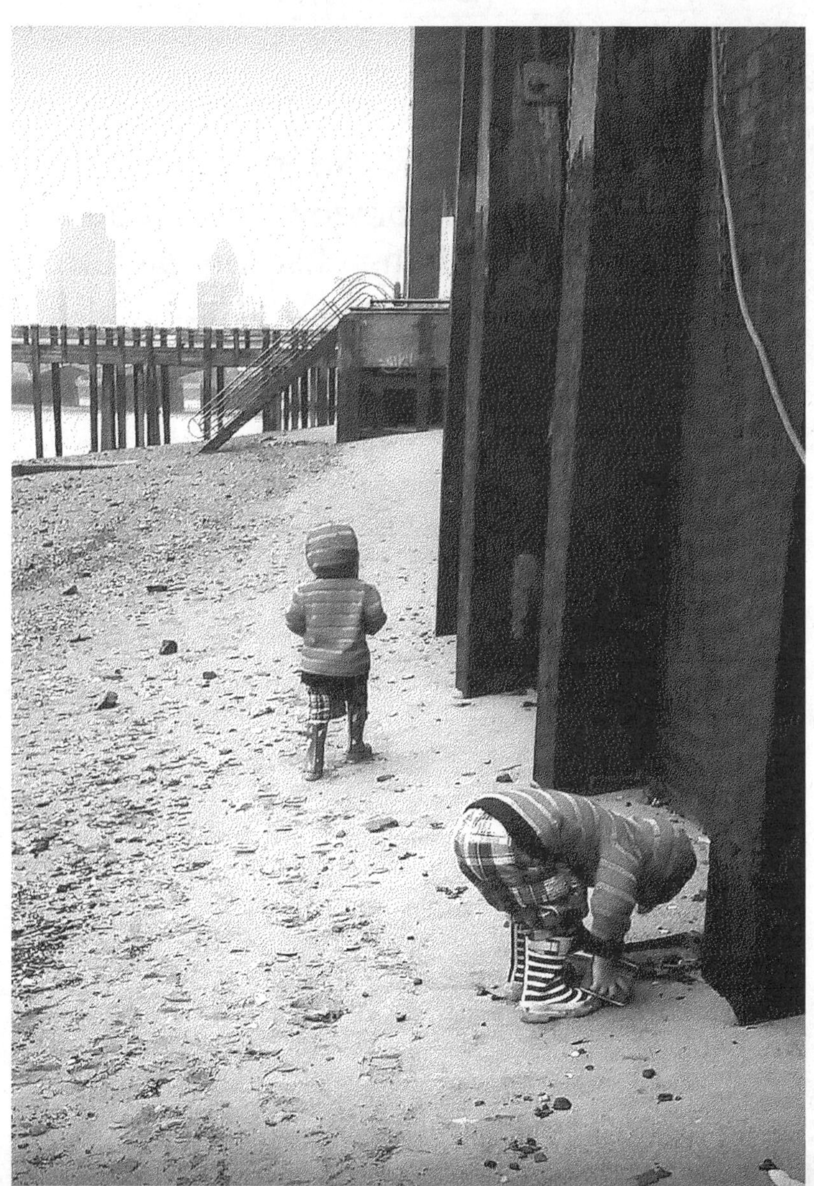

may 1	marissa	domestic worker & coordinator	london
may 2	realizza	domestic worker & visual artist	london
may 3	realizza	domestic worker & visual artist	london
may 4	trenton	publisher	london
may 5	daniela	artist	barcelona
may 6	trenton	publisher	london
may 7	pinky & bunny	cats	the desert
may 8	maria	artist, researcher, & teacher	barcelona
may 9	scott	artist	glasgow
may 10	thomas	designer	bruxelles
may 11	pilar	architect	castellón
may 12	bernardo	artist	amsterdam
may 13	tessa	visual artist	nowhere
may 14	lucia	artist	bogotá
may 15	luciana	photographer	bologna
may 16	christian	artist	london
may 17	project 181	collaborators	atlanta
may 18	sindihogar	union of domestic and care workers	barcelona
may 19	adam	landscape architect	nowhere
may 20	esmee	artist	amsterdam
may 21	stas	graphic designer	brussels
may 22	anacoreta	domestic worker	london
may 23	sohrab	artist	london
may 24	sebastien	civil servant	paris
may 25	marc	artist	amsterdam
may 26	ernst	artist	berlin
may 27	ariella	philosopher	tel aviv
may 28	kim	artist & curator	new york
may 29	al fadhil	artist	lebanon
may 30	sabrina	communication consultant	amsterdam
may 31	laura jane	cinema worker & print maker	hackney
jun. 1	denise	graphic designer	tokyo
jun. 2	agne	artist	amsterdam
jun. 3	flavia	filmaker	amsterdam
jun. 4	vika	artist	amsterdam
jun. 5	luciana	photographer	amsterdam
jun. 6	emily	mother & artist	toronto
jun. 7	angela	artist & student	madrid
jun. 8	jena	domestic worker	singapore
jun. 9	reinilde	student	curaçao
jun. 10	raquel	photographer	barcelona
jun. 11	mirari	photographer & babysitter	brooklyn
jun. 12	yuji	unknown	madrid
jun. 13	ariadna	artist & nighttime tour guide	barcelona
jun. 14	ronan	artist	brittany
jun. 15	wok the rock	visual artist	yogyakarta
jun. 16	rogier	artist	amsterdam
jun. 17	roman	producer	barcelona

Date	Name	Role	City
jun. 18	francesca	artist	london
jun. 19	erik	visual artist	amsterdam
jun. 20	la caníbal	bookstore clerks	barcelona
jun. 21	mercedes	artist	barcelona
jun. 22	leanne	graphic design student	london
jun. 23	valery	photographer	st. petersburg
jun. 24	marina		amsterdam
jun. 25	noemí	retoucher & image editor	barcelona
jun. 26	realizza	domestic worker & visual artist	london
jun. 27	jolanda	permanent student	madrid
jun. 28	benji	student	seattle
jun. 29	trenton	publisher	london
jun. 30	joão	designer	oslo
jul. 1	rafael	artist	camp largo
jul. 2	scott	artist	glasgow
jul. 3	pilar	architect	castellón
jul. 4	maría	artist, researcher, & teacher	barcelona
jul. 5	daniele	photographer	napoli
jul. 6	bernardo	artist	amsterdam
jul. 7	wilma	domestic worker & j4dw fundraiser	london
jul. 8	marilou	student	amsterdam
jul. 9	torkel	cultural analyst & writer	stockholm
jul. 10	pinky & bunny	cats	the desert
jul. 11	marissa	domestic worker & union coordinator	london
jul. 12	tessa	visual artist	berlin
jul. 13	lucía	artist	barcelona
jul. 14	anacoreta	domestic worker	amsterdam
jul. 15	serena	painter	milano
jul. 16	project 181	collaborators	atlanta
jul. 17	lucía	artist	barcelona
jul. 18	marc	artist	barcelona
jul. 19	adam	landscape architect	hong kong
jul. 20	roma	artists, activists, & architects	sheffield
jul. 21	sohrab	artist	london
jul. 22	sebastien	civil servant	den haag
jul. 23	ulla	artist	amsterdam
jul. 24	machiel	art student	amsterdam
jul. 25	al fadhil	artist	milano
jul. 26	sarah	student	amsterdam
jul. 27	flavia	filmmaker	amsterdam
jul. 28	denise	graphic designer	tokyo
jul. 29	carolina	graphic designer & student	bogotá
jul. 30	pierre-henri	cabinet du maire du 3e arrdt.	paris
jul. 31	reinilde	student	curaçao
aug. 1	robin	not-writer, maybe sculptor, student	amsterdam
aug. 2	katayoun	artworker	amsterdam
aug. 3	raquel	photographer	amsterdam
aug. 4	mario	unknown	madrid

aug. 5	cocco	fashion designer	paris
aug. 6	alicja	artist	warsaw
aug. 7	ben	bead maker	london
aug. 8	aitziber	cultural worker & filmmaker	barcelona
aug. 9	stephen	curator & artist	de pere
aug. 10	jesper	artist	stockholm
aug. 11	lorena	psychologist	móstoles
aug. 12	esmee	artist & student	eindhoven
aug. 13	marianna	curator	berlin
aug. 14	sinquenza	artist & curator	home
aug. 15	binna	curator	utrecht
aug. 16	ina	graphic designer	weimar
aug. 17	caro	photographer	ghent
aug. 18	isabel	artist	amsterdam
aug. 19	neodoze	designer	madrid
aug. 20	anacoreta	domestic worker	amsterdam
aug. 21	realizza	domestic worker & visual artist	london
aug. 22	maría	artist, researcher, & teacher	barcelona
aug. 23	daniela	artist	barcelona
aug. 24	scott	artist	glasgow
aug. 25	marissa	domestic worker & union coordinator	london
aug. 26	pinky & bunny	cats	the desert
aug. 27	pilar	architect	castellón
aug. 28	zoe & eira	artist collaborative	glasgow
aug. 29	lucía	artist	barcelona
aug. 30	thomas	designer	bruxelles
aug. 31	lucía	artist	barcelona
sept. 1	marissa	domestic worker & union coordinator	london
sept. 2	laura jane	cinema worker & print maker	hackney
sept. 3	roma	artists, activists, architects	sheffield
sept. 4	diet	poet & journalist	utrecht
sept. 5	sebastien	civil servant	den haag
sept. 6	camilla	antiques dealer	verona
sept. 7	machiel	art student	amsterdam
sept. 8	margarita		amsterdam
sept. 9	emily	mother & artist	toronto
sept. 10	agne	artist	amsterdam
sept. 11	luciana	photographer	amsterdam
sept. 12	angela	artist & student	madrid
sept. 13	luciana	photographer	amsterdam
sept. 14	andrea	writer & part-time bookseller	barcelona
sept. 15	tessie	domestic helper	singapore
sept. 16	flavia	graphic designer & illustrator	toronto
sept. 17	alice	journalist	toulouse
sept. 18	jason	writer, invigilator, work from home	london
sept. 19	marta	documentarist	barcelona
sept. 20	micheál	autonomous artist	london
sept. 21	jan	art student	amsterdam

Date	Name	Role	City
sept. 22	maiko	curator	amsterdam
sept. 23	marcel	graphic artist	
sept. 24	sarah	fine art student	rotterdam
sept. 25	felipe	artist	bogotá
sept. 26	catherine	graphic artist	são paulo
sept. 27	neme		madrid
sept. 28	annie	teacher	amsterdam
sept. 29	marissa	domestic worker & union coordinator	london
sept. 30	jenny	producer	st. martí vell
oct. 1	trenton	publisher	london
oct. 2	realizza	domestic worker & visual artist	london
oct. 3	pinky & bunny	cats	the desert
oct. 4	daniela	artist	barcelona
oct. 5	scott	artist	glasgow
oct. 6	pilard	architect	castellón
oct. 7	lamis	housework, practitioner	london
oct. 8	thomas	designer	bruxelles
oct. 9	project 181	collaborators	atlanta
oct. 10	anacoreta	domestic worker	amsterdam
oct. 11	stas	graphic designer	prague
oct. 12	merve	artist	new york
oct. 13	sebastien	civil servant	den haag
oct. 14	esmee	artist & student	eindhoven
oct. 15	camilla	antiques dealer	verona
oct. 16	machiel	art student	amsterdam
oct. 17	margarita		amsterdam
oct. 18	dooho	artist	amsterdam
oct. 19	agne	artist	amsterdam
oct. 20	luciana	photographer	amsterdam
may 21	reinilde	student	amsterdam
oct. 22	juan carlos	vividor	madrid
oct. 23	rogier	graphic designer & artist	amsterdam
oct. 24	realizza	domestic worker & visual artist	london
oct. 25	andrea	writer & part-time bookseller	shanghai
oct. 26	ariadna	artist & nighttime tourguide	barcelona
oct. 27	oriol	artist	barcelona
oct. 28	astroboi	artist & part-time porn actor	barcelona
oct. 29	anna	interdisciplinary artist	barcelona
oct. 30	jort	visual artist	amsterdam
oct. 31	anacoreta	domestic worker	amsterdam
nov. 1	nadine	artist	berlin
nov. 2	manu	graphic designer	zurich
nov. 3	marieke	artist	amsterdam
nov. 4	christina	multidisciplinary designer	belgrade
nov. 5	will	writer	amsterdam
nov. 6	marissa	domestic worker & j4dw coordinator	london
nov. 7	realizza	domestic worker & visual artist	london
nov. 8	pinky & bunny	cats	the desert

nov. 9	daniela	artist	barcelona
nov. 10	sindihogar	union of domestic & care workers	barcelona
nov. 11	bernardo	artist	amsterdam
nov. 12	lucía	artist	barcelona
nov. 13	project 181	collaborators	atlanta
nov. 14	esmee	artist & student	eindhoven
nov. 15	stas	graphic designer	prague
nov. 16	sohrab	artist	london
nov. 17	marc	artist	amsterdam
nov. 18	machiel	art student	amsterdam
nov. 19	margarita		amsterdam
nov. 20	emily	mother & artist	toronto
nov. 21	elsa	artist	amsterdam
nov. 22	maiko	curator	amsterdam
nov. 23	juan carlos	vividor	madrid
nov. 24	katayoun	art worker	amsterdam
nov. 25	yuji	student	madrid
nov. 26	ronan	artist	brittany
nov. 27	mathias	graphic designer	amsterdam
nov. 28	jeleton	unemployed	bilbao
nov. 29	jameson	teacher & journalist	draycott
nov. 30	iza	student	amsterdam
dec. 1	constança	artist	lisbon
dec. 2	catoo	art student	amsterdam
dec. 3	elsa	student	besançon
dec. 4	marissa	domestic worker & j4dw coordinator	london
dec. 5	trenton	publisher	london
dec. 6	maría	artist, researcher, & teacher	barcelona
dec. 7	scott	artist	glasgow
dec. 8	zoe & eira	artist collaborative	glasgow
dec. 9	thomas	designer	bruxelles
dec. 10	stas	graphic designer	prague
dec. 11	esmee	artist & student	eindhoven
dec. 12	sebastien	civil servant	den haag
dec. 13	ernst	artist	amsterdam
dec. 14	jenny	producer	miami
dec. 15	dooho	artist	amsterdam
dec. 16	elsa	artist	amsterdam
dec. 17	raquel	photographer	barcelona
dec. 18	robin	not-writer, maybe-sculptor, student	amsterdam
dec. 19	cocco	fashion designer	paris
dec. 20	maiko	curator	amsterdam
dec. 21	francisco	philosopher	amsterdam
dec. 22	l'occasione	on/off hostess	bilbao
dec. 23	luciana	photographer	são paulo
dec. 24	dina	domestic worker	london
dec. 25	-jl	web designer & photographer	barcelona
dec. 26	fema		

dec. 27	antonia	designer	montréal
dec. 28	realizza	domestic worker & visual artist	london
dec. 29	pinky & bunny	cats	the desert
dec. 30	pilar	architect	castellón
dec. 31	torkel	cultural analyst & writer	stockholm
jan. 1	lucía	artist	barcelona
jan. 2	luciana	photographer	são paulo
jan. 3	daniele	photographer	napoli
jan. 4	marc	artist	amsterdam
jan. 5	minke	communication consultant	amsterdam
jan. 6	denise	graphic designer	tokyo
jan. 7	petrina & matt	artists & musicians	london
jan. 8	kim	artist, curator	st. louis
jan. 9	jena	domestic worker	singapore
jan. 10	luciana	photographer	amsterdam
jan. 11	felipe	artist	bogotá
jan. 12	sarai	graphic designer	amsterdam
jan. 13	johan	assistant professor	amsterdam
jan. 14	luca	graphic designer	amsterdam
jan. 15	alec	art student	amsterdam
jan. 16	info	unknown	berkley
jan. 17	marissa	domestic worker & j4dw coordinator	london
jan. 18	trenton	publisher	london
jan. 19	torkel	cultural analyst & writer	stockholm
may 20	zoe & eira	artist collaborative	glasgow
jan. 21	project 181	collaborators	atlanta
jan. 22	adam	landscape architect	hong kong
jan. 23	christian	artist	london
jan. 24	camilla	antiques dealer	verona
jan. 25	margarita		amsterdam
jan. 26	serena	painter	milano
jan. 27	jena	domestic worker	singapore
jan. 28	rogier	graphic designer & artist	amsterdam
jan. 29	fani	graphic designer & ceramist	barcelona
jan. 30	ainara	artist	barcelona
jan. 31	yolande	student & producer	utrecht
feb. 1	luisa	photographer	frankfurt
feb. 2	laura	teacher and artist	wolf
feb. 3	realizza	domestic worker & visual artist	london
feb. 4	maría	artist, researcher, & teacher	barcelona
feb. 5	pilar	architect	castellón
feb. 6	project 181	collaborators	atlanta
feb. 7	esmee	artist & student	eindhoven
feb. 8	sohrab	artist	london
feb. 9	emily	mother & artist	toronto
feb. 10	ariella	philosopher	tel aviv
feb. 11	maiko	curator	amsterdam
feb. 12	raquel	photographer	barcelona

feb. 13	annie	artist & designer	amsterdam
feb. 14	femke	designer	amsterdam
feb. 15	maurits	writer	amsterdam
feb. 16	nolwenn	student	amsterdam
feb. 17	jena	domestic worker	singapore
feb. 18	realizza	domestic worker & visual artist	london
feb. 19	maría	artist, researcher, & teacher	barcelona
feb. 20	pilar	architect	castellón
feb. 21	yuji	student	madrid
feb. 22	lucía	artist	barcelona
feb. 23	ernst	artist	amsterdam
feb. 24	edwin	graphic designer	amsterdam
feb. 25	sabine	artist	amsterdam
feb. 26	alexandra	musician & art student	amsterdam
feb. 27	simon	art worker	melbourne
feb. 28	marissa	domestic worker & j4dw coordinator	london
mar. 1	daniela	artist	barcelona
mar. 2	lucía	artist	barcelona
mar. 3	janneke	visual artist	amsterdam
mar. 4	marilou	student	amsterdam
mar. 5	marc	artist	amsterdam
mar. 6	emily	mother & artist	toronto
mar. 7	mirari	photographer & babysitter	brooklyn
mar. 8	flavia	graphic designer & illustrator	toronto
mar. 9	ocean	undefined	derbyshire
mar. 10	liane	art worker & writer	beirut
mar. 11	vika	artist	amsterdam
mar. 12	trenton	publisher	london
mar. 13	lamis	housework practitioner	london
mar. 14	anacoreta	domestic worker	amsterdam
mar. 15	ulla	artist	amsterdam
mar. 16	sarah	student	amsterdam
mar. 17	andrea	writer & part-time bookseller	barcelona
mar. 18	alejandro	curator	london
mar. 19	jenny	producer	st. martí vell
mar. 20	tatiana	artist & student	valencia
mar. 21	realizza	domestic worker & visual artist	london
mar. 22	sindihogar	union of domestic & care workers	barcelona
mar. 23	pierre-henri	cabinet du maire du 3e arrdt.	paris
mar. 24	marilou	student	amsterdam
mar. 25	esther	artist & researcher	london
mar. 26	derveloy	designer	arnhem
mar. 27	realizza	domestic worker & visual artist	london
mar. 28	lucía	artist	barcelona
mar. 29	merve	artist	new york
mar. 30	agne	artist	amsterdam
mar. 31	mario	unknown	madrid
apr. 1	emilio	artist	amsterdam

apr. 2	realizza	domestic worker & visual artist	london
apr. 3	project 181	collaborators	atlanta
apr. 4	nafisse	student	fès
apr. 5	rogier	graphic designer & artist	amsterdam
apr. 6	raquel	visual artist	london
apr. 7	maría	artist researcher & teacher	barcelona
apr. 8	roma	artistst, activistst, architects	sheffield
apr. 9	roland	psychologist	amsterdam
apr. 10	thomas	designer	bruxelles
apr. 11	matthijs	artist	amsterdam
apr. 12	pinky & bunny	cats	the desert
apr. 13	marc	artist	barcelona
apr. 14	alejandron	curator	london
apr. 15	anacoreta	domestic worker	amsterdam
apr. 16	neus	technical architect	barcelona
mar. 17	sindihogar	union of domestic & care workers	barcelona
apr. 18	mario	unknown	madrid
apr. 19	torkel	cultural analyst & writer	stockholm
apr. 20	angela	artist & student	madrid
apr. 21	luciana	photographer	são paulo
apr. 22	carolina	graphic designer & student	bogotá
apr. 23	flavia	filmmaker	amsterdam
apr. 24	sebastien	civil servant	den haag
apr. 25	margarita		amsterdam
apr. 26	denny	graphic designer	amsterdam
apr. 27	alicia	photographer	lima
apr. 28	maria	editor	barcelona
apr. 29	werker	art collective	amsterdam
apr. 30	realizza	domestic worker & visual artist	london

notes

notes